D1106188

International Refugee Law

International Refugee Law

A Reader

Edited by

B.S. Chimni

Sage Publications

New Delhi/Thousand Oaks/London

First published in 2000 by

Sage Publications India Pvt Ltd
M-32 Market, Greater Kailash, Part I
New Delhi 110 048

Sage Publications Inc.
2455 Teller Road
Thousand Oaks, California 91320

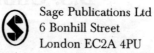

Sage Publications Ltd
6 Bonhill Street
London EC2A 4PU

Published by Tejeshwar Singh for Sage Publications India Pvt Ltd, lasertypeset by Line Arts, Pondicherry, and printed at Chaman Enterprises, Delhi.

Library of Congress Cataloging-in-Publication Data
International refugee law: a reader/edited by B.S. Chimni.
     p.   cm.   (cloth)
    Includes bibliographical references and index.
    1. Refugees—Legal status, laws, etc.   I. Chimni, B.S., 1952–
K3230.R45I55   341.4'86—dc21   1999   99–41686

ISBN: 0–7619–9362–2 (US-Hb)
      81–7036–853–7 (India-Hb)

Sage Production Team: Nilanjan Sarkar, R.A.M. Brown and Santosh Rawat

For my sons
Abhik and Sarthak

Contents

List of Abbreviations

AALCC	Asian–African Legal Consultative Committee
AAPSU	All Arunachal Pradesh Students Union
BIA	Board of Immigration Appeals
CABA	Cuban American Bar Association
CCRC	Committee for Citizenship Rights of the Chakmas
CHT	Chittagong Hill Tracts
CIA	Central Intelligence Agency
CIREFCA	International Conference on Central American Refugees
CJI	Chief Justice of India
CPA	Comprehensive Plan of Action
CRC	Convention on the Rights of the Child
CRPF	Central Reserve Police Force
DC	Deputy Collector
DHA	Department of Humanitarian Affairs
ECHA	Executive Committee on Humanitarian Affairs
ECOSOC	Economic and Social Council of United Nations
EPRS	Emergency Preparedness and Response Section (of UNHCR)
EXCOM	Executive Committee of UNHCR
HPF	Humanity Protection Forum
IASC	Inter-agency Standing Committee
ICA	International Coffee Agreement
ICARA	International Conference on Assistance to Refugees in Africa
ICEM	Intergovernmental Committee for European Migration
ICESR	International Covenant on Economic, Social and Cultural Rights

ICJ	International Court of Justice
ICPR	International Covenant on Civil and Political Rights
ICRC	International Committee of the Red Cross
ICVA	International Council of Voluntary Agencies
IDP	Internally Displaced Persons
IGCR	Intergovernmental Committee on Refugees
ILA	International Law Association
ILO	International Labour Organisation
IMF	International Monetary Fund
INA	Immigration and Nationality Act
IOM	International Organisation for Migration
IRCC	International Red Cross Committee
LIC	Low-intensity conflict
MOA	Memorandum of Agreement
NEFA	North Eastern Frontier Agency
NGO	Non-governmental Organisation
NHRC	National Human Rights Commission
NIEO	New International Economic Order
NLA	National Liberation Army
OAU	Organisation of African Unity
OCHA	Office for the Coordination of Humanitarian Affairs
ORC	Open Relief Centres
PARinAC	Partnership in Action
PCJSS	Parbottiya Chattogram Jana Shangati Samiti
SAARC	South Asian Association for Regional Cooperation
SAHRDC	South Asian Human Rights Documentation Centre
SPC	Special Political Committee of UNGA
UDHR	Universal Declaration of Human Rights
UNDP	United Nations Development Programme
UNGA	United Nations General Assembly
UNHCR	United Nations High Commissioner for Refugees
UNPROFOR	United Nations Protection Force
UNRRA	United Nations Relief and Rehabilitation Agency
UNRWA	United Nations Relief and Works Agency
UNTAC	United Nations Transitional Authority in Cambodia
UNV	United Nations Volunteers
USCR	United States Committee for Refugees

Foreword

The dissemination and promotion of refugee protection principles continue to be of the greatest importance for millions of people compelled by persecution and conflict to leave their homes and seek refuge in other countries. Asylum policies are increasingly restrictive—frequently for internal political reasons—and in many instances states retreat from their international obligations to the global asylum regime. Therefore, there is an urgent need to better inform and educate public opinion on refugee matters, and create support for refugee protection.

One of the most effective ways to build constituencies in support of refugees is through education and advocacy. This Reader edited by Professor B.S. Chimni is the first of its kind and offers a comprehensive introductory text on the subject.

Professor Chimni is a leading and distinguished scholar of refugee law in India, based at the Jawaharlal Nehru University in New Delhi. He has rendered his services and expertise to UNHCR as a member of the External Research Advisory Committee since 1996. He has also been a great supporter of UNHCR's promotional and training activities in India. Professor Chimni has been a strong voice and a critic of the current international refugee regime, in particular the restrictive practices of states on international protection. He is a firm advocate of the principle of equitable international burden-sharing in providing asylum and assistance to refugees.

This collection of readings will make a significant contribution to the teaching of international refugee law. Its publication is another milestone in our ongoing efforts to promote teaching and research on refugee issues and a better understanding of the global refugee problem and its solutions.

I wish to congratulate Professor Chimni for his dedication to the refugee cause and for this outstanding scholarly contribution which I trust will be used extensively throughout South Asia and other regions of the world.

Sadako Ogata
United Nations High Commissioner for Refugees
Geneva, August 1999

Preface

This book is intended as an introduction to international refugee law.

The status of the refugee in international law is constituted by a complex network of national, regional and international laws. The principal legal instruments on the international plane are the 1951 United Nations Convention on the Status of Refugees and the 1967 Protocol relating to the Status of Refugees which have been ratified by 134 states respectively. The 1951 Convention contains the most widely accepted definition of the term 'refugee'. It also incorporates the principle of *non-refoulement* (described as the cardinal principle of international refugee law) and outlines the minimum standard of treatment of refugees. The 1967 Protocol does away, albeit prospectively, with certain temporal and geographical limitations of the 1951 Convention.

At the regional level, there is the 1969 OAU Convention Governing the Specific Aspects of Refugee Problems in Africa which came into force in 1974. The OAU Convention goes further than the 1951 Convention in offering protection to refugees. It expands the definition of the term 'refugee' as well as gives the principle of *non-refoulement* a broader interpretation. It is also the first binding international instrument to contain an explicit provision on voluntary repatriation, the preferred solution to the global refugee problem.

Latin America has no regional convention. However, the Cartagena Declaration on Refugees, adopted by a group of government officials and jurists from Central America in 1984, has exercised considerable influence in the region despite being a non-binding instrument. It has been incorporated into the national legislation of several states in the region. The Cartagena Declaration follows the lead of the 1969 OAU Convention in broadening the definition of 'refugee'.

Insofar as Asia is concerned, mention may be made of the principles adopted by the Asian–African Legal Consultative Committee (AALCC) in 1966. These principles, also non-binding in character, have however exercised little influence in the region. Finally, a Group of Arab experts meeting in Cairo in November 1992 adopted a non-binding Declaration on the Protection of Refugees and Displaced Persons in the Arab world.

The focus of the Reader, insofar as international legal instruments go, is on the 1951 Convention even as it includes some material on regional conventions and declarations. The 1951 Convention is implemented through national laws and regulations. National jurisdictions often differ in their interpretation of the Convention obligations with the result that the status of the asylum-seeker and refugee may vary from country to country. While the readings which have been included take cognisance of the divergent practices of states, they make no attempt to describe or analyse the laws or case law of individual countries.

At the institutional level the Office of the United Nations High Commissioner for Refugees (UNHCR) is the principal international agency concerned with the assistance and protection of refugees. Its mandate and functions are spelt out in the Statute of the United Nations High Commissioner for Refugees adopted by the General Assembly in December 1950. Its primary responsibilities relate to 'providing international protection ... and ... seeking permanent solutions for the problem of refugees'. Among its key functions is the supervision of the application of the 1951 Convention whose Article 35 requires state parties to cooperate with it.

The Reader considers in some detail the mandate and functions of the UNHCR. However, with the exception of the International Committee of the Red Cross (ICRC), it does not deal with other international institutions concerned with providing assistance and protection to refugees. These include the United Nations Relief and Works Agency for Palestine Refugees in the Near East (UNRWA), the International Organisation on Migration (IOM), the International Labour Organisation (ILO), and regional organisations like the OAU Bureau for Refugees.

The Reader has been divided into eight chapters. The first four chapters deal with the definition of 'refugee', the law of asylum, the rights and duties of refugees, and the mandate and functions of the UNHCR respectively.

The subsequent three chapters consider the issue of the root causes of refugee flows and the law of state responsibility, durable solutions to the refugee condition, and the international law of internally displaced persons. These chapters address concerns which go beyond the 1951 Convention but are crucial to the understanding and resolution of the global refugee problem.

The final chapter deals with the legal condition of refugees in India, which is not a party to the 1951 Convention or the 1967 Protocol. However, since 1995 it has been a member of the Executive Committee of the UNHCR. It is hoped that the Reader will help familiarise those concerned with the fate of refugees in this country and elsewhere with the basic provisions of the 1951 Convention, as also with other relevant issues and problems, so that they can effectively participate in shaping India's national and international response to the global refugee problem.

Each chapter opens with an introduction which identifies the key issues and themes dealt with and the particular readings which address them. It also draws attention to ongoing debates and raises questions in a bid to encourage critical thinking. It may however be mentioned that on occasions issues have been touched upon to stimulate further reading and research but for which no particular readings have been included. I hope that this does not pose a problem to the reader.

Putting the Reader together has not been an easy task. It was rendered difficult by a number of factors which deserve brief mention.

First, reference may be made to the crisis that currently afflicts international refugee law. It is manifested above all in the growing tension between its language of protection and the ground reality of rejection. The crisis has its roots in the end of the Cold War (negating the principal political context of the 1951 Convention), the economic crisis which grips the industrialised world, the rise of regressive ideologies like xenophobia and the growing North–South divide. The industrialised world in particular has taken a series of restrictive administrative and legal measures—indicated in Chapter 2—to ensure that refugees do not end up at their door steps. Increasingly, attention is being focused on providing humanitarian assistance and protection inside countries and in this context pointing to the anachronistic nature of the concept of sovereignty.

The UNHCR is, not surprisingly, affected by these developments. Under pressure from the powerful and rich donor countries, it is presently being metamorphosed from a refugee to a humanitarian organisation reflected in its growing involvement with internally displaced persons (IDPs). Critics have expressed concern that this involvement with IDPs could be at the expense of providing assistance and protection to refugees. To put it differently, the nature and implications of the ongoing transformation of the principal agency concerned with the protection of refugees is far from clear.

Such a time of transition in the life of refugee law and institutions is a difficult moment to assemble a reader such as this. For you can either end up including materials exaggerating discontinuities or portray a static regime far removed from the uncertainties and changes which characterise the real world. To cite an example, even a few years back a book on international refugee law would not have contained much material on IDPs leave alone devote a separate chapter to it. Yet today, irrespective of the view one holds on the legitimacy and limits of international concern with IDPs—and I for one think that the countries of the third world are rightly concerned that it may provide a pretext to intervene in their internal and external affairs—the subject matter needs to be explored at some length.

Second, refugee law literature has an uneven quality about it. It is, among other things, characterised by considerable gaps. While much has been written on some issues (for example, on the elements which constitute the 1951 Convention definition of refugee), other areas of crucial concern (for example, the distinction between refugees and economic migrants, the rights of refugees, legal aspects of the solution of voluntary repatriation and the law of state responsibility for causing refugee flows) have not been adequately researched. It is only fair to warn readers that this unevenness may be reflected in the Reader.

Third, there is the absence of a tradition in the literature on refugee law of debating issues from a wider social science perspective. International refugee law scholarship has been dominated by a positivist tradition which affirms the fragmentation of social sciences.[1] This tradition views international law as an abstract system of rules which can be identified, objectively interpreted and enforced. The domain outside the system of rules is designated as politics which may assume the language of either power or morality. This failing to engage with the world beyond rules is rendered deeply problematic in the case of international refugee law by the fact that there are few rules in areas of critical importance like the responsibility of states causing refugee outflows or solutions to the global refugee problem.

I have attempted to fill these gaps through including readings which acquaint the reader with the interdisciplinary literature which constitutes the field of refugee studies. Till recently, however, there was a dearth of writings on different aspects of the global refugee problem and on the lifeworld of refugees. But the past decade has seen the arrival of a corpus of interdisciplinary literature which is in the midst of redefining the field of refugee studies.[2] Anthropologists, sociologists, political philosophers, political scientists and international relations specialists have brought their insights to bear on the global refugee problem and the everyday world of refugees. For example, anthropologists have done much to dispel the image of refugees as parasites and passive recipients of aid. Others have addressed the problem of root causes of refugee flows. It was important to include a sample of these writings in order to introduce the reader to the developments in the field of refugee studies, for these can have a direct bearing on the legal context.

---

[1] For a more detailed discussion of this tradition see B.S. Chimni, 'The Geopolitics of Refugee Studies: A View from the South', *Journal of Refugee Studies* (Vol. 11, 1998), pp. 350–75 at pp. 352–55.

[2] In the new edition of his book Guy Goodwin-Gill, a leading scholar of international refugee law, talks of 'the extraordinary growth in refugee studies, literature and case law'. Guy S. Goodwin-Gill, *The Refugee in International Law* (Clarendon Press, Oxford, 1996), second edition, p. xi. For a perspective on the evolution of refugee studies see Chimni, ibid.

Moreover, an understanding of the wider global environment—economic, political, cultural—which has shaped international refugee law is critical for those approaching it for the first time. In view of its humanitarian language it is often difficult to appreciate in the beginning its deeply political character. In this context, readers will do well to remember that powerful states exercise dominance in the international system not by means of brute force, but through the medium of language, with the language of the law playing a crucial role. International laws, to put it differently, do not evolve in a vacuum but reflect the power relations which inform the international system. The dominant actors in it are able to write their interests into law.[3] International refugee law, notwithstanding its humanitarian core, is no exception to this systemic reality.

Consequently, the terrain of international law is a key site for contesting ideas which reinforce structural inequities in the international system. Where international refugee law is concerned, the critical task is to ensure that it is not mobilised in favour of a language of exclusion and rejection, as it deals with the fate of the truly wretched of the earth. It concerns the destiny of individuals and groups who flee the more brutal moments in which the structural inequities manifest themselves in their lives. Empathy and solidarity with their pain and sufferings dictates a language of protection.

But contestation at the site of international refugee law is not an easy task. It is rendered complex by a number of factors. At least two of these may be mentioned to illustrate the point. First, the discourse of power often uses the goodwill of institutions like the UNHCR to preempt its critique, for a negative appraisal of the institution has to confront the enormous personal sacrifices of its staff and the undoubted relief and protection it offers to those who have lost a world. It is not always easy to explain to those who jump to its defense that a critique of the UNHCR is not directed at its enviable record in relief and protection or at its personnel—albeit this cannot at times be avoided—but at the powerful donor states which seek to either use it for non-humanitarian ends or to avoid fulfilling their international obligations.

Second, there is the insatiable demand for contextual criticism, be it of state policies or the UNHCR. For example, a critique of the policies of a state which abandons established principles of protection in favour of some form of principleless pragmatism is required to come to terms with a range of opposing arguments which *inter alia* relate to national security interests, state of the economy, concerns of host communities (demographic, cultural, economic, etc.), issues of environmental protection, the scale of

[3] For the author's perspective see B.S. Chimni, *International Law and World Order: A Critique of Contemporary Approaches* (Sage Publications, New Delhi, 1993).

influx, the extent of international burden sharing, the actions of other states in a similar situation, particular interpretations of international obligations and the response (or lack of it) of the United Nations system. In other words, states always appear to be able to cite reasons to make out a case for the exclusion of asylum-seekers or to deny refugees a life of dignity. On the other hand, critics are most often portrayed as starry eyed idealists with little understanding of the complex realities which shape national refugee policies.

These remarks should not be interpreted in any way to mean that the cause of refugees is advanced by being dismissive of the concerns of states, including powerful states in the international system. The language of protection does not demand that the legitimate interests of states be disregarded. Indeed, as a product of the states system these concerns are recognised by international refugee law. But more often than not states cite them as a pretext to deny protection and assistance to asylum-seekers and refugees. There is a constant need to be alert to this practice.

Much as I would have liked to include more readings which explore these dimensions of international refugee law the need to be sensitive to the economics of publishing meant leaving out a lot of interesting material. Indeed, there are many areas of refugee studies which find little or no place in this Reader. These *inter alia* include ethics of national and global refugee policy, security dimensions of global refugee flows, refugee aid and development, and the impact of refugee flows on the environment. The Reader also excludes reference to international principles and norms which apply to aliens in general (refugees being a special class of aliens), or to the international human rights laws or humanitarian laws whose violation is most often the reason which forces individuals to flee their countries in search of refuge.

For the interested reader a list of further readings has been appended; it contains references to some of the key writings on these subjects. Where the texts of relevant international and regional conventions and declarations are concerned readers are referred to the indispensable two-volume *Collection of International Instruments and Other Legal Texts Concerning Refugees and Displaced Persons* published by the UNHCR in 1995. For reasons of space only the texts of the 1951 Convention, the 1967 Protocol and the Statute of the Office of the United Nations High Commissioner for Refugees have been reproduced in the annex. The texts of the conclusions adopted by the Executive Committee of the UNHCR, frequently cited in the literature, along with the texts of relevant international instruments and refugee case law are readily available at the UNHCR's website: *http://www.unhcr.ch*. Reference may also be made to *Refworld*, which is an authoritative resource of refugee-related information in full text developed by the Centre for Documentation and Research of the

UNHCR. It contains a veritable mine of information cross-indexed for ready reference and can be accessed at the website of UNHCR. It is also available in CD format. *Refworld* should be an essential tool in the teaching of international refugee law.

The Reader is intended for a wide and varied audience: students, researchers, judges, policy-makers, and personnel of non-governmental organisations. This meant striking a balance between materials of interest to the academia and those which could be useful for individuals involved in the policy-making and conflict resolution processes or concerned with the everyday world of refugees. Whether the balance strived for has been achieved is of course for readers to judge.

In the end one or two details about the editing style need to be mentioned. I have deleted footnotes from reprinted materials without giving an indication. Where footnotes have been retained these have been renumbered, albeit the original style has been maintained. Certain headings have also been deleted, and in almost all cases their original numbering, without signalling the omission. I hope these will not inconvenience the reader in any way.

Acknowledgements

The idea of doing a reader on international refugee law came up in 1995 in a conversation with Shamsul Bari who was then the head of the UNHCR mission in India. He not only persuaded me to do the Reader but gave me all the necessary assistance and encouragement. I remain indebted to him for this.

I found the idea of preparing a reader appealing for two reasons: First, the lack of access to relevant literature has been a major hurdle in the introduction and teaching of international refugee law in India and elsewhere in South Asia. A reader, I believe, will go a long way in overcoming it. Second, there was the felt absence of any text which presented international refugee law from a third world perspective. It is a different matter that in view of the constraints of space, and the fact that the Reader is intended to be an introductory text, I have not been able to bring out as sharply or comprehensively as I would have liked a Southern perspective on international refugee law. For example, I have not been able to include readings which record at length the restrictive practices of the industrialised world which go to constituting what has been termed the *non-entrée* regime.

In the process of assembling the Reader I have incurred many debts. A book usually bears the name of an individual author even when knowledge production is inevitably a collective process. In the case of a reader it is even more so. Therefore, above all, I am indebted to the authors through whose work I converse with my readers. I would like to take this opportunity to thank the concerned publishers for giving permission, in many cases waiving any fee involved, to reproduce extracts.

I am extremely grateful to the United Nations High Commissioner for Refugees Mrs Sadako Ogata for agreeing to contribute a foreword. I hope that the Reader will further the ongoing efforts of the UNHCR to disseminate and promote refugee protection principles in India and the rest of South Asia.

I would like to thank Irene Khan, who succeeded Shamsul Bari at the New Delhi mission, and her successor Augustine Mahiga, for taking keen interest in the Reader.

I would also like to thank Wei Ming Lim, formerly Senior Legal Officer at the Mission, and her successor Brian Gorlick, as well as Rajiv Kapur, formerly Deputy Chief of the Mission in India, for the help I received from them. Brian Gorlick deserves special thanks for undertaking the tedious task of obtaining permission from different publishers.

Narsimha Rao, a former student and at present UNHCR Liaison Officer at Chennai, never refused a call for assistance. Many thanks to him.

Judith Orland and Debashish Krishan, interns at the Mission, deserve my thanks for reading through the draft of the Reader and giving some helpful comments. I am also grateful in this respect to my colleague V.S. Mani.

A Fulbright Fellowship allowed me to spend, albeit for a different project, the academic year 1995–96 at Harvard University which allowed me to consult its rich libraries. I am indebted to the United States Educational Foundation in India (USEFI) in this regard.

I also used a number of other libraries to collect material for the book. These include the library of the Jawaharlal Nehru University, New Delhi, the library of the Centre for Refugee Studies, York University, Canada, and the resource centre of the Refugee Studies Programme, Oxford University. My thanks to the staff of all these libraries.

Finally, I would like to thank my wife Maitrayee and two sons Abhik and Sarthak for their love and encouragement without which I could not have completed this Reader.

In the end I would be failing in my duty if I did not lay sole claim to the shortcomings of the book. It also provides me with the opportunity to mention that the time lag between assembling the Reader and its publication has meant that I have not been able to include some of the more recent writings. I hope this will not affect in any way the quality and usefulness of the Reader. However, I have tried to rectify matters by referring to these writings in the bibliography.

Every effort has been made to contact the copyright holders of the readings reproduced here. In the absence of a reply, permission has been assumed.

- James C. Hathaway, *The Law of Refugee Status* (Butterworths, Toronto, 1991), pp. vi–vii, 2–10, 24–27, 29–33, 65, 74, 80, 105, 107–8, 116–17. Reprinted by permission of Butterworths Canada Ltd.

- *Handbook on Procedures and Criteria for Determining Refugee Status* (UNHCR, Geneva, September 1979), paras 37, 38, 40–42, 51, 52, 62–64, 68–86.

- Patricia Tuitt, *False Images—Law's Construction of the Refugee* (Pluto Press, London, 1996), pp. 80–83, 85–86. Reprinted by permission of Pluto Press.

- Costas Douzinas and Ronnie Warrington, 'A Well-founded Fear of Justice: Law and Ethics in Postmodernity', in Jerry Leonard, ed., *Legal Studies as Cultural Studies: A Reader in (Post)Modern Critical Theory* (State University of New York Press, New York, 1995), pp. 197–99, 204–9. Reprinted by permission of the State University of New York Press.

- T. Alexander Aleinikoff, 'The Meaning of "Persecution" in U.S. Asylum Law', in Harold Adelman, ed., *Refugee Policy: Canada and the United States* (York Lanes Press, Toronto, 1991), pp. 296–98. Reprinted by permission of the Centre for Refugee Studies, York University, Toronto.

- Jacqueline Greatbatch, 'The Gender Difference: Feminist Critiques of Refugee Discourse', *International Journal of Refugee Law,* (Vol. 1, No. 4, 1989), pp. 518–26. Reprinted by permission of Oxford University Press, Oxford, UK.

- United States INS Gender Guidelines, *Considerations for Asylum Officers Adjudicating Asylum Claims from Women*, Memorandum, 26 May 1995. Reprinted from *Refworld*, CD-ROM released by UNHCR, January 1999.

- *Refugee Children: Guidelines on Protection and Care* (UNHCR, Geneva, 1994), pp. 18–25, 97–107, 137–48, 163–74.

- UNHCR, EC/47/SC/CRP. 29, 30 May 1997, 'Note on the Exclusion Clauses', 8th Meeting, Standing Committee, Executive Committee of the High Commissioner's Programme, paras 1, 3–7, 16–19.

- UNHCR, EC/47/SC/CRP. 30, 30 May 1997, 'Note on the Cessation Clauses', 8th Meeting, Standing Committee, Executive Committee of the High Commissioner's Programme, paras 3–6, 8.

- James C. Hathaway, 'A Reconsideration of the Underlying Premise of Refugee Law', *Harvard Journal of International Law* (Vol. 31, 1990), pp. 162–64. Reprinted by permission of the *Harvard Journal of International Law*.

- Eduardo Arboleda, 'Refugee Definition in Africa and Latin America: The Lessons of Pragmatism', *International Journal of Refugee Law* (Vol. 3, No. 2, 1991), pp. 186–205. Reprinted by permission of Oxford University Press, Oxford, UK.

- Principles Concerning Treatment of Refugees as Adopted by the Asian-African Legal Consultative Committee at its Eighth Session, Bangkok, 1966, Article I, Definition of the Term 'Refugee', in *Collection of International Instruments Concerning Refugees*, second edition (UNHCR, Geneva, 1979), pp. 201–2.

- Carol A. Batchelor, 'Stateless Persons: Some Gaps in International Protection', *International Journal of Refugee Law* (Vol. 7, 1995), pp. 232–34,

239–41, 258–59. Reprinted by permission of Oxford University Press, Oxford, UK.

- Daniel Warner, 'We are All Refugees', *International Journal of Refugee Law* (Vol. 4, No. 3, 1992), pp. 366–72. Reprinted by permission of Oxford University Press, Oxford, UK.

- Aristide R. Zolberg, 'International Migrants and Refugees in Historical Perspective', *Refugees* (December 1992), pp. 37–39, and *Refugees* (April 1993), pp. 41–42.

- Astri Suhrke, 'Refugees and Asylum in the Muslim World', in Robin Cohen, ed., *The Cambridge Survey of World Migration* (Cambridge University Press, Cambridge, 1995), pp. 457–60. Reprinted by permission of Cambridge University Press, Cambridge, UK, and Astri Suhrke.

- David Kennedy, 'International Refugee Protection', *Human Rights Quarterly* (Vol. 8, No. 1, 1986), pp. 42–46, 57–65. Reprinted by permission of the Johns Hopkins University Press. © The Johns Hopkins University Press.

- Claudena M. Skran, *Refugees in Inter-war Europe: The Emergence of a Regime* (Clarendon Press, Oxford, 1995), pp. 3–6. Reprinted by permission of Oxford University Press, Oxford, UK.

- Guy S. Goodwin-Gill, '*Non-refoulement* and the New Asylum Seekers', in David Martin, ed., *The New Asylum Seekers: Refugee Law in the 1980s* (Martinus Nijhoff Publishers, Dordrecht, 1988), pp. 103, 105–6. Reprinted by kind permission of Kluwer Law International.

- Kay Hailbronner, '*Non-refoulement* and "Humanitarian" Refugees: Customary International Law or Wishful Legal Thinking?' in David Martin, ed., *The New Asylum Seekers: Refugee Law in the 1980s* (Martinus Nijhoff Publishers, Dordrecht, 1988), pp. 128–36. Reprinted by kind permission of Kluwer Law International.

- James C. Hathaway and John A. Dent, *Refugee Rights: Report on a Comparative Survey* (York Lanes Press, Toronto, 1995), pp. 5–17, 18–42, 43–48. Reprinted by permission of the Centre for Refugee Studies, York University, Toronto.

- Supreme Court of the United States: Chris Sale, Acting Commissioner, Immigration and Naturalisation Service, et al., Petitioners v. Haitian Centers Council, Inc., et al., On Writ of Certiorari to the United States Court of Appeals for the Second Circuit (21 June 1993).

- Anthony H. Richmond, *Global Apartheid: Refugees, Racism and the New World Order* (Oxford University Press, Toronto, 1994), pp. xii–xv, 206–8, 210–11. Reprinted by permission of Oxford University Press, Canada.

- United Nations High Commissioner for Refugees, *The State of the World's Refugees—In Search of Solutions* (Oxford University Press, Oxford, 1995), pp. 85–90. Reprinted by permission of Oxford University Press, Oxford, UK.

- Arthur C. Helton, 'The Case of Zhang Zhenhai: Reconciling the International Responsibilities of Punishing Air Hijacking and Protecting Refugees', *Loyola of Los Angeles International and Comparative Law Journal* (Vol. 13, No. 4, June 1991), pp. 841–49. Reprinted by permission of *Loyola of Los Angeles International and Comparative Law Journal*, Los Angeles, California.

- UNHCR, Conclusion No. 17: Problems of Extradition Affecting Refugees.

- Emanuel Marx, 'The Social World of Refugees: A Conceptual Framework', *Journal of Refugee Studies* (Vol. 3, 1990), pp. 190, 196–98. Reprinted by permission of Oxford University Press, Oxford, UK.

- Robin Needham, 'Refugee Participation', in *Refugee Participation Network* 17 (Oxford University Press, Oxford, August 1994), p. 17. Reprinted by permission of Oxford University Press, Oxford, UK.

- Observations and Conclusions on Detention of the Working Group of the International Institute of Humanitarian Law held under the auspices of UNHCR, 1984.

- Harold Hongjhu Koh, 'America's Offshore Refugee Camps', *University of Richmond Law Review* (Vol. 29, No. 1, 1994), pp. 139–41. Originally published in 29 U. RICH. L. REV. 139 (1994). Reprinted by permission of the University of Richmond Law Review Association. © University of Richmond Law Review Association 1994.

- Elly Elikunda-Mtango, 'Military and Armed Attacks on Refugee Camps', in Gil Loescher and Laila Monahan, eds, *Refugees and International Relations* (Clarendon Press, Oxford, 1989), pp. 87–88, 102, 113–18. Reprinted by permission of Oxford University Press, Oxford, UK.

- UNHCR, Executive Committee Conclusion No. 22 (1981): Protection of Asylum Seekers in Situation of Large-scale Influx.

- *Guidelines on the Protection of Refugee Women* (UNHCR, Geneva, July 1991), pp. 8–11.

- Anders B. Johnsson, 'The Duties of Refugees', *International Journal of Refugee Law* (Vol. 3, No. 3, 1991), pp. 579–83. Reprinted by permission of Oxford University Press, Oxford, UK.

- Louise W. Holborn, *The International Refugee Organisation: A Specialised Agency of the United Nations—its History and Work 1946–1952* (Oxford University Press, London, 1956), pp. 3–18.

- John George Stoessinger, *The Refugee and the World Community* (The University of Minnesota Press, Minneapolis, 1956), pp. 61–62, 64–66, 81, 111–13, 197–200. Reprinted by permission of John George Stoessinger.

- Kim Salomon, 'The Cold War Heritage: UNRRA and the IRO as Predecessors of UNHCR', in Goran Rystad, ed., *The Uprooted* (Lund University Press, Lund, 1990), pp. 175–76. Reprinted by permission of Kim Salomon.

- Guy S. Goodwin-Gill, *The Refugee in International Law* (Clarendon Press, Oxford, 1983), pp. 129–36. Reprinted by permission of Oxford University Press, Oxford, UK.

- Sadruddin Aga Khan, Lectures on Legal Problems Relating to Refugees and Displaced Persons delivered at The Hague Academy of International Law, 4–6 August 1976, pp. 44–50. Reprinted from *Refworld*, CD-ROM released by UNHCR, January 1999.

- Anders B. Johnsson, 'UNHCR's Protection Role Continually Evolving', *Refugees* (No. 92, April 1993), pp. 15–16.

- David Rieff, *Slaughterhouse: Bosnia and the Failure of the West* (Simon and Schuster, New York, 1995), pp. 190, 195–96, 198, 200–202, 206–12. Reprinted by permission of Random House, London.

- Guy Goodwin-Gill, 'New Mandate? What New Mandate?' *Refugees* (No. 88, January 1992), pp. 38–40.

- Guy S. Goodwin-Gill, 'Asylum: The Law and Politics of Change', *International Journal of Refugee Law* (Vol. 7, No. 1, 1995), pp. 10, 12–13. Reprinted by permission of Oxford University Press, Oxford, UK.

- Hiram A. Ruiz, 'Emergencies: International Response to Refugee Flows and Complex Emergencies', *International Journal of Refugee Law* (Special Issue, 1995), pp. 155–58. Reprinted by permission of Oxford University Press, Oxford, UK.

- Roger P. Winter, *Assisting the World's Unprotected People: The Unique Role of Non-governmental Agencies* (The Danish Centre for Human Rights, Copenhagen, 1993), pp. 105–10. Reprinted by permission of The Danish Centre for Human Rights.

- Louise W. Holborn, *Refugees—A Problem of Our Time: The Work of the United Nations High Commissioner for Refugees, 1951–1972* (Scarecrow Press Inc., Metuchen, 1975), Vol. 1, pp. 119–20. Reprinted by permission of Scarecrow Press Inc., Lanham, Maryland.

- Santiago Romero-Perez, 'Partnership in Action', *Refugees* (No. 97, 1994), pp. 8–9.

- Jean-Philippe Lavoyer, 'Refugees and Internally Displaced Persons: International Humanitarian Law and the Role of the ICRC', *International Review of the Red Cross* (No. 305, March–April 1995), pp. 167–70. Reprinted by permission of the International Committee of the Red Cross, Geneva.

- *The State of the World's Refugees: The Challenge of Protection* (Penguin, New York, 1993), pp. 14–24.

- Aristide R. Zolberg, Astri Suhrke and Sergio Aguayo, *Escape from Violence: Conflict and the Refugee Crisis in the Developing World* (Oxford University Press, New York, 1989), pp. 260–63. Reprinted by permission of Oxford University Press, Inc. Copyright © Oxford University Press, Inc., 1989.

- Michel Chossudovsky, 'Hidden Hands behind Rwandan Holocaust', *Health for the Millions* (Vol. 22, No. 2, March–April 1996), pp. 33–34. Reprinted by permission of the Voluntary Health Association of India.

- James Petras and Steve Vieux, 'Bosnia and the Revival of US Hegemony', *New Left Review* (No. 218, July–August 1996), pp. 9–12. Reprinted by permission of *New Left Review*, London.

- Mark Gibney, 'US Foreign Policy and the Creation of Refugee Flows', in Howard Adelman, ed., *Refugee Policy: Canada and the United States* (York Lanes Press, Toronto, 1991), pp. 81, 87–90, 93–100. Reprinted by permission of the Centre for Refugee Studies, York University, Toronto.

- Chaloka Beyani, 'State Responsibility for the Prevention and Resolution of Forced Population Displacements in International Law', *International Journal of Refugee Law* (Special Issue, 1995), pp. 131–37. Reprinted by permission of Oxford University Press, Oxford, UK.

- Payam Akkavan and Morten Bergsmo, 'The Application of the Doctrine of State Responsibility to Refugee Creating States', *Nordic Journal of International Law* (Vol. 58, Nos 3–4, 1989), pp. 252–54.

- Jack I. Garvey, 'The New Asylum Seekers: Addressing their Origin', in David A. Martin, ed., *The New Asylum Seekers: Refugee Law in the 1980s* (Martinus Nijhoff Publishers, Dordrecht, 1988), pp. 187–91. Reprinted by kind permission of Kluwer Law International.

- Luke T. Lee, 'The Right to Compensation: Refugees and Countries of Asylum', *American Journal of International Law* (Vol. 80, 1986), pp. 533, 537–39, 545–66. Reprinted with permission from 80 A.J.I.L. 532 (1986). © The American Society of International Law.

- Christian Tomuschat, 'State Responsibility and the Country of Origin', in Vera Gowlland-Debbas, ed., *The Problem of Refugees in the Light of*

Contemporary International Law Issues (Martinus Nijhoff Publishers, The Hague, 1995), pp. 60, 64–68, 70–71, 74–79. Reprinted by kind permission of Kluwer Law International.

- International Law Association, 'The Cairo Declaration of Principles of International Law on Compensation to Refugees', *American Journal of International Law* (Vol. 87, No. 1, 1993), pp. 157–59. Reprinted with permission from 87 A.J.I.L. 157 (1993). © The American Society of International Law.

- Rupert Colville, 'Resettlement: Still Vital after All These Years', *Refugees* (No. 94, December 1993), pp. 4–8.

- Tom Kuhlman, *Asylum or Aid? The Economic Integration of Ethiopian and Eritrean Refugees in the Sudan* (African Studies Centre, Leiden, 1994), pp. 51–52, 56–57. Reprinted by permission of African Studies Centre, Leiden.

- Gervase Coles, 'Approaching the Refugee Problem Today', in Gil Loescher and Laila Monahan, eds, *Refugees and International Relations* (Clarendon Press, Oxford, 1989), pp. 387–93, 403–4. Reprinted by permission of Oxford University Press, Oxford, UK.

- Jonathan Bascom, 'The Dynamics of Refugee Repatriation: The Case of Eritreans in Eastern Sudan', in W.T.S. Gould and A.M. Findlay, eds, *Population Migration and the Changing World Order* (John Wiley and Sons, New York, 1994), pp. 226–28, 244–46. Reprinted by permission of John Wiley and Sons, East Sussex, England, W.T.S. Gould and A.M. Findlay.

- John R. Rogge, 'Repatriation of Refugees', in Tim Allen and Hubert Morsink, eds, *When Refugees Go Home: African Experiences* (UNRISD, Geneva, 1994), pp. 14, 24, 31–34, 43–46. Reprinted by permission of the United Nations Research Institute for Social Development.

- UNHCR, Executive Committee Conclusion No. 18 (1980): Voluntary Repatriation.

- UNHCR, Executive Committee Conclusion No. 40 (1985): Voluntary Repatriation.

- Article V of the OAU Convention Governing the Specific Aspects of Refugee Problems in Africa, 1969.

- US Committee for Refugees, *'Something Like Home Again': The Repatriation of Cambodian Refugees* (May 1994), pp. 62–64, 67. Reprinted by permission of the US Committee for Refugees, Washington, D.C.

- International Conference on Central American Refugees (CIREFCA), Guatemala City, 29–31 May 1989, Declaration and Concerted Plan of

Action in Favour of Central American Refugees (CIREFCA/89/14, 31 May 1989), pp. 1–15.

- Barry N. Stein and Fred C. Cuny, 'Repatriation under Conflict', *World Refugee Survey 1991*, pp. 15–21. Reprinted by permission of US Committee for Refugees.

- *Handbook on Voluntary Repatriation: International Protection* (UNHCR, Geneva, 1996), pp. 17–18.

- UN Doc. E/CN.4/1994/44, 25 January 1994, 'Internally Displaced Persons: Report of the Representative of the Secretary-General, Mr Francis Deng, Submitted Pursuant to Commission on Human Rights Resolution 1993/95', paras 19–28.

- Roberta Cohen, 'Protecting the Internally Displaced', *World Refugee Survey 1996*, pp. 21–25. Reprinted by permission of US Committee for Refugees.

- Michael W. Reisman, 'Sovereignty and Human Rights in Contemporary International Law', *American Journal of International Law* (Vol. 84, 1990), pp. 866, 869–70, 872–74. Reprinted with permission from 84 A.J.I.L. 866 (1990). © The American Society of International Law.

- International Court of Justice, Case Concerning Military and Paramilitary Activities in and against Nicaragua (*Nicaragua v. United States of America*), Judgement of 27 June 1986, paragraphs 202, 203, 205, 206, 209, 246, 263, 267, 268.

- G.A. Res 46/182: Strengthening of the Coordination of Humanitarian Emergency Assistance of the United Nations, 19 December 1991, adopted without a vote.

- *For a Strong and Democratic United Nations: A South Perspective on UN Reform* (South Centre, Geneva, 1996), pp. 18–21.

- Denise Plattner, 'ICRC Neutrality and Neutrality in Humanitarian Assistance', *International Review of the Red Cross* (No. 311, March–April 1996), pp. 171–73, 175–77. Reprinted by permission of the International Committee of the Red Cross, Geneva.

- Office for the Coordination of Humanitarian Affairs (OCHA), *Guiding Principles on Internal Displacement*.

- UNHCR, Executive Committee, 45th Session, EC/SCP/87, 17 August 1994, 'Protection Aspects of UNHCR Activities on Behalf of Internally Displaced Persons', pp. 176–91.

- B.S. Chimni, 'The Incarceration of Victims: Deconstructing Safety Zones', in N. Al-Nauimi and R. Meese, eds, *International Legal Issues*

Arising under the United Nations Decade of International Law (Kluwer Law International, The Hague, 1995), pp. 823–54. Reprinted by kind permission of Kluwer Law International.

- Bill Clarance, 'Protective Structure, Strategy and Tactics: International Protection in Ethnic Conflicts', *International Journal of Refugee Law* (Vol. 5, No. 4, 1993), pp. 586–92. Reprinted by permission of Oxford University Press, Oxford, UK.

- Joseph B. Schechtman, *The Refugee in the World: Displacement and Integration* (A.S. Barnes and Co., New York, 1963), pp. 103–5.

- Nilanjana Chatterjee, 'The East Bengal Refugees: A Lesson in Survival', in Sukanta Chaudhuri, ed., *Calcutta: The Living City*, Vol. II: *The Present and the Future* (Oxford University Press, Delhi, 1990), pp. 70–76. Reprinted by permission of Oxford University Press, New Delhi.

- Kanti B. Pakrasi, *The Uprooted: A Sociological Study of the Refugees of West Bengal, India* (S. Ghatack, Calcutta, 1971), pp. 49–52.

- Jacques Vernant, *The Refugee in the Post-war World* (Yale University Press, New Haven, 1953), pp. 740–41.

- U. Bhaskar Rao, *The Story of Rehabilitation* (Department of Rehabilitation, Government of India, New Delhi, 1967), pp. 112–15, 121–25, 128–34.

- B.S. Chimni, 'The Legal Condition of Refugees in India', *Journal of Refugee Studies* (Vol. 7, No. 4, 1994), pp. 378–83, 389–98. Reprinted by permission of Oxford University Press, Oxford, UK.

- Justice J.S. Verma, former Chief Justice of India, Inaugural Address delivered at the Conference on Refugees in SAARC Region: Building a Legal Framework, New Delhi, 2 May 1997, pp. 3–9. Reprinted by permission of Justice J.S. Verma.

- K.C. Saha, 'Landmark Chakma Peace Accord—A Model for Permanent Solution of Refugee Problem', *Bulletin on IHL and Refugee Law* (Vol. 3, Nó. 2, 1998), pp. 255, 265–68.

- In the Supreme Court of India Original Civil Jurisdiction, Writ Petition (Civil) No. 720 of 1995. (1) Supreme Court 295, 1996, 49435, pp. 1–20.

- Nirmala Chandrahasan, 'A Precarious Refuge: A Study of the Reception of Tamil Asylum Seekers into Europe, North America and India', *Harvard Human Rights Yearbook* (Vol. 2, 1989), pp. 92–94. Reprinted by permission of *Harvard Journal of International Law*.

- Asha Hans, 'Repatriation of the Sri Lankan Refugees from India', *Bulletin on IHL and Refugee Law* (Vol. 2, No. 1, January–June 1997), pp. 96–108.

- *P. Nedumaran and Dr. S. Ramadoss v. The Union of India* and another Unreported Judgement in the High Court of Judicature at Madras, dt. 27.8.1992.

- *Digvijay Mote v. Government of India and Government of Karnataka*, Unreported Decision in the High Court of Karnataka at Bangalore dt. 17.2.1994.

- UN Secretary-General's Aide Memoire of 19 July 1971, to Governments of India and Pakistan. *Bangladesh Documents* (Ministry of External Affairs, New Delhi, n.d.), p. 657.

- India's Reply to UN Secretary-General's Aide Memoire, delivered on 2 August 1971. *Bangladesh Documents* (Ministry of External Affairs, New Delhi, n.d.), pp. 660–63.

- US Committee for Refugees, *World Refugee Survey 1997* (Washington, D.C., 1997). Reprinted by permission of US Committee for Refugees.

Chapter 1

Who is a Refugee?

The definition of a 'refugee' in international law is of critical importance for it can mean the difference between life and death for an individual seeking asylum. Definitions in international law, it may be noted, depart from the ordinary meaning of the word 'refugee'. In everyday speech, the word 'refugee' is used to describe a person who is forced to flee his or her home for any reason for which the individual is not responsible, be it persecution, public disorder, civil war, famine, earthquake or environmental degradation.[1] However, in international law, a 'refugee' is a person who is forced to leave home for certain specified reasons and who, furthermore, is outside the country of his or her origin and does not have its protection. Persons who are compelled to move but do not cross international borders are classified as 'internally displaced persons'.[2]

Different Definitions

Several attempts to define the term 'refugee' have been made in the course of the twentieth century. The definitions contained in different international instruments during the period of the League of Nations is the subject of **Reading I.A.** It provides the historical backdrop against which contemporary definitions need to be considered.[3] These include

---

[1] 'A refugee can be defined in three ways: legally (as stipulated in national or international law); politically (as interpreted to meet political exigencies); and sociologically (as reflecting an empirical reality).' Astri Suhrke, 'Global Refugee Movements and Strategies of Response', in M. Kritz, ed., *US Immigration and Refugee Policy: Global and Domestic Issues* (1983), pp. 157–62.

[2] For a review of the historical and practical reasons which justify alienage as a criterion to define a refugee, see the introduction to and **Reading I.A** of Chapter 7.

[3] For a review of the role of international refugee organisations in the League period see **Reading I.A** of Chapter 4.

the definitions contained in the 1951 Convention on the Status of Refugees (hereafter the 1951 Convention), the 1969 OAU Convention Governing the Specific Aspects of Refugee Problems in Africa (hereafter the OAU Convention), and the Cartagena Declaration on Refugees, 1984 (hereafter the Cartagena Declaration).

In studying the different definitions readers should bear in mind the observation that while definitions help 'impose finite limits on human problems' they often 'tend to raise form over substance, class over need, [and] characterization over purpose'.[4] At this point they become ideological or political devices to arbitrarily delimit or extend the problem.

The 1951 Convention Definition

The most widely accepted definition of a 'refugee' is that contained in the 1951 Convention.[5] The mandate of the Convention extends to any person who

> as a result of events occurring before 1 January 1951 and owing to well-founded fear of being persecuted for reasons of race, religion, nationality, membership of a particular social group or political opinion, is outside the country of his nationality and is unable or, owing to such fear, is unwilling to avail himself of the protection of that country; or who, not having a nationality and being outside the country of his former habitual residence as a result of such events, is unable or, owing to such fear, is unwilling to return to it.

However, despite the fact that this definition is widely accepted there is no avoiding, as **Reading II.1.A** points out, the Cold War origins of the 1951 Convention definition and its Eurocentric focus. **Reading II.2.B**, on the other hand, identifies the essential elements of the definition. The subsequent readings of Section II examine in detail the meaning of some of the key words or phrases in the Convention definition.

---

[4] Guy Goodwin-Gill, 'The Benigno Aquino Lecture in Human Rights. Refugees and Human Rights: Challenges for the 1990s', *International Journal of Refugee Law* (Special Issue, September 1990), pp. 29–38 at p. 34.

[5] As Hathaway puts it: 'The Convention refugee definition is of singular importance because it has been subscribed to by more than one hundred nations in the only refugee accords of global scope. Many nations have also chosen to import this standard into their domestic immigration legislation as the basis upon which asylum and other protection decisions are made.' James C. Hathaway, *The Law of Refugee Status* (Butterworths, Toronto, 1991), p. v.

Well-founded Fear: Subjective or Objective Test?

Readings II.3.C to **II.3.F** consider the meaning of the crucial phrase 'well-founded fear' which occurs in the definition. Its interpretation has generated a debate on whether the subjective or the objective test should be applied in determining 'well-founded fear' of being persecuted. In **Reading II.3.C** the UNHCR's *Handbook on Procedures and Criteria for Determining Refugee Status* (hereafter the UNHCR *Handbook*) recommends the use of both the subjective and the objective tests. However, a leading scholar of international refugee law, James Hathaway, emphasises the objective test in **Reading II.3.D.** He contends that granting refugee status has little to do with the state of mind of the individual concerned.

The problem with advocating the sole use of the objective test is the underlying assumption that the 'subjective' perception of the individual represents an arbitrary evaluation of events. On the other hand, it is perhaps legitimate to ask if an 'objective' determination is possible at all. Are there really 'objective' facts out there waiting to be discovered? Do they allow the possibility of arriving at an ethical judgement on the pain and fear an individual experiences?[6] Does the availability of a huge quantity of information on the human rights record of the country of origin offer a foolproof method of determining 'well-founded fear'? Or, is the goal of arriving at an 'objective' determination a pretext to impose the 'subjective' determination of status-determining authorities and courts on the asylum-seeker? Any determination is, after all, an interpretation and, where government agencies are concerned, deeply influenced by state policies. Thus, in a paranoid world the sole application of the objective test could mean, as **Readings II.3.E** and **II.3.F** strive to point out, the increasing disenfranchisement of the refugee claimant.[7] These are somewhat difficult readings but will repay careful study.

Persecution

It is widely accepted that the drafters of the Convention deliberately left the meaning of 'persecution' undefined as it was an impossible task to

---

[6] See Elaine Scarry, *The Body in Pain: The Making and Unmaking of the World* (Oxford University Press, Oxford, 1987).

[7] In **Reading II.3.F** Douzinas and Warrington rely on post-modern scholarship to show how reliance on an objective test may lead to the commission of an ethical tort. For an introduction to post-modern scholarship and its critique see Steven Seidman, ed., *The Postmodern Turn: New Perspectives on Social Theory* (Cambridge University Press, Cambridge, 1994); Stuart Hall et al., eds, *Modernity and its Futures* (Polity Press in Association with Open University, Cambridge, 1992); Alex Callinicos, *Against Postmodernism: A Marxist Critique* (Polity Press, Cambridge, 1989).

enumerate in advance the myriad forms it might assume. But this omission also gave states a large measure of discretion, resulting in the absence of a 'coherent or consistent jurisprudence'.[8] **Readings II.4.G to II.4.I** consider against this backdrop the meaning of the word 'persecution'. **Reading II.4.G** reproduces two brief sections on the subject from the UNHCR *Handbook*. In **Reading II.4.H** Aleinikoff reflects on the intention of the drafters of the Convention and examines the interpretation offered by the UNHCR *Handbook*. In the final reading Hathaway attempts a definition of 'persecution' by linking it to wider developments in the field of human rights. He distinguishes his position from those who would link the meaning of 'persecution' to a narrow subset of human rights.[9]

Nexus with Civil or Political Status

The 1951 Convention mandates protection only for those whose civil and political rights are violated, without protecting persons whose socio-economic rights are at risk. It extends to persons who have been disenfranchised on the basis of race, religion, nationality, membership of a particular social group, or political opinion. **Reading II.5.J** examines the different civil and political rights which must be at risk.

Hathaway has described the 1951 Convention mandate as 'the lopsided and politically biased human rights rationale for refugee law'.[10] The historical reason for reference to civil and political rights alone, as **Reading II.1.A** noted, was to embarrass the former Soviet Union and its allies whose record in the sphere of political and civil rights was less than wholesome. However, in the final analysis, the problem of defining a refugee is a debate about the epistemological principles which inform its elaboration. The Convention definition merely illustrates the point that definitions are not neutral devices but embody particular, usually partial, interpretations of social reality. Thus, the concept of a 'refugee' may be described as 'an essentially contested concept', i.e., a concept of which competing definitions may be advanced on the basis of different epistemological principles.[11]

[8] Guy S. Goodwin-Gill, *The Refugee in International Law* (Clarendon Press, Oxford, 1996), second edition, p. 67.

[9] The interpretation of the term 'persecution' raises a number of other significant questions which cannot, for reasons of space, be addressed here. These include the questions of 'agents of persecution' and the availability of an internal flight alternative (IFA) to deny refugee status. For a discussion of these issues see Goodwin-Gill, ibid., pp. 69ff; and Karin Landgren, 'The Future of Refugee Protection: Four Challenges', *Journal of Refugee Studies* (Vol. 11, 1998), pp. 416–32 at pp. 417–20.

[10] It may be traced to the distinction between negative and positive liberty made famous by Isaiah Berlin.

[11] For a discussion of the meaning of 'essentially contested concepts' see W.B. Gallie, *Philosophy and Historical Understanding* (Chatto and Windus, London, 1964), pp. 157–91.

Membership of a Particular Social Group: Gender Guidelines

In the last decade the literature on refugees has come to concern itself with the different experience of refugee women as compared to their male counterparts; they often fear persecution for different reasons than men, and face a different set of problems on becoming refugees. **Reading II.6.K** offers a critical introduction to feminist perspectives on the definition of refugee and considers the appropriateness of including gender as an enumerated basis for persecution in the Convention definition.[12]

In 1985, the UNHCR Executive Committee adopted Conclusion No. 39 which noted that refugee women and girls constituted the majority of the world's refugee population and that many of them were exposed to special problems.[13] The Conclusion also recognised that states were free to adopt the interpretation that women asylum-seekers faced with harsh or inhuman treatment for having transgressed the social mores of the society in which they lived could be considered a 'particular social group' within the 1951 Convention definition. In October 1993, the UNHCR Executive Committee adopted Conclusion No. 73 on Refugee Protection and Sexual Violence. It recognised that asylum-seekers who have suffered sexual violence should be treated with particular sensitivity, and recommended the establishment of training programmes designed to ensure that those involved in the determination of refugee status are adequately sensitised to issues of gender and culture. In 1991, the UNHCR issued its 'Guidelines on the Protection of Refugee Women' which essentially addressed issues relating to women in refugee camps. However, the Guidelines also addressed gender-related persecution and recommended procedures to make the refugee adjudication process more accessible to women.

In March 1993, Canada issued its *Guidelines on Women Refugee Claimants Fearing Gender-related Persecution*, and became the first country to establish formal procedures for the adjudication of refugee claims made by women. The *Guidelines* formally recognise that women fleeing persecution because of their gender can be found to be refugees. In May 1995, the United States became the second country in the world to adopt formal guidelines recognising that women may experience discrimination unique to their gender, and that in some cases, such discrimination can meet the standards for refugee status. **Reading II.6.L** reproduces Section III of the US INS Guidelines entitled 'Legal Analysis of Claims', which serves as an introduction to a range of issues and considerations involved

---

[12] On the gender question in general see *The Polity Reader in Gender Studies* (Polity Press, Cambridge, 1994).

[13] The Conclusions adopted by the Executive Committee of the UNHCR each year are not binding on state parties. They are mere recommendations but often have great value in practice.

in determining gender-based refugee status.[14] While the establishment of these guidelines by Canada and the United States represents substantial progress, it is important to remember that they coexist with a host of restrictive practices—mentioned in Chapter 2—which all but ensure that women will not be able to access them. The deference with which status-determining authorities treat national asylum policies also makes it difficult to believe that the gender guidelines will translate into justice on the ground. The negative experience of Bosnian refugee women in the courts in Europe attests to this scepticism.[15]

The special concerns relating to the determination of refugee status of children are outlined in **Reading II.7.M** which reproduces an extract from the UNHCR guidelines for the protection and care of children.

Economic Migrants

The 1951 Convention does not, as we have seen, mandate protection for those whose socio-economic rights are at risk. But can a neat distinction be made between 'political' and 'economic' refugees? As **Reading II.8.N** points out, a sharp distinction between 'political' and 'economic' refugees is difficult to sustain. It is more likely that the political and economic causes of flight are so inextricably intertwined as to resist any simplistic classification as one or the other.[16]

[14] For an introduction in general to United States law and practice see D.E. Anker, *The Law of Asylum in the United States: A Manual for Practitioners and Adjudicators* (American Immigration Lawyers' Association, Washington, D.C., 1989); T.A. Aleinikoff et al., eds, *Immigration: Process and Policy* (West Publishing House, Minnesota, 1995), third edition.

[15] See U. David, 'Refugees from Bosnia and Herzegovina: Are they Genuine', *Suffolk International Law Review* (Vol. 28, 1995), pp. 53–131.

On the other hand, as has been pointed out by Deborah Anker and Nancy Kelly, 'while these guidances will affect only a small number of women, they are important, not only for those few who arrive ... who should have an equal chance with men to obtain protection—but because they establish the principle that human rights instruments cannot exclude women, and that the harms women face because of their gender must be recognized and taken seriously.' *Harvard Law School News* (26 May 1995).

[16] Prince Sadruddin Aga Khan, the former High Commissioner for Refugees, has rightly stressed that 'it would be wrong to draw too fine a distinction between the two, since political persecution and economic oppression can easily overlap. It is often the poorest members of society who are discriminated against (on grounds of race, religion or politics), and people flee from economic conditions which are the direct result of a political failure to guarantee distribution of food, land, jobs or education.' Sadruddin Aga Khan, 'Looking into the 1990s: Afghanistan and Other Refugee Crises', *International Journal of Refugee Law* (Special Issue, September 1990), pp. 14–28 at p. 24.

Readers would do well to return to this issue after studying Chapter 6 which deals with the causes of refugee flows. This chapter reveals the complexity of the problem, and in particular highlights the international dimension of the causes of refugee flows. The latter assumes importance in the North–South context, because states responsible for creating

However, because the Convention does not mandate protection for those whose socio-economic rights are at risk, states can regard individuals with such claims as economic migrants. This is often justified on the grounds that extending protection to such individuals could mean offering asylum to every poor person in the world. But, as Hathaway clarifies in **Reading II.8.O**, the right to seek asylum is carefully circumscribed in this regard. Mandating protection for those whose social and economic rights are at risk certainly does not mean that every poor person can claim refugee status.

Exclusion and Cessation Clauses

Not everyone who applies for refugee status deserves protection. The application of the 1951 Convention is subject to what have been termed 'exclusion clauses' embodied in Sections D to F of Article 1. They list certain categories of persons who do not deserve international protection. Clause F is of note for it excludes those who have committed crimes against peace and security, serious common law criminals and individuals who have acted in contravention of the principles and purposes of the United Nations. **Reading II.9.P** outlines the framework within which exclusion clauses are to be applied and briefly discusses the case of serious common law criminals.

Reading II.9.Q discusses the 'cessation clauses' contained in Clause C of Article 1 which lists the circumstances in which international protection may cease. Among other things, it makes the important point that the cessation clauses are exhaustive in their enumeration.[17]

The 1967 Protocol

The key feature of the Protocol of 31 January 1967 relating to the Status of Refugees (hereafter the 1967 Protocol) was that it removed the temporal and geographical limitations contained in the 1951 Convention. However, as **Reading III.A** points out, there was no attempt to reconsider the definition of the term 'refugee'. This meant that most third world refugees continued to remain *de facto* excluded, as their flight is frequently

---

the conditions in which socio-economic rights come to be at risk then turn round to classify those who seek to escape such conditions as economic migrants.

[17] 'It is generally agreed that the enumeration of cessation clauses in Article 1C of the Refugee Convention and in the second section of Paragraph A of the UNHCR Statute is exhaustive. In other words, once a person has become a refugee as defined in Article 1 of the Convention or Paragraph 6A of the Statute, he continues to be a refugee until he falls under any of those cessation clauses.' Atle Grahl-Madsen, *The Status of Refugees in International Law* (A.W. Sijthoff, Leyden, 1966), Vol. 1, p. 369.

prompted by natural disaster, war, or political and economic turmoil rather than by 'persecution', at least as that term is understood in the Western context.

Regional Instruments: The OAU Convention and the Cartagena Declaration

At the regional level different definitions of 'refugee' have been adopted, namely, the OAU Convention and the Cartagena Declaration. **Reading IV.A** examines the conditions under which the different definitions were adopted in Africa and Latin America and their salient features.

The definition of 'refugee' contained in the 1951 Convention was expanded by the OAU Convention to meet specific aspects of refugee problems in Africa. It defines the term 'refugee' to include persons fleeing their country of origin due to external aggression, occupation, foreign domination, or events seriously disturbing public order in either a part or the whole of the country of origin or nationality. The addition implies a move away from the 1951 Convention's 'well-founded fear' of persecution standard, stressing that refugees included persons fleeing civil disturbances, violence and war irrespective of whether or not they have a well-founded fear of persecution. Thus, the OAU definition leaves open the possibility that the basis for the harm may be indeterminate, and also goes back to the pre–World War II practice of recognising group disenfranchisement. Another feature of the definition is that it extends protection to persons who seek to escape serious disruption of public order 'in either a part or whole' of their country of origin. Therefore, a person is not required to seek refuge in a safe part of his or her own country before seeking it outside.[18]

The Cartagena Declaration recommends a definition very similar to that contained in the OAU Convention.

For two decades after the adoption of the OAU Convention academics argued for the need to bring the 1951 definition in line with it. It was *inter alia* contended that the 1951 definition of refugee was not a moral definition.[19] However, no sooner was the Cold War over that Western states jettisoned the debate on definitions; it was made clear that the definition contained in the 1951 Convention would not be revised. But is the West justified in resisting the expansion of the definition of refugee after states in Africa and Latin America have expanded it?

---

[18] For recent practice relating to the 1951 Convention on this question see footnote 9 earlier.

[19] Eugene Kamenka, 'On Being a Refugee', in Amin Saikal, ed., *Refugees in the Modern World* (Australian National University, Canberra, 1989), pp. 11–15 at p. 15.

Asia

In so far as Asia is concerned, mention must be made of the Bangkok Principles adopted by the Asian African Legal Consultative Committee (AALCC) in 1966. These Principles—reproduced as **Reading V.A**—are non-binding and have, as noted in the Preface, not exercised the kind of influence that the Cartagena Declaration has in Latin America.[20]

An Arab Convention?

In November 1992, a Group of Arab Experts meeting in Cairo adopted the 'Declaration on the Protection of Refugees and Displaced Persons in the Arab World'.[21] Article 6 of the Declaration recommended that 'pending the elaboration of an Arab Convention relating to refugees, Arab States adopt a broad concept of "refugee" and "displaced person"....'

Stateless Persons

'Refugees' are to be distinguished from stateless persons, whether or not this distinction stands to reason. While the 1951 Convention addresses the problem of 'refugees' alone, the international legal rights of stateless persons are addressed in the Convention Relating to the Status of Stateless Persons, 1954, which came into force in 1960.[22] It defines a 'stateless person' as a 'person who is not considered as a national by any State under the operation of its law'. The 1954 Convention was followed by the adoption of the Convention on the Reduction of Statelessness, 1961, which came into force in 1975.[23]

[20] Readers should also refer to the *Report of the Working Group on Current Problems in the International Protection of Refugees and Displaced Persons in Asia* which adopted certain conclusions and recommendations for the Asian region in 1981. It recommended a definition akin to the one embodied in the OAU Convention. *Report of the Working Group on Current Problems in the International Protection of Refugees and Displaced Persons in Asia*, 19–22 January 1981 (under the Auspices of the Office of the United Nations High Commissioner for Refugees, Geneva, March 1981).

[21] For the text of the Declaration see *Collection of International Instruments and Other Legal Texts Concerning Refugees and Displaced Persons* (UNHCR, Geneva, 1995), Vol. II, p. 116. More recently, in March 1997, 'steps have been taken to develop a forum for regional consultations on the problems of refugees and displaced persons in Central Asia, South West Asia and the Middle East . . . with the participation of 13 governments.' *Opening Statement by the United Nations High Commissioner for Refugees at the Forty-eighth Session of the Executive Committee of the High Commissioner's Programme*, p. 8.

[22] For the text of the Convention Relating to the Status of Stateless Persons, 1954, see *Collection of International Instruments and Other Legal Texts Concerning Refugees and Displaced Persons* (UNHCR, Geneva, 1995), Vol. I, p. 75.

[23] For the text of the agreement see ibid., p. 99.

In the League of Nations period refugees and stateless persons were not sharply differentiated, with both categories receiving assistance from international refugee organisations. However, at the time the 1951 Convention was drafted, France and the United States insisted that the problems of stateless persons were not only less urgent than those of the refugees but also gave rise to fewer social problems than in the case of refugees. The former Soviet Union, on the other hand, had tried to extend protection to stateless persons. In recent years, the problem of statelessness has arisen in several parts of the world, thus renewing interest in filling the gaps in the prevailing regime of international protection. **Reading VI.A** offers an introduction to some of the issues involved.

Are We All Refugees?

The final reading of Chapter 1 is included to encourage reflection on the 'striking similarities between the universal condition and the plight of refugees'. It is perhaps important to emphasise that Warner is not questioning the usefulness of the legal category of 'refugee' but merely pointing towards certain parallels between the refugee condition and the existential condition of humankind. **Reading VII.A** also calls for an imaginative rethinking of the idea of 'solutions' to the refugee problem, a matter which is the subject of Chapter 6. But readers should consider the criticism that Warner's thesis only connects with the existential condition of the affluent and the post-modern North rather than with the poor and predominantly pre-modern South.

* * *

I. EARLY DEFINITIONS

A. James C. Hathaway, *The Law of Refugee Status* (Butterworths, Toronto, 1991), pp. 2–6.

Analysis of the international refugee accords entered into between 1920 and 1950 reveals three distinct approaches to refugee definition. Each of these perspectives—juridical, social, and individualist—was dominant during a part of the initial decades of refugee law.

The Juridical Perspective

From 1920 until 1935, refugees were defined in largely juridical terms, which meant that they were treated as refugees because of their membership in a group of persons effectively deprived of the formal protection of the government of its state of origin. The purpose of refugee status conceived in juridical terms is to facilitate the international movement of persons who find themselves abroad and unable to resettle because no nation is prepared to assume responsibility for them.

These first refugee definitions were formulated in response to the international legal dilemma caused by the denial of state protection. The withdrawal of *de jure* protection by a state, whether by way of denaturalisation or the withholding of diplomatic facilities such as travel documents and consular representation, results in a malfunction in the international legal system. Because the then existing international law did not recognise individuals as subjects of international rights and obligations, the determination of responsibilities on the international plane fell to the sovereign state whose protection one enjoyed. When the bond of protection between citizen and state was severed, no international entity could be held accountable for the individual's actions. The result was that states were reluctant to admit to their territory individuals who were not the legal responsibility of another country. The refugee definitions adopted between 1920 and 1935 were designed to correct this breakdown in the international order, and accordingly embraced persons who wished to have freedom of international movement but found themselves in the anomalous situation of not enjoying the legal protection of any state.

The most fundamental form of *de jure* withdrawal of state protection is, of course, denaturalisation. It was the general policy of the League of Nations to extend protection to groups of persons whose nationality had been involuntarily withdrawn. As well, the League recognised that persons who could not obtain valid passports were entitled to international protection. Both of these groups received League of Nations identity certificates which contracting states agreed to recognise as the functional equivalent of passports.

The definitions of this era contained a criterion of ethnic or territorial origin, coupled with a stipulation that the applicant not enjoy *de jure* national protection. Only persons applying from outside their country of origin were eligible for refugee recognition. This is consistent with the notion of the refugee as an international anomaly: while the unprotected individual remained within the boundaries of her home state, there was no question of another country being confronted with a person outside the bounds of international accountability and, accordingly, no need to include her within the scope of League of Nations protection.

The Social Perspective

In contrast to the initial juridical focus, the refugee agreements adopted between 1935 and 1939 embodied a *social* approach to refugee definition. Refugees defined from the social perspective are the helpless casualties of broadly based social or political occurrences which separate them from their home society. Assistance in migration is afforded refugees not, as from the juridical perspective, with a view to correcting an anomaly in the international legal system, but rather in order to ensure the refugees' safety or well-being. The categories of persons eligible for international assistance encompassed groups adversely affected by a particular social or political event, not just those united by a common status vis-à-vis the international legal system.

The essence of this second definitional approach was to continue to assist persons without formal national legal protection, but to assist as well the victims of social and political events which resulted in a *de facto*, if not a *de jure*, loss of state protection. For the most part, these agreements sought to protect persons caught up in the upheaval and dislocation caused by the National Socialist regime in Germany. The substantive scope of this era's definitions was defined by an *en bloc* reference to general, situation-specific categories of persons affected by adverse social or political phenomena.

The Individualist Perspective

The third phase of international refugee protection, comprising the accords of the 1938–1950 era, was revolutionary in its rejection of group determination of refugee status. A refugee by individualist standards is a person in search of an escape from perceived injustice or fundamental incompatibility with her home state. She distrusts the authorities who have rendered continued residence in her country of origin either impossible or intolerable, and desires the opportunity to build a new life abroad. Refugee status viewed from this perspective is a means of facilitating international movement for those in search of personal freedom.

This individualist approach first affected the determination procedure: the decision as to whether or not a person was a refugee was no longer made strictly on the basis of political and social categories. Rather, the accords of the immediate post-war era prescribed an examination of the merits of each applicant's case. Moreover, the move to a more personal conception of refugeehood altered substantive notions. The essence of refugee status came to be discord between the individual refugee applicant's personal characteristics and convictions and the tenets of the political system in her country of origin.

The subjective concept of a refugee was not universally embraced by the international community. During debate in the United Nations in 1946, for example, the socialist states asserted the impropriety of including political dissidents among the ranks of refugees protected by international law. It was argued unsuccessfully that political emigres who had suffered no personal prejudice ought not be protected as refugees under the auspices of the international community as a whole, but should instead seek the assistance of those states sympathetic to their political views. The voting strength and influence of Western alliance, however, led to a movement away from a focus on group *de jure* or *de facto* disfranchisement, and toward a personalised evaluation of incompatibility between state of origin and refugee claimant in search of personal freedom and liberty. This initiative to define the refugee concept in a manner consistent with the ideology of the more powerful states set the stage for the development of contemporary international refugee law.

II. THE 1951 CONVENTION DEFINITION

1. The Political Context

A. James C. Hathaway, *The Law of Refugee Status*
(Butterworths, Toronto, 1991) pp. 6–10.

The primary standard of refugee status today is that derived from the 1951 *Convention relating to the Status of Refugees....*

The Convention was drafted between 1948 and 1951 by a combination of United Nations organs, *ad hoc* committees, and a conference of plenipotentiaries. The two main characteristics of the Convention definition are its strategic conceptualisation and its Eurocentric focus.

The strategic dimension of the definition comes from successful efforts of Western states to give priority in protection matters to persons whose flight was motivated by pro-Western political values. As anxious as the Soviets had been to exclude political emigres from the scope of the Convention for fear of exposing their weak flank, so the more numerous and more powerful Western states were preoccupied to maximise the international visibility of that migration. In the result, it was agreed to restrict the scope of protection in much the same way as had been done in the post-World War II refugee instruments: only persons who feared 'persecution' because of their civil or political status would fall within the international protection mandate. This apparently neutral formulation facilitated the condemnation of Soviet bloc politics through international law in two ways.

First, the persecution standard was a known quantity, having already been employed to embrace Soviet bloc dissidents in the immediate postwar years. It was understood that the concept of 'fear of persecution' was sufficiently open-ended to allow the West to continue to admit ideological dissidents to international protection.

Second, the precise formulation of the persecution standard meant that refugee law could not readily be turned to the political advantage of the Soviet bloc. The refugee definition was carefully phrased to include only persons who have been disfranchised by their state on the basis of race, religion, nationality, membership of a particular social group, or political opinion, matters in regard to which East-bloc practice has historically been problematic. Western vulnerability in the area of respect for human rights, in contrast, centres more on the guarantee of socio-economic human rights than on respect for civil and political rights. Unlike the victims of civil and political oppression, however, persons denied even such basic rights as food, health care, or education are excluded from the international refugee regime (unless that deprivation stems from civil or political status). By mandating protection for those whose (Western inspired) civil and political rights are jeopardised, without at the same time protecting persons whose (socialist inspired) socio-economic rights are at risk, the Convention adopted an incomplete and politically partisan human rights rationale.

In addition to their desire for the refugee definition to serve strategic political objectives, the majority of the states that drafted the Convention sought to create a rights regime conducive to the redistribution of the post-war refugee burden from European shoulders. The Europeans complained that they had been forced to cope with the bulk of the human displacement caused by the Second World War, and that the time had come for all members of the United Nations to contribute to the resettlement of both the remaining war refugees and the influx of refugees from the Soviet bloc. Refugees would be more inclined to move beyond Europe if there were guarantees that their traditional expectations in terms of rights and benefits would be respected abroad. The Convention, then, was designed to create secure conditions such as would facilitate the sharing of the European refugee burden.

Notwithstanding the vigorous objections of several delegates from developing countries faced with responsibility for their own refugee populations, the Eurocentric goal of the Western states was achieved by limiting the scope of mandatory international protection under the Convention to refugees whose flight was prompted by a pre-1951 event within Europe. While states might opt to extend protection to refugees from other parts of the world, the definition adopted was intended to distribute the European refugee burden without any binding obligation to reciprocate by way of the establishment of rights for, or the provision of assistance to, non-European refugees. It was not until more than fifteen years later that the *Protocol relating to the Status of Refugees* expanded the scope of the Convention definition to include refugees from all regions of the world.

2. Five Essential Elements

B. James C. Hathaway, *The Law of Refugee Status* (Butterworths, Toronto, 1991), pp. vi–vii.

The Convention refugee definition may be viewed as comprising five essential elements, each of which must be established before status is appropriately recognised....

The first essential definitional element, comprehending a range of contextual concerns, is referred to here as alienage. The Convention definition includes only persons who have left their country of nationality, or in the case of stateless persons, their country of former habitual residence....

Second, the refugee claimant must be *genuinely at risk*. It is not enough that she truly believe herself to be in jeopardy. Rather, there must be objective facts to provide a concrete foundation for the concern which induces her to seek protection in another state....

Third, the claimant's flight must be motivated by the prospect of 'persecution', that is, *risk of serious harm* against which the state of origin is *unwilling or unable to offer protection*....

Fourth, the risk faced by the refugee claimant must have some nexus to her race, religion, nationality, membership in a particular social group, or political opinion. The critical question is whether but for her *civil or political status* she could reasonably be said to be at risk of serious harm....

Fifth and finally, there must be a genuine need for and legitimate claim to protection.

3. Well-founded Fear

C. Handbook on Procedures and Criteria for Determining Refugee Status (UNHCR, Geneva, September 1979), paras 37, 38, 40–42.

37. The phrase 'well-founded fear of being persecuted' is the key phrase of the definition. It reflects the views of its authors as to the main elements of refugee character. It replaces the earlier method of defining refugees by categories (i.e., persons of a certain origin not enjoying the protection of their country) by the general concept of 'fear' for a relevant motive. Since fear is subjective, the definition involves a subjective element in the person applying for recognition as a refugee. Determination of refugee status will therefore primarily require an evaluation of the applicant's statements rather than a judgement on the situation prevailing in his country of region.

38. To the element of fear—a state of mind and a subjective condition—is added the qualification 'well-founded'. This implies that it is not only the frame of mind of the person concerned that determines his refugee status, but that this frame of mind must be supported by an objective situation. The term 'well-founded fear' therefore contains a subjective and an objective element, and in determining whether well-founded fear exists, both elements must be taken into consideration.

40. An evaluation of the subjective element is inseparable from an assessment of the personality of the applicant, since psychological reactions of different individuals may not be the same in identical conditions. One person may have strong political or religious convictions, the disregard of which would make his life intolerable; another may have no such strong convictions. One person may make an impulsive decision to escape; another may carefully plan his departure.

41. Due to the importance that the definition attaches to the subjective element, an assessment of credibility is indispensable where the case is not sufficiently clear from the facts on record. It will be necessary to take into account the personal and family background of the applicant, his membership of a particular racial, religious, national, social or political group, his own interpretation of his situation, and his personal experiences—in other words, everything that may serve to indicate that the predominant motive for his application is fear. Fear must be reasonable. Exaggerated fear, however, may be well-founded if, in all the circumstances of the case, such a state of mind can be regarded as justified.

42. As regards the objective element, it is necessary to evaluate the statements made by the applicant. The competent authorities that are called upon to determine refugee status are not required to pass judgement on conditions in the applicant's country of origin. The applicant's statements cannot, however, be considered in the abstract, and must be viewed in the context of the relevant background situation. A knowledge of conditions in the applicant's country of origin—while not a primary objective—is an important element in assessing the applicant's credibility. In general, the applicant's fear should be considered well-founded if he can establish, to a reasonable degree, that his continued stay in his country of origin has become intolerable to him for the reasons stated in the definition, or would for the same reasons be intolerable if he returned there.

D. James C. Hathaway, *The Law of Refugee Status* (Butterworths, Toronto, 1991), pp. 65, 74, 80.

The hallmark of a Convention refugee is the inability or unwillingness to return home due to a 'well-founded fear of being persecuted'. Not all involuntary migrants qualify as refugees in law: only those who face a genuine risk of persecution in their state of origin are entitled to the protections established by the Convention. . . .

It is generally asserted that 'well-founded fear' entails two requirements. The *first* criterion is that the refugee claimant perceive herself to stand in 'terror of persecution', her very personal response to the prospect of return to her home country must be an extreme form of anxiety that is neither feigned nor overstated, but is rather sincere and reasonable. *Second*, the subjective perception of risk must be consistent with available information on conditions in the state of origin, as only those persons whose fear is reasonable can be said to stand in need of international protection. This chapter argues that this two-pronged approach to the definition of 'well-founded fear' is neither historically defensible nor practically meaningful. Well-founded fear has nothing to do with the state of mind of the applicant for refugee status, except insofar as the claimant's testimony may provide some evidence of the state of affairs in her home country. The concept of well-founded fear is rather inherently objective, and was intended to restrict the scope of protection to persons who can demonstrate a present or prospective risk of persecution, irrespective of the extent or nature of mistreatment, if any, that they have suffered in the past....

The [...] decision of the British House of Lords in *Sivakumaran*[24] provides a thorough analysis of the meaning of the phrase 'well-founded fear', drawing richly on the drafting history and internal context of the Convention. Lord Keith refutes the notion that the appropriate test is anything other than objective:

> ... the general purpose of the convention is surely to afford protection and fair treatment to those for whom neither is available in their own country *and does not extend to the allaying of fears not objectively justified, however reasonable these fears may appear from the point of view of the individual in question*.... Fear of persecution, in the sense of the convention, is not to be assimilated to a fear of instant personal danger arising out of an immediately presented predicament.... *The question is what might happen if he were to return to the country of his nationality.* He fears that he might be persecuted there. Whether that might happen can only be determined by examining the actual state of affairs in that country [emphasis added].[25]

In a concurring judgement, Lord Goff states succinctly:

> ... the true object of the convention is not just to assuage fear, however reasonably and plausibly entertained, but to provide a safe haven for those unfortunate people whose fear of persecution is in reality well founded.[26]

... The appropriate starting point for an analysis of objective conditions within the refugee claimant's state of origin is an examination of that country's general human rights record. Because the insufficiency of state protection is the *sine qua non* for recognition as a refugee, persons who flee countries that are known to commit or acquiesce in persecutory

---

[24] *R v. Secretary of State for the Home Department*, ex parte Sivakumaran [1988], 1 All E.R. 193 (H.L.).

[25] Id., at 196–97, per Lord Keith of Kinkel.

[26] Id., at 202, per Lord Goff of Chieveley.

behaviour should benefit from a rebuttable presumption that they have a genuine need for protection.

E. Patricia Tuitt, *False Images—Law's Construction of the Refugee* (Pluto Press, London, 1996), pp. 80–83, 85–86.

The well-founded fear concept has evolved from a relatively simple inquiry within which the refugee's subjective feelings of 'terror' were prominent, to a much more complex and wide-ranging inquiry within which concepts such as the 'safe state' will increasingly be sole determinants of the issue of the well-founded fear.

It is argued here that the refugee claimant is becoming increasingly disenfranchised from the decision-making process relating to this legal inquiry. This chapter examines the evolution of the well-founded fear concept, and attempts to explore the processes which have led to the refugee's increasing invisibility in the determination process in favour of generalised concepts as founding the basis of refugeehood. It argues that the shift in emphasis is due to the inability of refugee-receiving structures to cope with the challenge to settled notions of reasonability which is presented in individual case inquiries, and examines how the response to these challenges has portrayed the refugee as being a fundamentally unreliable base point of inquiry such as to justify the shift to a generalised or group-based evaluation of a well-founded fear.

The Subjective Fear Approach

The House of Lords decision in *R v. Secretary of State ex parte Sivakumaran* (1988) was one of a number of landmark decisions within jurisdictions of Western states which heralded the present phrase in the evaluation of the well-founded fear criterion. This, it is argued, clearly favours evidence extraneous to the refugee. *Sivakumaran* established that whether a fear was well-founded was to be determined largely on the basis of the objective circumstances relevant to the refugee's claim, with particular emphasis on the conditions found to prevail within the country from which asylum is being sought. For all practical, if not academic, purposes it has put paid to the view which previously dominated academic discourse as well as judicial authority—that the definition of the refugee under Article 1.A (2) of the Geneva Convention was constructed of mainly subjective elements. According to this school of thought, the well-founded fear test was one which looked mainly to the refugee's emotional reaction to persecutory events. This is to be qualified only by the fact that the objective circumstances of the case must not contradict or render unlikely the refugee's subjective assessment of risk.

This approach pervaded judicial decisions in the United Kingdom. Indeed, right up until the House of Lords judgement in *Sivakumaran*, it was still being argued that 'the adjectival phrase "well-founded" qualifies but cannot transform, the subjective nature of the emotion....' The Court of Appeal in *Sivakumaran* favoured a test within which proof of the claimant's 'actual fear' of persecution could only be impeached if there was no good reason for that fear 'looking at the situation from the point of view of one of reasonable courage circumstanced as was the applicant for refugee status'.

... It appears to be widely accepted that the subjective test approach originated by attributing the popular (the term literal would be inappropriate) usage of the term 'fear' to its usage within the refugee definition. According to the popular interpretation, 'fear' connotes 'terror', fright or whatever term most conjures up the various shades of feeling that the 'person of ordinary fortitude' (per Sir John Donaldson in *Sivakumaran*) may feel when confronted with the real possibility that she might suffer persecution.

Hathaway rightly takes issue with this popular reading of the term 'fear' as being inappropriate to an interpretation of the Convention meaning of 'well-founded fear' which he argues is, in the context of the drafting history of the Convention, historically indefensible. He also argues that the interpretation is not 'practically meaningful' in the sense that few judgements bore evidence of a wholehearted slant towards the refugee's emotional reactions, which the statements of principle appear to suggest. While I would tend to agree that in the same way that objective is seldom objective in law, so too subjective is seldom subjective, the subjective fears approach did allow the refugee her highest point of visibility within the process of determination.

Undoubtedly there is substance in the criticisms levelled at the subjective fears approach. It is accepted that an overemphasis on the refugee's subjective fears would result in inequalities between the treatment accorded to refugees on the basis of their varying emotional strengths.

Lord Keith, giving the leading judgement in *Sivakumaran*, had this to say about the subjective fears approach: '... the fears of some, but not those of others would be allayed, and it might be by no means easy to decide what degree of courage a person of ordinary fortitude might be expected to display.'[27] Yet it must also be said that the recognition of the refugee as an individual within this aspect of the decision-making process redressed some of the inherent inequalities which the refugee faces within most determination structures.

In the United Kingdom the refugee is weak at every level of the process, from entry to eventual expulsion—in terms, for example, of their access to representation. These weaknesses, although woefully apparent even when the refugee was a principal focus of inquiry, are becoming

[27] Id., at p. 151.

increasingly so as the focus shifts from individual examination of the well-founded fear criterion to group determination based mainly upon an assessment of the country from which the refugee claims asylum or has arrived in the receiving state....

The status of the *Sivakumaran* decision is well-nigh unassailable as other countries have gone through a similar (sometimes greater) revolution of thought before arriving at the objective fear test. While an evaluation of the arguments for and against an objective or subjective assessment of a well-founded fear is necessary to an understanding of its present development stage, it is not here argued that either represents the ideal position. Given the important interest that the refugee seeks to preserve, the real challenge is to establish a test wherein she is given sufficient standing. Arguably both the subjective and objective tests fail in their emphasis, seeming as they appear little more than broad descriptions denoting the greater or lesser focus or role given to the refugee within such inquiries. The objective test ought to have promoted an approach to decision-making which assesses all the relevant evidence in a fair and balanced manner. The contrary appears to be the case ... the range of acceptable or cogent evidence in refugee inquiries of this kind is increasingly restrained, leading almost inevitably to an increasingly narrow identity of refugees in Europe.

The Application of the Objective Test

While an objective test would not per se result in the refugee's disenfranchisement within the determination process, it is argued here that this has been the practical effect of the test for two main reasons. First, in case-by-case individualistic inquiries into a well-founded fear, the concept of reasonableness, the basis upon which an objective evaluation of the refugee's circumstances is made, is tainted with local perceptions and thus often fails to be context-sensitive. In particular it is argued that parochial notions of reasonability are imported into decisions which are determined mainly or substantially upon the Tribunal's findings relating to the applicant's credibility, and where she seeks to found her claim partly or substantially on the basis of political activities engaged in within the host country, before or pending examination of her claim to refugee status.

Second, it is argued that determining authorities are increasingly abandoning individualistic case-by-case inquiry into the well-founded fear in favour of group determinations which focus primarily on the country from which asylum is sought. Within such inquiries the refugee has little or no visibility, first because she is unable effectively to challenge or contradict the evidence in most cases and second, where she seeks to challenge the evidence, refugee evidence is accorded low weight.

F. Costas Douzinas and Ronnie Warrington, 'A Well-founded Fear of Justice: Law and Ethics in Postmodernity', in Jerry Leonard, ed., *Legal Studies as Cultural Studies: A Reader in (Post)Modern Critical Theory* (State University of New York Press, New York, 1995), pp. 197–99, 204–9.

'Does he know his sentence?' 'No' said the officer. 'He doesn't know his own sentence?' 'No' the officer said again: he was still for a moment as if expecting the traveller to volunteer some reason for his question, then he said, 'There would be no sense in telling him. He experiences it on his own body.'

— Kafka, *In the Penal Colony*

Interpretation and Action

Legal judgements are both statements and deeds. They both interpret the law and act on the world. A conviction and sentence at the end of a criminal trial is the outcome of the judicial act of legal interpretation. But it is also the authorisation and beginning of a variety of violent acts. The defendant is taken away to a place of imprisonment or of execution, acts immediately related to, indeed flowing from, the judicial pronouncement. Again, as a result of civil judgements people lose their homes, their children, their property, or they may be sent to a place of persecution and torture....

Legal interpretations and judgements cannot be understood independently of this inescapable imbrication with—often violent—action. In this sense, legal interpretation is a practical activity other-oriented and designed to lead to effective threats and—often violent—deeds. This violence is evident at each level of the judicial act. The architecture of the courtroom and the choreography of the trial process converge to restrain and physically subdue the body of the defendant. From the latter's perspective, the common but fragile facade of civility of the legal process expresses a recognition 'of the overwhelming array of violence ranged against him and of the helplessness of resistance or outcry'.[28] But for the judge too, legal interpretation is never free of the need to maintain links with the effective official behaviour that will enforce the statement of the law. Indeed the expression 'the law is enforced' recognises that force and its application lies at the heart of the judicial act. Legal sentences are both propositions of law and acts of sentencing. Judges, whatever else they do, deal in fear and pain and death. If this is the case, any aspiration to coherent and shared legal meaning will flounder on the inescapable and

---

[28] Cover, 'Violence and the Word', *Yale Law Journal* (Vol. 95, 1986), p. 1607.

tragic line that distinguishes those who mete out violence from those who receive it.

This necessary distinction and linkage between the constative and performative aspects of legal judgements has passed without much comment in jurisprudence. Hermeneutically orientated legal theory assumes that the rightness, fairness or justice of the interpretative enterprise will bestow its blessing on the active component of the judgement and justify its violence. Theory and practice, word and deed are seen as belonging to the same field, as successive points on an unproblematic continuum. A just interpretation and statement of the law is accepted without more as just action. But is this assumption justified? Does the correct interpretation of the law—if it exists—and the 'right answer' to a legal problem—if we can find it—lead to more and just praxis? Is the law because it is just or is the law just because it is the law?

To do justice to such questions we turn to some paradigmatic tests which explicitly or impliedly address ethics and the problem of justice. Our reference will be [to] ... cases from the canon of postmodern philosophy.... The stakes behind the confrontation are high. Can there be a postmodern ethics that while accepting the pragmatic, epistemological and ontological critiques of modern moral philosophy, is not condemned to cynicism or passivity?....

The Refugee Cases

Our first two cases are very similar.[29] They involved a number of Tamils seeking asylum in Britain. The refugees were fleeing Sri Lanka in 1987 as a result of an offensive by the majority Sinhalese government and the Indian army against the guerilla Tamil forces in the north of the island. According to the court, parts of the country 'have been in a serious state of civil disorder, amounting at times to civil war. The authorities have taken steps [which] have naturally resulted in painful and distressing experiences for many persons innocently caught up in the troubles.... [The] Tamils are the people who have suffered most.'[30]

In both cases the applicants were refused asylum by the immigration authorities and challenged the refusal in proceedings for judicial review. In the first case the material question was under what circumstances is someone a refugee entitled to asylum; in the second, what can one do to challenge the decision that refused him/her refugee status.

[29] *R v. Secretary of State for the Home Department*, ex parte Sivakumaran and conjoined appeals (see footnote 24 earlier); *Bugdaycay v. Secretary of State for the Home Department* and related appeals [1987], 1 All E.R. 940 (H.L.).

[30] *R v. Secretary of State for the Home Department*, ex parte Sivakumaran and conjoined appeals (see footnote 24 earlier), p. 198.

... In the first case, the sole point for consideration before the House of Lords was the proper basis for the determination of a 'well-founded fear of persecution'. The Court of Appeal had held that the test for a 'well-founded fear' was qualifiedly subjective. It would be satisfied by showing (*a*) actual fear and (*b*) good reason for this fear, looking at the situation from the point of view of one of reasonable courage. Unless an applicant's fear could be dismissed as 'paranoid', 'fear is clearly an entirely subjective state and should be judged accordingly'.[31]

The House of Lords reversed, reinstated the immigration decisions and as a result the refugees were sent back to Sri Lanka. The Court held that a genuine fear of persecution could not suffice. The fears should have an 'objective basis' which could be 'objectively determined'.[32] Such fears to be justified should be based on 'true', 'objective facts' that could be ascertained by an objective observer like the Home Secretary or the immigration officers and not solely 'on the basis of the facts known to the applicant or believed by him to be true'.[33] Once that was accepted the Secretary of State was entitled to have regard to facts 'unknown to the applicant' in order to assess whether 'subjective fear was objectively justified'. The Secretary indeed had taken into account such 'unknown facts', reports of the refugee unit of this department compiled from press articles, 'journals and Amnesty International publications, and also information supplied to him by the Foreign Office and as a result of recent visits to Sri Lanka by ministers'.[34] He had concluded that the army activities, 'that amounted to civil war' and 'occurred principally in areas inhabited by Tamils... do not constitute evidence of persecution of Tamils as such[35]... nor of any groups of Tamils'. As no 'real risk' of persecution of the group in general existed, nor a risk 'on the balance of possibilities', the Secretary was justified to conclude that none of the applicants had been or was likely to be subjected to persecution.

Lord Goff rounded off by assuring the UN High Commissioner for Refugees who had intervened in favour of the applicants that he need have 'no well-founded fear that, in this country, the authorities will feel in any way inhibited from carrying out the UK's obligations under the convention by reason of their having to make objective assessments of conditions prevailing in other countries overseas.'[36] The UK would continue to apply the law and give sanctuary to refugees. The objective test was necessary to ensure that this country—regarded as a suitable haven by

[31] Ibid., p. 195.
[32] Ibid., p. 196.
[33] Ibid., p. 200.
[34] Ibid., p. 198.
[35] Ibid., p. 199.
[36] Ibid., p. 203.

many applicants for refugee status—would not be 'flooded' with persons who objectively experienced no fear of persecution.[37]

The second case involved four applicants who were refused asylum by the immigration authorities and wanted to challenge that decision. They claimed that they met the criteria for asylum and that they should not be removed to a country where they feared persecution unless they had exercised a right of appeal against the initial refusal. Now, under the Immigration Act 1971, illegal entrants and those refused leave at a port of entry have a right of appeal against refusal to the immigration adjudicator and further to the Immigration Appeals Tribunal, but only after they have left the country. With the beginning of the troubles in Sri Lanka, a visa requirement was imposed upon all those arriving from that country. Both those without visa and those refused refugee status at a port of entry should leave the country and appeal against the refusal from abroad. One suspects that people fleeing persecution will experience some difficulty in acquiring genuine travel documents and visas.

The appellants had been designated illegal entrants because they had obtained temporary leave to enter on various grounds and later applied for refugee status. They claimed that under the UN Handbook on Refugee Determination Procedures, they had a right to appeal against refusal and that their removal—a precondition for appealing under the Act— would frustrate that right. The House of Lords ruled first that the Handbook had 'no binding force in either municipal or international law'.[38] It went on to endorse the applicants' designation as illegal entrants. At the time of arrival they had misrepresented to the immigration authorities the 'true nature and purpose of their visit... by making statements— which they knew to be false or did not believe to be true'.[39] Such being the case, to allow the applicants to stay, while all visitors denied leave to enter could appeal after leaving 'would be plainly untenable'.[40] It was prohibited by law, and it would discriminate in favour of illegal entrants.

Criteria of (In)Justice (I): Fear and Truth

> Before the Law stands a doorkeeper. To this doorkeeper there comes a man from the country who begs admittance to the Law. But the doorkeeper says that he cannot admit the man at the moment. The man, on reflection, asks if he will be allowed, then, to enter later. 'It is possible,' answers the doorkeeper, 'but not at this moment'.
>
> Kafka, *Before the Law*

[37] Ibid., p. 201.
[38] *Bugdaycay v. Secretary of State for the Home Department* and related appeals (see footnote 29 earlier), p. 946.
[39] Ibid., p. 947.
[40] Ibid.

The Tamils' cases are (legal) judgements on (administrative) judgements. Are the judgements just? Can we judge their justice? Can we ever be just when facing the refugee? Justice requires that we must read the judgements carefully and justly, do justice to their word.

A foreigner comes along to the house of the law. He says: 'I am in fear.' He asks to be admitted and to be given sanctuary. The immigration officer/judge demands: 'Justify your fear, give reasons for it.' He answers: 'My father has been killed by the policy of my country. My two sisters have been harassed. One of my cousins was arrested, taken to a barracks where he died of injuries. Before dying he gave particulars of my friends and relatives including myself. My other cousin has since been arrested and killed.' 'Ah', says the judge, 'you must accept that fear is valid when it is based on the facts. And facts being what they are I can find them out as well as you can. Indeed better. I know the true facts from my newspapers and from reports by my agents and informers on "the current political, social and law and order position at present pertaining"[41] in your country. Let us have a look at the facts. People are being killed in your part of the world, some Tamils in particular. But then people are always killed in your part of the world. On the basis of the true facts as I know them I can find no systematic persecution of Tamils or of any group amongst you. There is no objective basis for your fear as you are under no "real and substantial risk". I cannot admit you at the moment.'

In this encounter with the refugee the role of the judge has gradually changed. He started as the recipient of the refugee's request but in asking for grounds and reasons and in stating the facts he now claims to be on the same plane as the refugee, able to understand his predicament. In other words, the past pain of the refugee and his fear of future torture have been translated into an interpretable, understandable reality that like all reality is potentially shareable by judge and victim. But if interpretation is the possibility of constructing interpersonal realities in language, pain, death and their fear bring interpretations to an end.

> For the person in pain [or fear of pain], so incontestably and unnegotiably present is it that 'having pain [or fear of pain]' may come to be thought as the most vibrant example of what it is 'to have certainty' while for the other person it is so elusive that hearing about pain [or its fear] may exist as the primary model of what it is to 'have doubt'. Thus pain [and fear of pain] comes unshareably into our midst as at once that which cannot be denied and that which cannot be confirmed. Whatever pain [and its fear] achieves, it achieves through its unshareability, and it ensures this unshareability in part though its resistance to language.[42]

[41] Ibid., p. 949.
[42] Scarry, *The Body in Pain* (see footnote 6), p. 4.

The claim that fear and pain can be rationalised through the shared understanding of their cause puts the victim in a double bind. Either he is in fear or he is not. If he is, he should be able to give facts and reasons for it which, as they belong to the genre of truth, should match up to the assessment of the judge. If they do not, the refugee is lying. If, on the other hand, he cannot give 'objective' justifications for his fear the refugee is again lying. Similarly, when the refugee is inarticulate and cannot explain the 'objective basis' of his fear, he is not in fear. But when he can do so, the immigration officer 'formed the view that the Applicant, who appeared in good health, was alert and confident at interview, was moving away from Uganda because a better life awaited him somewhere else and that this was not a genuine application for asylum.'[43]

In the idiom of cognition, fear is either reasonable and can be understood by the judge or is unreasonable and therefore non-existent. In the first instance it is the excess of knowledge and reason on the part of the judge that disqualifies the fear, in the second it is the excess of fear that disqualifies itself. But this translation of fear into knowledge and of the style into reasons and causes assumes that the judge can occupy the place of the refugee and share his pain. Fear, pain and death, however, are radically singular; they resist and at the limit destroy language and its ability to construct shared worlds.

Lyotard has called this violent double bind an ethical tort (differend); it is an extreme form of injustice in which the injury suffered by the victim is accompanied by a deprivation of the means to prove it.

> This is the case if the victim is deprived of life, or of all liberties, or of the freedom to make his or her ideas or opinions public, or simply of the right to testify to the damage, or even more simply if the testifying phrase is itself deprived of authority.... Should the victim seek to bypass this impossibility and testify anyway to the wrong done to her, she comes up against the following argumentation, either the damage you complain about never took place, and your testimony is false; or else they took place, and since you are able to testify to them, it is not an ethical tort that has been done to you.[44]

When an ethical tort has been committed the conflict between the parties cannot be decided equitably because no rule of judgement exists that could be applied to both arguments. The genre judged and the outcome will be necessarily unjust. The violence of injustice begins when the judge and the judged do not share a language or idiom. It continues when all

---

[43] *Bugdaycay v. Secretary of State* (see footnote 29 earlier), p. 949.

[44] Jean Francois Lyotard, *The Differend: Phrases in Dispute* (Manchester University Press, Manchester, 1978), p. 5.

traces òf particularity and otherness are reduced to a register of sameness and cognition mastered by the judge. Indeed all legal interpretation and judgement presuppose that the Other, the victim of the language's injustice, is capable of language in general, is man as a speaking animal, in the sense that we, men give to the word language. And as Derrida reminds us, 'there was a time not long ago and not yet over, in which "we, men" meant "we adult" white male Europeans, carnivorous and capable of sacrifice.'[45] But our communities have long lost any aspirations to a common idiom. We should not forget, therefore, that justice may turn out to be impossible, just a shibboleth.

4. Persecution

G. *Handbook on Procedures and Criteria for Determining Refugee Status* (UNHCR, Geneva, September 1979), paras 51, 52.

51. There is no universally accepted definition of 'persecution', and various attempts to formulate such a definition have met with little success. From Article 33 of the 1951 Convention, it may be inferred that a threat to life or freedom on account of race, religion, nationality, political opinion or membership of a particular social group is always persecution. Other serious violations of human rights—for the same reasons—would also constitute persecution.

52. Whether other prejudicial actions or threats would amount to persecution will depend on the circumstances of each case, including the subjective element.... The subjective character of fear of persecution requires an evaluation of the opinions and feelings of the person concerned. It is also in the light of such opinions and feelings that any actual or anticipated measures against him must necessarily be viewed. Due to variations in the psychological make-up of individuals and in the circumstances of each case, interpretations of what amounts to persecution are bound to vary.

H. T. Alexander Aleinikoff, 'The Meaning of "Persecution" in U. S. Asylum Law', in Howard Adelman, ed., *Refugee Policy: Canada and the United States* (York Lanes Press, Toronto, 1991), pp. 296–98.

Rethinking 'Persecution'

Reading through the BIA's (US Board of Immigration Appeals) asylum cases, one is struck by the Board's focus on whether the persecution likely

---

[45] Jacques Derrida, 'Force of Law: The Mystical Foundation of Authority', *Cardozo Law Review* (Vol. 11, 1990), p. 951.

to be suffered by the applicant is based on one of the five grounds specified in the definition of refugee. To some degree this is understandable;
after all, the definition does appear to single out particular kinds of persecution as giving rise to claims for asylum. An approach to the statute
that would grant asylum to anyone with a well-founded fear of persecution, with no regard to the source of the persecution, could expand statutory coverage considerably.

Yet it seems peculiar for adjudicators to adopt narrow and technical
readings of the specified grounds for persecution once an applicant has
demonstrated the likelihood, in fact, of persecution if returned home. It
is as if the Board had reconstructed the original intention of the drafters
of the 1951 Convention (and, by implication, the Congress that enacted
the 1980 Refugee Act) in the following manner: The Convention drafters
faced a post-World War II Europe overflowing with displaced persons
who feared returning home based on dozens of different grounds. From
all the possible grounds for fear, the drafters selected just five: race, religion, nationality, political opinion, and membership in a social group....
Thus, to be true to the Convention (and Congressional intent to adopt
the Convention's definition), the Board must ensure that applicants come
within one of the preferred categories. Other forms of persecution may
be unfortunate, but they are beyond the purview of the relevant legal
texts.

In fact, this is not the proper story to tell about the drafting of the Convention. A review of the *travaux preparatoires* does indeed disclose lengthy
debates about the definition of refugee; perhaps no other topic received
as much consideration. The discussions, however, did not focus on the
kinds of persecution that ought to give rise to refugee status. Rather, they
dealt with the geographical and temporal limitations in the definition.
Some delegates sought to limit the Convention to events occurring in
Europe prior to 1951, out of concern for the willingness of states to sign
on to a document that would otherwise impose unpredictable obligations
in the future; other delegates thought that the definition should be
broader in order to provide protection to future refugee flows; but there
is virtually no discussion of the kinds of persecution that would qualify an
individual for refugee status.

My best reading of the *travaux* is that the Convention was written with
the intent of protecting all persons (and groups) then existing in Europe
who had been or were likely to be the victims of persecution. No forms of
persecution were intentionally excluded (although various other exclusions were written into the Convention).

This non-exclusionary intent is clearly evidenced by the manner in
which the category of 'membership in a particular social group' came into
the Convention. For most of the deliberations, the definition of refugee
was limited to four categories (political opinion, race, religion, and

nationality). Late in the discussions, the Conference of Plenipotentiaries accepted the proposal of the Swedish delegation that 'membership in a particular social group' be added to the definition 'apparently with no other motive than "to stop a possible gap" in the coverage afforded by the other, more specific categories.'[46] The proposal was adopted without discussion or dissent.[47] In short, the history of the Convention provides no support for a narrow reading of the grounds of persecution. Rather, it displays an intent to write a definition of refugee sufficiently broad to cover then existing victims of persecution. Beginning this way—that is, with a concern for the victims of likely persecution—focuses attention first on the meaning of persecution.

Courts and commentators tend to see the persecution issue primarily in terms of the level of harm imposed on an individual. The UNHCR Handbook on Procedures and Criteria for Determining Refugee Status is typical. In its brief discussion, it notes that

> [t]here is no universally accepted definition of 'persecution', and various attempts to formulate such a definition have met with little success. From Article 33 of the 1951 Convention, it may be inferred that a threat to life or freedom on account of race, religion, nationality, political opinion or membership in a particular social group is always persecution. Other serious violations of human rights—for the same reasons—would also constitute persecution.

Two considerations are at work in this paragraph: (1) the harm imposed must be of a serious nature; and (2) to qualify as persecution within the terms of the Convention, the harm must be imposed for one of the designated reasons. The first point is sensible enough; surely neither international law nor the dramatic relief provided by US asylum law need concern itself with minor inconveniences inflicted upon individuals, regardless of the motive of the inflicter.

The second point, however, requires further reflection. Why is the definition of persecution necessarily linked to the five specified grounds? My sense is that this gets at something other than simply the level of harm; call it a 'qualitative' or 'normative' aspect of the definition of persecution. That is, persecution connotes unacceptable, unjustified, abhorrent infliction of harm, not simply a particular degree of harm. To see this, compare two legal cases: that of an individual sentenced to life imprisonment for having committed murder and that of a person sentenced to ten years in prison for having circulated a pamphlet opposing the government. The first case is unlikely to be seen as persecution; the second might well be.

---

[46] Aristide Zolberg et al., *Escape from Violence* (Oxford University Press, Oxford, 1989), p. 25, quoting Grahl-Madsen.

[47] Conference of Plenipotentiaries, Summary Records: UN Doc.A Conf.2/SR.23, p. 8.

The use by the Handbook of the five grounds in its explication of persecution, then, signals the unjustifiable, intolerable aspect of the infliction of harm. One's race or religion cannot provide an acceptable reason for the imposition of serious injury. But while one can understand how the existence of one of the five grounds might signal the qualitative aspect of the definition of persecution, it is not at all clear that persecution ought to be so limited—or, more importantly, that an applicant, to establish persecution, must be able to establish conclusively that one of the five grounds is at work. Persecution might well be given a 'free-standing' meaning that requires judgements about both the degree of and justifications for the harm, but not one that necessarily invokes the five grounds as the test of the qualitative aspect.

No black-letter guidelines could reasonably be provided for the qualitative aspect of the definition of persecution. . . .

I. James C. Hathaway, *The Law of Refugee Status* (Butterworths, Toronto, 1991), pp. 105, 107–8.

. . . persecution may be defined as the sustained or systemic violation of basic human rights demonstrative of a failure of state protection. A well-founded fear of persecution exists when one reasonably anticipates that remaining in the country may result in a form of serious harm which government cannot or will not prevent, including either 'specific hostile acts or. . . an accumulation of adverse circumstances such as discrimination existing in an atmosphere of insecurity and fear.'

. . . The use of a human rights standard for determining the existence of persecution is not accepted by all. The most conservative position, argued by Karl Zink, is that only a narrow subset of human rights violations can constitute persecution, namely, deprivation of life or physical freedom. This position is often inappropriately tied to a narrow and literal reading of Article 33 of the Convention, which prohibits the return of a refugee to 'the frontiers of territories where his life or freedom would be threatened. . .'. Atle Grahl-Madsen adopts only a slightly more liberal view, arguing without explanation that the restriction or denial of such rights as freedom of thought, conscience and religion, freedom of opinion and expression, and freedom of peaceful assembly and association are outside the ambit of persecution.[48]

The dominant view, however, is that refugee law ought to concern itself with actions which deny human dignity in any key way, and that the sustained or systemic denial of core human rights is the appropriate standard.[49]

[48] Grahl-Madsen, *The Status of Refugees in International Law* (see footnote 17 earlier), p. 195.

[49] G. Coles, 'The Human Rights Approach to the Solution of the Refugee Problem: A Theoretical and Practical Enquiry', in A. Nash, ed., *Human Rights and the Protection of*

5. Nexus with Civil or Political Status

J. *Handbook on Procedures and Criteria for Determining Refugee Status* (UNHCR, Geneva, September 1979), paras 68–86.

Race

68. Race, in the present connexion, has to be understood in its widest sense to include all kinds of ethnic groups that are referred to as 'races' in common usage. Frequently it will also entail membership of a specific social group of common descent forming a minority within a larger population. Discrimination for reasons of race has found world-wide condemnation as one of the most striking violations of human rights. Racial discrimination, therefore, represents an important element in determining the existence of persecution.

69. Discrimination on racial grounds will frequently amount to persecution in the sense of the 1951 Convention. This will be the case if, as a result of racial discriminations, a person's human dignity is affected to such an extent as to be incompatible with the most elementary and inalienable human rights, or where the disregard of racial barriers is subject to serious consequences.

70. The mere fact of belonging to a certain racial group will normally not be enough to substantiate a claim to refugee status. There may, however, be situations where, due to particular circumstances affecting the group, such membership will in itself be sufficient ground to fear persecution.

Religion

71. The Universal Declaration of Human Rights and the Human Rights Covenant proclaim the right to freedom of thought, conscience and religion, which right includes the freedom of a person to change his religion and his freedom to manifest in public or private, in teaching, practice, worship and observance.

72. Persecution for 'reasons of religion' may assume various forms, e.g. prohibition of membership of a religious community, of worship in

---

Refugees under International Law (Canadian Human Rights Foundation, Montreal, 1988), p. 196; accord, e.g., J. Vernant, *The Refugee in the Post-war World* (Allen and Unwin, London, 1953), p. 8; G. Melander, *Eligibility Procedures in West European States* p. 7; Goodwin-Gill, *The Refugee in International Law* (Clarendon Press, Oxford, 1983), p. 38; A. Ghoshal and T. Crowley, 'Refugees and Immigrants: A Human Rights Dilemma', *Human Rights Quarterly* (Vol. 5, 1983), p. 329.

For a discussion of what rights are to be considered basic and inalienable see Hathaway, *The Law of Refugee Status* (see footnote 5), pp. 108–12.

private or in public, of religious instruction, or serious measures of discrimination imposed on persons because they practice their religion or belong to a particular religious community.

73. Mere membership of a particular religious community will normally not be enough to substantiate a claim to refugees status. There may, however, be special circumstances where mere membership can be a sufficient ground.

Nationality

74. The term 'nationality' in this context is not to be understood only as 'citizenship'. It refers also to membership of an ethnic or linguistic group and may occasionally overlap with the term 'race'. Persecution for reasons of nationality may consist of adverse attitudes and measures directed against a national (ethnic, linguistic) minority and in certain circumstances the fact of belonging to such a minority may in itself give rise to well-founded fear of persecution.

75. The co-existence within the boundaries of a State of two or more national (ethnic, linguistic) groups may create situations of conflict and also situations of persecution or danger of persecution. It may not always be easy to distinguish between persecution for reasons of nationality and persecution for reasons of political opinion when a conflict between national groups is combined with political movements identified with a specific 'nationality'.

76. Whereas in most cases persecution for reason of nationality is feared by persons belonging to a national minority, there have been many cases in various continents where a person belonging to a majority group may fear persecution by a dominant minority.

Membership of a Particular Social Group

77. A 'particular social group' normally comprises 'persons of similar background, habits or social status'. A claim to fear of persecution under this heading may frequently overlap with a claim to fear of persecution on other grounds, i.e. race, religion or nationality.

78. Membership of such a particular social group may be at the root of persecution because there is no confidence in the group's loyalty to the Government or because the political outlook, antecedents or economic activity of its members, or the very existence of the social group as such, is held to be an obstacle to the Government's policies.

79. Mere membership of a particular social group will not normally be enough to substantiate a claim to refugee status. There may, however, be special circumstances where mere membership can be a sufficient ground to fear persecution.

Political Opinion

80. Holding political opinions different from those of the Government is not in itself a ground for claiming refugee status, and an applicant must show that he has a fear of persecution for holding such opinions. This pre-supposes that the applicant holds opinions not tolerated by the authorities, which are critical of their policies or methods. It also presupposes that such opinions have come to the notice of the authorities or are attributed by them to the applicant. The political opinions of a teacher or writer may be more manifest than those of a person in a less exposed position. The relative importance or tenacity of the applicant's opinions—in so far as this can be established from all the circumstance of the case—will also be relevant.

81. While the definition speaks of persecution 'for reasons of political opinion' it may not always be possible to establish a causal link between the opinion expressed and the related measures suffered or feared by the applicant. Such measures have only rarely been based expressly on 'opinion'. More frequently, such measures take the form of sanctions for alleged criminal acts against the ruling power. It will, therefore, be necessary to establish the applicant's political opinion, which is at the root of his behaviour, and the fact that it has led or may lead to the persecution that he claims to fear.

82. As indicated above, persecution 'for reasons of political opinion' implies that an applicant holds an opinion that either has been expressed or has come to the attention of the authorities. There may, however, also be situations in which the applicant has not given any expression to his opinions. Due to the strength of his convictions, however, it may be reasonable to assume that his opinions will sooner or later find expression and that the applicant will, as a result, come into conflict with the authorities. Where this can reasonably be assumed, the applicant can be considered to have fear of persecution for reasons of political opinion.

83. An applicant claiming fear of persecution because of political opinion need not show that the authorities of his country of origin knew of his opinions before he left the country. He may have concealed his political opinion and never have suffered any discrimination or persecution. However, the mere fact of refusing to avail himself of the protection of his Government, or a refusal to return, may disclose the applicant's true state of mind and give rise to fear of persecution. In such circumstances the test of well-founded fear would be based on an assessment of the consequences that an applicant having certain political dispositions would have to face if he returned. This applies particularly to the so-called refugee 'sur place'.

84. Where a person is subject to prosecution or punishment for a political offence, a distinction may have to be drawn according to whether the prosecution is for political opinion or for politically-motivated acts. If the prosecution pertains to a punishable act committed out of political motives, and if the anticipated punishment is in conformity with the general law of the country concerned, fear of such prosecution will not in itself make the applicant a refugee.

85. Whether a political offender can also be considered a refugee will depend upon various other factors. Prosecution for an offence may, depending upon the circumstances, be a pretext for punishing the offender for his political opinions or the expression thereof. Again, there may be reason to believe that a political offender would be exposed to excessive or arbitrary punishment for the alleged offence. Such excessive or arbitrary punishment will amount to persecution.

86. In determining whether a political offender can be considered a refugee, regard should also be had to the following elements: personality of the applicant, his political opinion, the motive behind the act, the nature of the act committed, the nature of the prosecution and its motives; finally, also, the nature of the law on which the prosecution is based. These elements may go to show that the person concerned has a fear of persecution and not merely a fear of prosecution and punishment— within the law—for an act committed by him.

6. Social Group: Gender

K. Jacqueline Greatbatch, 'The Gender Difference: Feminist Critiques of Refugee Discourse', *International Journal of Refugee Law* (Vol. 1, No. 4, 1989), pp. 518–26.

Feminist Perspectives on the Refugee Definition

The Geneva Convention definition of refugee has recently come under fire from feminists for its 'neglect of gender as a critical consideration'[50] in refugee determination. By portraying as universal that which is in fact a male paradigm, it is argued, women refugees face rejection of their claims because their experiences of persecution go unrecognised. Doreen Indra cites the omission of 'gender' from the enumerated grounds of persecution as an illustration of the 'the depth of gender delegitimation in refugee contexts'.

The absence of gender as an enumerated basis for fear of persecution in the Convention definition is an omission which ideally requires amelioration. However, feminist complaints go far beyond the language of the definition, to the root of what gender-based claims to persecution would look like, were it possible to make them.

---

[50] D. Indra, 'Gender: A Key Dimension of the Refugee Experience', *Refuge* (Vol. 6, February 1987).

Indra and others[51] call for a definition of persecution which acknowledges the feminist theory of social bifurcation: that society is divided into public and private spheres of activity; that the public sphere is male-dominated and women are relegated to the private sphere. Radical feminist theorists such as Catherine MacKinnon[52] and Margaret Thornton[53] propounded a distinct 'women's experience' of the private sphere which, it is claimed, is the site of gender oppression. Law, history and epistemology are dismissed as 'phallocentrism masquerading as universalism'. The experience of women's oppression is viewed as trans-historical and trans-cultural. Objectivity is rejected as a method of enquiry and theory is derived instead from 'women's experiences'.

This theory of women's oppression is reflected in the views of feminist critics of the refugee convention, as exemplified by Indra's thesis that women's experiences of persecution are ignored because,

> the key criteria for being a refugee are drawn primarily from the realm of public sphere activities dominated by men. With regard to private sphere activities where women's presence is more strongly felt, there is primarily silence—silence compounded by an unconscious calculus that assigns the critical quality 'political' to many public activities but few private ones. Thus, state oppression of a religious minority is political, while gender oppression at home is not.

In Indra's view, the addition of 'gender' as a basis upon which to found a claim to refugee status would do little to improve the position of refugee women without a redefinition of 'persecution' to give credibility to women's private-sphere experiences. Marika Meijer continues the critique when she posits the existence of a form of resistance to oppression unique to women, and unrecognised in refugee discourse:

> It should be realised that the resistance of women against their oppressed state is often not recognised and therefore is difficult to prove. Women's resistance is as a rule not organised. The position to which women are delegated (*sic*) does not give them the opportunity to organise.

This analysis founders on its ahistoric, acultural approach to women's oppression, in addition to its inattention to key aspects of the Convention

[51] See, for example, L. Van Willigen, 'Women Refugees and Sexual Violence', and M. Meijer, 'Oppression of Women and Refugee Status', discussion papers presented at a seminar on refugee women at Soesterberg, The Netherlands, 22–24 May 1985.

[52] C.A. MacKinnon, 'Feminism, Marxism; Method and the State: Toward Feminist Jurisprudence', *Signs* (Vol. 8, Summer 1983), p. 635.

[53] M. Thornton, 'Feminist Jurisprudence: Illusion or Reality', *Australian Journal of Law and Society* (Vol. 3, 1986), pp. 5–29.

definition and its overarching limitations. The bifurcated version of society itself ignores the realm of women's lives outside domesticity, and creates a rhetorical and theoretical wall between domestic and social culture. It roots women's oppression in sexuality and private life, thereby disregarding oppression experienced in non-domestic circumstances, and the interconnections of the public and private spheres.

In its call for a shift in emphasis in defining what makes a refugee, this analysis does not address the crucial question of a refugee's relationship to her State. It ignores shortcomings of the Convention definition not exclusively predicated on gender, because it has no room to acknowledge that women's experiences of oppression may sometimes overlap with those of men. This note reconsiders feminist critiques of the Convention's definition and its application. Relying on case studies of women in post-revolutionary Iran and under the Pinochet regime in Chile, it proposes an alternative feminist critique which takes account of historical and cultural context, and places the question of gender within a broader analysis of the limitations of the refugee definition.

Women in Post-revolutionary Iran

> The position of women within the Islamic Republic of Iran is a surprising one in the sense that it is not the position typically accorded individuals who have just helped to bring about a revolutionary change in government . . . . Implicit in this objective is the understanding that such change is progressive in nature.[54]

As suggested by Zolan and other Iranian feminists, there was widespread support among women for the Islamic revolution, and anti-feminist fundamentalist policies implemented by the Khomeini regime came as something of a shock to many of the middle-class. Economic expansion under the Shah had provided new educational and employment opportunities, and progressive family legislation which benefitted women. Codification of Islamic customary law, resulting from a resurgence of fundamentalism, removed many of those gains. The Iranian Constitution reflects the fundamentalist notion that woman's role is at the centre of the family. Family legislation which reformed customary marriage practices including polygamy, child marriage and unequal rights in divorce and child custody was repealed. Women were removed from participation in large segments of the workforce, and social services, such as day care, were cut back.

Symbolic to the Iranian revolution was the donning of the chador by women. A practice which was adopted before the overthrow of the Shah,

---

[54] A.S. Zolan, 'The Effect of Islamicization on the Legal and Social Status of Women in Iran', *Boston College Third World Law Journal* (Vol. 7, 1987), p. 183.

its significance goes beyond any notions of female sexuality. Refusal to wear the chador is viewed as an expression of political dissent, and may result in harsh punishment, both physical and economic. Segregated education and the restriction of women's entry into certain fields of higher education were reintroduced. Women were denied the right to practice law and fields of medicine not viewed as pertaining specifically to women.

However, women retain the right to vote and do participate in public life. Opponents of the fundamentalist regime, such as Afshar, concede that there is substantial support for the government among poor women, who have seen economic benefits from the revolution.

Women's resistance in the recent history of Iran has taken both unique and familiar forms, which are inextricably tied to the historical and cultural context. The position of women against the backdrop of a fundamentalist revolution, as the case of Iran shows, will inevitably be coloured by the precepts upon which the revolution itself is founded. Similarly, the forms of resistance to oppression which arise out of that revolution will be coloured by it. In Iran, for instance, the chador has taken on ideological proportions.

As the chador symbolises Islamic nationalism in the eyes of the Iranian state, so it has also become a symbol of oppression for women who oppose the regime. When the first edicts regarding female dress and appearance were made, women participated in public demonstrations of their opposition. Latterly, with the quelling of organised opposition and widespread persecution of public dissidents, refusal to wear the chador became a form of silent, individual resistance when little else was possible. However, in media reports concerning the formation of an external opposition force (the National Liberation Army), much was made of women in combat roles. Ironically, it is claimed that a woman commander of the NLA relies on the chador as an effective disguise during her recruiting forays into Tehran.

Chilean Women under Pinochet

> The backward hands of the clock. . . have thrust women into darkness, back into a period where they are no longer even second or third class citizens, but rather society's pariahs.[55]

Repression in Chile after the 1973 coup d'état included measures directly aimed at women. The overall position of women had improved under

[55] 'Roles and Contradictions of Chilean Women in the Resistance and in Exile: Collective Reflections of a Group of Military Prisoners', unpublished paper, Latin-American Working Group Library, Toronto (1979).

the Frei and Allende governments, coincidental to the expansion of the Chilean economy and the institution of general social reforms. Women won the right to maternity leave, and contraception was decriminalised. Under the Popular Unity regime, President Allende had declared his support for the legal equality of women, and established a National Secretariat for Women. Women in poor and working-class communities began to participate in public life around community issues in ways they had never done before.

The new regime's monetarist economic policies, however, called for the dismantling of public sector services and the jobs that went with them. Promotion of a 'family policy' emphasising the 'traditional role' of women as wife and mother provided a compatible ideology for the removal of women from the workforce. The National Secretariat, now under the tutelage of Mrs. Pinochet, was devoted to 'propagating national and family values to form a consciousness and a correct comprehension of the dignity of women and their mission within the family.'

Hand-in-hand with the regime's ideological campaign went legal measures that effectively reversed the gains women had made over the previous decade. Shutdowns of public educational facilities and social services limited women's access to education and health care to those who could afford to pay. The regime severely reduced public sector jobs commonly filled by women and, in addition, labour legislation giving job protection to pregnant women was removed. Women who had to work were increasingly forced into underpaid domestic work and prostitution. Finally, with the imposition of a state of siege and the suspension of civil and political rights, women lost the right to protest the measures which so detrimentally affected them.

Resistance in Chile took on a female voice which, like the case of Iran, has a historical and cultural context particular to that country. The sweeping arrests and detentions immediately following the coup d'état mostly involved men. But the first openly organised opposition group was the 'Relatives of the Disappeared', founded in 1978 by women who had come together as a result of their common search for missing relatives.

The loss of male breadwinners due to detention or unemployment signalled greater responsibilities for women. In response, women established communal kitchens and co-operative nurseries and took the lead in reorganising their demoralised communities. Just as the individual protests of women in Iran are viewed by the State as expressions of political dissent, so have communal efforts to assist one's neighbours been interpreted as forms of dissent in Chile.

In the latter half of the 1980s, with the growth of organised public opposition in Chile, women have remained at the forefront of the resistance movements.

Women and Persecution

Indra contends that the site of women's oppression is the private sphere, and that the necessarily political label which refugee discourse assigns to public sphere activities is therefore not applied to gender oppression. The cases of Chile and Iran, however, shed doubt on the theoretical portrait of a society rigidly divided into gender-determined spheres of activity, which locate the site of oppression and dictate its form.

Measures to limit women's economic power and their access to education affect women in their roles as workers and as students, as well as in their roles as wives and mothers. The disruption of these public sphere activities illustrates that women's oppression is not limited to domestic life. The political nature of oppression rests upon its relation to the State, rather than the realm of human endeavour affected. It is this crucial element which is a key determinant of persecution.

Thus the contention that a non-gender specific definition of refugee 'obscure(s) the divergent relationships to the state' of women and men is doubtful. The more relevant inquiry is whether a link can be established between a particular form of oppression and the State. The cases of Iran and Chile illustrate that restrictions on women's autonomy can be tied to their respective States, and thus satisfy that criterion.

Aside from its necessarily political quality, the term 'persecution' has an elastic meaning which will vary according to the particular circumstances in each case. The UNHCR Handbook on Procedures and Criteria for Determining Refugee Status only identifies threats to life or freedom on account of one of the prohibited grounds to be certain instances. Without specific reference, it suggests that '(o)ther serious violations of human rights' or various measures in combination may constitute persecution. With such a loosely circumscribed concept, Indra's contention that gender-specific forms of oppression cannot amount to persecution is untenable. Certainly it is because of the forms and possible combinations which persecution may take that no definite meaning has been ascribed to the term.

As suggested in the Handbook and by commentators on refugee law, reference to international human rights concepts can provide further guidance. Goodwin-Gill proposes as a comprehensive definition:

> measures, taken on the basis of one or more of the stated grounds, which threaten: deprivation of life or liberty; torture or cruel, inhumane or degrading treatment; subjection to slavery or servitude; non-recognition as a person (particularly where the consequences of such non-recognition impinge directly on an individual's life, liberty, livelihood, security or integrity); and oppression, discrimination or harassment of a person in his or her private, home or family life.[56]

---

[56] Goodwin-Gill, *The Refugee in International Law* (see footnote 49 earlier), p. 40.

It is unpersuasive to contend that gender-specific forms of persecution, even in a private-sphere framework, cannot be brought within such a conceptualisation of the term. The question left unmasked by that writer, however, and by the Handbook, is how to frame a claim to gender-based persecution in the absence of gender as a prohibited ground.

The second aspect of the radical feminist characterisation of bifurcated refugee experiences is Meijer's characterisation of women's resistance. The cases of Iran and Chile show that the form resistance takes is shaped by the cultural and historical moment. Again, it is unhelpful to suggest that there exists a form of resistance peculiar to women, or that women's resistance is often not recognised. The enquiry must instead consider what consequences an act of resistance might bring about to determine, first, the relationship to the State, and secondly, whether the measures taken amount to persecution. The enquiry then arrives at the troublesome point of the ground upon which such a fear of persecution may be founded.

Gender: A Basis for Persecution

Certainly many claims to Convention refugee status by women can be framed upon one of the existing grounds: race, religion, nationality, membership of a particular social group or political opinion. It must be acknowledged, however, that in many cases women face a barrier to protection, even though their claims to a well-founded fear of persecution are comparable in every other way to those of members of the delineated groups.

In response to feminist critics, the European Parliament, followed by the UNHCR, has urged the recognition as a particular social group of 'women who face harsh and inhuman treatment because they are considered to have transgressed the social mores of their society.' This formulation capitalises on the elasticity of the definition of persecution by incorporating the phrase 'harsh and inhuman treatment'. Further, it imbues political qualities to individual acts of resistance. In short, it goes a considerable way to address the concerns of critics such as Indra and Meijer.

Innovative use of the under-utilised social group category promises some amelioration for the absence of gender as a specified ground, but there are at least two stumbling blocks to its providing a complete solution: the problematic nature of claims to persecution of an economic or social nature; and the trend in third-country resettlement States to restrict entry into their domestic determination systems.

The most problematic claims to Convention refugee status are those where the nature of the feared persecution is economic or social. The UNHCR Handbook distinguishes economic migrants as those who 'voluntarily' leave their country of origin for exclusively economic considerations. It also acknowledges, however, that the

> distinction between an economic migrant and a refugee is. . . sometimes blurred in the same way as the distinction between economic and political measures in an applicant's country of origin is not always clear. Behind economic measures affecting a person's livelihood there may be racial, religious or political aims. . .'

The Handbook does not address the question of what amounts to persecution of a social nature, although some guidance may be taken from the description of 'social group' as a ground for persecution: 'Mere membership of a particular social group will not normally be enough to substantiate a claim to refugee status.'

It is in respect of claims to persecution of an economic or social nature that the absence of gender as an enumerated ground most significantly harms women, although the difficulty in establishing such claims ultimately lies in the nature of the right violated. Economic and social rights, as formulated in the 1966 Covenant, are generally viewed as future rights, which states should strive to provide in an unspecified time frame. Moreover, despite the humanitarian rhetoric of resettlement States, which eschews both political and immigration considerations in refugee determination, both issues factor into the domestically regulated determination systems.

As the cases of Iran and Chile illustrate, women are among the first victims of economic and social repression. However, the proclivity of States of all political stripes to the oppression of women, coupled with the vagueness with which economic and social rights are proclaimed in international law, suggests that successful use of the 'particular social group' category for claims to persecution of an economic or social nature will be minimal.

Finally, as States which traditionally offer permanent resettlement to refugees tighten controls on entry into their domestic determination systems, bearing the additional burden of establishing the existence of a particular social group is an unenviable prospect. Screening provisions and reduced appeal rights will jeopardise the chance of effectively utilising this ground.

The answer to adequate protection for women refugees then lies not merely in creating a separate 'female paradigm' for gender-based claims to persecution. A human rights based approach to defining persecution, the recognition of women as a particular social group, documentation of discriminatory and repressive measures aimed at or particularly affecting women, access to full and fair determination procedures, and a liberal reading of the Convention definition, would provide the basis for the development of a profile of gender-based refugee claims, and for recognition of the difference gender makes.

L. United States INS Gender Guidelines, *Considerations for Asylum Officers Adjudicating Asylum Claims from Women*, Memorandum, 26 May 1995.

Legal Analysis of Claims

Women make up a large percentage of the world's refugees. In order to qualify as a refugee under our laws, female applicants must—like any applicant—show that they cannot return home and cannot avail themselves of the protection of their country because of 'persecution or a well-founded fear of persecution on account of race, religion, nationality, membership in a particular social group, or political opinion. . .'. Often, of course, the asylum claim of a female applicant will have nothing to do with her gender. In other cases, though, the applicant's gender may bear on the claim in significant ways to which the adjudicator should be attentive. For example, the applicant may assert a particular kind of harm, like rape, that either is unique to women or befalls women more commonly than men. Or an applicant may assert that she has suffered persecution on account of her gender or because of her membership in a social group constituted by women. She might also assert that her alleged persecutors seek to harm her on account of a political or religious belief concerning gender. Such claims must be analysed within the terms of United States law, but gender-related claims can raise issues of particular complexity, and it is important that United States asylum adjudicators understand those complexities and give proper consideration to gender-related claims.

This section will describe how such claims should be analysed within the framework of US law. As with asylum cases in general, which can be among the most complicated adjudications in US administrative law, there are no special 'bright line' tests for evaluating claims that are based on the applicant's gender. This is a developing area, and adjudicators should freely seek legal counsel regarding these issues as the decisional law evolves.

Persecution: How Serious is the Harm?

As in all asylum cases, the asylum officer must assess whether the harm that the applicant fears or has suffered is serious enough to be regarded as 'persecution' as that term is understood under the relevant international and domestic law. . . . The Board of Immigration Appeals has interpreted persecution to include threats to life, confinement, torture, and economic restrictions so severe that they constitute a threat to life or freedom. *Matter of Acosta*, 19 I&N Dec. 211, 222 (BIA 1985), overruled on other grounds by *Matter of Mogharrabi*, 19 I&N Dec., 439 (BIA 1987). 'Generally harsh conditions shared by many other persons' do not amount to persecution. Id. See also *Kovac v. INS*, 407 F. 2d 107 (9th Cir. 1969) (persecution involves 'the infliction of suffering or harm upon those who differ... in a manner regarded as offensive'); *Hernandez-Ortiz v. INS*, 77 F. 2d 509, 516 (9th Cir. 1985) (persecution can occur where 'there is a difference between the persecutor's views or status and that of the victim; it is oppression which is inflicted because of a difference the persecutor will not tolerate'). In addition, though discriminatory practices and experiences are not generally regarded by themselves as persecution, they 'can accumulate over time or increase in intensity so that they may rise to the level of persecution.' *Basic Law Manual* at 22.

The forms of harm that women suffer around the world, and that therefore will arise in asylum claims, are varied. Forms of harm that have arisen in asylum claims and that are unique to or more commonly befall women have included sexual abuse, rape, infanticide, genital mutilation, forced marriage, slavery, domestic violence, and forced abortion. The form of harm or punishment may be selected because of the gender of the victim, but the analysis of the claim should not vary based on the gender of the victim. Asylum adjudicators should assess whether an instance of harm amounts to persecution on the basis of the general principles. . . .

A. Rape and Other Forms of Sexual Violence as Persecution

Serious physical harm consistently has been held to constitute persecution. Rape and other forms of severe sexual violence clearly can fall within this rule. See *Lazo-Majano v. INS*, 813 F. 2d 1432, 1434 (9th Cir. 1987) (Salvadoran woman raped and brutalised by army sergeant who denounced her as subversive had been 'persecuted' within the terms of the Act). In *Matter of*—, Krome (BIA May 25, 1993. . .), it was determined that the gang rape and beating of a Haitian woman in retaliation for her political activities was 'grievous harm' amounting to persecution. Severe sexual abuse does not differ analytically from beatings, torture, or other forms of physical violence that are commonly held to amount to persecution. The appearance of sexual violence in a claim should not lead adjudicators to conclude automatically that the claim is an instance of purely personal harm. As in all cases, the determination that sexual abuse may be serious enough to amount to persecution does not by itself make out a claim to asylum. The applicant must still demonstrate that the fear of persecution is well-founded and that the persecution was threatened or inflicted on account of a protected ground.

B. Violation of Fundamental Beliefs as Persecution

The Third Circuit has considered whether an Iranian woman faced with having to wear the traditional Islamic veil and to comply with other harsh rules imposed on women in Iran risked 'persecution' as the Board has defined it. *Fatin v. INS*, 12 F. 3d 1233 (3d Cir. 1993). The record included evidence about the possibility of physical harm. The applicant had asserted in her brief that the routine penalty for women who break the moral code in Iran is 174 lashes, a year's imprisonment, and in many cases brutal rapes and death. Id. at 1241. These, the court stated, would constitute persecution. The court went on to assume that 'the concept of persecution is broad enough to include governmental measures that compel an individual to engage in conduct that is not physically painful or harmful but is abhorrent to that individual's deepest beliefs.' Id. at 1242. Having to renounce religious beliefs or to desecrate an object of religious importance might, for example, be persecution if the victim held strong religious beliefs. Noting that the administrative record was 'sparse', the court found that the applicant before it did not risk persecution because she had not shown either that she would disobey the rules and risk the consequences or that obeying the rules would be 'so profoundly abhorrent' as to amount to persecution. Id.

The court did not specify how 'profoundly abhorrent' to one's beliefs forced behaviour must be to constitute persecution. It did note that 'the concept of persecution does not encompass all treatment that our society regards as unfair, unjust, or even unlawful or unconstitutional.' Id. at 1240. The degree of abhorrence an applicant claims to feel at such forced behaviour must be objectively reasonable—that is, it would have to be a degree of abhorrence that a reasonable person in the circumstances of the applicant could share. Id. at 1242 n.11.

Fisher v. INS, 37 F. 3d 1371 (9th Cir. 1994) rehearing *en banc* pending, also concerned an Iranian woman whose claim was based on failure to conform to fundamentalist religious and cultural norms. The *Fisher* court emphasised that persecution should not be evaluated 'solely on the basis of the physical sanction. . .' 37 F. 3d at 1379. Citing *Fatin*, the court stated that 'when a person with religious views different from those espoused by a religious regime is required to conform to, or is punished for failing to comply with laws that fundamentally are abhorrent to that person's deeply held religious convictions, the resulting anguish should be considered in determining whether the authorities have engaged in "extreme conduct" that is "tantamount to persecution".' 37 F. 3d at 1381.

Nexus: The 'On Account of' Requirement

Some of the most difficult issues in asylum law arise over whether a gender-based asylum claim involves persecution 'on account of' one of the five statutory grounds. This is a critical part of the analysis under US law. *INS v. Elias-Zacarias,*—U.S.—, 112 S.Ct. 812 (1991). Discussing this requirement in the context of a political opinion claim based on forced recruitment, the Supreme Court emphasised that persecution must be threatened or inflicted 'on account of the *victim's* political opinion, not the persecutor's. If a Nazi regime persecutes Jews, it is not, within the ordinary meaning of language, engaging in persecution on account of political opinion; and if a fundamentalist Moslem regime persecutes democrats, it is not engaging in persecution on account of religion.' Id. at 816. Thus harm must be inflicted in order to punish the victim for having one or more of the characteristics protected under the statute. *See Acosta,* 19 I&N Dec. at 226.

A. Actual or Imputed Political Opinion

Asylum claims may often raise assertions of fear on account of a political opinion having to do with gender-related issues. The Third Circuit in *Fatin* had 'little doubt that feminism qualifies, as a political opinion within the meaning of the relevant statutes'. 12 F. 3d at 1242. The political opinion of the applicant in that case did not, however, provide a basis for refugee status. Though she had shown that she generally possessed political beliefs about the role of women in society that collided with those prevailing in Iran, she had not shown that she would risk severe enough punishment simply for holding such views. Nor had she shown that she actually possessed the narrower political opinion that Iran's gender-specific laws and repressive social norms must be disobeyed on grounds of conscience, although the court had indicated that the penalties for disobedience were harsh enough to amount to persecution. Id. at 1242–43. However, the case does make clear that an applicant who could demonstrate a well-founded fear of persecution on account of her (or his) beliefs about the role and status of women in society could be eligible for refugee status on account of political opinion.

Some tribunals have held or suggested that an applicant can establish eligibility for refugee status by demonstrating that he or she is at risk on account of a political opinion that the persecutor believes the applicant to have, whether or not the applicant actually possesses that political opinion. This is the doctrine of 'imputed political opinion'. See, e.g., *Ravindran v. INS,* 976 F. 2d 754 (1st #3195 (BIA 1992). . . . Thus, in addition to the question whether views on issues that relate to gender can constitute a 'political opinion' under the INA, asylum claims sometimes raise the question whether a woman has been persecuted because of a political opinion (regardless of its substance) that has been imputed to her.

In *Campos-Guardado v. INS,* 809 F. 2d 285, 289 (5th Cir, 1987), for example, the Fifth Circuit considered the claim of a woman whose family members had been politically active in El Salvador. Armed attackers came to her home, bound the applicant and other female family members and forced them to watch while the attackers murdered male family members. The attackers then raped the applicant and the other female family members while one attacker chanted political slogans. In what might appear to be an extreme assessment of the evidence, the court affirmed the Board's determination that the applicant had not established that the attackers were motivated by a political opinion they imputed to the victim. Reasonable minds could differ over this record. The court might reasonably have concluded that the chanting of political slogans during the rape indicated not merely that the attackers were politically motivated, but more specifically that they believed the petitioner to have contrary political views and that they punished her because of it. In any case, *Campos-Guardado* illustrates the need for an adjudicator to carefully ascertain all the facts surrounding an allegation of persecution in order to assess whether there are indicia that the act was committed or threatened on account of a protected characteristic.

B. Membership in a Particular Social Group

(1)   General

'Membership in a particular social group' is perhaps the least clearly defined ground for eligibility as a refugee. See e.g., *Fatin*, 12 F. 3d at 1238 & n. 4, 5, citing courts and commentators who have 'struggled' with the concept. An applicant may, of course, have a claim based on more than one ground; 'this heading may frequently overlap with a claim to fear of persecution on other grounds, i.e., race, religion or nationality.' UNHCR *Handbook on Procedures and Criteria for Determining Refugee Status* ('Handbook') para. 77. Nevertheless, the Convention . . . clearly set forth membership in a particular social group as an independent basis of refugee status.

The Board of Immigration Appeals has stated that:

> 'persecution on account of membership in a particular social group' encompasses persecution that is directed toward an individual who is a member of a group of persons all of whom share a common, immutable characteristic. The shared characteristic might be an image one such as sex, color, or kinship ties, or in some circumstances it might be a shared past experience such as military leadership or land ownership. The particular kind of group characteristic that will qualify under this construction remains to be determined on a case-by-case basis. However, whatever the common characteristic that defines the group, it must be one that the members of the group either cannot change, or should not be required to change because it is fundamental to their individual identities or consciences. *Acosta*, 19 I&N Dec. at 233.

According to the Ninth Circuit, an adjudicator considering a claim of persecution on account of membership in a particular social group must determine:

1) whether the class of people identified by the asylum applicant is cognisable as a particular social group under the applicable laws;
2) whether the applicant qualifies as a member of the group;
3) whether the group has in fact been targeted for persecution on account of the characteristics of the group members; and
4) whether 'special circumstances' are present that would justify regarding mere membership in the group in itself as sufficient to recognise the applicant as a refugee.

Sanchez-Trujillo v. INS, 801 F. 2d 1572, 1574–75 (9th Cir. 1986). The requirement of 'special circumstances' apparently applies only when the applicant's claim is based on mere membership in the social group.

(2) Social Group Defined by Gender

An increasing number of asylum applicants claim that gender, alone or along with other characteristics, can define a 'particular social group'. The Second Circuit has stated that gender alone cannot. 'Possession of broadly-based characteristics such as youth and gender will not by itself endow individuals with membership in a particular group.' *Gomez v. INS*, 947 F. 2d 660, 664 (2nd Cir 1991). The Third Circuit has taken a different view. In *Fatin*, the court emphasised that an Iranian applicant who feared persecution because she is a woman would be a member of a particular social group under the INA. Ms. Fatin was not eligible for asylum, however, because she had not shown that persecutors would seek to harm her 'based *solely* on her gender'. 12 F. 3d at 1240 (emphasis added).

Thus, while some courts have concluded as a legal matter that gender can define a particular social group, no court has concluded as a factual matter that an applicant has demonstrated that the government (or a persecutor the government could not or would not control) would seek to harm her solely on account of her gender. The courts have then considered whether gender might be one characteristic that combines with others to define the particular social group.

In *Fatin*, for example, the applicant's primary argument was not that she risked harm simply for being female. Rather, she argued that she risked harm as a member of a 'very visible and specific subgroup; Iranian women who *refuse to conform* to the government's gender specific laws and social norms'. 12 F. 3d at 1241, quoting petitioner's brief. . . . This group, the court noted, is not made up of all Iranian women who hold feminist views, nor even of all those who object to the rules that govern women in that country. It is limited to the smaller group of women who so strongly object that they refuse to conform, despite the risk of severe punishment. If a person would choose to suffer severe consequences rather than to comply with rules contrary to her beliefs, the court reasoned, then those beliefs might well be so fundamental to her identity or conscience that she ought not have to change them. The subgroup that the applicant asserted therefore could be seen as a particular social group. Moreover, the record indicated that the punishment facing the members of that group is severe enough to constitute persecution. The applicant was not a refugee, though, because she had not shown that she was a member of such a group. She had testified only that she would try to avoid as much as she could the strictures that she objected to. Id.

Thus the *Fatin* court found that women in Iran could constitute a 'particular social group' and recognised the applicant's membership, but found that the members were not at risk of persecution. The court also seemed to recognise the narrower subgroup of Iranian women who find their country's gender-specific laws offensive and do not wish to comply with them, but similarly found no evidence that people in this narrower group faced harm serious enough to constitute persecution. Last, the court recognised the narrowest subgroup of Iranian women whose opposition to Iran's gender-specific laws is so profound that they would disobey at serious peril; it held that the possible consequences of disobedience were extreme enough to be persecution but found that petitioner was not in the particular social group. In each scenario the court regarded gender, either alone or as part of a combination, as a characteristic that could define a particular social group within the meaning of the INA. *Accord, Safaie*, 25 F. 3d at 640, citing *Fatin* (although 'a group of women, who refuse to conform [with moral code in Iran] and whose opposition is so profound that they would choose to suffer the severe consequences of noncompliance, may well satisfy the definition,' the applicant had failed to show that she fell within that group).

This is consistent with the statement of the Board in *Acosta* that 'sex' might be the sort of shared characteristic that could define a particular social group. It is also consistent with the view taken by the UNHCR Executive Committee, of which the United States is a member. In 1985 the Executive Committee

> recognized that States, in the exercise of their sovereignty, are free to adopt the interpretation that women asylum-seekers who face harsh or inhuman treatment due to their having transgressed the social mores of the society in which they live may be considered as a 'particular social group' within the meaning of Article 1 A(2) of the 1951 United Nations Refugee Convention.

Conclusions on the International Protection of Refugees adopted by the Executive Committee of the UNHCR Program, No. 39(k) (36th Session 1985).

When considering whether gender might combine with other characteristics to define a particular social group, asylum adjudicators should consider whether such additional characteristics are likely to be ascertainable by persecutors. In *Gomez*, the applicant argued—in line with the suggestion in *Acosta* that a shared past experience might define a particular social group—that she was a refugee based on her membership in the class of women who had been previously battered and raped by Salvadoran guerrillas. The court denied her claim, finding that she had failed to produce evidence that persons in this group could be identified as members by would be persecutors and would be targeted for further harm on the basis of their common characteristic—that is, having been harmed by the guerrillas in the past. For this reason, the group could not be recognised as a 'particular social group' within the meaning of the INA. *Gomez*, 947 F. 2d at 664.

(3) Social Group Defined by Family Membership

Asylum seekers often claim to have suffered harm or to face the risk of harm because of a family relationship. In *Gebremichael v. INSA*, 10 F. 3d 28, 36 (1st Cir. 1993), the court concluded: 'There can, in fact, be no plainer example of a social group based on common, identifiable and immutable characteristics than that of a nuclear family.' This appears to follow the pronouncement of the BIA in *Matter of Acosta* that 'kinship ties' could be the shared characteristic defining a particular social group. *Gebremichael* concerned an Ethiopian applicant who had been imprisoned and tortured by Dergue government officials seeking information about the applicant's brother. The court found that

> the link between family membership and persecution is manifest . . .
> the Ethiopian security forces applied to petitioner the 'time-honored
> theory of *cherchez la famille* ("look for the family"),' the terrorization
> of one family member to extract information about the location of
> another family member or to force the family member to come for-
> ward. As a result, we are compelled to conclude that no reasonable
> fact finder could fail to find that petitioner was singled out for mis-
> treatment because of his relationship to his brother. Thus, this is a
> clear case of '[past] persecution on account of. . . membership in a
> particular social group.'

10 F. 3d at 36. See also *Ravindran v. INS*, 976 F. 2D 754, 761 N. 5 (1ST CIR. 1992), *Quoting Sanchez-Trujillo*, 801 F. 2D at 1576 ('a prototypical example of a "particular social group" would consist of the immediate members of a certain family, the family being the focus of fundamental affiliational concerns and common interests for most people'). Without mentioning *Sanchez Trujillo*, however, or exploring the question in depth,

the Ninth Circuit later held that the concept of persecution on account of membership in a particular social group does not extend to the persecution of a family. *Estrada-Posadas v. INS*, 924 F. 2d 916, 919 (9th Cir. 1991).

While the state of the law is therefore uncertain in the Ninth Circuit, there is nevertheless Board and federal court support for the principle that family membership could define a 'particular social group' under the asylum laws. Obviously all other elements of the definition must be satisfied for this to be the basis of eligibility as a refugee. There must be past persecution or a well-founded fear of future persecution, and the harm must be threatened or inflicted on account of the applicant's membership in the group. Adjudicators should also note that the applicant's gender need not play any role in whether family membership can define a particular social group in the context of a particular case; Gebremichael, for example, was male. But claims based on family membership are frequently asserted by female applicants, particularly in countries where men tend to be more active politically than women. Thus, adjudicators should be aware of the Caselaw on this point.

Public versus Private Acts

(1) Is the Persecutor the Government or Someone the Government is Unable or Unwilling to Control?

After the adjudicator has examined the degree of harm and whether it has been threatened or inflicted on account of one or more of the five grounds, it is still necessary to inquire about the availability of protection within the country of claimed persecution. This is based on the notion that international protection becomes appropriate where national protection is unavailable. . . . Caselaw establishes that this means, in part, that the persecutor can be either the government or a non-government entity that the government is unable or unwilling to control. *See Matter of Villalta*, Int. Dec. No. 3126 (BIA 1990).

In the usual case, the government will be the alleged persecutor. The question may arise, however, whether an act committed or threatened by a government official was nevertheless a purely private one. The Ninth Circuit considered whether a woman who was 'singled out to be bullied, beaten, injured, raped, and enslaved' was persecuted by an agent of the government for political or for personal reasons in *Lazo-Majano v. INS*, 813 F. 2d 1432, 1434 (9th Cir 1987). There the persecutor, a member of the Salvadoran military, threatened to accuse the applicants of subversion. He then did so, to a friend in the police force. Based on evidence of severe treatment of subversives by Salvadoran authorities, the court determined that the applicant was a refugee on account of the political opinion that could be imputed to her because of the public accusation, even without evidence that she actually held subversive political views. In *Lazo-Majano*, therefore, an act that might have been regarded as personal violence not covered by the INA was held to have become persecution on account of a protected characteristic because of the conduct of the persecutor. *Cf. Matter of Pierre*, 15 I&N Dec. 461 (BIA 1975) (husband's status as a legislator in Haiti did not by itself make abuse of his wife persecution on account of political opinion even though the Haitian government would not restrain the husband).

The Sixth Circuit considered the distinction between public and private acts in a claim based on sexual harassment in *Klawitter v. INS*, 970 F. 2d 149 (6th Cir. 1992). There the applicant claimed that she feared the unwanted sexual advances of a colonel in the Polish secret police. The court agreed with the position of the Board that '[h]owever distasteful his apparent treatment of the respondent may have been, such harm or threats arising from a personal dispute of this nature, even one taking place with an individual in a high governmental position, is not a ground for asylum.' . . . Although petitioner's testimony recounts an unfortunate situation, harm or threats of harm based solely on sexual attraction do not constitute "persecution" under the Act.' 970 F. 2d at 152.

These cases involve public officials who commit what is commonly seen as a private act. In such situations adjudicators must determine whether a reasonable basis exists for regarding the act as a 'public' one that can be attributed to the government or an agent the government is unable or unwilling to control. *Compare Klawitter* (sexual abuse by officer of Polish secret police was a purely private act) *with Lazo-Majano* (otherwise private acts of brutality by military officer treated as having become 'public' when officer falsely accused victim in public of political opposition, putting her at risk of harm from other military officers). Adjudicators must also determine, as always, whether the applicant faces harm 'on account of' a protected characteristic. *Elias-Zacarias*.

As mentioned above, the persecutor might also be a person or group outside the government that the government is unable or unwilling to control. If the applicant asserts a threat of harm from a non-government source, the applicant must show that the government is unwilling or unable to protect its citizens. *See Matter of Villalta*, Int. Dec. 3126 (BIA 1990); *Rodriguez-Rivera v. INS*, 848 F. 2d 998, 1005 (9th Cir. 1988). It will be important in this regard, though not conclusive, to determine whether the applicant has actually sought help from government authorities. Id. Evidence that such an effort would be futile would also be relevant.

(2) Is State Protection Possible Elsewhere in the Country?

The principle that international protection becomes appropriate where national protection is unavailable also means that, to be eligible for international protection, an applicant must generally demonstrate that the danger of persecution exists nationwide. See *Acosta*, 19 I&N Dec. 211; *Matter of Fuentes*, 19 I&N De. 658 (BIA 1988); *Matter of R-*, Int. Dec. 3195 at 7–9 (BIA 1992); *Quintanilla-Tjcas v. INS*, 783 F. 2d 955 (9th Cir. 1986). If there is evidence that the applicant can avoid the threat by relocating to a different part of the country or that a government would offer protection from otherwise private acts of harm elsewhere in the country than the locality where those acts take place, then normally the applicant will not qualify for asylum. See *Beltran-Zavala v. INS*, 912 F. 2d 1027, 1030 (9th Cir. 1990).

This principle becomes crucial where the applicant alleges private actions—such as domestic violence—that the state will not protect against. In such situations the officer must explore the extent to which the government can or does offer protection or redress, and the extent to which the risk of harm extends nationwide. According to the UNHCR *Handbook*, 'a person will not be excluded from refugee status merely because he could have sought refuge in another part of the same country, if under all the circumstances it would not have been reasonable to expect him to do so.' UNHCR *Handbook*, para. 91. Whether it is 'reasonable under all the circumstances' to expect an applicant to have sought refuge from acts of domestic violence or other seemingly 'private' acts will of course depend on the facts of the case. Asylum adjudicators should carefully explore the circumstances giving rise to the harm or risk of harm, as well as the extent to which government protection would have been available in other parts of the country. The adjudicator must consider whether protection was available as a factual matter as well as in the law of the country and whether, under all the circumstances, it would be reasonable to expect a woman to seek residency elsewhere in her country. This underscores the general need to develop the record fully, with respect to both the applicant's particular circumstances and the conditions prevailing in the country of origin.

7. Determination of Refugee Status of Children

M. *Refugee Children: Guidelines on Protection and Care* (UNHCR, Geneva, 1994), pp. 97–107.

Determination of Refugee Status

The 1951 Convention and 1967 Protocol relating to the Status of Refugees define a refugee regardless of age, and make no special provision for the status of refugee children. Applying the criterion of 'well-founded' fear of persecution to children does not normally give rise to any problem when, as in the majority of cases, they are accompanied by one or both of their parents. Determining the refugee status of unaccompanied children is more difficult and requires special consideration.

Depending on the law of the State, a child seeking asylum may be granted:

- Refugee status for having a 'well-founded fear of being persecuted', as defined in the 1951 Convention and the 1967 Protocol;
- refugee status as defined in the 1969 OAU Convention or the 1984 Cartagena Declaration;
- if the refugee claim is denied, the child might be permitted to stay with an immigration status granted for another humanitarian reason, or receive rejection or a deportation order.

Regardless of what law a child may be seeking asylum under, there will be a procedure to determine the claim. The three basic methods are: (1) group determination, (2) determination based on an adult's claim, and (3) determination based on the child's own claim.

- **Group determination.** If a refugee movement is too large to make individual status determinations possible, the State might grant refugee status to all members of the group. Each child in the group would automatically receive refugee status.
- **Determination based on an adult's claim.** When the head of a household is granted refugee status, the common practice of States is to grant refugee status to the dependents. This is not required under any article of the refugee treaties, but States do it in order to promote family unity. . . .
  When a child is with one or both parents, the family unity principle clearly applies and, in most cases, a dependent child will be accorded the parent's status. However, when the child is with an uncle, cousin or other relative a State might not consider the relatives to be a 'family', and might therefore require each person, including the child, to make an individual claim. This could result in the relative being granted refugee status, based on their own well-founded fear, but the child's claim being denied. When this happens, the child is split apart from the relative, and may become an unaccompanied minor. In practice, dependents should be considered if they are living in the same household. . . . A claim of 'family unity' might also be made by a child in the care of a non-relative when the quality of the relationship is equivalent to a family. In some cases, the claim might describe the relationship as an informal, traditional or de facto adoption.
- **A child's individual claim.** If a child who is in the care of a parent, relative or other adult care-taker makes an individual claim, the adult can be of great assistance by giving factual information to

document the claim, speaking on behalf of the child, helping the child understand the procedures, giving emotional support, offering advice, or making a decision on behalf of the child.

By contrast, an unaccompanied child will have none of this support when making an individual claim.

Unaccompanied Children

Although procedures for status determination exist in many countries, they do not normally take into account the special situation of unaccompanied children. . . .

Considering the effects that a prolonged stay in camp or camp-like situations may have on children's physical and psychological developments, the refugee status determination or decision-making on the child's best interests must be made quickly, and with the appropriate special attention and procedures. Keeping children in limbo regarding their status, hence their security and their future, can be harmful to them.

Determinations of the status of unaccompanied children should be guided by the following:

(a) The question of how to determine whether an unaccompanied refugee child qualifies for refugee status will depend on the child's degree of mental development and maturity. An expert with sufficient knowledge of the psychological, emotional and physical development and behaviour of children should be called upon to make the necessary assessment, bearing in mind that children may manifest their fears in ways different from adults. When possible, such an expert should have the same cultural background and mother tongue as the child. . . .

(b) Where it is decided that the child is mature enough to have and to express a well-founded fear of persecution, the case may be treated in a manner similar to that of an adult.

(c) Where the child has not reached a sufficient degree of maturity to make it possible to establish a well-founded fear in the same way as for an adult, it is necessary to examine in more detail objective factors, such as the characteristics of the group the child is left with, the situation prevailing in the country of origin and the circumstances of family members, inside or outside the country of origin.

(d) As children are not legally independent, they should be represented by an adult whose task it would be to promote a decision that will be in the child's best interests. In some situations, this function may be performed by persons carefully selected from within the refugee community.

(e) The problem of 'proof' is great in every refugee status determination. It is compounded in the case of children. For this reason, the decision on a child's refugee status calls for a liberal application of the principle of the benefit of the doubt. This means that should there be some hesitation regarding the credibility of the child's story, the burden is not on the child to provide proof, but the child should be given the benefit of the doubt.

(f) Considering the special vulnerability of children, the determination of appropriate durable solutions in their best interests may be established following the refugee status determination.

8. Economic Migrants

N. *Handbook on Procedures and Criteria for Determining Refugee Status* (UNHCR, Geneva, September 1979), paras 62–64.

62. A migrant is a person who, for reasons other than those contained in the definition, voluntarily leaves his country in order to take up residence elsewhere. He may be moved by the desire for change or adventure, or by family or other reasons of a personal nature. If he is moved exclusively by economic considerations, he is an economic migrant and not a refugee.

63. The distinction between an economic migrant and a refugee is, however, sometimes blurred in the same way as the distinction between economic and political measures in an applicant's country of origin is not always clear. Behind economic measures affecting a person's livelihood there may be racial, religious or political aims or intentions directed against a particular group. Where economic measures destroy the economic existence of a particular section of the population (e.g., withdrawal of trading rights from, or discriminatory or excessive taxation of, a specific ethnic or religious group), the victims may according to the circumstances become refugees on leaving the country.

64. Whether the same would apply to victims of general economic measures (i.e., those that are applied to the whole population without discrimination) would depend on the circumstances of the case. Objections to general economic measures are not by themselves good reasons for claiming refugee status. On the other hand, what appears at first sight to be primarily an economic motive for departure may in reality also involve a political element, and it may be the political opinions of the individual that expose him to serious consequences, rather than his objections to the economic measures themselves.

O. **James C. Hathaway, *The Law of Refugee Status* (Butterworths, Toronto, 1991), pp. 116–17.**

Risk to Economic, Social, and Cultural Rights

Just as the serious risk of violation of civil and political liberties indicates a lack of state protection, so too does failure to respect social, economic, and cultural rights. This position is often misunderstood to imply that every one who is poor, or who leads a life with few material advantages, can successfully advance a claim to refugee status. For example, Scott Burke has challenged the propriety of refugee claims grounded in the denial of socio-economic rights on the basis that '. . .hundreds of millions of people, including the entire Third World. . . suffer the deprivation of the "rights" set forth in the Covenant [on Economic, Social, and Cultural Rights],' thus implying a right to asylum 'for anyone from an economically backward society'.[57] Kenneth Brill has pointedly observed that '[o]ne of the main reasons for not expanding the refugee definition to encompass others besides political persecutees is that this would open the floodgates to the kind of economic migrants that our immigration system has sought to exclude.'[58] These characterisations demonstrate a fundamental misperception of the nature of economic, social, and cultural human rights.

Unlike the Civil and Political Covenant, the International Covenant on Economic, Social, and Cultural Rights [ICESCR] does not create obligations that states are required to fulfil immediately upon accession. Rather, the duty of each state party is simply 'to take steps, individually and through international assistance and cooperation, especially economic and technical to the maximum of its available resources, with a view to achieving progressively the full realisation of the rights recognised', and to 'guarantee that the rights enunciated. . . will be exercised without discrimination of any kind. . .'. Thus, the Covenant creates two kinds of duty. *First*, a government must marshal national and international resources and give priority to the expenditure of those resources in achieving the full realisation of human rights. *Second*, and more commonly related to refugee claims, states must implement socio-economic rights on a non-discriminatory basis, and may not, for example, limit basic educational opportunities to members of certain minority groups, or deny the right to work to members of an opposition political party. It must be emphasised, however, that the persistence of non-discriminatory poverty or hardship does not constitute *per se* a violation of the Covenant.

In addition to this carefully circumscribed duty, the substantive scope of most socio-economic rights is far from a guarantee of prosperity for all. By way of example, the mandatory scope of the right to health only obligates states to work to reduce infant mortality, improve hygiene, control diseases, and establish basic medical services. Similarly, the right to education requires universal access only to primary education, with further opportunities conditioned by circumstances.

Taken together, these carefully crafted qualifications within the ICESCR mean that an absence of state protection can be said to exist only where a

---

[57] S. Burke, 'Compassion versus Self-interest: Who Should Be Given Asylum in the United States?' *Fletcher Forum* (Vol. 8, 1984), pp. 319, 320.

[58] K. Brill, 'The Endless Debate', *Cleveland State Law Review* (Vol. 32, 1983), p. 117.

government fails to ensure the non-discriminatory allocation of available resources to meet the most basic of socio-economic needs. It is in this context that refugee protection becomes relevant—not as a means of guaranteeing access to 'the good life', but rather only to vindicate the right to everyone to those social, economic, and cultural attributes which are essential to human dignity.

9. Persons who Do Not Deserve Protection: Exclusion and Cessation Clauses

P. UNHCR, EC/47/SC/CRP. 29, 30 May 1997, 'Note on the Exclusion Clauses', 8th Meeting, Standing Committee, Executive Committee of the High Commissioner's Programme, paras 1, 3–7, 16–19.

The international refugee instruments governing refugee law lay out criteria for the recognition of refugees. They also establish criteria by which individuals may be excluded from international protection. The term 'exclusion clauses' refers to legal provisions designed to achieve this effect. Article 1F of the 1951 Convention includes a number of exclusion clauses. . . .

. . . The exclusion clauses enumerated in Article 1F of the 1951 Convention operate to disqualify persons from the benefits of refugee status by reason of serious transgressions committed, in principle, prior to seeking asylum. The idea of an individual 'not deserving' protection as a refugee is related to the intrinsic links between ideas of humanity, equity, and the concept of refuge. The primary purpose of these exclusion clauses are to deprive the perpetrators of heinous acts and serious common crimes of such protection, and to safeguard the receiving country from criminals who present a danger to that country's security. If the protection provided by refugee law were permitted to afford protection to perpetrators of grave offence, the practice of international protection would be in direct conflict with national and international law, and would contradict the humanitarian and peaceful nature of the concept of asylum. From this perspective, exclusion clauses help to preserve the integrity of the asylum concept.

General Principles Governing Application of Exclusion Clauses

Under the 1951 Convention, responsibility for establishing exclusion lies with states. The UNHCR is competent in this regard, under its Statute. According to Article 1F of the 1951 Convention, persons are excludable where 'there are serious reasons for considering' that they have committed the offenses in question. States should, therefore, have substantially demonstrable grounds for invoking an exclusion clause. Decisions on exclusion should be clear and reasoned, and the claimant should be afforded a fair hearing in view of the inherently serious effect of invoking exclusion clauses. In principle, decision on exclusion may properly be made only in the context of a full examination of the grounds for a refugee claim.

The exclusion clauses are carefully enumerated in the 1951 Convention, and describe those situations in which persons who fulfil the positive requirements of recognition as refugees are nonetheless constrained from being recognised as such. Denying protection against return to the country of origin to someone with a well-founded fear of persecution can result in their continued persecution, or even worse. Use of these exclusion clauses is, therefore, an extreme measure. Exclusion clauses must be interpreted within narrow limits and in a manner which does not undermine the integrity of international protection.

Exclusion from refugee status will not always result in the individual's expulsion from the country of asylum, as the excluded person is still entitled to the protection of relevant municipal and international laws. For example, the person may still be protected against *refoulement* by Article 3(1) of the 1984 Convention Against Torture and Other Cruel, Inhuman and Degrading Treatment or Punishment.... The excluded person is also covered by relevant State laws governing due process and the rights of aliens.

The Categories of Excludable Offences and Individual Liability

The three categories of excludable acts and crimes specified in Article 1F of the Convention are: crimes against peace, war crimes and crimes against humanity, serious non-political crimes, and acts contrary to the purposes and principles of the United Nations....

Serious Non-political Crimes—Article 1F(b)

This Article excludes persons whose past criminal acts in another jurisdiction are especially egregious. The 'seriousness' of a crime may depend on such factors as the extent of physical or property harm it causes, and the type of penal sentence it attracts within the particular legal system. Rape, homicide, armed robbery, and arson are examples of offenses which are likely to be considered serious in most States. It is important to recall that the intention of this Article is to reconcile the aims of rendering due justice to a refugee, even if he or she has committed a crime, and to protect the community in the country of asylum from the danger posed by criminal elements fleeing justice. This Article should be seen in parallel with Article 33 of the 1951 Convention, which permits the return of a refugee if there are reasonable grounds for regarding the refugee as a danger to the security of the country or who, having been convicted by a final judgement of a particularly serious crime, constitutes a danger to the security of that country.

The serious crime must also be non-political, which implies that other motives, such as personal reasons or gain, predominate. Increasingly, extradition treaties specify that certain crimes, notably acts of terrorism, are to be regarded as non-political for the purpose of those treaties, although they typically also contain protective clauses in respect of refugees. For a crime to be regarded as political, its political objective must also, for purposes of this analysis, be consistent with the exercise of human rights and fundamental freedoms. Crimes which deliberately inflict extreme human suffering, or which violate *jus cogens* rules of international law, cannot possibly be justified by any political objective.

Even if the serious and non-political nature of a crime is established, a 'balancing test' must be applied before this exclusion clause may be invoked. This test ensures that exclusion does not result in greater harm to the offender than is warranted by the alleged crime. Thus, its seriousness should be weighed against the level of persecution likely to be faced by the offender in the country of origin. If the persecution feared is so severe as to endanger the offender's life or liberty, then only an extremely grave offence will justify the application of this exclusion clause.

Article 1F(b) requires that the crime in question was committed 'outside the country of refuge. . .prior to his admission' to the country of asylum. This could be the country of origin, or another country. It can never be the country where the applicant seeks recognition as a refugee. Refugees who commit serious crimes within the country of refuge are not subject to the exclusion clauses. They are subject to that country's criminal law process and to Articles 32 and 33(2) of the 1951 Convention, in the case of particularly serious crimes. While Article 1F(b) offers no guidance as to the role of expiation, practice has been to interpret it as applying chiefly to fugitives from justice, and not to those who have already served their sentences, unless they are regarded as continuing to constitute a menace to a new community.

Q. UNHCR, EC/47/SC/CRP. 30, 30 May 1997, 'Note on the Cessation Clauses', 8th Meeting, Standing Committee, Executive Committee of the High Commissioner's Programme, paras 3–6, 8.

General Principles

All the basic international refugee instruments, including the 1951 Convention and its Protocol, the 1969 Organisation of African Unity (OAU) Convention and the Statute of UNHCR, contain clauses setting out the specific situations in which those instruments and the competence of the

High Commissioner, respectively, cease to apply. These are the cessation clauses.

The underlying rationale for the cessation clauses was expressed to the Conference of Plenipotentiaries in the drafting of the 1951 Convention by the first United Nations High Commissioner for Refugees, G.J. Van Heuven Goedhart, who stated that refugee status should 'not be granted for a day longer than was absolutely necessary, and should come to an end . . . if, in accordance with the terms of the Convention or the Statute, a person had the status of de facto citizenship, that is to say, if he really had the rights and obligations of a citizen of a given country'. Cessation of refugee status therefore applies when the refugee, having secured or being able to secure national protection, either of the country of origin or of another country, no longer needs international protection. This linkage of international protection to the duration for which it is needed distinguishes the cessation clauses from the exclusion clauses in Article 1F of the 1951 Convention, which address situations in which the refugee does not deserve the benefits of international refugee protection. For analytical purpose, it is helpful to divide the cessation clauses into two broad sets. The first set comprises the four clauses which relate to a change in personal circumstances of the refugee, brought about by the refugee's own act, and which results in the acquisition of national protection so that international protection is no longer necessary. The second set comprises the clauses which relate to change in the objective circumstances in connection with which the refugee has been recognised, so that international protection is no longer justified (the 'ceased circumstances' cessation clause).

The cessation clauses are exhaustive. This means that the refugee's status is maintained until one of the cessation clauses can be invoked: in any case, refugees should not be subjected to constant or regular reviews of their refugee status. In principle, the application of the cessation clauses is declaratory in nature, acknowledging that international refugee protection is no longer required. It operates to withdraw refugee status, and brings to an end related rights and benefits. Such a withdrawal should, however, be distinguished from cancellation of refugee status, which is not specifically covered by the international refugee instruments. Such cancellation is undertaken where it emerges that status was obtained by a misrepresentation of material facts or where there is subsequent discovery of material facts which clearly indicate that, had these been known at the time of status determination, the individual would not have been recognised as a refugee. . . .

Given that the application of the cessation clauses would result in the withdrawal of refugee status, the clauses should be interpreted in a restrictive way, taking into account the guidance contained in the UNHCR *Handbook on Procedures and Criteria for Determining Refugee Status* and in the Executive Committee's Conclusion 69. A premature or insufficiently grounded application of the cessation clauses can have extremely serious consequences as refugees who need to remain in the country of asylum may be forced to do so illegally, or may be threatened with *refoulement.*

III. THE 1967 PROTOCOL: REMOVAL OF TEMPORAL AND GEOGRAPHICAL LIMITATIONS

A. James C. Hathaway, 'A Reconsideration of the Underlying Premise of Refugee Law', *Harvard Journal of International Law* (Vol. 31, 1990), pp. 162–64.

Although a Protocol was adopted in 1967 which updated the Convention by removing the temporal and geographical limitations, the Protocol failed to review the substantive content of the definitions it embraced. Specifically, even after the 'universalisation' effected by the 1967 Protocol, only persons whose migration is prompted by a fear of persecution in relation to civil and political rights come within the scope of Convention-based refugee protection. This means that most Third World refugees remain *de facto* excluded, as their flight is more often prompted by natural disaster, war, or broadly-based political and economic turmoil than by 'persecution', at least as that term is understood in the European context.

The adoption of the Protocol was therefore something of a Pyrrhic victory for the less developed world: while modern refugees from outside Europe were formally included within the international protection scheme, very few Third World refugees can in fact lay claim to the range of rights stipulated in the Convention. The retention of a fundamentally European and increasingly outmoded refugee definition as the accepted international standard for refugee protection was at the least a tacit recognition of the priority of European and analogous claims to a guarantee of basic rights within the international community.

It is difficult to argue that the drafters of the Protocol were consciously motivated by a desire to exclude refugees from less developed states. Indeed, the driving force behind the Protocol was the UNHCR's determination to harmonise the refugee definition in the Convention-based scheme with its own, already universal mandate. The drafting history nonetheless reveals a determination to avoid the discussion of fundamental issues of refugee protection, and particularly to steer clear of a strategy that would give rise to 'political discussion' of refugee issues in the General Assembly. There was clearly a risk that detailed discussion of the scope of refugee protection in the non-Western dominated General Assembly could have resulted in a broadening of the conceptualisation of refugee status in line with regional shifts in the less developed world. This danger was successfully avoided by the submission to the General

Assembly of a short, technical Protocol that neither reproduced nor made explicit reference to the terms of the Convention, but merely noted the extension of protection to refugees on a universal and enduring basis.

Whatever the intentions of the architects of the Protocol, its advent has proved to be of great importance in the maintenance of a dualistic approach in refugee law. As the number of Third World refugees has increased and transportation links to the developed world have improved, a small minority of these refugees have made asylum claims in Western states. The refugee definition established by the Protocol has enabled authorities in developed states to avoid the provision of adequate protection to Third World asylum claimants while escaping the political embarrassment entailed by use of an overtly Eurocentric refugee policy. While not drafted as a standard for refugee determination per se, the Convention-derived definition has been adopted by an increasing number of Western states as the basis upon which asylum or protection decisions are made. Because the definition has the imprimatur of international law, and because it has been specifically approved by more than one hundred states, it is difficult to argue the inappropriateness of this transmutation. But because the definition fails to reflect the full range of phenomena that give rise to involuntary migration, particularly in the less developed world, its minimal protection against *refoulement* works a pernicious injustice against many genuine refugees. Most Third World refugees find themselves turned away by Western states or offered something less than durable protection.

IV. THE OAU CONVENTION AND THE CARTAGENA DECLARATION

A. Eduardo Arboleda, 'Refugee Definition in Africa and Latin America: The Lessons of Pragmatism', *International Journal of Refugee Law* (Vol. 3, No. 2, 1991), pp. 186–205.

The internationally accepted refugee definition has proven inadequate to deal with the problems posed by the millions of externally displaced persons in the third world. . . . Broader refugee definitions, therefore, have been advanced at the regional level. The 1969 Organisation of African Unity Convention Governing the Specific Aspects of Refugee Problems in Africa (OAU Convention) adopted a definition more closely reflecting the realities of Africa during a period of violent struggle for self-determination and national development. The 1984 Cartagena Declaration on Refugees (Cartagena Declaration) broadened the definition still further recognising the special attention deserved by the Central American situation.

... This article outlines the evolution of the broader refugee definitions in the OAU Convention and the Cartagena Declaration. It presents historical synopses of asylum and refugee in Africa and Latin America, and recounts the circumstances and conditions which led to the revision, in these third world regions, of the refugee definitions set by the international community in the early fifties. ...

The general definitions of refugee status contained in the Statute of the UNHCR and the 1951 Convention have been rendered obsolete by evolving realities in the third world. With hindsight, this was inevitable. Elaborated in the special atmosphere of the post-war years, the restrictive nature of the early definitions did not adequately respond to the variety of situations in the sixties and seventies; for the drafters of the early definitions neither considered nor anticipated the problems of the less developed world.

Africa and Central America are prime examples of regions where the internationally accepted definitions of refugee have proven inadequate. ... Africa and Central America have been characterised by a large exodus of people, mostly destitute, among neighbouring nations. It is debatable whether, as a matter of law, the majority of those fleeing their home countries would qualify under the 'well-founded fear of persecution' requirement set forth in the 1951 Convention and interpreted in the UNHCR Handbook.

The first broader definition of refugee was advanced in the 1969 OAU Convention. Article 1 of the OAU Convention definition incorporated the earlier definitions and added:

> The term 'refugee' shall also apply to every person who, owing to external aggression, occupation, foreign domination or events seriously disturbing public order in either part or the whole of his country of origin or nationality, is compelled to leave his place of habitual residence in order to seek refuge in another place outside his country of origin or nationality.

For the first time the legal term 'refugee', albeit at regional level, was extended to individuals forced to leave their countries owing to aggression by another State and/or as a result of an invasion. The OAU Convention marked the beginning of a refugee protection system which directly addressed the causes of mass refugee influxes, by emphasising objective conditions in the country of origin.

An even broader definition of refugee was advanced in 1984 in the Cartagena Declaration on Refugees, Section III.3 of which provides:

> ... in view of the experience gained from the massive flows of refugees in the Central American area, it is necessary to consider

enlarging the concept of a refugee.... Hence the definition or concept of a refugee to be recommended for the region is one which, in
addition to containing the elements of the 1951 Convention and the
1967 Protocol, includes among refugees persons who have fled their
country because their lives, safety, or freedom have been threatened
by generalized violence, foreign aggression, internal conflicts, massive violation of human rights or other circumstances which have
seriously disturbed public order.

The Cartagena Declaration was the first document in the Latin American
context to establish guidelines for States faced with mass inflows of refugees. It was also the first international declaration recognising that the
victims of generalised violence, internal conflicts, and massive human
rights violations deserved refugee status. Although, unlike the OAU Convention, the Cartagena Declaration is not a formally binding legal instrument, its broader definition has gradually become the established norm
throughout Central America.

The 1969 OAU Convention: Historical Perspective

The refugee problem in Africa was the product of the 1960s, the decade
of maximum decolonisation and of the intensification of the struggles for
independence by African nations. Refugees came primarily from two
main groups of States: the colonial and dependent States, and the independent African States. Over half of all refugees came from the former,
and of these most came from the Portuguese colonies. Less than fifty percent came from the remaining thirty-eight independent African States.

   The enormous refugee problem in dependent and colonial territories
in Africa stemmed primarily from oppression and racism. The intensification in the 1960s of the struggles in places like Angola, Mozambique,
and Portuguese Guinea produced stringent and brutal measures of
repression on the part of the Portuguese Government. Similar struggles
for independence in South Africa and Rhodesia precipitated a more rigid
enforcement of the policies of apartheid and the introduction of harsher
measures of racial discrimination which eroded the black majority's freedom of speech, movement, and even of education.

   The root causes of the refugee problem in independent African States
are even more complex. Partly they stem from the colonial legacy: as a
result of the rather arbitrary manner in which the continent of Africa
was carved up among the colonial powers, most African States today consist of a medley of different ethnic, cultural and tribal groups; refugees
are often the product of clashes between these groups. The continued
interference of former colonial and other external powers in the internal affairs of the recently formed States, and levels of neo-colonial

involvements, also explain at times the exodus of nationals from their home countries. The problems associated with the establishment of viable and sovereign States are yet another contributing factor; refugees are at times a product of the attempts by the new States to ensure external and internal security, internal stability, and economic and social reconstruction. The refugee problem in independent African States is also exacerbated by the impatience and possible over-enthusiasm of the new governments, and intolerance of any ideologies but their own. . . .

A Broader Concept of Refugee in Africa: Calls for a Broader Definition

From the very beginning of the drafting of the OAU Convention most African States agreed that the meaning of 'refugee' had to be expanded. There was consensus that the definition in the 1951 Convention was not sufficiently broad to cover all the situations of African refugees and various OAU member States criticised the limits of the OAU Convention throughout its various drafts. Despite their acceptance of the 1951 Convention, many States felt that an African Convention merely reiterating its provisions and making only a few modifications was not justified. . . .

Features of Broader Regional Definition

The broader definition of refugee adopted by the 1969 OAU Convention contained a number of unprecedented stipulations. Paragraph 2 of Article 1 made the term 'refugee' applicable to asylum seekers who left their country of origin owing to external aggression, occupation, foreign domination, or events seriously disturbing the public order. Individuals in these situations would acquire, *ipso facto*, the status of refugee. They would not have to justify their fear of persecution, as would have been required under the 1951 Convention.

The new definition of refugee is qualitatively different from the classical definitions for it considers situations where the qualities of deliberateness and discrimination need not be present. These more far reaching provisions reflected the reality of the armed conflicts so pervasive in Africa before and during the period of the drafting of the 1969 OAU Convention. They allowed the grant of refugee status to nonetheless dangerous consequences of intensive fighting and associated random lawlessness in their countries of origin.

Significance of Broader Terminology

The terminology utilised in the refugee definition of the OAU Convention, which reflected the urgency of responding to the African reality, established an important precedent in international law. The new terminology responded to obvious humanitarian concerns and sought to provide a practical solution to the problem of determining refugee status; the massive migrations occurring at the time made individual determinations quite impractical. Unlike developed countries, where the existence of refugee determination procedures allowing case by case determination is assumed, the absence of decision-making infrastructures in Africa demanded not only a humanitarian but also a pragmatic approach. In responding to the real and urgent African needs, the drafters of the new definition gave secondary consideration to the strict legal meaning of its terminology and to case law.

The characterisation of refugee agreed in the 1969 OAU Convention included terms that lacked a firm definition under international law. Terms such as 'external aggression', 'occupation', and 'foreign domination' were not yet established in international law practice and today there is still no consensus on the meaning of intervention in international law. The basic concept of 'aggression' had been discussed extensively in international forums before 1969, but a formal definition was not adopted until 1974...:

> Aggression is the use of armed force by a State against the sovereignty, territorial integrity or political independence of another State, or in any other manner inconsistent with the Charter of the United Nations as set out in this definition.

The use of 'aggression' in defining refugee status in the 1969 OAU Convention may have assisted in the acceptance of an international standard for this term....

The 1984 Cartagena Declaration: Historical Perspective

Latin American countries have espoused the concepts of asylum and refuge, throughout their history as Independent States. Indeed, several of the leaders, in the wars of independence, had the opportunity to experience first hand the rigours of forced exile. Jose de San Martin, liberator of the southern nations of South America, died penniless in forced exile in France. Simon Bolivar, his counterpart in northern South America, was forced to take refuge outside Venezuela several times during and after his liberation campaigns.

The legal concept of asylum dates back to 1889; an entire chapter of the Montevideo Treaty on International Penal Law signed on 23 January 1889, is devoted to asylum, which is affirmed as an inviolable right of those persecuted for their political beliefs. The Treaty reflected the political instability of Latin America at the time and the need to protect the inevitable victims of political persecution.

The 1889 Montevideo Treaty was followed by a series of regional conventions dealing specifically with the subject. Conventions were concluded in February 1928 in Havana; December 1933 and March 1940 in Montevideo; March 1954 in Caracas; and November 1969 in San Jose, Costa Rica. These conventions dealt with both 'territorial' and 'diplomatic' asylum, and 'asylees' were defined as persons seeking refuge due to persecution by virtue of their imputed or real 'political delinquency'.

Traditional Latin American Definition of Refugee

As defined in the Latin American Conventions, territorial asylum is narrower in scope than the refugee concept advanced by the 1951 Convention. Although both concepts share the same underlying promise, namely the protection of persecuted individuals, the Latin American Conventions limited asylum rights to those persecuted for political reasons, excluding by omission non-political reasons such as race and religion.

Consolidation of Concepts of Asylum and Refuge

The various Latin American Conventions use the terms 'refugee' and 'territorial asylee' interchangeably, which suited the historical circumstances of the first part of this century. Both Latin American and European citizens sought asylum in Central and South American countries before 1951. In the 1930s, Spaniards fleeing the Spanish Civil War found asylum primarily in Mexico. During and after the Second World War, Europeans of other nationalities were generously granted asylum in a number of South American countries. Although the Europeans seeking refuge constituted a large group of people, they were a relatively homogeneous group. Their needs, as well as those of the few individual cases from other Latin American countries, were resolved within the context of the regional asylum instruments.

But these instruments were designed to respond to individual cases under very specific circumstances. With the ever-increasing number of persons fleeing Caribbean countries in the sixties, and with the political turmoil in the southern cone of Latin America in the seventies, the region was faced for the first time with the phenomenon of massive internal population shifts.

Latin Americans became aware of the need to complement their generous asylum tradition with adherence to the internationally accepted 1951 Convention and 1967 Protocol definition of refugee. Refugee experts viewed the latter definition as more precise, and realised that it presented an opportunity to address more adequately the problems and necessities posed by the new waves of displaced persons. Although the refugee definition of the 1951 Convention required a 'well founded fear of persecution', it still presented a more flexible interpretation than the regional asylum instruments, which required proof of actual or anticipated persecution. The newer definition also considered other grounds for persecution, such as race and religion, making it possible for every 'territorial asylee' to be considered a 'refugee', while the converse was not necessarily the case. . . .

A Broader Concept of Refugee in Latin America: Crisis—The Catalyst for Change

The Latin American tradition of asylum was put to a severe test in the 1980s. The outbreak of violence throughout the Central American region forced hundreds of thousands of people to flee their homes, and the established rules of asylum were ill-suited to handle this massive regional displacement. The Latin American instruments focused primarily on relationships between the States concerned, not on the individuals in need of protection. Though the later asylum treaties, such as the 1969 American Convention on Human Rights, provided protection to individuals, the Latin American tradition perceived protection only in terms of a safe reception in the asylum country of those fleeing direct political persecution. Since the inter-American asylum treaties did not foresee unprecedented displacements, assistance was not an issue in a regional asylum system established to benefit individuals whose survival was not at stake, and whose burden on the receiving community was easily bearable. Voluntary repatriation was also not part of the asylum system, since it was presumed that asylees would return to their countries of origin once the motives for persecution disappeared. Even the broader and more precise refugee definitions of the 1951 Convention and 1967 Protocol, which were fast gaining acceptance throughout Latin America, were too rigid to define adequately the externally displaced type of refugee created by the massive Central American exodus.

The characteristics of the new refugees were also problematic. These were not high-profile or well-known individuals, as was the case up to the 1970s. No longer were the refugees primarily from urban centres, nor were they strictly representative members of social or political elites like the politicians, labour leaders, and intellectuals who had fled what they perceived as repressive regimes. The new wave of Central American asylum seekers were mostly rural, ethnically mixed people, who concentrated in remote areas bordering their country of origin. In some instances, particularly among Salvadoran and Guatemalan asylum-seekers, whole villages fled together in search of protection.

Central American countries, including Mexico, had to revitalise their long standing asylum traditions to deal humanely with the plight of these unexpected victims, mostly peasants who did not fit the mould of an asylee in the traditional Latin American context. Tolerance and eventual acceptance of this massive influx of individuals in refugee situations was slow in coming, but it was partially facilitated by a highly visible UNHCR role in the region, protecting and assisting these refugees....

Beginnings of a Broader Refugee Definition: The 1981 Colloquium on Asylum and International Protection of Refugees in Latin America

The Central American crisis, which created serious problems for both the displaced people and the States trying to absorb them, in 1981 brought interested nations to a Colloquium in Mexico held by the Mexican Secretariat of Foreign Affairs, in co-operation with the Institute for Legal Research of the National University of Mexico, under the auspices of the Office of the United Nations High Commissioner for Refugees. The primary purpose of this Colloquium on Asylum and the International Protection of Refugees in Latin America was to discuss the most immediate and delicate problems presented by the regional crisis in Central America. It also sought to examine the inadequacies of international refugee law and the respective national refugee legislation.

The 1981 Colloquium made several important determinations. It recognised that asylum law was still evolving and that it could not be treated in a vacuum; tradition, the social and political circumstances of a region, and, hopefully, the pragmatic response to these circumstances by the receiving States were among the ways to concretise asylum law. The Colloquium also determined that the regional refugee reality had surpassed the capacity of the existing legal framework.

For the first time in a regional forum, a broader refugee definition was proposed for Latin America. Conclusion No. 4 of the Colloquium's Conclusions and Recommendations specified the need for a more encompassing refugee definition to deal with the consequences of the rapidly deteriorating situation. This conclusion basically reiterated the language of the 1969 OAU Convention and added 'massive violations of human rights' to the conditions defining a refugee. It is significant that the broader definition of refugee proposed at the 1981 Colloquium was not restricted to Central America, but was offered for all Latin America.

In the context of Latin America and particularly Central America, 'refugee status' does not necessarily entail the grant of individual rights outlined in the 1951 Convention. It does, however, connote for States the unquestionable need for international protection of those in search of asylum. So far as protection is concerned, no distinction is made between 'broader definition' refugees and '1951 Convention' refugees. Moreover, though many signatory States do not generally extend all the individual rights under the Convention, there is a presumption that all refugees, whether falling under the 'Convention' or 'broader definition', have certain basic rights, for example, the right to work, or to education, which States grant whenever it is feasible for them to do so.

Formulation of a More Encompassing Refugee Definition: The 1984 Cartagena Declaration

In the three years following the 1981 Colloquium in Mexico, Central American refugee problems became more acute. Salvadorans and Guatemalans left their countries in unprecedented numbers; Cubans and Haitians in search of better opportunities also contributed to the refugee problem, which affected the entire area from Panama to Mexico and eventually Canada and the United States as well.

The severity of the situation prompted another regional meeting in 1984. From 19–22 November, experts and representatives from ten governments (Belize, Colombia, Costa Rica, El Salvador, Guatemala, Honduras, Mexico, Nicaragua, Panama and Venezuela) met in Cartagena, Colombia, and held a Colloquium entitled 'Coloquio sobre la Protection International de los Refugiados en America Central, Mexico y Panama: Problemas Juridicos y Humanitarios'. The Colloquium was sponsored by the University of Cartagena, the Regional Centre for Third World Studies, and the UNHCR, and was held under the auspices of the Colombian government.

It was this 1984 Colloquium that resulted in the most encompassing definition of refugee for Latin America to date. The '1984 Cartagena Declaration' calls for consideration of the objective situation in the country of origin and the particular situation of the person or groups of persons seeking protection as refugees. This definition requires that two conditions be met to be declared a refugee: that there exist a threat to life, security, or liberty; and that the threat result from one of five factors: generalised violence; foreign aggression; international conflicts; massive violations of human rights; or circumstances seriously disturbing public order.

The third conclusion of the Cartagena Declaration adopts terminology not established either in the 1951 Convention/1967 Protocol or in any other international instrument relating to refugees. The far-reaching phrases such as 'generalised violence', 'internal conflicts' and 'massive violations of human rights', which constitute the most expansive language so far used to define refugees, go further even than the language used in the OAU Convention.

The terminology used in the Cartagena Declaration reflects the deep rooted and generous tradition of asylum in Latin America. It also introduced new and pragmatic principles for the region at an opportune moment.

V. ASIA: AALCC PRINCIPLES

A. Principles Concerning Treatment of Refugees as Adopted by the Asian-African Legal Consultative Committee at its Eighth Session, Bangkok, 1966, Article I, Definition of the Term 'Refugee', in *Collection of International Instruments Concerning Refugees*, second edition (UNHCR, Geneva, 1979), pp. 201–2.

A refugee is a person who, owing to persecution or well-founded fear of persecution for reasons of race, colour, religion, political belief or membership of a particular social group:

(a) leaves the State of which he is a national, or the Country of his nationality, or, if he has no nationality, the State or Country of which he is a habitual resident; or

(b) being outside such State or Country, is unable or unwilling to return to it or to avail himself of its protection.

Exceptions

(1) A person having more than one nationality shall not be a refugee if he is in a position to avail himself of the protection of any State or Country of which he is a national.

(2) A person who prior to his admission into the Country of refuge, has committed a crime against peace, a war crime, or a crime against humanity or a serious non-political crime or has committed acts contrary to the purposes and principles of the United Nations shall not be a refugee.

Explanation

The dependents of a refugee shall be deemed to be refugees.

Explanation

The expression 'leaves' includes voluntary as well as involuntary leaving.

Notes

i) The Delegation of Ghana reserved its position on this Article.

ii) The Delegations of Iraq, Pakistan and the United Arab Republic expressed the view that, in other opinion, the definition of the term 'Refugee' includes a person who is obliged to leave the State of which he is a national under the pressure of an illegal act or as a result of invasion of such State, wholly or partially, by an alien with a view to occupying the State.

iii) The Delegations of Ceylon and Japan expressed the view that in their opinion the expression 'persecution' means something more than discrimination or unfair treatment but includes such conduct as shocks the conscience of civilised nations.

iv) The Delegations of Japan and Thailand expressed the view that the word 'and' should be substituted for the word 'or' in the last line of paragraph (a).

v) In Exception (2) the words 'prior to his admission into the Country of refuge' were inserted by way of amendment to the original text of the Draft Article on the proposal of the Delegation of Ceylon and accepted by the Delegations of India, Indonesia, Japan and Pakistan. The Delegations of Iraq and Thailand did not accept the amendment.

vi) The Delegation of Japan proposed insertion of the following additional paragraph in the Article in relation to proposal under note (iv):

A person who was outside of the State of which he is a national or the Country of his nationality, or if he has no nationality, the State or the Country of which he is a habitual resident, at the time of the events which caused him to have a well-founded fear of above-mentioned persecution and is unable or unwilling to return to it or to avail himself of its protection shall be considered a refugee.

The Delegations of Ceylon, India, Indonesia, Iraq and Pakistan were of the view that this additional paragraph was unnecessary. The Delegation of Thailand reserved its position on this paragraph.

VI. STATELESS PERSONS

A. Carol A. Batchelor, 'Stateless Persons: Some Gaps in International Protection', *International Journal of Refugee Law* (Vol. 7, 1995), pp. 232–34, 239–41, 258–59.

Introduction

The prominence of statelessness as an area of international concern rises as a correlative of the number of people who either have no nationality or have no effective nationality. As defined in article 1 of the 1954 Convention relating to the Status of Stateless Persons, statelessness means a 'person who is not considered as a national by any State under the operation of its law'. This is concise and to the point. It defines a specific group of people, the *de jure* stateless, because it delineates a specific, quantifiable fact: either one is, or one is not a national by operation of a State's law. This clear definition is stated in the 1954 Convention and presumed in the 1961 Convention on the Reduction of Statelessness.

A problem arises, however, in that the definition itself precludes full realisation of an effective nationality because it is a technical, legal definition which can address only technical, legal problems. Quality and attributes of citizenship are not included, even implicitly, in the definition. Human rights principles relating to citizenship are not delineated, despite the inspiration of the Conventions themselves by article 15 of the Universal Declaration of Human Rights. The definition is not one of quality, simply one of fact.

In the case of stateless persons, history has shown that the question of nationality is not merely a legal one, not merely one of whether or not a nationality has been ascribed. In certain cases, having a nationality may push individuals to seek a different status, may itself lead to statelessness. This was, in effect, the case for *de facto* stateless German Jews who were, under the Reich laws, classed as nationals and non-citizens. Although legally still holding a nationality, the lack of the usual attributes of nationality, including effective protection, was evident. It is from this epoch that the term *de facto* stateless traces its origins. At that time, however, the terminology was more encompassing for the criterion was not lack of citizenship but, rather, lack of effective protection.[59]

... The crucial question is that of an effective nationality. The attributes of nationality, the rights and responsibilities which generally flow from an effective nationality, are stabilising factors. Clearly there is a gap between the technical question of being ascribed a nationality and the question of effective national protection. The gap is all the more significant because not all those who lack effective protection qualify as refugees, even if they are outside their place of habitual residence. The protection of the stateless thus reveals a gap in definition between those who are stateless refugees, and as such protected as refugees, and those who are legally or *de jure* stateless and, therefore, covered by the statelessness conventions. As Manley Hudson, Special Rapporteur for the International Law Commission on the subjects of nationality and statelessness, commented,

> Purely formal solutions ... might reduce the number of stateless persons but not the number of unprotected persons. They might lead to a shifting from statelessness 'de jure' to statelessness 'de facto'.[60]

[59] Provisional Arrangement of 4th July 1936 concerning the Status of Refugees coming from Germany: '[T]he term *refugee coming from Germany* shall be deemed to apply to any person who was settled in that country, who does not possess any nationality other than the German nationality, and in respect of whom it is established that in law or in fact he or she does not enjoy the protection of the Government of the Reich.'

[60] Manley O. Hudson, *Report on Nationality Including Statelessness*, International Law Commission 4th Session: UN Doc.A/CN.4/50, 21 February 1952, p. 49.

There is a need to address the issue as a question of protection rather than one simply of recognition under the law as either a national or a non-national. Efforts may then be made to prevent unnecessary dislocation and hardship.

The United Nations High Commissioner for Refugees (UNHCR) has a mandate to assist refugees. The High Commissioner's Office has also been charged with responsibilities under article 11 of the 1961 Convention on the Reduction of Statelessness. Issues which relate to actual or potential movement of persons are necessarily of concern to the High Commissioner's Office and in this sense, the appointment is logical. UNHCR is concerned with facilitating the realisation of an effective nationality, not only as a means of prevention of displacement, but also as a means of reintegration or local integration once movement has occurred. There remain, however, a large number of people who are without effective national protection, but for whom neither the refugee nor the statelessness conventions apply. . . .

Refugees and Stateless Persons: No Distinctions

Stateless persons have not always comprised a distinct group. Previously, refugees and stateless persons,

> [W]alked hand in hand, and after the First World War, their numbers condition were almost coterminous. Later, their paths diverged, with refugees being identified principally by reference to the reasons for their flight, and their statelessness, if it existed, being seen as incidental to the primary cause.[61]

Despite historical developments, however, the fact remains that refugees and stateless persons are similarly situated, for they both suffer from a lack of national protection. While initially no distinction was made between refugees and stateless persons, later the stateless were included in the group receiving international protection only if they could fit into the narrower definition of refugee; statelessness alone was not decisive. However, before the First World War, certain assumptions were made in relation to nationality which largely precluded the matter of statelessness from arising. In essence, the inhabitants of a territory were deemed to be part of the land and were thought to be disposed of together with the territory.[62] Later, when treaties were used to regulate the transfer of

[61] G.S. Goodwin-Gill, 'The Rights of Refugees and Stateless Persons: Problems of Stateless Persons and the Need for International Measures for Protection', in K.P. Saksena, ed., *Human Rights Perspective and Challenges (In 1990 and Beyond)* (Lancer Books, New Delhi, 1994), pp. 378, 389–90.

[62] Y. Onuma, 'Nationality and Territorial Change: In Search of the State of the Law', *Yale Journal of World Public Order* (Vol. 8, 1981).

territory, the principle of domicile was assumed to establish an effective link between the individual and the territory. Following the First World War, the presumption of effective link was no longer so evident in the treaties concluded, in that certain groups were excluded from acquisition of the new nationality regardless of residence.[63] Ethnicity, race and language became relevant factors, although domicile was still employed as a safety-net in instances where statelessness might otherwise result.[64]

The concept of attachment to the land through residency or domicile is also implicit in early responses to the large-scale movement of people. Under the auspices of the League of Nations, several multilateral treaties were concluded to address the situations of Russian, Armenian and later other specific groups of refugees.[65] The definition encompassed stateless persons by reference to those 'who [do] not enjoy or who no longer [enjoy] the protection of the Government . . . and who [have] not acquired another nationality'.[66] Underlying this was the assumption that the individual was outside his or her habitual country of residence, and was therefore without the traditional domiciliary link and without the protection which that link generally afforded. This definition was later elaborated in reference to stateless Germans as applying to,

Stateless persons not covered by previous Conventions or Agreements who have left German territory after being established therein and who are proved not to enjoy, in law or in fact, the protection of the German Government.[67]

Refugees were defined by the fact that they were without national protection, one criterion of which was their physical location. No particular distinction was made between the stateless and refugees, both being defined as outside their place of residence and lacking protection. Of course, this definition was not universal, but applied only to specific groups of interest. One cannot say that there was a purposeful approach to the stateless per se. What is of interest is that the question of protection and location was definite, it not being deemed necessary to distinguish the legal position of refugees and stateless persons on any other level.

[63] Treaty of Versailles, Art. 91, *2 Major Peace Treaties of Modern History 1648–1967*, at 1332; Treaty of St. Germain, Art. 76, ibid., vol. 3, 1564; Treaty of Trianon, Art. 62, ibid., 1888; Treaty of Neuilly, Art. 39, ibid., 1739. See also Intergovernmental Committee on Refugees, *Statelessness and Some of Its Causes: An Outline* (March 1946), in which the faulty administration of tests for establishing the right to nationality is described as statelessness which the treaty drafters had sought to avoid.

[64] Onuma 'Nationality and Territorial Change' (see footnote 62 earlier), pp. 8–10.

[65] See P. Mutharika, *The Regulation of Statelessness under International Law and National Law* (1989).

[66] LNTS NO. 2004 (1926), quoted in Mutharika, ibid., p. 7.

[67] 192 LNTS 59 (No. 4461), Art. 1(b).

Stateless persons outside their country of habitual residence and without national protection, qualified as refugees and, as such, for the assistance of whichever international organisation was responsible for refugees at the time, from the League of Nations High Commissioners for Refugees, to the Intergovernmental Committee on Refugees, and finally to the International Refugee Organisation. Stateless individuals were dealt with in turn by each of these entities but under the rubric of their position as refugees. A progressive narrowing in the definition of 'refugee' can be followed during this time. The Intergovernmental Committee on Refugees took the following position in relation to stateless persons:

> [The] mandate of the Intergovernmental Committee does not mention statelessness at all, while policy decisions in respect of groups recognized as coming under the 'current and authorized operations' of the Committee, regard de jure and de facto statelessness merely as one of the criteria of eligibility in conjunction with others, e.g., flight into another State as a result of racial, political or religious persecution.[68]

It was no longer sufficient to be outside of one's country of habitual residence and without effective protection. The reasons for flight became paramount and statelessness, in turn, marginalised as merely one of many symptoms to be analysed in considering a refugee claim. *De jure* and *de facto* stateless were, nonetheless, still factored into the equation by the organisations appointed to assist refugees.

... Refugees and stateless persons were once treated in like manner. The divergence of their paths ... cannot be interpreted as an intention to deny international protection to those who lack national protection. Further, the division of *de jure* and *de facto* stateless persons was a result of two things. The first was the desire to extend protection to those who legally had a nationality but had none of the attributes of a nationality. The second was a misconception regarding who would qualify at the time and over the years, as a refugee. The assumption was that *de facto* stateless persons were refugees. As such, they were already granted international protection.

VII. ARE WE ALL REFUGEES?

A. Daniel Warner, 'We are all Refugees', *International Journal of Refugee Law* (Vol. 4, No. 3, 1992), pp. 366–72.

... For the purpose of asylum, the legal differentiation between refugees and non-refugees is crucial, which explains continuing debate about the

[68] Intergovernmental Committee on Refugees (see footnote 63 earlier), p. 2.

refugee definition. . . . The act of categorisation necessarily implies that refugees possess certain characteristics, or are in a certain position, that clearly separates them from others, if only for legal purposes.

But how valid is the. . . . 'separation' of refugees from others into a specific category? The definitions of refugees highlight the otherness of refugees, for which there are certainly valid historical and political reasons. People were placed in a specific category as refugees at a time when many were defenceless. Refugees were not separated as much as they were recognised as being in a situation without adequate protection. But this otherness, this opposition to those who were able to protect themselves (or to avail themselves of government protection), was part of a specific upheaval that occurred in a particular time and place. The physical situation of those categorised as refugees after World War Two was strikingly different from that of those who were able to avail themselves of government protection. The differences between insiders and outsiders were manifest and the legal necessity of recognising the separateness of a group was obvious.

Without prejudicing the necessity of placing certain persons in the category of refugees because of the manifest differences between those who do and those who do not have protection, and the legal importance of differentiating between refugee and non-refugee for reasons of asylum, an opposite track in the relationship between refugees and non-refugees is nevertheless feasible, and there are implications beyond legal definitions. Although refugees were and are recognised as a specific category of people distinct from others, current literature on our (post)modern situation shows striking similarities between the universal condition and the plight of refugees. Going beyond the specificity of the legal definitions, we can discern the universality of the refugee situation, and how the otherness of refugees can be refuted without prejudicing the need of certain people for international legal protection. This does not entail our reintegrating refugees into a universal category, but seeing how those outside the refugee category are similar to refugees. The situation of the refugee becomes the basic norm and we, the outsiders, disclose our similarity. The differentiation between refugees and non-refugees diminishes as we see the important ways in which we are all refugees.

Homesickness and Homelessness

William Connolly describes one aspect of modernity, homesickness, and its relation to politics through the writings of Nietzsche. Connolly states quite forthrightly that 'Modern thinkers . . . demand a solution to homesickness',[69] and in explaining the basis of this homesickness, he points to

---

[69] W.E. Connolly, *Political Theory and Modernity* (Basil Blackwell, Oxford, 1989), p. 137.

certain basic aspects of the human condition that have been unfulfilled since the death of God. Connolly points this modern predicament, as defined by Nietzsche, in terms that are very close to the outsiders' traditional understanding of the discontinuity of the refugee experience:

> The drive to establish commonalities and to seal them in truth is well grounded in the human condition as Nietzsche defines it. It is grounded, first, in the essential incompleteness of the human before it is given social form; second, in the practical requirements of coordination among beings whose activities would not mesh without social rules enforced by moral and civil sanctions; third, in the restrictive provision of socially established identities in any structured way of life; fourth, in the character of beings who must reduce much of the common life to implicit rules, routines, habits, traditions and recipes to avoid overloading their limited capacities of conscious reflection with too many explicit rules and conventions; fifth, in the dense medium of language through which a common world of standards and judgements is crystallized; *sixth, in the psychic disturbance which wells up when the conventional character of socially established identities, implicit standards and explicit norms is exposed.*[70]

The problem which intrigues Connolly, and on which he focuses his discussion of Nietzsche, is the extent to which the posited basic urge to find a home in the world can be called into question. That is, the modern search for community may be a nostalgic search that has no solution. I have previously criticised Gervase Coles for his lack of clarity in defining the community referred to when he speaks of the refugee's right to community; here the criticism is that the very notion of community as an ultimate solution may be wrong, as indeed may be the very notion of an ultimate solution and the search for it.

Connolly goes on to say:

> These requirements and demands demarcate the human as the 'herd animal'. They join with one additional feature to fix it as the 'sick animal'. For if the human is the animal which requires social formation and coordination to fix itself and its conduct, it also encounters elements of resistance in itself to any specific form imposed upon it. It thus becomes the animal which requires reasons to live this way rather than that and then demands that these reasons too have their reasons. *Its sickness resides in its quest to reach the end of a trail which has no terminus.*[71]

---

[70] Ibid., p. 138. Emphasis added.
[71] Ibid.

Thus, whereas we feel that we should have a home or be at home, just as people feel that the best solution for refugees is repatriation, the search for a home is infinitely more complex than a territorial integration. The search for a home and shelter in refugee language is usually a physical problem. But the search for a home is a more profound search, that is not necessarily tied to a specific place. Connolly quotes Nietzsche on the modern wish to find a home in the world and the separation of the physical sense of home from the feeling of being at home:

> *We who are homeless*—Among Europeans today there is no lack of those who are entitled to call themselves homeless in distinctive and honorable senses; it is to them that I especially commend my secret wisdom and gaya scienze. . . . We children of the future how could we be at home in this today? We feel disfavor for all ideals that might lead one to feel at home even in this fragile, broken time of transition. The ice that still supports people today has become very thin; the wind that brings the thaw is blowing; we ourselves who are homeless constitute a force that breaks open ice and other all too thin 'realities'.[72]

The homeless, therefore, are not necessarily those without territorial place, although the two can be easily confused. As Connolly stated concerning homesickness in another context, 'It is a homesickness that construes correspondence between the scope of troubles and a territorial place of action to form the essence of democratic politics. It is nostalgia for a politics of place.'[73] In his essay on Nietzsche, Connolly further develops this nostalgia by redefining it in these terms: 'The demand for self-knowledge presupposes a fit between inner life and the public resources of language, between the structure of desire and the logic of articulation.'[74] The transposition of the territorial place takes place when the mind/body dualism is theoretically realised within one's own community. That is the nostalgia in Coles' version of community, apparently a community wherein the desire for self-knowledge can be most easily integrated and fulfilled.

Connolly examines Nietzsche's position that this drive for integration/self-knowledge can never be fulfilled, either by remaining in or returning to a specific place, or in some individual search for self-knowledge. In Connolly's exegesis of Nietzsche, the situation of modernity is such that even if we were able to remain within the pre-modern understanding of

[72] F. Nietzsche, *The Gay Science*, translated by W. Kaufmann (Vintage Books, New York, 1974), p. 338.
[73] W.E. Connolly, 'Democracy and Territoriality', *Millennium: Journal of International Studies* (Vol. 20, No. 3, Winter 1991), p. 464.
[74] Connolly, *Political Theory and Modernity* (see footnote 69 earlier), p. 148.

community, we would still be strangers to ourselves. Connolly cites Nietzsche:

> 'Self-knowledge' simultaneously lifts the self to a more complex level of social subtlety and subdues that which does not fit into the elevator: 'So we are necessarily strangers to ourselves, we do not comprehend ourselves, we have to misunderstand ourselves, for us the law, 'Each is furthest from himself' applies to all eternity—we are not 'men of knowledge' with respect to ourselves.[75]

It is this notion of 'strangers to ourselves' that characterises Nietzsche's description of the modern condition that is so similar to discussions of the refugee situation. When we talk of durable solutions for refugees, in terms of voluntary repatriation or integration and adaptation in exile, we assume that there has been some form of disjuncture between a 'normal life' and the refugee situation. Once the durable solution has been enacted, we assume that there is some form of finality to the situation, that normalcy has returned. We assume that the return to place through repatriation will naturally lead to fulfilment through articulation and integration, just as we assume that integration and adaptation will serve the same function in a foreign country after exile and asylum. Connolly, through Nietzsche, is saying that this is not so. Even though the refugee has been disjoined from his or her traditional place, the disjuncture between self and 'home' existed before flight and will exist after flight, whether there is voluntary repatriation or asylum. It is this disjuncture which causes the refugee and non-refugee to be similar. If the refugee is searching for a 'home', so are we all, 'we' being those who have not been forced into exile.

Connolly's analysis of Nietzsche and the politics of homesickness opens up new avenues of reflection. It questions the radical split between the situation of the refugee and the non-refugee by allowing us to see that we all have a certain homesickness that cannot be fulfilled. No matter where we are, even in our countries of origin, we are all strangers to ourselves. But where does this realisation lead us? On the one hand, it should lead non-refugees to have more compassion for refugees, in that instead of having sympathy for them, we can empathise with them. Secondly, in terms of solutions, it allows us to realise that while certain physical solutions are preferable, namely, voluntary repatriation, the situation of the individual today in longing for a 'politics of place' is not a final solution to homesickness. Durable solutions are one crucial level of protection that cannot be underestimated. But, in Nietzsche's terms, we should not stop

---

[75] F. Nietzsche, *On the Genealogy of Morals*, translated by W. Kaufmann and R.J. Hollingdale (Random House, New York, 1969), section 1, p. 15.

at these 'solutions' in our analysis of the refugee situation, for the very nature of solutions is more complex than traditional refugee vocabulary allows. Durable solutions are solutions to one level of problem, just as legal definitions serve one level of problem, such as asylum. We should recognise the limitations of these solutions.

All this may be comforting to the refugee, but it should be frightening to the non-refugee. If we realise that we are similar to refugees, we also must realise that the protected home that distinguishes us from refugees is only an illusion. I repeat Connolly's description of the sixth grounding of the drive to establish commonalities according to Nietzsche: 'The psychic disturbance which wells up when the conventional character of socially established identities, implicit standards and explicit norms is exposed'. The finiteness of identity is at the core of the modern identity crisis. If we are to take the situation of the refugee seriously, as we take our own situations seriously, then we should not be condescending to those who have been physically uprooted. We are all caught within the tensions and uncertainties of modernity, whether we are categorised as refugees or not. The categorisation of others as refugees allows us to ignore the dynamics and uncertainties of our own existence. We explain certain psychic trauma by the refugee experience, and, in a way, cast off the demons which exist in each of us. 'They' have these insecurities or syndromes because of their experiences; I should not have them because I have not had similar experiences. I can only sympathise with the refugee; I cannot empathise.

What would happen if the refugee interviewed the government official? Would the official be able to comprehend that many of his or her deepest longings were the same as those of the refugees, but without the physical dislocation? Would UNHCR field officers understand that their own doubts were the same as the refugees'? Perhaps the government official and the UNHCR field officer do understand, and that is why they have chosen their professions.

To say that we are all refugees is to say that we are all strangers to ourselves. To categorise certain people as refugees suggests that we deny the refugeeness inside us all, or deny the 'normalcy' that is part of all refugees. Categorising people as refugees serves an important legal function. It allows millions of people the right to international protection which they may otherwise not enjoy. On the other hand, the categorisation delimits one group from another, creating insiders and outsiders. This brief essay has argued that the bridge between the two groups is shorter than one may imagine, and that the solution to the 'refugee experience' may be more complex, as, indeed, is the solution to our own existence.

Chapter 2

Asylum

This chapter considers the history of the concept and institution of asylum and discusses its core principle, viz., the principle of *non-refoulement*.

History

The concept of asylum has a long history. It has been 'in existence for at least 3,500 years and is found, in one form or another, in the texts and traditions of many different ancient societies'.[1] For example, with reference to ancient India, Nagendra Singh writes:

> It was the right of every sovereign state who felt strong enough to maintain its position among the community of states to give protection to anyone who had surrendered and taken refuge or shelter for the sake of his life. Both secular and sacred literature abound in legends which establish that it was the sacred duty of the king whose shelter any individual took, to protect the refugee or *saranagat* at all times. The *Mahabharatha* also speaks of the sacred duty of refusing to surrender a fugitive or a refugee to the enemy.[2]

As is to be expected, the shape and content of the institution of asylum has varied at different points of time and in different cultures. **Readings I.A** and **I.B** offer a glimpse of this history. While **Reading I.A** provides an overview of the history of 'international migrants and refugees' in the last

---

[1] *The State of the World's Refugees: The Challenge of Protection* (Penguin, New York, 1993), p. 33.

[2] Nagendra Singh, *India and International Law: Ancient and Medieval* (S. Chand, Delhi, 1973), Vol. 1, p. 48.

four centuries, **Reading I.B** examines the Islamic concepts of refugee and asylum.[3]

Reading I.C generates suspicion about linear and progressive accounts of the institution of asylum. For, as Kennedy notes in it, prior to the nineteenth century, 'authors were not concerned about ascertaining an obligation but about elaborating the conditions of justice.' It is only in the modern period, with its emphasis on sovereign discretion, that the view has come to prevail that 'to be beyond legal status is to be nothing. . . .' In this context it may be noted that states have consistently refused to undertake an obligation to accept a right of asylum enforceable at the instance of an individual. The frequently cited Article 14 of the Universal Declaration of Human Rights (UDHR) merely provides that 'everyone has the right to seek' but not be granted asylum.[4] The 1977 United Nations Conference on Territorial Asylum convened to consider such a possibility 'was an abject failure'.[5]

[3] The essay by Suhrke on 'Refugees and Asylum in the Muslim World' is reproduced in its entirety here because, as she notes, 'by the opening of the 1990s, about two-thirds of the world's estimated 18 million refugees were Muslims or refugees in Muslim states.'

[4] The right of asylum was not included in the International Covenant on Civil and Political Rights, 1966, or the International Covenant on Economic, Social and Cultural Rights, 1966.

[5] Guy S. Goodwin-Gill, *The Refugee in International Law* (Clarendon Press, Oxford, 1996), second edition, p. 181. See further A. Grahl-Madsen, *Territorial Asylum* (Swedish Institute of International Affairs, 1980); and P. Weis, 'The Draft United Nations Convention on Territorial Asylum', *British Yearbook of International Law*, (Vol. 50, 1980), p. 151.

In the context of the assertion of sovereign discretion to offer or deny asylum, a question is often asked as to whether a state should have a monopoly of the protection function. After all, the argument goes, the practice of asylum 'originated in sanctuaries offered by the holy places'. S.P. Sinha, *Asylum and International Law* (Martinus Nijhoff, The Hague, 1971), p. 1. In the West, the church continues to claim the privilege of granting asylum to individuals. C.S. Milligan, 'Ethical Aspects of Refugee Issues and US Policy', in Ved P. Nanda, ed., *Refugee Law and Policy: International and US Responses* (Greenwood Press, New York, 1989), pp. 165–85; Tom Gerety, 'Sanctuary: A Comment on the Ironic Relation between Law and Morality', in D.A. Martin, ed., *The New Asylum Seekers: Refugee Law in the 1980s* (Martinus Nijhoff, Dordrecht, 1988), pp. 159–80. According to the philosopher Adelman:

if institutions, such as churches, have played a historic role in protection—in this case, of providing sanctuary to those whose lives are in danger—then the sovereignty of the state cannot limit the protection those institutions offer to non-members; the state may not have the absolute sovereign authority to deny to those individuals protection by institutions which may historically predate the creation of the state.

Howard Adelman, 'Refuge or Asylum: A Philosophical Perspective', in H. Adelman and C.M. Lanphier, eds, *Refuge or Asylum: A Choice for Canada* (York University Press, Toronto, 1990), pp. 12–27 at p. 22.

The question of non-sovereign protection functions is a delicate and complex matter. While in some societies it helps carve out progressive space to offer refuge to those in need, in others it may give rise to certain problems. Four points may be made here. First, it is not

In **Reading I.D** Kennedy questions the usefulness of a debate on the concept of asylum which hopes to reconcile national discretion with the individual right to be granted asylum. There is the predictable inability of such a discourse to reach closure. The reading is of interest inasmuch as the argument for obligation is said to fail, among other things, because of the 'vagueness of the institution'.[6] But is the institution of asylum 'vague'? Or is its 'vagueness' the function of the nature and character of the contemporary international system? Readers may address this issue in the matrix of the history of the institution of asylum.

It is often contended by Western states and scholars that the nature and character of refugee flows in the third world are radically different from refugee flows in Europe since the end of World War I. This is a highly debatable proposition. To begin with, as **Reading I.A** shows, the European belief that the present rate of intercontinental movements is unprecedented in history is clearly wrong. To quote Widgren:

Taking a 200-year perspective from 1800 to 2000, by far the peak of migration was reached during the years 1845–1924, when 50 million people, mainly Europeans, moved to the Western Hemisphere at a time when world population counted only somewhat more than one billion. The total number of Africans and Asians who moved (or moved as seven million slaves) to other continents during the period 1500–1960 is estimated at only 15 million.... Europe's role as a major sending partner compared with other continents was maintained up to the 1970s.... Thus it is only in the last two decades that the OECD region as a whole has started to experience net immigration and each of the non-OECD regions net emigration.[7]

In **Reading I.E** Skran goes further and questions the view that refugee problems have undergone a radical transformation in the post-1945 period. Her thesis is significant because the unique nature of the contemporary global refugee problem is advanced as a key reason by the

---

certain if religious asylum was practised in all cultures. According to Sinha, 'Religious asylum was practised among the ancient civilizations of Jews, Greeks, Roman and Christians, although it had no place in the legal schemes of the more developed of the ancient civilizations as, for example, of the Hindus or the Egyptians.' Sinha, *Asylum and International Law* (see above), p. 275. Second, 'it was often abused', and, in the third world context, has the potential of being seriously abused by forces which threaten the security and territorial integrity of states. Third, it may give rise to the practice of selective humanitarianism. Fourth, the answer perhaps lies not in carving out small spaces for religious institutions but to bring public opinion to bear on states to redefine their attitude towards the institution of asylum.

[6] Goodwin-Gill, *The Refugee in International Law* (see footnote 5 earlier), p. 174.

[7] J. Widgren, 'International Migration and Regional Stability', *International Affairs* (Vol. 65, 1990), p. 752.

Western countries to justify the institutionalisation of what Hathaway has called the *non-entrée* regime.[8]

Principle of *Non-refoulement*: Customary International Law?

While states have refused to recognise a right of asylum, they have accepted the obligation of *non-refoulement* in Article 33 (1) of the 1951 Convention. Broadly speaking, it prescribes that 'no refugee should be returned to any country where he or she is likely to face persecution or torture.'[9] The principle of *non-refoulement* has also come to be embodied in other international instruments. For example, Article 3 of the 1984 Convention against Torture states:

1. No State Party shall expel, return (*'refouler'*) or extradite a person to another State where there are substantial grounds for believing that he would be in danger of being subjected to torture.

2. For the purpose of determining whether there are such grounds, the competent authorities shall take into account all relevant considerations including, where applicable, the existence in the State concerned of a consistent pattern of gross, flagrant or mass violations on human rights.[10]

The principle of *non-refoulement* is not, however, an absolute principle. Article 33 (2) of the 1951 Convention states:

The benefit of the present provision may not, however, be claimed by a refugee whom there are reasonable grounds for regarding as a danger to the security of the country in which he is, or who, having been convicted by a final judgement of a particularly serious crime, constitutes a danger to the community of that country.

The 1951 Convention was drafted with the individual asylum-seeker in mind. It does not quite deal with a situation of mass influx of asylum-seekers which could either preclude formal determination of refugee

[8] For a detailed discussion of what I have termed the 'myth of difference', see B.S. Chimni, 'The Geopolitics of Refugee Studies: A View from the South', *Journal of Refugee Studies* (Vol. 11, 1998), pp. 350–75 at pp. 355–60.

[9] Goodwin-Gill, *The Refugee in International Law* (see footnote 5 earlier), p. 117.

[10] See also Article II(3) of the 1969 OAU Convention, Article 12(3) of the African Charter of Human and People's Rights, 1981, Article 22(8) of the 1969 American Convention on Human Rights, Article 3 of the 1950 European Convention on Human Rights and Article 45 of the 1949 Geneva Convention relative to the Protection of Civilian Persons in Time of War. For the text of these treaties see *Collection of International Instruments and Other Legal Texts Concerning Refugees and Displaced Persons* (UNHCR, Geneva, 1995), Vols I and II.

status or/and exclude a lasting solution. Moreover, the asylum-seekers may include those who fall within the broader definition of refugee contained in the OAU Convention and the Cartagena Declaration. In the context of 'protection of asylum-seekers in situations of large-scale influx' the Executive Committee of the United Nations High Commissioner for Refugees (UNHCR) adopted Conclusion No. 22 in 1981 which insists on the provision of temporary refuge through the act of admission:

1. In situations of large-scale influx, asylum-seekers should be admitted to the State in which they first seek refuge and if that State is unable to admit them on a durable basis, it should always admit them at least on a temporary basis.... They should be admitted without any discrimination as to race, religion, political opinion, nationality, country of origin or physical incapacity.

2. In all cases the fundamental principle of *non-refoulement*—including non-rejection at the frontier—must be scrupulously observed.

A key question which arises with respect to the the principle of *non-refoulement* is whether it forms a part of customary international law. If so, does its scope extend to non-Convention refugees? Arriving at a determination that a principle or norm has evolved into a customary law principle or norm is an inherently difficult exercise, for it turns on the evaluation of material and psychological evidence which lends itself to diverse interpretations.[11] In **Readings II.A** to **II.C** Goodwin-Gill argues the case for customary status and its extension to non-Convention refugees, Hailbronner against, and Hathaway aspires to occupy middle ground.[12]

More recently, Goodwin-Gill has modified his approach. In the second edition of his book *The Refugee in International Law* (1996) he writes:

In a 1986 paper ... the present writer argued that while customary international law had incorporated the core meaning of Article 33, it had also 'extend[ed] the principle of *non-refoulement* to include displaced persons who do not enjoy the protection of the government

---

[11] See David Kennedy, *International Legal Structures* (Baden Baden, 1987); and Martii Koskenniemi, *From Apology to Utopia: The Structure of International Legal Argument* (Lakmiesliiton Kustannus, Helsinki, 1989). More generally, see Ian Brownlie, *Principles of Public International Law* (Clarendon Press, Oxford, 1990), third edition, pp. 4ff, and the references he lists.

[12] On the question see also F.P. Feliciano, 'The Principle of *Non-Refoulement*: A Note on International Legal Protection of Refugees and Displaced Persons', *Phillipine Law Journal* (Vol. 57, 1982), p. 598; P. Hyndman, 'Asylum and Non-Refoulement—Are these Obligations Owed to Refugees under International Law?' *Phillipine Law Journal* (Vol. 57, 1982), p. 43; and D.A. Martin, 'Large Scale Migrations of Asylum Seekers', *American Journal of International Law* (Vol. 76, 1982), p. 598.

of their country of origin'. Although framed with specific reference to danger caused by civil disorder, internal conflicts or human rights violations, the argument in terms of *non-refoulement* was not well chosen, particularly given States' perceptions linking the principle closely to Convention refugees and asylum. Rather, the impact on State competence of the broader developments relating to human rights and displacement would have been better served by characterising State responsibilities in terms of a general principle of *refuge*.[13]

This understanding raises a number of questions.[14] What are the implications of framing the issue in terms of an 'analogous principle of refuge'? Is it in any way more restrictive than extending the scope of the customary international law principle of *non-refoulement* to non-Convention refugees? What difference will couching the 'analogous principle' in the language of duty and state responsibility make? If the emergence of a principle of refuge were to be questioned, what would its implications be for states in relation to non-Convention refugees? Lastly, what if it is contended that there is no customary international law principle of *non-refoulement* which extends even to Convention refugees?

Principle of *Non-refoulement*: Practice and Implications

Readings contained in Section III note the increasing threats to the principle of *non-refoulement* in recent years. In **Reading III.A** Hathaway and Dent discuss three types of state practice that may offend the basic principle of *non-refoulement*: the return of refugees physically present in the territory of the state, the return of refugees at or near the border, and the evolution of arms-length *non-entrée* policies in the industrialised world.

In so far as the return of refugees from a state's frontiers is concerned, the decision of the US Supreme Court in *Sale v. Haitian Centers Council* (1993) represents a particularly regressive step. In it the Supreme Court upheld the view that interdicting asylum-seekers on the High Seas was not violative of the letter and spirit of the 1951 Convention. The decision has been described by the High Commissioner for Refugees 'as a setback to modern international refugee law'. **Reading III.B** reproduces parts of the judgement along with Justice Blackmun's persuasive dissenting opinion. The case has been discussed by Hathaway and Dent in **Reading III.A.**

[13] Goodwin-Gill, *The Refugee in International Law* (see footnote 5 earlier), p. 136.

[14] I would recommend that readers carefully read Chapter 4 of the second edition of Goodwin-Gill's book to understand the reasons why he has modified his approach. See also D. Perluss and J. Hartman, 'Temporary Refuge: Emergence of a Customary International Law Norm', *Virginia Journal of International Law* (Vol. 26, 1986), p. 551; B.S. Chimni, 'The Language of Protection and the Reality of Rejection: End of Cold War and Crisis in Refugee Law', in K.P. Saksena, ed., *Human Rights: Perspective and Challenges* (Lancer Books, New Delhi, 1994), pp. 322–37, especially p. 333.

A major source of threat to the principle of *non-refoulement* comes from a whole host of measures which the industrialised countries have taken to construct a *non-entrée* regime. It would require a separate tome to review these measures, some of which Hathaway and Dent discuss briefly such as imposition of visa requirements, carrier sanctions, the concept of safe third country and the designation of international zones at airports. Hathaway and Dent also touch upon the negative implications of the process of harmonising asylum procedures in Europe through *inter alia* the Schengen and the Dublin Conventions.[15] Readers would do well to consult the growing literature on these issues.[16]

In **Reading III.C** Richmond contends that the growing North–South divide and the increasing restrictive practices of Northern states with respect to asylum point towards the construction of apartheid on a global scale. While this may seem a provocative thesis, the evidence for it is growing.

[15] The Convention Determining the State Responsible for Examining Applications for Asylum Lodged in One of the Member States of the European Communities (Dublin Convention) of 15 June 1990; the European Agreement on the Gradual Abolition of Controls at the Common Frontiers (Schengen Agreement); and Schengen Implementation Convention. For the texts of these agreements see *Collection of International Instruments and Other Legal Texts Concerning Refugees and Displaced Persons* (UNHCR, Geneva, 1995), Vol. II.

[16] J.J. Bolten, 'From Schengen to Dublin: The New Frontiers of Refugee Law', in H. Meijers et al., eds, *Schengen: Internationalization of Central Chapters of the Law on Aliens, Refugees, Privacy, Security and the Police* (Kluwer Law and Taxation, W.E.J. Tjeenk Willink, 1991), pp. 8–36; J. Hathaway, 'Harmonizing for Whom? The Devaluation of Refugee Protection in the Era of European Economic Integration', *Cornell International Law Journal* (Vol. 26, 1993), pp. 719–35; A. Shacknove, 'From Asylum to Containment', *International Journal of Refugee Law* (Vol. 5, 1993), pp. 516–33; G.L. Neuman, 'Buffer Zones Against Refugees: Dublin, Schengen, and the German Asylum Amendment', *Virginia Journal of International Law* (Vol. 33, 1993), pp. 503–26; E. Kjaergaard, 'The Concept of "Safe Third Country" in Contemporary European Refugee Law', *International Journal of Refugee Law* (Vol. 6, 1994), pp. 649–55; UNHCR, Regional Bureau for Europe, *An Overview of Protection Issues in Western Europe: Legislative Trends and Positions Taken by UNHCR* (Vol. 1, No. 3, September 1995); A. Cruz, *Shifting Responsibility: Carriers' Liability in the Member States of the European Union and North America* (Trentham Books, Staffordshire, 1995); M. Spencer, *States of Injustice: A Guide to Human Rights and Civil Liberties in the European Union* (Pluto Press, London, 1995); S. Mahmood, 'The Schengen Information System: An Inequitable Data Protection Regime', *International Journal of Refugee Law* (Vol. 7, 1995), pp. 188–200; K.E. McCarron, 'The Schengen Agreement as a Violation of International Law and the Need for Centralized Adjudication on the Validity of National Asylum Policies for Members of the United Nations', *Boston College International and Comparative Law Review* (Vol. 17, 1995), pp. 401–28; A. Achermann and M. Gattiker, 'Safe Third Countries: European Developments', *International Journal of Refugee Law* (Vol. 7, 1995), pp. 19–37; P. Tuitt, *False Images: Law's Construction of the Refugee* (Pluto Press, London, 1996); and *At Fortress Europe's Moat: The 'Safe Third Country' Concept* (USCR, Washington, D.C., 1997); S. Lavenex, *Safe Third Countries* (Central European University Press, Budapest, 1999).

Concept of Temporary Protection

Part IV deals with the 'new' concept of temporary protection.[17] While it can be argued that protection was always conceived as temporary, vide Article I(C) of the 1951 Convention which contains the cessation clause, international refugee law was in practice firmly wedded to an exile bias.[18] As Goodwin-Gill has noted, the Convention 'was drafted at a time when voluntary repatriation was effectively obsolete. There was no talk then of temporary protection, temporary refuge, dealing with causes, promoting the condition for safe return, or preventing the necessity for flight.'[19]

The emergence of the contemporary concept of temporary protection in the North can be traced to a paradigm shift in the post–Cold War era. More than 90 per cent of those given asylum in the West in the course of the Cold War came from the former communist countries. With the Cold War dissipated, refugees have lost ideological and geopolitical value causing international refugee law to move away from the exile bias.

The concept of temporary protection was conceived in the context of refugees fleeing the conflict in former Yugoslavia. Three features, among others, distinguish the *practise* of temporary protection. First, even those refugees who fall squarely within the definition of the 1951 Convention may only receive, as pointed out in **Reading III.A**, temporary protection.[20] Second, the concept coexists with a *non-entrée* regime which makes access to the industrialised world difficult. Third, it is premised on a notion of return in which the wishes of the refugee are not paramount.[21] **Reading IV.A** discusses the possible advantages of a temporary protection regime and the accompanying problems. In its light, one may ask whether the temporary protection regime is just and can be introduced elsewhere in the world. Readers may also compare the practice of 'temporary protection' in the North and in the South.

---

[17] On the concept of temporary protection see Goodwin-Gill, *The Refugee in International Law* (footnote 5 earlier), pp. 199–202; M. Kjaerum, 'Temporary Protection in Europe in the 1990s', *International Journal of Refugee Law* (Vol. 6, 1994), p. 444; D. Luca, 'Questioning Temporary Protection, Together with a Selected Bibliography on Temporary Refuge/Temporary Protection', *International Journal of Refugee Law* (Vol. 6, 1994), p. 535; and J. Thorburn, 'Transcending Boundaries: Temporary Protection and Burden-sharing in Europe', *International Journal of Refugee Law* (Vol. 7, 1995), p. 459.

[18] On the cessation clause see Chapter 1 **Reading II.9.Q.**

[19] Guy Goodwin-Gill, 'Editorial', *International Journal of Refugee Law* (Vol. 7, 1995), p. 8.

[20] U. David, 'Refugees from Bosnia and Herzegovina: Are They Genuine?', *Suffolk International Law Review* (Vol. 18, 1995), pp. 53–131.

[21] See in this regard James Hathaway, 'The Meaning of Repatriation', *International Journal of Refugee Law* (Vol. 9, No. 4, 1997), pp. 551–58. For a critique of Hathaway see B.S. Chimni, 'From Resettlement to Repatriation: Toward a Critical History of Durable Solutions', Recent Issues in Refugee Research, UNHCR Working Paper No. 2 (Geneva, May 1999). For a discussion of the solution of voluntary repatriation see Chapter 6.

The Principle of Burden-sharing

In the period of the Cold War the industrialised world emphasised the principle of burden-sharing in the context of refugee flows. It has now given way, as we have seen, to the practice of burden-shifting. The practices which constitute burden-shifting violate the principle of burden-sharing which is arguably a customary international law principle. **Reading V.A** considers some of the evidence in this regard. In its light, we may address the following questions: Is the evidence for the emergence of a customary international law principle of burden-sharing any less than that for the principle of *non-refoulement*? What are the implications for state practice if it is deemed a principle of customary international law? What impact would the principle have on the behaviour of states if it were instead to be classified as a soft law principle?[22]

Readers may also reflect on the links of the principle of burden-sharing with the principle of *non-refoulement*. While the absence of burden-sharing can never be a pretext to violate the principle of *non-refoulement*, the willingness of the international community to share the burden of the global refugee problem will encourage greater respect for it. The concept of temporary refuge, in other words, is linked to the observance of the principle of burden-sharing at the level of asylum.[23]

Extradition and Asylum

Part V deals with the problem of extradition and asylum. **Reading V.A** poses the question of reconciling the international consensus against the crime of hijacking with the obligations undertaken under the 1951 Convention which is silent on the question of extradition. In this context Helton examines the decision of the Tokyo High Court in the famous case of Zhang Zhenhai who was extradited to China. He contends that the Japanese court failed to appreciate fully Zhang's claim under international refugee law. Would readers agree? **Reading V.B** reproduces Conclusion No. 17 adopted by the Executive Committee of UNHCR on the matter of extradition and asylum.[24]

---

[22] On the distinction between hard and soft law see R.R. Baxter, 'International Law in "Her Infinite Variety"', *International and Comparative Law Quarterly* (Vol. 29, 1980), pp. 549–66; Prosper Weil, 'Towards Relative Normativity in International Law', *American Journal of International Law* (Vol. 74, 1980), pp. 413–42; and H.L.A. Hart, *The Concept of Law* (Oxford University Press, Oxford, 1961), Chapter 10.

[23] This was the model which informed, for example, the resettlement of the Indo-Chinese refugees in a large number of industrialised states.

[24] See further, Goodwin-Gill, *The Refugee in International Law*, (footnote 5 earlier), pp. 147–50.

I. HISTORY

A. Aristide R. Zolberg, 'International Migrants and Refugees in Historical Perspective', *Refugees* (December 1992), pp. 37–39, and *Refugees* (April 1993), pp. 41–42.

The emergence of powerful European states in the 15th century inaugurated a distinctive era in the history of human migrations. The conquest by the Europeans of the New World, their success in linking all the world's oceans into a continuous network of transportation, and their aggressive pursuit of commercial hegemony, had the effect of incorporating the world's population into a single migratory system, bringing about unprecedented encounters between very different groups widely separated in space. This process steadily expanded geographically and quantitatively, down to our own time. Its history can be divided into three epochs, each of which produced distinctive patterns of economic and political migrations.

In the era of absolutism and mercantilism (16th to 18th centuries), population grew very slowly and was considered a scarce economic and military resource. European rulers sought to confine their subjects within their territory, but at the same time tried to acquire valuable populations from other states, or from what constituted for them the external world. The primitive conditions of long-distance transportation rendered independent undertakings to relocate very difficult.

There was little international movement of labour within Europe, but its outward expansion produced two large transoceanic migrations: the relocation of some 2 to 3 million Europeans in the New World colonies, most as bound labourers, and the importation of an estimated 7.5 million West Africans as plantation slaves, initially to islands adjoining Europe itself, and then to the New World as well. Africa was already the major source of slave labour for the Islamic world, and continued to play this role well into the 20th century. . . .

Despite the positive value placed on human resources, the pursuit of religious uniformity as an instrument of state hegemony occasionally prompted rulers to eject populations, or to persecute them to the point of precipitating their flight. The new element was not persecution, but rather the targeting of large groups. The series began with the expulsion of the unconverted Jews from Spain in 1492, and continued in the next century with that of the *moriscos* of Arab descent. From the 1560s onwards Spanish authorities attempted to contain a rebellion in the southern Low Countries (today's Belgium) by exiling Protestants, many of whom were prominent in the region's manufacturing and commerce. The Tudors exiled Irish Catholic lites while Cromwell deported many Irish to the West Indies; and the application of the principle *cuius regio, eius religio* triggered innumerable forced population exchanges among the German principalities. The last massive wave consisted of some 200,000 Huguenots who fled France when Louis XIV revoked the Edict of Nantes in 1685.

Second Epoch

The second epoch was inaugurated by the industrial, democratic and demographic revolutions of the late 18th century. The interaction of rapid population growth with the dynamics of capitalism massively propelled Europe's rural populations in search of work. Overseas, there were now a number of independent countries or self-governing colonies under the control of people of European descent, eager to secure settlers and workers. On the European side, these developments prompted governments to relinquish traditional prohibitions on emigration, which came to be viewed as a way of lowering welfare burdens and as a safety valve in the face of social unrest. Concomitantly, 'freedom to leave' was recognised as a human right.

Overall, gross emigration from Europe overseas grew from a mere 120,000 in the first decade of the 19th century to about 8.5 million in the last, for a total of some 29 million. Initially the major source was the United Kingdom, but in 1854 arrivals in the United States from Germany surpassed those originating in the British Isles, and by the 1870s many were coming from southern and eastern Europe as well....

The conflicts associated with the democratic and national revolutions fostered a distinctive type of refugees based on political opinion and class affiliation. The most notorious of the early waves are the *emigrés* who escaped the French Terror. But the American Revolution triggered a much larger flow in relation to population size, involving 'Tory' partisans of continued British rule, many of whom were relocated in Canada. The comings and goings of political refugees became commonplace throughout the 19th century, mostly from the ranks of defeated revolutionary and nationalist movements. These exiles, who consisted usually of small numbers of educated professionals, easily found asylum among the emerging liberal regimes of Europe and America.

Third Epoch

The principal features of our own world began to emerge in the final decades of the 19th century. A major characteristic of this third epoch was the formation of a growing gap between a small number of capital-rich, technologically advanced, and militarily powerful countries—European or of European origin plus Japan—and the rest of the world. Concurrently, the demographic expansion of the advanced countries slowed

down, whereas that of the others speeded up; Europe reached its historical maximum proportion of world population around World War I, and
the United States and Japan around 1950....

In response to what they perceived as a threat of invasion by a multitude of poor strangers, many of whom belonged to what prevailing ideologies defined as 'undesirable' or 'racially inferior' groups, the affluent
states instituted more effective border controls and imposed severe limits
on entry for purposes of permanent settlement. Around the turn of the
20th century, the overseas countries governed by people of European
descent adopted draconian measures to prevent further immigration of
any kind from Asia, while Germany and Britain undertook to prevent
the entry of Jews from eastern Europe. Although in the United States
attempts were also launched at this time to deter immigrants from eastern and southern Europe, who were said to be unwilling or unable to
become American, the restrictionists took nearly a quarter of a century to
achieve their objectives. Meanwhile, the transatlantic traffic reached unprecedented heights.

World War I and the Soviet Revolution prompted a further reinforcement of controls and restrictions on grounds of national security. By the
1920s, most receiving states in Europe and overseas had erected solid
walls, with well-policed narrow gates to provide for temporary workers,
and in the case of the overseas countries, family members of the previous
immigrants as well as a small number of new settlers, preferably from the
'founding' nationalities. Taken together, these enactments formed a worldwide international migration regime, still largely in effect today. An additional feature of the regime was the elaboration by the 20th century's
authoritarian states of draconian barriers against exit, to prevent their
populations from 'voting with their feet' against the political regime and
from undermining its economic policies....

... In the first half of the century, the refugees originated mostly in
Europe. In the 1930s, with the onset of the depression and mounting
international tensions, the gates were everywhere shut even tighter, making it almost impossible for the persecuted to find a haven. The inability
to expel the Jews from Europe contributed to the Nazi's decision to
undertake instead their mass murder. The Nazis also forcibly relocated
very large numbers of workers throughout occupied Europe. Huge populations were further uprooted at the end of the war, including this time
Germans who had previously migrated to eastern Europe, as well as
masses of people fleeing the advancing Russian armies, the imposition of
Polish and Soviet control over the eastern parts of Germany, or the establishment of Soviet-dominated regimes. Most of these were relocated in
West Germany, the United States and Canada....

In the early post-war period, the western countries undertook to
atone for recent tragedies by providing international mechanisms for

protecting and assisting refugees. Although these were initially destined to deal only with the sequels of past persecution, subsequently, most western states also welcomed people escaping from European countries under communist rule. But except for Germany until 1960 and Hungary in 1956, the numbers were quite small. Meanwhile, however, the processes that had generated refugees in Europe for many centuries began to engulf other parts of the world, starting with the partition of India and Pakistan in 1947 and of Palestine the following year. There were also massive displacements from continental China to Taiwan, from North to South Korea, and from North to South Vietnam. Most of the refugees from this period were relatively quickly resettled within the Third World itself, with the notable exception of the Palestinians. However, in the 1960s the wars of national liberation in southern Africa as well as internal crises among the continent's new states also began to generate large-scale displacements, and in the course of the following decade, the number of internationally displaced persons in need of assistance worldwide escalated from an annual level of about 5 million to some 15 million. This crisis was attributable mostly to an exacerbation of internal conflicts by direct or indirect intervention of the superpowers, resulting in the expansion of these conflicts in both time and space.

Most of the Third World's new refugees continued to remain in their region of origin, but now tended to be confined in camps where they had little or no opportunity to fend for themselves, and were therefore dependent on intermittent assistance from international agencies. A very small number, mostly Indochinese, were invited to resettle in western countries. Some others ventured farther afield and came knocking at the door of the rich just as hard times set in. Concurrently, the proliferation of barriers against immigration also prompted some migrants to try their luck by filling an asylum claim. Existing mechanisms for processing applications were rapidly overwhelmed, and the appearance of large numbers of questionable refugees further fuelled xenophobic fires. This led to a tightening of procedures, with deleterious consequences for some genuine refugees.

B. Astri Suhrke, 'Refugees and Asylum in the Muslim World', in Robin Cohen, ed., *The Cambridge Survey of World Migration* (Cambridge University Press, Cambridge, 1995), pp. 457–60.

By the opening of the 1990s, about two-thirds of the world's estimated 18 million refugees were Muslims or refugees in Muslim states. The trend was expected to continue, with upheavals in Central Asia, the Caucasus and the Balkans contributing their part. This situation has generated growing interest in the subject of Islamic concepts of refugee and asylum.

What are the formal concepts and how do they relate to the practice of states? Is there a case for closer ties between the Islamic world and the international refugee regime anchored in the United Nations? This essay will approach these questions by examining Islamic concepts of refugee and asylum, and the main historical events that have shaped them.

Formal Concepts

While Western traditions of refugee and asylum in part have religious origins, the equivalent Muslim concepts are central to the genesis of Islam itself. The flight of the Prophet Muhammad and his followers from hostile Mecca to friendly Medina in A.D. 622 came to be known as the *hijra*—the migration. Medina's welcome enabled the Prophet to regroup and successfully lead a holy war (*jihad*) against Mecca. From this point onwards, Islam developed as a global religion. The flight and battle which made this possible became the defining elements of Islamic thought regarding refugees. A generic Arabic term for migration, *hijra* came to signify movement from a land of infidelity or oppress to the land of Islam, from *dar al-harb* to *dar al-Islam*. The process could involve a *jihad* and triumphant return to the liberated land of Islam, or an expansion of the frontiers of *dar al-Islam* by establishing a new Muslim community, or yet a third alternative of settling in an existing Muslim state.

The model for receiving refugees—i.e., granting asylum—likewise was determined by the Prophet's experience when he reached Medina and was warmly welcomed. Formalised in the fourth *surah* of the Koran, the obligations of the receiving society (*ansar*, i.e., host) are derived from the characteristic nature of the migration itself: 'He who emigrates in the path of God will find frequent refuge and abundance.'

While Western concepts of refugee emphasise the involuntary nature of the movement, and contemporary international law defines a 'refugee' with respect to the nature of abuse feared or inflicted, the Islamic tradition clearly differs. In its classic sense, flight is a sacred duty to be undertaken by Muslims who live in non-Muslim societies regardless of the kind of oppression to which they might be subjected. The obligation is premised on the indivisibility between state and society, which holds that a Muslim society cannot exist in a non-Muslim state. The notion of 'persecution', which figures so prominently in Western jurisprudence governing refugee status, thus becomes secondary as does the common sociological distinction between voluntary (migration) and involuntary (refugee) movements. *Hijra* is simply a duty.

Time and a changing world modified the classic concepts. Yet the evolution of Islamic doctrines continued to centre on obligations to exit (in contrast to the Western focus on conditions of entry). The pre-occupation reflected the stagnation and eventual retrenchment of secular Muslim power in the late medieval period and again from the eighteenth century onwards.

As Christian states started to conquer Muslim lands, the question of flight was posed more often and in stark terms: must Muslims flee from land that once had been, but now had ceased to be *dar al-Islam*? The dominant theological interpretation in the late medieval period upheld the obligation to perform *hijra*, but conditions which permitted exceptions were later enumerated by Islamic scholars, and some—mainly the Sufi—interpreted *hijra* as a spiritual withdrawal from a hostile society rather than a physical movement.

The Refugee in History

In practice, the *hijra* command was rarely followed, and all but one took place in the context of immediate violence. When Granada fell in A.D. 1492, many Muslims did indeed leave the Iberian peninsula as called for by Islamic doctrine, but persecution and eventual expulsion left them little choice. Centuries later, when millions of Muslims in the Middle East and Africa came under European colonial rule, only one major case of *hijra* is recorded. Thousands of Algerians left their homes from Libya in protest against French colonialism, but also to escape repression after the failed Abdulqadir revolt (1832–47).

Other population movements commonly referred to as *hijra* in the nineteenth and early twentieth centuries occurred as the Ottoman empire was pushed back, as were millions of Muslims who mostly fled to the interior regions of the Ottoman realm. When the Russians conquered Crimea and most of the Caucasus, Muslims were pushed out to make room for Christian Slav settlers. From all sides, the Muslims were pressured: 'The destruction of native social and political institutions, the implementation of a land policy intended to favour Russian ownership and its attendant serf agriculture, and concern that most Muslim natives posed security problems for the state, all combined to produce pressure on [them] ... to leave.' Russian officials spoke of the 'cleansing' of Crimea already in 1837. Later, the Tartars were deemed doubly undesirable by virtue of their suspected collaboration with the Ottoman forces during the Crimean War. In the Caucasus, the Russians needed three years and some 100,000 soldiers to subdue an armed rebellion led by the Sufi Naqshbandi order. Large-scale out-migration of the defeated Muslims followed.

As the line of conflict between the Christian and Muslim worlds shifted southward, the exodus reached massive proportions. At its height (1855–60), between 700,000 and 900,000 Muslims moved from the Crimea and the Caucasus towards the inner regions of the Ottoman empire. Moving on their own without assistance from the humanitarian organisations, which only later developed to aid refugees, the migrants suffered severe deprivations and thousands died on the way from smallpox, dysentery, fever or exhaustion.

The other main migration into the Ottoman realm in this period was the *hijra* from the Balkans after the Turco–Russian war (1877–8) and the Balkan wars of 1912–13. The wars further decimated the Ottoman empire, breaking off chunks that were reconstituted as independent states. The Muslims were fragmented by new state boundaries and transformed into minorities in various non-Muslim states. Immediately, they were 'encouraged or forced to emigrate'.

Russian penetration of the independent Muslim khanates on the Ottoman periphery in Central Asia also provoked armed resistance and flight—a pattern continued for almost a decade after the Bolshevik revolution of 1917. Most fled to neighbouring Muslim territory—Afghanistan and the nominally Chinese ruled part of Turkestan—from where the resistance continued. Emphasising the religious nature of their refugee condition, some referred to themselves as *muhajir*, i.e., one that performs the *hijra*.

The principal *hijra* that was initiated as a protest rather than an escape took place in India after the First World War. Calling for self-determination for Indian Muslims and simultaneously the recognition of the Ottoman sultan as the head of the entire Islamic world, some 20,000–30,000 Muslims proclaimed a *hijra* and *jihad*, and marched to neighbouring Afghanistan to seek support for the war. The quixotic march ended in defeat as hundreds died of exhaustion on the way and the survivors failed to get support or recognition either in Afghanistan, Turkey or the Middle East.

By the early twentieth century, foreign rule, failed rebellions and ultimate displacement of Muslim peoples had come to define the reality of the refugee experience in the Islamic world. The original concept of *hijra* as a sacred duty leading to the victorious expansion, or restoration, of the Islamic realm had been overtaken by historical events. Moreover, millions of Muslims continued to live in secular states under colonial rule, or as minorities in Christian, Hindu or Buddhist societies. Few had any realistic alternative. Unlike in medieval times and in the Ottoman period—when Muslims could freely settle anywhere in the realm—an emerging world of national states with formal border controls increasingly posed barriers to migration also in the Muslim world.

While the option of settling freely anywhere in *dar al-Islam* narrowed, a reverse movement simultaneously became more attractive. Increasingly, Muslims sought to migrate to non-Muslim countries for educational and economic advancement. Scholars posed new questions to redefine *hijra*. From where does one not need to migrate? To where can one migrate?

The image of the Muslim refugee as someone forcefully displaced by non-Muslim powers was reinforced during the second half of the

twentieth century as three prominent refugee populations appeared—
the Palestinians, the Afghans and the Bosnian Muslims. The Palestinians
clearly were subjected to expulsion during the partition of Palestine and
its aftermath, as were the Bosnian Muslims forty years later when the former Yugoslavia dissolved into war. The Afghan case was more a matter of
escaping the violence of war brought on by a local revolution (1978) and
Soviet intervention, but there was also the element of withdrawal from
enemy-ruled territory to regroup and fight on. The liberation struggle
called for in the classic linking of *jihad* to *hijra* was launched. To emphasise the point, many Afghan refugees referred to themselves as both
muhajir and *mujahedin* (i.e., the noun for participants in both activities).
The Palestinians tenaciously fought displacement by making the 'right of
return'—however defined—central to their political and military struggle
and, by some factions, defined in classic Islamic terms. In the former
Yugoslavia, the culturally European Muslims of Bosnia rarely depicted
their refugee condition in Islamic terms, at least not during the first two
years of the war. Until the war, their religious identity had limited
saliency compared with language and kinship identities.

Asylum

While Islamic theories of asylum are not highly developed, the core is
clear. To provide asylum is a precondition for *hijra* and thus a sacred duty.
But also others—non-Muslims and Muslims who flee from Muslims—
have a right to protection according to the Koran: in effect, all who 'emigrate in the path of God' (the Koran, *surah* 4,100). For Muslims, the right
is also derived from their common membership in the Islamic community (*umma*).

By this standard, the asylum policy of the principal receiving entity for
many centuries—the Ottoman empire—was exemplary. In the late medieval period, both Muslims and Jews expelled from Spain were welcome,
and the door remained open for Muslims and non-Muslims alike. Only
towards the end of the nineteenth century did the sultan emphasise the
religious element by declaring the empire open to all Muslims who would
come to settle—a shift shaped by the intensified conflict with Russia and
the European powers.

The population movement from the periphery to the centre of the
Ottoman empire has been estimated at between five and seven million in
the period between 1860 and 1914. Demand for manpower in thinly
populated regions helped sustain the liberal immigration policy. New settlers were given tax and other incentives, as well as assistance upon
arrival. The influx also led the Ottomans to codify admissions practice.
The first civil refugee code in the Muslim world, the law of 1857, probably made no distinction between migrants and refugees, but used the term
muhacir—equivalent to the Arabic *muhajir*—to denote all subjects.

By the mid-twentieth century, nation states had replaced empires, demographic conditions had changed, and the successor Muslim states brought entirely different perspectives to asylum and immigration issues. Apart from the Gulf states, most were poor countries with a large labour surplus. While most governments recognised in principle their Islamic duty to provide asylum, practice was clearly influenced by economic and political constraints. As in most countries, refugee policy was a multi-dimensional and often multi-purpose process. Iran, for example, gave extremely liberal asylum to Afghan refugees, but variously opened and closed its borders to Kurdish refugees in the 1970s. Pakistan had welcomed over three million Afghan refugees as long as the war in Afghanistan was internationalised (1979–89), but closed its borders in 1993 when it feared that international aid to refugees would cease.

More generally, a dual tension is apparent in the asylum policy of Muslim states. The tension between humanitarian ideals and political realism is a universal phenomenon shared by all reasonable governments. Particular to Muslim states is the form this tension takes, shaped on the one hand by traditional principles of asylum—which are broad and generous, derived from Islamic canons as well as pre-Islamic tradition in many areas—and the demands on the modern state to ration benefits to 'non-members'. Asylum ... has passed from the traditional stage as an act of protection generally accorded by individuals and leaders to anyone seeking it, to the modern stage where asylum has become exclusively a state function to be precisely defined. Since few Muslim states have civil laws to regulate modern asylum, practice tends to be random or restrictive, and, some fear, could be influenced by the restrictive European example.

International Cooperation

The predominant image of Muslim refugees as victims of advancing non-Muslim power had by the second half of the twentieth century clearly given way to more varied movements. Many were the result of conflict in or between Muslim states. Protracted warfare in the Horn of Africa produced several million refugees, revolution in Iran and the subsequent war with Iraq led to massive outflows, as did the Gulf War of 1990–91. Civil war in Central Asia caused large displacements in the early 1990s. Two decades earlier, the break-up of Pakistan had generated perhaps nine million refugees.

Recognising the need for international cooperation to deal with the complexities of forced migration, African Muslim states and most Afro–Arab states signed the refugee convention of the Organisation of African Unity (1969) as well as the UN Convention on Refugees, or its 1967 Protocol. The Arab world, however, was weakly tied to the international refugee regime. Except for Tunisia, Algeria and Morocco, no Arab state had signed the 1951 Convention or the 1967 Protocol. For years, rich Arab Gulf states gave only symbolic financial contributions to the United Nations High Commissioner for Refugees (UNHCR). Change did not come until the refugee crisis during the Gulf War and the close political cooperation between Saudi Arabia and the West during that conflict. The Saudi-initiated Organisation of the Islamic Conference subsequently signed agreements with UNHCR to promote cooperation in all matters concerning refugee assistance in the Muslim world. In a related development, efforts were underway in the early 1990s to establish cooperation among Arab League states for the protection and support of refugees.

C. David Kennedy, 'International Refugee Protection', *Human Rights Quarterly* (Vol. 8, No. 1, 1986), pp. 42–46.

The contingency of contemporary notions about asylum as a solution emerges sharply when contrasted with European notions of asylum before 1700 and during the late nineteenth century era of high positivism. Texts from the early period delimit no coherent doctrinal notion of asylum, let alone one of a particularly national discretionary or political form. Scholars wrote of various hospitalities and protections accorded by princes or other authorities to one another and to citizens in various situations, but there was no uniformly recognised status by the name 'asylum' or any other name whose content could be assessed and whose attributes could be measured.[25] The protections and hospitalities of which they wrote were thought to be binding, but were neither uniform nor integrated into a single doctrinal category. On the contrary, they seemed to be responses to the particular needs of those requesting protection. Doctrinally, these texts speak less of a single status to be granted, which entailed particular rights and duties, than of a variety of protective activities encouraged by considerations of a universal legal and moral fabric for people who, for one or another reason, were 'unfortunate'.[26] Thus, historically, those who were protected by states had little of importance in common. One found merchants fleeing debts, peasants seeking to escape feudal bonds or replace collapsing allegiances, children of mixed-class parentage seeking licence to trade, members of religious orders and their flocks seeking princely support or freedom to practice their faith, and

[25] One might collect bits and pieces of doctrine from various places in the work of Grotius or Gentili which described protections accorded people who might today be regarded as refugees and call this resulting collection the 'origins' of modern asylum law, but such a collection would not do justice to these earlier scholars. Neither Suarez nor Vitoria considered the issue.

[26] See, for example, H. Grotius, *On the Law of War and Peace* (1625) (De Jure Belli ac Pacis, Libri Tres) in J.B. Scott, ed., *The Classics of International Law* (1925), Book II, Section V, p. 550.

traders seeking military assistance against pirates or in recovery of property at sea. Many of these individuals received the protection they sought merely by being present elsewhere, for example in a different religious area, while others received special assistance.

In this early period, these people were referred to as 'exiles' (voluntary and involuntary) and 'suppliants', but these were not status categories.[27] Exiles were those who had left their home, seeking to resettle elsewhere, as a result of some fear of disaster. The reasons mentioned *en passant* for their exile included religious persecution, criminal prosecution (just and unjust), war, slavery and general misfortune. It is important to note that these conditions did not trigger a legitimate 'exile' status, but merely described some of the reasons people might flee. Princes welcome exiles, not because their status triggered a duty, but because it was just to do so unless there was some reason rendering it unjust to do so. Since the welcome granted was not triggered by the doctrinal structure of the exile, it was never doctrinally elaborated.

'Suppliants' referred to people requesting that a sovereign right a wrong or protect an interest. A suppliant, for example, might be an exile requesting assistance in recovering property. Although the texts reflect a general sense that such requests should be granted unless it is unjust to do so, the crucial point is that these authors were not concerned about ascertaining an obligation but about elaborating the conditions of justice. Thus, the practice of protecting exiles from the claims of their home sovereign is discussed, not as an aspect of asylum but as one of a number of limits upon a sovereign's ability justly to acquire and sustain rights over subjects. The granting of immunities to suppliants against prosecution is taken up in the elaboration of the justice of sharing punishments among rulers and ruled, that is, as a consequence of guilt, not discretion.

... The early European tradition differed remarkably from the vision of asylum which we see through the lenses of an internationalised notion of refugee status. Neither defines 'asylum' as a condition with specific international legal attributes. For moderns, this seems to be a failure, an absence of legal status, a deficiency in the elaboration of international law. It seems so because, in this modern vision, to be beyond legal status is to be nothing, to be whimsy or politics. In the early vision, however, this lack of a definition was not a deficiency. The need for a legal status simply did not arise in a world which neither placed the sovereign at its centre nor distinguished law from politics and morality. Rather, a wider range of people received as a matter of their just due a wide variety of solutions in unfortunate circumstances.

[27] See, for example, Grotius, ibid., pp. 232, 530–35; Vattel, *Le droit des Gens* (1758) at pp. 228–31; C. Wolff, *The Law of Nations* (1764).

The nineteenth century positivist typically viewed asylum as a sovereign right of states, a vision at odds with both our own and its predecessor. This notion developed progressively as scholars differentiated international from municipal law and positive law from morality and politics. As earlier, more integrated notions of international society were transformed into legal rights, capacities and statuses, asylum was classified in different ways. In the writings of Wolff, it appeared as a normatively obligatory, if modified, capacity of states. In those of Pufendorf it was viewed as a humanitarian obligation which states remained legally free to disregard. All these traditional texts reflected the sense that asylum, regardless of its legal status, was normally to be granted.

The development of a unified notion of a unilateral sovereign capacity to grant asylum did not reflect so much a hardening of attitudes about exiles as a reorientation of the vision of sovereignty. Attempts to square the practice of asylum with growing notions of sovereign independence and authority were directed not to diminishing the force of asylum or the frequency of its being granted, but rather to account for its continued viability in an era in which sovereigns were understood to have complete authority over their nationals. The important part of the nineteenth century sovereign 'right to asylum' was not that it was a sovereign rather than an individual right but that it was a right against the home rather than the host state. In other words, this approach was primarily concerned to resolve conflicting assimilation claims by host and home sovereigns and did so in favour of the institution of asylum.

This was done by treating asylum as the result of the priority of territorial jurisdiction over other claims by a sovereign upon his subjects. The 'asylum' itself was simply the result of this priority. Oppenheim, beginning his seemingly more modern discussion of the 'so-called right of asylum', echoes this vision of asylum as the consequence of jurisdictional conflict by saying:

> The fact that every State exercises territorial supremacy over all persons on its territory, whether they are its subjects or aliens, excludes the prosecution of aliens thereon by foreign States. Thus, a foreign State *is*, provisionally at least, an asylum for every individual who, being prosecuted at home, crossed its frontier.[28]

Yet, merely because asylum was doctrinally understood to depend upon national boundaries did not mean that it resulted from them in any historical or substantive sense. This approach to asylum was a way for positivists to account for a pre-existing institution which had its own substantive content within their vision of sovereignty.

[28] L. Oppenheim, *International Law* 551 (McNair, ed., fourth edition, 1928). Emphasis added.

Nevertheless, as asylum was assimilated to a system of bounded sovereign authorities, it began to take on a more uniform and limited quality. Gone from view was the variety of protection activities accorded and employed in the pre-1700 period. One now thought only of protection which could be doctrinally derived from sovereign boundaries: primarily protection from capture and prosecution or extradition. In this sense, asylum derived a uniform meaning in response to its assimilation to an image of the sovereignty against which it could be invoked rather than from the diverse needs and protections of exiles. Although this reorientation of asylum, by making it dependent upon a picture of sovereignty, brought it closer to our image of asylum, it should be stressed that this did not yet mean that asylum could be given no international content or have no legal force. Nineteenth century asylum was neither uniformly national nor unpredictable. It remained a condition whose contours could be seen from the international doctrinal boundaries which enabled it.

In this, asylum came to be defined in a way which was dependent upon international theories of sovereignty rather than responsive to the needs of refugees. Nevertheless, the positivist vision of asylum was based on an ongoing practice of hospitality and took a uniform shape in response to asylum's internationalisation, not to its exclusion from international law. The increasing tendency to consider asylum as something to be granted was associated with a regularisation of the conditions under which it would be granted and a clarification of what it consisted of, both of which reflected its position in an international doctrinal structure.

Moreover, unlike both modern and earlier notions of asylum, nineteenth century asylum doctrine was completely unconnected to the notion of 'refugee'. For earlier scholars, both the situation of the suppliant and his treatment were matters of justice. For the modern, even if asylum and refugee are imagined to be one another's opposite, created and sustained on different levels, it remains true that the one is regarded as the response to the other. In high positivist literature, asylum grew as a protection separate both from uniform notions of its justice or injustice in particular situations and from a particular qualifying status. This independence of asylum in positivist literature poised it to become the discretionary other of a regularised international refugee status, but this later development was in no sense required by the doctrinal notion of asylum as a sovereign right. Thinking of asylum as dependent upon a set of jurisdictional boundaries instead of a set of notions about justice enabled asylum to take many forms, but did not at that time signify anything about a state's ability to refuse to grant asylum or to grant it on any terms. In fact, as to the latter point, the dependency of respect for asylum upon international notions of jurisdiction suggested that the protection granted, to be respected, would have to be of a particular type, rather than of any type.

D. David Kennedy, 'International Refugee Protection', *Human Rights Quarterly* (Vol. 8, No. 1, 1986), pp. 57–65.

Most contemporary treatments of asylum begin with, and many are devoted exclusively to, consideration of a right to asylum. Scholars who think that this is an important question for investigation carefully distinguish the right *of* asylum (or the 'right to grant asylum'), which is acknowledged to be the *sine qua non* of the institution asylum, from a right *to* asylum (or the 'right to be granted asylum') which, all acknowledge, is more controversial. These two rights are treated as compatible dimensions of an international law of asylum. Because one is seen to be a right of one sovereign against another sovereign and the other is seen to be an individual's right against a sovereign, they do not seem inconsistent. Moreover, were the legal system 'complete', we would have both. The controversy about the right to asylum is, for both supporters and detractors, a 'deficiency' in the legal fabric. It appears that a legal regime, properly articulated, could fulfil both the aspiration to protect sovereign autonomy (the right of asylum) and an international scheme of refugee protection (right to asylum). . . .

However, this distinction has not been successfully translated into distinguishable legal categories. Rather, scholars have recognised that an individual's right to be granted asylum can conflict with a sovereign right to grant asylum if that sovereign right is understood to imply not simply the expectation of international recognition of asylums granted, but also unfettered discretion to refuse to grant asylum. As a result, given the relationship between asylum and national sovereign authority, when these two rights have been seen to conflict, the right of asylum has prevailed. But international law scholars seem uncomfortable with a doctrinal corpus which contains only the right of asylum, understood to be the symbol of absolute discretion. A wholly discretionary right of asylum threatens the international legal character of that right by depriving it of any grounding in mutual sovereign respect. As a result, scholars have continued to discuss the right to asylum, seeking either to rehabilitate it within a regime dominated by the right of asylum or to strengthen it by scholarly advocacy, convention drafting or practice.

The debates about the right to asylum which have ensued are familiar. Most commentators have concluded that there is no right to asylum, although they recognise that there may be other obligations (such as municipal rights, non-extradition, *non-refoulement*, humanitarian duties) protecting asylum-seekers. A minority of commentators argue that there is now a right to asylum, although they recognise that the right may be a qualified one—progressively developing, subject to exceptions, or not fully enforceable or accepted. Those of the majority take a harder line with respect to the qualifications acknowledged by the minority, arguing that there can be no right until it has been fully developed and accepted, is associated with a correlative duty, or is enforceable. Those of the minority take a harder line with respect to the exceptions acknowledged by the majority, arguing that international law can be composed of municipal legal principles and that the humanitarian obligations which make up the penumbra of human rights law are developing into valid rights.

The majority tends to confine its image of international law to the world of sovereigns. The majority tends to rely upon traditional positivist notions about the consensual and formal sources of international legal obligations, the distinction between law and morality, and the primacy of sovereign autonomy. The minority supports, both historically and doctrinally, the possibility of international legal rights and duties for individuals. The minority tends to rely upon recently rehabilitated naturalist notions of sovereign cooperation and the interdependence of law and morality and tends to take a more liberal view of soft, informal, non-consensual or instant sources of law. These tendencies are obviously not absolute. There are, for example, those who acknowledge that individuals may have international legal rights or that 'soft law' may exist, but argue that the right to asylum does not yet make the grade.

The fascinating aspect of this debate, however, is its inconclusive and parallel structure. Both sides accept the basic division of asylum into a sovereign capacity and an individual benefit. Both accept the basic structure of international legal obligation and treat the existence of an obligation as the *sine qua non* of protection. Each develops a position qualified by exceptions designed to meet the objections of the other, yet neither can account for the capacity of its acknowledged exceptions to devour its position when confronted by the challenge of the other. Most importantly, neither alone is able to account for sovereign autonomy and co-operation simultaneously. . . .

Thinking of the debate about a right to asylum as an irresolvable repetition ... reveals how distracting the debate can be. If the task of protection is to get asylum for people, seeking a 'right to asylum' distracts protection lawyers into either wishful thinking or resigned scepticism. Until there is a right, nothing can be done and yet no right seems defensible or achievable which does not comfort us with a new manifestation of sovereign discretion. Moreover, and most disturbingly, this debate, by accepting and reinforcing the disjuncture between international law and national discretion, prevents the UNHCR from capitalising on the new roles thrust upon it by changing conceptions of its mandate for asylum situations and its ability to participate with states in developing flexible solutions for the divergent problems of refugees. To continue this debate places faith in an infinite legal process rather than institutional action.

The Debate about 'Non-refoulement' and 'Admission'

... Like the debate about the right to asylum, discussion of *non-refoulement* begins with an assumption about the distinctiveness of asylum and refugee law.... Legal scholars discussing *non-refoulement* proceed in several stages. The first step is to develop *non-refoulement* as an international legal obligation. International lawyers have devoted a great deal of energy to developing and strengthening the principle of 'non-refoulement', not as the source of a right to asylum coterminous with it, nor as the source for asylum's substantive content, but as an independent obligation of refugee law. As a result, the practice of *non-refoulement* has, over the last hundred and fifty years, been transformed into the 'principle of *non-refoulement*', which is seen by scholars as a 'fundamental' international legal obligation forming the cornerstone of refugee law. Of course, there are exceptions, and state practice, particularly as to *opinio juris*, is anything but conclusive. Nevertheless, scholars continue to insist that the principle of *non-refoulement* has become binding as a matter of both treaty and customary law if not also as a so-called peremptory norm or *jus cogens*.

The important point is not whether these scholars are correct in their assertions about the status of the *non-refoulement* principle, but the strength of their insistence and its consequences for the structure of further debate about *non-refoulement*. Whether correct or not, these assertions reflect a strong sense that *non-refoulement*, as opposed to other aspects of the treatment of refugees, is to be thought of as an international matter of law. Indeed, it is on the basis of this quality of *non-refoulement*, regardless of its particular strength, status or content, that one thinks of refugee law as law at all on the international plane. If one manages to think that the key point about *non-refoulement* is its international legal character, one can think of refugee law as a legitimate subspecies of international law even if one eventually concludes that *non-refoulement* has not (yet) acquired binding force. *Non-refoulement*, like refugee law as a whole, has taken a leap towards international legalisation through the process of its transformation into a 'principle'.

In the process, of course, other aspects of refugee treatment have been left behind or, more accurately, have come to be thought of as matters of national discretion. The various protections beyond non-return which add up to asylum now contrast starkly with the internationalised legal principle of *non-refoulement*. Indeed, sometimes scholars develop the international legal nature of the 'principle' of *non-refoulement* in express contrast to the 'institution' of asylum. This contrast helps preserve the notion that both national discretion and international cooperation can be preserved in the system of refugee protection as a whole. States will be required to do something—not return refugees—as a matter of international law, but their sovereign discretion to refuse asylum will not be disturbed....

... The only compelling aspect of the debate is its inability to achieve closure and its grounding in a fundamental disjuncture between international and national competencies which cannot be overcome by an imaginative but doctrinal craft.... As a result, this debate, while central to much literature about asylum and refugee protection seems, finally, not to matter very much and, like the debate about a right to asylum, to be a matter of preference. It is not surprising, then, that the term of the debate remain murky, for not only does its resolution remain forever out of reach, there is no great incentive to clarify, for to do so would be to abandon the enterprise of doctrinal mediation altogether.

E. Claudena M. Skran, *Refugees in Inter-war Europe: The Emergence of a Regime* (Clarendon Press, Oxford, 1995), pp. 3–6.

The major argument ... is that international assistance efforts of the inter-war era constituted an international regime, and this regime had— and continues to have—a significant impact on refugee policy.... In linking inter-war and contemporary refugee movements, this work challenges the popularly held notion that refugee problems have significantly changed since 1945. Contemporary refugee crises are said to be worse than those of the past because unprecedented numbers of refugees face long periods of exile, primarily in Third World countries. American diplomat William Smyser, for instance, contends that 'the second half of the twentieth century has witnessed an unprecedented explosion in the number and impact of refugees'.[29] In a comprehensive study of refugees and world politics, Leon Gordenker argues that recent refugee movements present 'a contrast with earlier migrations' because of unparalleled numbers of refugees, their location in the developing world, and the growth of transnational networks to assist them.[30]

It is true that in the last decade of the Cold War era the majority of people considered to be refugees were located in the developing world of Asia, Africa, and Latin America. But the notion that the contemporary refugee crisis is unique lacks a historical perspective and neglects this important fact: mass refugee movements are neither new nor exclusive to specific regions. They have been an enduring and global issue throughout the twentieth century. Before the Second World War, the European continent experienced refugee flows similar to those taking place in

[29] Smyser also argues that refugee problems are different from those of the past because of the extended period of time they spend in exile, and because their location has moved from Europe to the Third World. W.R. Smyser, 'Refugees: A Never-ending Story', *Foreign Affairs* (Vol. 64, Fall 1985), pp. 154–68.

[30] Leon Gordenker, *Refugees in International Politics* (Columbia University Press, New York, 1987), pp. 49–59.

Eastern Europe and the developing world today. Those refugee movements began in the early twentieth century, when the Balkan wars forced several hundred thousand people to flee their homes.[31] The two World Wars caused even more disruption. The Second World War alone displaced a staggering number of people—more than thirty million. Even during the relatively peaceful inter-war period, millions of people became refugees, including Germans, Poles, Hungarians, Russians, Greeks, Turks, Armenians, Bulgarians, Jews, Italians and Spaniards.[32] In 1926, for instance, an estimated 9.5 million were considered refugees. While the number of refugees is approximately the same as that of the refugee population of 1980, it is a proportionally larger figure because the world's population doubled in the meantime.[33]

Even when pre-1945 refugee movements are considered, it is often with the stipulation that European refugees are fundamentally different from non-European ones. In particular, the typical European refugee is said to have been an individual escaping political persecution or interstate war, while his or her Third World counterpart is part of a mass movement fleeing political and economic breakdown brought on by civil war or social unrest. While it is true to say that each refugee movement—and each refugee—is distinct, the differences between European and non-European refugees have been greatly exaggerated. Certainly, Cold War refugees tend to fit the profile of an individual facing political persecution. These refugees, however, constituted only a fraction of European refugees in the twentieth century. In fact, there are remarkable similarities between the refugee movements of inter-war Europe and those taking place in the developing world since 1945 and in former Communist countries since the collapse of the Soviet Union.

First, mass refugee movements of this century have been generated primarily by common historical processes which have affected the entire international system. The development of highly destructive military technology and the advent of total war have meant that international conflicts have affected entire populations, not just soldiers. As a result, modern conflicts—be they interstate wars, such as the First and Second World Wars, or internationalised civil wars, such as the Salvadorean or Nicaraguan civil wars—are very likely to produce large numbers of refugees. In addition, throughout this century, when multi-ethnic empires have been transformed into homogeneous nation-states, mass refugee

[31] Sir John Hope Simpson, *The Refugee Problem: Report of a Survey* (Oxford University Press, London, 1939), p. 551.

[32] Michael R. Marrus, *The Unwanted: European Refugees in the Twentieth Century* (Oxford University Press, New York, 1985), pp. 51 and 297.

[33] In 1930 the world's population was approximately 2 billion while by 1980 the population had more than doubled to 4.4 billion. *Encyclopedia Americana* (Grolier, Danbury, 1988), p. 403; *Information Please Almanac* (Houghton Mifflin, Boston, 1991), p. 136.

movements have been an unfortunate by-product. This process often involves a combination of economic pressure and political persecution, thus prompting refugees to leave for a variety of reasons. After the First World War, attempts to create new national states forced millions to become refugees, and the Nazis' attempt to achieve purity forced thousands of Jews into exile. The Serbian policy of 'ethnic cleansing' is not unlike these earlier policies, and the results have been similar: refugees. In the developing world, ethnic violence, civil war and refugee flows have all been a part of the nation-building process after decolonisation.

II. THE PRINCIPLE OF *NON-REFOULEMENT*:
A NORM OF CUSTOMARY INTERNATIONAL LAW?

A. Guy S. Goodwin–Gill, '*Non-refoulement* and the New Asylum Seekers', in David Martin, ed., *The New Asylum Seekers: Refugee Law in the 1980s* (Martinus Nijhoff Publishers, Dordrecht, 1988), pp. 103, 105–6.

... The central thesis of this essay is that the essentially moral obligation to assist refugees and to provide them with refuge or safe haven has, over time and in certain contexts, developed into a legal obligation (albeit at a relatively low level of commitment). The principle of *non-refoulement* must now be understood as applying beyond the narrow confines of Articles 1 and 33 of the 1951 Refugee Convention. It must be emphasised that *non-refoulement* is not about returning refugees to intermediate countries or so-called countries of first asylum. Nor is *non-refoulement* about the failure to provide durable solutions. The central, if not the only valid question in the *non-refoulement* debate is that of risk to refugees.

... State practice has broadened the scope of Article 33. First, it has confirmed that the duty of *non-refoulement* extends beyond expulsion and return and applies to measures such as rejection at the frontier[34] and even extradition. Second, it has further established the principle of *non-refoulement* in international law by extending its application to a broader category of refugees.[35] The 1951 Refugee Convention and 1967 Refugee Protocol define 'refugee' as a person with a well-founded fear of persecution for reasons of race, religion, nationality, membership of a particular social group or political opinion. Customary international law incorporates this core meaning, but extends the principle of *non-refoulement* to include displaced persons who do not enjoy the protection of the government of the country of origin.

[34] See Article II, para. 3 of the OAU Convention. See also Declaration on Territorial Asylum, Art. 3, G.A. Res. 2312, 22 UN GAOR Supp. (No.16) at 81, UN Doc.A/6716 (1967).
[35] See the OAU Convention and the Cartagena Declaration.

The application of the principle of *non-refoulement* is independent of any formal determination of refugee status by a state or an international organisation.[36] *Non-refoulement* is applicable as soon as certain objective conditions occur. A state which returns foreign nationals to a country known to produce refugees, or to have a consistently poor human rights record, or to be in a civil war or a situation of disorder, must therefore justify its actions in light of the conditions prevailing in the country of origin. The very existence of a programme of involuntary return should shift the burden of proof to the returning state when the facts indicate the possibility of some harm befalling those returned for any of the above reasons. Moreover, a state may be liable for a breach of the duty of *non-refoulement* regardless of notions of fault, either directly for the acts and omissions of its officials, or indirectly where its legal and administrative systems fail to provide a remedy or guarantee which is required by an applicable international standard.[37]

The binding obligations associated with the principle of *non-refoulement* are derived from conventional and customary international law. While the principle may not necessarily entail asylum, admission, residence, or indeed any particular solution, it does enjoin any action on the part of a state which returns or has the effect of returning refugees to territories where their lives or freedom may be threatened.

B. Kay Hailbronner, '*Non-refoulement* and "Humanitarian" Refugees: Customary International Law or Wishful Legal Thinking?' in David Martin, ed., *The New Asylum Seekers: Refugee Law in the 1980s* (Martinus Nijhoff Publishers, Dordrecht, 1988), pp. 128–36.

Commentators have taken the view that the principle of *non-refoulement* must be considered today as a rule of customary international law.[38] Whether this view finds sufficient support in a virtually uniform and extensive state practice accompanied by the necessary *opinio juris*[39] is

[36] Report of the United Nations High Commissioner for Refugees, paras 22–23, UN Doc.E/1985/62 (1985); Report on the Twenty-eighth Session of the Executive Committee of the High Commission's Programme, para. 53(4)(c), UN Doc. A/AC. 96/549 (1977).

[37] See generally, I. Brownlie, *System of the Law of Nations: State Responsibility* (1983), Part I, pp. 132–58.

[38] See Goodwin-Gill, *The Refugee in International Law* (Clarendon Press, Oxford, 1983), first edition, pp. 97–98.

[39] In the *North Sea Continental Shelf* cases (*W. Ger. v. Den.; W. Ger. v. Neth.*), 1969 I.C.J. 3, 43, the International Court of Justice stated that

an indispensable requirement [for determining customary international law] would be that within the period in question, short though it might be, State practice, including that of States whose interests are specially affected, should have been both extensive

doubtful. Although the 1951 Refugee Convention has been ratified by a large number of countries, almost all states of Eastern Europe, Asia and the Near East have consistently refused to ratify refugee agreements containing *non-refoulement* clauses. The drafting history of the United Nations Declaration on Territorial Asylum, as well as the statements made during the 1977 Conference on Territorial Asylum, show a reluctance to enter into legally binding obligations to admit a large number of refugees even on the basis of a temporary stay. On the other hand, states have never claimed a general right to return refugees to a country where they may face severe persecution on account of race, religion or political opinion. For this reason, the principle of *non-refoulement* has been described as universal customary law in the making, and regional customary law in Western Europe, the American Continent and Africa.

The 'Peremptory Norm' of Non-refoulement

Despite the reluctance of states to bind themselves through treaties, the UNHCR has sought to have the principle of *non-refoulement* characterised as a peremptory norm of customary international law....[40] It is unclear whether UNHCR's plea for an extended version of the principle of *non-refoulement* need be understood as a proposal *de lege ferenda* or as a statement *de lege lata*.

... Typifying this view, Goodwin-Gill casts the principle of *non-refoulement* of humanitarian refugees as part of customary international law. Relying on state practice as persuasive evidence of a customary rule of international law, even in the absence of any formal judicial pronouncements, Goodwin-Gill finds that states are enjoined from taking any action which returns or has the effect of returning humanitarian refugees to persecution or danger to life or limb.

The proponents of a customary international norm, however, ignore the fact that a rule of customary international law requires proof of

---

and virtually uniform in the sense of the provision invoked; and should moreover have occurred in such a way as to show a general recognition that a rule of law or legal obligation is involved.

See also R. Bernhardt, 'Customary International Law', in 7 *Encyclopaedia of Public International Law* 61, 64 (R. Bernhardt, ed., 1984) (asserting that the Court's view is 'now widely accepted').

[40] See 1985 Note on International Protection, Thirty-sixth Session of the Executive Committee of the High Commissioner's Programme, para. 17, UN Doc.A/AC.96/660 (1985) ('The fundamental principle of *non-refoulement* ... is an overriding legal principle having a normative character independent of international instruments'); Note on International Protection, Thirty-fifth Session of the Executive Committee of the High Commissioner's Programme, para. 15, UN Doc.A/AC.96/643 (1984) (*non-refoulement* 'is progressively acquiring the character of a peremptory norm of international law').

consistent state practice. Neither the UNHCR's extended mandate nor its repeated recommendations that *de facto* refugees should at least be protected against *refoulement* and be permitted to remain in the territory of refuge until an appropriate solution is found for them provides sufficient evidence of the emergence of a customary international law covering humanitarian refugees. The UNHCR, under its extended mandate, protects the interests of Convention and *de facto* refugees, including the improvement of their legal status. It is within the UNHCR's mandate to represent the interests of the refugees and request states to grant temporary refuge. These efforts have resulted in demands for a wider understanding of the principle of *non-refoulement* as well as for financial assistance and generous admission of *de facto* refugees by states.

The activities of the UNHCR, however, must not be confused with state practice. Although the UNHCR fulfils its functions with the agreement of states, it remains a special body entrusted with humanitarian tasks. In addition, it is charged with proposing solutions to the urgent humanitarian problems or refugees, whether they are considered refugees in the sense of the 1951 Refugee Convention or whether they have left their home country due to civil war, severe internal upheavals or natural disasters.

Furthermore, the fact that the UNHCR continues to care for the interests of *de facto* refugees cannot be considered evidence of an *opinio juris* by states. State practice resulting from the UNHCR's recommendations may eventually lead to a customary international law. UNHCR's proposals as such, however, provide little help to decide the crucial question of whether temporary refuge of victims of armed conflict can be considered as a legal requirement or simply as a commendable humanitarian policy when circumstances permit.

... The point at which the UNHCR's view of *non-refoulement* diverges from state practice is the point at which wishful legal thinking replaces careful factual and legal analysis. The requirements for the existence of customary international law—consistent state practice and *opinio juris*—simply are not met....

The 'Emerging Norm' of Temporary Refuge

Temporary refuge for humanitarian refugees has similarly been claimed as a customary rule of international law by Professors Perluss and Hartman.[41] A customary norm of temporary refuge,[42] they argue, 'emerged

---

[41] Perluss and Hartmann, 'Temporary Refuge: Emergence of a Customary Norm', *Vanderbilt Journal of International Law* (Vol. 26), p. 551.

[42] Perluss and Hartmann define 'temporary refuge' as a customary norm which 'prohibits a state from forcibly repatriating foreign nationals who find themselves in its territory

out of the principle of balance between necessity and humanity which is the essence of humanitarian law'.[43] Under this view, temporary refuge is understood as a civil right of a person fleeing internal armed conflict to be left alone and not be forcibly repatriated by the state of refugee. A state, they argue, 'is forbidden to repatriate the alien back to a state engaged in an internal armed conflict regardless of the nationality of the alien and regardless of the lack of reciprocity in adherence to the norm or the unavailability of burden-sharing arrangements with other states'.[44]

Perluss and Hartman do not treat sufficiently the critical issue of whether temporary refuge or *non-refoulement* carries with it a right to non-rejection at the frontier. Moreover, the extent of the rising obligation itself remains rather obscure. On the one hand, Perluss and Hartman emphasise that the norm imposes only a passive obligation on states.[45] On the other hand, they argue that 'its effective implementation may also entail some active participation by the refuge state'.[46] Part of this rising obligation must logically require states of temporary refuge to provide the basic necessities of life.[47] As the obligations of the norm become clearer, the futility of describing it as passive grows obvious. It necessarily entails affirmative action.

To support the emergence of a rule of temporary refugee, its proponents have invoked the practice of states in granting permanent or at least temporary shelter to large numbers of persons not qualifying as refugees under the 1951 Refugee Convention.[48] A close examination of state practice, however, reveals a somewhat more ambiguous picture. There are admittedly numerous examples of assistance provided by states to humanitarian refugees. The array of protection afforded, however, differs considerably from state to state. In many instances, states have simply admitted all refugees presenting themselves at the border. In other instances, states have been more cautious by granting parole or temporary or permanent residence to those deemed deserving of special protection. The term 'temporary refuge' has never been consistently applied as a distinct concept of domestic refugee law.

Temporary refuge as a legal concept seems to obscure the real issue of a state's obligation to shelter an indefinite number of aliens. Although the definition of temporary shelter, asylum or refuge is broad in Africa and

---

after having fled generalized violence and other threats to their lives and security caused by internal armed conflict within their own state'. Ibid. at 554.

[43] Ibid. at 602.

[44] Ibid. at 616.

[45] Ibid. at 618.

[46] Ibid.

[47] Ibid.

[48] Ibid. at 558–75.

Asia, where millions of refugees have fled 'temporarily' across frontiers to find shelter in border camps, the situation in Europe is different.…

The question critical to the temporary refuge notion that often arises is whether an alien is to be admitted or granted a prolonged stay. Admission alone does not imply a right of immigration. Thus, 'temporary' does not always have a useful meaning. For example, the residence of refugees recognised under the 1951 Refugee Convention may be terminated if the political conditions change in the refugees' home countries. Moreover, opportunity for third country resettlement is not assured once an alien has been admitted. An indefinite stay results, therefore, whenever third country resettlement cannot be secured and where the refugee's home country does not experience political change.

Although generally recognising the need to participate in the solution of problems of humanitarian refugees, states have not yet developed any binding legal standards. Faced with situations of large-scale influx of aliens, states have felt free to determine, according to their own laws, whether and under what conditions large numbers of refugees should be granted refuge. In some cases, states have refused the landing of boat people on their shores. The United States has adopted a similar policy.… Other states have taken recourse to strategies such as introducing strict standards of granting asylum or detaining asylum seekers. In other cases, refugees have even been repatriated against their will, although in general the voluntary character of repatriation of large numbers of refugees has been recognised.

In individual cases, there is no indication in the practice of states that deportation or expulsion could be challenged based on status as a humanitarian refugee. As a further restriction, temporary refuge has recently been made dependent upon third country resettlement arrangements and financial assistance. In 1979, the Foreign Ministers of the Association of Southeast Asian Nations announced that refugees would be admitted only on the basis of firm commitments from third countries that they would be resettled within a reasonable time.

The practice of many states indicates that temporary or permanent refuge is granted to large groups of refugees on a purely humanitarian basis without accepting any firm legal obligations. There is no evidence of a general recognition of an individual right of temporary refuge for any humanitarian refugee in case of return. Domestic law indicates that states have granted temporary refuge on the basis of general decisions to admit certain categories of refugees. The criteria, however, under which certain groups of aliens may be tolerated vary considerably. In some countries, the government is authorised to suspend deportation generally for 'humanitarian' reasons which may include a general pattern of gross and persistent violations of human rights, famine and natural disasters or civil wars. Other countries will shelter aliens from states besieged by civil war or severe internal disturbances regardless of evidence of individual risk. In short, there is no consensus on the definition of a 'humanitarian' refugee who would otherwise deserve some form of temporary refuge.

Like the practice of states, international legal instruments, resolutions and declarations of international bodies do not provide evidence for finding a customary international norm of temporary refuge. The ... OAU Convention is the sole international convention explicitly providing for an extended definition of the term 'refugee'.... Although little is known about the exact domestic application of the OAU Convention in the contracting states, the OAU Convention has served as a legal basis for a number of African states to provide temporary refuge to nationals of neighbouring countries who fled violence or civil strife. Notably, however, Nigeria and Ghana do not grant an individual the right to rely on the extended definition of the OAU Convention. Since the OAU Convention does not have the force of law within the municipal sphere, an alien has no legal protection directed specifically against deportation or refusal of an application of asylum.

In addition, Article I of the OAU Convention provides for a wide range of exceptions. Accordingly, the OAU Convention does not apply to any refugee if 'he has seriously infringed the purposes and objectives of this Convention', or if 'he has been guilty of acts contrary to the purposes and principles of the Organisation of African Unity' or 'of the United Nations'. Finally, it is explicitly up to each of the contracting states to determine whether an applicant is in fact a refugee. These provisions offer contracting states wide discretion. It is doubtful, therefore, whether the OAU Convention really does lend support to the supposition that a civil right of temporary refuge triggered by armed conflict can be considered as regional customary international law. The practice of contracting states in cases of mass influx of persons also seems to be far from certain. Several African states have expelled large numbers of aliens notwithstanding internal conditions approaching outright civil war or serious internal upheavals.

C. James C. Hathaway, *The Law of Refugee Status* (Butterworths, Toronto, 1991), pp. 24–27.

Taking into account the consensus on the extension of the mandate of the UNHCR, the agreement reached on broadening the refugee concept at the Conference on Territorial Asylum, the conceptual advances of the three regional refugee accords, and the consequent shifts in the practice of states, can it be said that modern international law recognises any duty toward a class of refugees more broad than as defined in the Convention and Protocol?

Guy Goodwin-Gill has argued that a new class of refugees is recognised in customary international law. He believes that the obligation of states to observe the principle of '*non-refoulement*', implying at least temporary refuge in the face of imminent danger, now extends to persons outside the Convention refugee definition insofar as they may be said to lack governmental protection against harmful events beyond their choosing or control. Persons who flee situations of civil disorder, domestic conflict or human rights violations should benefit from a presumption of humanitarian need, and may not be returned unless the state of refuge can rebut the presumed risk of danger.

On the other hand, Kay Hailbronner characterises such views as 'wishful legal thinking' on the basis that there is neither extensive and uniform state practice nor *opinio juris* sufficient to warrant an assertion of international rights for refugees outside the scope of the Convention. Hailbronner notes that most of the international practice in favour of the expanded class of refugees is in fact UNHCR institutional practice, which cannot be said to bind states in their own actions. Moreover, regional standards have not been codified in binding terms, and national efforts on behalf of humanitarian refugees have been carefully defined as discretionary exercises of prerogative over immigration.

Insofar as there is an international legal consensus on an expanded conceptualisation of refugee status based upon custom, it surely is, as Goodwin-Gill concedes, 'at a relatively low level of commitment'. In my view, Goodwin-Gill's assertion of a *right* to protection against 'refoulement' overstates the extant scope of customary law in regard to non-Convention refugees. As noted by Hailbronner, developed states have felt free to reject members of the broader class of asylum seekers by the imposition of visa requirements, penalties on transportation companies, naval blockades and the establishment of strictly discretionary mechanisms to cope with those asylum seekers who do reach their territory. Developing states have conditioned their willingness to protect humanitarian refugees on the agreement of the international community to underwrite the costs of temporary asylum and to relocate the refugees to states of permanent resettlement. Even the UNHCR has been tentative in its assertion of an expanded scope for the refugee definition applicable in the context of legal protection decisions.

On the other hand, Hailbronner overlooks the consensus at the global, regional and national levels in favour of *addressing in some way* the claims of those persons in one's territory or at one's borders who fear harm in their country of origin as a result of serious disturbances of public order. No aspect of international practice has questioned the duty to examine their need for protection. The nature of the special consideration has varied, and the avoidance of 'refoulement' has not been universal. Nonetheless, UNHCR practice, the international consensus at the Conference on Territorial Asylum, all three regional refugee accords and relatively consistent state practice agree in their extension of *some opportunity for special consideration* to persons within a state's territory who have been victimised by serious disturbances of public order in their country of origin.

The level of commitment is lower than that suggested by Goodwin-Gill, but an intermediate category of refugee protection does now exist. The customary norm rooted in international usage is a right to be considered for temporary admission, whether by formal procedure or administrative discretion, *on the basis of a need for protection.* That is, customary international law precludes the making of decision to reject or expel persons who come from nations in which there are serious disturbances of public order without explicit attention being paid to their humanitarian needs. This duty may be met through the granting of formal status as is contemplated by the three regional refugee accords, through the discretionary programs ̕of 'B' status, special measures, or extended voluntary departure that exist in Western developed states, or by seeking the assistance of other states or the international community to share the burden of actual or impending refugee flows. The obligation is simply to do *something* which provides a meaningful response to the humanitarian needs of the victims of serious disruptions of public order. We have not yet reached the point, though, of assimilating such persons to Convention refugees for the purpose of stipulating a duty to avert return in all cases.

III. THE PRINCIPLE OF *NON-REFOULEMENT* AND STATE PRACTICE

A. James C. Hathaway and John A. Dent, *Refugee Rights: Report on a Comparative Survey* (York Lanes Press, Toronto, 1995), pp. 5–17.

Non-refoulement is the cardinal principle of international refugee law. Yet, while almost all states join the UNHCR and refugee rights advocates in promulgating this ideal through their rhetoric, the principle of *non-refoulement* is undeniably under increasing attack in state practice.... [T]his section discusses three types of state practice that may offend the basic principle of *non-refoulement*: the return of refugees physically present in the territory of the state, the return of refugees at or near the border, and the evolution of arms-length *non-entrée* policies.[49]

[49] The Report on Refugee Rights from which this reading has been drawn is based (to quote the Report) 'on the insights of nearly thirty scholars from all regions of the world, who each prepared a *National Report on the Legal Condition of the Refugee* for their respective countries...' (p. 2). The countries were Argentina, Australia, Austria, Belgium, Burundi,

Refoulement *from Within State Territory*

In light of the massive refugee crises often facing frontline states in the less developed world, it is remarkable that the principle of *non-refoulement* is in fact respected by most of these states most of the time. Instances of refoulement of refugees from within a state's territory do, however, occur, especially in the context of large influxes of refugees. In 1982–83, for example, thousands of Rwandans, including many refugees, were 'chased' from western Uganda back to Rwanda. In Pakistan, non-Afghan refugees have not enjoyed official recognition by the government, and some have been summarily returned to their countries of persecution as illegal immigrants. In India, where the Supreme Court has advocated an unfettered right to deport aliens, the 'voluntary' nature of some Sri Lankan repatriations has been questioned amidst allegations of coercive measures by the Indian state. Beyond the violation of the prohibition of *non-refoulement*, the return of a refugee, lawfully in the host state, without due process, or for reasons other than a fair determination that the refugee poses an individuated risk to national security or public order, also violates Article 32 of the Convention regulating the expulsion of refugees.

Refoulement of refugees from within the territory of developed states most often occurs in a less direct form, namely by application of an excessively restrictive interpretation of the Convention definition, leading to the rejection of genuine refugees who may face persecution upon their return. In what some have called an attempt to define refugees out of existence, states have relied excessively on the internal flight rule, refused to acknowledge as refugees persons in flight due to the failure of state protection, and erroneously insisted on personalised evidence of a fear of persecution. In Austria, asylum-seekers who face persecution on any grounds other than political opinion, or who are persecuted as a group rather than individually, are not considered Convention refugees. The Norwegian National Report cites an example in which the absence of individuated evidence of persecution was relied upon to return ethnic Albanians to their native province of Kosovo in Serbia, where they faced systemic racial discrimination by Serbian authorities, including genuine risks of disappearance, arbitrary arrest, inhumane treatment and torture.

Many developed states also channel refugees into discretionary categories such as 'de facto', 'humanitarian', or 'temporary' protection status. For example, many European states have granted only 'temporary' or 'humanitarian' protection to refugees fleeing ethnic persecution in the

Canada, Denmark, Finland, France, Germany, Ghana, Greece, India, Italy, Japan, Malta, Nepal, Netherlands, New Zealand, Norway, Pakistan, Romania, Sweden, Switzerland, Uganda, United Kingdom, United States, Zimbabwe. The National Report on India was written by B.S. Chimni.

former Yugoslavia. As noted by several national rapporteurs, the refusal to grant Convention status to these refugees is striking in view of the similarity of their cause for flight with that of the refugees of concern to the drafters of the Convention. While there is no violation inherent in the use of these alternative classifications, the risk of *refoulement* may escalate if it is not made abundantly clear to authorities that relabelled persons who meet the Convention refugee definition remain entitled to the full protection of the Convention, and in particular of Article 33. Devoid of international legal foundation, the purely administrative quality of these substitute classifications sometimes places refugee protection at the mercy of the potentially capricious discretion of states.

Refoulement *from a State's Frontiers*

In addition to actions that deny protection to refugees physically present within their territories, states have also violated Article 33 by repelling refugees who claim asylum at their frontiers. Techniques of interdicting refugees at the border continue, such as the push-backs executed most infamously by the Thai government in response to Vietnamese boat people, and the border interdictions noted in the National Report for Austria. Border guards in Austria have the authority to deny entry to refugees who do not come directly from the state in which they claim to fear persecution (a condition that is virtually impossible to meet given Austria's geographic positioning), who have been persecuted for reasons other than their political opinion, or who fear, but have not actually suffered, persecution. These border guards thus have responsibility for assessing the validity of asylum claims, based only on the limited evidence before them, without even the benefit of prescribed guidelines. As the Austrian Report includes, 'a refugee who attempts to enter Austria legally runs a very real risk of being denied access to the determination process at the border itself'. It is beyond question that such actions conflict with the essential premise that states must assume responsibility to avoid the *refoulement* of refugees within their ambit of effective jurisdiction. As Goodwin-Gill has pointedly observed, '[a]s a matter of fact, anyone presenting themselves at a frontier post, port or airport will already be within state territory and jurisdiction. . .'.[50]

A new variant of the problem of refusal to guarantee *non-refoulement* to refugees arriving at a state's frontiers is the dilemma presented by refugees who come into contact with the authorities of a state in areas of assumed jurisdiction beyond that state's formal frontiers. The American policy of summarily returning Haitian refugees interdicted in international

---

[50] Goodwin-Gill, *The Refugee in International Law* (see footnote 38 earlier), p. 75.

writers without screening, for example, was challenged domestically as being contrary to Article 33 of the Convention. In upholding the legality of the US policy of interdiction and return, the ruling of the US Supreme Court illustrates the potential ambiguity of the scope of Article 33 at or beyond a state's borders if the obligation of *non-refoulement* is considered in an ahistorical and technocratic manner.

The Supreme Court's decision in *Sale v. Haitian Centers Council* [51] held that there was an inherent territorial limitation on the prohibition of *refoulement* contained in Article 33(1). In part, this decision was based on the denial under American immigration law of protection to persons other than those previously admitted to American territory. More fundamentally, however, the Supreme Court reasoned that the framing of the exception of *non-refoulement* in Article 33(2) limited initial protection to persons physically present in the territory of a state party, and that the term '*non-refoulement*' was selected specifically to avoid the broad reading that might otherwise have been attributed to the prohibition on 'return'. In refusing to give extraterritorial scope to the duty of *non-refoulement*, the Supreme Court drew on the work of refugee law scholars such as Nehemiah Robinson and Atle Grahl-Madsen. Grahl-Madsen, for example, argued that the negotiating history of the Convention shows that Article 33 'may only be invoked in respect of persons who are already present—lawfully or unlawfully—in the territory of a Contracting State. . . . [I]t does not obligate the contracting states to admit any person who has not already set foot on their respective territories'.[52]

Interestingly, though, the illogical implications of distinguishing between refugees located on either side of a border are acknowledged by both Robinson and Grahl-Madsen. Robinson commented that 'if a refugee has succeeded in eluding the frontier guards, he is safe; if he has not, it is his hard luck'.[53] Grahl-Madsen posits the scenario of a refugee approaching a frontier control post some distance inside the actual frontier, who may be refused permission to proceed farther inland, but must be allowed to stay in the bit of the territory situated between the actual frontier line and the control post, because any other course of action would mean a violation of Article 33(1).[54] The purely formalistic rationale for denying

[51] (1993) 113 S.Ct. 2549.

[52] A. Grahl-Madsen, *The Status of Refugees in International Law* (A.W. Sijthoff, Leyden, 1972), p. 4. See also N. Robinson, *Convention Relating to the Status of Refugees: Its History, Contents, and Interpretation* (Institute of Jewish Affairs, New York, 1953) at p. 163: 'Art. 33 concerns refugees who have gained entry into the territory of a Contracting State, legally or illegally, but not to refugees who seek entrance into this territory.'

[53] Ibid. at p. 163.

[54] A. Grahl-Madsen, 'Commentary on the Refugee Convention, 1951' (Unpublished, 1963), Vol. 3, at p. 390. Available in the Collections of the Refugee Law Research Unit, Centre for Refugee Studies, York University.

responsibility towards unadmitted refugees was noted in the UNCHR *amicus curiae* brief in the *Sale* case:

> [The U.S. Government's] interpretation of Article 33 ... extinguishes the most basic right enshrined in the treaty—the right of non-return—for an entire class of refugees, those who have fled their own countries but have not yet entered the territory of another State. Under [the U.S. Government's] reading, the availability of the most fundamental protection afforded refugees turns not on the refugee's need for protection, but on his or her own ability to enter clandestinely the territory of another country.[55]

Other arguments for interpreting Article 33 to proscribe denial of responsibility to refugees at or beyond the frontier include the 'plain meaning' interpretation of Article 33, the consistency of this interpretation with the possible existence of an internationally recognised customary norm of *non-refoulement*, and an alternative interpretation of the Conventions drafting history.

More fundamentally, though, the US Supreme Court's decontextualised reliance on the Convention's drafting history is problematic. It cannot be maintained that the drafters envisioned, let alone would have sanctioned, interdiction and return as it has been practised on the high seas by the United States. There was certainly no historical precedent of a policy of proactive deterrence, encompassing affirmative steps intended specifically to take jurisdiction over refugees (such as forcing them onto US ships and destroying their boats), without a concomitant assumption of responsibility. General principles of international law deny states the possibility of technocratic defence to harms occasioned by their assumption of jurisdiction.[56] It is in this broader sense that the territorial scope of the *non-refoulement* rule must be understood. While Article 33 was not intended to compel states to take protective steps in the world at large, it was meant fundamentally to constrain national treatment of refugees within the scope of each state's authority. Putting to one side the basic question of the legality of the Americans' unilateral assumption of jurisdiction on the high seas, there can surely be no question of allowing a government to insulate itself from its international legal obligations by selective reliance on its lack of formal authority, its own actions to the contrary notwithstanding.

---

[55] UNHCR, 'The Haitian Interdiction Case 1993: Brief *amicus curiae*', reprinted in *International Journal of Refugee Law* (Vol. 6, No. 1, 1994), p. 92.

[56] P. Sieghart, *The International Law of Human Rights* (Clarendon Press, Oxford, 1983), at p. 58.

Refoulement *by Policies of Non-entrée*

It may be, however, that the gravest contemporary threat to refugee protection is grounded in a third variant of *refoulement*, namely the pernicious new practices of *non-entrée*, which aim to exclude unwanted migrants through preventive, arms-length measures.[57] *Non-entrée* tactics include the imposition of visa requirements on the nationals of genuine refugee-producing countries enforced through carrier sanctions; first host country and safe third country rules applying to refugees who do not travel directly to the country where they seek asylum; safe country of origin exclusions that discriminate against refugees from non-traditional refugee-producing states; and the refusal to accept refugee claims made in so-called 'international zones', such as the transit lounges of international airports.

Although many of these policies are increasingly in use in North America and Oceania, it is in Europe that they are most highly formalised. Under the Schengen Agreement[58] and the draft Convention on the Crossing of External Borders,[59] member states are required to impose visa requirements systematically on the nationals of most migrant-generating, less developed countries, and to enforce this policy by sanctioning carriers that transport asylum-seekers and others not in possession of the requisite visa.[60] This restrictive visa policy is required of states in order to secure unrestricted freedom of movement for their own nationals within the European Union. It creates an almost complete barrier to the right to seek asylum from persecution, since even if refugees are able safely to access a European consular authority in their state of origin, no visa will be issued to an individual for the purpose of making a claim to protection in Europe.

Visa requirements and carrier sanctions are crude instruments that bar genuine refugees from exercising their right to see protection. The risk to refugees is inevitable given that the enforcement of the indiscriminate visa requirements is wholly outside the realm of legal accountability: forcing carriers to verify travel documentation places the protection of individuals in the hands of those who are unauthorised to make asylum

---

[57] The norm of *non-entrée* ('the refugee shall not access our community') is elaborated in J. Hathaway, 'The Emerging Politics of *Non-entree*', *Refugees* (Vol. 91, 1992) p. 40.

[58] Convention Applying the Schengen Agreement of 14 June 1985 between the Governments of the States of The Benelux Economic Union, The Federal Republic of Germany and the French Republic on the Gradual Abolition of Checks at their Common Borders, 19 June 1990, 30 *International Legal Materials* 84 (1991) ('Schengen II'), Art. 26(2).

[59] Draft Convention on the Crossing of External Borders, Doc. SN 2528/91 (WGI 822), 24 June 1991, Art. 14(2).

[60] These points are elaborated more fully in Hathaway, 'Harmonizing for Whom?' (see footnote 16 earlier), pp. 722–28.

determinations, who are untrained in refugee and asylum principles, and who are motivated solely by economic considerations in their desire to avoid financial penalties. Although they may not violate Article 33 directly, visa requirements and carrier sanctions increase the risk of *refoulement*, and effectively undermine the most fundamental purposes of the Convention.

Other policies of *non-entrée* that have proven effective in keeping out genuine refugees are first host country and safe third country provisions. Under first host country rules, as developed in Europe, the country that either issued the refugee claimant a visa or first came into contact with the claimant normally has sole responsibility for considering the claim and executing the resultant decision.[61] Safe third country provisions similarly restrict protection options by authorising the removal to non-European transit of claimants who have not travelled directly to the country where they requested asylum. While Article 33 does not explicitly exclude either of these policies aimed at returning the refugee claimant to a country in which there is no discernible threat of *refoulement*, it is clear that if the second country returns the claimant to a country in which she fears persecution, then the precipitating removal by the first state constitutes a breach of the Convention.[62] Indeed, indirect *refoulement* has occurred in situations such as the return of refugees by Greece to Turkey, Libya, and the Sudan, from where some were then returned to their countries of origin, as well as the return by Norway of Kosovo–Albanian asylum-seekers to Sweden (where their claims had already been rejected), with the knowledge that they would be returned by Sweden to Serbia. On a broader level, the assumption that the treatment of a refugee claimant in one contracting state discharges the duty of all participating governments is dangerous for refugees, and is in direct conflict with the international legal duty of each state to implement independently its obligations under the Refugee Convention.

The 'safe country of origin' concept is emerging as a new form of *non-entrée*, in that European immigration ministers have recently sanctioned its use as a tool for *en bloc* exclusion of nationally defined groups.[63] As practice evolves towards the making of pre-emptive negative status determinations that take little or no account of individuated circumstances, the risk of *refoulement* is particularly acute unless states prove willing to

[61] Convention Determining the State Responsible for Examining Applications for Asylum Lodged in One of the Member States of the European Communities, 15 June 1990, 30 *International Legal Materials* 425 (1991) ('Dublin Convention'), at Arts. 4–8, and 'Schengen II' (see footnote 58 earlier), Art. 30.

[62] Grahl-Madsen, 'Commentary on the Refugee Convention, 1951' (see footnote 54 earlier), at p. 395.

[63] 'Resolution on Manifestly Unfounded Applications for Asylum', Ad Hoc Group on Immigration, Doc. SN4822/1/92 (WGI 1282), 1992.

abandon current, loose definitions of 'safe'. In Switzerland, for example, all of India is considered 'safe', while Germany regards Ghana, Romania and Senegal in the same manner. If the designation of such countries as 'safe' is used to deny protection on a wholesale basis, there is reason to believe that genuine refugees stand at risk of *refoulement*.

A particularly insidious mechanism of *non-entrée* is the designation by some states of part of their airports as a so-called 'international zone', in which neither domestic nor international law is said to apply. Invoking this mechanism, governments have argued that the removal of refugee claimants from an "international zone" does not infringe the duty of *non-refoulement*, since there has been no entry into their territory. This is clearly a legal fiction. Persons present in an 'international zone' are in fact within state jurisdiction, and are validly subject to the exercise of authority by the territorial state. They are in this sense clearly within the sphere of that state's legal competence. In the absence of an explicit limitation to the contrary, therefore, the general principle of reciprocity of rights and obligations requires states simultaneously to guarantee Convention rights to all refugees within their jurisdiction.[64] It would be duplicitous in the extreme for a state to assert its prerogative to impose control over refugees, even while disavowing any duty to live up to its freely assumed obligations towards them.

B. Supreme Court of the United States: Chris Sale, Acting Commissioner, Immigration and Naturalisation Service, et al., Petitioners v. Haitian Centers Council, Inc., et al., On Writ of Certiorari to the United States Court of Appeals for the Second Circuit (21 June 1993).

Justice Stevens delivered the opinion of the Court.

The President has directed the Coast Guard to intercept vessels illegally transporting passengers from Haiti to the United States and to return those passengers to Haiti without first determining whether they may qualify as refugees. The question presented in this case is whether such forced repatriation, ('authorised to be undertaken only beyond the territorial sea of the United States') violates 243(h)(1) of the Immigration and Nationality Act of 1952 (INA or Act). We hold that neither 243(h) nor Article 33 of the United Nations Protocol Relating to the Status of Refugees applies to action taken by the Coast Guard on the high seas.

---

[64] 'Responsibility is the necessary corollary of a right. All rights of an international character involve international responsibility. If the obligation in question is not met, responsibility entails the duty to make reparation.' Judge Huber in *Spanish Zone of Morocco Claims*, 6 R.I.A.A 615, at p. 641, quoted in I. Brownlie, *Principles of Public International Law* (see footnote 11 earlier), at p. 433.

Aliens residing illegally in the United States are subject to deportation after a formal hearing. Aliens arriving at the border, or those who are temporarily paroled into the country, are subject to an exclusion hearing, the less formal process by which they, too, may eventually be removed from the United States. In either a deportation or exclusion proceeding the alien may seek asylum as a political refugee for whom removal to a particular country may threaten his life or freedom. Requests that the Attorney General grant asylum or withhold deportation to a particular country are typically, but not necessarily, advanced as parallel claims in either a deportation or an exclusion proceeding. When an alien proves that he is a 'refugee', the Attorney General has discretion to grant him asylum pursuant to 208 of the Act. If the proof shows that it is more likely than not that the alien's life or freedom would be threatened in a particular country because of his political or religious beliefs, under 243(h) the Attorney General must not send him to that country. The INA offers these statutory protections only to aliens who reside in or have arrived at the border of the United States. For 12 years, in one form or another, the interdiction program challenged here has prevented Haitians such as respondents from reaching our shores and invoking those protections.

On September 23, 1981, the United States and the Republic of Haiti entered into an agreement authorising the United States Coast Guard to intercept vessels engaged in the illegal transportation of undocumented aliens to our shores. While the parties agreed to prosecute 'illegal traffickers', the Haitian Government also guaranteed that its repatriated citizens would not be punished for their illegal departure. The agreement also established that the United States Government would not return any passengers 'whom the United States authorities determine[d] to qualify for refugee status'.

On September 29, 1981, President Reagan issued a proclamation in which he characterised 'the continuing illegal migration by sea of large numbers of undocumented aliens into the southeastern United States' as 'a serious national problem detrimental to the interests of the United States'. He therefore suspended the entry of undocumented aliens from the high seas and ordered the Coast Guard to intercept vessels carrying such aliens and to return them to their point of origin. His executive order expressly 'provided, however, that no person who is a refugee will be returned without his consent'.

In the ensuing decade, the Coast Guard interdicted approximately 25,000 Haitian migrants. After interviews conducted on board Coast Guard cutters, aliens who were identified as economic migrants were 'screened out' and promptly repatriated. Those who made a credible showing of political refugee status were 'screened in' and transported to the United States to file formal applications for asylum.

On September 30, 1991, a group of military leaders displaced the government of Jean Bertrand Aristide, the first democratically elected president in Haitian history. As the District Court stated in an uncontested finding of fact, since the military coup 'hundreds of Haitians have been killed, tortured, detained without a warrant, or subjected to violence and the destruction of their property because of their political beliefs. Thousands have been forced into hiding.' Following the coup the Coast Guard suspended repatriations for a period of several weeks, and the United States imposed economic sanctions on Haiti.

On November 18, 1991, the Coast Guard announced that it would resume the program of interdiction and forced repatriation. The following day, the Haitian Refugee Center, Inc., representing a class of interdicted Haitians, filed a complaint in the United States District Court for the Southern District of Florida alleging that the Government had failed to establish and implement adequate procedures to protect Haitians who qualified for asylum. The District Court granted temporary relief that precluded any repatriations until February 4, 1992, when a reversal on appeal in the Court of Appeals for the Eleventh Circuit and a denial of *certiorari* by this Court effectively terminated that litigation. See *Haitian Refugee Center, Inc. v. Baker,* 949 F. 2d 1109 (1991) *(per curiam),* cert. denied, 502 U.S.—(1992).

In the meantime the Haitian exodus expanded dramatically. During the six months after October 1991, the Coast Guard interdicted over 34,000 Haitians. Because so many interdicted Haitians could not be safely processed on Coast Guard cutters, the Department of Defense established temporary facilities at the United States Naval Base in Guantanamo, Cuba, to accommodate them during the screening process. Those temporary facilities, however, had a capacity of only about 12,500 persons. In the first three weeks of May 1992, the Coast Guard intercepted 127 vessels (many of which were considered unseaworthy, overcrowded and unsafe); those vessels carried 10,497 undocumented aliens. On May 22, 1992, the United States navy determined that no additional migrants could safely be accommodated at Guantanamo.

With both the facilities at Guantanamo and available Coast Guard cutters saturated, and with the number of Haitian emigrants in unseaworthy craft increasing (many had drowned as they attempted the trip to Florida), the Government could no longer both protect our borders and offer the Haitians even a modified screening process. It had to choose between allowing Haitians into the United States for the screening process or repatriating them without giving them any opportunity to establish their qualifications as refugees. In the judgement of the President's advisors, the first choice not only would have defeated the original purpose of the program (controlling illegal immigration), but also would have impeded diplomatic efforts to restore democratic government in

Haiti and would have posed a life-threatening danger to thousands of persons embarking on long voyages in dangerous craft. The second choice would have advanced those policies but deprived the fleeing Haitians of any screening process at a time when a significant minority of them were being screened in.

On May 23, 1992, President Bush adopted the second choice. After assuming office, President Clinton decided not to modify that order; it remains in effect today. The wisdom of the policy choices made by Presidents Reagan, Bush and Clinton is not a matter for our consideration. We must decide only whether Executive Order No. 12807, 57 Fed. Reg. 23133 (1992), which reflects and implements those choices, is consistent with 243(h) of the INA.

... Both parties argue that the plain language of 243(h)(I) is dispositive. It reads as follows:

> The Attorney General shall not deport or return any alien (other than an alien described in section 1251(a)(4)(D) of this title) to a country if the Attorney General determines that such alien's life or freedom would be threatened in such country on account of race, religion, nationality, membership in a particular social group or political opinion. 8 USC 1253(h)(I) (1988 ed., Supp. IV).

Respondents emphasise the words 'any alien' and 'return'; neither term is limited to aliens within the United States. Respondents also contend that the 1980 amendment deleting the words 'within the United States' from the prior text of 243(h) obviously gave the statute an extraterritorial effect. This change, they further argue, was required in order to conform the statute to the text of Article 33.1 of the Convention, which they find as unambiguous as the present statutory text.

Petitioners' response is that a fair reading of the INA as a whole demonstrates that 243(h) does not apply to actions taken by the President or Coast Guard outside the United States; that the legislative history of the 1980 amendment supports their reading; and that both the text and the negotiating history of Article 33 of the Convention indicate that it was not intended to have any extraterritorial effect.

... [T]he text and negotiating history of Article 33 of the United Nations Conventions are both completely silent with respect to the Article's possible application to actions taken by a country outside its own borders. Respondents argue that the Protocol's broad remedial goals require that a nation be prevented from repatriating refugees to their potential oppressors whether or not the refugees are within that nation's borders. In spite of the moral weight of that argument, both the text and negotiating history of Article 33 affirmatively indicate that it was not intended to have extraterritorial effect.

The Text of the Convention

Two aspects of Article 33's text are persuasive. The first is the explicit reference in Article 33.2 to the country in which the alien is located; the second is the parallel use of the terms 'expel or return', the latter term explained by the French word *'refouler'*. . . .

Under the second paragraph of Article 33 an alien may not claim the benefit of the first paragraph if he poses a danger to the country in which he is located. If the first paragraph did apply on the high seas, no nation could invoke the second paragraph's exception with respect to an alien there: an alien intercepted on the high seas is in no country at all. If Article 33.1 applied extraterritorially, therefore, Article 33.2 would create an absurd anomaly: dangerous aliens on the high seas would be entitled to the benefits of 33.1 while those residing in the country that sought to expel them would not. It is more reasonable to assume that the coverage of 33.2 was limited to those already in the country because it was understood that 33.1 obligated the signatory state only with respect to aliens within its territory.

Article 33.1 uses the words 'expel or return (*refouler*) as an obvious parallel to the words 'deport or return' in 243(h)(1). There is no dispute that 'expel' has the same meaning as 'deport'; it refers to the deportation or expulsion of an alien who is already present in the host country. The dual reference identified and explained in our opinion in *Leng May Ma v. Barber* suggests that the term 'return (*refouler*)' refers to the exclusion of aliens who are merely '"on the threshold of initial entry"'. 357 U.S. at 187 (quoting *Shaughnessy v. United States ex rel. Mezei*, 345 U.S. 206, 212 (1953)).

This suggestion—that 'return' has a legal meaning narrower than its common meaning—is reinforced by the parenthetical reference to *refouler*, a French word that is not an exact synonym for the English word 'return'. Indeed, neither of two respected English–French Dictionaries mentions *refouler* as one of many possible French translations of 'return'. Conversely, the English translations of *refouler* do not include the word 'return'. They do, however, include words like 'repulse', 'repel', 'drive back', and even 'expel'. To the extent that they are relevant, these translations imply that 'return' means a defensive act of resistance or exclusion at a border rather than an act of transporting someone to a particular destination. In the context of the Convention, to 'return' means to 'repulse' rather than to 'reinstate'.

The text of Article 33 thus fits with Judge Edwards' understanding 'that "expulsion" would refer to a "refugee already admitted into a country" and that "return" would refer to a "refugee already within the territory but not yet resident there." Thus, the Protocol was not intended to govern parties' conduct outside of their national borders.' *Haitian Refugee Center v. Gracey*, 257 U.S. App. D.C., at 413, 809 F. 2d, at 840. From the time of the Convention, commentators have consistently agreed with this view.[65]

The drafters of the Convention and the parties to the Protocol—like the drafters of §243(h)—may not have contemplated that any nation would gather fleeing refugees and return them to the one country they had desperately sought to escape; such actions may even violate the spirit of Article 33; but a treaty cannot impose uncontemplated extraterritorial obligations on those who ratify it through no more than its general humanitarian intent. Because the text of Article 33 cannot reasonably be read to say anything at all about a nation's actions toward aliens outside its own territory, it does not prohibit such actions.[66]

[65] See, for example, Robinson, *Convention Relating to the Status of Refugees* (see footnote 52 earlier), pp. 162-63. ('The Study on Statelessness [UN Dept. of Social Affairs 60 (1949)] defined "expulsion" as "the juridical decision taken by the judicial or administrative authorities whereby an individual is ordered to leave the territory of the country" and "reconduction" [which is the equivalent of "refoulement" and was changed by the Ad Hoc Committee to the word "return"] as "the mere physical act of ejecting from the national territory a person resident therein who has gained entry or is residing regularly or irregularly".... Art. 33 concerns refugees who have gained entry into the territory of a Contracting State, legally or illegally, but not to refugees who seek entrance into [the] territory'); A. Grahl-Madsen, *The Status of Refugees in International Law* (see footnote 52 earlier), p. 94 (['*Non-refoulement*] may only be invoked in respect of persons who are already present—lawfully or unlawfully—in the territory of a Contracting State. Article 33 only prohibits the expulsion or return (*refoulement*) of refugees to territories where they are likely to suffer persecution; it does not obligate the Contracting State to admit any person who has not already set foot on their respective territories'). A more recent work describes the evolution of *non-refoulement* into the international (and possibly extraterritorial) duty of non-return relied on by respondents, but it also admits that in 1951 *non-refoulement* had a narrower meaning, and did not encompass extraterritorial obligations. Moreover, it describes both 'expel' and 'return' as terms referring to one nation's transportation of an alien out of its own territory and into another. See Goodwin-Gill, *The Refugee in International Law* (see footnote 38 earlier), pp. 74–76.

Even the United Nations High Commissioner for Refugees has implicitly acknowledged that the Convention has no extraterritorial application. While conceding that the Convention does not mandate any specific procedure by which to determine whether an alien qualifies as a refugee, the 'basic requirements' his office has established impose an exclusively territorial burden, and announce that any alien protected by the Convention (and by its promise of *non-refoulement*) will be found either 'at the border or in the territory of a Contracting State'. Office of United Nations High Commissioner for Refugees, *Handbook on Procedures and Criteria for Determining Refugee Status* 46 (Geneva, September 1979) (quoting Official Records of the General Assembly, Thirty-second Session, Supplement No. 12 [A/32/12/Add. 1], para. 53 [6] [e]). Those basic requirements also establish the right of an applicant for refugee status 'to remain *in the country* pending a decision on his initial request'. Emphasis added. *Handbook*, at p. 460.)

[66] The Convention's failure to prevent the extraterritorial reconduction of aliens has been generally acknowledged (and regretted). See Aga Khan, 'Legal Problems Relating to Refugees and Displaced Persons', *Hague Academy of International Law*, 149 Recueil des Cours, 287, 318 (1976) ('Does the *non-refoulement* rule ... apply ... only to those already within the territory of the Contracting State?... There is thus a serious gap in refugee law as established by the 1951 Convention and other related instruments and it is high time

The Negotiating History of the Convention

In early drafts of the Convention, what finally emerged as Article 33 was numbered 28. At a negotiating conference of plenipotentiaries held in Geneva, Switzerland on July 11, 1951, the Swiss delegate explained his understanding that the words 'expel' and 'return' covered only refugees who had entered the host country. He stated:

> Mr. ZUTTER (Switzerland) said that the Swiss Federal Government saw no reason why article 28 should not be adopted as it stood; for the article was a necessary one. He thought, however, that its wording left room for various interpretations, particularly as to the meaning to be attached to the words 'expel' and 'return'. In the Swiss Government's view, the term 'expulsion' applied to a refugee who had already been admitted to the territory of a country. The term 're-foulement', on the other hand, had a vaguer meaning; *it could not, however, be applied to a refugee who had not yet entered the territory of a country.* The word 'return', used in the English text, gave that idea exactly. Yet, article 28 implied the existence of two categories of refugee: refugees who were liable to be expelled, and those who were liable to be returned. In any case, the States represented at the Conference should take a definite position with regard to the meaning to be attached to the word 'return'. The Swiss Government considered that in the present instance *the word applied solely to refugees who had already entered a country, but were not yet resident there.* According to that interpretation, States were not compelled to allow large groups of persons claiming refugee status to cross its frontiers. He would be glad to know whether the States represented at the Conference accepted his interpretations of the two terms in question. If they did, Switzerland would be willing to accept article 28, which was one of the articles in respect of which States could not, under Article 36 of the draft Convention, enter a reservation. (Emphasis added.)

No one expressed disagreement with the position of the Swiss delegate on that day or at the session two weeks later when Article 28 was again discussed. At that session, the delegate of the Netherlands recalled the Swiss delegate's earlier position.

> Baron van BOETZELAER (Netherlands) recalled that at the first reading the Swiss representative had expressed the opinion that the

---

that this gap should be filled'); Robinson, *Convention Relating to the Status of Refugees* (see footnote 52 earlier), at p. 163 ('[I]f a refugee has succeeded in eluding the frontier guards, he is safe; if he has not, it is his hard luck. It cannot be said that this is a satisfactory solution of the problem of asylum'); Goodwin-Gill, *The Refugee in International Law*, at 87 ('A categorical refusal of disembarkation cannot be equated with breach of the principle of *non-refoulement*, even though it may result in serious consequences for asylum-seekers').

word 'expulsion' related to a refugee already admitted into a country, whereas the word 'return' ('refoulement') related to a refugee *already within the territory but not yet resident there.* According to that interpretation, article 28 would not have involved any obligations in the possible case of mass migrations across frontiers or of attempted mass migrations.

He wished to revert to that point, because the Netherlands Government attached very great importance to the scope of the provision now contained in article 33. The Netherlands could not accept any legal obligations in respect of large groups of refugees seeking access to its territory.

At the first reading the representatives of Belgium, the Federal Republic of Germany, Italy, the Netherlands and Sweden had supported the Swiss interpretation. From conversations he had since had with other representatives, he had gathered that the general consensus of opinion was in favour of the Swiss interpretation.

In order to dispel any possible ambiguity and to reassure his Government, he wished to have it placed on record that the Conference was in agreement with the interpretation that the possibility of mass migrations across frontiers or of attempted mass migrations was not covered by article 33.

There being no objection, the PRESIDENT ruled that the interpretation given by the Netherlands representative should be placed on record.

Mr. HOARE (United Kingdom) remarked that the Style Committee had considered that the word 'return' was the nearest equivalent in English to the French term 'refoulement' (*refouler* in verbal uses) should be included in brackets and between inverted commas after the English word 'return' wherever the latter occurred in the text.

The PRESIDENT suggested that in accordance with the practice followed in previous Conventions, the French word *'refoulement'* (*'refouler'* in verbal uses) should be included in brackets and between inverted commas after the English word 'return' wherever the latter occurred in the text. (Emphasis added.)

Although the significance of the President's comment that the remarks should be 'placed on record' is not entirely clear, this much cannot be denied: at one time there was a 'general consensus', and, in July of 1951 several delegates understood the right of *non-refoulement* to apply only to aliens physically present in the host country. There is no record of any later disagreement with that position. Moreover, the term *refouler* was included in the English version of the text to avoid the expressed concern about an inappropriately broad reading of the English word 'return'.

Therefore, even if we believed that Executive Order 12807 violated the intent of some signatory states to protect all aliens, wherever they might be found, from being transported to potential oppressors, we must acknowledge that other signatory states carefully—and successfully—sought to avoid just that implication. The negotiating history, which suggests that the Convention's limited reach resulted from a deliberate bargain, is not dispositive, but it solidly supports our reluctance to interpret Article 33 to impose obligations on the contracting parties that are broader than the text commands. We do not read that text to apply to aliens interdicted on the high seas. . . .

. . . It is perfectly clear that 8 U.S.C. §1182(f), grants the President ample power to establish a naval blockade that would simply deny illegal Haitian migrants the ability to disembark on our shores. Whether the President's chosen method of preventing the 'attempted mass migration' of thousands of Haitians—to use the Dutch delegate's phrase—poses a greater risk of harm to Haitians who might otherwise face a long and dangerous return voyage, is irrelevant to the scope of his authority to take action that neither the Convention nor the statute clearly prohibits. As we have already noted, Acts of Congress normally do not have extra-territorial application unless such an intent is clearly manifested. The presumption has special force when we are construing treaty and statutory provisions that may involve foreign and military affairs for which the President has unique responsibility. Cf. *United States v. Curtiss Wright Export Corp.*, 299 U.S. 304 (1936). We therefore find ourselves in agreement with the conclusion expressed in Judge Edwards' concurring opinion in *Gracey*, 257 U.S. App. D.C. , at 414, 809 F. 2d, at 841:

> This case presents a painfully common situation in which desperate people, convinced that they can no longer remain in their homeland, take desperate measures to escape. Although the human crisis is compelling, there is no solution to be found in a judicial remedy.

The judgement of the Court of Appeals is reversed.

It is so ordered.

Justice Blackmun, Dissenting

When, in 1968, the United States acceded to the United Nations Protocol Relating to the Status of Refugees, Jan. 31, 1967, (1968) 19 U.S.T. 6223, T.I.A.S. 6577, it pledged not to 'return (*'refouler'*) a refugee in any manner whatsoever' to a place where he would face political persecution. In 1980, Congress amended our immigration law to reflect the Protocol's directives. Refugee Act of 1980, 94 Stat. 102. See *INS v. Cardoza–Fonseca*, 480 U.S. 421, 429, 436–437, 440 (1987); *INS v. Stevic*, 467 U.S. 407, 418, 421 (1984). Today's majority nevertheless decides that the forced repatriation of the Haitian refugees is perfectly legal, because the word 'return' does not mean return ... because the opposite of 'within the United States' is not outside the United States ... and because the official charged with controlling immigration has no role in enforcing an order to control immigration....

I believe that the duty of nonreturn expressed in both the Protocol and the statute is clear. The majority finds it 'extraordinary', ... that Congress would have intended the ban on returning 'any alien' to apply to aliens at sea. That Congress would have meant what it said is not remarkable. What is extraordinary in this case is that the Executive, in disregard of the law, would take to the seas to intercept fleeing refugees and force them back to their persecutors—and that the Court would strain to sanction that conduct.

I begin with the Convention, for it is undisputed that the Refugee Act of 1980 was passed to conform our law to Article 33, and that 'the non-discretionary duty imposed by 243(h) parallels the United States' mandator *non-refoulement* obligations under Article 33.1...' *INS v. Doherty*, —U.S.—, (1992) (slip op., at 3) (SCALLA, J. concurring in the judgement in part and dissenting in part). See also *Cardoza-Fonseca*, 480 U.S., at 429, 436–437, 440; *Stevic*, 467 U.S., at 418, 421. The Convention thus constitutes the backdrop against which the statute must be understood.

Article 33.1 of the Convention states categorically and without geographical limitation:

> No Contracting State shall expel or return (*'refouler'*) a refugee in any manner whatsoever to the frontiers of territories where his life or freedom would be threatened on account of his race, religion, nationality, membership of a particular social group or political opinion.

The terms are unambiguous. Vulnerable refugees shall not be returned. The language is clear, and the command is straightforward; that should be the end of the inquiry. Indeed, until litigation ensued, see *Haitian Refugee Center v. Gracey*, 257 U.S. App. D.C. 367, 809 F. 2d 794 (1987), the Government consistently acknowledged that the Convention applied on the high seas.

The majority, however, has difficulty with the Treaty's use of the term 'return (*'refouler'*)'. 'Return', it claims, does not mean return, but instead has a distinctive legal meaning.... For this proposition the Court relies almost entirely on the fact that American law makes a general distinction between deportation and exclusion. Without explanation, the majority asserts that in light of this distinction the word 'return' as used in the Treaty somehow must refer only to 'the exclusion of aliens who are ... "on the threshold of initial entry"'.

Setting aside for the moment the fact that respondents in this case seem very much 'on the threshold of initial entry'—at least in the eyes of the

Government that has ordered them seized for 'attempting to come to the United States by sea without necessary documentation', Preamble to Executive Order No. 12,807, 57 Fed. Reg. 23133 (1992)—I find this tortured reading unsupported and unnecessary. The text of the Convention does not ban the 'exclusion' of aliens who have reached some indeterminate 'threshold'; it bans their 'return'. It is well settled that a treaty must first be construed according to its 'ordinary meaning'. Article 31.1 of the Vienna Convention on the Law of Treaties, 1155 U.N.T.S. 331, T.S. No. 58 (1980), 8 I.L.M. 679 (1969). The ordinary meaning of 'return' is 'to bring, send, or put (a person or thing) back to or in a former position'. *Webster's Third New International Dictionary* 1941 (1986). That describes precisely what petitioners are doing to the Haitians. By dispensing with ordinary meaning at the outset, and by taking instead as its starting point the assumption that 'return', as used in the Treaty, 'has a legal meaning narrower than its common meaning', ante, at 24, the majority leads itself astray.

The straightforward interpretation of the duty of non-return is strongly reinforced by the Convention's use of the French term *refouler.* The ordinary meaning of *'refouler'*, as the majority concedes, is '[t]o repulse, . . .; to drive back, to repel'. *Dictionnaire Larousse* 63 (1981). Thus construed, Article 33.1 of the Convention reads: 'No contracting state shall expel or [repulse, drive back, or repel] a refugee in any manner whatsoever to the frontiers of territories where his life or freedom would be threatened. . .'. That, of course, is exactly what the Government is doing. It thus is no surprise that when the French press has described the very policy challenged here, the term it has used is *'refouler'*. See, e.g., Le bourbier hattien, *Le Monde*, May 31–June 1 1992 (*'[L]es Etats-Unis ont decide [de* refouler] *directement les refugies recueillis par la grade cotiere.'* (The United States has decided [*de refouler*] directly the refugees picked up by the Coast Guard).

And yet the majority insists that what has occurred is not, in fact, 'refoulement'. It reaches this conclusion in a peculiar fashion. After acknowledging that the ordinary meaning of *'refouler'* is 'repulse', 'repel', and 'drive back', the majority without elaboration declares: 'To the extent that they are relevant, these translations imply that 'return' means a defensive act of resistance or exclusion at a border. . . .' I am at a loss to find the narrow notion of 'exclusion at a border' in broad terms like 're- pulse', 'repel', and 'drive back'. Gage was repulsed (initially) at Bunker Hill. Lee was repelled at Gettysburg. Rommel was driven back across North Africa. The majority's puzzling progression (*'refouler'* means repel or drive back; therefore 'return' means only exclude at a border; there- fore, the treaty does not apply) hardly justifies a departure from the path of ordinary meaning. The text of Article 33.1 is clear, and whether the operative term is 'return' or *'refouler'*, it prohibits the Government's actions.

Article 33.1 is clear not only in what it says, but also in what it does not say: it does not include any geographical limitation. It limits only where a refugee may be sent 'to', not where he may be sent from. This is not surprising, given that the aim of the provision is to protect refugees against persecution.

Article 33.2, by contrast, does contain a geographical reference, and the majority seizes upon this as evidence that the section as a whole applies only within a signatory's borders. That inference is flawed. Article 33.2 states that the benefit of Article 33.1

> may not ... be claimed by a refugee whom there are reasonable grounds for regarding as a danger to the security of the country in which he is, or who, having been convicted by a final judgement of a particularly serious crime, constitutes a danger to the community of that country.

The signatories' understandable decision to allow nations to deport criminal aliens who have entered their territory hardly suggests an intent to permit the apprehension and return of noncriminal aliens who have not entered their territory, and who may have no desire ever to enter it. One wonders what the majority would make of an exception that removed from the Article's protection all refugees who 'constitute a danger to their families'. By the majority's logic, the inclusion of such an exception presumably would render Article 33.1 applicable only to refugees with families.

Far from constituting 'an absurd anomaly', the fact that a state is permitted to 'expel or return' a small class of refugees found within its territory but may not seize and return refugees who remain outside its frontiers expresses precisely the objectives and concerns of the Convention. Nonreturn is the rule; the sole exception (neither applicable nor invoked here) is that a nation endangered by a refugee's very presence may 'expel or return' him to an unsafe country if it chooses. The tautological observation that only a refugee already in a country can pose a danger to the country 'in which he is' proves nothing.

The majority further relies on a remark by Baron van Boetzelaer, the Netherlands' delegate at the Convention's negotiating conference, to support its contention that Article 33 does not apply extraterritorially. This reliance, for two reasons, is misplaced. First, the isolated statement of a delegate to the Convention cannot alter the plain meaning of the Treaty itself. Second, placed in its proper context, van Boetzelaer's comment does not support the majority's position.

It is axiomatic that a treaty's plain language must control absent 'extraordinarily strong contrary evidence'. *Sumitomo Shoji America, Inc. v. Avagliano*, 457 U.S. 176, 185 (1982). See also *United States v. Stuart*, 489 U.S. 353, 371 (1989) (SCALLA, J., concurring in the judgement); id., at 370 (KENNEDY, J. concurring in part and concurring in judgement). Reliance on a treaty's negotiating history (*travaux preparatoires*) is a disfavoured alternative of last resort, appropriate only where the terms of the document are obscure or lead to 'manifestly absurd or unreasonable' results. See Vienna Convention on the Law of Treaties, Art. 32, 1155 U.N.T.S., at 340, 8 I.L.M., at 692 (1969). Moreover, even the general rule of treaty construction allowing limited resort to *travaux preparatoires* 'has no application to oral statements made by those engaged in negotiating the treaty which were not embodied in any writing and were not communicated to the government of the negotiator or to its ratifying body'. *Arizona v. California*, 292 U.S. 341, 360 (1934). There is no evidence that the comment on which the majority relies was ever communicated to the United States' Government or to the Senate in connection with the ratification of the Protocol.

The pitfalls of relying on the negotiating record are underscored by the fact that Baron van Boetzelaer's remarks almost certainly represent, in the words of the United Nations High Commissioner for Refugees, a mere 'parliamentary gesture by a delegate whose views did *not* prevail upon the negotiating conference as a whole' (emphasis in original). Brief for Office of the United Nations High Commissioner for Refugees as *Amicus Curiae* 24. The Baron, like the Swiss delegate whose sentiments he restated, expressed a desire to reserve the right to *close borders to large groups of refugees*. 'According to [the Swiss delegate's] interpretation, States were not compelled to allow large groups of persons claiming refugee status to cross [their] frontiers.' Conference of Plenipotentiaries on the Status of Refugees and Stateless Persons, Summary Record of the Sixteenth Meeting, U.N. Doc. A/CONF. 2/SR. 16, p. 6 (July 11, 1951). Article 33, van Boetzelaer maintained, 'would not have involved any obligations in the possible case of mass migrations across frontiers or of attempted mass migrations' and this was important because '[t]he Netherlands could not accept any legal obligations in respect of large groups of refugees seeking access to its territory'. Conference of Plenipotentiaries on the Status of Refugees and Stateless Persons, Summary Record of the Thirty-Fifth Meeting, U.N. Doc. A/CONF.2/SR.35, pp. 21–22 (Dec. 3, 1951). Yet no one seriously contends that the Treaty's protections depend on the number of refugees who are fleeing persecution. Allowing a state to disavow 'any obligations' in the case of mass migrations or attempted mass migrations would eviscerate Article 33, leaving it applicable only to 'small' migrations and 'small' attempted migrations.

There is strong evidence as well that the Conference rejected the right to close land borders where to do so would trap refugees in the persecutors' territory. Indeed, the majority agrees that the Convention *does* apply to refugees who have reached the border. The majority thus cannot maintain that van Boetzelaer's interpretation prevailed.

That it did not is evidenced by the fact that Baron van Boetzelaer's interpretation was merely 'placed on record', unlike formal amendments to the Convention which were 'agreed to' or 'adopted'. It should not be assumed that other delegates agreed with the comment simply because they did not object to their colleague's request to memorialise it, and the majority's statement that 'this much cannot be denied: at one time there was a "general consensus"', is wrong. All that can be said is that at one time Baron van Boetzelaer remarked that 'he had gathered' that there was a general consensus, and that his interpretation was placed on record.

In any event, even if van Boetzelaer's statement *had* been 'agreed to' as reflecting the dominant view, this is not a case about the right of a nation to close its borders. This is a case in which a Nation has gone forth to *seize* aliens who are *not* at its borders and *return* them to persecution. Nothing in the comments relied on by the majority even hints at an intention on the part of the drafters to countenance a course of conduct so at odds with the Convention's basic purpose.

In sum, the fragments of negotiating history upon which the majority relies are not entitled to defence, were never voted on or adopted, probably represent a minority view, and in any event do not address the issue in this case. It goes without saying, therefore, that they do not provide the 'extraordinarily strong contrary evidence', *Sumitomo Shoji America, Inc.*, 457 U.S., at 185, required to overcome the Convention's plain statement: 'No Contracting State shall expel or return (*'refouler'*) a refugee in any manner whatsoever to the frontiers of territories where his life or freedom would be threatened....'

The Convention that the Refugee Act embodies was enacted largely in response to the experience of Jewish refugees in Europe during the period of World War II. The tragic consequences of the world's indifference at that time are well known. The resulting ban on *refoulement*, as broad as the humanitarian purpose that inspired it, is easily applicable here, the Court's protestations of impotence and regret notwithstanding.

The refugees attempting to escape from Haiti do not claim a right of admission to this country. They do not even argue that the Government has no right to intercept their boats. They demand only that the United States, land of refugees and guardian of freedom, cease forcibly driving them back to detention, abuse and death. That is a modest plea, vindicated by the Treaty and the statute. We should not close our ears to it.

I dissent.

C. Anthony H. Richmond, *Global Apartheid: Refugees, Racism, and the New World Order* (Oxford University Press, Toronto, 1994), pp. xii–xv, 206–8, 210–11.

Apartheid

In 1955, just six years after the nationalist government came to power in South Africa, I wrote a book, *The Colour Problem*, which examined

racial relations in various countries. At that time, I suggested that two elementary processes of social organisation are involved in the examination
of migration, race and ethnic relations. The first is the principle of *super-
ordination/subordination*. The second is the principle of *separation/integra-
tion*. Each is a continuum involving varying levels of inequality in the distribution of status and power, together with degrees of segregation and
dispersion of the populations concerned. When these two bases of social
organisation are combined, four main types of system are possible, although
there are many variations when other factors, such as demographic
ratios, levels of economic development and degrees of similarity and
difference in language and culture are taken into account. Extreme differences in power and status, combined with geographic and social separation, lead to apartheid....

The Colour Problem (1955) contained a chapter entitled 'Apartheid and
White Supremacy in South Africa'. The book was banned in that country,
although a few copies were smuggled in by travellers who disguised it as a
novel. I wrote 'in South Africa a large majority of the European population appears to be determined to hold on to, if not extend, its own privileged position and to exclude non-Europeans from a full share in the
government of the country, now or in the future. For this reason racial
relationships in South Africa are bound to deteriorate until the pressure
on non-Europeans becomes so great that a major upheaval ensues. The
only alternative would appear to be a widespread change of attitude on
the part of Europeans, when and if the grim consequence of present policies is fully appreciated'.[67] Six years later when a revised edition of the
book went to press, the treason trials started and Nelson Mandela began
his long period of detention. I wrote then: 'Afrikaner nationalism, as a
sociological phenomenon is understandable enough. But it is obvious
that the problems of a plural society cannot be solved by means of the
unbridled assertiveness and unlimited pretension of a single racial group,
reinforced by fear and relying purely on violence. For a time Europeans
in South Africa will be able to maintain their supremacy through political
oppression backed by tanks and machine guns such as those used at
Sharpeville in 1960. But Nemesis is bound to follow'.[68]

More than thirty years later, and after much more violence and blood-
shed, the 'White' South African government finally recognised the impossibility of maintaining its exclusive power.... The end of official apartheid
in South Africa coincides with growing fears elsewhere in the world concerning the impact of mass migration and consequent conflicts in poly-
ethnic and multiracial societies.... Increasingly repressive and restrictive
measures to restrain the flows of migrant labourers and refugees from

[67] Anthony Richmond, *The Colour Problem* (Penguin, Hammondsworth, 1955), at p. 81.
[68] Richmond, revised edition (1961), at pp. 134–35.

Africa, Asia, the Caribbean and Latin America are being imposed. Today we guard our airports, interdict undocumented travellers, build electronic fences, maintain coastguard patrols and use computerised data banks to ensure that our borders are not infringed. Armed guards patrol frontiers 'and gunboats turn back ships loaded with asylum seekers and so-called 'illegal' immigrants. Advanced technologies, including infrared surveillance, fingerprinting, and computer data banks are being used to exclude unwanted persons. In some countries, voting rights and citizenship are denied even to long-term residents, unless they are of the same ethnic origin as the majority group....

... It now seems that a generous policy towards refugees was a cold luxury, and even then one mainly reserved for Europeans. That is why new policies can be described as a form of *global apartheid*....

Global Apartheid: Migration, Racism and the World System

It may seem strange to juxtapose terms such as 'apartheid', 'asylum', and 'refuge' and to link them to concepts such as 'ethnic cleansing', 'reservation', 'prison', and 'hospital'. However, from a sociological perspective, these are all actions, structures and institutions associated with forcible isolation of people who are different. Because of the differences, they are perceived as having actually (or potentially) conflicting relationships. Distancing is used to deal with the conflict. When separation is imposed by a dominant group upon a less powerful one, the conflict is only temporarily resolved. In the long run, the opposition is generally exacerbated. Restitution and retribution may be delayed for generations, but the power struggle continues. As processes of structuration, apartheid and asylum have much in common.

The word 'apartheid' literally means 'apart*hood*' (c.f. neighbourhood), that is, the separation of people into different areas. The term 'asylum' (literally meaning non-seizure) originated with the Church's refusal to allow wanted criminals and others sought by the authorities to be forcibly removed from the altar. Later the term was applied to mental hospitals, sanatoria and other institutions where anyone who might contaminate others, disturb the peace or in some way come into conflict with the general public could be kept apart. As Michel Foucault (1973) showed in his study of *Madness and Civilization*, the nineteenth-century insane asylum brought to bear on the mentally ill all the means of social control in the power of 'keepers'. They used segregation, surveillance, subordination and silencing as instruments. These replaced physical coercion with self-restraint, judgement and the patriarchal authority of the medical profession.

Totalitarian states have long used the device of exile or forcible confinement in prisons or hospitals as a means of dealing with dissidents and political enemies. Thus 'asylum' acquired a dual meaning. On the one hand, it is a way in which a more powerful (or majority) group segregates 'others' who do not conform or who are seen as threatening. On the other hand, the asylum offers sanctuary and some protection for the minority or outcast who might otherwise face death. The term 'refugee' (from the Latin *refugium*, meaning to flee back) was first applied to the Protestant Huguenots escaping the threat of death and persecution in France, following the revocation of the Edict of Nantes in 1685.

... As far as immigration is concerned, the question becomes, are we creating a system of global apartheid based on discrimination against migrants and refugees from poorer developing countries? Or are we simply acting rationally to protect the integrity of our social systems and harmonise our immigration policies? Will the emerging new world order ensure justice and equality of treatment for immigrants and refugees, or will it create a system that privileges some and deprives others of their rights?....

Racism Outside South Africa

... as apartheid in South Africa is gradually giving way to political reform and social change, the rest of the world appears to be moving in a different direction. In eastern and central Europe, following the collapse of the Soviet empire, nationalism and irredentism have revived, causing widespread violence. Ethnic cleansing provides the ideological rationale for civil war in the former Yugoslavia. The idea that only one dominant racial or ethnoreligious group should be allowed to occupy a particular territory is precisely the meaning of apartheid. When military force is used to bring about such territorial separation, killing or displacing hundreds of thousands (possibly millions) of people in the process, it is no exaggeration to speak of 'apartheid'.

Faced with the prospect of mass migration from poorer to richer countries, from those where governmental systems have collapsed to those with more stable political environments (and with huge refugee flows from Bosnia–Herzegovina) coordinated efforts are being made to stem the potential flow into western Europe. The legislation used and the regulative institutions created have a remarkable similarity to those that South Africa adopted to control the movement of people from outside and within its borders. Furthermore, the ideological justifications used to defend these measures echo those adopted by the dominant 'White' minority in South Africa to defend their actions in imposing the system of apartheid on the non-'White' majority. As well as explicit racism and claims to 'superiority', they include an obligation to limit intertribal conflict, the need to preserve ethnic identity, expressions of religious fanaticism, the defence of existing cultural and social institutions, state security, the maintenance of law and order, preservation of economic privilege and the need to regulate and manage population movements. These themes, which were constantly repeated by defenders of the South African system, are now recurring in the rhetoric of those who wish to restrict immigration into western Europe, North America and Australia.

IV. CONCEPT OF TEMPORARY PROTECTION

A. United Nations High Commissioner for Refugees, *The State of the World's Refugees—In Search of Solutions* (Oxford University Press, Oxford, 1995), pp. 85–90.

Temporary Protection or Permanent Asylum?

Whether asylum should lead to integration, or whether it should be a means of providing protection until repatriation is possible, has become a particularly pertinent issue in relation to former Yugoslavia, where, it was initially assumed, the international community would succeed in finding a speedy solution to the war. On the basis of this assumption and in the context of a broader range of measures intended to address the humanitarian crisis in the region, the concept of 'temporary protection' was devised.

This notion is not an entirely new one. It was used by the states of South-East Asia when they agreed to admit the Vietnamese boat on a provisional basis, pending their resettlement in third countries. Pakistan has always insisted that the many Afghan refugees living on its territory have been granted only temporary asylum, and will be expected to go home once conditions have improved in their homeland. A related concept is also referred to in the 1990 US Immigration Act, which offers the possibility of granting 'temporary protected status' to citizens of countries experiencing armed conflict and other extraordinary conditions.

It is in the context of former Yugoslavia, however, that the notion of temporary protection has been developed most systematically as a means of resolving refugee problems. On 29 July 1992, at the first UNHCR-sponsored conference on former Yugoslavia, the High Commissioner for Refugees formally requested governments to give temporary protection to people fleeing from the conflict and associated human rights violations in former Yugoslavia.

There were three key elements to this proposal. First, former Yugoslavs were to be admitted to countries of refuge and guaranteed protection against a forcible return to any country where their life or liberty would be at risk. Second, in relation to their rights and entitlements while in the country of refuge, the beneficiaries of this arrangement were to be treated 'in accordance with internationally recognised humanitarian standards'. And third, the former Yugoslavs would be allowed to remain in the country which had admitted them until the time when a safe return to their country of origin became possible. At that point, they would generally be expected to repatriate with assistance from the international community. Some 700,000 people from former Yugoslavia had been granted temporary protection in Europe by the first quarter of 1995, the largest number of them in Germany.

As the following paragraph indicates, the temporary protection arrangement has a number of actual and potential advantages, both for the beneficiaries themselves and for the countries which have admitted them.

Providing Immediate Security

The former Yugoslavs who have been granted temporary protection in Western Europe have generally not been obliged to go through the lengthy procedures which European governments normally use to approve or reject individual applications for asylum. As a result of this dispensation, the beneficiaries have enjoyed an immediate guarantee of security and have been spared the anxiety of waiting to find out whether their request for refugee status has been successful.

Recognising Protection Needs

Faced with a steady increase in the number of people seeking asylum on their territory, the world's more prosperous countries have in recent years tended to adopt increasingly restrictive interpretations of the criteria for refugee status. In many instances, people fleeing from armed conflict have been refused refugee status on the grounds that they cannot demonstrate an individual fear of persecution in their country of origin. The temporary protection approach has circumvented this difficulty, and has helped to establish a consensus that international protection should be given to people whose safety is at risk, whether or not they fall within a particular interpretation of the refugee definition.

Simplifying Procedures

The procedures employed to assess individual asylum applications in the industrialised states have in recent years been overwhelmed by the number of people claiming refugee status. By granting temporary protection to the many former Yugoslavs seeking refuge on their territory, governments have been spared the task of dealing with a potentially unmanageable number of individual applications.

Encouraging Generosity

As suggested already, one of the principal reasons why politicians and the public in the industrialised states have hardened their attitude towards asylum seekers is the perception that refugees have no real desire to return to their homeland, even if conditions become safe there, but would rather remain and enjoy the material benefits of life in the western world. By limiting asylum to the period when a safe refuge is actually required, the temporary protection approach promises to allay such fears. As experience with the former Yugoslav has demonstrated, governments may feel that they can afford to be more generous to a group of asylum seekers if their presence will not become a permanent one.

Facilitating Repatriation

Temporary protection, or 'return-focused protection', as one European government has called it, obliges all of the parties concerned to give serious consideration to the question of an eventual repatriation. Knowing from the beginning that they will be expected to return to their homeland when conditions have improved, beneficiaries of temporary protection can prepare themselves psychologically and in more practical ways for the day when safe return becomes possible. At the same time, the temporary protection approach will oblige host governments and UNHCR alike to consider the neglected question of how repatriation from the industrialised states can most effectively be facilitated.

Resolving the Conflict

The temporary protection approach provides host governments with a tangible incentive to address refugee problems at their source, in the country of origin. Expressed more simply, if states want to see the speedy return of the people they have temporarily admitted to their territory, then they must use all of the means which they have at their disposal to create the conditions necessary in the country of origin for safe repatriation to take place.

The Question of Entitlements

Given the relatively short period of time since the introduction of temporary protection for former Yugoslav citizens, it is difficult to say whether all of the potential advantages identified above will be realised, particularly those relating to the longer-term future of the beneficiaries. Nevertheless, it is possible to identify some of the key questions which have been raised by the introduction of temporary protection in Europe, and which must be addressed more systematically if similar approaches are to be introduced elsewhere.

First, what entitlements should be accorded to the beneficiaries of temporary protection? As indicated already, one of the reasons why refugees tend to stay indefinitely in the industrialised states is because they very quickly develop social connections there, adapt to the way of life and become accustomed to the standard of living which such societies have to offer. Should people with temporary protection be prevented or discouraged from establishing such ties to their country of refuge? And if so, can that objective be achieved without violating their human rights?

If social and economic integration really is a disincentive to voluntary repatriation, as some governments appear to believe, then the most rational means of ensuring the eventual repatriation of people granted temporary protection would be to accommodate them in isolated camps, to bar them from seeking employment, to discourage them from learning the local language and to prevent their family members from joining them. While such measures have already been employed in a number of states, these strategies are likely to prove politically unacceptable if maintained over an extended period of time.

Some of the measures which can be taken to discourage integration can also be challenged on legal and ethical grounds. Given that at least some of the people who are granted temporary protection would qualify for refugee status if their request for asylum was to be considered on an individual basis, they cannot be arbitrarily deprived of the rights to which they are entitled under the UN Refugee Convention. And as they have already been recognised as people who are in need of international protection, it seems perverse to treat them in a less generous manner than asylum seekers from other countries, many of whom will ultimately be refused refugee status.

How Temporary is Temporary?

Second, in view of the fact that conditions in a country of origin may not improve as quickly as initially anticipated, at what point should the beneficiaries of temporary protection have their asylum claims examined on an individual basis, or, alternatively, be offered the full range of rights and entitlements enjoyed by people who are recognised as refugees under the 1951 Convention?

When the temporary protection approach was introduced in 1992, there were hopes that the war in former Yugoslavia might not be prolonged. Now, however, three years later, there is still no certain prospect that conditions will improve sufficiently to permit the safe return of many people who have fled from the war, especially those originating from areas where their ethnic or religious group was not, or is no longer, in the majority.

At some stage, therefore, host governments will have to recognise that people with temporary protection must be offered greater certainty about their future and offered a standard or treatment which may make them less inclined to repatriate, even if it becomes safe for them to do so.

Clearly, conditions which are appropriate for a period of several weeks cannot be prolonged for months or years without prejudicing the human rights of the people concerned. Moreover, in some cases, beneficiaries of temporary protection may have suffered such grievous abuses in their country of origin that the prospect of voluntary repatriation should not be entertained at all.

Safe Return

A third set of issues relates to the withdrawal of temporary protection and the notion of safe return. With regard to these topics, it may simply suffice to list some of the questions which arise in connection with the future of the former Yugoslavs, and to which there are currently no definite answers. Who, for example, will determine whether it is safe for these people to go home? How much time must elapse after the hostilities and associated human rights violations have ceased before it can be deemed safe for people to return? What will happen to people who lose their temporary protection but who do not want to go home? And what solution will be found for those whose homes like in areas which have been occupied by members of another ethnic group, or which have come under the control of another government as a result of a negotiated settlement to the conflict?

Fourth, to what extent will temporary protection—like the right to remain—be misused by states who wish to limit their obligations to refugees? When the temporary protection proposal was introduced in 1992, it was as part of a broader package of measures which was intended to provide asylum seekers with both the immediate protection they required and an eventual solution to their plight. One important element of this package was that receiving countries should maintain open borders for new arrivals from former Yugoslavia. That principle has not been fully respected.

People escaping from war affected areas of former Yugoslavia, particularly Bosnia and Herzegovina, have encountered serious difficulties in gaining access to countries of refuge.... Even when departure is not blocked by fighting or hostile local elements, entry into neighbouring states is often refused for lack of required documentation.... Most of the countries that provide temporary protection ... have imposed visa requirements or similar restrictions on Bosnians.

Resolving Root Causes

Fifth and finally, certain questions arise with regard to the claim that the temporary protection approach will provide countries of refuge with an incentive to address the root causes of refugee movements in the country of origin. It could not be regarded as somewhat fanciful to suggest that the states of Western Europe have tried any harder to resolve the war in former Yugoslavia, simply because of their desire to witness the return of people to whom they have granted temporary protection.

The governments of Western Europe have many reasons—economic, political, military and diplomatic—to bring the war in former Yugoslavia to an end, all of which loom far larger in the mind of key decision-makers than the refugee question. And yet, even these important strategic interests have not motivated the governments concerned to take the kind of decisive action that might have halted the fighting and human rights abuse which have provoked such massive displacements, and which are now preventing those refugees from returning to their homes.

V. THE PRINCIPLE OF BURDEN-SHARING

A. B.S. Chimni, 'The Principle of Burden-sharing' (Unpublished paper).

The principle of burden-sharing which requires states to cooperate in dealing with the global refugee problem is not merely a moral but a legal principle. It is arguably a principle of customary international law. Such a characterisation can be sustained by weighing the following chain of evidence:

   i. Provisions of universal and regional conventions and declarations on refugees;
   ii. Conclusions adopted by the Executive Committee of the UNHCR Programme;
   iii. General Assembly resolutions on the problem of refugees;
   iv. The texts of different plans and programmes of action adopted by the international community, in particular the Declaration and Programme of Action of the First and Second International Conference on Assistance to Refugees in Africa ICARA I and II, the Comprehensive Plan of Action on Indo-Chinese Refugees, 1989 (CPA), and the Declaration and Concerted Plan of Action in favour of Central American Refugees, Returnees and Displaced Persons, 1989 (CIREFCA).
   v. A host of conventions and declarations which endorse the general principle of international cooperation in diverse fields of international life. These *inter alia* include the Charter of the United Nations, the Declaration on Principles of International Law Concerning Friendly Relations and Cooperation among States in accordance with the Charter of the United Nations, the Charter of

Economic Rights and Duties of States, the Declaration on the Right
to Development, 1986, and the Paris Declaration on the Least
Developed Countries, 1990.

vi. State practice relating to resettlement and local integration as well
as financial asssitance to host states and institutions such as the
UNHCR, UNRWA, etc.

The origin of the principle of burden-sharing in the post-war period, and
in a refugee specific context, can possibly be traced to the 1951 Convention relating to the Status of Refugees which states in its preamble that:

the grant of asylum may place unduly heavy burdens on certain
countries, and that a satisfactory solution of a problem of which the
United Nations has recognised the international scope and nature
cannot therefore be achieved without international cooperation.

There was, however, no substantive provision devoted to the principle.

The first substantive formulation on burden-sharing was contained in
Article 2 para (2) of the 1967 Declaration on Territorial Asylum which
states that:

where a state finds difficulty in granting or continuing to grant asylum, States individually or jointly or through the United Nations
shall consider, in a spirit of international solidarity, appropriate measures to lighten the burden on that State.

At the regional level, the OAU Convention contains an important provision on burden-sharing. Article 2 para (4) states:

Where a Member State finds difficulty in continuing to grant asylum
to refugees, such Member State may appeal directly to other Member States and through the OAU, and such other Member States
shall in the spirit of African solidarity and international cooperation
take appropriate measures to lighten the burden of the Member
State granting asylum.[69]

The Cartagena Declaration also emphasises the need for burden-sharing.
In the preambular paragraphs it underlines the need

To request immediate assistance from the international community
for Central American refugees, to be provided either directly, through

[69] See also OAU Doc. BR/COM/XV/55.90, Khartoum Declaration on Africa's Refugee
Crisis, 1990. Reproduced in *International Journal of Refugee Law* (Vol. 3, 1991), pp. 153–57.

bilateral or multilateral agreements, or through UNHCR and other organisations and agencies.[70]

The Asian–African Legal Consultative Committee (AALCC) adopted in 1987 an addendum to its 1966 principles calling for greater international burden-sharing. The Report of the AALCC on the adoption of the addendum states:

> In the light of the exchange of views and the material placed before the Committee ... the conclusion could be drawn that the principle of international solidarity in dealing with the refugee situations and the concept of burden sharing in that context appear by now to be firmly established in the practice of States.[71]

The additional principles adopted are:

I. The refugee phenomenon continues to be a matter of global concern and needs the support of the international community as a whole for its solution and as such the principle of burden sharing should be viewed in that context.

II. The principle of international solidarity and burden sharing needs to be applied progressively to facilitate the process of durable solutions for refugees whether within or outside a particular region, keeping in perspective that durable solutions in certain situations may need to be found by allowing access to refugees in countries outside the region due to political, social and economic considerations.

III. The principle of international solidarity and burden sharing should be seen as applying to all aspects of the refugee situation, including the development and strengthening of the standards of treatment of refugees, support to States in protecting and assisting refugees, the provision of durable solution and the support of international bodies with responsibilities for the protection and assistance of refugees.

IV. International solidarity and cooperation in burden sharing should be manifested whenever necessary, through effective concrete measures in support of States requiring assistance, whether through financial or material aid or through resettlement opportunities.

---

[70] Conclusion 11 of the Declaration also stresses the need:

> To make a study, in countries in the area which have a large number of refugees, of the possibilities of integrating them into the productive life of the country by allocating to the creation or generation of employment the resources made available by the international community through UNHCR, thus making it possible for refugees to enjoy their economic, social and cultural rights.

[71] See *Collection of International Instruments and Other Legal Texts Concerning Refugees and Displaced Persons* (UNHCR, Geneva, 1995), Vol. II, pp. 63–64.

The conclusions of the Executive Committee of the UNHCR contain a large number of references to the principle of burden-sharing. For example, Conclusion No. 22 on *Protection of Asylum-Seekers in Situations of Large-Scale Influx* stresses the need 'to establish effective arrangements in the context of international solidarity and burden-sharing for assisting countries which receive large numbers of asylum-seekers'. In the section entitled 'International Solidarity, burden-sharing and duties of States' the Conclusion states that:

> A mass influx may place unduly heavy burdens on certain countries; a satisfactory solution of a problem, international in scope and nature, cannot be achieved without international cooperation. States shall, within the framework of international solidarity and burden-sharing, take all necessary measures to assist, at their request, States which have admitted asylum seekers in large-scale influx situations.

These conclusions have been, in one form or another, reiterated by the Executive Committee since.[72] They also find place in General Assembly resolutions dealing with the problem of refugees.[73]

[72] For example, in 1988 the Executive Committee adopted Conclusion No. 52 (XXXIX) entitled 'International Solidarity and Refugee Protection' in which it reaffirmed:

> that refugee problems are the concern of the international community and their resolution is dependent on the will and capacity of States to respond in concert and whole-heartedly, in a spirit of true humanitarianism and international solidarity.

It went on to stress that:

> the principle of international solidarity has a fundamental role to play in encouraging a humanitarian approach to the grant of asylum and in the effective implementation of international protection in general.

And finally recalled that:

> in all circumstances, the respect for fundamental humanitarian principles is an obligation for all members of the international community, it being understood that the principle of solidarity is of utmost importance to the satisfactory implementation of these principles.

More recently, in Conclusion No. 79 (XLVII), adopted in 1996, the Executive Committee recognised that:

> countries of asylum carry a heavy burden, including in particular developing countries with limited resources and those which, due to their location, host large numbers of refugees and asylum-seekers; reiterates in this regard its commitment to uphold the principles of international solidarity and burden-sharing and calls on Governments and UNHCR to continue to respond to the assistance needs of refugees till durable solutions are found.

[73] To take an example, G.A. Res. 46/106,16 December 1991, on the Office of the United

Likewise the various plans of actions—ICARA I and II, CPA and CIREFCA—confirm the principle of burden-sharing.[74] The ICARA II Final Declaration and Program of Action states, for example, that:

> The Conference recognises that the condition of refugees is a global responsibility of the international community and emphasises the need for equitable burden sharing by all its members, taking into consideration particularly the case of the least developed countries. More significantly, in these plans the principle has been actualised through implementing concrete measures.[75]

The Declaration adopting the CPA notes the preoccupation of the concerned parties with 'the burden imposed, particularly on the neighbouring countries and territories, as a result of the continuation of the outflow and the presence of large numbers of asylum-seekers still in camps'.[76] Finally, the Declaration adopting the Concerted Plan of Action in favour of Central American Refugees notes that it approves the Plan 'in accordance with the principle of international solidarity'.[77]

Lastly, there is the vast practice of states, manifested in the provision of resettlement opportunities, local integration, and financial assistance, either bilaterally or through international institutions, which corroborates the emergence of a customary international law principle of burden-sharing.

Nations High Commissioner for Refugees stresses the need to find 'ways in which ... burden sharing mechanisms might be strengthened', and goes on to urge:

> the international community, including non-governmental organisations, in accordance with the principle of international solidarity and in the spirit of burden-sharing, to continue to assist the countries referred to in paragraph 16 above and the High Commissioner in order to enable them to cope with the additional burden that the care for refugees and asylum-seekers represents;

Para. 16:

> *expresses deep appreciation* for the valuable material and humanitarian response of receiving countries, in particular those developing countries that, despite limited resources, continue to admit large numbers of refugees and asylum-seekers on a permanent or temporary basis.

[74] The Text of the Final Declaration and Program of Action is reproduced in Robert F. Gorman, *Coping with Africa's Refugee Burden: A Time for Solutions* (Martinus Nijhoff, Dordrecht, 1987), Appendix IV.

[75] See Gorman, ibid., and Joseph B. Stern, *Review of the Comprehensive Plan of Action for Indo-Chinese Refugees*, Report submitted to the Canadian International Development Agency, International Humanitarian Assistance Division, November 1991.

[76] A/44/523,22 September 1989, International Conference on Indo-Chinese Refugees, Annex.

[77] CIREFCA/89/14, 31 May 1989, Declaration and Concerted Plan of Action in Favour of Central American Refugees, Returnees, and Displaced Persons.

The element of *opinio juris* is clearly present inasmuch as no state rejects the idea of burden-sharing. While the current practice of burden-shifting (by Western states in particular) appears to suggest otherwise, they do not involve a rejection of the principle of burden-sharing but its violation (or one could say a controversial and illegitimate interpretation of it). A rejection of the principle would, in the final analysis, involve the denial of the core principle of *non-refoulement*. The links of the principle of burden-sharing with the principle of *non-refoulement* have been noted by a number of established scholars. Atle Grahl-Madsen has observed that:

> the principle of *non-refoulement* is part of a sacred trust, but the principle does not stand alone; it is indeed closely connected with the principle of burden sharing.[78]

Goodwin-Gill writes that:

> the peremptory character of *non-refoulement* makes it independent of principles of solidarity and burden-sharing, but these cannot be ignored in a society of inter-dependent States. In situations of large-scale influx, protection cannot cease with the fact of admission; on the contrary, it must move towards solutions in full knowledge of the political and practical consequences which result from a State abiding by *non-refoulement*.[79]

This sketchy overview may be concluded by emphasising the need to take cognisance of the above pieces of refugee-specific evidence in the matrix of the general principle of cooperation outlined in relevant charters and declarations, some of which have been mentioned earlier.[80] Such an exercise would place in perspective our characterisation of the principle of international burden-sharing as a customary principle of international law.

---

[78] Atle Grahl-Madsen, 'Refuge in Canada: The Legal Background', in H. Adelman and C.M. Lanphier, eds, *Refuge or Asylum: A Choice for Canada* (York Lanes Press, Toronto, 1991), pp. 1–12 at p. 8.

[79] Goodwin-Gill, *The Refugee in International Law* (see footnote 5 earlier), p. 201.

[80] Besides Articles 55 and 56 of the Charter of the United Nations, particular mention may be made of the following:

(i) The duty of States to cooperate with one another in accordance with the fourth principle contained in the Declaration on Principles of International Law Concerning Friendly Relations and Cooperation among States in Accordance with the Charter of the United Nations. It *inter alia* states that:

States have the duty to co-operate with one another, irrespective of the differences in their political, economic and social systems, in the various spheres of international relations, in order to maintain international peace and security and to promote international economic stability and progress, the general welfare of

VI. EXTRADITION AND *NON-REFOULEMENT*

A. Arthur C. Helton, 'The Case of Zhang Zhenhai: Reconciling the International Responsibilities of Punishing Air Hijacking and Protecting Refugees', *Loyola of Los Angeles International and Comparative Law Journal* (Vol. 13, No. 4, June 1991), pp. 841–49.

Introduction

Concern over the dangers posed by aircraft hijacking has led the international community to address and specifically prohibit such acts.[81] At the

---

nations and international co-operation free from discrimination based on such differences.

GA Res. 2625 (xxv) adopted on 24 October 1970.

(ii) The Charter of Economic Rights and Duties of States lists 'International co-operation for development' and 'Promotion of international social justice' as among the fundamental principles of international economic relations. Articles 8, 9 and 17 of the Charter reinforce these duties.

GA Res. 3281 (xxix), 1974.

(iii) Article 4 of the Declaration on the Right to Development, 1986 states:

1. States have the duty to take steps, individually or collectively, to formulate international development policies with a view to facilitating the full realisation of the right to development.
2. Sustained action is required to promote more rapid development of developing countries. As a complement to the efforts of developing countries, effective international co-operation is essential in providing these countries with appropriate means and facilities to foster their comprehensive development.

G.A. Resolution 41/128 of 4 December 1986.

(iv) Finally, reference may be made to the Paris Declaration on the Least Developed Countries, 1990 for it captures the spirit in which the principles of co-operation and burden-sharing need to be approached and also because it is these poorest of poor countries which are carrying on behalf of the international community a substantial part of the burden of refugees. The Paris Declaration appropriately states that:

Refusal to accept the marginalisation of the least developed countries is an ethical imperative. It also corresponds to the long-term interests of the international community. In an increasingly interdependent world, the maintenance or deepening of the gap between the rich and poor nations contains serious seeds of tension. Our world will not enjoy lasting peace without respect for the United Nations Charter, international commitments and shared development.

UNCTAD/RDP/LDC/58, Paris Declaration on the Least Developed Countries.

[81] See Convention on Offenses and Certain Other Acts Committed on Board Aircraft, 14 September 1963, 20 U.S.T. 2941, T.I.A.S. No. 6768, 704 U.N.T.S. 219; Convention for the

same time, the international community has long sought to ensure the protection of displaced refugees who have a well founded fear of persecution on account of race, religion, nationality, membership in a particular social group, or political opinion upon return to their countries. Conflicts between these two international responsibilities are relatively rare. However, the celebrated case of Zhang Zhenhai presents such a situation. The case involved a request by the People's Republic of China to Japan for the extradition of a Chinese national who hijacked an aircraft and requested asylum in Japan.[82]

This article discusses the circumstances of the case of Zhang Zhenhai, the decision of the Japanese High Court on the extradition request, and the Japanese law relating to extradition and refugee protection. The Article analyses the relevant law and discusses how the Japanese court should have resolved the case.

Statement of the Case

The Hijacking

Zhang Zhenhai, a 36-year-old Chinese citizen and manager of a textile machinery factory in Hubei Province, participated in the [...] pro-democracy activities in China. Specifically, Zhang Zhenhai demonstrated in Tiananmen Square in June of 1989. While Zhang was arrested and detained by the Chinese police on unrelated charges, the Chinese police interrogated him about his involvement in Tiananmen Square. After bribing government officials, Zhang was released and sought to leave China.

After an unsuccessful land escape, Zhang resorted to hijacking an Air China jetliner bound for New York through Shanghai and San Francisco on December 16, 1989. His wife and 13-year-old son accompanied him. The hijacking began when Zhang handed over a piece of Chinese paper money to a stewardess on which he had written: 'Please go to South Korea. If my request is not accepted in three minutes, I will blow up the airplane.' The South Korean authorities denied permission to land, and the plane subsequently landed at Fukuoka Airport in Japan. Zhang had no weapons, nor did he commit any act of violence in connection with the hijacking.

After landing, a flight attendant led Zhang to a door at the rear of the airplane. When Zhang looked outside through the open door, he was pushed out of the plane and seriously injured, requiring his hospitalisation.

Suppression of Unlawful Seizure of Aircraft (Hijacking), Dec. 16, 1970, 22 U.S.T. 1641, T.I.A.S. No. 7192; Convention for the Suppression of Unlawful Acts Against the Safety of Civil Aviation, 26 January 1973, 24 U.S.T. 564, T.I.A.S. No. 7570.

[82] Decision of 20 April 1990 (Kosai) (High Court), Tokyo, Japan [hereafter Decision].

The same day, December 16, 1989, the hijacked airplane flew back to China with Zhang's wife and son aboard. Shortly thereafter, the Japanese government announced that it would extradite Zhang to China at a later time. The Japanese government transferred Zhang from the hospital to a prison in Fukuoka and then to the Tokyo Detention House on January 11, 1990. He was extradited to China on April 28, 1990, after the Chinese government assured Japanese authorities that Zhang would not receive the death penalty. Upon extradition on July 18, 1990, a Chinese court in Beijing, after a one-day trial, sentenced Zhang to a term of eight years imprisonment and a two-year suspension of civil rights.

The Tokyo High Court Decision

While in Japan, Zhang applied for asylum as a refugee. With the assistance of counsel, he also sought to avoid extradition through a judicial challenge, *inter alia*, on the grounds that the offense he had committed was political in nature. On April 20, 1990, the Tokyo High Court upheld the extradition.

The Tokyo High Court recognised that extradition decisions are the responsibility of the Japanese Minister of Justice, but held that such decisions are subject 'to judicial evaluation by the court as to the question of whether there is a contradiction to the prohibitive clause of the Law'. It explained:

> When the Court entertains this question, it is only concerned with the judgement as to whether the case under consideration falls within the range of protection clauses of Article 2 of the Law of Extradition ... or not, hence it does not include the decision with regard to the appropriateness of the extradition.

The court next addressed the question of whether the offense in question was political in nature, thus exempting the offender from extradition. It held:

> Generally speaking, a political offence is defined as a crime which aims at changing the political regime of a State, or a crime which tries to influence on [*sic*] the internal and external policy of a State, and also is in contravention to the penal law of the State concerned. As to the question of whether a relative political crime, namely those cases in which the political offence comprises at the same time an ordinary crime that is socially and morally culpable, should be recognized as a political offence or not, must be decided by the casebycase principle. However, on deciding this question, there should be some measuring-rods such as, whether or not it has a direct and important relationship to the achievement of political purposes, and whether

or not the nature of the offence, the seriousness of the offence are disproportionate to the intended purposes, and lastly, whether or not as a whole it deserves protection.

The court then examined Zhang's specific situation. The court stated that it could not overlook the 'fundamental character of the present case as a crime of hijacking against a civil aircraft'. Even if the court believed Zhang was involved in the demonstrations in Tiananmen Square, it stated that it could not consider his role as anything other than a 'mere passive participant'.

The court also discussed the general policy question of whether air hijacking could constitute a 'political offence' so as to render an offender exempt from return. It explained:

This case is an offence in which the suspect hijacked a civil aircraft and exposed more than 220 passengers to risk. The Air China jet-liner could not obtain permission to land from any airports in the Republic of Korea to which it requested permission, was driven away by four Korean jet fighters and was forced to make an emergency landing at Fukuoka Airport, fac[ed] with the danger of running out of fuel. These facts should not be overlooked. Moreover, the Court must take into account ... passengers who were terrified and felt their lives were in danger.

In order to eradicate the occurrence of future hijackings, which ex-posed [innocent] civil passengers ... to terror, and which was attempted by an individual for his personal gain—fleeing from his country—there should be established an international agreement for the pun-ishment of an act of hijacking. Moreover in order to justify non-extradition at the sacrifice of this requirement, there need[s] to be a recognition of the public good which deserves better protection at the cost of any inconveniences experienced by passengers. In the present case, the suspect did not try to change the political regime or to influence internal and external policy of the State by his offence. The direct aim of the offence was to escape from his country. Hence it does not bear any special resemblance [sic] as a political offence, which is committed against the State.

The court also briefly addressed the question of return under interna-tional refugee law. It stated that 'Article 1F(b) of the Convention relating to the Status of Refugees provides as follows; ... "the provisions of the Convention shall not apply to any person... [who] has committed a seri-ous non-political crime outside the country of refuge prior to his admis-sion to that country as a refugee".' The court once again noted that the present case is a case of hijacking a civil aircraft, and this is not considered to be a political offense. Hence the court found that the provision of article 1F(b) of the Convention could not be applied.

Refugee and Extradition Law in Japan

Refugee Law

On January 1, 1982, Japan acceded to two multilateral United Nations treaties, the 1951 Convention relating to the Status of Refugees ('Refugee Convention') and the 1967 Protocol relating to the Status of Refugees ('Protocol').

Article 33 of the 1951 Convention, as amended by the 1967 Protocol, provides: 'No Contracting State shall expel or return ('*refouler*') a refugee in any manner whatsoever to the frontiers of territory where his life or freedom would be threatened on account of his race, religion, nationality, membership of a particular social group of political opinion.' However, as the High Court in Zhang's case recognised, article 1F(b) of the same convention states that the provisions of the Refugee Convention do not apply to a person if there are serious reasons to believe that, prior to admission as a refugee, that person committed a serious non-political crime outside the country of refuge.

The Immigration Control and Refugee Recognition Act in Japan incorporates by reference criteria set forth in the Refugee Convention and Protocol regarding the recognition of refugee status. The Immigration Bureau of the Ministry of Justice has established procedures to determine refugee status.

The ... UNHCR oversees the Refugee Convention's administration. The Executive Committee of the High Commissioner's Programme, a committee of governments that oversees the work of UNHCR, examined the problem of extradition as it affected refugees in 1980. In response, the Executive Committee adopted Conclusion No. 17 (XXXI) which emphasised the fundamental character of the *non-refoulement* principle and recognised the need to protect refugees from extradition to a country where they have a well-founded reason to fear persecution. In 1977, the Executive Committee, in Conclusion No. 6 (XXVIII) on *non-refoulement*, reaffirmed the fundamental importance of the observance of this principle irrespective of whether or not the individuals in question have been formally recognised as refugees. The Executive Committee's Conclusion No. 8 (XXVIII), promulgated that same year, recognised that it was essential that an applicant for refugee status 'be permitted to remain in the country while an appeal to a higher administrative authority or to the courts is pending'.

Extradition Law

As the Tokyo High Court recognised, a person against whom extradition is requested is generally permitted to defend against extradition on the ground that the offense in question was political in character.[83] No precise definition of what constitutes a political offense exists. In legal theory, however, a political offense generally has been characterised as either a 'pure political offense' or a 'relative political offense'.[84] A pure political offense is an act that is 'directed against the state [but which] contains none of the elements of ordinary crime',[85] such as sedition, treason and espionage. A relative political offense is one in which 'a common crime is so connected with a political act that the entire offense is regarded as political'.[86] Either type of political offense can be raised as a defense to extradition.

One commentator has stated that air hijacking is an international offense that constitutes a categorical exception to the political offense exception to extradition.[87] Another, however, has argued that the political offense exception may still be available to forestall the return of a refugee who has committed air hijacking to flee persecution, depending upon the particular circumstances of an individual's case.[88]

Analysis

Standards of international refugee law should govern extradition decisions. The 1979 Handbook on Procedures and Criteria for Determining Refugee Status Under the 1951 Convention and the 1967 Protocol relating to the Status of Refugees (Handbook), sets forth relevant criteria for determining when an individual claiming refugee status may be subject to extradition. The Handbook, in explicating the 'serious non-political crime' exclusionary language of article 1F(b) of the Refugee Convention, states:

> it is also necessary to strike a balance between the nature of offence presumed to have been committed by the applicant and the degree of persecution feared. If a person has a well-founded fear of very

[83] See generally Garcia-Mora, 'The Nature of Political Offenses: A Knotty Problem of Extradition Law', *Vanderbilt Law Review* (48, 1962), p. 1226.

[84] Ibid. at pp. 1231, 1239.

[85] Ibid. at pp. 1230, 1237.

[86] Ibid. at pp. 1230–31.

[87] M.C. Bassiouni, *International Extradition: United States Law and Practice*, VIII (1983), pp. 2–86.

[88] Arthur Helton, 'Harmonizing Political Asylum and International Extradition: Avoiding Analytical Cacophony', *Georgetown Immigration Law Journal* (Vol. 1, No. 457, 1986), pp. 475–80.

severe persecution, e.g., persecution endangering his life or free-dom, a crime must be very grave in order to exclude him.[89]

The Handbook adds that in evaluating the nature of the alleged crime, all relevant factors, including mitigating circumstances, must be considered.[90] Specifically addressing the issue of the refugee status of individuals accused of hijacking, the Handbook refers to two reports leading to the adoption of international treaties concerning the unlawful seizure of aircraft. These reports state that 'the adoption of the draft Resolution cannot prejudice any international legal rights or duties of States under instruments relating to the status of refugees and stateless persons[s]', and 'the adoption of the draft Resolution cannot prejudice any international legal rights or duties of States with respect to asylum'.[91]
The Handbook further specifies that:

[t]he various conventions adopted in this connection deal mainly with the manner in which the perpetrators of such acts have to be treated. They invariably give Contracting States the alternative of extraditing such persons or instituting penal proceedings for the act on their own territory, *which implies the right to grant asylum*.[92]

The Handbook concludes:

[w]hile there is thus a possibility of granting asylum, the gravity of the persecution of which the offender may have been in fear, and the extent to which such fear is well-founded, will have to be duly considered in determining his possible refugee status under the 1951 Convention. The question of the exclusion under Article 1F(b) of an applicant who has committed an unlawful seizure of an aircraft will also have to be carefully examined in each individual case.[93]

An individual should not be extradited to a country where he will face serious persecution, if the individual's only crime is that he hijacked an airplane in order to escape persecution, and the actions taken were proportionate to those ends. In essence, a balancing of aggravating, mitigating and persecutory circumstances is required. The determination of whether there is a possibility of persecution upon his return and other factors affecting the individual's asylum status are governed by the standards set forth under the Refugee Convention and Protocol. The

---

[89] *Handbook* (see footnote 65 earlier), at p. 156.
[90] Ibid. at p. 157.
[91] Ibid. at p. 159.
[92] Ibid. at p. 160.
[93] Ibid. at p. 161.

methods of flight condemned under international law, absent aggravating circumstances, do not preclude granting asylum to deserving individuals. Thus, the execution of an extradition order must be suspended until a final decision on refugee status is made. This is necessary because after the application has been examined, the individual may prove to be a refugee entitled to benefit from the principle of *non-refoulement*.

Conclusion

There is an undeniable international consensus against air hijacking. There is also a well-established legal principle to protect refugees and not return them to places where they may face persecution.[94] The Japanese court in the case of Zhang Zhenhai was highly solicitous of the former principle, but gave insufficient consideration to the latter. It found Zhang undeserving of protection under extradition law, but failed to fully appreciate the nature of his claim under refugee law. That he utilised air hijacking in his flight from persecution did not preclude his recognition as a refugee. This merely begins the inquiry. The court's failure to inquire further deprived Zhang of the individualised justice to which refugee law entitles him. Zhang's claim for protection should have been fully addressed under the relevant asylum procedures and criteria. Had such an analysis occurred, Zhang most likely would have been declared a refugee and granted asylum.

B. UNHCR, Conclusion No. 17: Problems of Extradition Affecting Refugees.

The Executive Committee

(a) Considered that cases in which the extradition of a refugee or of a person who may qualify as a refugee is requested may give rise to special problems;

(b) Reaffirmed the fundamental character of the generally recognised principle of *non-refoulement*;

(c) Recognised that refuges should be protected in regard to extradition to a country where they have well-founded reasons to fear persecution on the grounds enumerated in Article 1(A) (2) of the 1951 United Nations Convention relating to the Status of Refugees;

(d) Called upon States to ensure that the principle of *non-refoulement* is duly taken into account in treaties relating to extradition and as appropriate in national legislation on the subject;

---

[94] Extradition is by no means an inevitable outcome under current state practice when these principles conflict. See 'India Won't Extradite Hijackers to Burma', *The Nation*, Bangalore (13 November 1990), at p. A2.

   (e) Expressed the hope that due regard be had to the principle of *non-refoulement* in the application of existing treaties relating to extradition;

   (f) Stressed that nothing in the present conclusions should be considered as affecting the necessity for States to ensure, on the basis of national legislation and international instruments, punishment for serious offences, such as the unlawful seizure of aircraft, the taking of hostages and murder;

   (g) Stressed that protection in regard to extradition applies to persons who fulfil the criteria of the refugee definition and who are not excluded from refugee status by virtue of Article 1(F)(b) of the 1951 United Nations Convention relating to the Status of Refugees.

Chapter 3

Rights and Duties of Refugees

The 1951 Convention details the civic and socio-economic rights of refugees which must be respected.[1] In addition, there are the regional and universal human rights instruments which, read in conjunction with the refugee-specific rights regime, 'set a wide-ranging, if perhaps not fully adequate or integrated' measure of respect for the basic dignity of refugees.[2] The network of instruments is of significance particularly where states are not parties to the 1951 Convention or have entered reservations permitted by Article 42. In such an event human rights instruments can be invoked to guarantee the basic rights of refugees.[3]

Negative Developments

The importance of using the language of rights to provide refugees with an opportunity to reconstruct their lives cannot be overstated. But the promotion and defence of refugee rights is no easy task today. First, as already seen in Chapter 2, the attitude of states to refugees has hardened. Second, as Emanuel Marx, looking at the social world of refugees in **Reading I.A** suggests, often those (including governments, NGOs and refugee leadership) who are in a position to help refugees reconstruct their lives seek to deny them basic rights such as mobility, work, education and housing in a bid to 'retain' them as refugees.

[1] In considering the rights of refugees in this chapter, the principle of *non-refoulement* is not examined as it was discussed in Chapter 2. Instead, this chapter focuses on a set of other rights of refugees which need to be be respected.

[2] James C. Hathaway and John A. Dent, *Refugee Rights: Report on a Comparative Survey* (York Lanes Press, Toronto, 1995), p. 1.

[3] See *Human Rights and Refugee Protection* (UNHCR, Geneva, 1995), Parts I and II.

Stereotype Images

The stereotype image of refugees as individuals devoid of will and resources to rebuild their lives is another serious hurdle to promoting a rights-based approach. As **Reading I.B** notes, refugees are viewed as helpless creatures, as mere statistics, to be enumerated and counted, rather than as active participants in remaking their lives. Whereas for a rights-based approach to be promoted, it is imperative that refugee voices be heard, particularly those of refugee women, in the assistance and protection process.[4]

Detention

The 1951 Convention permits the detention of a refugee under certain circumstances. Article 9 of the Convention provides that 'in time of war or other grave and exceptional circumstances' a state may take 'provisional measures' which it considers 'essential to the national security in the case of a particular person'. These measures can be taken pending a determination that the person is in fact a refugee and that the continuance of the provisional measures 'is necessary in his case...'. Mention may also be made of Article 31(2) of the 1951 Convention which allows certain restrictions to be placed on the movements of refugees 'unlawfully in the country of refuge'. But these restrictions must be 'those which are necessary' and 'shall only be applied until their status in the country is regularised or they obtain admission into another country'.

There is a widespread consensus that detention should be viewed as an exceptional measure.[5] **Reading II.A** reproduces the observations and conclusions of a Working Group of the International Institute of Humanitarian Law in 1984 on the question of detention. Readers may also refer to Conclusion No. 44 adopted by the Executive Committee of the UNHCR in 1986. It clarifies *inter alia* the situations in which detention may be deemed appropriate:

if necessary, detention may be resorted to only on grounds prescribed by law to verify identity; to determine the elements on which the claim to refugee status or asylum is based; to deal with cases

---

[4] This point is also made in **Reading II.F** which deals with the special assistance and protection needs of women.

[5] Guy S. Goodwin-Gill, *The Refugee in International Law* (Clarendon Press, Oxford, 1996), second edition, p. 248; L. Takkenberg, 'Detention and Other Restrictions of the Freedom of Movement of Refugees and Asylum-seekers: The European Perspective', in J. Bhabha and G. Coll, eds, *Asylum Law and Practice in Europe and America* (Federal Publications Inc., Washington, D.C., 1992), pp. 180–84.

where refugees or asylum seekers have destroyed their travel and/or identity documents or have used fraudulent documents in order to mislead the authorities of the State in which they intend to claim asylum; or to protect national security or public order.

In considering the conditions in which detention is lawful under the 1951 Convention, the attention of readers is drawn to the fact that international human rights law goes further in offering protection against arbitrary arrest and detention.[6] Under human rights law, as Goodwin-Gill has pointed out, 'arbitrary embraces not only what is illegal, but also what is unjust.'[7]

In the case of mass influx of refugees a key question is whether keeping refugees in closed or restricted camp conditions amounts to detention. Much would appear to depend upon the circumstances of the particular case and the nature of the restrictions which have been imposed on the freedom of movement of refugees.[8] This issue is briefly discussed in **Reading II.D.**

Recent years have seen the disturbing practice of detention of asylum-seekers in the industrialised countries. A UNHCR survey reveals that 'countries in Western Europe are increasingly resorting to detention of asylum-seekers.'[9] The situation is no different where the United States is concerned.[10] **Reading II.B** reproduces a brief extract from an article by Koh on 'America's Offshore Refugee Camps' in which he mentions the startling decision of US Courts (see, for instance, *Cuban American Bar Association [CABA] v. Christopher*)[11] to declare offshore refugee camps a 'rights-free zone' for asylum-seekers. According to Bill Frelick of the USCR, decisions like *CABA v. Christopher* suggest 'that the very purpose of establishing a center offshore is to insulate it from the reach of US law and to

---

[6] Ibid. See, for example, Article 9 of the 1966 Covenant on Civil and Political Rights and Article 5, 1985 United Nations Declaration on the Human Rights of Individuals who are Not Nationals of the Country in which they Live. For the texts of these instruments see *Collection of International Instruments and Other Legal Texts Concerning Refugees and Displaced Persons*, vol. I (UNHCR, Geneva, 1995).

[7] Goodwin-Gill, *The Refugee in International Law* (footnote 5 earlier), p. 248.

[8] See generally in this regard Richard Black, 'Putting Refugees in Camps', *Forced Migration Review* (No. 2, August 1998), pp. 4–7; Jeff Crisp and Karen Jacobsen, 'Refugee Camps Reconsidered', *Forced Migration Review* (No. 3, December 1998), pp. 27–30; and Richard Black, 'Refugee Camps Not Really Reconsidered: A Reply to Crisp and Jacobsen', ibid., p. 31.

[9] UNHCR, European Series, *Detention of Asylum-seekers in Europe* (Vol. 1, No. 4, October 1995), p. 7.

[10] Arthur C. Helton, 'The Detention of Asylum-seekers in the United States and Canada', in H. Adelman, ed., *Refugee Policy: Canada and the United States* (York Lanes Press, Toronto, 1991), pp. 253–68.

[11] 43 F.3d 1412 (11th Cir. 1995).

minimise the due process rights of asylum seekers'.[12] In other words, the price which an asylum-seeker must pay for temporary asylum is detention.[13]

Physical Security of Refugees

Reading II.C considers the problem of military and armed attacks on refugee camps which violate the most basic right of refugees, *viz.*, the right to physical security. It notes the absence of explicit provisions in international refugee law concerning the physical safety of refugees and emphasises the need to adopt an international convention on the subject. In this context, it proceeds to articulate the principles which should form a part of such a convention, as also make a series of other recommendations. At the level of 'soft law', the Executive Committee of the UNHCR has adopted two Conclusions on the subject, *viz.*, Conclusions No. 45 and No. 48. They condemn 'all violations of the rights and safety of refugees and asylum-seekers and in particular military or armed attacks on refugee camps and establishments', and underline the need to ensure the civilian and humanitarian character of refugee camps and settlements.

Civil and Socio-economic Rights

Reading II.D takes a look at the state practice with regard to three crucial rights contained in the 1951 Convention: freedom of internal movement, the right to employment and the right to public assistance. Among other things, it discloses certain differences in the state practice of the industrialised and the third world countries and the reasons for these. Readers may query if the reasons advanced by the third world countries to justify their different practices are persuasive. In evaluating the reasons put forward by these countries there is a need to carefully balance the concerns of poor societies with scarce resources even for their citizens and the rights of refugees to live their lives with dignity.[14] **Reading II.D** also contains a critical analysis of the 1951 Convention rights regime.

Reading II.E reproduces excerpts from Executive Committee Conclusion No. 22 which lists the basic rights of refugees in situations of mass influx.

[12] Bill Frelick, 'Safe Haven: Safe for Whom', *World Refugee Survey 1995*, pp. 18–27 at p. 27.

[13] Ibid., p. 25. I would urge readers to read the series of articles written on the subject by Professor Harold Koh of Yale Law School. Harold Hongjhu Koh, 'The Human Face of the Haitian Interdiction Program', *Virginia Journal of International Law* (Vol. 33, 1993), pp. 483–90; 'Refugees, the Courts, and the New World Order', *Utah Law Review* (No. 3, 1994), pp. 999–1027; 'America's Offshore Refugee Camps', *University of Richmond Law Review* (Vol. 29, 1995), pp. 139–73.

[14] In this context readers may like to turn to Chapter 8 and review the practice in India.

Special Needs of Refugee Women and Children

Two decades after feminist writings have made their presence felt in the social sciences, it is still not sufficiently appreciated that refugee women, who constitute a majority of the world refugee population, have special needs. In 1991, the UNHCR adopted the *Guidelines on the Protection of Refugee Women* from which **Reading II.F** reproduces a brief excerpt. It outlines the international legal framework for the protection of refugee women and the measures needed at the level of assistance and protection, in particular the need for women refugees to be involved in the planning and delivery of assistance activities. Subsequently, in 1993, the year the UNGA adopted the Declaration on the Elimination of Violence against Women, the Executive Committee of the UNHCR adopted Conclusion No. 73 on 'Refugee Protection and Sexual Violence'.

Readings II.G and **II.H** reproduce two extracts from UNHCR's *Refugee Children: Guidelines on Protection and Care*. **Reading II.G** attempts to identify the special needs of children for protection and care. The guidelines fill an important gap in the 1951 Convention which merely stresses family unity and access to primary education.

Reading II.H briefly reviews certain rights available to children under the 1989 Convention on the Rights of the Child (CRC). Readers may, in its light, address the important question as to whether the CRC deals with the specific problems of refugee children, that is, as opposed to children in general?[15] If the answer is in the negative, there is a need to determine the steps which should be taken to fill the gaps.[16]

Future of a Refugee-specific Rights Regime

At the time of the drafting of the 1951 Convention, the only comprehensive standard for international human rights law was the unenforceable UDHR. But the subsequent adoption of a number of conventions at the regional and international levels raises the question of the relationship of the specific refugee rights regime contained in the 1951 Convention and international human rights law. Indeed, the question arises as to whether in view of the enormous developments in international human rights law there is any longer a need to retain a refugee-specific rights regime. Only a careful comparison of the relevant texts can help answer this question. **Reading III.A** offers a beginning in this regard.

[15] According to Goodwin-Gill, the CRC does not offer an 'entirely satisfactory legal basis' for action for it does not address the situation of children as refugees. Goodwin-Gill, *The Refugee in International Law* (see footnote 5 earlier), p. 257. For the text of CRC see UNHCR, *Collection of International Instruments* (footnote 6 earlier).

[16] See Goodwin-Gill, *The Refugee in International Law* (footnote 5 earlier), pp. 257ff.

Duties of Refugees

It is often forgotten that refugees are no different from other individuals and have certain duties to fulfil. Article 2 of the 1951 Convention states:

> Every refugee has duties to the country in which he finds himself, which require in particular that he conform to its laws and regulations as well as to measures taken for the maintenance of public order.

In the single reading in Part IV, Johnsson discusses the duties refugees owe to host communities.

* * *

I. LIFEWORLD OF REFUGEES

A. Emanuel Marx, 'The Social World of Refugees: A Conceptual Framework', *Journal of Refugee Studies* (Vol. 3, 1990), pp. 190, 196–98.

[The view that] a refugee is a person whose social world has been disturbed ... can contribute to our understanding in at least two ways. First, it offers a meaningful classification of refugees, on a continuum that runs from total destruction of the refugee's social world to its persistence even as he or she moves. At one extreme there are refugees whose social world almost collapsed in flight, who lost relatives and livelihood. Such were the survivors of Nazi concentration camps, who had no one left in the world and no home to return to. Then there are those refugees whose social world became more circumscribed as a result of flight, but were able to maintain some links or establish new ones. Most Afghan and Ethiopian refugees might fall into this category. At the other extreme are refugees who maintained or quickly established full-fledged networks in a new environment. ...

Second, the concept enables us to follow the movement of refugees and to chart the transformations of their social worlds. Where a social world is constructed around a person, all the person's movements and all the changes in his or her condition can be attended to. One can dispense altogether with a territorial base. The various stages of the person's career, from the destruction of his or her social world, through camp life, to the growth of a diversified social network, can all be encompassed in the framework of a study. ...

Social World of Migrants

These abstract statements can be illustrated from the findings of research in related fields. Particularly revealing are studies of total institutions, the early socialisation of children and the growth of their social networks, and the adaptation of immigrants to life in a new environment. Let us first see how these studies help us to understand the growth of a network of relationships. Whenever a refugee's social networks have been severely disrupted, he or she suffers loss of social competence. Their situation is similar to that of a newborn baby, as described in sociological studies of socialisation. Some time after birth, the child becomes aware that he or she is distinct from the mother and recognises her as the person on whom he depends. He must communicate his needs to the mother, and for that purpose learns more, and more specific, signs. He also learns to relate to a growing number of persons and to differentiate between them. As each of them takes on some of the mother's tasks, as well as quite new ones, the relationship with the mother loses some of its totality, yet remains central and multiplex. A growing number of new and often very specialised relationships provide for an ever widening range of needs.

Social anthropologists encounter complexities and variations in their studies, which do not permit them to conceive of socialisation as a unilineal development. The child's social development is often obstructed at numerous points, so that he or she may never realise their full potential. Judging from the studies of initiation, which supposedly turns children into adults, one would conclude that the obstructions to the child's development are quite systematic. Adults everywhere, including the child's own parents, have a vested interest in holding up his or her development. An outstanding example would be the Maasai initiation which, manifestly, turns young men into fighters, and women into the companions of fighters. The young people who have just become 'adults' are then prevented from owning property, from marrying and from settling down for another decade. They become almost unpaid herdsmen of their elders' cattle and protectors of their property. When translated into the refugee situation, we find that social networks develop in a variety of ways, and suffer all kinds of mischief en route. Development may be obstructed by policies of segregation, such as keeping refugees in closed camps, or by treating them as wards of state of welfare agencies.

The first stages of the refugee experience, the sensation of loss, disorientation and numbness, have been recorded in the memories of many. But this stage has not easily lent itself to study in the field. The closest we can come towards understanding these situations are studies of the induction of mental patients into asylums, and of prisoners into gaols. The inmates end up in institutions because they have become a burden to their associates or relatives, and not so much because of their affliction.

The loss of social relationships is in these cases intensified by a sense of betrayal. They realise that the outside world, and especially their closest associates, have left them without protection. This theme is taken up by the staff of the total institution. They sharply remind inmates of their helplessness by stripping them of the remaining vestiges of the old life, their clothing and belongings. They seek to prolong this defenceless state by isolating them from the other inmates. This is done by physically isolating the inmates for some time, and teaching them the rules and regulations of the institution, while impressing on them that these must be observed implicitly. At this stage, inmates bow to the inevitable, identify with the rules and hesitate to collaborate with other inmates. The efforts of the managers to apply the regulations on a permanent basis, to treat inmates as completely lacking in power, continue unabated, even when they eventually begin to establish relationship with other inmates. This development leads to a series of secondary accommodations, or forms of institutional 'underlife'. A facade of deference to regulations and segregation between staff and inmates is formally maintained, both towards the institution's management and the outside world. But in daily life the institutional order is continually negotiated, producing various forms of collaboration between staff and inmates. Is not the fate of many refugees similar to the situation described here? The competent authorities rarely concede that the helpless refugees they met on arrival gradually acquire some power of their own, and that they integrate in society.

B. Robin Needham, 'Refugee Participation', in *Refugee Participation Network* 17 (Oxford, August 1994), p. 17.

The world has acquired a fairly stereotyped impression of refugees. Unfortunately, these stereotypes also affect those of us who work with refugees and prevent participation by refugees in decisions that affect them and their future.

Firstly, refugees are assumed to be completely helpless and crying out for any assistance that can be given to them. A condition such as this is seen to require direct action and intervention, independent of the participation of, or consultation with, the refugees themselves.

Secondly, refugees are treated as statistics and numbers. The operation of working with them is regarded as a logistical exercise. Refugees are recipients for objects and items. Successful progress in a refugee operation is measured in terms of x houses built, y tons of food provided, z patients treated. There is little consideration of social factors or refugee values because the whole basis of so many refugee relief efforts rests on objects, not on people; on what is available, not on what is needed.

Thirdly, 'he who pays the piper, calls the tune'. The donors are usually the ones calling the tune so the agencies serving refugees see themselves as being more accountable to the donors than to the beneficiaries. It is the donors who—to a great extent—dictate the nature of response by consciously or sub-consciously expecting their will to be done. Basic needs may be being met, but whose basic needs? The donors, the assisting agencies or those of the recipients?

Fourthly, assisting agencies sometimes develop a highly specialised but rather inflexible approach to the provision of that assistance. Specialisation and models developed in community health care, food distribution, camp layout and services, etc. in one refugee assistance programme become the blueprint for the work of that agency in any and all other refugee settings.

Fifthly, many agencies and donors provide high-tech, high profile, capital-intensive, photogenic types of assistance such as sophisticated field hospitals, imported machinery and equipment, new technology and 'appropriate' housing and sanitation. Many of these appliances and applications are beyond the knowledge and experience of refugees and thus widen the cultural and social gap between the intervenor and the refugee.

Sixthly, the decision-making apparatus in many international organisations or voluntary agencies does not have the provision for a major local input. Overall policy and programming is decided in Geneva, London or Washington and directives are handed down in such a way that questioning them is often difficult or unwise. Policy formulated at these levels may commit an organisation to a course of action that can become outmoded or impractical in the light of subsequent developments.

Seventhly, many agencies have no history of real provision for a participatory approach within their own organisations; power sharing with or participation by those outside the agencies—such as beneficiaries—is consequently unthinkable.

These various constraints to the participation of refugees have led refugee assistance programme to be described as:

> ... the last bastion of the ultra-paternalistic approach to aid and development. It is hard to think of another area where the blinkered nonsense of the 'we know what is best for them' approach survives so unchallenged.
>
> (Malloch Brown)

II. RIGHTS OF REFUGEES

A. Observations and Conclusions on Detention of the Working Group of the International Institute of Humanitarian Law held under the auspices of UNHCR, 1984.

The problems related to the detention of refugees and asylum-seekers was examined by a Working Group convened in Florence in June 1984 by the International Institute of Humanitarian Law and held under the auspices of the Office of the United Nations High Commissioner for Refugees. The report of the Working Group was noted with approval by the participants of the Tenth Round Table on Current Problems of International Humanitarian Law which was held by the Institute in San Remo from September 17–20, 1984. The Round Table commended the following observations and conclusions for the consideration of governments and international organisations:

1. The automatic or indiscriminate detention by State, without valid reasons, of refugees and asylum-seekers who are under their jurisdiction is at fundamental variance with the notion of protection. The detention of refugees and asylum-seekers should only be resorted to as an exceptional measure and should only be maintained for as long as strictly required by the exigencies of the situation.

2. Entry in search of refuge on account of persecution, armed conflict or other event seriously disturbing public order does not constitute an unlawful act. Detention in such circumstances solely on the ground of illegal entry or presence is, therefore, unjustifiable.

3. In the case of individual asylum-seekers, a reasonable initial period of deprivation of liberty may be unavoidable to establish identity and the *bona fide* nature of the asylum claim. Otherwise detention should only be envisaged in cases where action is being taken with a view to lawful deportation or extradition and where there are serious grounds such as criminal association or intent or a reasonable apprehension that the person is likely to abscond.

4. In all cases, detention of refugees or asylum-seekers would be subject to administrative re-examination and judicial review in accordance with national law and relevant international obligations. All such persons should be notified of their legal rights in a manner that they can understand and they should also have access to legal counsel and to a representative of the United Nations High Commissioner for Refugees. Where justified, they should be granted provisional liberty on suitable conditions.

5. The observations in paragraphs 3 and 4 do not affect the question of detention in cases of arrest in general criminal proceedings or administrative detention arising from other provisions of national law which are not in violation of international law.

6. In situations of large-scale influx, restrictions on freedom of movement might also be unavoidable, but should similarly be strictly limited to the requirements of the circumstances. The conditions of such restrictions, however, should in no case fall below the basic minimum standards identified by the Executive Committee of the United Nations High Commissioner for Refugees' Program at its 32nd Session in 1981.

7. In order to ensure that they are not exposed to unjustified measures of detention, it is essential that refugees be identified as such. In situations of large-scale influx where individual determination of status may not be feasible group determination should be made. In the case of individual asylum-seekers, appropriate procedure for the determination of refugee status should be established. Such procedures should be as expeditious as possible so as to ensure that any measures of detention are not unduly prolonged.

8. Measures of detention should not be applied in a manner which violates the principle of non-discrimination, nor should detention be resorted to in order to deter further refugee movements.

9. Refugees and asylum-seekers should never be used as a buffer in cases of armed conflict or confined to areas where their physical safety is threatened.

10. In cases of detention, refugees and asylum-seekers whose status has not yet been determined should continue to benefit from the principle of *non-refoulement* and their human rights should be respected. Refugees and asylum-seekers should not be subject to forced or compulsory labour. Whenever possible, national authorities—if necessary with international assistance—should provide suitable opportunities for work and education, as well as conditions which respect their religious and cultural identity and personal dignity.

11. Competent national authorities should inform UNHCR promptly of all cases of detention of refugees and asylum-seekers and allow access to such detainees; they should also permit UNHCR to supervise the well-being and protection of the inhabitants of refugee camps. UNHCR, intergovernmental agencies and other non-governmental agencies concerned with the welfare of refugees should be afforded an effective role based upon close cooperation with States of refuge.

12. International solidarity and cooperation are of paramount importance in refugee situation. The effective implementation of the principle of solidarity may facilitate the solution of problems of detention of refugees, in particular in cases of large-scale influx. All States, therefore, should promote appropriate solutions by way of voluntary repatriation, local integration or third country resettlement.

B. Harold Hongjhu Koh, 'America's Offshore Refugee Camps', *University of Richmond Law Review* (Vol. 29, No. 1, 1994), pp. 139–41.

America's offshore refugee camps rank among the most startling, yet invisible, features of United States foreign policy in the post-Cold War era.

Since 1991, our Government has almost continuously maintained tent cities holding thousands of men, women and children, surrounded by rolls of razor-barbed wire, amid the sweltering heat of the US Naval Base at Guantanamo Bay, Cuba, and the former Panama Canal Zone. Those incarcerated in the camps have witnessed birth and death, hope and despair, and untold waves of frustration and tedium.

Sadly, American detention camps are hardly new. Volumes have been written about the ten internment camps into which more than 110,000 Japanese-Americans were relocated and detained during World War II, camps condoned by such civil libertarian heroes as Franklin Delano Roosevelt, Earl Warren and Hugo Black. Nor has the territorial United States lacked its share of refugee camps, particularly in the last quarter of the twentieth century. In the mid-1970s, the US government employed several military bases within the United States as sites for emergency housing, processing and resettlement of thousands of refugees fleeing Vietnam. The 1980 Mariel 'Freedom Flotilla' brought 125,000 Cubans to our shores, some of whom still, incredibly, linger in long-term detention in various federal penitentiaries. Since the late 1980s, the INS has detained thousands of Central American refugees in border facilities and tent-shelters in rural areas in Arizona, California, South Texas, as well as in federal detention facilities in Louisiana and Florida.

As horrific as these experiences have been, three unique features characterise the offshore captivity of Haitians and Cubans in the 1990s. First, these refugees have been intercepted on the high seas and held offshore as part of a conscious 'buffer zone' strategy adopted by the United States government to prevent refugees from reaching US territory and asserting rights under US law. Second, refugees have been detained at these offshore sites indefinitely, without regard to whether they might be able to assert or establish individual claims of political asylum. Third and most stunning, the US government has consistently asserted—and some courts have agreed—that these offshore locations constitute 'rights-free zones', where refugees lack any legal rights cognisable under US law and American citizens lack First Amendment rights to communicate with them.

What brought us to this? How did these offshore refugee camps evolve? What is their human face, and if they are to exist, how should they be run? Remarkably, the vast American immigration literature includes no single history of these refugee camps, or of how they came into being.

C. Elly-Elikunda Mtango, 'Military and Armed Attacks on Refugee Camps', in Gil Loescher and Laila Monahan, eds, *Refugees and International Relations* (Clarendon Press, Oxford, 1989), pp. 87–88, 102, 113–18.

The Statute of the Office of the United Nations High Commissioner for Refugees (UNHCR Statute) and the 1951 Convention Relating to the

Status of Refugees (Refugee Convention) refer to the protection mandate and function of the United Nations High Commissioner for Refugees (UNHCR) without specifically mentioning his competence on matters relating to the physical safety of refugees. A possible explanation for this omission could be that these instruments were drafted at a time when the serious threat to physical safety during World War II had passed. The war was over, the United Nations had been established to ensure durable peace, and the 1949 Geneva Conventions already agreed to regulate the conduct of war. The drafters of the two refugee instruments would have felt, therefore, that the United Nations mechanism, the law of armed conflicts and the national laws of asylum would be adequate to ensure the physical integrity of refugees. They thus concentrated on issues relating to the economic and social well-being of refugees. States were left free to negotiate and agree on additional provisions for the protection of refugees and the UNHCR had to promote such agreements (Statute, Article 8(a)). Only the 1969 OAU Convention covers specific measures relating to the security of refugees, countries of asylum and countries of origin. This Convention, however, applies only to its signatories inter se within Africa. . . .

It is necessary, therefore, to search for legal principles proscribing armed attacks on refugees in the Law of Armed Conflicts, human rights law and fundamental principles of international law contained primarily in the United Nations Charter and the relevant resolutions of the United Nations General Assembly, such as resolution A/Res. 2625 (XXV). The fact that the relevant legal instruments and declarations of the General Assembly largely reflect established rules of customary international law makes it possible to suggest that the problem is not so much one of lack of rules but lack of will by governments to recognise the applicability of the law and the obligation to abide by international law.

Today, however, armed attacks on refugees take various forms in various parts of the world. The culprits can be countries of origin, countries of asylum or armed groups within these countries. Attacks may be simply indiscriminate or may be directed at specific refugee camps or locations. In one region, states of asylum may separate armed refugees from non-combatant refugees, while in another region combatants and civilians may exist side by side in the same camp.

. . . The problem of determining which principles of international law are applicable to the problem of armed attacks on refugees has also caused a lot of confusion. There is no single body of law that deals adequately with the problem. Refugee law does not cover the question of physical protection of refugees, and the law of armed conflicts expressed in the Geneva Conventions of 1949 and its additional Protocols of 1977 covers situations facing refugees in other circumstances and has little to do with armed attacks on refugee camps and settlements. The international law relating to the use of force, human rights or protection of aliens can be applied to this problem only by analogy since the concepts were developed before the phenomenon of military and armed attacks on refugees manifested itself and became a matter of great concern to the international community....

... The UNHCR Statute refers to international protection in general terms, suggesting that the main concern is legal rather than physical protection. The applicability of the Statute in relation to the security of refugees only arose during the debate preceding the adoption of the Statute by the United Nations General Assembly. At that time, a view was expressed that 'it would be the duty of the High Commissioner to intervene with governments in order that refugees might be afforded minimum rights and privileges essential to their existence and security'.[17] Similarly, the 1951 Refugee Convention and the 1967 Protocol did not contain explicit reference to the physical safety of refugees in their enumeration of the rights to be accorded either on an equal basis with nationals or with other aliens. Although refugees should be entitled to the same treatment as ordinary aliens, in regard to the protection of physical safety, the law applicable to aliens is unsatisfactory since the duty to protect aliens is owed by the alien's national state. The situation of refugees is thus anomalous since they do not enjoy the protection of the country of their nationality.

A central provision of the 1967 Declaration on Territorial Asylum is that the granting of asylum is a humanitarian, non-political act and that, once asylum is granted, it must be respected by all other states, including the state from whose territory the refugees have fled. This provision is intended to ensure the security of refugees and countries of asylum. In practice, however, countries of origin of refugees do not perceive the granting of asylum in that way. Refugee policy is often an intensely political matter, and refugee problems, therefore, are a major source of tension between states....

It is necessary to draw up a new international convention dealing with the problem of the physical safety of refugees, and particularly with the prohibition of armed attacks on refugees.... The new instrument to be drawn up should clarify, specify and consolidate the principles and rules of international law applicable to the whole question of the security of refugees in order to improve the understanding and acceptance of such principles and rules. It should specifically strengthen the competence of the High Commissioner on all issues pertaining to physical safety, including the importance of maintaining an international presence in refugee camps and settlements to guarantee their civilian character. The High Commissioner's mandate in this respect should extend to all refugees,

[17] GAOR, C. III, p. 363 (1950), Mrs Roosevelt (USA).

whether or not they fall under the notion of 'refugee' provided under the 1951 Refugee Convention. The instrument should clarify the international responsibility of all forces attacking refugees, including organisations other than states. It should also underline the collective responsibility of all in the protection of refugees, including the duty of international solidarity and burden-sharing in responding to the needs of the victims of attacks.

... the Executive Committee should focus its attention on the following principles and recommendations....

Principles

1. Refugees, including those in camps and settlements, shall not be an object of a military or armed attack. Such attacks must be condemned by the international community if and when they occur.

   Explanation: This principle is in line with Article 51 of Protocol I and Article 13(1) and (2) of Protocol II additional to the 1949 Geneva Conventions. Although the principle is not specific on whether under existing principles of international law military or armed attacks on refugee camps and settlements are proscribed, such a conclusion is inevitable once the principle is agreed. A further elaboration of this principle may spell out the right of the country of asylum and of refugees themselves to demand compensation for damages caused, as well as to demand punishment of the individual culprits.

2. Refugee camps and settlements are civilian places. Their civilian character shall not be abused by anyone.

   Explanation: This principle prohibits any state, group, or individual from abusing the non-military character of refugee camps and settlements. It is a safeguard for those states that allege that certain refugee camps and settlements could be used for military purposes.

3. The UNHCR's access to all refugee camps and settlements of its concern shall be facilitated, taking into account the importance of maintaining the highest degree of co-operation with the country of asylum or refuge.

   Explanation: This principle provides a further safeguard that refugee establishments will remain non-military. UNHCR's presence would enable it to monitor refugee activities which appear suspicious to the country of origin. The UNHCR would also be empowered to demand the removal of any military elements whenever they were identified. In doing so, however, UNHCR must co-operate with countries of asylum which are naturally sensitive on matters bearing on their sovereignty.

4. Reprisal attacks on refugee camps and settlements or indiscriminate attacks or acts of terrorism against refugees shall be forbidden.

   Explanation: This principle is in line with the rules of international humanitarian law. It is based on the premise that refugee camps and settlements are civilian places and actions by refugees against their countries of origin do not justify reprisal attacks on civilians. States make reprisal attacks on refugees in neighbouring countries in order to appease public opinion in the country of origin or to create an appearance of invincibility.

5. No state shall tolerate, condone, or encourage any state, or agents thereof, to launch attacks on refugees or to give any other form of assistance to an attacking force. This also includes the obligation of all states to take measures to prevent such attacks.

6. States shall respect all the humanitarian principles and ideals, and in particular abide by the applicable rules of international law, including international humanitarian law.

   Explanation: This is a 'catch-all' clause intended to strengthen the respect for international law and encourage its implementation. It is based on the concept that a solution to the problem of military and armed attacks can only be the result of strict compliance with the principles of international law.

Recommendations

Several pragmatic considerations which, though not legal obligations per se, are nevertheless essential for the promotion of the physical safety of refugees in countries of asylum or refuge. They are listed only as recommendations since they are matters falling essentially within the realm of national sovereignty and in certain cases could only be observed where the state concerned has the means and is able to do so. The idea of specific recommendations has not been considered in the past, although attempts have been made to frame some provisions in a non-mandatory format. A clear distinction between obligations and recommendations is useful to the extent that it may allay unnecessary fears of encroachment on matters strictly within the national sovereignty of states. Such a clarification may render the draft declaration of principles more easily acceptable to governments. The following recommendations are proposed.

1. Refugee camps and settlements should be established at a reasonable distance from the border of the country from which the refugees have fled.

2. Countries of asylum or refuge should not tolerate within their borders activities of refugees which are contrary to the purpose and principles of the United Nations.

3. The UNHCR and other international agencies should assist countries of asylum or refuge to promote conditions of safety for refugees.
4. The international community shares with countries of asylum or refuge the moral obligations to protect refugees from attacks endangering their physical integrity and well-being.
5. Refugees have a duty to abide by the laws and regulations of the countries of asylum or refuge, including the duty to respect rules for the protection of national security which encompass their own security.

General

The above principles and recommendations should form the basis of a solemn declaration to be adopted by the United Nations General Assembly. The adoption of the declaration should be followed by a diplomatic conference to negotiate an international treaty or convention on the physical safety of refugees which will transform the agreed principles into concrete legal norms to bind all states....

Postscript

As this paper was being completed, the UNHCR Executive Committee adopted a Conclusion on a set of principles on Military and Armed Attacks on Refugee Camps and Settlements (Doc. A/AC.96/702, of 12 October 1987). The Conclusion declares that military or armed attacks on refugees are indiscriminate in nature, unlawful and deserve condemnation in the strongest terms. It goes on to condemn all violations of the rights and safety of refugees and asylum-seekers, and in particular military or armed attacks on refugee camps and settlements, stating that such attacks violate the principles of international law and cannot be justified. States and international organisations are called upon to assist victims of attacks if ever they occur. It recommends that the states of refuge should do all within their power to ensure that the civilian character of refugee camps and settlements is maintained, and that other states and international organisations be asked to assist in that regard. It further recommends that states should co-operate in granting the High Commissioner access to camps and settlements of concern to him, particularly when he cannot effectively accomplish his functions without such access.

My main criticism of this Conclusion is that it is predicated on the assumption that refugee camps and settlements are exclusively civilian and humanitarian. Few camps and settlements around the world correspond to this precise definition, and even if these did exist, the precise language used could be twisted to provide a pretext for reprisals or other politically motivated attacks. The language used falls short of the absolute prohibition of attacks on refugee camps and settlements demanded by countries of refuge and envisaged in the principles recommended above. Furthermore, there was no decision to submit the agreed set of principles to the United Nations General Assembly for adoption as a solemn declaration.... It is submitted, therefore, that the result of the deliberations in the UNHCR Executive Committee has been unsatisfactory, and hence the pursuit of specific action at the United Nations General Assembly should continue. The ultimate goal of a solemn declaration and an international legal instrument on the physical security of refugees remains a pressing necessity.

D. James C. Hathaway and John A. Dent, *Refugee Rights: Report on a Comparative Survey* (York Lanes Press, Toronto, 1995), pp. 18–42.[18]

Freedom of Internal Movement

State parties to the Convention are obliged not to unduly restrict the internal movement of refugees in their territory. Article 31(2) governs restrictions on the freedom of movement of refugees 'unlawfully' in the territory of a contracting state,[19] encompassing asylum-seekers whose status is not regularised.[20] The freedom of movement of refugees 'lawfully' in the territory is guaranteed by Article 26.... [It] regulates the right to freedom of movement of refugees formally recognised as such by a contracting state, logically including all refugees whose status is not contested by a contracting state.[21] It provides in part that

[18] The Report is based 'on the insights of nearly thirty scholars from all regions of the world, who each prepared a *National Report on the Legal Condition of the Refugee* for their respective countries...'. The countries were Argentina, Australia, Austria, Belgium, Burundi, Canada, Denmark, Finland, France, Germany, Ghana, Greece, India, Italy, Japan, Malta, Nepal, The Netherlands, New Zealand, Norway, Pakistan, Romania, Sweden, Switzerland, Uganda, United Kingdom, United States, Zimbabwe. The footnote references to these reports have been deleted. These reports are available in the library of the Centre for Refugee Studies, York University, Canada.

[19] The phrase 'unlawfully' in the territory refers to 'present in [a state's] territory without authorization', as defined in paragraph 1 of Article 31. Article 31(1) provides that '[t]he Contracting States shall not impose penalties, on account of their illegal entry or presence, on refugees who, coming directly from a territory where their life or freedom was threatened in the sense of Article 1, enter or are present in their territory without authorization, provided they present themselves without delay to the authorities and show good cause for their illegal entry or presence.'

[20] See A. Grahl-Madsen, 'Commentary on the Refugee Convention, 1951' (unpublished, 1963), Vol. 3, at pp. 304, 306. Available in the Collections of the Refugee Law Research Unit, Centre for Refugee Studies, York University.

[21] In states that do not employ a status determination system for refugees, *prima facie* refugees must be accepted as such and granted their full rights under the Convention. The

[e]ach Contracting State shall accord to refugees lawfully in its territory the right to ... move freely within the territory subject to any regulations applicable to aliens generally in the same circumstances.

In considering the restriction of movement by reason of 'any regulations applicable to aliens generally in the same circumstances', the *Ad Hoc* Committee that prepared the Refugee Convention had in mind restrictions on access by aliens generally to frontier zones, strategic zones, areas of natural catastrophe, areas of rebellion, of civil war and of large-scale police operations.[22]

Once recognised, refugees in industrialised states rarely face restrictions on their freedom of movement. This is, however, not always the case in less developed countries which typically host significantly larger refugee populations. While some Southern countries, such as Pakistan, allow refugees in camps considerable *de facto* freedom of movement, many less developed states force even recognised refugees to live in closed camps, primarily for reasons of security or administrative ease in delivering services to them....

As Article 26 does not allow refugee-specific exceptions to the right to freedom of movement for reasons of national security[23] or for administrative convenience (unless such regulations are 'applicable to aliens generally in the same circumstances'), closed-camp policies directed towards refugees whose status has either been recognised or is not contested are *prima facie* in contravention of the Convention. Some latitude may, however, be afforded by EXCOM Conclusion No. 22 on the 'Protection of Asylum-seekers in Situations of Large-scale Influx', which does allow states to restrict the movement of large-scale influxes under certain extenuating circumstances. Specifically, Part II (B)(2)(a) of the Conclusion elaborates the premise of Article 31(2) of the Convention to permit the detention of asylum-seekers who have been temporarily admitted to a country pending arrangements for a durable solution, but only if the restrictions on freedom of movement are necessary in the interest of public health and public order. EXCOM Conclusion No. 22 thus provides some flexibility to, for example, frontline states participating in a

---

denial to refugees of an opportunity to confirm their status does not represent a legitimate ground for denying them access to their Convention rights. Rather, if states wish to restrict protection to only those asylum-seekers whom they consider meet the Convention definition, they must necessarily establish a system for the determination of refugee status. Accord P. Hyndman, 'The 1951 Convention and its Implications for Procedural Questions', *International Journal of Refugee Law* (Vol. 6, No. 2, 1994), p. 249.

[22] UN Doc. E/AC.32/SR.15, at p. 14, 27 January 1950.

[23] In contrast, Article 12 of the International Covenant on Civil and Political Rights, which also deals with liberty of movement, does include an exemption based on the protection of national security.

responsibility-sharing arrangement, such as the Comprehensive Plan of Action for Indochinese Refugees. This narrow exception does not, however, vindicate the predilection for long-term confinement cited in the National Reports of Uganda and Zimbabwe. As a situation-specific exception to the general duty of freedom of movement set by Article 26, detention as a temporary measure bridging the gap to durable protection as authorised by Article 31(2) and EXCOM Conclusion No. 22 must, of course, be strictly interpreted.

In sum, restrictions on the freedom of movement of both asylum-seekers and refugees remain common. Such problems as exist in industrialised states tend to involve unduly harsh restrictions on the freedom of movement of refugee claimants pending a determination of their claim. Rarely, though, is there any issue of Northern states seeking to limit the liberty rights of recognised refugees. The situation is more complex in less developed states, where formal status determination systems are not always employed. Here, restrictions on the mobility rights of *prima facie* refugees are more commonly encountered. Policies such as closed camps violate Article 26 of the Convention unless they are in conformity with the minimally intrusive and situation-specific exceptions authorised by Article 31(2) and relevant resolutions of the UNHCR's Executive Committee.

Socioeconomic Rights

Employment

Not surprisingly, the issue of refugee employment rights arises quite frequently in the National Reports. Whereas protection of the national labour market has always been a priority of states, recent recessionary pressures have contributed to calls in many industrialised states for a tightening of restrictions on foreign labour. Employment rights for recognised Convention refugees in most developed states are nonetheless generally superior to Convention requirements, with problems for refugees arising more often from the implementation of legislation than from deficiencies in statutory provisions themselves. It is in the granting of the right to work to asylum-seekers whose status remains undetermined that Northern state practice varies more widely. The countries of the less developed South, facing challenging economic circumstances of another degree, have adopted differing approaches to the employment rights of refugees, as these states are wary not to undermine development objectives or scarce economic opportunities for their own nationals.

According to Article 17 of the Convention, a contracting state is obliged to grant refugees lawfully staying in its territory the most favourable treatment accorded nationals of a foreign country regarding the right to engage in wage-earning employment.[24] Furthermore, restrictive measures imposed on aliens for the protection of the national labour market are not to be applied to refugees who have resided in the country for three years or more, or who have a spouse or child possessing the nationality of the host country. Sympathetic consideration is also to be given to granting refugees the same employment rights as those afforded nationals. Article 17 is thus designed to secure for refugees access to wage-earning employment, which has historically been reserved exclusively for the host country's citizens, or aliens benefitting from a reciprocity agreement. It is intended to 'obtain for refugees the advantages which Governments sought to have granted to their own [nationals]',[25] because refugees by their very nature are denied the support of their governments and cannot rely on intercession by their state of formal nationality to negotiate a bilateral arrangement. Articles 18 and 19 of the Convention regulate self-employment[26] and the liberal professions,[27] and oblige signatory states to accord to refugees treatment in these areas at least as favourable as that accorded to aliens generally.

As it appears that the drafters of the Convention intended the provisions on employment to be limited to refugees authorised by the national authorities to be in the territory on an ongoing basis,[28] asylum-seekers whose status is not regularised are likely excluded from these Convention guarantees. Nonetheless, in states that utilise a status determination system, the treatment of asylum-seekers whose claims have not yet been determined varies tremendously, with several states granting refugee claimants full employment rights. Such policy decisions are presumably driven by pragmatic calculations, rather than by perceived international obligations. Whatever the legalities, states are faced with a *de facto* policy choice: unless they are prepared to allow asylum-seekers literally to

---

[24] Although the term 'wage-earning employment' is not defined in the 1951 Refugee Convention, it must be understood in its broadest sense to include all those kinds of employment that cannot properly be described as self-employment or liberal professions. Grahl-Madsen, 'Commentary on the Refugee Convention, 1951' (footnote 20 earlier), p. 390.

[25] UN Doc. E/AC.32/SR.13, at pp. 2–3, 26 January 1950.

[26] Self-employment is defined in Article 18 as including agriculture, industry, handicrafts and commerce, and the establishment of commercial and industrial companies.

[27] The 'liberal professions' are understood to encompass practitioners of law (barristers or solicitors); physicians or surgeons, dentists, veterinarians, engineers and architects, as well as accountants, authorised translators, and interpreters. Grahl-Madsen, 'Commentary on the Refugee Convention, 1951' (footnote 20 earlier), p. 126.

[28] 'It results from the *travaux préparatoires* that any refugee who with the authorization of the authorities is in the territory of a Contracting State otherwise than purely temporarily, is to be considered as lawfully staying ("residant regulierement").' P. Weis, 'Commentary on the Convention Relating to the Status of Refugees of 28 July 1951' (unpublished), at p. 469. Available in the Collections of the Refugee Law Research Unit, Centre for Refugee Studies, York University.

starve, their subsistence needs must either be met through employment earnings or through public assistance. Whereas the latter option increases state expenditures, access to employment is perceived by many states to increase job competition for nationals, and/or increase the 'pull factor' for asylum-seekers.

... In contrast with the wide-ranging practices of states regarding employment for asylum-seekers awaiting status determination, most industrialised states grant Convention employment rights to recognised refugees. Indeed, many states, including Switzerland, Finland, Denmark, the Netherlands, the United States and Canada exceed their duties by granting recognised refugees the legal right to engage in wage-earning employment on par with nationals, though employment in the civil service may be excluded. Exceptions to countries adopting this approach include Greece, which by way of reservation limits its undertaking such that refugees are only accorded treatment equivalent to aliens generally....

Even where refugees are legally guaranteed their Convention right to seek employment, they may still encounter obstacles in realising this right due to a restrictive interpretation of the scope of Article 17. For instance, Germany does not consider the obligation to treat refugees on par with the 'most favourable treatment accorded to nationals of a foreign country' to entail treatment of refugees equivalent to 'privileged aliens', such as nationals of European Union states. As states increasingly conclude bilateral and multilateral arrangements that include provisions concerning access to employment in member states, the actual benefits of the 'most favourable treatment' provisions may, through such restrictive interpretation, be indirectly eroded.

Social conditions such as a lack of employment opportunities, racial barriers and bureaucratic obstacles may also inhibit refugees from realising their right to seek employment. Beyond the general scarcity of employment opportunities in many countries of the world, refugees typically suffer from even higher unemployment rates than nationals. The National Report for Sweden notes that refugees from Asia and Africa suffer from higher levels of unemployment than those from Eastern Europe and Latin America, perhaps indicating a 'concealed discrimination' against refugees from certain areas of the world. In addition to xenophobia, obstacles to refugee participation in the labour market include language difficulties, educational differences and cultural barriers. Some countries, such as the United States, present refugees with a different kind of labour market problem: the heavy pressure placed on them to find employment as soon as possible may force refugees to accept work for which they are not suited, potentially retarding their career development. Lastly, bureaucratic obstacles can prevent refugees from realising their right to employment, and are often particularly daunting with respect to self-employment and the liberal professions. Greece's perennial delay in issuing permits for self-employment is an example of this problem. Many states also take an unduly narrow approach to the recognition of the validity of foreign qualifications, severely limiting the access of refugees to the liberal professions.

Non-industrialised states of the South hosting large refugee populations face a difficult dilemma concerning how best to provide for refugees' basic needs. The common practice in Africa of accepting all forced migrants as refugees is rightly hailed as generous and fair minded, but a policy of granting employment rights to such large numbers of refugees is seen by some countries as a potential threat to the scarce opportunities for work available to nationals. As noted in the National Report for Zimbabwe, 'it could not be expected that the Zimbabwean Government would be compelled to implement those particular articles in regard to refugees when they are not able to satisfy their own nationals on the same issues.' The Ghanaian rapporteur concurs that under such conditions 'it is simply very difficult for a host country to encourage refugees [to enter] the national labour market.' The National Report for Uganda similarly observes that the fear of engendering local hostility towards refugees may also discourage host countries from providing employment opportunities to refugees, such as land for farming. Indeed, this dilemma may account for some of the reluctance of Asian states to accede to the Convention. . . .

In summary, state practice towards asylum-seekers whose status has not been regularised varies considerably among developed countries, reflecting different conclusions on the advantages of meeting the subsistence needs of asylum-seekers through a policy of legal employment as opposed to one of direct public assistance. With respect to Convention refugees lawfully staying in their territory, industrialised states are fairly consistent in granting employment rights which meet or exceed Convention standards. Obstacles to employment for refugees residing in these states thus more frequently arise from inadequate implementation of statutory provisions or from inhospitable social conditions than from explicit non-compliance with the Convention. Southern states facing large refugee influxes and scarce employment opportunities for their own citizens are, not surprisingly, more reluctant to grant full employment rights to refugees for fear of displacing nationals in search of employment, thereby engendering local hostility.

Public Assistance

If refugees are unable to secure, or are prohibited from seeking employment in order to sustain themselves, the Convention foresees the possibility that their basic needs be met through public assistance. Almost all refugees require public assistance at some point, at least as a temporary measure until they are able to adapt to the host society sufficiently to achieve success in the labour force. Given the obstacles that refugees face in finding work, many remain dependent on social assistance for some time. The Convention provisions on public assistance and social security are thus of utmost importance to refugees' well-being. Although policies vary, refugees and even asylum-seekers in industrialised states generally receive national treatment in regard to social assistance. Evaluating compliance in the less developed world, however, is more difficult due both to the absence of national social security schemes in many host countries and to their generally depressed economies.

Article 23 of the Convention obliges contracting states to accord to refugees lawfully staying in their territory national treatment (i.e., the treatment a state gives its nationals) with respect to public relief and assistance. This obligation is not dependent upon whether such relief is provided out of national, regional or local funds, or through agencies other than those that provide relief and assistance to nationals.[29] Article 24 of the Convention further provides that contracting states shall accord refugees lawfully staying in their territory national treatment in matters of social security such as compensation in the event of occupational injuries and diseases, maternity leave, sickness, disability, old age pension, unemployment and family responsibilities.

The *Ad Hoc* Committee that prepared the Convention did not enumerate the instances in which refugees should be entitled to public relief under Article 23 because 'a complete enumeration [is] always difficult to achieve'.[30] It is the view of Grahl-Madsen that the drafters of the Convention thus intended these provisions on public relief to be given a wide interpretation, covering at least such areas as medical attendance and hospital treatment, measures of relief for the blind, emergency relief and the like.[31]

Whereas the Convention rights to public assistance are limited to refugees 'lawfully staying' in the territory of the contracting state, most states surveyed do grant asylum-seekers national treatment in access to social assistance, and virtually all provide some form of assistance....

Most industrialised states comply with the provisions on social assistance once refugee status has been formally recognised. Several states actually exceed Convention requirements, granting to refugees special assistance programmes intended to offset their disadvantages, and to facilitate their adaptation....

Even in industrialised countries, however, refugees can suffer from inadequate access to general public assistance programmes. Concerns

---

[29] Cf. UN Doc. E/AC.32/SR.38, at p. 5, 26 September 1950.

[30] As cited in Grahl-Madsen, 'Commentary on the Refugee Convention, 1951' (footnote 20 earlier), at p. 147.

[31] Ibid., at p. 147, with reference to UN Doc. E/AC.32/SR.15, at pp. 5–8, 27 January 1950.

regarding full compliance with the national treatment provisions have been raised in Denmark, where language requirements for social welfare benefits may disadvantage refugees. In Belgium, refugees must fulfil a five-year residency requirement before receiving social assistance. In the United States, the heavy emphasis placed on employment as the means of subsistence for refugees has been accompanied by severe cutbacks to refugees' social assistance entitlement....

An evaluation of compliance with the public assistance provisions of the Convention must take cognisance of the fact that the poorer countries of the South, which host the vast majority of the world's refugees, simply lack the resources to provide for their sustenance. With some exceptions, such as India's historic determination to finance refugee relief operations independently, it is international relief organisations, particularly the UNHCR, which collaborate with Southern host states to deliver basic services to refugees.

It must be remembered that nationals in many countries of Africa and Asia do not themselves have access to the type of formal social assistance scheme envisioned in the Convention. Moreover, conditions in these regions typically demand that priority attention be given simply and directly to attempting to meet basic survival needs. For instance, UNHCR programmes for Afghan refugees in Pakistan provided relief assistance such as cash, tents, construction material for mud huts, food, household items, blankets, cooking utensils, fuel, water and medical dispensaries.

Under the Convention, states are not only obliged to equate resident refugees to nationals in the operation of all forms of public assistance, but also must not discriminate among and between refugee populations in the granting of relief, whatever the number of refugees or limitation of resources. India provides an example of non-conforming conduct in that, in contrast to the generous assistance provided to refugees from Tibet, East Pakistan and Sri Lanka, India's treatment of Chakma refugees is substandard by any measure. Their camps are described as 'squalid' and 'ill-equipped'; food rations consist merely of rice and salt; and health care is virtually non-existent.[32]

... the stringency of the standard for compliance with the Convention's socioeconomic rights guarantees is a source of concern to the national rapporteurs of some less developed states. There is legitimate anxiety that the UNHCR and other aid is less than fully guaranteed, and frequently inadequate. As presently structured, however, state parties to the Convention are expected to treat all refugees as part of their own community for purposes of public relief, however much this may tax their resources.

[32] See in this regard the introduction to Chapter 8.

Critical Analysis of the Refugee Convention's Rights Regime

The second part of this report moves from the discussion of empirical patterns to a critical analysis of the Convention rights regime itself. The national rapporteurs have identified many shortcomings of the Convention, including rights that fail to respond to the real human rights dilemmas faced by refugees, rights framed such that they are irreconcilable with states' legitimate self-interest, rights that should be included but are not, and rights that need not be included at all. These critiques of the Convention can, for the most part, be traced to one of three factors: furtherance of the migration management goals of Convention was drafted in 1951, or the evolution of international human rights law over the more than four decades since the Refugee Convention's entry into force.

An examination of the history of refugee law reveals that it is founded not on pure principles of humanitarianism or advancement of human rights, but on compromises designed to reconcile the sovereign prerogative of states to control immigration with the reality of forced migrations of people at risk.[33] It has been designed not so much to meet the needs of refugees themselves, but to govern the disruptions of regulated international migration without jeopardising the interests of states. Many of the perceived shortcomings of the Convention regime are therefore actually reflections of the resistance of states to cede to any significant degree their right to sovereignty over immigration matters.

This factor is relevant to criticisms of the Convention regime's under-inclusiveness in terms of international supervisory mechanisms. Several national reports found the lack of an enforcement mechanism for refugee rights to be a serious shortcoming of the Convention. Perhaps most significant is the fact that the procedures governing the determination of refugee status are untouched by the Convention, falling wholly within the purview of national sovereignty.[34] While contracting states are expected to cooperate with the UNHCR and to provide it with information on measures taken to implement the Convention, the international agency has no role in either the design or implementation of state protection systems. The lack of any meaningful international scrutiny of the procedural dimensions of refugee protection has resulted in a wide range of protection practices and interpretations of the Convention definition.... This

---

[33] For an elaboration of these arguments, see James C. Hathaway, 'A Reconsideration of the Underlying Premise of Refugee Law', *Harvard International Law Journal* (Vol. 31, No. 1, 1990), 129, at pp. 143 ff.

[34] This approach is in contrast with that of international refugee accords preceding the 1951 Convention which, in some cases, authorised international coordinating agencies to make determinations of refugee status on behalf of participating states. Ibid., pp. 166–68.

weakness in the protection system is aptly noted in the National Reports for Belgium, Finland and Switzerland, while the high degree of discretion delegated to domestic officials in the design and implementation of refugee protection systems is the subject of specific criticism in the National Report for the United Kingdom.

... A second factor precipitating criticism of the Convention is the changing nature of the refugee phenomenon since the enactment of the Convention in 1951. Whereas the refugees of concern to the delegates at the Conference of Plenipotentiaries in 1951 were racial and religious minorities in Europe and dissidents from the Soviet bloc, the contemporary mandate of universal refugee protection obviously encompasses a refugee problem vastly different in scope and nature. Rather than originating solely in Europe, the majority of refugees today flee from the poor nations of the South, and present a range of needs that differ substantially from those of the stereotypical refugees of the Cold War era. For example, the European refugees for whom the Convention was drafted were considered to be primarily in need of legal protection, rather than material assistance.[35] The Convention therefore provides rights in such areas as personal status and intellectual property, while failing to address the more salient modern problems of physical security and the fulfilment of basic survival needs in the context of large-scale refugee influxes. To paraphrase from the Ugandan National Report, the Convention's focus on individual rights does not translate easily into the actual protection of large numbers of refugees, whose basic needs include food, shelter, clean water, sanitation, group rights and protection from cruel, inhuman and degrading treatment.

Another implication of the major changes since the Convention came into force is that whereas refugees of concern to its drafters were usually moving from a European country to another Western state, the vast majority of contemporary refugees originate in and are protected by the poor countries of the South. Assumptions built into the Convention rights regime about the prosperity of countries of asylum, and the kinds of rights typically enjoyed within them, are therefore no longer valid. That the Convention rights regime as a whole is too expensive for a poor country is noted in several national reports, with employment rights and welfare rights singled out as the most costly. The Zimbabwean and Ghanaian Reports in particular emphasise the difficulty of a less developed state providing for the economic needs of a large refugee population

[35] See, for example, the statement of the French delegate, who argued that European refugees '[w]ere the only refugees in respect of whom international protection without international financial assistance had any meaning'. 11 UN ESCOR (161st mtg.) at p. 8, UN Doc. E/AC.7/SR.161 (1950).

when the needs of its own citizens are not met. In such situations, the survival rights of refugees can only be ensured through international assistance, a policy not without serious drawbacks of its own, including the lack of predictable and adequate funding of international relief enterprises, the possibility of hostility from the indigenous population of the host state if refugees are perceived to be better off or to be exploiting communal resources, and the tendency of such assistance schemes to be dependency-producing and short-term.

The obligation of states to facilitate the assimilation and naturalisation of refugees[36] is considered by some national rapporteurs to represent another example of the Convention's Eurocentric bias. Whereas such an obligation may have been realistic within the historical context of comparatively small numbers of refugees arriving in wealthy industrialised states, the expectation that poor Southern states permanently absorb massive numbers of refugees currently enjoying asylum in their territories is considered to be impractical, unnecessary and potentially destructive of communal rights to self-determination.

Other Convention rights argued to be in conflict with the interests of poor states that are host to large numbers of refugees include property rights and the right to freedom of movement. Property rights are mentioned as a potential inhibitor of the theoretically preferred solution of repatriation, as refugees who become more settled and acquire property may be reluctant to abandon everything in favour of an uncertain future in the homeland. Property rights may also bring refugees into conflict with local populations anxious to access scarce resources, such as land. The perceived conflict with the right to freedom of movement is mainly tied to security concerns that legitimately preoccupy many frontline states, particularly where mobility may facilitate the involvement of refugees in armed activities against their country of origin, thereby exposing the host country's population to the risk of attack from the armed forces of the refugees' country of origin. It has not been unusual for countries of asylum to respond to these security concerns by confining refugees in camps. While Article 26 of the Convention makes no allowance for such restrictions of movement, the exemptions of EXCOM Conclusion No. 22[37] may reflect the beginnings of an attempt to attenuate the Convention's rigidity in recognition of legitimate state concerns.

---

[36] Article 34 of the Convention provides that '[t]he Contracting States shall as far as possible facilitate the assimilation and naturalization of refugees. They shall in particular make every effort to expedite naturalization proceedings and to reduce as far as possible the charges and costs of such proceedings.'

[37] EXCOM Conclusion No. 22 applies to temporary asylum policies for mass influxes of asylum-seekers, pending a durable solution.

E. UNHCR, Executive Committee Conclusion No. 22(1981): Protection of Asylum Seekers in Situation of Large-scale Influx.

B. Treatment of asylum seekers who have been temporarily admitted to a country pending arrangements for a durable solution.

1. Article 31 of the 1951 United Nations Convention relating to the Status of Refugees contains provisions regarding the treatment of refugees who have entered a country without authorisation and whose situation in that country has not yet been regularised. The standards defined in this Article do not, however, cover all aspects of the treatment of asylum seekers in large-scale influx situations.

2. It is therefore essential that asylum seekers who have been temporarily admitted pending arrangements for a durable solution should be treated in accordance with the following minimum basic human standards:

(a) they should not be penalised or exposed to any unfavourable treatment solely on the ground that their presence in the country is considered unlawful; they should not be subjected to restrictions on their movements other than those which are necessary in the interest of public health and public order;

(b) they should enjoy the fundamental civil rights internationally recognised, in particular those set out in the Universal Declaration of Human Rights;

(c) they should receive all necessary assistance and be provided with the basic necessities of life including food, shelter and basic sanitary and health facilities; in this respect the international community should conform with the principles of international solidarity and burden-sharing;

(d) they should be treated as persons whose tragic plight requires special understanding and sympathy. They should not be subjected to cruel, inhuman or degrading treatment;

(e) there should be no discrimination on the grounds of race, religion, political opinion, nationality, country of origin or physical incapacity;

(f) they are to be considered as persons before the law, enjoying free access to courts of law and other competent administrative authorities;

(g) the location of asylum seekers should be determined by their safety and well-being as well as by the security needs of the receiving State. Asylum seekers should, as far as possible, be located at a reasonable distance from the frontier of their country of origin. They should not become involved in subversive activities against their country of origin or any other State;

(*h*)   family unity should be respected;

(*i*)   all possible assistance should be given for the tracing of relatives;

(*j*)   adequate provision should be made for the protection of minors and unaccompanied children;

(*k*)   the sending and receiving of mail should be allowed;

(*l*)   material assistance from friends or relatives should be permitted;

(*m*)   appropriate arrangements should be made, where possible, for the registration of births, deaths and marriages;

(*n*)   they should be granted all the necessary facilities to enable them to obtain a satisfactory durable solution;

(*o*)   they should be permitted to transfer assets which they have brought into a territory to the country where the durable solution is obtained; and

(*p*)   all steps should be taken to facilitate voluntary repatriation.

F. *Guidelines on the Protection of Refugee Women* (UNHCR, Geneva, July 1991), pp. 8–11.

Ensuring the protection of refugee women requires adherence not only to the 1951 Convention and its 1967 Protocol but also to other relevant international instruments such as the Universal Declaration of Human Rights; the 1949 Geneva Conventions and the two Additional Protocols of 1977; the 1966 Human Rights Covenants; the Convention on the Elimination of All Forms of Discrimination Against Women; the Declaration on the Protection of Women and Children in Emergency and Armed Conflict; the Convention on Consent to Marriage, Minimum Age for Marriage and Registration of Marriages; the Convention on the Nationality of Married Women; and the Convention on the Rights of the Child. While individual States may not be parties to all of these instruments, they do provide a framework of international human rights standards for carrying out protection and assistance activities related to refugee women.

From these various international instruments can be drawn principles of equity that should underlie all politics and programmes established for refugees by UNHCR. To quote from Article 1 of the UN Convention on the Elimination of All Forms of Discrimination Against Women, no distinction, exclusion or restriction is to be made on the basis of sex which has the effect or purpose of impairing or nullifying the recognition, enjoyment or exercise by women, irrespective of their marital status, on a basis of equality of men and women, of human rights and fundamental freedoms in the political, social, cultural, civil or any other field.

In addition to international law, the national law of the country of asylum governs the protection of refugee women. Signatories to the 1951

Convention or the 1967 Protocol agree to cooperate with UNHCR in the exercise of its functions and, in particular, its duty of supervising the application of the provisions of the Convention and Protocol (Articles 35 and II, respectively). Further, national laws and policies determine what legal status an individual receives, where she will live and what assistance will be provided. Also, many of the offences against women, such as rape and physical attack, are punishable by national law. A further legal framework, within the national framework, is provided by the legal codes and processes adopted for international use in refugee camps. It is particularly important that these instruments of self-governance have provided for the protection of refugee women.

Beyond Legal Measures

International protection goes beyond adherence to legal principles. Equally important, the protection of refugee women requires planning and a great deal of common sense in establishing programmes and enforcing priorities that support their safety and well-being. Thus, international protection of refugee women must be understood in its widest sense. Refugee women who are unable to feed, clothe and shelter themselves and their children will be more vulnerable to manipulation and to physical and sexual abuse in order to obtain such necessities. Refugee women who are detained among strangers and/or where traditional social protection systems no longer exist, will face greater dangers than those living among family and friends. Refugee women who must bribe guards to obtain firewood, water or other essential goods will be more susceptible to sexual harassment. Moreover, refugee women who formerly had a means of expressing their views in the community may find themselves unable to do so in the camp management committees established by assistance organisations.

As these examples indicate, the intrinsic relationship which exists between protection and assistance is particularly evident in relation to refugee women, female adolescents and children. Protection concerns can often be best addressed through assistance-related measures. Conversely, the planning and implementation of assistance programmes can have direct, and sometimes adverse, consequences for the protection of refugee women if they ignore their special needs.

To understand fully and address the protection concerns of refugee women, they themselves must participate in planning protection and assistance activities. Programmes which are not planned in consultation with the beneficiaries, nor implemented with their participation, cannot be effective. Since a large proportion of refugees are women, many solely responsible for their dependent children, it is essential that they be involved in planning and delivery of assistance activities if these are to be properly focused on their needs.

Participation itself promotes protection. Internal protection problems are often due as much to people's feelings of isolation, frustration, lack of belonging to a structured society and lack of control over their own future as they are to any other form of social problem. This may be particularly evident in overcrowded camp conditions. Refugee participation helps build the values and sense of community that contribute to reducing protection problems.

Relief officials often point to cultural constraints in involving women in decision-making, particularly where women have had a limited role in the country of origin. Looking to women as decision-makers under these circumstances, they argue, amounts to tampering with the culture of the group.

These relief officials may, however, have only a superficial understanding of the socio-cultural roles of women. Their concerns may reflect the cultural biases of the officials and/or inadequate understanding of both the traditional cultures and the new circumstances in which refugee women find themselves. Prior to flight, women typically have opportunities to express their concerns and needs, sometimes through their husbands and other times through traditional support networks. In refugee camps, however, many women are unable to participate through such traditional mechanisms as these have broken down. Alternative arrangements must be made to ensure that their voices are heard and the perspectives that they have to offer are included in decision-making. It is essential, therefore, that organisations working with refugees recognise that special initiatives may be needed so that refugee women have the opportunity to contribute to activities being planned.

G. *Refugee Children: Guidelines on Protection and Care* (UNHCR, Geneva, 1994), pp. 163–74, paras 1–3, 10–28.

1. Approximately half of the world's refugees are children. Action by the Office of the United Nations High Commissioner for Refugees (UNHCR) to protect and care for these children is central to the fulfilment of its mandate. This paper presents the policy framework that UNHCR will use to guide its action on behalf of refugee children.

2. Although the policy implies, first and foremost, the duty of UNHCR staff to act, it is hoped that it will also guide the endeavours of others concerned with refugee children, such as governments, other United Nations bodies, international and national non-governmental organisations (NGOs), as well as refugee groups. This is a key manner in which the policy is intended to promote appropriate, collaborative action among all parties to ensure the protection and care of refugee children.

3. In keeping with the Convention on the Rights of the Child, UNHCR considers a child to be a person 'below the age of 18 years, unless, under the law applicable to the child, majority is attained earlier'.... Unless otherwise specified, the term 'refugee child' when used in this policy may be understood to mean any child of concern to the High Commissioner, including those children who are refugees, returnees, asylum-seekers and displaced persons of concern to UNHCR.

10. Three interrelated factors contribute to the special needs of refugee children: their dependence, their vulnerability and their developmental needs (i.e., their requirements for healthy growth and development at different ages). Children, particularly in their early years, are dependent upon their parents or other adults to provide the basic necessities for their survival. Moreover, they are recognised in national and international law as being legally dependent on their parents or guardians for appropriate guidance and direction.

11. Children's vulnerability results in part from this dependence. They are physically and psychologically less able than adults to provide for their own needs or to protect themselves from harm. Consequently, they must rely on the care and protection of adults. They are psychologically at great risk from the trauma inherent in situations which cause uprooting, and from the uprooting itself. Younger children are physically less able than adults and adolescents to survive illness, malnutrition or deprivation of basic necessities. When resources are scarce, they are the first to die.

12. Refugee girls are often even more vulnerable than refugee boys. In some cultural and social contexts, girls are less valued than boys and, consequently, are more often subject to neglect and abuse. Their participation in education programmes is often prematurely curtailed. They are subject to sexual abuse, assault and exploitation in greater numbers than are boys.

13. Vulnerable in normal circumstances, in numerous situations currently confronting UNHCR, children's lives, health and safety are at extreme risk. Living conditions, particularly in the emergency stage, are often precarious. In some situations, the survival of children must be assured in the midst of armed conflict. Not only are children frequently the unintended casualties of war, they are sometimes a direct target. In many situations, military and armed groups recruit children. Extraordinary efforts are required to protect them in situations of armed conflict.

14. Among refugee children, the most vulnerable are those who are not accompanied by an adult recognised by law as being responsible for their care. In the absence of special efforts to monitor and protect their well-being, the basic needs of unaccompanied refugee children often go unmet and their rights are frequently violated. Indeed, the presence of unaccompanied children and the need for special actions on their behalf must be anticipated in every refugee situation.

15. Children's developmental needs are a fundamental reality often not considered in relief efforts. In order to grow and develop normally, a child has certain age-specific requirements which must be satisfied. Basic health care, nutrition and education are generally recognised as necessary for the physical and intellectual development of children. Beyond these, however, healthy psychosocial development depends in large measure on the nurturing and stimulation that children receive as they grow, and on the opportunities that they have to learn and master new skills. For refugee children, healthy psychosocial development also requires coping effectively with the multiple traumas of loss, uprooting and often more damaging experiences. In short, tragic long-term consequences may result where children's developmental needs are not adequately met.

16. The grounds for special action on behalf of refugee children are well-established in both national and international law. Refugee children share certain universal rights with all other people, have additional rights as children and particular rights as refugees. Because of their dependence, vulnerability and developmental needs, children are accorded specific civil, economic, social and cultural rights in national and international law. Refugee children are also entitled to the international protection and assistance of UNHCR.

17. The Convention on the Rights of the Child provides a comprehensive framework for the responsibilities of its States Parties to all children within their borders, including those who are of concern to UNHCR. Moreover, as a United Nations convention, it constitutes a normative frame of reference for UNHCR's action....

18. A principle of international law fundamental to this policy is the primary responsibility of parents or legal guardians to care for children. Moreover, States are responsible for protecting the human rights of all persons within their territory, including refugee children, and for providing the adults accountable for these children with the support necessary to fulfil their own responsibilities.

19. The Office of the United Nations High Commissioner for Refugees is committed to protecting and providing adequately for the needs of all children within its competence. Expanding on the measures taken by the Office and outlined in the background information provided above, UNHCR's Executive Committee has adopted two Conclusions specifically regarding refugee children. The first, Conclusion No. 47 (XXXVIII) adopted in 1987, urged action aimed at addressing the human rights and needs of children who are refugees; highlighted the particular vulnerability of unaccompanied and disabled refugee children and the need for action by UNHCR to protect and assist them; recommended regular and timely, people-oriented assessment and review of the needs of refugee children; recognized the need to promote cooperation between the Office and other concerned agencies and bodies; and acknowledged the

importance of further study to identify additional support programmes and the reorientation of existing ones as necessary.

20. In 1989, in its Conclusion No. 59, the Executive Committee reaffirmed and expanded upon the need for particular attention to refugee children; gave examples of how these needs could be assessed, monitored and met; drew special attention to UNHCR's particular need to endeavour to ensure the right of refugee children to education, as well as their protection from military recruitment and irregular adoption. It urged UNHCR to intensify its efforts in the area of public awareness of these issues—in particular the effects of persecution and armed conflict on refugee children—as well as in the development of training materials to improve the capacity of field staff to identify and address refugee children's protection and assistance needs. Finally, it reiterated its request that the High Commissioner report regularly to the Executive Committee on the needs of refugee children, and on existing and proposed programmes for their benefit.

21. UNHCR's effective management of refugee protection and assistance requires that the actions of its staff be tailored to the different needs and potentials of refugee children, women, men, disabled persons, the elderly and other groups with distinct requirements. Their needs are not well served when, particularly in emergencies, refugees are treated as an undifferentiated mass of humanity.

22. Children share with adult refugees needs for protection and assistance. Children, however, have needs and rights additional to those of adults. Care must be taken to ensure that these special needs and rights are perceived, understood and attended to by those who seek to protect and assist refugees generally. Until this becomes a matter of course for all actors working with refugees, specific directives regarding refugee children are required.

23. Children's needs, however, must not be addressed in isolation. They are normally met most effectively within the context of family and community. Moreover, a child's welfare is closely linked to the health and security of the primary care-giver, who is usually the mother. Consequently, UNHCR staff need to strengthen the capacities of refugee families to meet their own needs and improve the participation and situation of refugee women, thereby contributing significantly to the welfare of their children. Staff members must ensure effective implementation of the High Commissioner's Policy on Refugee Women and UNHCR's Guidelines on the Protection of Refugee Women in order to improve the situation of refugee children. As the High Commissioner's policies on children and on women are complementary, their implementation needs to be coordinated. Moreover, the components of the policy on refugee children must be integrated within an overall programme of protection and assistance for refugees generally.

24. UNHCR staff need to redouble their efforts to integrate children themselves into the protection and programming processes. Although vulnerable, children are also a resource with much to offer. The potential contributions of children must not be overlooked. They are people in their own right, with suggestions, opinions and abilities to participate in decisions and activities that affect their lives. Efforts on behalf of refugee children fall short if they are perceived only as individuals to be fed, immunised or sheltered, rather than treated as participating members of their community.

25. UNHCR's primary goals with regard to refugee children are as follows:

(a) To ensure the protection and healthy development of refugee children.

(b) To achieve durable solutions which are appropriate to the immediate and long-term developmental needs of refugee children.

26. The following are the central principles which will guide the pursuit of these goals by UNHCR staff:

(a) In all actions taken concerning refugee children, the human rights of the child, in particular his or her best interests, are to be given primary consideration.

(b) Preserving and restoring family unity are of fundamental concern.

(c) Actions to benefit refugee children should be directed primarily at enabling their primary care-givers to fulfil their principal responsibility to meet their children's needs.

(d) Where the special needs of refugee children can only be met effectively through child-focused activities, these should be carried out with the full participation of their families and communities.

(e) Refugee girls and boys must be assured protection and assistance on a basis of equality.

(f) Unaccompanied refugee children must be the particular focus of protection and care.

(g) UNHCR staff are required to make their best efforts both to prevent risk to refugee children and to take additional action to ensure the survival and safety of refugee children at particular risk.

27. On the basis of these principles, UNHCR staff should endeavour to ensure that the protection of children's rights as recognised under national and international law, including their rights to personal security and special assistance, are adequately and consistently addressed in the Office's protection and assistance activities. To this effect, UNHCR staff will pursue the following specific objectives:

(*a*) the protection of refugee children at risk from detention, armed conflict, military recruitment, sexual assault or abuse, prostitution, torture, hazardous working conditions or any other form of violence, abuse or neglect;

(*b*) the diligent enforcement of national laws regarding all forms of violence and abuse against refugee children, in accordance with the relevant international legal obligations of the States concerned;

(*c*) the consistent incorporation, from the beginning of a refugee situation, of protection and assistance criteria for assessing, monitoring and addressing the needs and vulnerabilities of refugee children;

(*d*) the compilation and updating of a statistical profile on each refugee population of concern to the High Commissioner, including age/gender disaggregation and identification of unaccompanied minors, for use in planning protection and assistance measures;

(*e*) the identification, and provision for the special protection and care, of unaccompanied children in every refugee situation, as well as their reunification with their families;

(*f*) the training of UNHCR and implementing partner staff to understand and address appropriately within their areas of competence the particular needs of refugee children in ways consistent with this policy and the UNHCR Guidelines on Refugee Children;

(*g*) the training of police and military forces, other Government employees involved with refugee protection and assistance, adults and leaders regarding the specific human rights most relevant to the well-being of refugee children;

(*h*) the sensitisation of refugee children themselves to their specific rights;

(*i*) the promotion of awareness of, and response to, the particular needs of refugee children through information strategies directed at the Governments of both countries of asylum and countries of origin, donors, NGOs, other United Nations bodies and the public at large;

(*j*) the promotion and facilitation by UNHCR of the cooperation of technically competent governmental and non-governmental organisations and other United Nations bodies in providing for the protection and care of refugee children.

28. No set of goals or objectives is definitive. A continual process or review and upgrading is necessary to ensure that UNHCR's protection and programme related actions remain relevant and practical. Such a process requires an ongoing exchange of information and experience amongst all those concerned with the rights and welfare of refugee children.

H. *Refugee Children: Guidelines on Protection and Care* (UNHCR, Geneva, 1994), pp. 18–25, 103–4.

... The treaty which sets the most standards concerning children is the 1989 Convention on the Rights of the Child (CRC). While the CRC is not a refugee treaty, refugee children are covered because all CRC rights are to be granted to all persons under 18 years of age (Article 1) without discrimination of any kind (Article 2).

The Convention on the Rights of the Child is important to refugee children because it sets comprehensive standards. Virtually every aspect of a child's life is covered, from health and education to social and political rights. Some of the standards are specific, for example the articles on juvenile justice (Articles 37 and 40), adoption (Article 21) and family rights (Articles 5, 9 and 14.2). Some social welfare rights are expressly qualified by the State's financial capability. Rights to health (Article 24), education (Article 28), and to an adequate standard of living (Article 27) are called 'progressive rights' because they increase along with the State's economic development. However, these social welfare rights are not just principles or abstract goals. Because they are 'rights', the prohibition against discrimination (Article 2) means that whatever benefits a State gives to the children who are its citizens, it must give to all children, including those who are refugees on its territory. The Convention on the Rights of the Child has gained importance to refugee children because of the near-universal ratification of the treaty.... The CRC standards have been agreed to by countries in every region of the world, countries of every population and geographical size and stage of economic development, and representing every type of political system and religious tradition. Because the standards are universal, the CRC can be used as a powerful tool for advocacy: a country cannot claim its uniqueness as an excuse for not living up to universal standards....

Overview of the Convention on the Rights of the Child

The 'Triangle of Rights'

The CRC's major innovation is that it gives rights to children. We are used to thinking of children as having needs that should be met, rather than as having legal rights. Because of the CRC, children now have internationally recognised human rights.

Although the rights in the CRC cover almost every aspect of a child's life, there are three rights that are so fundamental that they can be thought of as underlying the entire CRC: the 'best interests' rule, non-discrimination, and the right to participate. These three rights are so important and so interrelated that it is helpful to think of them as a 'triangle of rights'. The three rights of the triangle reinforce each other to reach the objective: 'the survival and development' of children (Article 6).

'Best Interests' Rule

The 'best interests' rule has two main applications: government policy-making and decisions made about children on an individual basis.

Policy decisions: Article 3 requires that 'In all actions concerning children' the State shall make 'the best interests of the child a primary consideration'. This article requires States to analyse how each course of action may affect children. Because the interests of children are not always identical to adults' interests, and can at times even conflict, the State must carefully separate out the various interests at stake. The government does not have to take the course of action that is best for children, but if any conflicts are identified, the State must make the 'best interests' of children 'a primary consideration'. This rule applies in budget allocations, in the making of laws, and in the administration of the government.

Individual children: When a decision is being made about an individual child, then the child's best interests must be, at a minimum, 'a primary consideration'. There are some situations where the child's welfare gets higher consideration. For example, in a case of abuse or neglect, a child can be separated from parents if it 'is necessary for the best interests of the child' (Article 7). In an adoption case, the 'best interests of the child shall be the paramount consideration' (Article 21). In these cases, how a course of action might affect the child must be looked at closely, which is a requirement similar to that in policy decisions. What can be different in individual cases is that under some CRC articles a child's welfare must be given priority over an adult's. For example, making a long term plan for an unaccompanied minor requires a decision about a child's best interests. A child might be an orphan living in a refugee camp, with grandparents in the country of origin, an uncle in a second country asylum, and with an unrelated family in another country that would like to adopt the child. In deciding what is best for the child many factors would have to be considered, including 'the desirability of continuity' of culture and language (Article 20), the preservation of family and nationality (Article 8), and the child's own desires, which must be considered according to the child's 'age and maturity' (Article 12). The objective is to allow the child to 'grow up in a family environment, in an atmosphere of happiness, love and understanding' (Preamble). The decision about a child's best interests can often be difficult; no single answer may be obviously and indisputably correct. (In the example, not enough 'facts' were given to make a decision.

More information would be needed: does the child have the legal status of 'refugee'? How old is the child? What are the conditions in the home country? Are the grandparents able to raise the child? And so on). The best interests rule underlies the CRC; each article is a variation on the theme of the best interests of children.

Non-discrimination

The non-discrimination article, Article 2, requires States to 'respect and ensure the rights set forth in the present Convention to each child within their jurisdiction without discrimination of any kind, irrespective of the child's ... national, ethnic or social origin ... or other status.' In other words, every child within a State's jurisdiction holds all CRC rights without regard to citizenship, immigration status or any other status. Refugee children, asylum seekers, and rejected asylum seekers are entitled to all the rights of the CRC.

Participation

Participation is a theme that runs throughout the CRC. Article 12 provides that: 'States Parties shall assure to the child who is capable of forming his or her views the right to express those views freely in all matters affecting the child, the views of the child being given due weight in accordance with the age and maturity of the child.' In one way or another, nearly every article concerns some aspect of children's participation in society.

There are many forms of participation. For example, there is social participation in family (Articles 7.1, 10) and community life (Articles 15, 17), and participation of those with special needs, such as disabled children (Article 23).

The participation of children in decision-making helps adults make better choices because they are better informed of the thoughts, feelings and needs of the children. But participation also meets a developmental need. It is through participation that children learn decision-making skills and gain the confidence to use those skills wisely.

As children age and mature they have greater participation in decision-making. Three forms of participation in decision-making are:

Information input: When primary school children draw pictures, the activity can be just recreation and self-expression. But it can also be participation, provided that adults use the pictures as a source of information about the children's thoughts and feelings in their decision-making.

Dialogue: Children have opinions and can discuss them with adults. When adults give the opinions 'due weight', according to the child's age and maturity, then the children are participating in the decision-making process, according to the CRC.

Decision-making: At an older age, young people can make some of their own decisions. For example, under national law adolescents may have the right to get married or to join the army. Even though these choices are usually subject to the approval of parents, the right of adolescents to decide what is in their own best interests shows that participation is a continuum: with an increase in age and maturity comes an increase in control over one's life.

Birth Registration, Nationality and Statelessness

As prescribed by Article 24 of the International Covenant on Civil and Political Rights and Article 7 of the Convention on the Rights of the Child, every child shall be registered immediately after birth and has the right to acquire a nationality. Birth registration is essential to enable date and place of birth to be conclusively established, thereby activating certain rights, including those rights which are dependent upon nationality and personal status. Those basic human rights can be violated in refugee situations unless particular attention is given to ensuring the proper documentation of children.

A stateless child lacks the guaranteed protection of any state. His or her basic rights, legal status, security in the country of residence and travel outside that country are subject to state discretion. Statelessness is often caused by states' deliberate policies not to confer nationality to children born to refugees. It may also be caused by the existence of conflicting laws regarding nationality. Some countries grant their nationality to children born on their territory (*jus solis*), while others confer their nationality exclusively to children born of parents who are their nationals (*jus sanguinis*). Thus, for example, a refugee child born in a country that applies the *jus sanguinis* principle to nationals of another country that applies the *jus solis* principle, will not be able to benefit from either nationality.

Pursuant to Article 1(A) (2) of the 1951 Convention relating to the Status of Refugees and/or paragraph 6 (A) (ii) of its Statute, UNHCR is formally empowered to exercise the full range of its responsibilities on behalf of stateless persons (and refugees). Stateless persons are also entitled, in countries who are parties to the 1951 Convention or to the Organization of African Unity (OAU) 1969 Convention governing the specific aspects of Refugee Problems in Africa (Article I(1)), to enjoy the rights recognized in these instruments. In addition, UNHCR has specific responsibilities as the body to which a stateless person should turn to for assistance in connection with reduction of statelessness through its designation by the General Assembly pursuant to Article 11 of the 1961 Convention on the Reduction of Statelessness.

III. FUTURE OF THE REFUGEE RIGHTS REGIME

A. James C. Hathaway and John A. Dent, *Refugee Rights: Report on a Comparative Survey* (York Lanes Press, Toronto, 1995), pp. 43–48.

Reflections on the Future of Refugee Rights

The flowering of international human rights law since the drafting of the Refugee Convention, so that two overlapping yet distinct rights regimes now coexist, raises important questions concerning the relation between refugee rights and human rights, and the future role of a refugee-specific rights regime. A reasonable point of departure in the examination of the relation between international human rights and refugee rights is a review of the purpose and historical context of the 1951 Refugee Convention. Prior to the development of international human rights law in the post-World War II period, traditional international law was exclusively a 'law of nations' rather than a 'law of people'. The individual was subsumed into the nation-state framework through the 'bond of nationality'. A wrong committed by a state against an alien was interpreted as a wrong against the alien's state of nationality. The alien herself, in most cases, had no individual rights that were enforceable against the host state. The position of the refugee was thus particularly precarious as, lacking a state of nationality to champion her case, she was utterly without protection. Due to their inability to obtain protection from their country of origin and their consequent involuntary separation from that state, refugees were identified as individuals in need of special protection. Surrogate protection was required from the international community.

In addressing the dilemma of the refugee through the establishment of a particularised rights regime, the approach embodied in the Convention relating to the Status of Refugees can legitimately be considered progressive in international law. To place the Convention in context, it should be remembered that, at the time of its drafting, the only comprehensive standard for international human rights law was the Universal Declaration, a simple, unenforceable General Assembly resolution. Over the next twenty-five years, pending the entry into force of binding human rights covenants, the guarantees of the Refugee Convention were among the very few international norms upon which refugees could depend.

Today, in contrast, international human rights law comprises not only the International Covenants of 1966, but also a range of specialised universal accords, and regional human rights regimes in Europe, Africa and the Americas. In consequence, the individual is today clearly a subject of international law, and the holder of an impressive range of human rights.

It is of particular significance to refugees that most civil rights are not subject to requirements of nationality. The International Covenant on

Civil and Political Rights extends its protection to 'everyone' or 'all persons'. Each contracting state undertakes in Article 2(1) to ensure the rights in the Covenant 'to all individuals within its territory and subject to its jurisdiction ... without distinction of any kind, such as race, colour, sex, language, religion, political or other opinion, national or social origin, property, birth or other status.' While nationality is not included in this illustrative list, it is logically embraced by the residual category of 'distinction of any kind'. That the Civil and Political Covenant generally applies to aliens is further established through contrast of this inclusive wording with the two articles that explicitly extend to a more limited class of beneficiaries, namely Article 25's extension of freedom of movement only to persons 'lawfully in the territory of the contracting state'. Although the Covenant does not govern admission to or residence in a State party, the UN Human Rights Committee has determined that an alien may enjoy its protection in relation to entry and residence when considerations of non-discrimination, prohibition of inhuman treatment, or respect for family life arise.

The International Covenant on Economic, Social and Cultural Rights is, however, less generous to aliens. The most obvious limitation is Article 2(3), which permits developing countries to determine, in light of their economic situation, the extent to which they guarantee the economic rights of the Convention to non-nationals. As such, the economic rights guaranteed by the Refugee Convention may be of greater practical importance than their civil rights counterparts. Whereas refugees would be entitled to benefit from civil rights in the majority of states that are parties to the International Covenant on Civil and Political Rights, the attenuation of their economic rights authorised under conventional human rights law is mitigated by the more categorical provisions of the Refugee Convention.

The maturation of human rights law over the past four decades, then, has to a certain extent filled the vacuum of protection that necessitated the development of a refugee-specific rights regime in 1951. Human rights law has evolved beyond the norms of the refugee regime, so that refugees now derive protection of their basic human rights from both the refugee-specific 1951 Convention and from general human rights instruments. As these rights regimes overlap and contain different standards in many areas, questions arise as to how they should logically be reconciled. How should a holistic sense of obligation towards refugees be defined? In recognition of their situation-specific vulnerability, should refugees be afforded rights superior to those afforded by general human rights law? Are the special needs of refugees adequately addressed in the present Refugee Convention? Need a refugee rights regime reiterate rights contained in general human rights instruments?

A starting point in answering these questions is a more careful examination of the areas of overlap and competing standards of the regimes. National rapporteurs have noted several areas of overlap between human rights law and refugee law, including rights to employment, social assistance, education, freedom of movement, nondiscrimination, and freedom from expulsion. Generally speaking, refugee-specific rights aspire to a lower standard of treatment. Because the rights in the Refugee Convention are often framed differently from their counterparts in conventional human rights law, however, it can be difficult to determine which of the standards affords a stronger basis for protection. For example, the socio-economic rights in the Economic Covenant appear superior to those of the Refugee Convention in that, unlike the Refugee Convention's Articles 17, 18, and 19, they are not limited to a guarantee of treatment afforded aliens, but arguably mandate treatment akin to that granted to nationals. However, the proviso in the Economic Covenant's Article 2(3) permitting developing countries to determine, in light of economic conditions, the extent to which they will grant economic rights to non-nationals could be potentially fatal to the employment rights of the vast majority of the world's refugees located in the less-developed world. Moreover, the entire Economic Covenant is enforceable only at the level of nondiscriminatory progressive implementation, whereas the Refugee Convention appears to set absolute, if less exigent, expectations of states.

A similar difficulty arises in comparing the differing formulations of the right to freedom of movement of recognised refugees. While Article 12 of the Civil and Political Covenant is open to limitations to accommodate, among other things, national security and public order concerns, Article 26 of the Refugee Convention subjects this right only to regulations applicable to aliens generally in the same circumstances, and arguably to the situation-specific limits suggested by the Conclusions of the Executive Committee.

While they overlap in several areas, the comparison of refugee law with human rights law reveals a number of rights unique to one or the other regime. That the protections established by the Refugee Convention extended beyond general human rights is not surprising, given the particularly vulnerable situation of refugees. Refugee-specific rights are needed to address unique dilemmas relating to personal status, naturalisation, illegal entry, the need for travel and other identity documents and especially the threats of expulsion and refoulement. What is perhaps surprising is the absence from the Refugee Convention of basic civil rights such as the right to life, liberty and security of person; the rights to protection from slavery, torture and arbitrary arrest, detention or imprisonment; the right to equal protection before the law; and the right to freedom of thought, opinion, and expression. The right to family reunification is, moreover, not formally guaranteed by the Refugee Convention, but is included only at the level of a nonbinding resolution in the drafting conference's Final Act.

The Refugee Convention's lack of protection of some critical civil rights is curious in that the omissions render the Convention a somewhat incomplete document and put into question the intent of its drafters. It would appear that the participants at the drafting conference did not intend the Convention to be limited to situation-specific rights required by the precarious nature of refugeehood, on the assumption that all other rights would be protected by general human rights law. Otherwise, the Refugee Convention would not address subjects already recognised as legitimate aspects of general human rights protection, such as rights to employment, social assistance, education, and freedom of movement. Yet neither did its drafters intend the Convention to be an exhaustive elaboration of refugee rights independent of general human rights law, as they surely would have included such critical human rights as the right to life, liberty, and security. To posit otherwise would imply that the Convention's drafters did not consider refugees' most basic security interests as warranting protection.

Given the enigmatic relationship between the 1951 Refugee Convention and contemporary human rights law, what should be done to clarify and to consolidate the rights to which refugees are entitled? Should a refugee-specific regime be maintained, and if so, what form should it take, with what substantive focus? In appraising the utility of a refugee-specific rights regime in an era of widely applicable international human rights, one might consider three factors: first, whether the existence of a refugee-specific system enhances the enforceability of generally guaranteed rights; second, whether the refugee rights regime breaks new substantive ground as compared with general human rights law, resulting in a more comprehensive enumeration of rights; and third, whether the refugee-specific regime aids in the clarification or reinforcement of generally accepted rights so as more effectively to coincide with the real needs of refugees.

IV. DUTIES OF REFUGEES

A. Anders B. Johnsson, 'The Duties of Refugees', *International Journal of Refugee Law* (Vol. 3, No. 3, 1991), pp. 579–83.

Introduction

Much has been written on the rights of refugees; less so on their duties. And yet, refugees are no different from other individuals. They must conform to the laws and regulations of the country in which they find themselves. The question arises, however, whether refugees have any duties over and above such general obligations and what conflicts, if any, may exist with respect to their fundamental rights....

Subversive Activities

It is a universally recognised principle that the grant of asylum and the recognition of refugee status have a peaceful, non-political and humanitarian character. It follows that refugees, at least for the purpose of protection under international instruments, are civilians. Persons actively engaged as combatants in military and armed conflicts benefit from the special protection afforded under applicable international humanitarian law.

As regards refugees, some of the relevant international instruments call upon States to do everything within their power to prevent the refugee problem from becoming a source of tension between States. The corresponding provision in the preamble to the 1951 Convention is based upon a proposal submitted by the delegation of Yugoslavia, according to which States should forbid 'all hostile activity the part of political or other refugee organisations directed against the country of origin ... (and all) ... activity designed to exploit the difficult position or refugees, with a view to using it for political ends contrary to the principles and purposes of the United Nations Charter'.[38] They should also forbid the creation of refugee military formations. So as not to compromise the essentially humanitarian nature of the Convention, the drafters finally agreed to express the wish that 'all States, recognising the social and humanitarian nature of the problem of refugees, will do everything within their power to prevent this problem from becoming a cause of tension between States'.[39]

The 1969 OAU Convention Governing the Specific Aspects of Refugee Problems in Africa takes the provisions of the 1951 Convention relating to the duties of refugees several steps further. After recalling the general duties of refugees, the Convention declares that refugees shall also abstain from any subversive activities against any Member State of the OAU. In addition, States parties undertake to prohibit refugees residing in their respective territories from attacking any State Member of the OAU, by any activity likely to cause tension between Member States, and in particular by use of arms, through the press, or by radio.

Other international instruments contain provisions relating to the duties of refugees. The 1928 Havana Convention on Asylum provides

[38] UN Doc. A/CONF.2/96.
[39] GAOR, fifth session, Supplement No. 20 (A/1775), p. 48.

that refugees shall not be allowed to perform acts contrary to the public peace while enjoying asylum.[40] The 1939 Montevideo Treaty on Asylum and Political Refuge declares that territorial asylum shall be inviolable, but that it is the duty of the State granting asylum to prevent refugees from committing acts within its territory which may endanger the public peace of the State from which they came.[41] The 1967 United Nations Declaration on Territorial Asylum holds that States granting asylum shall not permit persons who have received asylum to engage in activities contrary to the purposes and principles of the United Nations.[42]

States have also addressed the issue of subversive activities of refugees in various fora. In 1981, the Executive Committee of the High Commissioner's Programme declared that asylum-seekers should not become involved in subversive activities against their country of origin or any other State.[43] Six years later, the Executive Committee considered that refugees have a duty to abstain from any activity likely to detract from the exclusively civilian and humanitarian character of refugee camps and settlements. For their part, seven African Heads of State and Government meeting in Rwanda in November 1986 declared that States should commit themselves to prohibiting refugees from all political, military and propaganda activities likely to prejudice good relations between the country of refuge and that of origin.[44]

Similarly, States meeting at the International Conference on Central American Refugees confirmed the obligation of refugees to avoid any activities which might affect the strictly civilian and humanitarian nature of camps and settlements, 'as well as any activity that is incompatible with the regional peace process'.[45]

Duties and Fundamental Human Rights

The parameters for the duties of refugees are clear. They have a general obligation to respect the laws and regulations of the country in which they find themselves. In this they are no different from the citizens of that country, or for that matter, any other foreigner. This obligation includes a duty to refrain from engaging in subversive activities directed against their country of origin, such as armed insurrection. What is less clear is the delimitation between these obligations and the right of refugees (as

[40] OAS Official Records, OEA/Ser.X/1, Treaty Series 34.
[41] Ibid.
[42] UNGA res. 2321 (XXIII), 10 December 1967.
[43] Executive Committee Conclusion No. 22 (XXXII) on the Protection of Asylum-seekers in Situations of Large-scale Influx.
[44] Bangui Declaration Adopted by Seven African Heads of State and Government, November 1986.
[45] CIREFCA/89/14, 31 May 1989, p. 3.

others) to enjoy fundamental human rights such as freedom of opinion and expression.

That there can be a conflict is clear. Suffice to recall the French amendment to the 1951 Convention, the effect of which would have been to forbid refugees even to express political opinions, and which 'would certainly deny them access to an area of human activity in which they should have as much right to engage as any other alien'.[46] The Cartagena Declaration on Refugees acknowledges the conflict in different terms through its commitment to institute appropriate measures in the receiving countries to prevent the participation of refugees in activities directed against the country of origin, 'while at all times respecting the human rights of refugees'.

How best to protect the right to freedom of opinion and expression? One very minor effort was undertaken by insisting that the measures taken for the maintenance of public order be lawful,[47] and consequently not themselves in violation of a State's responsibilities to uphold human rights. More express provisions are contained in the 1954 Caracas Convention on Territorial Asylum.[48] Article VII provides that freedom of expression of thought, recognised by domestic law for all inhabitants of a State, may not be grounds for complaint by a third State on the basis of opinions expressed publicly against it or its government by asylees or refugees, 'except when these concepts constitute systematic propaganda through which they incite to the use of force or violence against the government of the complaining State.' Similarly, Article VIII provides that no State has the right to request that another State restrict political asylees' or refugees' freedom of assembly or association, which the latter State's internal legislation grants to all aliens within its territory, 'unless such assembly or association has as its purpose formenting the use of force or violence against the government of the soliciting State.'

Conclusion

Refugees are persons whose fundamental rights have been violated. They seek refuge abroad precisely in order to be able to continue to enjoy their basic human rights, including the right to freedom of opinion and expression. While they are clearly no different from other individuals, so far as they must respect the laws and regulations in the country in which they find themselves, this obligation must not be taken to deprive them of their fundamental human rights. Thus, the repeated call by States that refugees have a duty not to engage in subversive activities, should not

[46] UN Doc. E/AC.32/SR.10, p. 10.

[47] Executive Committee Conclusion No. 48 (XXXVIII) para. 4(a); CIREFCA/89/14, 31 May 1989, para. 7.

[48] OAS Official Records, OEA/Ser.X/1, Treaty Series 34.

prohibit them from enjoying such rights. The only permissible limit would be when, for example, in the exercise of the right to freedom of opinion and expression, refugees incite violence or the use of force.

Chapter 4

The United Nations High Commissioner for Refugees (UNHCR)

Historical Background: The League of Nations Period (1919–46)

The history of an organised response to the refugee problem can be
traced to the birth of the League of Nations. By 1920 it became increasingly clear that large-scale refugee movements in Europe could not be
dealt with without intergovernmental cooperation.[1] In 1921 Dr Fridtjof
Nansen assumed the office of the High Commissioner for Russian Refugees. Subsequently his services were used to deal with other refugee
flows. In 1929, the Assembly set up the Nansen International Office for
Refugees which was liquidated in 1938. An Intergovernmental Committee on Refugees (IGCR) was established in 1938 as an independent international refugee organisation outside the framework of the League of
Nations. The initiative came from the United States. The Committee was
to take care of Jewish refugees from Germany and Austria. In 1939 a
High Commissioner for the League of Nations was appointed to take
care of the refugee problem. In 1946 he transferred the duty of protection of refugees to the IGCR which acted until the International Refugee
Organisation (IRO) took over the responsibilities in 1947. Meanwhile, the
United Nations Relief and Rehabilitation Agency (UNRRA) was established in 1943 when 44 participating states signed the charter of the new
international organisation. Its objective was to make 'preparations and
arrangements ... for the return of prisoners and exiles to their homes'.

In **Reading I.A** Holborn provides an overview of the efforts between
1920 and 1947 to institutionalise the response to the growing refugee

---

[1] For a history of developments in this period see Claudena M. Skran, *Refugees in Inter-
war Europe: The Emergence of a Regime* (Clarendon Press, Oxford, 1995).

problem. Further, along with Stoessinger in **Reading I.B**, Holborn identifies a number of key features of the organised response and briefly assesses the role of the League of Nations in refugee assistance. Holborn writes that 'the amount and extent of the work accomplished through the international cooperation of governments and voluntary organisations under the guidance of the League of Nations and the use of its machinery was considerable.' Others have portrayed its record in a negative light. For example, Walters concludes that 'the League's record [on refugees] was regrettably inadequate and confused.'[2] Skran has recently challenged this view and contended that 'contrary to the position put forward by Walters and others, the League of Nations played a valuable part in refugee assistance in inter-War Europe.'[3] According to her, 'Walter's claim that the League never built up a well-defined organisation in the field of refugee assistance is inaccurate.'[4] This is a debate which interested readers may pursue further.

International Refugee Organisation (IRO) (1946–52)

The IRO was established in 1946. It had a life of five years and was liquidated in 1952. It differed from the UNRRA and IGCR in the fact that 'it did not merely provide supplies and a place to live, but was coupled to the resettlement programme.'[5] It represented 'the culmination of earlier more piecemeal efforts on behalf of refugees which dated back to the end of the First World War'.[6] In **Reading I.B** Stoessinger contrasts its 'unified and integrated' approach with other efforts before it.

In **Reading I.C** Salomon discusses the Cold War influences on the operation of the IRO. There is much that can be learnt from the experience of the IRO regarding the role political and economic interests play in shaping global refugee policies and the institutions which oversee them. For example, the Western emphasis on the solution of resettlement—

[2] F.P. Walters, *A History of the League of Nations* (Oxford University Press, London, 1960), pp. 187–89.

[3] Skran, *Refugees in Inter-war Europe* (see footnote 1 earlier), p. 283. Salomon takes the middle-of-the-road position and talks about the partial failure of the refugee policy of the League of Nations. According to him, 'the international refugee work of the 1920s and 1930s under the auspices of the League of Nations bore the stamp of half-hearted commitment.' Kim Salomon, *Refugees in the Cold War: Toward a New International Refugee Regime* (Lund University Press, Lund, 1991), p. 37.

[4] Ibid.

[5] Louise W. Holborn, *The International Refugee Organisation: A Specialised Agency of the United Nations—its History and Work, 1946–1952* (Oxford University Press, London, 1956), p. 2.

[6] Ibid., p. 24. Holborn quotes the last Director General of the organisation as saying that it was 'the most successful example of large-scale international co-operation for humanitarian purposes in history'. Ibid., p. 1.

dictated by Cold War interests and labour shortage—as opposed to the official policy of repatriation crucially influenced the working of the organisation.[7] Among other things, it caused 'a growing cleavage between the officers responsible for repatriation and the officers responsible for resettlement'.[8] Salomon also notes the complete unconcern of Western states at this stage with the refugee movements in the third world. The history of the IRO points towards the following broad institutional lessons: first, the defining policy feature of an organisation affects all aspects of its operation. Second, the dominance of one division of an organisation can prove detrimental to its work. Finally, if an organisation pursues contradictory policies it can lead to friction within the organisation. Readers may, in the light of the later readings, reflect on the significance of these lessons for the UNHCR at a time when it is being transformed into a humanitarian organisation with its increasing involvement with IDPs.

UNHCR: Cold War Origins

The demise of IRO was followed in 1951 by the establishment of the Office of the UNHCR. Its mandate, like the 1951 Convention, was shaped by the Cold War. As Salomon has noted, 'there was a political logic in the development from UNRRA and the IRO to the UNHCR.'[9] Refugees are defined by the Statute of the UNHCR using the same ideological criteria as in the (subsequently arrived at) 1951 Convention, albeit without placing temporal or geographical limitations. But did the UNHCR serve as an instrument of Western powers during the Cold War? And if so, what were the different ways in which it served Western interests? These are questions which have still not been adequately researched by the academic community.[10] The answers to these questions are of not merely

---

[7] As Salomon writes elsewhere in the essay reproduced: 'A new mentality was prevailing among the IRO staff. Even though the constitution bound the Organisation to a definite priority policy in favor of repatriation, the problem of repatriation had been lost sight of in the rush of enthusiasm toward the resettlement goal . . . repatriation became almost a dead letter. It might even be said that repatriation continued in spite of rather than because of the activities of the IRO.' Salomon, *Refugees in the Cold War* (see footnote 3 earlier), p. 127. Readers should also consult **Reading I.A** in Chapter 6.

[8] Ibid., p. 126.

[9] Ibid., p. 244. Indeed, it is Salomon's basic thesis that 'the Cold War had a decisive influence on the form of international refugee policies. Conflicts about the international refugee policy, which in turn led to changes of regime, can . . . be interpreted in large measure in terms of East-West differences.' Ibid., p. 242–43.

[10] However, see generally Gil Loescher, *Beyond Charity: International Cooperation and the Global Refugee Crisis* (Oxford University Press, Oxford, 1993), Chapter 3.

A fuller evaluation requires that the UNHCR archives be made available to researchers. The archives are presently being arranged and classified. But the UNHCR has yet to develop a policy on throwing it open to researchers.

historical but also of contemporary significance. For if the UNHCR did play the alleged role in the Cold War, it would be legitimate to ask about the place it has been assigned in the post–Cold War strategy of Western powers. Further, what would be its meaning and implications for the non-political character of the Office of the High Commissioner?

Be that as it may, the UNHCR performed an important humanitarian role during the Cold War through offering assistance and protection to those in need. It is noteworthy that it was twice awarded the Nobel Prize for Peace, in 1954 and 1981 respectively.

UNHCR: Standing and Relationship with UN

Readings II.A to **II.F** offer excerpts which explore the legal standing and evolution and growth of the Office of the High Commissioner. In **Reading II.A**, Goodwin-Gill discusses the status of the UNHCR in international law, its relationship with the General Assembly of the United Nations, and the establishment of the Executive Committee (popularly known as EXCOM) to advise the Office of the High Commissioner. Readers may note that while the conclusions adopted by the Executive Committee are not legally binding on member states, they have exercised considerable influence on the practice of states.

Evolution and Growth of the Office

In **Reading II.B**, Sadruddin Aga Khan, the former High Commissioner for Refugees, narrates how the Office gradually evolved in the first decades in relation to its competence *rationae personae* and the need to offer material assistance.[11]

The end of the Cold War has had, as was to be expected, a profound impact on the organisation. It is said that the 'UNHCR has been transformed from a refugee organisation into a more broadly-based humanitarian agency.'[12] It has been compelled by a variety of factors to develop new areas of competence and to undertake a number of non-traditional activities. The most significant factor is that refugees are no longer welcome in the Western world.[13] Instead, Western states have sought to persuade the UNHCR to concern itself increasingly with providing assistance

---

[11] An important role of the Office of the High Commissioner is to promote durable solutions to the refugee problem. This aspect of the functioning of the UNHCR is considered in Chapter 6 which deals with the question of durable solutions.

[12] UNHCR, *The State of the World's Refugees: In Search of Solutions* (Oxford University Press, Oxford, 1995), p. 48.

[13] Chapter 2 discusses the host of restrictive measures that states in the Western world have taken to stop asylum-seekers from reaching their territory.

and protection to displaced persons within states. The ongoing transform-ation of the UNHCR raises a series of questions. Should the UNHCR involve itself in non-traditional activities? What are the implications of this involvement for the non-political character of the organisation which its Statute mandates? Would not the assumption of a political stance, as its increasing involvement with the IDPs could demand, undermine the credibility of the organisation with governments? What are the organisa-tional changes this involvement in non-traditional activities call for? While the role of UNHCR with respect to IDPs is examined in greater detail in Chapter 7, **Reading II.C** reproduces an early expression of scep-ticism of the possible metamorphosis of UNHCR.[14]

Some delicate problems the UNHCR may have to confront in the pro-cess of being transformed into a humanitarian organisation is the subject of **Reading II.D**. In it, Rieff discusses the role of the UNHCR in former Yugoslavia and notes the dilemma in which the UNHCR found itself: either to leave people to die or to be 'complicit' in ethnic cleansing by arranging for their transport out of the danger zone.

Need for a New Mandate?

Readings II.E and **II.F** raise the question of whether recent develop-ments call for the adoption of a new mandate for the Office of the High Commissioner. It is interesting that in the first Reading Goodwin-Gill appears to answer the question in the negative, but only three years later modifies his approach. The debate over a new mandate is useful in exam-ining and evaluating the changes which have visited the UNHCR.

Funding UNHCR: Need for a Regular Budget?

In **Readings II.E** and **II.F** Goodwin-Gill also underlines the need for the UNHCR to have a regular budget. At present, however, with the excep-tion of a very limited subsidy from the United Nations Regular Budget, to be assigned exclusively to meeting administrative costs, UNHCR's assist-ance programmes are funded by voluntary contributions from govern-ments, intergovernmental and non-governmental organisations, and individuals. This dependence on voluntary contributions to carry out its programmes is said to be the 'most significant weakness of the UNHCR'.[15] For it compels the UNHCR to adopt policies that reflect the interests and priorities of the major donor countries.[16] The absence of a

[14] Readers may recall here once again the organisational lessons learnt from the opera-tion of the IRO and consider what they have to offer to UNHCR by way of guidance.

[15] Loescher, *Beyond Charity* (footnote 10 earlier), p. 131.

[16] Ibid. 'During the 1980s, for example, international aid levels per Afghan refugee in pro-Western Pakistan were more than three times higher than those allocated to Afghan

regular budget compromises its independence as criticism of the practices of donor countries is met with threats to cut off funding. The proposal of a regular budget therefore deserves serious consideration. The key questions for consideration in this regard are: would a regular budget really help insulate the UNHCR from donor politics? Does the experience of other United Nations agencies lend support to this proposal? Would it constrain the UNHCR thereafter in seeking voluntary contributions?

Emergency Preparedness

Reading II.G traces the evolution of emergency response of the UNHCR. Criticisms from states and NGOs of its emergency preparedness role in several situations led it to establish in 1992 the Emergency Preparedness and Response Section (EPRS). The Reading elaborates on the structure and objectives of the EPRS.

UNHCR and Non-governmental Organisations (NGOs)

Non-governmental organisations are today playing a significant role in dealing with the global refugee problem. **Reading III.A** considers the diverse nature of NGOs and the different roles they are expected to play in meeting the assistance and protection needs of refugees in the contemporary world.

It is important not to idealise the world of NGOs. From the very beginning, their operation has had several problematic aspects. For example, in the inter-War period, selective humanitarianism was the norm.[17] Contemporary NGOs have their own set of problems. They are often subservient to donor priorities, insensitive to local conditions, have inadequate trained or equipped personnel, are media-hungry, indulge in narrow

refugees in anti-Western Iran. Similarly, during the 1991 Gulf crisis, international aid to Iraqi refugees in Iran was substantially less than that to Kurds who fled to Turkey and other areas.'

[17] '... the private voluntary organizations participating in the international refugee regime were unable to live up to the humanitarian principle. These organizations seemed to unleash their humanitarian passions on behalf of refugees with whom they shared a common religion and culture more often than they did for refugees who were noticeably different. British and American philanthropic groups, for instance, primarily helped Christian refugees living in the Muslim Middle East. In response to the German refugee crisis, sectarianism was even more pronounced: Jewish organizations helped Jewish refugees, Catholic organizations helped Catholic refugees, Socialist organizations helped Socialist refugees, and Communist organizations helped Communist refugees.' Skran, *Refugees in Inter-war Europe* (see footnote 1 earlier), p. 276. However, there were exceptions, as Skran notes, even 'in this environment of selective humanitarianism, the Quakers stand out as one of the few organizations (possibly the only) which helped all types of refugees, be they Christian, Jew, Socialist, or Communist' (ibid.).

politics and resist coordination in a bid to protect their turf. Readers may also note that humanitarian assistance has now become a multi-billion-dollar industry and NGOs certainly have a stake in it.[18] As one observer has put it: 'What would be called profits in any other sector have enabled NGOs to grow and proliferate.'[19] These problems are mentioned not to deny the contribution of NGOs in providing relief and protection to refugees but to caution against taking a simplistic view of their role, as also to stress the need for accountability.[20]

The UNHCR's Statute mandates it to work with NGOs. **Reading III.B** reproduces a short excerpt on the relationship of UNHCR with NGOs. The UNHCR is said to be a non-operational agency for it does not implement assistance programmes directly but through governmental and non-governmental organisations. It works with nearly 300 NGOs throughout the world. These include large international organisations such as Medicins Sans Frontiers, CARE, OXFAM, Caritas, Save the Children and some small and local NGOs.

The relations of the UNHCR with the NGOs are not always smooth. In recent years there is growing criticism from the NGO community that the UNHCR has given short shrift to principles of protection in favour of some form of pragmatism.[21] While the difference of being an intergovernmental organisation is not sufficiently appreciated by the NGO community, its criticism of the UNHCR policies and practices is not always without merit. On the other hand, faced with legitimate criticisms, it is not unknown for the UNHCR to flex its muscles.[22]

---

[18] Antonio Donini, 'The Future of Humanitarian Assistance', paper presented at the UNU Symposium on the UN System in the 21st Century, Tokyo, 21–22 November 1995, pp. 5–6. Donini observes that 'a contract culture has emerged, with media and dollar-hungry NGOs competing for finite resources of the international community.' He then goes on to note 'the exponential growth of humanitarian assistance ... from barely $845 million a year in 1989 to close to $5 billion a year'. See also Robert Lacville, 'There's Money in Disaster', *The Guardian Weekly* (13 October 1996).

[19] Lindsey Hilsum, 'Save Us from Our Saviours', *The Observer* (31 December 1995).

[20] See, generally, P. Gassmann, 'International Humanitarian Action: Growing Dilemmas and New Perspectives for the Twenty-first Century', in Medicins Sans Frontiers, *World in Crisis* (Routledge, London, 1997), pp. 37–41; Rakiya Omaar and Alex de Waal, 'Humanitarianism Unbound? Current Dilemmas facing Multi-mandate Relief Operations in Political Emergencies', Discussion Paper No. 5, *African Rights* (1994); Joanna Macrae and Anthony Zwi, *War and Hunger: Rethinking International Responses to Complex Emergencies* (Zed Books, London, 1994).

[21] See, for example, Amnesty International, *Refugees Have No Borders* (March 1997); and Human Rights Watch, *Uncertain Refuge: International Failure to Protect Refugees* (April 1997).

[22] The competition for power among the principal actors involved in the assistance process, viz., the UNHCR, NGOs, the donor and the host governments, often leads to a situation where each seeks to enhance its power vis-à-vis the other actors in order to realise its own goals, but often at the expense of the welfare of refugees. Eftihia Voutira and Barbara E. Harrell-Bond, 'In Search of the Locus of Trust: The Social World of the Refugee Camp',

In recent years, the UNHCR has entered into a series of dialogues with the NGO community concerning their future partnership. In 1994 The PARinAc (Partnership in Action) Global Conference held in Oslo adopted the Oslo Declaration and Plan of Action which includes 134 recommendations. In **Reading III.C**, Romero-Perez discusses the process leading up to the adoption of the Oslo Declaration and the underlying rationale.

Refugees and the Role of ICRC

Finally, **Reading IV.A** examines the extent to which refugees are protected by international humanitarian law and discusses in this context the role of the ICRC.[23]

* * *

I. PREDECESSORS

A. Louise W. Holborn, *The International Refugee Organisation: A Specialised Agency of the United Nations—its History and Work 1946–1952* (Oxford University Press, London, 1956), pp. 3–18.

League of Nations Work for Refugees, 1919–46

... Following the First World War, League of Nations' agencies had grappled with some of the most obvious needs of the waves of refugees caused from 1912 on by the dislocations of war, the impact of violent nationalisms and the arbitrary action of dictatorial regimes. When German National Socialism, through its intolerance and racial legislation, created a huge exodus after 1933 and placed great numbers of individuals in an intolerable position, special intergovernmental action was organised from 1938 on under the initiative of President Roosevelt, resulting in the establishment of the Intergovernmental Committee for Refugees. This intergovernmental action, under the direction of the United States and Great Britain, was continued and broadened during the Second World War to deal with new emergencies. In the third place were the large-scale efforts on behalf of displaced persons by the military authorities once liberation

---

in E.V. Daniel and C.K. Knudsen, eds, *Mistrusting Refugees* (University of California Press, Berkeley, 1995), p. 214.

[23] For an introduction to international humanitarian law see Frits Kalshoven, *Constraints on the Waging of War* (International Committee of the Red Cross, Geneva, 1991), second edition; and Jean Pictet, *Development and Principles of International Humanitarian Law* (Martinus Nijhoff Publishers, Dordrecht, 1985).

of the Continent began with the second front in June 1944. These efforts were supplemented by those of relief agencies, notably UNRRA ... whose work, along with that of IGCR, form(ed) the immediate background to the establishment of IRO.

Large-scale refugee movements began with the Balkan wars of 1912–14, when tens of thousands of Greeks, Bulgars and Turks were driven from their homes. Millions more were displaced during the First World War. Many of these people, however, were repatriated after the war, and resettled as in earlier post-war periods. Civilian populations which had fled or were evacuated from the eastern fronts into Russia (estimated as 3 million by the spring of 1916) were able to return to their homes in states like Poland and the new Baltic countries. Peoples who had left the western front for Great Britain, France, and other places were able to return after the defeat of the enemy. Magyar refugees driven out of Rumania, Yugoslavia and Czechoslovakia found refuge and final settlement in Hungary, while about 600,000 persons of German extraction, who left Poland under pressure, were settled in Germany itself.

Other refugee movements that arose during the First World War and the post-war period were more difficult to handle however, and contributed to the political unrest and tensions in central and eastern Europe and the Near East in the inter-war period.

1. About 1.5 million Russian nationals were dispersed and left stranded mainly in north, central and southern Europe and in the Far East in the years 1918–22 as a result of the Bolshevik revolution of November 1917, the rout of the anti-Bolshevik armies in European Russia in 1919–20, the famine of 1921 and the breakdown of White Russian resistance in Siberian Russia in 1922.

2. By 1923 an estimated 320,000 Armenian refugees were scattered throughout the Near East, the Balkans and other European countries after they had fled from persecutions and massacres in Asia Minor following the collapse of the Ottoman Empire and the nationalistic policy adopted by Turkey.

3. Under the provisions of the Treaty of Lausanne of 1923, 1,300,000 Greeks were transferred from Asia Minor to Greece, while 400,000 Turks were moved from the Balkans to Turkey.

4. More than 220,000 Bulgars moved between 1913 and 1925 into the truncated territories of Bulgaria.

5. Thirty thousand Assyrian refugees, who had fought against the Turks, escaped after the Russian collapse in 1917 to the Caucasus, Greece and Iraq, and some later to Syria.

6. The ranks of refugees from the First World War and the inter-war period for whom a full solution had not yet been found were swelled by refugees from Greater Germany, following the establishment of the National Socialist regime in 1933. Three main waves,

encompassing 400,000 refugees, left Germany in consequence of this country's racial legislation, of the annexation of Austria, and the pogroms of November 1938.

7. Of the 450,000 Spanish refugees in France between 1938 and 1939, 140,000 remained in France after the end of the Civil War.

All these groups had more or less in common the fact that they did not leave their country of their own volition. They became uprooted and dis-possessed by wars and their aftermath, political changes and social up-heavals, massacres, persecutions and fear. They were no longer protected by their native governments and did not or could not return to their country of origin. . . .

In 1920 it became clear for the first time in history that international action was the only means which could solve the refugee problem inher-ited from the First World War. Collaboration among the governments concerned was needed to reconcile the often conflicting interests of the countries of first refuge and those of final reception. It was imperative to provide for an international authority which would co-ordinate the vari-ous efforts already undertaken for the material relief of the refugees, develop plans for enabling them to become self-supporting and help them to be repatriated to their country of origin or to resettle in overseas coun-tries. Another important function that could be carried out only by an international authority was to grant political and legal protection as long as the refugees had to live in a 'no man's land' between state jurisdictions.

By the end of 1920 some governments and voluntary philanthropic agencies could no longer cope with the refugee problem which had assumed vast dimensions. They appealed to some technical organs of the League of Nations to undertake the work which they found to be beyond their scope and capability. On 20 February 1921, the President of the International Red Cross Committee (IRCC), on behalf of a large number of voluntary organisations, approached the Council stating that the League of Nations was 'the only super-national authority capable of solving a problem which is beyond the power of exclusively humanitarian organ-isations'.

War and post-war experience had proved the greater effectiveness of co-ordinated efforts, especially in the repatriation of the prisoners of war from Siberia which had been carried out so successfully under the direc-tion of Dr. Fridtjof Nansen, who had acted as the High Commissioner for the League of Nations. In response to the appeal, the Council agreed to put its machinery at the disposal of the governments with the under-standing that it would take no responsibility for the organisation or financing or relief and that its work should be considered temporary. On the request of the Council, Dr. Nansen assumed the office of High Com-missioner for Russian Refugees on 1 September 1921. The League of

Nations also availed itself of the relief services of the High Commissioner to solve some emergency problems connected with the influx of Greek and Armenian refugees from Asia Minor into Constantinople (Istanbul) in 1921, and in 1923 to improve the situation of the Bulgarians who had been turned out of western Thrace. In September 1923 the Council also transferred the protection and care of the Armenian refugees to the High Commissioner and, four years later, the Assyrian, Assyro-Chaldean, Turkish (friends of Allies) and assimilated refugees.

During his period of office from 1921 to his death early in 1930, Dr. Nansen was constantly concerned with the question of the final disposition of the refugees either by repatriation, employment in the countries of refuge, or settlement in overseas countries.

From 1921 to 1924 the preparatory work for achieving final settlements was made. Since the High Commissioner was not provided by the League of Nations with a general authority or with financial resources except for limited administrative expenses, Dr. Nansen undertook first of all to organise machinery for co-ordinating the efforts which were being made for relief and settlement by the humanitarian organisations and national governments. He kept contact through his own representatives with the refugees, and consulted with the representatives of the interested governments in intergovernmental conferences and with the representatives of the private organisations which formed an advisory committee under his chairmanship. The office of the High Commissioner thus became a clearing house for information to fit the individual efforts into a general plan and to present it to the League of Nations. During this period the work concentrated mainly on immediate relief and care in order to mitigate the tremendous stress and need of the refugees. A census was carried out and the legal status was regulated so that refugees could be dispersed from congested areas and attempt to secure employment.

From 1921 to 1929 technical aspects of the work for refugees like employment, emigration and settlement were transferred to the International Labour Organisation (ILO) as they fell within the scope of its activity. The High Commissioner retained the responsibility for legal and political questions. By the middle of 1928 the number of unemployed refugees had been reduced from about 400,000 to approximately 200,000. The majority of these unemployed were neither agricultural workers nor equipped to accept industrial contracts. Therefore, at the request of the ILO, since the problem had reached another stage, the refugee administration was reconsidered in 1928. The process of assimilation and absorption of these groups in the country of residence was seen to be the main emphasis of the work and it was recognised that this would take a considerable period of time.

In view of the situation as it presented itself in 1929, Dr. Nansen believed that the work for refugees could be wound up in ten years under an organisation with a definite status and possibility of planning for that period. He suggested keeping the work under the League by incorporating it in the Secretariat, but this was not approved. Instead, the Assembly set up the Nansen International Office for Refugees, which was to wind up the refugee work and be liquidated by 31 December 1938. The post of High Commissioner was abolished. The supreme authority in the Office was exercised by a governing body of which the President was nominated by the League Assembly.[24] The League voted grants for administrative expenses on a scale progressively diminishing to the date of final liquidation.

After the Assembly had approved the division of services for refugees, only the humanitarian work was referred to the Nansen Office, while the Secretariat of the League of Nations retained the legal and political protection of the refugees which it had exercised during the interim period 1929–30. In practice the Nansen Office undertook all phases of the work. The fact that the League kept the function of legal and political protection was of great significance, however, when the termination of refugee services was discussed in 1937. The financing of the operational work of the Nansen Office came from the sale of Nansen stamps and from surcharged postage stamps sold in France and Norway, as well as from contributions by private organisations.

Four unforeseen problems arose during the Nansen Office's period of activity, and these made it impossible for it to carry out its original plans. The first was the economic depression which drastically affected the employment of Nansen refugees. Labour permits became increasingly difficult to secure, and refugees were forced to relinquish their positions in favour of nationals. Refugees were expelled from countries for having no means of support, and at the same time were refused entry permits into other states. Moreover, the capital of charitable organisations was affected and direct relief almost ceased. The second factor was the decline of the League's moral influence owing to the setbacks which the system of collective security suffered after 1931. This inevitably reacted on the measure of protection which the League could give to the refugees. Third, there had already been a tendency noticeable in the League which operated in favour of reducing League activities on behalf of refugees. The entrance of the Union of Soviet Socialist Republics into the League strengthened this sentiment, since the Russian representatives bent their efforts to restricting the work being done for Russian refugees. The last factor was the new refugee problem which arose in Germany.

The German National Socialist Government created an acute problem, which made necessary a changed approach to the refugee problem as a whole. The German refugee problem was first brought to the attention of

[24] The members of the Governing Body were to be appointed by the League, the ILO, and by private relief organisations. Refugees could become members.

the Council of the League of Nations in May and July 1933 in the form of a minority petition. At the ILO conference in June, Dutch, Belgian and French representatives pointed out that the influx of German refugees threatened to disturb the labour markets in their countries, and the conference decided that the ILO should study the means of settlement of refugees and submit resolutions to the League. The German refugee question was brought before the League Assembly by the Netherlands delegation in September 1933. Because of objections made by the German delegate to direct action by the League, a compromise was formulated and the High Commission for Refugees (Jewish and others) coming from Germany was set up as an autonomous organisation, created by the League, but responsible to its own Governing Body, not to the League Council. The funds for the settlement of refugees as well as those for the administration of the Commission were provided by private contributions.

This compromise made it even more difficult for the new High Commissioner, Mr. J.G. McDonald, an American, to solve the German refugee problem, especially since, because of the exclusion and persecution of 'non-Aryan' people and of political opponents, the number of German refugees increased continually. The administration was further complicated by the fact that in May 1935 the Council entrusted the protection of the Saar refugees to the Nansen Office. When he resigned in December 1935, Mr. McDonald pointed out that the work for refugees from Germany needed the authority of the League. In June 1935 the Norwegian Government suggested a centralised scheme under the League of Nations and an extension of assistance to all groups of refugees (Croats, Macedonians, Italians, Slovenes, Spaniards and Portuguese). Also, the voluntary organisations unanimously expressed their desire for a centralisation of the work under the League. On the other hand, some governments felt that this would lead to a delicate political situation in the League because it would strain the relations between the countries of origin and those of asylum for the refugees. Also financial considerations helped to influence the decisions of the members of the League to reject these suggestions.

The Assembly of the League of Nations set up a committee of experts to examine the problem of refugees under the mandate of the Nansen Office and under the High Commissioner for Refugees Coming from Germany. However, it was not empowered to consider the extension of the Nansen Office beyond 1939, and no additional funds of the League could be made available 'without explicit permission from the Assembly'.[25]

In February 1936 Sir Neill Malcolm was appointed by the Council as High Commissioner for Refugees from Germany. His position corresponded to that of Dr. Nansen as High Commissioner for Russian and Armenian Refugees. His mandate was extended in May 1938 to include

---

[25] League of Nations Doc. A. 64, 1935, XII.

the refugees coming from Austria. It not only included the tasks of his predecessor—to negotiate and direct the international collaboration necessary to solve the economic, financial and social problems of the refugees—but also entrusted him with their legal and political protection and the handling of their employment questions. He was a League official, obtained administrative expenses from the League to which he was responsible, and had the assistance of the Secretariat.

The work of the League of Nations for refugees was subsequently reorganised on the basis of resolutions adopted by the Assembly on 30 September 1938. The Nansen International Office for Refugees and the Office of the High Commissioner for Refugees Coming from Germany were replaced by a High Commissioner of the League of Nations who had his headquarters in London and who took over on 1 January 1939 the protection of all groups of refugees who had been under the two former organisations (about 600,000 persons). By Council decision of 17 January 1939 the Czechoslovak refugees coming from the Sudetenland were added to these refugees.

Sir Herbert Emerson, an Englishman, was chosen as High Commissioner for a period of five years. He was responsible for the legal protection of the refugees, the co-ordination of material assistance, and extension of aid to governments and private organisations in their endeavours for emigration and settlement. The great difficulties caused by the war crippled his activities, however, as did the virtual liquidation of the League of Nations.

At the end of 1946, the High Commissioner of the League of Nations transferred the duty of protection to the Intergovernmental Committee on Refugees (IGCR), which acted until the International Refugee Organisation (IRO) took over all responsibilities for refugees on 1 July 1947.

In studying the work of the League of Nations on behalf of refugees in the period from 1919 to 1939, it is clear that the handling of the refugee problem, although it was fundamentally a humanitarian one, was constantly complicated and often hamstrung by political, economic and social factors which demanded an international authority. Only the League of Nations, including among its members most of the countries affected and concerned with the refugee problem, could co-ordinate the efforts of governments and non-governmental organisations, negotiate with the countries of origin, and conciliate the divergent economic and social interests of different countries. It is also obvious that only an international authority could represent the moral conscience of mankind.

Certain facts about its efforts are particularly instructive. Each time the League put a new group under its guardianship the initiative came from individuals or private organisations or governments which believed in international collaboration and stood for the recognition and protection of human rights. Without the leadership of such humanitarians and statesmen as the Swiss Mr. Ador, the Norwegian Fridtjof Nansen, the

British Lord Rober Cecil, Gilber Murray and Philip Noel-Baker, the Belgian M. Hyman, to mention only a few, the interest and imagination of the League Council and the Assembly would not have been inspired nor world public opinion stirred to action.

The very fact furthermore that the League of Nations existed made it possible to use its facilities. When the terrible disaster of the Greeks and Armenians happened in the Autumn of 1921, in Asia Minor, general and quick aid was possible only because Dr. Nansen could appeal to the Assembly of the League of Nations, then in session in Geneva. The governments were more willing to accept his plan for help immediately since their actions were in the public eye.

Immediately after the First World War repatriation of most of the Russian refugees was generally looked upon as the proper solution. Nansen and the Czechoslovak Government tried to connect repatriation schemes with their plans for the economic reconstruction of Russia as an integral part of the European economic system. It became clear, however, that the political division was too serious to be bridged. Nansen secured only the repatriation of about 6,000 Cossacks, and his efforts in 1923 to reach a general arrangement with the Soviet Union for repatriation similar to the Balkan schemes were not successful. From that time, repatriation as a general solution had to be abandoned. Attempts to repatriate Spanish refugees from France, and also German refugees, again failed due to the fact that no agreement could be secured between the countries of origin and those of temporary refuge.

Thus were left only assimilation and integration in the country of refuge or, as an alternative, emigration and settlement in overseas countries. For the period before final settlement the League of Nations assumed the legal and political protection of the refugees, since these people had become stateless *de jure* or *de facto* by the negation of protection and withdrawal of citizenship rights by their countries of origin. The experience of the League's work for refugees indicated the importance of securing an adequate legal status for refugees as a basis for all other efforts which are made on their behalf. However, the League of Nations was able neither to develop large-scale migration or colonisation schemes nor to influence the policies of the countries of origin. This made necessary intergovernmental action outside the League....

It remains to sum up the achievements and limitations of the League's work for refugees. In the first place, the League accepted the responsibility only for certain groups. It provided machinery outside its own administration and only on a temporary basis. It accepted limited and specific tasks for the sole purpose of aiding these uprooted and homeless people in their transition from a refugee status to a new national status, that is to say, of dealing with the problem in such a way that it could be brought to a final settlement on the national level by the governments of final residence.

Since the refugee administration was not vested with real authority nor furnished with the necessary operational means, it served mainly as a co-ordinating and stimulating agency both for short-range or temporary functions such as care, maintenance, health and other social welfare, and for long-range plans for final solutions like repatriation, emigration and integration. The operational tasks were predominantly carried out by private and voluntary agencies which were served by a large group of dedicated people much experienced in relief and social welfare work.

At the same time, the amount and extent of the work accomplished through the international co-operation of governments and voluntary organisations under the guidance of the League of Nations and the use of its machinery was very considerable. Many uprooted people were saved from starvation through its efforts and helped to find a new homeland in which to settle. The work also helped to release tensions in trouble spots which otherwise might have led to more incidents endangering peace. It was, in effect, the first truly functional approach in peace-time to 'promote international co-operation'.

Intergovernmental Organisation for Refugees, 1938–47

The intergovernmental efforts on behalf of refugees, which were at first supplementary to, and then virtually superseded those of the League of Nations, arose out of the tragic impasse of tens of thousands of victims of Nazi intolerance who could find no permanent asylum because of the impact of economic depression both on the countries of temporary refuge and those overseas. This situation led President Roosevelt to call a conference in July 1938, held at Evian-les-Bains in France, to consider what steps could be taken to facilitate the settlement in other countries of refugees from Germany (including Austria). This conference considered the problem of persons 'who desired to leave Germany, as well as those who had already done so',[26] thus introducing the new conception of a planned migration. 'It is essential', stated the delegates, 'that a long-range program should be envisaged, whereby assistance to involuntary emigrants, actual and potential, may be co-ordinated within the framework of existing migration laws and practices of Governments'.[27]

To undertake this comprehensive programme, the Evian conference established a permanent Intergovernmental Committee on Refugees (IGCR). The first Director, Mr. George Rublee, an American, was appointed by the Committee at its first meeting in August 1938; he was succeeded in February 1939 by Sir Herbert Emerson who combined this office with that of High Commissioner under the League of Nations. The work of the Director was threefold in character: to negotiate with Germany to

---

[26] For the full text see Eric Estorick, 'The Evian Conference and the Intergovernmental Committee', *The Annals* (Philadelphia, May 1939), pp. 136–41.
[27] Ibid., p. 138.

improve the conditions of exodus so that they would facilitate orderly emigration; to attempt to develop opportunities for permanent settlement through negotiations with the governments of countries of refuge and settlement; and to undertake migration studies in co-operation with existing refugee services of the League of Nations and the ILO.

The efforts of the Director were mainly diplomatic in character since his tasks were more difficult to perform. The countries of temporary refuge, like France, had virtually exhausted their resources in extending hospitality, while the British felt that for economic and social reasons they could extend political asylum only within narrow limits. Overseas countries were similarly reluctant for economic, social and political reasons to welcome large groups of immigrants, most of whom were Jewish. Above all, the negotiations with the German Government proved highly precarious, and had few, if any, conclusive results. German aggression in September 1939, in any case, brought the efforts at negotiation to an abrupt end.

A further difficulty was that during the period from 1938 to 1943 the funds of the IGCR, obtained through contributions from member governments, were used exclusively for administrative expenses. There were no operational expenditures for direct assistance to refugees at the disposal of the Committee. Thus, the maintenance and assistance of refugees had to be provided by Jewish and other private organisations, by friends and relatives, or by funds granted by individual or group guarantors.

The greatest problems were presented naturally by wartime conditions. All Allied efforts were directed towards stemming the onslaught of the Nazi aggression. At the same time, as the German army advanced, and Nazi rule expanded over western and eastern Europe, the number of refugees increased vastly.

Early in 1943 the British and American governments made another attempt to expand refugee aid on the international level. Public opinion in both countries was horrified at the systematic persecution of the Jewish populations in Nazi-occupied countries. After an exchange of notes and consultations, an Anglo-American conference was held at Bermuda from 19 to 29 April 1943. The two governments declared their readiness 'to investigate all possibilities for refugee havens, to give financial aid to any country caring for refugees, and to use available shipping facilities for the use of refugees'. Maintaining that they would 'aid war refugees of any race or creed wherever such measures did not interfere with war operations', they recommended a broadening of the activities of IGCR.

At an executive meeting of IGCR in August 1943, its mandate, which had previously referred only to refugees from Germany and Austria and the Sudeten area, was widened 'so as to include, as far as practicable also those persons, wherever they may be, who, as a result of events in Europe, have had to leave, or may have to leave, their countries of residence because of the danger to their lives or liberties on account of their race, religion or political beliefs'. Its functions were extended from the purely diplomatic one of co-ordinating the efforts of governments to an operational task, namely, 'to preserve, maintain and transport' persons coming within its mandate, 'so far as this may be necessary and desirable'.[28] Thus the IGCR now had responsibility for the legal protection, maintenance and resettlement of refugees.

The Committee was enlarged to thirty-six members, and the administrative budget increased.[29] Though public opinion was disappointed that the conference had not been able to produce 'concrete results', the British and American governments did what they could, underwriting in equal shares the operational expenditures of IGCR which gradually increased from that time on.

This was a departure from practices under the League, when governments expected private agencies to finance the humanitarian work for refugees. The governments now stepped in with public funds, since the means of private organisations had become utterly exhausted.

Further, the Committee made every endeavour to co-ordinate its activities with those of the High Commission of the League of Nations, the ILO, and later with the War Refugee Board of the US and UNRRA. Though no Allied agency could stop the development of the Jewish tragedy, the IGCR, by its support of Jewish benevolent societies in neutral countries and assisting underground movements especially in France, Hungary, Italy and Rumania, managed to bring some thousands to safety. Others escaping across the Pyrenees were helped by Allied agencies through Spain to North Africa.

As parts of Europe were liberated from 1944 on, the Committee appointed representatives to assist in those countries; Belgium, France, Italy, Portugal, Spain and the Middle East being the main areas of work. In addition to providing material assistance, mainly by subsidising the relief programmes of voluntary agencies, the IGCR arranged and paid for the migration of thousands of refugees and protected the interests of persons who did not enjoy, in law or in fact, the protection of a home government. This protection was both formal and informal; it included, from 1945 onwards, the protection of Spanish Republican refugees as well as the initiative and arrangements for the conclusion, in October 1946, of an intergovernmental agreement on the issue of travel documents for refugees. . . .

Inter-allied Military and Civilian Work for Displaced Persons and Refugees, 1943–47

The background to the more comprehensive approach to refugees and displaced persons was the magnitude of the problem, for the Second

---

[28] See Rules for the Constitution and Procedure of the IGCR, Article 2, in Louise W. Holborn, *War and Peace Aims of the United Nations* (Boston, 1948), Vol. 2, pp. 151f.

[29] The Soviet Union, Czechoslovakia, Egypt, Greece, Iceland, India, Luxembourg, Poland and the Union of South Africa became additional members. IGCR, Fourth Session of the Committee held in London, 15–17 August 1944.

World War caused the most formidable displacements of population ever experienced. At its outbreak, there had been more than a million refugees in various parts of Europe and Asia. This number was swelled almost beyond calculation by mass movements which brought vast human misery and suffering in their wake.

In Europe, the principal displacements were those of Germans within Greater Germany. These were caused by various factors: the transfer of ethnic Germans into Germany, mainly from the eastern European countries; the dispersal of industry within Germany; the bombing of urban centres; and the dislocations of the German population during the rout of the Nazi armies. By early 1945 the total figure was estimated at from 21 to 30 million. In addition there were in Germany more than 8.5 million nationals of other European countries including civilians and prisoners of war. Both groups were forced to join the ranks of labourers.

Beyond these groups were about 20 million non-German displaced persons partly the result of mass expulsions from the defeated countries, partly of population transfers and exchanges agreed upon by treaties, and partly of the systematic deportation and persecution of non-German Jews. Many of the latter group were dispersed as far as India, Africa and the Western Hemisphere. In Asia, about 20 million Chinese were uprooted, and at the end of the war there were some 12 million refugees and displaced persons in Japan, of whom 2 million were Koreans....

Consultations between the Allied governments between May and October 1943 led to the decision to put relief and rehabilitation on a UN basis to provide an international approach to what was seen to be an issue intimately associated with the establishment of eventual peace. On 9 November 1943, an Agreement Creating the United Nations Relief and Rehabilitation Administration (UNRRA) was signed at the White House in Washington by representatives of forty-four United Nations. The purpose of this newly established organisation was 'to plan and administer a relief programme supplementary to that of the Allied Military Forces', and to make 'preparations and arrangements ... for the return of prisoners and exiles to their homes'.[30]

At its First Session, immediately following the signing of the Agreement, the General Council, UNRRA's policy-making organ, also considered the role which UNRRA would have to assume in regard to displaced persons. On the basis of the Report of the Sub-committee on Policies with Respect to Assistance to Displaced Persons, it agreed that the Administration should help to care for and repatriate certain categories of displaced people with the agreement of the governments concerned and the military authorities.

Two studies on the nature and scope of the dislocation of people provided basic data for defining the eligibility of displaced persons for UNRRA

---

[30] George Woodbridge, *UNRRA: The History of the United Nations Relief and Rehabilitation Administration* (New York, 1950), pp. iii, 23, 31–33.

assistance. One of these studies, *The Statistical Statement on the Problems of Displaced Persons*, prepared under the auspices of the Leith-Ross Committee in London and finished in October 1943, estimated there would be about 22 million displaced persons not including 6 million Germans who had been moved from Western Germany. The other survey prepared by the ILO and published in 1943 in Montreal, Canada, dealt with the whole problem of the *Displacement of Populations in Europe*. This study estimated there would be 30 million displaced persons.

According to the classification in the latter study, the displaced persons fell into four broad categories which in practice were difficult to keep separate. The first group comprised the war refugees, i.e., the civilian victims of modern total war, the prisoners of war and the civilian internees. The second group, the result of ideological policies or divisions, were the refugees who for political, religious or racial reasons were stateless, in law or in fact, and thus were a responsibility of IGCR. In the third place were the labourers from both western and eastern Europe drawn into Germany by persuasion or force. Lastly were the Germans, both those who had been settled on occupied or annexed territory, and those 'called home' from the Baltic countries, eastern Poland and from some of the Balkan states.

With the exception of prisoners of war, who would be taken care of by the military authorities, and persons of enemy or ex-enemy nationality 'intruded into' the territories of member governments, all these groups were declared eligible for UNRRA aid under the definition adopted by the General Council. The latter also accepted a working scheme of ten specific duties to guide the work of the Administration.

This plan was not implemented under UNRRA's jurisdiction and control, however, as the military authorities carried out the repatriation of almost all UN displaced persons. Not until later did UNRRA assume the care of displaced persons, mostly in enemy territory, 'who did not wish to return or did not wish immediately to do so'.

B. John George Stoessinger, *The Refugee and the World Community* (The University of Minnesota Press, Minneapolis, 1956), pp. 197–200.

Every parting is a foretaste of death but every coming together is a glimpse of the resurrection.

Schopenhauer

Since the inception of the League of Nations, governments have consistently attempted to deal with the refugee problem, though, as a rule, within rather narrowly defined limits of time and space. Parading through the annals of international organisation is an uninterrupted procession of temporary agencies, each established to solve what is essentially a long-range problem. Not only have all these agencies been limited in time, but each has had jurisdiction over only specific parts of the world's refugee population. Although very diversified in international apparatus, international organisations dealing with refugees have remained essentially within this pattern and differences among them have been in degree rather than kind.

In addition to the spatial and temporal limitations, there has also been among the refugee agencies a rather clear-cut division of labour regarding the various aspects of refugee work. With one exception, the International Refugee Organisation, each agency has exercised responsibility in only one major activity. Thus, the Nansen Office concentrated mainly on matters of legal protection similar to the function of the present United Nations High Commissioner's Office for Refugees. UNRRA's responsibility has been primarily relief and repatriation, while the Inter-Governmental Committee for Refugees has been interested mainly in the exploration of resettlement opportunities. Only the International Refugee Organisation, while also limited like the other agencies in time and space, has combined all the above activities under one roof and treated the refugee problem in totality.

In view of such a division of labour, it is not surprising that the problem of coordination has always loomed large in the work of refugee agencies on the international scene. Generally, the relationships of the various organizations to their parent bodies, whether the League of Nations, as in the case of the Nansen Office, or the United Nations, as in the case of the International Refugee Organisation, have been rather tenuous and in practice have tended toward even greater decentralisation of efforts. Some agencies, like the Inter-Governmental Committee for European Migration [ICEM], have been dissociated completely from the world organisation. Coordination among the diverse international refugee organs has been sporadic and lacking in institutional basis.

Instances of duplication and overlapping resulting from such a decentralised approach have detracted markedly from operational and administrative efficiency. The lack of coordination among the Nansen Office, the Inter-Governmental Committee for Refugees, and the International Labour Office was partly to blame for the failure of international organisation to use its resources to the fullest during the League period.... In contrast, the International Refugee Organisation which, for a time at least, was the sole agency dealing with the refugee problem internationally by coordinating all intergovernmental activities on behalf of displaced persons attained a remarkable degree of efficiency.

This integrated approach by IRO probably accounts in part for the comparatively greater bargaining power with refugee-receiving states which the Organisation possessed, and neither prestige nor funds were dispersed in many different directions....

Intimately connected with the problem of coordinating international refugee agencies is the necessity for international organisations to co-ordinate their policies with those of national governments. In this con-nection, the problem of national leadership has recently come into focus. While during the League period no one state occupied the limelight in refugee work, this picture has changed significantly since World War II. International refugee activity under the League was dominated by an individual, Fridtjof Nansen, but in the United Nations this role has ac-crued to a national state, the United States.

This development has given rise to some weighty implications. While in the League there was no single arbiter of the refugees' fate among the member states, all post-World War II international refugee agencies have, in fact, been the creatures of the United States. The United States, by footing by far the largest part of the bill, has enjoyed a veto power over their life and death. The success of the International Refugee Organisa-tion would have been impossible without American leadership and, con-versely, the hardships of the United Nations High Commissioner's Office are, in large part, due to American reluctance to grant support.

An important corollary of this development has been the direct influ-ence which domestic political considerations have had upon international refugee work. Thus, the fortuitous circumstance whereby the majority of postwar displaced persons were concentrated in the United States zones of Germany and Austria prompted the American Senate to ratify the IRO Constitution and by this act breathe life into the Organisation. Also, in 1947, the Congress was still in favour of a United Nations organ includ-ing Communist representatives. On the other hand, by 1950, the mood of the Congress had changed to such an extent that it would not permit the creation of an international refugee organ on whose policy-making body representatives from the Iron Curtain countries would have a voice. The conviction that the Soviet and its satellites should not be included in any refugee organisation, coupled with the unexamined yet widely prev-alent assumption that a United Nations organ would *ipso facto* be ineffi-cient, prompted the Congress to insist upon ICEM's establishment outside the United Nations framework and persuaded it to withhold all financial support from the United Nations High Commissioner's Office.

The one permanent factor on the scene has been the work of the vol-untary agencies. For this reason, coordination among them and the gov-ernmental organs has been playing a very important part and is steadily gaining in significance. The most fruitful of such relationships was that during IRO's operation, when more than a hundred voluntary agencies were trained not only to perform complementary functions, but to assume primary responsibilities, as exemplified in the migration movements to Israel and in the securing of assurances basic to the administration of the

United States Displaced Persons Act. To a considerable extent, these voluntary agencies are ... shouldering the operational burden of international refugee work.

In sum, it may be said that the unified and integrated approach of IRO resulted in a more efficient and more economical attack upon the refugee problem than the decentralised approaches of both the League and the post-IRO periods. ...

C. Kim Salomon, 'The Cold War Heritage: UNRRA and the IRO as Predecessors of UNHCR', in Goran Rystad, ed., *The Uprooted* (Lund University Press, Lund, 1990), pp. 175–76.

The international attempts to resolve the refugee situation born out of World War II followed the pattern set in the inter-war period, with short-term measures aimed at solving an emergency situation. The refugee problem was seen as a direct result of the war, and the immediate response was a call for repatriation. At a very early stage, however, it became clear to the Western nations that the refugee problem must be judged in the light of the political changes that were taking place in Eastern Europe during, and immediately after, the war. A large number of the DPs [displaced persons] who remained in the camps a year after the end of the war were there as refugees, not from the war but from Communism and the Soviet Union. What was originally seen as the refugee problem of World War II turned out to be a refugee problem of a much wider, political nature. The Eastern bloc nations with the Soviet Union in the vanguard refused to accept the political implications of the refugee problem and insisted on continued repatriation, regardless of the wishes of the DPs themselves. In order to bypass the resulting stalemate, the IRO was founded by the Western nations as a venue for a mutual refugee policy.

Even if the Western powers maintained their support of repatriation in formal terms, the situation became problematic in practice. The military authorities of the Western occupied zones did not turn out to be particularly interested in the repatriation programme. In fact, the military were actively engaged in blocking this programme, a policy which seems to have been sanctioned by the American and British governments. The reasons for this are varied. For one example, in the propaganda war against Communism, the refugee situation provided an excellent opportunity to show that the people did not want to live in the East. Furthermore, there was a great interest, not least in the United Kingdom, in recruiting cheap labour among the refugees, an interest which was obviously incompatible with an active repatriation policy. ...

With the creation of the IRO, the refugee programme was expanded to include, not only World War II DPs, but also political refugees from the Soviet Union and other Communist states. The international refugee relief effort thereby acquired a more general character. It remained IRO policy to treat the refugee problem as a product of the war, however, making it difficult for new refugee categories to qualify for international aid except on a strict case-by-case basis. Following the influx of Czech refugees in 1948, however, a more liberal refugee policy began to make headway in the United States and the United Kingdom, and consequently also in the IRO.

The IRO's response to the Czech refugee movement was the first indication that the Western nations had begun to regard the refugee problem as a permanent issue. Another indication was the increasingly liberal interpretation of eligibility criteria in the case of Baltic and Ukrainian DPs. The Western powers felt a moral and political responsibility to receive refugees from Eastern Europe. The United States and the Western European nations differed somewhat on how future aid programmes could best be organised. The Western European nations pushed for a relief organisation within the United Nations structure, while the United States preferred setting up an organisation of its own. Even so, both sides shared the same goals of, on the one hand, assisting those war-time refugees still remaining in the DP camps, and, on the other hand, receiving the new refugee categories from Eastern Europe. The structuring of the UNHCR and the formulation of the UN Convention on Refugees should both be seen in the light of these common goals.

Even if the Western powers had recognised the refugee problem as being a permanent one by the late forties, they still preferred to regard it as European—not a global one. The UNHCR was primarily stuck with the task of dealing with European refugees. Nevertheless, leading Western governments were aware of the global character of the problem. At an informal meeting with the American UN delegation, held before the UN vote on the UNHCR charter, the leader of the Pakistani delegation explained why his nation would not vote in favour of the charter. Since in 1949 Pakistan had on its soil some 7 million Muslims who had fled India, the delegate wanted to know why such international relief measures as were taken under the United Nations' auspices should not also be available to his country. The response of the American delegation was that the United States neither wanted to solve nor was capable of solving the whole world's refugee problems.

... The relief effort was sponsored and dominated by the Western powers and exclusively geared at assisting refugees from Eastern Europe. There appears to have been no interest in offering any assistance to the refugees movement originating in the Third World. It was not until several years later that the international community began to address this issue.

II. UNHCR: STRUCTURE, MANDATE AND FUNCTIONS

A. Guy S. Goodwin-Gill, *The Refugee in International Law* (Clarendon Press, Oxford, 1983), pp. 129–36.

The Office of The United Nations High Commissioner for Refugees (UNHCR)

At its 1950 session, the General Assembly formally adopted the Statute of UNHCR as an annexe to Resolution 428 (V), in which it also called upon governments to co-operate with the Office. The functions of UNHCR encompass 'providing international protection' and 'seeking permanent solutions' to the problems of refugees by way of voluntary repatriation or assimilation in new national communities. The Statute expressly provides that 'the work of the High Commissioner shall be of an entirely non-political character; it shall be humanitarian and social and shall relate, as a rule, to groups and categories of refugees.' Of the two functions, the provisions of international protection is of primary importance, for without protection, such as intervention by the Office to secure admission of refugees, there can be no possibility of finding lasting solutions. Besides defining refugees the UNHCR Statute prescribes the relationship of the High Commissioner with the General Assembly and the Economic and Social Council (ECOSOC), makes provision for organisation and finance, and identifies ways in which the High Commissioner is to provide for protection. These develop the functions engaged in by predecessor organisations and include: (*i*) promoting the conclusion of international conventions for the protection of refugees, supervising their application and proposing amendments thereto; (*ii*) promoting through special agreements with governments the execution of any measures calculated to improve the situation of refugees and to reduce the number requiring protection; and (*iii*) promoting the admission of refugees.[31]

Notwithstanding the statutory injunction that the work of the Office shall relate, as a rule, to groups and categories of refugees, a major part of UNHCR's protection work is concerned with individual cases, as was that of its predecessor organisations. No state has objected to UNHCR taking up individual cases as such, although states may, and do, question whether an individual is indeed a refugee. Nevertheless, the individual

---

[31] In addition to the declared functions, the UNHCR's indirect or promotional activities encompass the enforcement of national laws and regulations benefiting refugees, the development and adoption of appropriate national laws, regulations and procedures, promotion of accession to international instruments, and the development of new legal instruments. Latterly, the Executive Committee has also included with approval the dissemination of refugee law in the list of activities; see, for example, UN Doc.A/AC.96/588, para. 48(1)(k), report of the 31st Session of the Executive Committee, 1980.

dimension to the protection function is a natural corollary to the declared task of supervising the application of international conventions. Such instruments define refugees in essentially individualistic terms and provide rights on behalf of refugees which can only be understood in the sense of the particular. The acquiescence of states in the individual protection function of UNHCR, however, significantly delineates both the competence of the Office and the status of the individual refugee in international law.

Relation of UNHCR to the General Assembly and its Standing in General International Law

UNHCR was established by the General Assembly as a subsidiary organ under Article 22 of the UN Charter, and the parent body has continued to play an active role in expanding the mandate of the Office. The relationship of the two organisations is clarified in the Statute, which declares that UNHCR acts 'under the authority of the General Assembly', that it shall 'follow policy directives given by [that body] or the Economic and Social Council', and that it 'shall engage in such additional activities, including repatriation and resettlement, as the General Assembly may determine'. The High Commissioner is further required to report annually to the General Assembly, through the Economic and Social Council, and the report is to be considered as a separate item on the agenda of the former. Finally, the Statute calls upon the High Commissioner, particularly where difficulties arise, to request the opinion of the advisory committee on refugees, if it is created. Such a committee was first established in 1951,[32] and replaced four years later by the UN Refugee Fund Executive Committee,[33] whose functions included supervision of material assistance programmes financed by the fund. The General Assembly called for its replacement in turn by the Executive Committee of the High Commissioner's Programme, which was set up by the Economic and Social Council in 1958.[34] Originally made of twenty-four states, it has been progressively enlarged....[35] The Committee's terms of reference include advising the High Commissioner, on request, in the exercise of the Office's statutory functions; and advising on the appropriateness of providing international assistance through the Office in order to solve any specific refugee problems. In 1975, the Executive Committee decided to

[32] ECOSOC Res. 393B (XIII), 10 September 1951.
[33] ECOSOC Res. 565 (XIX), 31 March 1955, further to GA Res. 832 (IX), 21 October 1954.
[34] GA Res. 1166 (XII), 26 November 1957, and ECOSOC Res. 672 (XXV), 30 April 1958.
[35] Its present membership is 56 states. India became a member of the Executive Committee in 1995.

set up a Subcommittee of the Whole on International Protection,[36] which makes a continuing contribution to the development and strengthening of refugee law.

Each of the above elements involves the participation of states, at varying levels, in the international institutions protecting refugees. The practice of such organisations is relevant in assessing the standing both of UNHCR and of the rules benefitting refugees in general international law. An international organisation such as UNHCR is not only a forum in which the views of states may be represented; it is also, as a subject of international law, an actor in the relevant field whose actions count in the process of law formation. Specific authority to involve itself in the protection of refugees has been accorded to the Office by states parties to the 1951 Convention and/or the 1967 Protocol relating to the Status of Refugees. Article 35 of the Convention, for example, provides: 'The contracting States undertake to co-operate with the Office of the United Nations High Commissioner for Refugees ... in the exercise of its functions, and shall in particular facilitate its duty of supervising the application of the provisions of this Convention.' The 1969 OAU Convention requires member states to co-operate similarly, while declaring itself to be the 'effective regional complement in Africa' of the 1951 Convention. UNHCR, however, is not itself a party to those instruments, and its standing must be located in more general principles.

Clearly, by derivation and intention, UNHCR does enjoy international personality. As a subsidiary organ of the General Assembly, its 'personality' (its capacity to possess international rights and duties) can be traced to the United Nations at large.[37] Moreover, its Statute shows that the Office was intended by the General Assembly to act on the international plane.[38] Its standing in regard to protection has been further reinforced by successive General Assembly resolutions urging all states to support the High Commissioner's activities, for example, by granting asylum, observing the principle of *non-refoulement* and acceding to the relevant international treaties. While it is trite knowledge that General Assembly resolutions are not legally binding, 'it is another thing', as Judge Lauterpacht noted in the *Voting Procedure* case, 'to give currency to the view that they have no force at all, whether legal or other, and that therefore they cannot be regarded as forming in any sense part of a legal system of supervision.'[39]

---

[36] Report of the Executive Committee, 26th Session, 1975, UN Doc. A/AC.96/521, para. 69 (h).

[37] See generally, *Reparations* case, ICJ Reports (1949), pp. 178–79 at p. 174.

[38] For example, the Statute refers to the High Commissioner supervising the application of international conventions, promoting certain measures through special agreements with governments, and consulting governments on the need to appoint local representatives: paras 8 (a), (b), 16.

[39] See generally, *South West Africa, Voting Procedure*, advisory opinion, ICJ Rep. (1955), 67, at pp. 120–22 (separate opinion of Judge Lauterpacht). Judge Lauterpacht noted (at

On this occasion, the 'legal system of supervision' was the mandate in respect of South West Africa. In his separate opinion, Judge Lauterpacht noted that, while the mandatory had the right not to accept a recommendation of the supervising body, it was nevertheless bound to give it due consideration in good faith, which in turn entailed giving reasons for non-acceptance.

Admittedly, General Assembly resolutions with regard to refugees and to UNHCR do not have the same degree of particularity as a recommendation relating to the administration of a mandate. Nevertheless, against the background of the UN Charter and general international law, UNHCR, with its principal function of providing 'international protection' to refugees, can be seen to occupy the central role in an analogous legal system of supervision. Indeed, though discretions continue to favour states in certain of their dealings with refugees, the peremptory character of the principle of *non-refoulement* clearly puts it in a higher class than the 'intangible and almost nominal' obligation to consider in good faith a recommendation of a supervisory body, such as Judge Lauterpacht discerned in the *Voting Procedure* case.[40] The entitlement of UNHCR to exercise protection on the basis of a universal jurisdiction receives additional support from the decision of the International Court of Justice in the *Reparations* case. There the Court read into the rights and duties of the United Nations Organisation, as a 'necessary intendment', the capacity to exercise a measure of functional protection on behalf of its agents.[41] UNHCR, moreover, is *expressly* ascribed the function of providing international protection to refugees; state practice reflects 'recognition or acquiescence in the assumption of such jurisdiction universally, and without regard to any requirement of treaty ratification'. The 'effective discharge'[42] of this function evidently requires capacity to assert claims on behalf of individuals falling within the competence of the Office.

Given states obligations with regard to refugees, the question must yet be considered, to whom are they owed? The individual is still not considered to be a subject of international law, capable of enforcing his or her rights on the international plane, while the problems faced by refugees are not such as would prompt the exercise of the right of diplomatic protection on the part of the state of nationality. In the case of states parties to the 1951 Convention and the 1967 Protocol, the existence of obligations *inter se* is established. Both instruments expressly provide for the settlement of disputes relating to their interpretation or application, and

---

p. 122) that General Assembly Resolutions are 'one of the principal instrumentalities of the formation of the collective will and judgement of the community of nations represented by the United Nations'.

[40] *Voting Procedure* case, ICJ Rep. (1955), 67, at p. 119.
[41] *Reparations* case, ICJ Rep. (1949), 174, at p. 184.
[42] *Reparations* case, ICJ Rep. (1949), 174, at p. 180.

for reference to the International Court of Justice at the request of any of the parties to the dispute, should other means of settlement fail.[43] No litigation has resulted, and, in the absence of injury to an individual related to a claimant state by the link of nationality, the results of any such litigation are likely to be without practical consequence.[44] There are precedents, however, by which states may yet have legal interests in matters other than those which affect directly their material interests.[45]

Under Article 24 of the European Convention on Human Rights, for example, any contracting state may refer to the European Commission an alleged breach of the Convention by another party. The instrument itself thus provides for a 'European public order', a regime in which all states parties have a sufficient interest in the observance of the European Convention's provisions to allow for the assertion of claims. While there are similarities in the objectives of the European Convention and the refugee conventions—both call for certain standards of treatment to be accorded to certain groups of persons—the refugee convention lack effective investigation, adjudication, and enforcement procedures; they can hardly be considered to offer the same opportunity for judicial or quasi-judicial solutions. None the less, in view of the importance of the rights involved, it may be argued that all states have an interest in their protection;[46] and that UNHCR, by express agreement of some states and by the acquiescence of others, is the qualified representative of the 'international public order' in such matters. A cogent theory of responsibility remains to be developed to cover this situation, and the legal consequences that may flow from a breach of the international obligations in question are as yet unclear. International claims can take the form of protest, a call for an inquiry, negotiation or a request for submission to arbitration or to the International Court of Justice. Both the nature of breaches of obligation affecting refugees and the nature of the protecting organisation rule out certain types of claims, such as arbitration, while strictly legal considerations exclude, for example, recourse to the International Court of Justice. Currently, the simple existence of obligations owed at large may provide sufficient justification, not just for 'expressions of international concern', but also for formal protest on the part of

---

[43] 1951 Convention, Art. 38; 1967 Protocol, Art. IV. Under the Protocol, but not under the Convention, states are entitled to make reservations to the Article on settlement of disputes.

[44] See *Northern Cameroons* case, *Preliminary Objections*, ICJ Rep. (1963), 15, at pp. 34–35.

[45] See *South West Africa* cases, *Preliminary Objections*, ICJ Rep. (1962), 319, at pp. 424–33 (separate opinion of Judge Jessup). But cf. *South West Africa* cases, *Second Phase*, ICJ Rep. (1966), 6 at pp. 32–33, 47 (holding that individual states do not have a legal right to require the performance of South Africa's mandate over South West Africa).

[46] *Barcelona Traction* case, ICJ Rep. (1970), 3 at p. 32. See also 1967 Declaration on Territorial Asylum, Art. 2(1).

UNHCR. The significance of this development for individual's standing in general international law should not be underestimated.

B. Sadruddin Aga Khan, Lectures on Legal Problems Relating to Refugees and Displaced Persons delivered at The Hague Academy of International Law, 4–6 August 1976, pp. 44–50.

... In order to enable the High Commissioner's Office to continue to discharge its humanitarian mission fully, as Governments wished, the criteria for intervention by the Office have had to be modified in keeping with changing requirements. What we now intend to examine is the way in which those criteria have been altered and the outcome, in terms of law, of a process of evolution which has enabled it gradually to adapt its activities to the demands of the moment.

Competence Rationae Personae: Its Expansion and the Gradual Return to Unity of Competence

The general definition of the term 'refugee' contained in the Statute reflects the strictly individualistic thinking which prevailed at the time it was drafted: claiming personally to be the victim of persecution, which he is required to prove, each refugee must be screened in order to be eligible for assistance under the High Commissioner's mandate and the 1951 Convention. The ensuing decision governs first and foremost his entitlement to the right of asylum and also, in principle, the right of the High Commissioner's Office to intervene on his behalf. Strictly interpreted, this concept could be considered to exclude from the High Commissioner's mandate refugees or groups or refugees whose circumstances made it impossible to verify their eligibility individually. This exclusion, which would have meant a denial of justice to these groups, was certainly not desired, not even specifically envisaged by the Assembly; it was the unwitting result of a concept of 'refugee' inspired by the specific circumstances, and was certainly not linked to a deliberate will to prohibit the High Commissioner from collective action for the benefit of these groups. A prohibition of this kind would, moreover, have been at variance with the rule contained in article 2 of the Statute, whereby his work 'shall relate, as a rule, to groups and categories of refugees'. Short of amending the definition of the term 'refugee', which was certainly not in anyone's mind, the problem was therefore that of unravelling the juridical entanglement—a task which the Assembly alone, as the sole legislative body of the United Nations, could undertake.

First Stage—Refugees Not within the Competence of the United Nations: Use of Good Offices by the High Commissioner

In 1959 came the first step towards this goal: in General Assembly resolution 1388 (XIV) of 20 November 1959, a distinction was drawn for the first time between refugees within the mandate and 'refugees who do not come within the competence of the United Nations', in respect of whom the High Commissioner was authorised to use his good offices in the transmission of contributions designed to assist them. General Assembly resolution 1167 (XII) of 26 November 1957 had already mentioned the High commissioner's good offices as regards the Chinese refugees in Hong Kong. There, however, the action of the High Commissioner's Office had been strictly confined to a specific group, and had also been of clearly limited scope. Passing from the particular to the general, the 1959 resolution thus extended the use of the good offices, transforming their application into supplementary means of action whereby the High Commissioner could henceforth transmit contributions on behalf of any group of refugees not 'within the competence of the United Nations'.

The 1959 resolution does not say why such refugees were excluded from the General Assembly's original mandate to the High Commissioner's Office. On the occasion of the sudden and massive exodus of some 200,000 Hungarians in 1956, for whom no individual eligibility procedure was feasible, at least not immediately, the question whether or to what extent the High Commissioner's Office was competent to intervene had in fact arisen. The removal of the legal and institutional barrier to his action was accomplished by General Assembly resolutions expressly requesting the High Commissioner to intervene.

A similar difficulty confronted the General Assembly and the High Commissioner's Office when the Assembly invited the High Commissioner to intervene for the first time in Africa; this too was resolved by an express decision of the General Assembly. The general circumstances of developing countries and the total absence of the requisite administrative structures excluded, even more clearly than in the case of the Hungarians, any possibility of instituting a procedure for determining the individual eligibility of the 180,000 or so Algerians who had taken refuge in Tunisia and Morocco during Algeria's struggle for independence. Also the need for such a procedure was all the less apparent as the refugees in question were already benefitting from a right of asylum which had been granted to them *en masse* and which no one had any intention of disputing. What they did need, however, was large-scale assistance in the form of food, clothing, shelter and so on.

Second Stage: Expanded Use of the High Commissioner's Good Offices

In 1961, a new expression appeared in both the general resolution for that year and the resolution concerning the Angolan refugees. It reiterated in broader terms the notion of the High Commissioner's good offices. There is no longer any mention of 'refugees who do not come within the competence of the United Nations', nor is the use of good offices confined to the transmission of contributions. Hence resolution

1673 (XVI) of 18 December 1961 requested 'the United Nations High Commissioner for Refugees to pursue his activities on behalf of the refugees within his mandate or those for whom he extends his good offices.' Here we have side by side for the first time two categories of refugees whom the High Commissioner's Office may assist. The verbal distinction between groups of refugees for whom the High Commissioner 'extends his good offices' and those who come *strict sensu* within his mandate remained until 1964.

A concept of collective *prima facie* eligibility, prompted by events, thus gradually took shape. It departed from the individualistic concept linked to the definition of the term 'refugee' in the Statute and Convention, and progressed towards a more pragmatic and humane rather than legalistic approach to the refugee problem.

Third Stage: Integration of the High Commissioner's Good Offices, and of the Groups of Refugees Concerned, into the Regular Activities of the Office

The final integration of the High Commissioner's good offices and hence that of new groups of refugees, into the regular mandate was reached in 1965: in resolution 2039 (XX) the General Assembly, abandoning the distinction between refugees within the mandate and refugees covered by the High Commissioner's good offices, simply requested 'the United Nations High Commissioner for Refugees to pursue his efforts with a view to ensuring an adequate international protection of refugees and to providing satisfactory permanent solutions to the problems affecting the various groups of refugees within his competence.' The resolution of the following year confirmed this return to a unified responsibility for the different kinds of refugees by requesting the High Commissioner 'to continue to provide international protection to refugees who are his concern, within the limits of his competence, and to promote permanent solutions to their problems'. The explicit reference here to both protection and permanent solutions, a feature which is repeated in the corresponding resolutions for the next three years, leaves no room for doubt as to what the General Assembly had in mind: to eliminate the temporary distinction between two very closely related categories of refugees who, at least collectively, meet the essential criteria for treatment as refugees specified in the mandate. Henceforth, both categories were entitled to receive protection and assistance from the High Commissioner's Office, in as much of course as they needed them.

Fourth Stage—Displaced Persons: Their Gradual Integration into the High Commissioner's Mandate

Matters would probably have gone no further, at least for the time being, if an important problem had not arisen with regard to Sudanese refugees, for whom the Addis Ababa Agreement finally opened up prospects of the return to their own country. To facilitate the speediest possible repatriation of the 150,000 Sudanese who had taken refuge in neighbouring countries, and to help those who had fled to the interior to return to their homes, the General Assembly mentioned refugees and displaced persons side by side for the first time in the history of the High Commissioner's Office. That was in resolution 2958 (XXVII) of 12 December 1972. The fact that the General Assembly was again dealing with a specific group could not be taken to mean that it had at the time the intention of generalising from this case to that of displaced persons as a whole. However, as we will see later, circumstances required UNHCR to be called upon to provide assistance in various parts of the world to large groups of displaced persons—victims of events over which they had no control. The gap, in institutional terms, was bridged by resolution 3445 (XXX) of 9 December 1975 in which the preamble specifically reaffirmed 'the eminently humanitarian character of the activities of the High Commissioner for the benefit of refugees and displaced persons'. This resolution was thus intended to re-establish the comprehensive character of the competence which had been the feature of the United Nations' activities during the first years of its existence. Its terms infer that the High Commissioner's Office could take action on behalf of large groups of people who may not all conform to the conventional definition of a refugee but are in a situation analogous to that of refugees. For example, they are victims of man-made events over deprivation or uprootedness as the result of sudden upheaval and separation from their homes. The reasoning behind this evolution would appear to be that cut off from their origins and scattered or brought together again by circumstances in one place, or another, these displaced persons clearly need some form of international assistance.

The economic, social or demographic context of the country of reception, with the possibilities which it offers for, or the obstacles which it places in the way of, rapid and smooth integration is of fundamental importance.

It also involves a financial effort which may be well beyond the financial resources of the country concerned. What would happen if the country of asylum was unable to assume that burden itself and the international community refused to come to its assistance?

Material Assistance

... What would happen if the country of asylum was unable to assume the burden itself...?

Obviously, this problem can be solved only if a parallel and co-ordinated effort is made by other nations. It could be said to be a matter of fairness to the countries of reception, which are bound in observance of their laws, their commitments or their principles and out of regard for the international community, to receive in their territory refugees coming to their borders. For the refugees, it is a matter of humanity to which the universal conscience cannot remain indifferent. Unfortunately, although it is simple to define and justify in principle, this effort of international solidarity sometimes involves more difficulty in practice. This is particularly so when in order to solve a particular problem, extensive recourse has been had over many years to the assistance of what is, in effect, a limited number of countries. Although they are swift to respond when the tranquillity of their consciences is shaken by a serious and sudden upheaval, people tend to forget sufferings which are drawn out and lasting.

In order to comprehend the reasons for the quite secondary importance given to material assistance in the original Statute of UNHCR, one should recall the situation at the time the Office was established. As the heir of two organisations which had considerable financial resources and had been given the onerous task of housing, feeding, assisting and repatriating or resettling millions of persons who were refugees or were displaced as a result of the Second World War, UNHCR was given only a modest share of those numerous activities. The year was 1950 and the main contributing Governments were showing signs of impatience and weariness. They wished to put an end to measures which were by definition temporary and geared to an exceptional and urgent situation which they regarded as being largely past. To them the time seemed to have come for a return to traditional standards involving the basic, if not exclusive, responsibility of each State toward the refugees whom it was sheltering. Consequently, in the Statute of UNHCR, the role of the Office to provide financial help to countries of reception or, material assistance to refugees was minimised.

The door was, however, left open for occasional and limited material assistance, and article 10 of the Statute authorises the High Commissioner to administer any funds which he may receive from public or private sources. But it was specified that he could not appeal to Governments, in other words that nothing new or important could be undertaken in that sphere without the prior approval of the General Assembly.

As often happens, events very soon brought about a substantial change in that optimistic approach, when thousands of refugees still remained in camps. After some hesitation, marked by resolutions in which the existence of major and urgent assistance requirements was recognised without any practical consequences being drawn, the Assembly decided in 1954 to authorise the High Commissioner to undertake a programme of permanent solutions. To finance the programme, the High Commissioner was finally authorised to appeal for voluntary contributions from Governments. Three years later, an Emergency Fund was established to meet the most urgent needs and an Executive Committee was set up to advise the High Commissioner on his activities in that sphere. Material assistance, originally a 'poor relative', was gradually to assume the importance which human needs and common sense conferred upon it within the general context of UNHCR activities.

C. Anders B. Johnsson, 'UNHCR's Protection Role Continually Evolving', *Refugees* (No. 92, April 1993), pp. 15–16.

Over the past four decades, UNHCR's traditional protection role has become much broader in scope and significantly more operational. At the same time, its focus of action is gradually shifting from protection in countries of asylum and refuge towards activities in countries of origin....

The focus of the international refugee protection regime is exile and integration. But this is not to say that protection cannot occur in countries of origin.

Although the return of refugees took place under international arrangement in the early 1920s and again after World War II, it was not until 1980 that the international community, faced with the soaring costs of refugee programmes, began to re-focus on the issue of repatriation. That year, and again five years later, UNHCR's Executive Committee adopted recommendations which would formalise a protection function for UNHCR in countries of origin. In essence, it consists of monitoring the fulfilment of amnesties or other forms of guarantees that may have been offered to induce the return of the refugees.

Thus, over the last decade, UNHCR has gradually assumed a more systematic protection role in countries of origin. Teams have been set up in countries of origin which, in collaboration with national authorities and voluntary agencies, seek to ensure that effective protection is provided upon return and that no one is made to suffer retribution on account of previous political activities having sought asylum elsewhere. The practice has, however, by no means been uniform and much remains to be done to ensure impartial action and avoid the application of different standards in largely identical situations.

Welcome though it may be, extending UNHCR's protection function to countries of origin has paradoxically also introduced an element of instability in the international protection regime. Not only has 'protection' been provided there to persons who were never refugees in the first place but, based on the dictum that prevention is better than cure, activities have also been directed at displaced persons in their countries of origin.

Among the multitude of questions to which this development has given rise, at least two deserve attention from a protection perspective. First, assistance to displaced persons in their own country, although necessary, does not amount to protection. Thus, the danger if such activities are viewed—which is increasingly the case—as a substitute to asylum in other countries. Second, these types of operations require separate authorisations which have the effect of severely diminishing the control which UNHCR can exercise. This should be a cause of major concern since independence (together with predictability) has so far been a main precondition for successful protection action.

More damaging, as the focus is shifting toward action in countries of origin, the image is gradually being created of a UNHCR which is selective in its approach to protection tasks and increasingly unable to carry them out successfully.

D. David Rieff, *Slaughterhouse: Bosnia and the Failure of the West* (Simon and Schuster, New York, 1995), pp. 190, 195–96, 198, 200–202, 206–12.

The honour of the world was redeemed in Bosnia by those who worked for the NGOs, the nongovernmental aid organisations, the International Committee of the Red Cross and the Office of the United Nations High Commissioner for Refugees. They worked there without any hidden agendas, and steadfastly refused to accept the idea that the interests of the great powers from which they derived so much of their funding compelled them to carry out the political agendas of those powers.…

… UNHCR staffers, international and local alike, fought and improvised, and, in an impossible situation for which there were no precedents, time and again pulled off what seemed like miracles. According to established UN rules, most of the places in which the UNHCR operated *routinely* in Bosnia were too dangerous to consider operating in. And yet the UNHCR stayed anyway. With or without military escorts, their convoy drivers pushed the aid through, past the feral thugs at the check points, and often under fire. Unlike vehicles issued the UN Protection Force, most UNHCR vehicles were not armoured. And examples of the personal courage of the international staff were so numerous that even the people at UNHCR began themselves to take them for granted. If a Marc Vachon, the young French-Canadian logistics officer at the Sarajevo airport in the fall of 1992 and the winter of 1993, drove a soft-skinned fuel truck across the siege lines at a time when UN Protection Force personnel almost never ventured out except in armoured vehicles, that was normal. All he would say was, 'This war sure fucks up your adrenaline.' And if UNHCR protection officers, as they were called, like Pierre Ollier and Philippos Papaphilippou in Banja Luka would drive alone and unarmed into Priejdor to demand that the Mayor there do something to stop the ethnic cleansing—a journey that nearly got them killed countless times—then that, too, was just something that was part of their job. 'If they wanted to sell shoes', the chief of the UNHCR for the former Yugoslavia, Jose Maria Mendiluce, once insisted, his affectionate tone belying his words, 'then they should have stayed in Rio, New York, or Paris.' That was what Mendiluce's staff thought too.

... For all their skill and dedication in dealing with the effects of war, most of the UNHCR officials who were sent to Bosnia knew little about war itself. This was not just simply because so many of them had spent their professional lives filing asylum claims for refugees in Europe or running refugee camps in Africa and East Asia. No one at the UNHCR had any experience in providing aid during a war. And yet that was precisely what they had been mustered to do—first in Croatia, and then in Bosnia....

... When Jose Maria Mendiluce, the Basque diplomat who had served for years in Central America and had then gone on to be the number two UNHCR official in Kurdistan before coming to the former Yugoslavia, realised what was actually going on in Bosnia when he arrived as High Commissioner Ogata's Special Representative, he understood immediately that the lessons the UNHCR had learned in the Middle East were not going to work in the Balkans. 'Whatever else we do', he told his staff with that odd mix of gaiety and gloom that often seemed to animate him, 'we are going to have to throw away the Blue Book....'

... Mendiluce's first exposure to the realities of ethnic cleansing came by accident. In the early spring of 1992, he was driving back to his office in Sarjaevo (like UNPROFOR, the UNHCR ran its operations during the Serbo–Croat war from the supposedly neutral Bosnian capital) after a meeting in Belgrade. By coincidence, he arrived in the town of Zvornik, on the Bosnian side of the Drina River, just at the moment when it was overrun by a Serb irregular unit known as the White Eagles. 'I saw kids put under the treads of tanks, placed there by grown men, and then run over by other grown men,' he recalled with a shudder. 'Everywhere, people were shooting. The fighters were moving through the towns, systematically killing all the Muslims they could get their hands on. It was an intoxication, sure. The Serb media had been full of reports of Muslims expelling the Serbs from Zvornik, and of the atrocities that had been committed there. And although this may have been true occasionally, usually these Serbs were pushed to do so by local leaders.

'In any case, the Serbs doing the killing in Zvornik that day did not come from Zvornik. This crisis did not begin as a war between Serbs and Muslims but as a war between fanatical nationalists. These people had a coherent strategy. The whole point was to inflict as much terror on the civilian population as possible, to destroy as much property as possible, and to target as much of the violence as possible against women and kids. After the irregulars had done their work, then the established authorities—the Yugoslav National Army, or Karadzic's forces, or the local police—would come in, ostensibly to restore order. But, of course, that would mean that the ethnic cleansing of that particular place had been successful, and the White Eagles could move on.'

That day in Zvornik, Mendiluce said, he rounded up as many of the surviving Muslims as he could, declaring to the local Serb commanders that he was placing the townspeople under UNHCR protection. But what in retrospect seemed like foolhardy heroism had its price. For although Mendiluce did the miraculous and saved hundreds of lives by evacuating the Muslims from the town and arranging for their transport to Tuzla, he had, acting with the best motives, guaranteed that Zvornik would thenceforth be a Serb town—which had been the political purpose of the White Eagles' assault in the first place. Mendiluce himself all but conceded the point. 'We have no mechanisms to deal with ethnic cleansing', he told me. 'We can treat the symptoms of the disease, whether by improving security conditions in those areas where ethnic cleansing has not yet taken place, or by doing our best to alert the international community to the depth of the crisis, or by trying to arrange food distribution through relief convoys and aerial resupply to besieged areas. But it's not as if we can compel the parties to stop the war, or militarily intervene to prevent the ethnic cleansing from continuing.'

'It's an impossible situation,' he went on. 'People from the beginning have liked to simplify the problem with words. They speak of the Lebanisation of the Balkans today, just as a few years ago they spoke of the Balkanisation of Lebanon. But the reality is that at the moment, no side is defeated, including the Bosnians, no goodwill exists, no stalemate has been achieved, and despite all the efforts of Vance and Owen, no real international pressure exists.' Mendiluce said all this in the fall of 1992, when he was still comparatively optimistic. When he left, a little over a year later, heartbroken over what had happened and his health all but ruined, the situation was far worse....

... from the beginning, Mendiluce encouraged his staffers to reveal the horrors they witnessed, whatever the political consequences. Whether they were detailing the siege of Gorazde or the continuing ethnic cleansing in Banja Luka, UNHCR officials could be relied upon to tell the truth. Perhaps that was all they could do for Bosnia. It was not as if Louis Gentile could stop the ethnic cleansing of the Bosanska Krajina, or, during the siege of Gorazde, the Irish UNHCR doctor Mary McGloughlin could do much for the wounded. But telling the truth is no negligible accomplishment, and to its eternal credit, the UNHCR staffers told the truth unswervingly. Of course, then the UN Protection Force public information people, and sometimes its senior officials, would weigh in with assertions that the UNHCR reports were exaggerated, that actually the damage (or the death toll, or the number of displaced people, or the degree of want) was much less than had been first reported. Since the victims in such cases were almost always the Bosnians, the UNPROFOR people often would hint broadly, in quite the eerie echo of the propaganda coming out of Pale and Belgrade, that the Bosnians had manufactured these reports in order to con the West into intervening militarily....

Inevitably, the UNHCR itself had been compromised by what it had had to do in Bosnia. Although it was the organisation that had done more than any other to publicise the facts of ethnic cleansing, there had been times when it found itself having to in effect abet it. 'I prefer thirty thousand evacuees to thirty thousand bodies', Mendiluce said on one occasion. In 1993, in Srebrenica, the UNHCR had organised a massive evacuation of the civilian population through Serb-controlled areas and on to Tuzla. It was not that anyone was being pressured to leave. As one UNHCR worker put it at the time, 'Everyone wants to get the hell out of Srebrenica. They know there's no future there.' And yet, as a Bosnian soldier remarked bitterly as he watched the first convoy cross the no-man's-land and roll past his position toward Tuzla city, 'This is just ethnic cleansing. The UNHCR is doing the Serbs' work for them.'

The UNHCR official in charge of the evacuation insisted that he was fulfilling a 'purely humanitarian' evacuation. And he warned that although the Srebrenica operation had been the largest the UNHCR had mounted in Bosnia to date, it was unlikely to be the last. And, as people taking the apocalyptic view tended to be in Bosnia, he was right. In the spring of 1994, when it became clear to the UNHCR that the Serbs in the Bosanska Krajina, particularly in the Priejdor area, were again beginning a systematic campaign of murder and arson against the six thousand or so Muslims who remained, there was an attempt to evacuate them *en masse* to Croatia. It was not as if the Muslims could have fled on their own. In the bus station in Banja Luka, a sign went up in the fall of 1993 declaring that Muslims were forbidden to ride the buses. Outside, a graffito restated that pairing peculiar to racist signs the world over: 'No dogs or Muslims'.

Reluctantly, the UNHCR and the International Red Cross attempted to put the evacuation together. The rumour in Zagreb was that the money that was being offered, under the table, to the local Serb authorities was insufficient, and that was why in the end the evacuation had fallen through. But the precedent set in Srebrenica, repeated in the following year on a smaller scale in places all over Bosnia, and set in motion though not completed in the Bosanska Krajina was increasingly defining what the UNHCR's mandate to 'protect' refugees really amounted to. In effect, it had been put in the impossible position of either standing by and watching the murders go on, or itself facilitating the larger Serb war aim of the transfer of the non-Serb population out of Bosnian Serb Army-controlled parts of Bosnia. For UNHCR officials, who had dedicated their lives to caring for refugees, even making the choice was all but unbearable, however much they might recognise its inevitability.

E. Guy Goodwin-Gill, 'New Mandate? What New Mandate?' *Refugees* (No. 88, January 1992), pp. 38–40.

Moments of crisis and doubt are commonly also the occasion for new religions to arise, and even a heresy or two. When an international agency loses its sense of direction and its faith in principle begins to waver, it's only to be expected that eyes and expectations will find comfort in the dream of a new mandate, clearer instructions and once and future rules.

UNHCR, say some, needs fresh instruction from the General Assembly. Bound to obey its parent, UNHCR must yet live with rules that at base reflect the values and concerns of a bygone era. Today, walls fall, curtains rise, and States collapse to re-emerge, multiplied. The old, cold doctrine doesn't cut the mustard; or does it?

What doesn't work? Sure, its tough times for UNHCR, even tougher for refugees. States are talking loud and playing hard to get. And violence against the refugee and the foreigner is looked on with the blind eye of those, not just in the developed world, who once when it was fashionable preached protection on the high seas, first asylum and tolerance in distant lands.

For years unwilling to resource their systems—with dollars, staff time, training, information—governments too often now redefine efficiency as closing down and shutting out. As if suffering and flight might, like poverty or need, be legislated away. They are not and cannot be; the human plight of those who flee remains before us. And human ingenuity, intrinsically light years ahead of bureaucracy, will get there anyway, driven by risk and urgent necessity.

So what is wrong with the UNHCR mandate, the statute adopted by the General Assembly at its fifth session on 14 December 1950 and annexed to resolution 428? Is it paragraph 1, which requires the High Commissioner to assume responsibility to provide international protection to refugees? Or to work with governments to seek solutions? Is it the personal scope of the statute, with its ambiguous references to categories, groups, and individuals with a well-founded fear of persecution? Hardly, for States themselves, acting repeatedly through the General Assembly, have made it abundantly clear that they want international protection and assistance to be accorded to a broad range of people in distress, far exceeding the initial scope of UNHCR's mandate.

So perhaps it is some limit to the nature and extent of UNHCR's activities?

Repatriation and resettlement, originally subject to approval by the General Assembly under paragraph 9, have long since entered the regular programme. So may be it's the further requirement to obtain similar approval before the High Commissioner appeals for funds? But that too is now an accepted feature of UNHCR activities. So what's the problem? And what's the General Assembly to do? Obviously we know something's wrong. States, for one, do not seem to share with UNHCR a single sense of who is a refugee, or what that implies. What is more, they lack the modalities, national or international, for protecting those who don't fall within the Convention refugee category, but nonetheless have other valid reasons for flight. States have difficulty, too, implementing immigration decisions, such as removal. And often seem unable, individually or collectively, to take the necessary pro-active steps to moderate or remove the causes of flight, to promote the mediation of conflict and the resolution of disorder, or to open the windows of local opportunity.

So whose problem is it now? UNHCR's and its mandate? Or States, with all their sovereign capacity? More and more it looks like the latter.

Sure, UNHCR could be stronger; but no General Assembly resolution today will impose obligations on States. Sure, it could get involved at source; but step by step may be the way through this minefield, rather than grandiose general principle. Sure, UNHCR needs a regular budget, not one subject to voluntary contribution and the whims of national interest; and there's a point to focus.

But a new mandate? Just look at paragraph 8 of the Statute. Apply it and develop it with imagination and a programme of action stretches out promoting protection and solutions, initiating and facilitating international cooperation with and between States, inviting in and coordinating the complementary work of other international institutions and non-governmental organisations.

UNHCR's role is to be service to refugees, to provide them with protection and assistance; but it also has responsibilities towards States, upon whose territory and within whose jurisdiction solutions must be found, and the reasons for flight avoided.

A new mandate is not needed. That mandate is, can and should be, renewed every day—in every contact with a refugee, in every dealing with government, in being there.

What may be needed is refocus and return to principle. That doesn't come from preachy words, but only from action. That means reviewing the empty rhetoric, and filling it with the substance of protection as a working tool. It means showing the way to governments seemingly overwhelmed and lost in the mire of functional problems, actively and effectively helping them to reach the known goals of protection.

If, in the end, who shouts loudest owns the problem, that should not blind us to the scope for cooperative enterprise.

F. Guy S. Goodwin-Gill, 'Asylum: The Law and Politics of Change', *International Journal of Refugee Law* (Vol. 7, No. 1, 1995), pp. 10, 12–13.

It is often said that the High Commissioner's mandate is infinitely flexible. Certainly, it has expanded to embrace new groups and categories;

but certainly it has *not* expanded to include new solutions, new responses or even a capacity for medium to long-term thinking. The negative impact of not having a regular or assessed budget can be exaggerated, but a measure of regular financing might well contribute to more serious strategic planning.

It is no longer enough to call yet again for better inter-agency co-operation, and hope that somehow the needs of refugees, migrants, the internally displaced, countries in the course of development, human rights and democratic modes of government will somehow come to pass, and coalesce in a new co-operative Utopia. What is needed is the vision and the authority to make that happen.

Now is the time for a substantial review of both the mandate of UNHCR and the rationale for maintaining the 1951 Convention definition approach to refugee protection and refugee solutions. . . .

UNHCR's statute, adopted 44 years ago, is quite out of date. It should be rewritten to take account of the social realities of population displacements today, which are far less a consequence of individualised persecution than of generalised violence, and to reflect the full range of responsibilities and activities entrusted to UNHCR and associated agencies over the years.

The focus of a reformed agency should be on population displacements resulting from coercion or compulsion, including conflict. The issue of sovereignty and the impact of article 2 (7) of the Charter will need to be accommodated, but there is growing recognition within the UN of the international dimensions to displacement, particularly where it results from grave breaches of international humanitarian law or massive violations of human rights. Nowhere has this been clearer than in the case of former Yugoslavia.

In a new regime of protection, the fact of having or not having crossed an international frontier should have procedural significance, but not be a substantive obstacle to competence. That is, if no border has been crossed but a population has been internally displaced and needs protection and assistance, agency involvement might be subject to international decision-making, itself governed by accurate and trustworthy information. Action based on such findings would be clearly humanitarian and therefore limited. Provided decision-making and implementation remain open and accountable, such operations would constitute no threat to the territorial integrity or political independence of any State.

In other cases, the agency should be competent with respect to all instances of coerced displacement, not excluding the mass expulsion of foreign nationals or incidental issues of statelessness. In each case, the threshold for action should be the necessity for international protection, either in the short or the long term; and the provision of international protection should remain the primary aim.

G. Hiram A. Ruiz, 'Emergencies: International Response to Refugee Flows and Complex Emergencies', *International Journal of Refugee Law* (Special Issue, 1995), pp. 155–58.

Emergency Preparedness and Response

Despite the fact that refugee outflows repeatedly generated emergency situations, until very recently, international, and specifically UNHCR, response to emergencies was consistently poor.

In the case of UNHCR, it could be weeks if not months from the time that a refugee emergency began until UNHCR mounted a response. During that time, it was left up to local people, host governments and local and international NGOs to do whatever they could to deal with the emergency. This often resulted not only in unnecessary deaths, but time and time again it resulted in situations where the local people and NGOs, with their limited capacities, set up systems to assist the refugees that may not have been the best or most appropriate, and which UNHCR often dismantled and rebuilt once it did arrive.

Only in the late 1970s, following the onset of the Indochinese refugee crisis, did UNHCR first set up an emergency response team.[47] Unfortunately, not only was that action quite late, it was also quite inadequate; for many years that first emergency team in fact did very little by way of emergency response, leading to external and internal criticism of UNHCR's performance in emergencies.

That was the case as recently as the late 1980s and early 1990s. One example occurred in early 1990, when Liberian refugees fled to Guinea. According to a US State Department report on the situation, by June 1990, the refugees situation had become 'truly life-threatening'. The State Department said: 'Many factors have contributed to this poor state of affairs. However, lack of co-ordination and a shortage of experienced emergency UNHCR relief staff have been the most significant problems.'[48]

UNHCR's response when refugees fleeing Somalia began entering Kenya and Ethiopia in early 1991 was even poorer. A population that was largely in good health when it arrived quickly deteriorated once exposed to the sub-standard conditions in the refugee camps. In Ethiopia, malnutrition rates among the refugee reached 25 per cent by April 1991. At Liboi, the largest refugee camp in Kenya, disease became widespread and by June the malnutrition rate was 29 percent. The influx into Kenya

[47] Sylvie Gerard, 'Can a UN Bureaucracy Deal with Emergencies', *Refugees* (UNHCR, Geneva, December 1992).

[48] Cited in Hiram Ruiz, *Uprooted Liberians: Casualties of a Brutal War* (US Committee for Refugees, Washington, 1992).

increased in late 1991. By this time, however, most refugees were arriving in already weakened physical condition. Nevertheless, the response remained poor, causing further deaths and suffering....

At about the same time, in another corner of the world, UNHCR's emergency response was also failing. Refugees from Bhutan began arriving in Nepal in 1991. Their number increased dramatically in the first months of 1992. According to UNHCR's *Refugees* magazine, 'Only after UNHCR's Geneva-based technical and programme staff learned of exceptionally high mortality rates among the refugees was Nepal placed on the emergency agenda in mid-April 1992. Unfortunately, by the time UNHCR's senior epidemiologist was sent to the field, it was early June, and between 1,200 and 1,500 preventable deaths had occurred.'[49]

Since 1989, UNHCR's Executive Committee had been urging the agency to make substantive improvements in its emergency response capabilities. In early 1991, the Executive Committee doubled the amount of UNHCR's Emergency Fund, from $10 million to $20 million. But substantive change did not come about until after UNHCR's failings in the much-publicised Gulf War-associated Kurdish refugee crisis in the spring of 1991.

UNHCR's *Refugees* magazine said of the organisation's response on that occasion: 'According to many observers both within and outside the organisation, UNHCR staff arrived on the scene of the emergency too slowly, in insufficient numbers, and with inadequate experience. UNHCR's own review of the operation noted, 'in the Persian Gulf, UNHCR's capacity to act quickly and decisively was limited by the absence of structures, systems, and procedures designed to meet the specific needs of an emergency.'[50] The article went on to say:

> The magnitude of the Kurdish emergency prompted newly appointed High Commissioner Sadako Ogata to forcefully push for the implementation of concrete proposals for the quick mobilisation of funds, of personnel, and for the pre-positioning of relief items. In short, she called for the mobilisation of the entire organisation for effective emergency response.

UNHCR's Emergency Preparedness and Response Section

The result of the call by the Executive Committee and High Commissioner Ogata for action was the establishment, in February 1992, of the Emergency Preparedness and Response Section (EPRS) within UNHCR. According to a report prepared by the EPRS titled 'Update on UNHCR's

---

[49] Gerard, 'Can a UN Bureaucracy Deal with Emergencies' (see footnote 47 earlier).
[50] Ibid.

Capacity to Respond to Emergencies', the Section has a number of tools at its disposal.[51]

The first is a core group of five Emergency Preparedness and Response Officers. These officers, who are based in the Section, monitor regional developments, establish contingency plans, develop operational procedures for emergencies, identify training needs for personnel assigned to work on emergencies, and, most importantly, are deployed to the field to lead needs-assessment missions and emergency response teams as necessary. These offices are, in effect, the front line of UNHCR's emergency response.

The EPRS has also established a roster of UNHCR staff members who are given training in dealing with emergencies and who are available on a stand-by basis to join Emergency Response Teams. The section has established a standby roster of trained Senior Emergency Administrators and Emergency Finance and Administrative Assistants who can be deployed to emergency situations to ensure that appropriate administrative and financial procedures are put in place.

Besides these internal resources, the EPRS has negotiated agreements with the Danish and Norwegian Refugee Councils, Radda Barnen (Sweden), and the UN Volunteers (UNV) programme that provide for rapid deployment in emergency operations of personnel seconded from these organisations. The Nordic organisations have long placed emphasis on emergency response. As part of the arrangement with UNHCR, each organisation has trained or will train a number of individuals who already have relevant skills in the particular needs of emergency situations. These individuals, who are not on the staff of the three organisations but are otherwise employed in their home countries, can be called up on 72 hours notice for service with UNHCR for up to six months in emergency operations.

... Besides these staffing arrangements, the EPRS has stockpiled or made arrangements for the immediate availability of emergency food stocks, other relief suppliers, vehicles, communication equipment, and emergency field kits. It has negotiated an agreement with the government of the Russian Federation for two airplanes and a trucking fleet to be on standby for UNHCR emergency use. The EPRS has also established arrangements with various non-governmental organisations (NGOs) for the provision of experts in technical areas such as health, sanitation, water, site planning, logistics and social services to work with UNHCR emergency teams.[52]

[51] 'Update on UNHCR's Capacity to Respond to Emergencies', paper presented by the EPRS to the UNHCR Executive Committee, Sub-committee on Administrative and Financial Matters, UNHCR, Geneva, 15 September 1993.

[52] 'Report of the UN High Commissioner for Refugees to the UN Economic and Social Council', May 1994.

III. UNHCR AND NGOs

A. Roger P. Winter, *Assisting the World's Unprotected People: The Unique Role of Non-governmental Agencies* **(The Danish Centre for Human Rights, Copenhagen, 1993), pp. 105–10.**

Humane instincts have undoubtedly driven people to assist others in need since the dawn of civilisation. Today the process of providing humanitarian assistance has become a highly organised enterprise involving laws and regulations, defined roles and vested interests, major political implications, international organisations, and large sums of money. Nevertheless, refugee assistance efforts remain heavily imbued with idealism and humanitarian motivation, particularly noticeable in private religious and charitable agencies. The concept of rescuing victims of persecution and violence is central to this motivation.

Though governmental entities are usually rather clearly identifiable, it is not always clear who is and is not part of the nongovernmental portion of the refugee assistance network. The field incorporates aspects of human rights, generic charity, immigration services, social services, religious services, development, education, advocacy and a host of support and other functions.

'NGOs', a term widely and often officially used in international circles, refers to 'non-governmental organisations'. NGOs are a highly diverse group; several of the major elements of the diversity include:

Religion as a factor or nonfactor in the agency's existence and programme. Most major religious bodies in the developed world have a refugee resettlement arm and relate to an entity involved in international refugee relief and assistance.

Size, which ranges from organisations with no paid staff to those with hundreds. Some smaller agencies may in fact be built around a single, often charismatic or driven, individual. Size of budget is an obvious variable.

Scope of programme: Refugee NGOs may be involved in both domestic resettlement of refugees and services to asylum seekers, and in international refugee aid. They may specialise in advocacy, public education, legal services, development aid or provide a full range of medical, logistical and relief services. A few specialise in particular nationalities. All, however, offer services to refugees or displaced people as *the* or *one of the central* focuses of their programme; their involvement with refugees is not by chance.

Style of operation: Some agencies are activists with respect to government policy, seeking to affect policy content or programme resources. Commitment to advocacy does not seem to be determined by size of constituency or, surprisingly, even to degree of reliance on government funding, though both are relevant factors.

Source of funds: Some NGOs rely heavily on funding from governments—others will not accept such funds and rely only on private support such as individual contributions, grants from foundations, or allocations from church bodies.

NGOs by definition are not controlled by government. While relations with governments tend to vary considerably over time and with reference to the subject at hand, most NGOs constantly communicate with government. In many countries NGOs are part of an umbrella organisation which helps them collaborate in meeting their goals and coordinate their representations to governments. Many such NGOs are also among the nearly 100 members of the International Council of Voluntary Agencies (ICVA) headquartered in Geneva, which helps serve similar functions on an international level.

... A total inventory of NGO functions and services is probably not possible, but the following examples of broad functional areas, both formal and informal, show the importance of NGOs to the refugee assistance network....

Implementing partner to the UN and to governments: In most refugee assistance programmes [...], NGOs are the actual deliverers of services to refugees. There are, of course, exceptions, such as when governments prefer—for control purposes, or otherwise—to provide services directly. However, in their service delivery role NGOs are often the element of the refugee assistance network most in touch with refugees and their needs, even in cases where the funding may come from the UN or from government.

Early warning (sometimes the only warning): The fact that many NGOs function broadly in development distributes their presence widely, particularly in developing countries including many that are refugee producers or refugee receivers. This frequently positions NGOs well to alert authorities and assistance networks world wide to emergent refugee situations and crises.

Emergency assistance: NGOs and their personnel are often experienced in responding quickly to critical humanitarian developments. In an emergency mode, with links to and credibility with external response systems, they are often first to be able to assist communities to respond to the needs of refugees and the uprooted victims of violence and persecution.

Protection by presence: In many contexts, the presence of expatriate NGO personnel or, somewhat less so, indigenous personnel in positions within organisations with international links can constitute a form of protection for refugees. They represent a credible reporting presence with a standing that potentially abusive authorities must take into account. Thus, they sometimes serve as a deterrent to abuse.

Monitoring/whistle-blowing: In many situations around the world where local government officials tend toward abuse, incompetence or corruption, NGOs can informally—through private feedback to authorities, media, or donors—pinpoint problems in policy or practice.

Resettlement processing: Providing a buffer between refugees and official government systems in the resettlement process is one function that has often generated controversy. Most NGOs, while cognisant of their obligations toward governments, tend to view their role as one of within-the-system advocacy that assists refugees to attain their goal of admission to a resettlement country. Once resettlement has occurred, government pursues the goal of economic self-sufficiency as quickly as possible. NGOs, while recognising that priority, tend to pursue resettlement more comprehensively in terms of personal development as well as economic development.

Development: NGOs ... to a greater or lesser degree, view the full range of their activities as development. Generally, development is seen as empowering people to participate fully in shaping their lives and futures. Some NGOs view life-saving and emergency assistance as the critical pre-requisites for any further development of refugees. However, the fit of third-country refugee resettlement within the development context is a conceptually difficult one as it sometimes contributes to a 'brain drain' from countries much in need of skilled and educated people.

Development education/public education/constituency building: Refugees are not at the top of everyone's list of priorities, nor is their predicament well understood by many policy makers or the public. Such understanding is critical, e.g., in the competition for public and private resources to meet refugee need, the development of diplomatic support for international refugee protection, and the formulation of appropriate solutions for refugees. While many NGO efforts in these areas focus on promoting their own programmes, most also approach these matters generically.

Lobbying: In a democratic society where the visibility of an issue affects the politics of that issue, public education and advocacy do affect governmental resources and policy. It is humanitarian political action.

Asylum-seeker assistance: NGOs often provide assistance of a humanitarian or legal nature to asylum-seekers or potential asylum-seekers who are in legal limbo or who have 'gone underground'. Such services are often provided in an adversarial posture vis-à-vis the government.

B. Louise W. Holborn, *Refugees—A Problem of Our Time: The Work of the United Nations High Commissioner for Refugees, 1951–1972* (Scarecrow Press Inc., Metuchen, 1975), Vol. 1, pp. 119–20.

The Non-governmental (Voluntary) Agencies

No element has been more vital to the successful conduct of the programmes of the UNHCR than the close partnership between UNHCR and the non-governmental organisation, commonly referred to as the voluntary agencies. For while the UNHCR is the symbol and manifestation of the concern of the international community for the problem of refugees, the voluntary agencies have been the practitioners who, through their dedication and long experience, permit this concern to be translated into effective measures of aid. They have been, and still are, agents of the private conscience.

The voluntary agencies have been a permanent factor in refugee work since the early 1920s. Not only have they been a necessary adjunct to the work of public statutory organisations (internal and national) but they have had a great importance in their own right. Under his Statute, the HC is directed to seek permanent solutions to refugee problems by assisting governments and private organisations to facilitate the voluntary repatriation of refugees or their assimilation within new national communities. To implement this directive the HC is to establish contracts with private organisations in such manner as he may think best (Art. 8[h]) and facilitate the coordination of the efforts of private organisations concerned with refugees (Art. 8[i]). The Statute thus carries on the link forged in 1921 between official international agencies dealing with refugee problems and the voluntary agencies. But while the HC could take advantage of the experience of his immediate predecessors, UNRRA and the IRO, in working with voluntary agencies the nature of his relationship had to be different because his functions and the political setting in which he had to work were different. Whereas both UNRRA and the IRO were established as operational bodies, acting directly on refugee problems and with large budgets provided by governments, the UNHCR was required to be non-operational, with a small budget only for administrative expenses. While international protection was a function to be performed directly by the HC and his staff, when it came to seeking permanent solutions his role was to be that of stimulating, assisting, and coordinating efforts of governments and voluntary agencies. Thus, it was essential for the HC to find operational partners through which he could work to achieve the goals set forth in the Statute. And it was equally essential that he find sources of support that would make the fullest implementation of his purpose possible. It was to meet both these needs that the HC turned to the voluntary agencies.

C. Santiago Romero-Perez, 'Partnership in Action', *Refugees* (No. 97, 1994), pp. 8–9.

UNHCR's Statute, adopted by the UN General Assembly in December 1950, mandated UNHCR to work with NGOs. This far-sighted decision allowed the first High Commissioner to receive and disburse funds through governments and NGOs, giving them the responsibility for the use of these funds in specific projects.

From its creation, one of UNHCR's main responsibilities, to provide assistance towards durable solutions, was linked, in a statutory manner, with NGOs.

The new agency, non-political and humanitarian, began its task alongside NGOs, relying on their knowledge and expertise to carry out its refugee programmes. This relationship with NGOs became fundamental to the success of UNHCR's work.

The NGO role in relation to UNHCR's principal task, to provide international protection to refugees, is frequently misunderstood. NGOs are often seen as UNHCR's operational arm, as deliverers of assistance, rather than as a source of support for UNHCR's protection tasks. There was a tendency in UNHCR to think that because the responsibility to provide international protection cannot be delegated, NGOs were assigned to a narrowly defined realm of assistance.

The increasing complexity and size of the refugee problem, and the growing needs of displaced persons inside and outside their own countries, have required enormous changes for UNHCR. The new world 'disorder' has required new strategies and a search for association with a wider segment of society, interested and involved in the search for solutions. The relationship with NGOs has, therefore, grown in quantitative terms to a level where in 1993 UNHCR channelled some $300 million, directly or indirectly, through NGOs. This relationship has also grown in terms of the number of NGOs working with UNHCR—some 300 in 1993—and in the diversity of their involvement. UNHCR's strategy of prevention, preparedness and solutions has necessitated greater NGO involvement, not only as 'implementing partners' but as sources of information, advocates of refugee rights, and important voices in policy formulation.

How has UNHCR traditionally related to NGOs? As much of UNHCR's work is field-oriented, the choice of operational partners is entrusted to our field representatives, who liaise with local and international NGOs on a daily basis, and are well placed to assess the needs and determine which agencies are best suited for programme delivery.

The selection criteria has been from the beginning quite simple, based on operational capacity and accountability. The three basic conditions require NGOs:

- to be legally registered at the location of their headquarters and/or where they operate;
- to have authority to operate a bank account and keep separate records of expenditures incurred on UNHCR's behalf;
- and, to demonstrate, via official audit statements, financial audit statements, financial reliability.

The varied nature of refugee situations requires flexibility in the choice of partners; some additional considerations include past experience, local expertise, rapid response capacity and phase-out potential.

The United Nation's Economic and Social Council (ECOSOC) permits NGOs to which it has granted consultative status, as well as members of the Commission on Refugees of the International Council of Voluntary Agencies (ICVA), to submit statements and participate as observers in the annual session of UNHCR's Executive Committee.

As the challenges to refugee protection and assistance increased, so did the need to re-examine relations with NGOs, recognising our respective roles and mandates. In 1990, UNHCR embarked, together with ICVA, on a dialogue with NGOs to reappraise the fundamental nature of the partnership. This exercise, which involved some 200 NGOs and 20 UNHCR field offices, led to the recognition that NGOs were more than mere 'implementing partners' or 'deliverers of service', and emphasised UNHCR–NGO complementary capacities. It also resulted in a document entitled, 'UNHCR–NGO Partnership: Reference on Relationship Between UNHCR and NGOs'. This important document, while calling for improved cooperation at field and headquarters level, did not, however, cover every area of potential partnership. It lacked a broader input, especially from local NGOs.

In order to widen the dialogue and improve our actions, in 1993 UNHCR and ICVA initiated a partnership process known as PARinAC (Partnership in Action). A series of six regional consultations began in Caracas in June 1993, and was followed by others in Kathmandu, Tunis, Bangkok, Addis Ababa and Budapest. The process culminated in a Global Conference in Oslo in June 1994. Supplementary consultations with NGOs also took place in Tokyo, Toronto, Washington, London and New York.

Taking the 'show on the road', UNHCR went to the South, but also East, West and North. Common issues of concern were discussed with people in the field. Over 500 NGOs from every continent, especially local NGOs, took part in the process.

The consultations centred around five priority areas: refugee protection, internally displaced, emergency preparedness and response, the continuum from relief to rehabilitation to development, and UNHCR–NGO partnership. Each regional conference viewed these themes through the prism of their own regional or local specificities and produced sets of proposals on concrete measures to improve our relations and the response to refugees and displaced persons.

The PARinAC Global Conference in Oslo included 182 NGO representatives from 83 countries, as well as observers from UN and other intergovernmental bodies, and government members of our Executive Committee. The meeting adopted by consensus the Oslo Declaration and

Plan of Action and endorsed the regional proposals from all the conferences. We see the Plan of Action, which includes 134 recommendations, as the blueprint which will guide our response to present and future humanitarian challenges. The following examples illustrate the origins and aims of a few of the PARinAC recommendations.

- The growing recognition of NGOs' role as advocates of refugee protection, requires enhanced NGO participation in dialogue with governments and appropriate information sharing. This need is reflected in the introduction to the protection recommendations in the Oslo Plan of Action and more specifically in recommendations 1 and 2.
- An NGO presence before an emergency occurs or in its early phase is of great value in improving early warning and the initial emergency response. At present, local NGOs are often not able to become involved because of a series of financial, administrative and/or operational handicaps. Recommendation 75 addresses this situation.
- UNHCR and NGOs often complain about each other's 'deficiencies' when it comes to project implementation. Some in UNHCR believe that project agreements are the basis of partnership and that NGO delays in complying with agreed reporting requirements are the cause of many of our differences. The PARinAC process has started a reform dialogue; most concretely, some 35 NGO representatives from Africa met with UNHCR officials immediately after the PARinAC regional conference in Addis Ababa, to propose improvements. Oslo recommendations 65–72 refer to programme reform and NGO involvement in this process.
- The need for better coordination is clearly recognised. This applies not only to UNHCR–NGO relations but also to relations between NGOs. Recommendation 61 calls for the establishment of committees to assess specific requirements before, during and after a refugee crisis emerges.
- How long is UNHCR presence required in a given refugee or returnee situation? Often the absence of other organisations and lack of resources results in a prolonged UNHCR presence. Recommendation 106 calls for a smooth phase-out period in which local NGOs are supported and other partners—government authorities, development agencies and donors—are called to play an active role.
- The need for an appropriate response to the growing problem of the internally displaced was a priority issue during PARinAC. There is no agency with a mandate to protect and assist internally displaced people. Recommendation 41 addresses institutional arrangements and calls on the UN Secretary General to designate a lead agency in specific situations. More importantly, however, it calls for the broad,

coordinated involvement of UNHCR, governmental and intergovernmental authorities and NGOs to address the problem.

The High Commissioner, in her keynote address in Oslo, called for bold
initiatives to make this new partnership work. She offered to bring NGOs
into operational and programme discussions; to strengthen, through
training, local agencies' response capacity; to undertake joint needs assessment of regional training requirements and approach donors for the necessary funds; to involve NGOs in formulation of programmes in all
relevant areas, including emergency response, repatriation, protection
and internally displaced; to strengthen information sharing; and to co-
operate with NGOs in the incorporation of issues concerning refugee
women and children in all our programme activities.

The NGOs have already designated focal points at both regional and
national levels to begin turning the PARinAC recommendations into reality and are busy preparing the agenda for the first every consultation
between NGOs and States members of UNHCR's Executive Committee.

Structural changes will also take place in UNHCR headquarters, where
senior officials in each regional bureau will be responsible for discussing
operational matters with NGOs. On August 1st, a coordinator, responsible for policy matters related to NGOs replaced the NGO Liaison Section, created in 1975, within the division of external relations.

This new partnership will have to overcome old working habits. It will
require real commitment from both UNHCR and NGOs to address the
problems of refugees and displaced persons as a team. It will need the
involvement of other UN agencies and programmes, as well as political
and financial cooperation of governments.

The challenge is great, the agenda is set, the tools have been identified.
It is imperative that we succeed.

IV. REFUGEES AND THE ROLE OF ICRC

A. Jean-Philippe Lavoyer, 'Refugees and Internally Displaced
Persons: International Humanitarian Law and the Role of
the ICRC', *International Review of the Red Cross* (No. 305,
March–April 1995), pp. 167–70.

Refugees: Protection under International Humanitarian Law

Whereas refugee law contains a specific definition of refugee, humanitarian law is very vague and only rarely employs the term. All the same, this
does not mean that refugees are neglected by humanitarian law, since
they are protected by it when they are in the power of a party to conflict.

During international armed conflicts, nationals of a State who flee hostilities and enter the territory of an enemy State are protected by the Fourth Geneva Convention as aliens in the territory of a party to the conflict (Articles 35 to 46 of the Fourth Convention). This Convention requests *favourable treatment for refugees* on the part of the host country; since, as refugees, they do not enjoy the protection of any government, they must not be treated as enemy aliens solely on the basis of their nationality (Article 44 of the Fourth Convention). Protocol I reinforces this rule while also referring to the protection of stateless persons (Article 73 of Protocol I). Refugee nationals of a neutral State who find themselves in the territory of a belligerent State are protected by the Fourth Convention when there are no diplomatic relations between their State and the belligerent State. Article 73 of Protocol I maintains this protection even when diplomatic relations exist.

The Fourth Convention further stipulates that 'In no circumstances shall a protected person be transferred to a country where he or she may have reason to fear persecution for his or her political opinions or religious beliefs' (principle of *non-refoulement*, Article 45, para. 4 of the Fourth Convention).

If, during the occupation of a territory, refugees again fall into the power of a State of which they are nationals, they also enjoy special protection: the Fourth Convention prohibits the Occupying Power from arresting, prosecuting, or convicting them, or from deporting them from the occupied territory (Article 70, para. 2 of the Fourth Convention).

However, nationals of a State who flee from armed conflict to the territory of a State that is not taking part in an international conflict are not protected by international humanitarian law, unless this State is beset by internal armed conflict, in which case they are protected by Article 3 common to the Geneva Conventions and by Protocol II. The refugees in question are then the victims of two situations of conflict, one in their own country, and the other in the country receiving them.

The Office of the United Nations High Commissioner for Refugees (UNHCR) plays a role of paramount importance in work on behalf of refugees.

The ICRC considers itself to be directly concerned by the fate of refugees who are *civilian victims of armed conflicts or disturbances*, or of their direct results, i.e., situations covered by its mandate. ICRC action for these refugees depends *inter alia* on their protection under international humanitarian law.

In the case of *refugees covered by humanitarian law*, the ICRC steps in to encourage belligerents to apply the relevant provisions of the Fourth Geneva Convention. At the operational level, the ICRC seeks to obtain access to the said refugees on the basis of this same Convention, and to provide them with any protection and assistance they may need.

As mentioned above, refugees are often *not protected by humanitarian law*, i.e., when the host country is not party to an international armed conflict or is itself not engaged in conflict. In such cases they are protected only by refugee law and benefit from the activities of UNHCR. As a rule, the ICRC then acts only in a *subsidiary* capacity and if it is the sole organisation in the area concerned. It withdraws once UNHCR and other organisations take over so that it can carry out tasks more in keeping with its specific role. The ICRC may, however, offer refugees the services of its Central Tracing Agency at any time. It has also developed war surgery programmes for wounded refugees.

The ICRC does, however, feel concerned when refugees encounter major security problems in host countries, particularly when violence or even military operations are directed toward refugee camps near the border. In this case, the ICRC is well placed to perform its role as a neutral and independent intermediary, and has *concurrent competence* alongside that of UNHCR. With regard to security problems arising in refugee camps particular note should be taken of two factors: the location of such camps in dangerous areas close to the border where they are exposed to hostilities, and the presence of combatants in the camps. International humanitarian law provides some solutions to these problems, though it must first be respected.

When both the ICRC and UNHCR are competent to take action, work by the two organisations is carried out in a spirit of complementarity. Concerted efforts and close coordination result in optimum assistance for victims.

Attention is drawn here to the important role played by the National Red Cross and Red Crescent Societies and their Federation in assistance operations for refugees.

The *repatriation of refugees* is another area of considerable concern to the ICRC. Although it generally does not engage in such operations, the ICRC considers that the States and organisations involved must carefully check that the time and conditions for the refugees' return are right. Owing to its good knowledge of the refugees' country of origin, it can analyse the situation and make recommendations to ensure that refugees return home safely and in dignity. On several occasions the ICRC has warned against the risk of over-hasty repatriations in unstable areas or places where the infrastructure has been destroyed.

The problem of landmines must be borne in mind here, with their devastating injuries that most all affect the civilian population. These mines not only constitute a reason for displacement, they also seriously impede the reconstruction of war-stricken countries and represent a major obstacle to the return of refugees and displaced persons. The ICRC is of the opinion that only a total prohibition of anti-personnel mines can put an end to this scourge.

Chapter 5

Causes of Refugee Flows and the Law of State Responsibility

Causes of Refugee Flows

Till recently, the issue of causes of refugee flows received little attention, although the matter was discussed in the Special Political Committee (SPC) of the United Nations General Assembly (UNGA) in the 1980s.[1] An important reason for this was 'the political paralysis of the bipolar world':

In the receiving countries of the West, anyone arriving from the Soviet Union or one of its allies was automatically granted some form

[1] The debate on 'root causes' was initiated in the United Nations in 1980 in the SPC of the General Assembly. The UNGA, on the recommendation of the SPC (UN Doc. A/35/582), adopted Resolution 35/124, the operative part of which strongly condemned 'all policies and practices of oppressive and racist regimes as well as aggression, alien domination and foreign occupation, which are primarily responsible for the massive flows of refugees throughout the world and which result in inhuman suffering'. The Resolution was adopted by a recorded vote of 105 in favour, 16 against with 14 abstentions. The Resolution invited member states to convey to the Secretary-General their comments and suggestions on international cooperation to avert new flows of refugees and to facilitate the return of those refugees who wish to return. In pursuance of this request, a number of states submitted their observations (UN Doc. A/36/582 and A/37/416). There followed in 1981 a study of mass exoduses prepared by Prince Sadruddin Aga Khan, the former High Commissioner for Refugees. ECOSOC, E/CN.4/1503, 31 December 1981, *Study on Human Rights and Massive Exoduses*. In 1985, a Group of Experts was established (UNGA Res. 36/148) to study the problem and submitted their report in 1986. See UN Doc. A/41/324, 13 May 1986, *Report of the Group of Governmental Experts on International Co-operation to Avert New Flows of Refugees, 1986*. Meanwhile, in 1983, an Independent Commission on International Humanitarian Issues co-chaired by Aga Khan and the Crown Prince of Jordan, Hassan Bin Talal, was formed. It issued a report in 1986. See *Refugees: Dynamics of Displacement* (Zed Books, London, 1986).

of asylum; no detailed scrutiny of their reasons for leaving was felt necessary. In the Third World too, it was almost impossible to address the causes of flight if the source country could call on the protection of one of the superpowers—and almost all could to some degree.[2]

It is symptomatic that the 1951 Convention did not contain any specific reference to the responsibilities of the country of origin. However, with the end of the Cold War, Western states have averred that 'prevention is preferable to cure' throwing 'the spotlight on the conditions and events that force people to flee'.[3]

The subject of root causes of refugee flows is a complex one. **Reading I.A** offers an overview of the political, economic, environmental and ethnic causes of refugee flows. It also underlines the fact that refugee flows almost always involve the violation of human rights.

However, beyond the simple enumeration of factors which generate refugee flows, there are a number of critical issues which call for further research and analysis. First, there is a debate over whether underdevelopment is a principal cause of refugee flows. According to **Reading I.A**, 'it is too simple to say that poverty begets refugees.' In **Reading I.B** Zolberg, Suhrke and Aguayo endorse this view. However, this is done not to deny the role of 'structural violence' in generating refugee flows but to caution against taking a facile view of the relationship between refugee flows and underdevelopment. Furthermore, it is emphasised that to talk about averting all refugee flows is the equivalent of opposing social change, for social change almost always involves uprooting people. While the work of Zolberg and his colleagues marks an important beginning, it may be safely concluded that a proper conceptualisation of the relationship between underdevelopment and refugee flows is a challenge which refugee studies has yet to meet.

Second, there is the related question as to whether the causes of refugee flow are 'internal' or 'international'. **Reading I.A** notes that 'both play major parts.' But as Zolberg et al. point out:

> The international dimension of the causes of refugee movements has not been recognised in prevailing legal concepts and definitions ... factors internal to the country of origin predominate in conventional interpretations of persecution .... This not only is incorrect but also obscures the point that external parties by action—or inaction—can significantly influence the processes that generate refugees. Refugees do not appear simply because they are persecuted by government X

[2] *The State of the World's Refugees: The Challenge of Protection* (Penguin, New York, 1993), pp. 8–9.

[3] Ibid., p. 9.

or victimised by brutalising rulers in weak states; such governments and states exist within a necessary structure of international support. It follows that outside parties and humanitarian groups concerned with refugees must make foreign policy a matter of abiding concern.[4]

The next two readings highlight the role of international factors in causing refugee flows. In **Reading I.C** Michel Chossudovsky looks at the causes of the tragedy of Rwanda and notes how the Western media has sought to portray the genocide as an instance of ethnic conflict—and depicted it as such even in **Reading I.A**—instead of looking at the complex social and economic realities, produced in great part by external factors, which led to the mass killings. This is also the theme of **Reading I.D** in which Petras and Vieux contend that the policies recommended by international financial institutions created the conditions in which ethnic hatred could be mobilised in former Yugoslavia. Petras and Vieux also highlight the role played by Western diplomacy in creating conditions conducive to conflict in former Yugoslavia.

In **Reading I.E**, Gibney examines the reasons why scholars have failed to address the international dimension of the causes of refugee flows. He singles out 'the unexamined assumption in both international law and in political theory that has given nations license to treat their own citizens and citizens of other countries by vastly disparate standards'. Gibney expands on this theme through analysing 'the changing nature of force' in the international system, and through focusing on the role of the United States in creating refugee flows from Vietnam.

The last decade has seen a 'new agenda for democratic theory' which has come to question the central assumption that nationals of other states can be treated differently from ones own. Central to the new democratic theory is 'a critical enquiry into the necessity, desirability, and possibility of "global democracy"—that is, democracy beyond borders'.[5] It recognises, in the words of Held, that

> the heart or 'deep structure' of the modern system of nation-states can be characterised by a striking tension between the entrenchment of accountability and democratic legitimacy inside state boundaries and the pursuit of power politics outside such boundaries.[6]

The new democratic theory calls for 'the extension of democracy beyond the nation-state to bring to account those global and transnational forces

---

[4] A.R. Zolberg, A. Suhrke and S. Aguayo, *Escape from Violence: Conflict and the Refugee Crisis in the Developing World* (Oxford University Press, New York, 1989), pp. 264–65.

[5] Anthony McGrew, 'Democracy beyond Borders? Globalization and the Reconstruction of Democratic Theory and Politics', in A. McGrew, ed., *The Transformation of Democracy* (Polity Press, Cambridge, 1997), pp. 231–65 at p. 231.

[6] David Held, *Democracy and the Global Order* (Polity Press, Cambridge, 1995), p. 73.

which presently escape effective democratic control'.[7] It squarely rejects the internalist explanation for it is overly deferential to the boundaries of nation-states refusing to come to terms with the idea that external social forces often crucially shape internal policies of states. Interested readers may pursue this line of thinking further.

The Chossudovsky, Petras and Viex, and Gibney extracts underline the difficulties involved in arriving at a law of state responsibility with respect to the generation of refugee flows. To focus simply on the responsibility of the state of *physical* origin in generating refugee flows is to take an internalist view of the causes of refugee flows to the exclusion of the critical international dimension. Unfortunately, however, the incipient debate on the law of state responsibility for refugee flows appears to be directed solely towards identifying the legal obligations of the physical state of origin.

Law of State Responsibility: Key Issues

The international law of state responsibility 'is concerned with the incidence and consequences of illegal acts, and particularly the payment of compensation for loss caused'.[8]

In **Reading II.A** Beyani introduces the subject of state responsibility for displaced populations (used as a generic reference to refugees and persons displaced within states). Beyani, however, confines the scope of the study to the responsibility of the state of physical origin. In the readings to follow Garvey, Lee and Tomuschat follow suit. In **Reading II.B** Akkavan and Bergsmo review some of the problems involved in confining attention to the state of physical origin and note certain situations in which it would be unconscionable to hold it responsible for causing refugee flows. They also briefly discuss the remedies that may be available.

A second issue concerning the development of the law of state responsibility relates to whether a cooperative or a sanctions approach should be followed in dealing with the state of origin. In **Reading II.C**, Garvey suggests that 'the thrust of the substantive principles should be cooperative.' On the other hand, in **Reading II.D**, Lee appears to support a sanctions approach. The cooperative approach appears to be more reasonable when it is recalled that the causes of particular refugee flows may be entirely international in nature and in the circumstances it would be inappropriate, and perhaps counterproductive, to demand a pound of flesh of the state of physical origin. It would be a rewarding exercise for readers to reflect further on the merits and demerits of the two respective approaches.

---

[7] Ibid., p. 232.

[8] Ian Brownlie, *Principles of Public International Law* (Clarendon Press, Oxford, 1990), third edition, p. 433.

A third significant issue relates to the doctrinal basis on which to develop the law of state responsibility. Reference is often made to a 1938 article by Jennings which relied on the doctrine of abuse of rights to develop the law. But as Goodwin-Gill points out, 'with developments since 1939, the bases for the liability of source countries now lie not so much in the doctrine of abuse of rights, as Jennings then suggested, as in the breach of original obligations regarding human rights and fundamental freedoms.'[9] In **Reading II.E,** Tomuschat, among other things, supports this view. But does human rights law offer a sufficient basis for developing the law of state responsibility? According to Goodwin-Gill, legal theory 'remains imperfect, given the absence of clear correlative rights in favor of a subject of international law competent to exercise protection, and the uncertain consequences which follow where breach of obligations leads to a refugee exodus'.[10] Would the reader agree with this view?

A fourth issue is whether an individual right of reparation exists in favour of refugees. The law on the subject is at a formative stage. A key problem is whether a right of individual compensation can be applied to a situation of mass migration, even if it is assumed under international human rights law. In **Reading II.E,** Tomuschat points to the difficulties in this regard. This scepticism is shared by Goodwin-Gill who succinctly sums up the critique:

> The subject of damages for the expulsion of foreign nationals remains controversial, and there are few precedents concerning refugees. Although the principle of compensating the victims of violations of human rights has much to commend it, introducing a financial substitute for State and community obligations risks lending respectability to ethnic, religious and ideological cleansing.[11]

Can the reader envisage other difficulties or possible solutions to the problems these authors note?

A fifth issue concerns the articulation of relevant international law norms and the evaluation of past practices with reference to obligations owed by the state of origin to the receiving country. Tomuschat concludes that whereas a legal case can be made out there is little practice supporting the existence of a duty to pay compensation. The reader might consider whether Lee in **Reading II.D** evidences sufficient state practice to support a contrary view.

A final issue relates to obligations owed by the state of origin to the international community. In this case Tomuschat concurs with Lee that a

---

[9] Guy S. Goodwin-Gill, *The Refugee in International Law* (Clarendon Press, Oxford, 1996), second edition, p. vi.
[10] Ibid.
[11] Ibid., p. 269.

good case can be made out that the UNHCR has a right to recover the costs incurred in assisting refugees from the country of origin. Would the reader agree that the UNHCR has the legal standing to claim the costs of assisting refugees?

Reading II.F reproduces the 'Cairo Declaration of Principles of International Law on Compensation to Refugees' of the International Law Association (ILA). The Declaration articulates a set of relevant principles for the progressive development and codification of the law. The Declaration, primarily the work of Lee, has at best an educative value. At worst it appears to overlook the problem of international causes of refugee flows.

* * *

I. CAUSES OF REFUGEE FLOWS

A. *The State of the World's Refugees: The Challenge of Protection* (Penguin, New York, 1993), pp. 14–24.

The international system of refugee protection was consolidated in the aftermath of World War II and during the tense early stages of the Cold War. To negotiators looking back to the Nazi persecutions and over their shoulders at Stalinist repression, the causes of the contemporary refugee problems did not seem excessively complicated. The governments of the countries that produced refugees were assumed not to be susceptible to international pressure concerning the treatment of their citizens. There was little to debate. A political consensus among Western democracies that the people of Eastern Europe were persecuted by their governments meant that the limited numbers who managed to flee were automatically granted asylum.

Conflicts over decolonisation in the late 1950s and 1960s—such as those in Algeria, Angola, Rwanda and Zaire—generated large numbers of refugees but did not shake the disinclination to examine root causes. Again, the causes seemed self-evident. It was not until the numbers of refugees escalated sharply in the 1970s that the debate was joined. Some of the energy behind it was dissipated in argument over whether internal or external factors were chiefly to blame for refugee problems. It is now evident that both play major parts; further generalisation is pointless. But the debate provided the stimulus for an analytical effort that is still going on....

Political Roots

The 1951 Convention identified what is still a major root cause of refugee flows: persecution based on who the refugee is (race, nationality, membership of a particular social group) or what he or she believes (religion or political opinion). Persecution usually takes place in the context of fundamental political disputes over who controls the state, how society organises itself, and who commands the power, privileges, patronage and perks that go with political control. These disputes are at their most heated during periods of intense change—in the aftermath of a revolutionary struggle (successful or failed), at the moment of a far-reaching change of regime or upon the emergence of a new state.

Entire social classes or ethnic groups may be presumed to hold political opinions in opposition to the state, such as the professional classes in Cambodia under Pol Pot, or the Kurds in Iraq under Saddam Hussein. Although the state usually has privileged access to the instruments of violence and persecution, it is not only states who indulge in acts that generate refugees. Armed opposition groups, such as the Shining Path in Peru, Ranamo in Mozambique, the Khmer Rouge in Cambodia, and nationalist groups in Bosnia and Herzegovina, have also made life unbearable—or impossible—for their adversaries and for many innocent bystanders....

As the superpower rivalry of the Cold War all too clearly demonstrated, external political involvement of the partisan variety complicates internal conflict and raises the level of violence. The largest refugee flows of the last three decades—Afghanistan, Vietnam, Cambodia, the Horn of Africa, Angola, Mozambique—were exacerbated by superpower involvement. External intervention in local disputes often disrupts traditional processes of mediation by giving one party, clan or faction a definitive upper hand. Contenders are provided with additional firepower to enforce their will. An outside patron may prop up leaders who have little if any domestic legitimacy. An infusion of military aid increases the destructiveness of confrontation, while economic aid raises the stakes in the context for control of domestic institutions.

The vast majority of refugees today, as in the past, are fleeing not from targeted acts of individual persecution but from generalised violence that endangers civilians and radically disrupts everyday life. These conditions are the products of instability, internally or externally generated, and are fed by political opportunism that seeks to exploit social division for political gain.

Economic Roots

Economic tensions are among the major underlying causes of refugee flows, but the relationship is not as straightforward as might be assumed. It is too simple to say that poverty begets refugees. In relatively static situations, extreme deprivation is as likely to breed resignation as resistance. More combustible material springs from a deterioration of economic standing. Bitter disputes among national groups arise from efforts to preserve or advance the standing of one group at the relative expense of others. Disputes concerning the distribution of resources during general economic decline are the most politically explosive. Leaders, trying to avoid the blame for deteriorating economic conditions, frequently turn to scapegoating. Minority groups often provide the most convenient targets.

Poverty undoubtedly exacerbates ethnic and communal tensions. To know that the number of rural poor has doubled since 1950, that per capita incomes have fallen steadily in a number of regions and that malnutrition has risen, is to know that the stage is set for continuing refugee flows—but this is only one part of the dynamic of displacement. More than one billion people worldwide live in absolute poverty. Only a small proportion of them will become refugees. In fact, the total number of refugees worldwide amounts to less than 2 percent of the destitute. Nevertheless, economic deprivation interacts with other circumstances to heighten instability and aggravate conflicts.

In near-subsistence economies, violent conflict disrupts food production and distribution even as it displaces people. When the conditions of daily life, precarious to begin with, are disrupted by war, the ensuing famine and disease often become greater threats to the population than the fighting itself. In Sudan's civil war, for example, 600,000 people are thought to have died so far, many of whom have starved or succumbed to diseases that they would probably have been able to resist had the situation been more stable.

There is an obvious logic in the argument that stagnation and decline aggravate conflict. That rapid growth can have the same effect may be less apparent. Every process of change has winners and losers. The dislocations of development result in imbalances, with some classes, regions or ethnic groups benefitting disproportionately. They may become the targets of resentment, or themselves assert a claim for self-determination in order to be free of what they see as the drag of less progressive elements of society. Either reaction may provoke violent confrontation.

Environmental Roots

Millions of people have been forced to leave their homes because the land on which they live has become uninhabitable or is no longer able to support them. In some cases the cause is a natural disaster; in others, the catastrophe is caused by humans. The disruption to the habitat may be sudden, as at Chernobyl or Mount Pinatubo, or as gradual as the spread of a desert or the retreat of a forest.

The terminology for describing environmentally induced migration is controversial. For many observers, 'migration' does not convey the fact that the people affected are forcibly uprooted. To call them refugees seems to convey more accurately that they left their homes involuntarily, for reasons not of their own making. Accurate use of the term 'refugee', however, implies a need for international protection. For most people whose usual places of residence have become uninhabitable, the first recourse remains their own governments and societies. People displaced by environmental degradation or natural disaster undoubtedly need assistance. They do not necessarily require the kind of international protection implied in the word 'refugee'.

There are, nevertheless, clear links between environmental degradation and refugee flows. The deterioration of the natural resource base, coupled with demographic pressure and chronic poverty, can lead to or exacerbate political, ethnic, social and economic tensions which in turn result in conflicts that force people to flee. Africa, for example, accounts for 10 percent of the world's population and hosts over 29 percent of its refugees. It is no coincidence that those parts of the continent that are most affected by soil erosion, drought and other environmental problems are also the main theatres of armed conflicts, recurrent famine and consequent refugee movements.

In the Sahel and the Horn of Africa, the combination of rapidly expanding populations, drought and competition between nomads and settled agriculturalists has erupted into violence along a number of fronts. Disputes over irrigable land in the Senegal River basin have contributed to the flow of thousands of Senegalese and Mauritanians across their common border in both directions. In southern Ethiopia, incursions by certain clans into the traditional grazing lands of other clans have led to fierce and bloody clashes, and to a large, though temporary, flow of refugees into northern Kenya. Further south, in Mozambique, civilians already under severe pressure from the effects of civil war were pushed to the very edge of survival—and in many cases beyond it—by the effects of drought in 1992. More than 100,000 of them took refuge in neighbouring Malawi in that year alone.

Occasionally, the destruction of a habitat takes on the character of persecution—for example if it occurs as a result of deliberate governmental action or gross negligence and no effort is made to compensate or assist the people affected. Indigenous people are particularly vulnerable to this kind of assault, as their way of life is often closely connected to a particular terrain. In extreme cases, for example in Iraqi Kurdistan, destruction of habitat may be used as a deliberate weapon of war. People who are uprooted because of wilfully negligent or intentional destruction of the environment may indeed need international protection.

Long term strategies of prevention should address environmental damage as a potential contributor to refugee flows. There is no comfort in the fact that today only a minority of environmentally displaced people need international protection. The international community has every interest in responding to the need to preserve and rehabilitate the environment before degradation leads to violence and persecution—and a mass of displaced people who easily meet the conventional definition of refugees.

Ethnic Tensions

Conflicts between ethnic groups have proliferated in recent years. Armenia and Azerbaijan, Bhutan, Burma, Ethiopia, Georgia, Iraq, Sri Lanka, Sudan and, of course, the former Yugoslavia are among a long list of examples. Very few modern states are ethnically homogeneous. The 190 or so independent states currently in existence contain at least 5,000 ethnic groups. Ethnic diversity is part of human geography almost everywhere. As a consequence, the notion of an ethnically pure nation-state is almost everywhere a fantasy, which can only be realised at an unacceptably high human cost.

Ethnic tensions can be seen as a root cause of refugee flows for two reasons. First, they are highly susceptible to political exploitation. Factions seeking to mobilise support commonly seek to fan ethnic antagonisms for their own ends. Ethnic conflict is a likely outcome when control of the state is captured by a single ethnic group that uses its power to further its own interests at the expense of others.

Second, despite the fact that most states contain a variety of ethnic groups, the ethnic identity of a single group is all too often made into a defining characteristic of nationality. Some minority groups may be seen as an obstacle to nation-building, incapable of fitting into a homogenous national identity. Ethnic Albanians and Bosnian Muslims, for example, have no place in extreme nationalist visions of an Orthodox Christian 'Greater Serbia'. The ideology of apartheid in South Africa defined the non-White population out of citizenship. Members of groups other than the dominant one may be exposed first of all to discrimination, then to forced assimilation, persecution, expulsion or even genocide. In many refugee crises, ethnicity is the criterion according to which people are denied the protection of their national governments.

Recurrent conflict among ethnic or communal groups within a state calls for mediation by the central government. If the state is party to the conflict, or if it is otherwise unwilling or too weak to perform its mediating role effectively, 'ethnic cleansing' or other forms of forcible unmixing of populations may be the result, leading to very large flows of refugees—as in Palestine and the Punjab in 1948, and in Bosnia and Herzegovina, Armenia and Azerbaijan today.

Ethnic tensions are also vulnerable to manipulation by external forces. Irredentism—the attempt to unite all territories occupied by a single ethnic group into one political entity—is the most obvious form, and has played a large part in refugee-producing conflicts, in the Horn of Africa and the former Yugoslavia, to cite two examples. Somalia's ambition to incorporate Somali-inhabited areas of the Ethiopian Ogaden led to a war in 1977, and the population of much of the region remains unsettled to this day, owing to a combination of political instability, ethnic tension, economic collapse and recurring drought.

Throughout the Cold-War period, superpower rivalry was a source of patronage for ethnic factions in numerous conflicts. Like European colonialism before it, the Cold War fostered or even created ethnic tensions. The recruitment of local factions into strategic alliances with East or West disrupted historical balances between groups, and artificially strengthened the position of client groups by arming them, arranging sanctuaries and providing diplomatic support for them. Members of certain disaffected ethnic groups were systematically co-opted to act as preferred proxies, intermediaries or fighters—for example, the Hmong in Laos or the Miskitos in Nicaragua—thereby exposing the whole group to retribution. Local impulses toward accommodation or reconciliation were sometimes submerged by a powerful patron's interest in continuing the conflict. Refugee populations themselves became pawns in disputes remote from their own immediate concerns.

If the Cold-War era was dominated by ideological conflict, the fear is widespread that the 1990s may be the start of a new era of ethnic violence that will uproot additional millions of people from their homes. Already, refugees from dozens of ethnic conflicts look to the international community for material assistance and protection. Supposedly ancient hatreds, to which many people attribute the savagery of ethnic conflicts, can be invented, revived or kept from dying a natural death by opportunists who see in them a vehicle for personal or political profit.

The challenge for modern states is to alleviate ethnic tensions through mediation and to prevent them from turning into violent conflict. This preventive role is set within a more positive responsibility: to manage ethnic diversity in a way that promotes tolerance within and beyond national borders.

Human Rights and Refugee Flows

Coerced departure is a violation of the human right to remain peacefully in one's home. The direct denial of other basic rights, including the rights of civilians not to be targeted in military actions, often provides the immediate impetus for flight. Indirectly, protest about or resistance to human rights violations may provoke violent retaliation, or take a violent form itself. An accumulation of abuses accompanied by violence, which leads to further abuses and a generalised climate of fear, is a sequence that frequently produces mass exodus. In Iraq, Bosnia and Herzegovina,

Myanmar, Guatemala and elsewhere, human rights violations have been at the core of major humanitarian emergencies.

The rights that states are obliged to protect are codified in the Universal Declaration of Human Rights, and are translated into binding form in the International Covenant on Civil and Political Rights and the International Covenant on Economic, Social and Cultural rights. These instruments and others identify the sovereign state as the primary defender of rights such as the right not to be subjected to torture or to arbitrary detention and the rights to freedom of expression, thought and belief. The refugee's need for international protection arises from the violation of his or her rights combined with the state's palpable failure in its duty to defend citizens against such violations—which of course includes the duty to refrain from violations itself.

The responsibility of states towards their citizens is coming under closer scrutiny as refugee flows increase and come to be seen by many receiving states as a threat to international peace and security. Both humanitarian and security concerns have focused attention more sharply on the causes of mass exodus, bringing human rights out from behind the shield of national sovereignty. Indeed, the concept of the state's responsibility towards its citizens is being extended to encompass a responsibility towards the international community for the way those citizens are treated. Protection against the most threatening forms of abuse, such as arbitrary killings, detention, torture and disappearance can have a profound impact on the cycle of violence and fear that impels so many people to flee.

Human rights violations do not occur in a vacuum. Like other causes of refugee flows they exist in a complex environment of economic strains, political instability, a tradition of violence, ecological deterioration and ethnic tensions. One factor or another may dominate a particular situation while interacting with others. By the time serious and massive abuses of fundamental rights occur, the chances of averting refugee flows are slim indeed.

Catalysts

If it is possible to detect broad patterns in the root causes of refugee movements, the immediate triggers tend to be much more specific to the particular setting. In northern Iraq, the catalyst was a savage attack by government forces in response to a failed rebellion. In the former Yugoslavia, it was a series of localised (though co-ordinated) campaigns of terror against ethnic opponents, involving gross violations of human rights, forced displacement and indiscriminate destruction of lives and livelihoods. In Somalia, it was the disintegration of law and order, leading to the violent disruption of production and distribution, which left millions of people vulnerable to famine. In Sudan, the imposition of laws and regulations which were unacceptable to a large segment of the population in the south or the country reignited a long-running secessionist struggle. In Haiti, a military coup against an elected government prompted a crackdown on civil and political expression as well as a regional economic boycott. In Afghanistan, the intervention of the Soviet Union in support of a client raised the level of violence in a civil war, which was further exacerbated by Western intervention to equip and fund opposition forces in exile.

While the events that trigger refugee outflows are specific to each particular setting, certain common denominators are apparent. The immediate cause of flight is in most cases an imminent threat to life, liberty or security. Deliberate expulsion may present any or all of these threats. In situations of armed conflict, the periods to civilian life and security are not only accidental. Although non-combatants do inadvertently get caught in the crossfire between opposing forces, the main dangers posed to civilians like in the flagrant disregard of international humanitarian law (also known as the laws of war), which forbids attacks on the persons or livelihoods of non-combatants. The use of indiscriminate weapons, the adoption of scorched-earth policies in enemy territories and the denial of access to food supplies are among the violations of humanitarian law that have become major causes of contemporary refugee flows.

B. Aristide R. Zolberg, Astri Suhrke and Sergio Aguayo, *Escape from Violence: Conflict and the Refugee Crisis in the Developing World* (Oxford University Press, New York, 1989), pp. 260–63.

The emphasis on economic underdevelopment as a cause of refugees, and the need for a new international economic order in order to get at the roots of the current refugee problem, calls for a correction. Our findings indicate that contrary to UN debate, economic underdevelopment is by itself not a major cause of refugee flows.

The simple notion that poverty produces refugees is inconsistent with the fact that situations of extreme economic deprivation usually have not generated population outflows claiming international refugee status (e.g., the poor in India or Burkina Faso). Even poverty in the form of structural violence—that is, extreme, systematic, and sustained economic deprivation—by itself and in the first instance typically produces powerlessness. When migratory movement occurs, it is most likely to take the form of internal migration that requires few resources, or if it is international, the poorest will be the last to leave (as in the case of Haiti). International population movements attributed to severe food shortages caused by foolish policies and unfavourable weather, as is happening in parts of Africa, present problems different from those of refugees requiring protection and possibly resettlement and so are aided accordingly with international famine relief.

Under prevailing international definitions of refugees, victims of structural violence are not likely to be given refugee status; population flows making claim to such assistance therefore rarely materialise. Recognition policies in this respect have the characteristics of a self-fulfilling prophecy. In extreme cases, it is true, internal conditions are so appalling as to create a simple overflow of needy people seeking basic security elsewhere, as in the cases of people fleeing weak states with tyrannical regimes in Africa. In these situations, the distinction between flight from violence and flight from hunger is in practice erased.... In an earlier period when the international refugee regime was poorly developed in Africa, such flows were treated as migrants (e.g., the mass exodus from Sekou Toure's Guinea). Later there was a greater tendency to treat them as refugees (e.g., from Equatorial Guinea).

Considering the circumstances under which victims of poverty, or its more precise form, structural violence, appear in the international refugee queue, it appears that these are conditioned both by the expansion of an international refuge regime able to render assistance and the objective conditions in the country of origin. First, when structural violence coincides with politically directed, physical violence—wars, state repression, abuse against minorities, and the like—the needy can draw on asylum and relief programmes made available primarily in the context of the political nature of the strife (e.g., Chad, El Salvador). Second, and sometimes concurrently, the small margin of survival in many parts of the South ensures that war will create a compounded disaster of man-made and nature-made destruction that compels very large numbers of people to seek basic necessities elsewhere (e.g., the Mozambique region and the Horn of Africa). Third, victims of structural violence can successfully claim refugee status en masse when there is an opportunity for 'pairing' cases, that is, when they can claim on the basis of equitable treatment with another at least superficially similar group (e.g., Haitians with the Cubans in the United States in 1980).

In complex conflict situations, a root cause strategy attempting to improve economic conditions in the home country is relevant but has obvious limitations. In cases of famine and internationalised war, a root cause strategy must be formulated at the international political level to establish the prerequisites for peace and development. When massive internal poverty is related to the structure of political power and production, reforms without fundamental change in the political economy will have marginal results.

In special situations, economic hardship directly contributes to refugee flows.... Societies in a postrevolutionary or postliberation phase are particularly vulnerable. Problems of reconstruction and consolidation can easily be made worse by external punitive measures, generating internal pressures for the population at large to leave the country in the face of widespread economic deprivation or a radicalisation of the revolution (as seen in Cuba, Vietnam, Nicaragua and, with disastrous results, Mozambique). Because the flows originate in highly politicised situations, the people are likely to claim and often obtain refugee status. In such cases, the policy implications for outside states are clear: termination of support for the *contras*, and the creation of a more benign international environment, including rendering aid rather than instituting a blockade, would reduce internal pressures and the consequent population flows.

The role of economic underdevelopment as a cause of refugees must also be addressed from the broader perspective adopted by the Independent Commission on International Humanitarian Issues. To what extent have the characteristic imbalances of economic underdevelopment contributed to violent political conflicts of the kind that historically has caused large refugee flows?... The relationship between structured economic inequalities and violent social change is extraordinarily complex, whether it concerns the development of a revolutionary situation, patterns of ethnic conflict, or the foundations of authoritarian rule. A restructuring of international economic relations along NIEO lines is not a precise instrument to reduce such conflict and related refugee flows. In fact, most reforms demanded under NIEO could just as well sharpen as reduce internal conflict, by contributing to uneven development processes. The same applies to economic aid policies, which tend to have an uncertain or unexpected impact on the structure of social conflict unless carefully targeted.

This is not to deny that international redistributive agendas such as NIEO and a liberal aid policy are desirable *per se*. They should be supported for many reasons, but not because they are likely to reduce international refugee flows, especially in the short run. Thus, for the South to argue that more development aid, or a reshaped international economic order, is necessary to deal with the root causes of refugee flows, is to stretch the logic of social conflict. Equally tenuous are expectations in the prosperous North that more generous aid policies can buy insulation from the refugee fallout of conflicts in the South. Such policies can, however, help reduce the burden in developing countries that receive large and sudden influxes of refugees from neighbouring states. Here the costs of providing asylum are inflated by conditions of general underdevelopment and, without compensatory economic schemes, will certainly generate new conflicts.

Root Causes and Social Change

The UN debate underlined the essentially political nature of the refugee phenomenon. The receiving countries tended to take an 'internalist' perspective, blaming the countries of origin; the latter claimed that external forces ultimately were responsible. Both perspectives were coloured by the dominant ideological cleavages of the time, in the last instance because root causes in fact are the constituent elements of social change and historical development. Deep disagreements in this area are to be expected. A revolution, for instance, is a root cause with a well-defined range of enemies and supporters. It would be naive to expect that a broad, international front could be formed to attack the root causes of refugees generally, or even in a single conflict complex such as in South Africa. Attempts to create a consensus in the UN accordingly produced a rhetorical General Assembly resolution that concluded the root cause debate. The Expert Group, for its part, sought to escape the divisive issues of cause by dealing with the consequences of conflict, that is, by considering improved assistance for refugees.

A more realistic approach must start by recognising the essential political and normative nature of the root causes. For a start, the call for a root cause approach in itself has a conservative preventive implication. As the history of refugee movements demonstrates, refugees are a by product of social change, and only one item on a much broader canvas of suffering and progress. Orientation towards the fate of refugees must be tempered by an awareness of this larger picture. A revolution, for instance, should not be judged merely by the tragic but historically necessary fact that it produces refugees.

The point is not always appreciated by humanitarian organisations devoted to aiding refugees, which frequently complain that nations pursue their conflicting interests with little regard for the possibility that refugees may result. Though well motivated, this concern ignores the historical connection between social change and refugees. To avert flows would be the equivalent of trying to oppose social change. In the aggregate, this of course is impossible, and in particular cases it may well be undesirable. To stifle change may freeze a repressive social order or contribute to systemic social inequalities. In the longer run, both conditions are likely to produce their own refugees, in the form of individuals fleeing oppressive conditions or revolutionary upheavals. In some circumstances, also, violent change may be a necessary path toward a more just social order. As Barrington Moore's classic study of social change points out, even liberal democracy originated in violent change.[12] An emphasis on conflict prevention, like an uncritical stress on 'law and order', has legitimised repressive and socially reactionary regimes, in revolutionary movements in semifeudal societies, and violent resistance to repressive, authoritarian regimes. In these situations, an outflow of refugees is arguably the most humane form of adjustment.

[12] Barrington Moore Jr., *Social Origins of Dictatorship and Democracy* (Penguin Books, Hammondsworth, 1966).

From this perspective, the emphasis on 'averting flows' in the UN debate is unfortunate. It suggests opposition by the wealthy and powerful North to radical, and especially violent, social change in the South and, at any rate, unwillingness to accept the consequence in terms of providing support for asylees and refugees. The simplest way of 'averting flows', it will be recalled, is for both the sending and the receiving countries to slam the door shut.

Clearly, some approaches to reducing conflict can readily be identified. Whether they should be adopted in particular situations must be determined by a broader calculus of what constitutes a just and desirable development. Whatever is ultimately decided, however, action must be informed by an awareness of likely human suffering associated with various strategies.

C. Michel Chossudovsky, 'Hidden Hands behind Rwandan Holocaust', *Health for the Millions* (Vol. 22, No. 2, March–April 1996), pp. 33–34.

The Rwandan crisis has been presented by the Western media as a profuse narrative of human suffering, while neglecting to explain the underlying social and economic causes. As in other 'countries in transition', ethnic strife and the outbreak of civil war are increasingly depicted as something which is almost 'inevitable' and innate to these societies, constituting 'a painful stage in their evolution from a one-party State towards democracy and the free market....'

The brutality of the massacres has shocked the world community, but what the international press fails to mention is that the civil war was preceded by the flare-up of a deep-seated economic crisis. It was the restructuring of the agriculture system which precipitated the population into abject poverty and destitution. This deterioration of the economic environment which immediately followed the collapse of the international coffee market and the imposition of sweeping macro-economic reforms by the Bretton Woods institutions—exacerbated simmering ethnic tension and accelerated the process of political collapse....

In 1987, the system of quotas established under the International Coffee Agreement (ICA) started to fall apart.[13] World price plummeted, the *Fonds d'egalisation* (the State coffee stabilisation fund) which purchased coffee from Rwandan farmers at a fixed price started to accumulate a sizeable debt. A lethal blow to Rwanda's economy came in June 1989 when the ICA reached a deadlock as a result of political pressures from Washington on behalf of the large US coffee traders. At the conclusion of historic meeting of producers held in Florida, coffee prices plunged in a

---

[13] On international commodity agreements see B.S. Chimni, *International Commodity Agreements: A Legal Study* (Croom Helm, London, 1987) (editor).

matter of months by more than 50 percent. For Rwanda and several other African countries, the drop in price wreaked havoc. With retail prices more than 20 times than that paid to the African farmer, a tremendous amount of wealth was being appropriated in the rich countries.

The Legacy of Colonialism

What is the responsibility of the West in this tragedy? First, it is important to stress that the conflict between the Hutu and Tutsi was largely the product of the colonial system, many features of which still prevail today. From the late 19th century the early German colonial occupation had used the *Mwami* (King) of the Nyiginya monarchy installed at Nyanza as means of establishing its military posts.

However, it was largely the administrative reforms initiated in 1926 by the Belgians which were decisive in shaping socio-ethnic relations. The Belgians explicitly used dynastic conflicts to reinforce their territorial control. The traditional chiefs in each hill (colline) were used by the colonial administration to requisition forced labour. Routine beatings and corporal punishment were administered on behalf of the colonial masters by the traditional chiefs. The latter were under the direct supervision of a Belgian colonial administrator responsible for a particular portion of territory. A climate of fear and distrust was installed, communal solidarity broke down, traditional client relations were transformed to serve the interests of the coloniser.

Colonial historiographers were entrusted with the task of 'transcribing' as well as distorting Rwanda-Urundi's oral history. The historical record was falsified: the Mwami monarchy was identified exclusively with the Tutsi aristocratic dynasty. The Hutus were represented as a dominated caste. . . .

The Belgian colonialists developed a new social class, the so-called *negres evolues* recruited among the Tutsi aristocracy, the school system was put in place to educate the sons of the chiefs and provide the African personnel required by the Belgians. In turn, the various apostolic missions and vicariates received under Belgian colonial rule an almost political mandate, the clergy was often used to oblige the peasants to integrate the cash crop economy. These socio-ethnic divisions—which have been unfolding since the 1920s—have left a profound mark on contemporary Rwandan society.

The Rwandan crisis has become encapsulated in a continuous agenda of donor round tables ... cease-fire agreements, peace talks.... These various initiatives have been closely monitored and coordinated by the donor community in a tangled circuit of 'conditionalities' (and cross-conditionalities). The release of multilateral and bilateral loans since late 1990 was made conditional upon implementing a process of so-called 'democratisation' under the tight surveillance of the donor community. In turn, Western aid in support of multiparty democracy was made conditional (in an almost 'symbiotic' relationship) upon the government reaching an agreement with the International Monetary Fund (IMF), and so on.

The model of 'democratisation' based on an abstract model of inter-ethnic solidarity envisaged by the Arusha peace agreement signed in August 1993 was an impossibility from the outset and the donors knew it. The brutal impoverishment of the population which resulted from both the war and the IMF reforms, precluded a genuine process of democratisation. The objective was to meet the conditions of 'good governance' (a new term in the donors' glossary) and oversee the installation of the bogus multiparty coalition government under the trusteeship of Rwanda's external creditors. In fact multipartism as narrowly conceived by the donors, contributed to fuelling the various political factions of the regime. Not surprisingly, as soon as the peace negotiations entered a stalemate, the World Bank announced that it was interrupting the disbursements under its loan agreement.

The Economy since Independence

The evolution of the post-colonial economic system played a decisive role in the development of the Rwandan crisis. While progress was indeed recorded since independence in diversifying the national economy, the colonial-style export economy based on coffee (*les cultures obligatoires*) established under the Belgian administration was largely maintained providing Rwanda with more than 80% of its foreign exchange earnings. A rentier class with interests in coffee trade and with close ties to the seat of political power had developed. Level of poverty remained high, yet during the 1970s, and the rifts part of the 1980s, economic and social progress was nonetheless realised: real gross domestic product (GDP) growth was of the order of 4.9% per annum (1965–89), school enrolment increased markedly, recorded inflation was among the lowest in sub-Saharan Africa, less than 4 per cent per annum.

While the Rwandan rural economy remained fragile, marked by acute demographic pressures (3.2% per annum population growth), land fragmentation and soil erosion, local-level food self-sufficiency had, to some extent, been achieved alongside the development of the export economy. Coffee was cultivated by approximately 70% of rural households, yet it constituted only a fraction of total monetary income. A variety of other commercial activities had been developed including the sale of traditional food staples and banana beer in regional and urban markets.

The economic foundations of the post-independence Rwandan State remained extremely fragile, a large share of government revenues depended on coffee, with the risk that a collapse in commodity prices would precipitate a crisis in the State's public finances. The rural economy was the main source of funding of the State. As the debt crisis unfolded, a larger share of coffee and tea earnings had been earmarked for debt servicing, putting further pressure on small-scale farmers.

Export earnings declined by 50% between 1987 and 1991. The demise of State institutions unfolded thereafter. When coffee prices plummeted, famines erupted throughout the Rwandan countryside. According to World Bank data, the growth of the GDP per capita declined from 0.4% in 1981–86 to –5.5% in the period immediately following the slump of the coffee market (1987–91).

D. James Petras and Steve Vieux, 'Bosnia and the Revival of US Hegemony', *New Left Review* (No. 218, July–August 1996), pp. 9–12.

The Break-up of Yugoslavia: The European Initiative

Of all the Western mendacity and hypocrisy surrounding the plight of the ex-Yugoslav Republic, none is more obscene than the notion that the break-up was the result of 'age-old hatreds' and 'ancient' feuds in a violent and volatile Balkan region. This was a convenient lie covering up three basic facts.

First, that these 'hate-filled' peoples had lived, married, studied, struggled and worked peacefully together for almost a half century prior to the so-called ethnic war.

The second fact is the central role of the West, particularly international lending institutions such as the IMF and the World Bank, in generating the social and economic preconditions for explosive ethnic conflict. As one observer of the Balkan Wars put it:

> The conflict is not a result of historical animosities and it is not a return to the pre-communist past, it is the result of transforming a socialist society to a market economy and democracy. A critical element of this failure was economic decline, caused largely by a programme intended to resolve a foreign debt crisis. More than a decade of austerity and declining living standards corroded the social fabric and the rights and securities that individuals and families had come to rely on.[14]

Austerity measures designed by the Western lending institutions contributed to the war in the Balkans in three ways. First, IMF policies exacerbated inter-republican rivalries and animosities. Second, the austerity measures

[14] Susan Woodward, *Balkan Tragedy* (Washington, D.C., 1995), p. 15; see also Catherine Samary, *Yugoslavia Dismembered* (New York, 1995), pp. 61–65.

increased the inflammability of social relations throughout Yugoslavia as the measures increased misery and desperation. Finally, the measures themselves generated a layer of unemployed or under employed angry and frustrated youth of war-making age, ideal cannon-fodder for nationalist demagogues.

Like much of the Third World, Yugoslavia ran up sizeable debts in the 1970s as it sought to cope with the economic consequences of rising oil prices and the declining markets for its manufactured goods in the West.[15] Further hikes in the price of oil, and the cut-off of commercial lending, spurred the country to pursue IMF lending. With much local intellectual and political backing—including the support of one-time bank director and neo-liberal Slobodan Milosevic—an IMF-guided stabilisation programme was implemented in stop-and-go fashion during the 1980s, with long periods of austerity from 1982 to 1985 and from 1987 into the early 1990s.[16]

Stabilisation programmes attempt to improve the trade position of a country by reducing internal demand; invariably living standards suffer as the stabilising government cuts government employment, reduces consumption subsidies, privatises services and so on. Yugoslavia was no exception. Food subsidies were dropped in 1982. In 1983 the prices for gasoline, heating fuel, food and transportation rose by a third. The government froze investment in infrastructure and social services. Private firms were unable to take up the employment slack under the pressure of high interest rates. Family income fell to a twenty-year low. Unemployment rose to 14 percent on average, with 23 percent unemployed in Bosnia–Herzegovina and in parts of Serbia including Belgrade.[17] Under the impact of the plans, the rate of growth of industrial production averaged 2.8 percent in 1987–88 and fell to –10.6 percent in 1990. Real wages fell by 41 percent in the first six months of 1990; inflation was over 70 percent. Under the impact of the IMF programme in the first nine months of 1990, 600,000 workers out of a workforce of 2.7 million had been laid off.[18]

The misery of stabilisation made large masses of citizens available for political mobilisation at the same time as the wholehearted submission to IMF policy by 'communists' and 'socialists' undermined the credibility of the Left and the principles of social solidarity and fraternity. Demagogues, first and foremost Milosevic, were able to tap into popular anger over the 'reform' measures and channel it for chauvinist purposes. The demonstrations of Serbians in 1987–88 which Milosevic directed against the autonomous status of Voyvodina and Kosovo had in the beginning a powerful anti-austerity charge. As one author remarked: 'The

[15] Woodward, *Balkan Tragedy* (see footnote 14), pp. 46–47.

[16] Ibid., pp. 67–68, 82, 96; Michel Chossudovsky, 'Dismantling Former Yugoslavia: Recolonizing Bosnia', *Economic and Political Weekly* (Vol. 21, No. 9, 1996).

[17] Woodward, *Balkan Tragedy* (see footnote 14 earlier), p. 51.

[18] Chossudovsky, 'Dismantling Former Yugoslavia' (see footnote 16 earlier), pp. 521–22.

demonstrators were often paid by their employers to attend but increasingly came from among the unemployed, who needed a handout or had nothing else to do'.[19] The young and the unemployed contributed significant numbers of soldiers to the warring sides as the fighting began.[20] The economic policies promoted by the West in Yugoslavia during the 1980s helped create the social and psychological preconditions for war along with a ready pool of embittered potential combatants.

The IMF did not simply guide economic reforms. It also tried to promote political and institutional reforms that it considered necessary for the long-term economic health of the economy. These proposals sharpened conflict between the political components of the old Yugoslavia, accelerating the trend to political break-up and war. The IMF argued that a full-fledged market economy required that a powerful central bank set monetary policy in a unified domestic market in which labour, credit and commodities circulated freely. The IMF further insisted that federal decision-making had to be strengthened at the expense of the old-style consensual policy-making among republican representatives. The 1990 World Bank–IMF loans cut off transfer payments from the centre to the republics and provinces.[21] The trend of IMF policy was to undermine the complex 'balancing act' of the Tito period which had attempted to lessen inequalities between republics and peoples by means of subsidies, federal aid, federal support for troubled industries and so forth. IMF opposition to these norms stimulated suspicions between the republics and contributed to growing tension in Yugoslavia.[22]

The third fact obscured by the ethnic hatred thesis is that the internal conflicts and territorial break-ups were in large part fuelled and fomented by Western European and US politicians, intent on carving out spheres of influence in Central Europe and the disintegration of the former Soviet Union, Europe—but principally Germany—has been scrambling with the US to grab resources, lucrative firms, skilled scientists and market share. Early on West Germany annexed East Germany; the US quickly offered 'associate' NATO membership to the Czechs, Poles and Hungarians.

German Ambitions

The break-up of Yugoslavia falls into the same pattern of dissolving larger coherent units into smaller ones in which local satraps could be more easily converted into client regimes. In the beginning, the US 'played' the nationalist card as a way of undermining the communist legacy in

---

[19] Woodward, *Balkan Tragedy* (see footnote 14 earlier), pp. 92, 96; Misha Glenny, *The Fall of Yugoslavia* (New York, 1994), p. 34.

[20] Woodward, ibid., p. 249; Glenny, ibid., p. 121.

[21] Chossudovsky, footnote 16 earlier, p. 521.

[22] Woodward, 'Dismantling Former Yugoslavia' (see footnote 14 earlier), pp. 39–40, 69–70, 74–81.

Yugoslavia. The idea of a unified, stable, non-communist state under US—rather than Russian—direction appealed to Washington. Not the least appealing feature of such an outcome was the existence of a central authority responsible for paying back outstanding international debts; any division of Yugoslavia, and corresponding reapportioning of the debt on a republican basis, would probably result in default by the poorer republic. There were two problems with this tack that swiftly undermined the thrust of Washington's policy: German regional ambitions and Serbian hegemonic aspirations.

Germany forced the EC to follow its lead in recognising the 'independence' of Croatia and Slovenia—a policy that followed close German ties to the budding Croat and Slovenian politicians. Both countries for all intents and purposes were seen by Bonn as part of the New Germany's sphere of influence.[23] At the same time, the Serbs sought to establish their hegemonic rule by raising the issue of the fate of the minority Serbs within the new, ethnically diverse Croat state and elsewhere in the former Yugoslavia. This was an explosive issue in Croatia where hundreds of thousands of Serbs had been victims of genocide during World War II at the hands of the fascist Croatian Pavelic regime. The Europeans recognised Croatia without providing any guarantees to the Serbs in Croatia. They thus handed Serbian chauvinists and extremists a powerful mobilising issue.

As the de facto partitioning took place, the US sought to seize a 'remnant piece of the action' as leverage for any future settlement in the region by recognising the independence of Macedonia and Bosnia. Yugoslavia was transformed into a region of warring ethnic entities occupying the same territory and dependent on external patrons. Each of the patrons sought the moral high ground, spot-lighting the victims of their particular ethnic clients. Since the US ostensibly chose the weakest of the competing ethnic entities, it seemed to have the least political leverage but the most 'moral capital' because the Bosnians were more vulnerable to attack than either the Croats or Serbs.

E. Mark Gibney, 'US Foreign Policy and the Creation of Refugee Flows', in Howard Adelman, ed., *Refugee Policy: Canada and the United States* (York Lanes Press, Toronto, 1991), pp. 81, 87–90, 93–100.[24]

Scholars, policy-makers and critics of US refugee policy have generally focused on two related questions: the number of refugees that the United

[23] The British government abandoned its publicly stated opposition to diplomatic recognition of Croatia and Slovenia under German pressure on 16 December 1991, in exchange for German support for the British right to 'opt-out' from the European monetary union and the Social Chapter of the Maastricht Treaty. See John Sweeney, 'How Bosnia Paid the Price of Major's Maastricht Opt-Out Coup', *The Observer* (17 September 1995).

[24] While much has changed in the international political situation since Gibney wrote this article (the Soviet Union no longer exists as a political entity, the rule of force in

States admits, and whether there remains an ideological bias in US refugee admissions and in asylum adjudications. The nature of this inquiry has been to determine the extent to which the United States has met its obligations under both international and domestic law. Marking this approach is the view that the United States is solely a recipient of refugee flows, and subject to debate is the degree to which the United States has 'fulfilled its promises' to resettle refugees and grant asylum.

Largely ignored, however, has been the flip side: the degree to which the United States has created or brought about refugee flows in the first place, or has taken action that has perpetuated such flows while pursuing foreign policy objectives and national security goals. That is, rather than simply viewing the United States as a *recipient* of refugees, inquiry should focus on the United States as the *creator* of refugee flows.

Ignoring the Refugee Consequences of Superpower Intervention

In this section, I examine reasons that both scholars and policy-makers have focused on what Zolberg and his colleagues have described as an 'internalist' view of the creation of refugee flows, at the same time overlooking the international dimensions. The inattention by policy-makers is easier to explain. The rules of the game—the entire international system itself—would be changed drastically if nations were somehow forced to consider the human consequences of their pursuit of foreign policy objectives. Harder to understand is the lack of attention by scholars to the international causes of refugee flows. I suggest that there are at least three reasons.

The first is what I will call the cause and effect problem: the difficulty in tracing the ultimate causes of refugee flows, particularly given the use of surrogates to pursue foreign policy objectives. The second is based on the kinds of rationales that recently have been employed in defence of intervention. The third arises from a deeper problem, namely, the unexamined assumption in both international law and in political theory that has given nations license to treat their own citizens and citizens of other countries by vastly disparate standards. Lea Brilmayer challenges this, posing the issue in its essential form: 'Is there any way to explain why an action suddenly becomes legitimate when it is undertaken outside one's territory? Would support for death squads in El Salvador be any different from support for death squads in Miami?'[25] I suggest that, for most purposes, these two situations are very similar, and, because of that, they should be judged by the same ethical standards. Rarely, if ever, has this occurred. Instead, nations have treated (and been allowed to treat)

---

international affairs has undergone change, etc.), the issues he raises in it are of continuing relevance (editor).

[25] Lea Brilmayer, *Justifying International Acts* (Cornell University Press, Ithaca, 1989), p. 28.

citizens of other countries in a manner that would violate their own domestic standards. This, in turn, has helped lead to much of the human carnage that marks the world today.

Difficulty in Uncovering Superpower Activity

The Changing Nature of Force

Determining the immediate causes of refugee flows is difficult enough. Who, for example, is responsible for the flight of approximately 300,000 Nicaraguans since 1979? How many refugees are the *contras* responsible for, or the Sandinistas? Attempting to determine the culpability of the superpowers is often even more difficult: What role did the United States play in the creation and perpetuation of these flows through its support of the contras? To what extent did the Soviet Union's pursuit of foreign policy objectives in that region bring about such flows of civilians?

I do not mean to suggest that clearcut cases of superpower culpability do not exist. They do. For example, a very substantial portion of the Afghan refugee population is directly attributable to the Soviet military invasion of Afghanistan. What was unique about the Soviet action, however, was not that it brought about widespread death and destruction; instead, it was the fact that the Soviet Union found it necessary to intervene directly, rather than through surrogate means.

Two of the leading scholars on the subject of political terrorism, George Lopez and Michael Stohl, have argued that the nature of force in international affairs has changed dramatically in recent years.[26] In their view, the overt use of force ... generally has been displaced by other, less obvious, and ... far less costly means. Lopez and Stohl focus on three types of this 'new' intervention: coercive diplomacy, covert state terrorism, and low-intensity conflict (LIC).

Of these three, coercive diplomacy, or diplomacy backed by threats of force, is the most commonly used and the least likely to create refugee flows. That is, however, unless the threat of force is not sufficient to achieve the ends desired, in which case either direct intervention is employed, or more likely, there is intervention by a surrogate force.

Examples from this country of the second form of changing force, covert state terrorism, range from the involvement of the Central Intelligence Agency in the overthrow of Guatemalan President Arbenz in 1954, the minding of Nicaraguan harbours, the CIA's role in the overthrow of the Allende regime in Chile, the car bombing in Beirut, the supply of instruments of terror to countries with gross levels of human rights abuses,

[26] George Lopez and Michael Stohl, 'The Changing Character of the Use of Force in International Relations', paper presented at the conference on The Ethical Dimensions of the 'Changing Use of Force' in International Affairs, University of Notre Dame, 4–6 April.

and so on. Obviously, we are talking about power politics; what has been largely ignored, however, is that power politics at times had a very high human price. Consider that before the CIA-directed coup in Guatemala, that country enjoyed a certain measure of peace. No one could make that same claim now, or for the past few decades. Zolberg and his colleagues write:

> The overthrow of Arbenz in 1954 became a watershed in Guatemalan history because it eliminated the political center and polarised political life between left and right. The landed oligarchy and foreign investors took control by establishing a corporatist and repressive state that murdered between 30,000 and 100,000 persons between 1966 and 1982. In fact, for years Guatemala was consistently considered one of the worst human rights violators in the hemisphere.[27]

Despite the involvement of the US government, and despite the human carnage that soon ensued, very few analysts would attribute culpability for these horrors to the United States. The problem in this area, admittedly, is in imputing responsibility on this basis of what might have been a single act. On the other hand, it is important to underscore the fact that even so-called isolated acts might have human costs to them. Some, as in the case of Guatemala, will have very high costs.

LIC is the last type of the 'new' intervention described by Lopez and Stohl, and the connection with the creation of refugee flows is more obvious, although seldom commented on. They describe LIC as a halfway measure between a state employing terror strategies to achieve its ends and engaging directly in counterinsurgency war. There are a number of distinguishing features of LIC. For one, while policy is formulated in the First World, it is executed in the Third World by Third World peoples and it affects only (or, more accurately, harms only) those in the Third World. One of the keys to the success of LIC (by First World standards) is that it gives the appearance that there is no conflict. In the words of Richard Barnet, 'the whole idea of low-intensity warfare is to avoid "disturbing"—a euphemism for informing—public opinion.'

In theory, LIC is intended as an economy of force, designed to quickly control, if not end, the challenge to the hostile state. When an immediate victory is not achieved, as is often the case, the intensity of the conflict rises considerably and more, rather than less, external assistance is needed, and almost always given. As the conflict then drags on, increased reliance is placed on ill-trained and less-disciplined soldiers, and the accepted doctrine is to win by any means possible. This, in turn, has brought about many of the instances of gross levels of human rights

[27] Zolberg et al., *Escape From Violence* (see footnote 4 earlier), p. 207.

abuses that exist in the world today, which translate into a dramatic increase in civilian deaths and ever-increasing refugee flows. Beyond this, Lopez and Stohl argue that this human toll is no accident; instead, they maintain, these new forms of intervention—and LIC in particular—are designed to produce civilian casualties and suffering. The aim is to increase the civilian cost—collateral damage, it is called—to the other side until it capitulates.

Concomitant with the change in the nature of force in the world has been an increase in where this force is employed. Zolberg and his colleagues have written:

> The expansion of the political–strategic system to include the entire globe implies that even the poorest and geopolitically least significant states will have some value in the games of the major players and that internal government changes in the developing countries will tend to be perceived as having implications for the wider system and will therefore be likely to provoke some sort of response by outsiders.[28]

Ignoring Harm to Others

How is it that we live in a world where human rights norms and principles are so widely accepted, yet millions of people are either slaughtered each year or driven from their country? How does one explain the fact that we in the United States live in a country dedicated to constitutional principles, and yet we have supported some of the most repressive regimes in the world and pursued foreign policy objectives that have been devastating to civilian populations in other countries? Finally, why have so few scholars concerned themselves with the issue of the vastly disparate ways in which we treat our own and others?

In the two previous sections, I explored reasons that outside intervention as a cause of large-scale refugee flows—one form of harm to others—generally has been ignored by scholars working in this area. In this section, I will present a larger theory for this inattention. The contours of this argument have been presented by Lea Brilmayer (1989). The starting point for her analysis is that neither political theory nor international relations scholarship has addressed adequately the question of the relationship between one nation-state and the citizens of another. Instead, political theory has concerned itself in general with the question of the proper relationship between the state and its own citizens. Brilmayer terms this a vertical analysis. International relations, on the other hand, has primarily focused on state–state relations. Brilmayer terms this the horizontal analysis. Scholars in both fields have ignored what she calls the

[28] Ibid., p. 232.

diagonal analysis—the relationship between the government of one country and the citizens of another country (Chart 1).

Chart 1

State A		State B
	horizontal	
vertical		*diagonal*
Citizens of State A		Citizens of State B

Of particular concern to Brilmayer are coercive diagonal relationships; that is, situations where intervention by an óutside state will have severe negative consequences for individuals in the country where the intervention has taken place. Brilmayer takes the position that scholars have not developed any standards to guide these kinds of relationships, although it is presumed that domestic standards—the standards that guide a liberal democracy in the treatment of its own citizens, for example—do not apply. Brilmayer disagrees with this presumption.

> Presumably we would think that it was illegitimate for a nation to murder its own citizens to gain political advantage. Genocide and political assassination, as domestic policies, are surely ruled out. Why then is slaughter of innocent persons or political assassination immune to political evaluation when it comes to international law? And why shouldn't the legitimacy of such acts be as much a question of political theory as it is in the domestic context?[29]

Brilmayer takes the view that there is no philosophical justification for a nation to employ different standards for the treatment of its own citizens and those of other countries. Brilmayer is not suggesting that Nation A must always treat citizens of Nation B the same as it treats it own citizens. In fact, she maintains that different circumstances might well dictate disparate treatment. Nonetheless, she argues, the criteria employed in evaluating such actions must be the same. Thus, support for death squad activity in El Salvador should be justified (if it now can be justified) according to other same criteria that would be used in support of death squads in Miami. To choose another example, if it would not be permissible for the US government to kill several hundred Americans in pursuit of a drug dealer, it should not be permissible to kill several hundred

[29] Brilmayer, *Justifying International Acts* (see footnote 25 earlier), p. 92.

Panamanians for the same purpose. Similarly, if it would not be permissible to pursue policies at home that would somehow bring about large-scale refugee flows (or internal displacement), it should not be permissible to do so in other countries. The question then becomes how many foreign interventions engaged in by the United States could withstand scrutiny by our own domestic standards. We now turn to this question.

Causing Refugee Flows

Southeast Asia

Since 1975, more than two million refugees have fled Vietnam, Cambodia and Laos, and the United States has offered permanent resettlement to nearly half. Although the number of Indochinese refugees seeking resettlement has been severely reduced from its level a little more than a decade ago, there is still no end in sight, and if the civil war in Cambodia escalates (and there is every indication that it will), these numbers could jump considerably. Valerie Sutter concludes her exhaustive study of the refugee situation in Southeast Asia with this pessimistic prognosis:

> Regrettably, this investigation concludes without insight into a magic formula for resolving this most perplexing refugee dilemma. In fact, the potential for increases in the tragic elements of this ongoing saga appear all too evident in the precarious Cambodian situation and in the continuing isolation of Indo-China, which keeps those states chronically underdeveloped. There have been increases in the exodus, a deterioration of first asylum, proclivity toward abusing refugees who seek asylum, and a decline to resettlement opportunities. Perhaps of the greatest concern now are complacency regarding the status quo and a waning of interest in the Indo-China refugee issue altogether.[30]

The question that Sutter and most other analysts have asked is whether there is any end in sight, given the premise of realpolitik. The answer to this question, quite correctly I think, is not in the affirmative. There are, however, other questions that could and should be asked. One is whether it is possible for the United States to pursue policies that could help to avert further refugee flows (or even whether these flows necessarily had to occur in the first place). A second is whether the United States has adequately considered (if it has considered at all) the human consequences of its foreign policy pursuits in Southeast Asia. The answer to the first question answers the second. I would suggest that it is very possible for the

[30] Valerie O'Connor Sutter, *The Indochinese Refugee Dilemma* (Louisiana State University Press, Baton Rouge, 1990), p. 224.

United States to pursue policies in this region that would help to avert further flows of refugees. (In fact, I would go so far as to say that it would have been possible for refugee flows to have been a fraction of what they have been). One reason this has not occurred, however, is that the human consequences of US foreign policy have not been weighed sufficiently. Instead, individuals in these countries, and refugees in particular, have been used as pawns in a larger East–West conflict. This does not mean that US (and Soviet) policy ought to be condemned merely on this basis; what is essential to understand, however, is that the superpowers are culpable for creating a major part of these refugee flows.

We can begin this analysis with Vietnam. After the fall of Saigon in 1975, the United States doggedly pursued a policy of isolating Vietnam from the world community. Attempts at normalising relations between the two countries were made in the early years of the Carter administration, but an impasse was reached over the issue of US reparations. In 1976 there were approximately 5,000 Vietnamese refugees (excluding the 130,000 who fled in 1975). By 1977, these numbers had increased to 15,000 in the face of increased tension between China and Vietnam, economic mismanagement, and natural disasters. With Sino–Vietnam strains growing in 1978, demands for US reparations as a precondition for normalisation were dropped. By this time, however, the United States had decided to pursue a relationship with China rather than with its arch-enemy Vietnam. On December 15, 1978, the United States and China agreed to establish diplomatic ties. Ten days later, Vietnam declared war on the Khmer Rouge government in neighbouring Cambodia, where it has remained until recently.

Relations between the United States and Vietnam are no different—and no better—than they were ten to fifteen years ago. What was thought to be the final hurdle to normalised relations, the removal of Vietnamese troops from Cambodia, has finally been accomplished, but there is no evidence that US policy is about the change. Sutter explains why.

> Those who argue against promotion of improved American ties with Vietnam point to the low level of national interest in the region, the need to remain firm with Vietnam, and a general satisfaction with the status quo.[31]

What, exactly, is this 'status quo'? It is a bleak one for all concerned. Vietnam's economy has long been devastated. The country's gross national product is one of the lowest in the world, and yearly per capita income is less than US $200. In response to these and other factors, since 1975, more than one million individuals have fled the country, and several

[31] Ibid., pp. 91–92.

thousand have died attempting to do so. With few exceptions, the world community is growing far less receptive to refugees from Vietnam. The West has placed the blame for the current state of affairs squarely on the Vietnamese government and its 'oppressive policies'. Is this, however, really the case? For example, Michael Teitelbaum has pointed out how refugee flows from Vietnam have been used by the United States to 'embarrass and discredit' the Hanoi government.[32] Paul Kattenburg has gone even further. In 1983 he wrote: 'US policy toward Vietnam is still driven by a profound animus on the part of US policy makers toward a country they believe has embarrassed and humiliated the United States.'[33] Unfortunately, much the same is true today.

US policy has produced no winners and many losers.... Members of the Association of Southeast Asian Nations have had to provide temporary (or, in many cases, not so temporary) refuge for a million refugees, and the United States and other Western nations have had to resettle these individuals. As for the refugees themselves, it might be argued that the vast majority (those who have been safely resettled in the West) are actually better off than if they had stayed in Vietnam. This assumes, however, a Vietnam that is isolated from the world community and whose economy is teetering on the brink. This situation did not have to occur. While Vietnam certainly deserves its share of the blame for pursuing policies that have produced refugees, the West has not been blameless. Its policy of 'bleeding' Vietnam has had severe human consequences, among them the flow of refugees and it should be held accountable for these policies.

However sad the situation in Vietnam, the situation in Cambodia has been even worse. Since April 1975, an estimated half million Cambodians have fled their homeland, while several hundred thousand have been denied formal asylum in Thailand and are living precariously in makeshift camps at the border. This human tragedy, however, pales beside the one to two million Cambodians who were slaughtered during Pol Pot's reign of terror.

Unless one is fully sympathetic to US efforts to isolate Vietnam, US policy vis-à-vis Cambodia is very difficult to comprehend, let alone justify. At the present time the United States is providing support to the two non-communist guerrilla forces that are aligned with (many would say subservient to) the genocidal Khmer Rouge. With Vietnam's departure from Cambodia, the prospects for avoiding a civil war in that country are not hopeful. The schizophrenic role that the United States has played—at the same time both creating and resettling refugees—has been described by Senate aide Jerry Tinker.

[32] Michael Teitelbaum, 'Immigration, Refugees, and Foreign Policy', *International Organization* (Vol. 38, 1984), p. 439.

[33] Paul Kattenburg, 'Living with Hanoi', *Foreign Policy* (Winter 1983–84), pp. 131–49.

[O]ne arm of the United States Government is working in complicity with those who help fuel the fighting inside Kampuchea and which produces the refugees, while the other arm pleads on their behalf and urges some be settled in the United States.[34]

Perhaps more than any other example, US policy toward Cambodia indicates not only the subservience of humanitarian considerations to foreign policy objectives, but also how far removed our domestic standards are from our international pursuits. In an attempt to weaken Vietnam ... by any means possible, the United States is willing to support allies of the Khmer Rouge and help to bankroll a civil war that will only heap added misery onto an already battered and decimated people. Whatever the human costs—and these have already been very high—the United States shares a large part of the blame. ...

Much of the present tragedy in Southeast Asia is the result of a US obsession with ultimately winning the Vietnam war. Because military victory eluded the United States, this country has pursued the war by other means, most notably economic. While on some level this might be good foreign policy, on a human level it has been disastrous.

II. THE LAW OF STATE RESPONSIBILITY

A. Chaloka Beyani, 'State Responsibility for the Prevention and Resolution of Forced Population Displacements in International Law', *International Journal of Refugee Law* (Special Issue, 1995), pp. 131–37.

A high proportion of the rules of international law is concerned to establish a legal *regime* of public international order prescribing permissible spheres of action by States. When the behaviour of States exceeds such spheres, the basic problem confronting the international legal system is to determine the legality of the acts in question and, if they be wrongful, to apportion responsibility for the acts in question. In this way, State responsibility seeks to prevent recourse to illegal acts which give rise to a multitude of undesirable consequences on the international plane, including the forced displacement of populations.

Accountability for consequences generated by the unacceptable conduct of States in international relations is a major focus of the international legal system. In the *Corfu Channel* case (Merits), the International Court of Justice remarked with truism that according to international practice, a State on whose territory or in whose waters an act contrary to

---

[34] Quoted in Sutter, *The Indochinese Refugee Dilemma* (see footnote 30 earlier), p. 79.

international law has occurred, may be called upon to give an explanation and that such a State cannot evade such a request by limiting itself to a reply that it is ignorant of the circumstances of the act and its authors.[35]

Responsibility in this case arose from the danger created to navigation in the North Corfu Channel by the laying of mines of which no warning had been given. In the opinion of the Court, responsibility lay on the basis of knowledge on the part of Albania of the laying of mines. From this case, Professor Goodwin-Gill has correctly drawn the analogy that responsibility may be attributed whenever a State, within whose territory substantial transboundary harm is generated, has knowledge or means of knowledge of harm and the opportunity to act.[36]

The theory of State responsibility rests on a simplistic but complex practical proposition. It is that every State must be held responsible for the performance of its international obligations under the rules of international law, whether such rules derive from custom, treaty or other source of international law. Failure to discharge international obligations incumbent upon a State constitutes an international wrong, for the consequences of which the erring State is responsible. In *Nicaragua v. the United States* (Merits), the International Court of Justice found that the United States acted wrongfully by committing a *prima facie* violation of the principle of the non-use of force and was in breach of the principles of sovereignty and non-intervention by organising or encouraging the organisation of irregular forces or armed bands for incursion into the territory of Nicaragua and participating in acts of civil strife in Nicaragua.[37]

What has been stated so far shows the application of the law of State responsibility. Apart from its concern which the incidence and consequences of illegal acts, State responsibility also has a strong inclination towards liability for loss, injury or damage caused. Its underlying premise is encapsulated in the Draft Articles on State Responsibility prepared by the International Law Commission, in particular, article 1:

Every internationally wrongful act of a State entails the international responsibility of that State.

Further, under article 3,

There is an internationally wrongful act of a State when:

(a) conduct consisting of an action or omission is attributable to the State under international law; and

---

[35] *United Kingdom v. Albania*, ICJ Rep. (1949), p. 4.
[36] Guy S. Goodwin-Gill, *The Refugee in International Law* (Clarendon Press, Oxford, 1983), first edition, p. 228.
[37] ICJ Rep. (1986), p. 14.

(*b*) that conduct constitutes a breach of an international obligation of
the State.

... Legal developments brought about by human rights leave no doubt
that the conduct of a State with regard to the treatment of its own population is a matter of international law, rather than exclusive domestic
jurisdiction. In any case domestic jurisdiction in international law is an
essentially relative concept which depends upon developments in international relations. As such, it lacks a fixed content and its exercise must
be consistent with the performance of international obligations and legal
interests of other States. An important consequence of this development
is that, without losing its original form, the application of the theory of
State responsibility has to vary and extend to the consequences of illegal
conduct of a State in breach of human rights obligations.

This point is underscored by the Cairo Declaration of Principles of
International Law on Compensation to Refugees which was concluded by
International Law Association in 1992. Principle 2 of the Declaration
states that:

> Since Refugees are forced directly or indirectly out of their homes in
> their homelands, they are deprived of full and effective enjoyment of
> all articles in the Universal Declaration of Human Rights that pre-
> suppose a person's ability to live in the place chosen as home. Ac-
> cordingly, the State that turns a person into a refugee commits an
> internationally wrongful act, which creates the obligation to make
> good the wrong done.

... the nature of illegality connected with refugee flows has had a spate of
authoritative comment. In 1938, Jennings was of the view that there seems
to be good ground for stating that the wilful flooding of other States with
refugees constitutes not merely an inequitable act, but an illegal act, *a fortiori* where the refugees are compelled to enter a country of refuge in a
destitute condition.[38]

Now in the era of human rights it is clearly prohibited to displace population groups by subjecting them to practices amounting to genocide,
torture, cruel or degrading treatment, ethnic cleansing, or violence aimed
at dispersing minorities or other ethnic groups from their homeland. Ian
Brownlie, for example, has written:

> If a new State, relying on the absence of a municipal law, tried to
> deport a part of its permanent population, it would be acting in clear

---

[38] R.Y. Jennings, 'Some International Law Aspects of the Refugee Question', *British Yearbook of International Law* (1938), p. 111.

breach of its legal duties and might even involve its government in acts punishable as genocide.[39]

This passage, written in the context of the problem of nationality and new States in 1964, is equally valid today. Its true import is that deportation of a part of the permanent population of a State as an exercise of domestic jurisdiction is a clear breach of its legal duty which might entail responsibility on the basis of genocide.

Goodwin-Gill noted later in 1983 that the responsibility of States in relation to refugees springs from the fact of control over a territory and its inhabitants. He also acknowledges the effect of human rights by stating that States owe the international community the duty to accord to their nationals a certain standard of treatment in the matter of human rights. In his view, a State is bound in its exercise of domestic jurisdiction by the principle *sic utere tuo ut alienum non laedas*, and that an ambulatory principle which obliges States to exercise care in their domestic affairs in the light of other States' legal interests does operate.

Lee offered an affirmative response to the question whether persecution by a country of its own citizens *en masse*, forcing them to flee abroad as refugees and thus impose economic, social and other burdens upon other countries constitutes an international wrong, in addition to the compensable wrong *vis-à-vis* individual refugees.[40] Lee's survey of the basis for responsibility includes the rights and duties of States, the exercise of territorial jurisdiction in a manner which interferes with the exercise by other States of their respective jurisdiction, the sovereign equality of States, unlawful deprivation of nationality, and a quasi-contractual relationship which is involved in the protection of refugees.

A cogent question to pose is whether the presence of international obligations for the protection of refugees absolves the State of origin from responsibility. It may be argued that no wrong is committed against such a State if it acts in fulfilment of the international obligations to grant entry to refugees, and that the principle of burden-sharing may mitigate the liability of the State of origin.

However, this argument ignores the fact that the obligation to provide sanctuary to refugees does not ipso facto rectify the wrong arising from breach of the legal duties of the State. As Goodwin-Gill observed,

> *A priori*, individuals and groups ought to be free to enjoy human rights in the territory with which they are connected by the internationally relevant social fact of attachment. The right to seek asylum and the benefits due to refugees, including *non-refoulement* and a

[39] Ian Brownlie, 'The Relations of Nationality in Public International Law', *British Yearbook of International Law* (1964), p. 318.

[40] Luke Lee, 'The Right to Compensation: Refugees and Countries of Asylum', *American Journal of International Law* (Vol. 80, 1986), p. 535.

certain standard of treatment, may therefore be seen as consequence of the breakdown of the norm.[41]

Indeed, the international obligations concerning the protection of refugees may be likened to the laws of armed conflict which render protection during conflict but do not, for instance, legalise armed conflict. But more guidance may be sought from the International Law Association's Declaration of Principles of International Law on Compensation to Refugees. Principle 1 of that Declaration provides that:

> The responsibility for caring for the world's refugees rests ultimately upon countries that directly or indirectly force their own citizens to flee/or remain abroad as refugees. The discharge of such responsibility by countries of asylum, international organisations (e.g., UNHCR, UNRWA, IOM) and donors (both governmental and nongovernmental), pending the return of refugees, their settlement in place, or their settlement in third countries, shall not relieve the countries of origin of their basic responsibility, including that of paying adequate compensation to refugees.

The weight and consensus of opinion presented above clearly shows the legal basis for the responsibility of the State of origin for the forcible displacement of populations in international law. Emphasis placed on the breach of a legal duty in exercise of domestic jurisdiction may lend support to the proposition that the responsibility of the State of origin in the area of forced population displacement may fall within the category of general wrongs arising from an abuse of State competence.

The Inter-American Court of Human Rights has elaborated upon this doctrine in the context of human rights.[42] In its view, the State has the right and duty to guarantee its security without question, but its power is not unlimited. Nor may a State resort to any means to attain it ends; the State is subject to law and morality, and *disregard for human dignity cannot serve as a basis of any State action*.

B. Payam Akkavan and Morten Bergsmo, 'The Application of the Doctrine of State Responsibility to Refugee Creating States', *Nordic Journal of International Law* (Vol. 58, Nos 3–4, 1989), pp. 252–54.

The Formulation of a Doctrine of State Responsibility within a Refugee Context

Goodwin-Gill candidly acknowledges that while '[a] principle of responsibility for "creating" refugees is easy to state ... [the] more precise

---

[41] Goodwin-Gill, *The Refugee in International Law* (see footnote 36 earlier), p. 229.

[42] The case of *Velasquez Rodriguez*, Judgement, Inter-American Court on Human Rights, Series C. No. 4 (1988), pp. 178–79.

formulation of the underlying rights and duties remains problematic'.[43] The following section attempts to examine in a cursory manner ... the elements of such doctrine. In particular, the constituent elements of liability for refugee flows will be explored having regard to the specific instances in which a state of origin may be held responsible for what might otherwise be an 'innocent' flow of refugees. Furthermore, the utilisation of *mala fides*, *culpa lata* and *culpa* as a 'standard of care' will be assessed on the basis of efficacy, in other words, the likelihood of their acceptance by states—the *sine qua non* of any norm of international law. Throughout the discourse the recommendations will be made with a view to balancing the interests of refugee creating states on the one hand, and recipient states on the other.

It is evident from the outset that it would be unfair and unacceptable to posit liability on a state for outflows of refugees from its territory without having regard to the conditions that caused such an outflow. For instance, natural disasters such as heavy floods, prolonged drought, soil erosion, earthquakes and desertification, could hardly be causes or factors for which a state could be held liable. It would be manifestly absurd to suggest that African states whose population was driven across national boundaries by drought or spreading deserts are liable simply because these people are treated as refugees. However, it may be that the respective state or states have omitted to take steps to alleviate the situation once it has occurred. Of course, this is a very wide if not inappropriate application of the 'refugee' definition under the 1951 Convention. Accordingly, for the sake of clarity and stability ... this definition may not be suitable in the formulation of a legal doctrine.

... in providing latitude for circumstances which are beyond the control of states and for the sake of precision, socio-economic factors should also be omitted as a cause although they are essential factors. It is unequivocal that in some cases socio-economic factors may be utilised as an effective tool for persecution. However, this should be strictly construed and limited to cases of systematic socio-economic deprivation. Any other application would cause numerous difficulties. For instance, it may be unconscionable for an underdeveloped state to be held responsible for its underdevelopment or to set about the quixotic task of determining who is responsible for adverse socio-economic conditions within a world economy with systematic deficiencies. Moreover, a developing state could maintain that refugee flows are a direct result of neo-colonialistic practices although it would be somewhat difficult to hold any state in particular liable.

This may also be a problem for political causes of refugee flows such as 'wars and armed conflicts' resulting from 'acts of aggression, alien

---

[43] Goodwin-Gill, *The Refugee in International Law* (see footnote 36 earlier), p. 226.

domination, foreign armed intervention and occupation'. Once again, determining liability may prove to be difficult. For instance, it may not be realistic to say that the aggressor would compensate a third state for the flow of refugees as a direct consequence of its own actions. Furthermore, it may be exceedingly difficult to denigrate one state as an aggressor since the use of armed force is the product of many often indeterminable variables and considerations which have plagued international law from its very beginning. For example, an act of pre-emptive self-defence or even humanitarian intervention may easily take the form of aggression.

It is submitted that given the difficulty of precisely formulating such highly amorphous causes and factors, the general problem of auto-interpretation in international law and the provisions of the 1951 Convention as a reflection of international law dealing with the duty of recipient state to accommodate refugees, liability should be posted on states which persecute their general populace or segments thereof for reasons of race, religion, nationality, membership of a particular social group or political opinion. Adopting such criteria would foreclose the possibility of *culpa* or negligence as a standard of care.

Determining persecution would have to be based on either *culpa lata* or *mala fides*. As mentioned previously, *mala fides* is very difficult to prove because a state will rarely, if at all, manifest malice aforethought in its official policy. Furthermore, on the basis of past experience, it can easily deny any malicious intention on its part and justify its actions for a variety of reasons. But since there is a strong element of malice involved in the notion of persecution, *culpa lata* may be an appropriate standard. This may provide an equitable balance between the state of origin and the receiving state. On the one hand it may avoid fastidious claims or claims which seek compensation for acts which are not subject to easy control. On the other hand, it will provide the recipient state with a standard of proof which is not inordinately restrictive.

Another problem is determining whether, for instance, the state has de facto control over a part of its territory. If there is little or no control by state authorities of a region of its territory, it may not be sound policy to posit liability for acts perpetrated there. However, if it acquiesces to persecution perpetrated by segments of the ordinary civilian population, it would seem that the state in question should be held liable for consequential damages on the basis of *culpa lata*.

The foregoing is not intended as an exhaustive list. It merely touches upon some of the issues that have to be dealt with in formulating a doctrine of state responsibility within a refugee context. Evidently there are myriad considerations which are well beyond the scope of this paper. It is safe to assert, however, that mere negligence and the consideration of factors beyond outright persecution are not likely to be accepted by the international community, especially the refugee producing states. In order to make such a doctrine feasible in view of state practice, the foregoing should be the general framework within which it should be formulated.

Remedies

Even with the provision of a precise formulation of the doctrine of state responsibility with respect to refugees, the question of an appropriate remedy must still be addressed. In particular, the function of such a doctrine should be deterrence for the state of origin and compensation for the recipient state and accordingly, a remedy should be suited for this purpose.

Voluntary repatriation is of course, the ideal solution to any refugee problem. Unfortunately, this is usually not possible. The fact that individuals or groups have abandoned their homes is mute testimony to intolerable conditions which most probably cannot be alleviated immediately.

Orderly departure is also an important means of mitigating the potential embarrassment and costs to a state of receiving refugees. At the least, it can allow the receiving state to prepare itself in advance and to summon international assistance.

Reparation and *restitutio in integrum*, although they are the most substantial remedies, may create certain undesirable consequences. In the case of reparation, it is foreseeable that such a conventional practice may well develop into a convenient means of 'buying' the right to denationalise in contravention of well-established international norms. Such a remedy may establish a justification for a calculated move which can balance the actual cost of denationalising and creating refugees against the desired objective of eliminating an 'undesirable' segment of the population. Notwithstanding such deficiencies, however, this form of remedy may be preferable when compared with *restitutio in integrum*, especially from the viewpoint of safeguarding the freedom of the refugees from persecution. Reparation may adequately compensate the recipient state and create at least some deterrence for the refugee generating state without actually averting already existing refugee flows. A remedy such as *restitutio in integrum*, which may have the effect of either preventing escape from persecution, or subsequent forced repatriation, is in apparent conflict with the avowed purpose of the law in this field. Accordingly, when it involves compensation on the basis of coercion, it may serve to undermine the haven that international law has painstakingly won for the refugee.

C. Jack I. Garvey, 'The New Asylum Seekers: Addressing their Origin', in David A. Martin, ed., *The New Asylum Seekers: Refugee Law in the 1980s* (Martinus Nijhoff Publishers, Dordrecht, 1988), pp. 187–91.

Legal responsibility of the state of origin, while not articulated as such in the current corpus of international refugee law, is firmly supported by established principles of international law. There is ample authority for the proposition that a state is obligated to avoid the generation across its borders of damage to other states. We see the relevant principle reflected in many treaties and resolutions of international organisations. It has also been articulated in international arbitrations and adjudications, principally *The Trail Smelter Arbitration*. There the tribunal, in finding transnational pollution to be in breach of international law, declared that 'no state has the right to use or permit the use of its territory in such a manner as to cause injury . . . in or to the territory of another or the properties or persons therein. . . .'[44] The analogy to pollution is, of course, offensive and awkward, and takes no account of the right to seek asylum. But the right to seek asylum is not inconsistent with placing responsibility upon the state of origin. Indeed, that responsibility has been articulated explicitly in reference to refugee flow. For instance, Jennings, writing as early as 1939, stated that 'the wilful flooding of other states with refugees constitutes not merely an inequitable act, but an actual illegality, and *a fortiori* where the refugees are compelled to enter the country of refuge in a destitute condition'.[45]

It is in fact obvious—undeniable—that refugee flow imposes severe social and economic burdens on receiving states. Failing to pursue the legal implications of this, while insisting, as we must, on the principle of *non-refoulement*, ultimately undermines *non-refoulement*. Potential receiving states see themselves being asked for one-sided sacrifices, while a state that allows or actually induces the flow remains wholly unburdened.

The Beginnings of State Responsibility—Some Guidelines for Guidelines

. . . the thrust of the substantive principles should be cooperative, rather than prohibitive. How do we seize the potential that now exists relative to the state of origin? Prohibition will not succeed when the extreme political interests and social conditions that induce mass flow are at work. But advantage may still be gained by recognising and articulating the legal responsibility of the state of origin to which such movement gives rise. The legal task is to mitigate the asperities and chaos of the movement by engaging state of origin responsibility where it is not now commonly engaged. What can be established are obligations to cooperate in the prevention of flow, obligations to adhere to procedures for the amelioration and management of flow, and obligations to help secure voluntary repatriation. States of origin may respect procedural and substantive

---

[44] *The Trail Smelter Arbitration* (US v. Can.), Trail Smelter Arbitral Tribunal, 3 R. Int'l Arb. Awards 1938, 1965 (1941).

[45] Jennings, 'Some International Law Aspects of the Refugee Question' (see footnote 38 earlier), p. 111.

limitations they see as tolerable and advantageous in order to reduce the negative political fallout that results from outflow.

An example of such specific obligation would be a requirement of earliest notice of impending refugee flow. The earlier the warning, the better the chances for mitigation. We can begin by articulating legal duties to provide early warning. These duties can be described as duties of coordination and cooperation owed to an international apparatus charged with an early warning function. That function could be triggered first by a state of origin, or by a receiving state in cases where the political realities discourage early warning by the state of origin.

The same sort of elaboration can be achieved concerning the next part of the task—defining a framework for orderly departure and transit. Much of this work has already been done, though on an ad hoc basis. The crisis of the Vietnamese boat people involved precisely such development, though formulation of arrangements for orderly departure. In 1979, the Office of the United Nations High Commissioner for Refugees concluded with the government of Vietnam a Memorandum of Understanding on the Orderly Departure of Persons from Vietnam, in connection with a conference in Geneva of concerned governments. The conference resulted in a number of countries making pledges of asylum spaces, thereby undertaking the 'equitable burden sharing' that ended the crisis.

In the post-flow context, there is another guideline for guidelines that would serve us well—a principle that assistance should always be secondary to solution. It is imperative to minimise the institutionalisation of assistance and dependency of refugees that now often occurs at the expense of durable solution, epitomised by the Palestinian refugee camps. The Palestinian situation, of course, did not present the same options of cooperation with the state of origin nor possibilities of repatriation that usually do exist in massive flow contexts. But even as to the Palestinian problem, opportunities for ameliorating the refugee problem could have been seized had policy makers simply considered frameworks of obligation that were achievable without complete resolution of the greater Middle East conflict.

... the institutionalisation of engagement of the state of origin must be at least as important as the development of substantive principles of responsibility. We must aim to achieve an institutional apparatus adequate to the variety of critical functions that involve the state of origin. First, as already mentioned, comes the function of early warning and monitoring. Second is the need to provide management and aid functions in relation to the state of origin. Third, the institutional apparatus must be designed to stimulate the political processes that will secure the cooperation of the state of origin, and to orchestrate any appropriate *quid pro quo* of assistance from the international community that may be needed to promote resolutions such as voluntary repatriation. The 'good offices' activity of the Secretary General is one example. But we need a similar institutional capacity specifically and permanently geared to the problem of the refugee.

... Finally, the concept of legal responsibility of the state of origin for the burden imposed on other states can be elaborated as substantive principles and procedures for compensation. For instance, proceedings before the International Court of Justice or other international claims fora seem entirely appropriate as recourse for states affected by refugee flow. Moreover, to the extent that substantive developments improve the prospects of procedural recourse against the state of origin, deterrence of mass movement is enhanced.

D. Luke T. Lee, 'The Right to Compensation: Refugees and Countries of Asylum', *American Journal of International Law* (Vol. 80, 1986), pp. 533, 537–39, 545–66.

The entire burden of caring for millions of refugees has until now been assumed by the uprooted refugees themselves, their countries of asylum, their countries of resettlement and donors, whether directly or through international organisations. Overlooked are the responsibilities of the countries of origin both toward their own citizens now turned refugees and toward the countries of asylum saddled with the burden of caring for those refugees. This paper focuses on the responsibilities of the source countries under international law to compensate refugees and countries of asylum. It is hoped that clarification and fulfilment of these responsibilities will contribute not only to the well-being of refugees and the alleviation of the burdens on their hosts, but also to the reduction or eradication of the very phenomenon of 'refugees'.

As its points of departure, this paper takes the definition of 'refugee' adopted in the 1951 Convention Relating to the Status of Refugees....

The Right of Refugees to Compensation

Legal Bases

As individuals outside their own country but still bearing the nationality of that country, refugees face formidable substantive as well as procedural obstacles under traditional international law to seeking compensation from their government. Such obstacles derive, for example, from their status under international law and the lack of a forum in which they can institute proceedings against their government. However, this paper focuses on the practical problems that impede fulfilment of the refugees' right to compensation within the framework of the generally accepted principles of international law and under municipal law....

Municipal Law

From the standpoint of municipal law as well as international law, an act by a state that transforms its own citizens into refugees is *ipso facto* illegal. The municipal law of virtually all countries guarantees the rights of their citizens to life, liberty, equality, property, due process etc. The mere existence of refugees, as defined by the 1951 Convention Relating to the Status of Refugees and the 1967 Protocol, shows that their own governments have violated these rights.

Thus, a country that is ruled by law must refrain from turning its citizens into refugees. If refugees have already been created, it should provide them with the opportunity for voluntary repatriation and compensation, whether pursuant to the principle of torts, unjust enrichment, abuse of rights or unconstitutionality.... Germany has undertaken a large-scale programme of compensating Jews that were forced to leave Germany during the Nazi period for their loss of property, liberty and dignity. Shortly after the downfall of Idi Amin, the Ugandan Government appointed a committee to handle compensation claims by thousands of Ugandans of Indian descent who were expelled in 1972. Properties of some Chinese refugees taken over by the People's Republic of China have reportedly been restored to the owners or compensated for. These instances show that governments are increasingly sensitive to the need to comply with their own laws, rooted in justice and equity....

International Law

Human Rights Law: When a state forces its citizens into becoming refugees either directly or indirectly, it is violating such movement-related provisions of the Universal Declaration of Human Rights as: Article 9, 'No one shall be subjected to arbitrary arrest, detention or exile'; Article 13(1), 'Everyone has the right to freedom of movement and residence within the borders of each State'; Article 13(2), 'Everyone has the right to leave any country, including his own, and to return to his country'; Article 15(1), 'Everyone has the right to nationality'; and Article 15(2), 'No one shall be arbitrarily deprived of his nationality nor denied the right to change his nationality.' To the above may be added Article 14(1), 'Everyone has the right to seek and to enjoy in other countries asylum from persecution.' Although this article appears to encourage a citizen to become a refugee, its explicit linkage to 'persecution'—the most critical element in the definition of 'refugee'—makes the movement in effect a coerced one.

Making a person a 'refugee', however—someone who by definition is arbitrarily deprived of the right to live in his own country—does not violate merely the above movement—related rights. It also violates any rights, whatever their legal sources, that depend to any extent for their full and effective enjoyment on a person's ability to live in his own country. A review of the Universal Declaration shows that the full and effective enjoyment of all the rest of its articles hinges upon that ability. Certainly, making a person a 'refugee' would seriously affect his birthrights to 'life, liberty and security of person' (Article 3); employment (Article 23); education (Article 26); family (Article 17); property (Article 17); social security (Article 22); nondiscrimination (Article 2); dignity (Article 1); equality before the law (Article 7); freedom of opinion and expression (Article 19); freedom of peaceful assembly and association (Article 20); participation in government and public service (Article 21); and so forth. Thus, the country that turns its own citizens into refugees is in violation of all the articles of the Universal Declaration of Human Rights....

Scope and Content

The foregoing discussion clearly demonstrates that refugees have legal right to compensation. Ascertaining the scope and content of that right, however, requires further inquiry.

During the debate on the UK draft resolution that culminated in the adoption of General Assembly Resolution 194 (III), Egypt expressed the view that compensation should cover not only property losses, but also losses of family or political losses.[46] It regarded the entire refugee matter as a test of UN principles. Syria drew attention to three kinds of loss or damage to property: (1) land and property of those who did not return— to be compensated for by the new possessors; (2) personal property and merchandise which were looted—to be compensated for by the looters; and (3) property destroyed—to be compensated for by those who destroyed the property.[47]

In creating the UN Group of Governmental Experts on International Cooperation to Avert New Flows of Refugees, the General Assembly in Resolution 36/148 of December 16, 1981 also '[e]mphasises the right of refugees to return to their homes in their homelands and reaffirms the right, as contained in its previous resolutions, of those who do not wish to return to receive adequate compensation'.

This 1981 resolution differs from the 1948 resolution in two respects. First, whereas the former specified compensation only to those who do not wish to return to their homes, the latter calls for compensating both those refugees choosing not to return to their homes and those suffering loss or damage to their property, 'which, under principles of international law or in equity, should be made good by the Governments or

[46] 3 UN GAOR, pt.1, C.1 (226th mtg) at p. 912 (1948).
[47] Ibid. at pp. 908–9.

authorities responsible' (thus including even those who choose to return). Second, although the latter stipulates that compensation should be made for 'property' losses, the former mentions merely 'adequate compensation'—hence a broader coverage. Be that as it may, since the text of the former is admittedly based on that of the latter, any difference in interpretation should be resolved in favor of the latter. . . .

A pertinent question concerns a refugees' right to compensation for injuries other than property loss suffered in consequence of being made a refugee. By focusing on compensation only 'for the property of those choosing not to return and for loss or damage to property', the General Assembly has refrained from passing judgment on whether countries of origin are obliged to compensate refugees for such other losses as deaths; personal injuries and indignities; wrongful arrest, detention or imprisonment; and emotional or mental anguish. A strong case can be made that such losses should also be compensable; indeed, . . . Germany did include among compensable losses the infringement of personal liberty resulting from internment in concentration camps, the interruption of education, and even the humiliation of wearing the yellow star as identification, which was suffered by Jews in all German-occupied countries except France and Italy.

By stressing 'property' losses, however, the General Assembly has trod the more familiar ground of state responsibility for the nationalisation or illegal taking of property in general. Refugees specifically seeking compensation for property loss thus enjoy a certain legal advantage over refugees seeking redress for other losses in view of the numerous General Assembly resolutions reaffirming the former right. In addition, property losses lend themselves more readily than other losses to valuation, and are thus more amenable to compensation.

While these General Assembly resolutions strengthen the refugee's hand in seeking to establish a right under customary international law to receive compensation for property, the basic principles underlying such a right apply also to the right of refugees to receive compensation for other aspects of the injury as well.

Implementation: Proposed Measures for the United Nations

Affirmation or reaffirmation of the right of refugees to compensation under international law is one thing; implementation of such a right is quite another. In view of the absence of international enforcement machinery, implementation may best be effected by giving states incentives to comply with the law. Such incentives can easily be found if the refugee-generating countries happen also to be developing countries that are interested in receiving developmental assistance from the United

Nations and its agencies. General Assembly resolutions may contribute to generating incentives for implementing the refugees' right to compensation, just as in their recommendatory role they may contribute to establishing or reaffirming a right to compensation under customary international law. Three different uses of General Assembly resolutions are illustrated in the following three kinds of implementation measures that might be undertaken mainly through the United Nations.

Controlling Developmental or Other Forms of Assistance

The authority of the General Assembly over UN agencies holds significant potential for enforcing the right of refugees to compensation.... In the interest of universal compliance with international law or equity, the General Assembly or a specialised agency may require that no developmental assistance be rendered to a refugee-generating state unless that state has first ... compensat[ed] refugees for the loss of or damage to their property. Since the United Nations and its specialised agencies invariably attach conditions or safeguards to their aid programs—the imposition of some of which, e.g., currency revaluation and import restriction, falls under traditional sovereign prerogatives—the requirement that aid recipients honour principles of international law and human rights in dealing with their own citizens should not be regarded as onerous or unreasonable. Similarly, a donor country may also require compliance with principles of international law and human rights as a precondition to providing assistance to refugee generating countries....

Exercising a Guardianship Function

The Statute of the Office of the United Nations High Commissioner for Refugees, adopted by General Assembly Resolution 428 (V) of December 14, 1950, provides: 'The United Nations High Commissioner for Refugees, acting under the authority of the General Assembly, shall assume the function of providing international protection, under the auspices of the United Nations, to refugees who fall within the scope of the present statute....' Of special significance in providing such protection is the power of the High Commissioner to 'administer any funds, public or private, which he receives for assistance to refugees' and to 'distribute them among the private and as appropriate, public agencies which he deems best qualified to administer such assistance.' This competence is affirmed by the 1951 Convention Relating to the Status of Refugees and the 1967 Protocol....

The broad and generally accepted power of the High Commissioner to protect and assist refugees makes him guardian of the interests of refugees. This relationship between the High Commissioner and refugees under the United Nations is closer than that under the League of Nations, which has been characterised as 'quasi consular'. . . .

Crucial to its performance of protecting and assisting refugees is the capacity of the United Nations to bring a claim on their behalf against the source country for failure to compensate them for their losses. Does the United Nations have such a capacity?

In its Advisory Opinion on *Injuries Suffered in the Service of the United Nations*, the International Court of Justice held that the United Nations had the capacity to bring an international claim against a state with a view to obtaining reparation for damage caused to its agent, even though the latter was a national of the defendant state. For, as the Court stated:

> The action of the Organisation is in fact based not upon the nationality of the victim but upon his status as agent of the Organisation. Therefore it does not matter whether or not the State to which the claim is addressed regards him as its own national, because the question of nationality is not pertinent to the admissibility of the claim.[48]

This holding is especially relevant to claims by the United Nations on behalf of refugees since, legally, the latter may remain nationals of their country of origin.

More significantly, the Court affirmed the capacity of the United Nations to bring an international claim against a state for damage caused not only to its 'agent', but also 'to the interests of which it is the guardian'.[49] Since the United Nations is the guardian of the interests of refugees, the conclusion is inescapable that it has not only the capacity to bring an international claim against a refugee-generating country on behalf of refugees, but even the duty to do so as a guardian.

Facilitating the Payment of Compensation

A corollary of the rule that General Assembly resolutions dealing with the internal working of the United Nations are legally binding on the United Nations and its members is that the General Assembly may establish machinery for implementing its resolutions. In the case of refugee compensation, such machinery is indispensable because refugees lack the procedural capacity to institute proceedings against their own governments. Hence the creation of the Conciliation Commission for the purpose, inter alia, of facilitating the payment of compensation to Palestinian refugees. Although the intractable conditions in the Middle East have prevented this commission from accomplishing its objectives, there is no intrinsic reason why the General Assembly cannot create a special body to

---

[48] *Reparation for Injuries Suffered in the Service of the United Nations*, ICJ Rep. (1949), p. 186.
[49] Ibid., p. 180.

collect, process and distribute compensation funds due refugees world-wide, or assign this task to an existing body. Enhancing the awareness that refugees do have a right to compensation and that the source countries have a corresponding obligation to pay compensation should have a deterrent effect on the future creation of refugees. One way to increase the deterrent effect would be to tabulate and publish the claims of refugees—both satisfied and unsatisfied—for the appropriate use and consideration of UN developmental agencies and other donors.

The Right of Countries of Asylum to Compensation

Does persecution by a country of its own citizens en masse, forcing them to flee abroad as refugees and thus to impose economic, social and other burdens upon other countries, constitute an international wrong, in addition to the compensable wrong vis-à-vis the individual refugees discussed above? What are the legal bases for compensation to these other countries?

Legal Bases

Rights and Duties of States

We start with one of the most basic norms of international law, namely, that every state has the right to exercise jurisdiction over its territory and over all persons and things within it. Since right and duty are two sides of the same coin, the corresponding duty is to avoid interfering with the exercise by other countries of their respective jurisdiction. Such a duty includes refraining from acts that would cause injury or damage to persons or property situated in the territory of other states. If a state violates, or is delinquent in its duty toward, the right of other states, international responsibility is incurred. The *Trail Smelter* arbitration is instructive. In this case, the United States sued Canada for damage to land, crops and trees in the state of Washington that had been caused by sulphur dioxide fumes emitted by a Canadian ore-smelting company. The tribunal held Canada 'responsible in international law for the conduct of the Trail Smelter' on the grounds that,

> under the principles of international law, as well as the law of the United States, no State has the right to use or permit the use of its territory in such a manner as to cause injury by fumes in or to the territory of another or the properties or persons therein, when the case is of serious consequence and the injury is established by clear and convincing evidence.[50]

[50] *Trail Smelter* case (see footnote 44 earlier), p. 1965.

The tribunal concluded with the statement: 'It is therefore, the duty of the Government of the Dominion of Canada to see to it that this conduct should be in conformity with the obligation of the Dominion under international law as herein determined'.[51]

Refugees, of course, are not 'fumes'. Nevertheless, certain legal similarities exist: both may cross international boundaries from countries of origin; both such crossings are not made with the voluntary consent of the receiving states; and both such crossings may impose economic and social burdens upon the receiving states, for which the countries of origin will be responsible.

A major difference lies in the fact that, while a state cannot prevent fumes from drifting into its air and over its land territories, it can, except perhaps in mass expulsion cases, prevent or deter the entry of refugees into its territories through such devices as barricades, imprisonment or internment ('humanitarian deterrence'), *refoulement*, rejection at the border and 'pushoffs'. The exercise of such power, however, is increasingly being considered as inimical to respect for the minimum standards of humane treatment or human rights, which are epitomised in the Declaration on Territorial Asylum: 'No person ... shall be subjected to measures such as rejection at the frontier or, if he has already entered the territory in which he seeks asylum, expulsion or compulsory return to any State where he may be subjected to persecution'.

It would be deeply ironic if source states could evade responsibility for their own inhumanity by arguing that states of asylum could avoid their burdens by being equally inhumane.

Sovereign Equality of States

A direct and immediate result of the mass expulsion or persecution of nationals is to force them on the territories of other states as refugees regardless of the wishes of these states. ...

Principle of Nationality

When a state expels its own citizens, it undermines the very foundation on which relations among states and between states and their citizens are built. ... The unilateral termination of such rights and duties would incur responsibility if, as Professor Brownlie emphasised, 'it were shown that the withdrawal of nationality was itself a part of the delictual conduct facilitating the result'.[52]

International law does permit denationalisation in certain circumstances. However, states are prohibited from manipulating their competence in this regard so as to avoid their international obligations.

[51] Ibid., pp. 1965–66.
[52] Ian Brownlie, *Principles of Public International law* (Clarendon Press, Oxford, 1979), third edition, p. 396.

Quasi-contractual Relationship

... Since refugees are, by definition, those forced to leave their countries by their own governments, a quasi-contractual relationship exists between their governments and those of the countries of asylum. Any attempt at defining a quasi contract would fill pages. For our purpose, perhaps the illustration given by Corbin would be the best way: 'Under compulsion of law ... A makes payment of money that it was B's legal duty to pay. In spite of any express refusal, B is under a quasi contractual duty to reimburse A.'

The law referred to above includes, for example, the United Nations Charter, which is binding on all member states, and the 1951 Convention Relating to the Status of Refugees and the 1967 Protocol, which are binding on 97 states.[53] By transforming citizens into refugees abroad, and thus shifting the burden of their care and maintenance to the country of asylum, the source country creates a quasi-contractual relationship with the country of asylum, which must be reimbursed by it for the costs. In this regard, it is significant that the report of the Committee on International Assistance to Refugees, presented to the Council of the League of Nations on June 20, 1936, stated: 'In view of the heavy burden placed on the countries of refuge, the Committee considers it an international duty for the countries of origin of the refugees at least to alleviate to some extent, the burdens imposed by the presence of refugees in the territory of other states'.[54] Commenting on this recommendation, Jennings wrote in 1939: 'If the conduct of the state of origin be in the first place illegal, it seems to follow that it is under a duty to assist settlement states in the solution of the problem to which it has given rise.'[55]

Indirect Responsibility

It bears emphasising that a refugee-generating country is obligated to reimburse the country of asylum for the costs of caring for refugees it generated not only directly, but also indirectly; for example, through actual or threatened military intervention in the internal affairs of a state resulting in the flight of the latter's citizens for fear of persecution. Article 28 of the draft articles on state responsibility (part 1) expresses this obligation well:

1. An internationally wrongful act committed by a State in a field of activity in which that State is subject to the power of direction or control of another State entails the responsibility of that other State.

[53] The present membership is 134 states respectively.
[54] Quoted by Jennings, 'Some International Law Aspects of the Refugee Question' (see footnote 38 earlier), p. 113.
[55] Ibid.

2. An internationally wrongful act committed by a State as the result of coercion exerted by another State to secure the commission of that act entails the international responsibility of that other State.

3. Paragraphs 1 and 2 are without prejudice to the international responsibility, under the other articles of the present draft, of the State which has committed the internationally wrongful act.

In its commentary, the Commission expressed the opinion

> that a State which commits an internationally wrongful act under coercion by another State is in fact in a situation similar to that of State which in one area of its activity is subject to the direction or control of another State. Since in this latter case the State is not acting in the free exercise of its sovereignty, it is not acting with complete freedom of decision and action. The coercing State compels the other State to take the course of committing an international offence which in other circumstances it would probably not commit.[56]

Thus, the notion of coercion here, according to the Commission, might be even broader in scope than that underlying Article 52 of the Vienna Convention on the Law of Treaties concerning the invalidity of treaties concluded under the threat or use of force.

Assuming that Article 28 of the draft articles on state responsibility reflects customary international law, the pertinent question may be asked: if the presence of some 2,500,000 and 780,000 Afghan refugees in Pakistan and Iran, respectively, could be attributed to the Soviet politico-military intervention in Afghanistan, could the two asylum countries claim compensation from the USSR for the refugee burden thrust upon them? Providing that such a causal relationship could indeed be established, the answer would appear to be that Pakistan and Iran could justifiably claim compensation from the USSR and invoke the procedures outlined in the subsection entitled 'implementation' below. . . .

Implementation

Protests: The first step to be taken by a country of asylum wishing to implement its right to compensation for inflows of refugees is to lodge a protest to the country of origin. It is no coincidence that the International Court of Justice, in its Advisory Opinion on *Injuries Suffered in the Service of the United Nations*, listed 'protest' as the first among 'customary methods recognised by international law for the establishment, the

---

[56] For the text and commentary see [1979] 2 Y.B. INT'L L. COMM'N, pt.2 at pp. 94–106, UN Doc. A/CN.4/SER.A/1979/Add.1.

presentation and the settlement of claims'.[57] For failure to lodge timely protests may well be taken to signify acquiescence. A few examples of such protests follow.

The aftermath of widespread disorders in East Pakistan that culminated in the Indo–Pakistan war and the establishment of Bangladesh was a massive influx of refugees from East Pakistan to India. In a note to the Pakistan High Commission in Delhi on May 14, 1971, the Indian Government stated:

> As a result of the military action taken by the Government of Pakistan in East Bengal, nearly 2,000,000 Pakistanis have been forced to flee from their homes and to take shelter in adjoining areas of India. This deliberate expulsion of such a large number of people from their homes has created a human problem of unparalleled magnitude which is capable of producing serious repercussions in the area, leading to a threat to peace in the region....

> The Government of India therefore hold the Government of Pakistan fully responsible for creating such conditions forthwith as would facilitate the return of these refugees to their homes.... At the same time the Government of India reserve the right to claim from the Government of Pakistan full satisfaction in respect of additional financial and other burdens that the Government of India have had to shoulder for affording relief to these Pakistani nationals.[58]

... To be credible, the protestor must follow up its protest with enforcement measures if the protest is ignored. What might such measures be that the protestor could legitimately employ?

Pacific Settlement of Disputes

If protests are ignored, recourse may be had to the means employed in the pacific settlement of disputes, as provided by chapter VI of the United Nations Charter....

Sanctions

In the event that the pacific settlement of disputes fails, for example because the International Court of Justice lacks jurisdiction, the injured state should ... be 'entitled, by way of reprisal, to suspend the performance of its ... obligations towards the State which has committed the internationally wrongful act', subject to the principle of proportionality. Reprisals on this basis might include economic sanctions, e.g., the

[57] ICJ Rep. (1949), at p. 175.
[58] *Keesing's Contemporary Archives*, 3–10 July 1971, at pp. 24, 685.

suspension of treaties of trade or consular rights, or the revocation of most-favoured-nation treatment.

If the source state has committed an 'international crime', that is, a crime *erga omnes*, the appropriate response should be made by the international community as a whole....

Reimbursement of the United Nations

Since in many countries the United Nations, mainly through the UNHCR and the United Nations Relief and Works Agency (UNRWA), has assisted in the care and maintenance of refugees, may the United Nations claim reimbursement from countries of origin for expenditures incurred? An affirmative answer to this question would provide redress, at least in part, for any procedural incapacity of countries of asylum to obtain reimbursement from countries of origin through the pacific settlement of disputes. For affirmation of a UN right to claim reimbursement would enable the United Nations to expand its role in assisting refugees and would correspondingly reduce the expenditures of countries of asylum.

E. Christian Tomuschat, 'State Responsibility and the Country of Origin', in Vera Gowlland-Debbas, ed., *The Problem of Refugees in the Light of Contemporary International Law Issues* (Martinus Nijhoff Publishers, The Hague, 1995), pp. 60, 64–68, 70–71, 74–79.

State Responsibility

Responsibility towards Individuals

An examination of possible rights of individuals against a State of origin cannot take as its starting point the refugee as defined by the 1951 Geneva Convention. Article 1 of that instrument has created an extremely artful construct which, on the one hand, includes persons who may not have suffered any actual injury—because fear of persecution is sufficient to claim refugee status—and which, on the other hand, excludes persons whose human rights may have been seriously violated, for instance in a civil war. It would be extremely difficult for the purposes of the enquiry undertaken here to follow strictly the borderlines of that definition. In order to simplify matters, we shall confine ourselves to considering whether an individual who has been coerced into leaving his or her country may have a claim against that country under general rules on State responsibility. Most refugees will fall within this category....

AN INDIVIDUAL RIGHT TO REPARATION?

... even if one proceeds from the assumption that human rights constitute individual entitlements under international law, at least to the extent that they are supported by an international mechanism of individual complaint or that core entitlements of the individual are arbitrarily impaired, it is by no means sure what consequences are entailed by the violation of such a right. The general proposition that a breach of an international engagement involves an obligation to make reparation, as it was formulated by the Permanent Court of International Justice in the *Chorzow* case,[59] is well known and need not be repeated here. Similarly, it should be noted that under Article 6 bis of the draft articles elaborated by the ILC on the form and contents of State responsibility 'the injured State is entitled to obtain from the State which has committed an internationally wrongful act full reparation'.[60] However, the relevant rule has always been formulated as inter-State law governing legal relationships between States as subjects of international law. Indeed, it has never occurred to any of the Special Rapporteurs of the ILC on the topic of State responsibility that a State could incur responsibility vis-à-vis the individuals injured in case of a breach of a human rights obligation. This finding carries all the more weight since violation of human rights is specifically mentioned in the available drafts....

It is significant, in this connection, that the relevant human rights treaties remain largely silent on the issue of the consequences deriving from non-compliance with its obligations by a State. The premise is always that a State must fulfil what it has formally pledged to do. Thus, to the extent that one may assume the existence of an individual entitlement under international law, there exists a right to specific performance. The individual has the right to claim that the governmental machinery he or she is confronted with behave as set forth in the relevant provisions. As far as violations of a continuing character are concerned, one may therefore speak of a right to cessation. Yet, it is less clear—or even totally obscure—whether a right to reparation proper comes into being, a right that would be designed to 'wipe out' the consequences of the commission of the unlawful act.

The relevant stipulations of the European Convention of Human Rights are remarkably cautious. According to Article 50, the European Court of Human Rights (Court) shall, 'if necessary, afford just satisfaction to the injured party', if the internal law of the author State 'allows only partial reparation to be made for the consequences' of the unlawful conduct complained of and found to exist. First of all, the phrase 'if necessary' grants the Court a wide margin of discretion. Second, domestic law, which ordinarily is considered from the viewpoint of international law as a pure factual element, is recognised as an obstacle justifying the wrongdoing State to abstain from restitution in kind. Thirdly, one may note that

---

[59] Of 13 September 1928, *Collection of Judgements*, Series A No. 17, at pp. 29, 47.

[60] Report of the ILC on the Work of its Forty-fifth Session, 48 GAOR Suppl. No. 10. UN Doc. A/48/10 (1993), p. 130.

the individual is not openly recognised as the holder of a right to 'just satisfaction' in lieu of reparation in kind; what Article 50 does, instead, is authorise the Court to grant satisfaction as required under the circumstances. Lastly, in its jurisprudence the Court has constantly interpreted 'just satisfaction' as being tantamount to financial compensation. Attempts by applicants to obtain a pronouncement requiring the defendant State to make good in kind the consequences of its unlawful conduct have always been in vain. Thus, in the *Bozano* case, the applicant had insisted on *restitutio in integrum*, namely re-surrender to French territory from which he had been removed in disregard of applicable French extradition procedures and therefore also in disregard of Article 5 of the Convention (right of individual freedom). But the Court did not accede to this demand; by avoiding to give a clear-cut answer, it implicitly made clear that its competence was confined to granting financial compensation.[61]

The legal position under the American Convention on Human Rights can be described in terms slightly more favourable to the individual. Article 63 (1) enjoins the Inter-American Court of Human Rights (Court) to rule, if it has made a finding of a violation, 'that the injured party be ensured the enjoyment of his right or freedom that was violated'. Thus, the Court is required to bring about cessation of the wrongful conduct complained of and found to exist. Additionally, however, it is incumbent on the Court (it 'shall') to rule, 'if appropriate, that the consequences of the measure or situation that constituted the breach of such right or freedom be remedied and that fair compensation be paid to the injured party'. Judgements which fix compensatory damages are enforceable under the laws of the country concerned (Article 68 (2)). Some language in the first judgement on the merits of a case, the decision of the Court in *Velasquez Rodriguez* of 29 July 1988,[62] and in the subsequent judgement on compensatory damages in that case of 27 July 1989,[63] could be interpreted as conveying the message that the individual victim of a violation holds a true right to financial compensation. But nowhere do the judgements openly say so. Each time, they speak of a duty to make reparation which was incumbent on the defendant, the State of Honduras. In fact, one may harbour serious doubts as to whether the 'if-appropriate' clause permits to affirm the existence of an individual right proper—which could hardly be committed to the discretion of the Court. It is significant, in this regard, that the compensation due in the *Velasquez Rodriguez* case

---

[61] Judgement of 18 December 1986, *Publications of the European Court of Human Rights (PECHR)*, Series A, Vol. III, p. 28, para. 65.

[62] Inter-American Court of Human Rights, Series C: Decisions and Judgements, No. 4, p. 91 (English version).

[63] Inter-American Court of Human Rights, Series C: Decisions and Judgements, No. 7, p. 33 (English version).

was to be negotiated and agreed upon between the Inter-American Commission and the Government of Honduras, not by the beneficiaries themselves.

The body that has consistently shown a bold approach to the issue of reparation is the Human Rights Committee under the International Covenant on Civil and Political Rights. The Covenant itself mentions a right to compensation in two places, each time in relation to personal freedom. Article 9 (5) specifies that an individual who has been the victim of unlawful arrest or detention 'shall have an enforceable right to compensation'. Similarly, Article 14(6) sets forth that a person who has been the victim of a miscarriage of justice 'shall be compensated according to law'. Although these two provisions are primarily intended to enjoin States to establish individual rights under domestic law by enacting the requisite legislation, they shed nonetheless some light on the stand of the authors of the Covenant as to when a situation must be considered so serious as to warrant being remedied by some compensation in money—an assessment that would seem to permit appropriate conclusions *e contrario*.

Notwithstanding the restrictive conception enshrined in the Covenant itself, the Human Rights Committee has not felt prevented from expressing in its final views under Article 5(4) of the Optional protocol fairly far-reaching suggestions as to the way in which a wrong committed is to be corrected. Already in its first views on the merits of a case, brought against Uruguay, it held that the defendant State was under an obligation 'to provide effective remedies to the victims'.[64] In many instances, it has held that the victim of a violation was entitled to a remedy, including appropriate compensation.[65] A culmination point of its jurisprudence was reached in a series of views addressing trials resulting in the imposition of the death penalty that had not been conducted in conformity with the procedural standards laid down in Article 14 of the Covenant. In view of the gravity of some of the procedural defects found by it, the Human Rights Committee pronounced itself for the immediate release of the convicted persons.[66] These rulings are not understood by the Committee as the

[64] *Case of Bazzano/Massera*, 15 August 1979, in UN, ed., *Human Rights Committee. Selected Decisions under the Optional Protocol*, Doc. CCPR/C/OP/1 (1985), p. 40, at p. 43.

[65] See, for instance, from the 1993 Report (48 GAOR, Suppl. No. 40, UN Doc. A/48/40) the following cases (all contained in Part II): *Linton v. Jamaica*, 22 October 1992, p. 12, at 16 para. 10.; *Orihuela Valenzuela v. Peru*, 14 July 1993, p. 48, at 51 para. 8; *Chiiko Bwalaya v. Zambia*, 14 July 1993, p. 52, at 55 para. 8; *Francis v. Jamaica*, 24 March 1993, p. 62, at 67 para. 14; *Kalinga v. Zambia*, 27 July 1993, p. 68, at 71 para. 8; *Bailey v. Jamaica*, 31 March 1993, p. 72, at 76 para. 11.1; *Balkissoon Soogrim v. Trinidad and Tobago*, 8 April 1993, p. 110, at 115 para. 15.

[66] The following cases from the 1993 Report (ibid.) may be referred to: *Smith v. Jamaica*, 31 March 1993, p. 28, at 36 para. 12; *Campbell v. Jamaica*, 24 March 1993, p. 41, at 45 para. 8; *Francis v. Jamaica*, 22 March 1993, p. 62, at 67 para. 14; *Simmonds v. Jamaica*, 23

exercise of some jurisdiction *ex aequo et bono*. Rather, the Committee views its appeals for the liberation of the victims as a logical consequence of the breach of the obligations in issue. Indeed, one is confronted here with an ineluctable choice where questions concerning the true meaning of international human rights cannot be papered over any more by some vague formulae. If an individual injured by a human rights obligation cannot obtain any redress for the loss suffered, the 'right' at stake becomes almost meaningless. To buttress its line of reasoning, the Committee has taken to invoking Article 2(3) of the Covenant, which provides that an individual claiming that his or her rights under the Covenant have been violated must be given an effective remedy. This argument is hardly persuasive, however. As is shown by a perusal of the other language versions, which speak of 'recours' in French and 'recurso' in Spanish, Article 2(3) refers to a remedy of a kind which permits an individual to challenge in some formalised procedure State conduct adversely affecting his or her rights. The reading of the Committee, according to which 'remedy' is equated with remedial action for the reparation of the wrong done, cannot be maintained in the light of the French and the Spanish texts, whose words do not have the same double connotation as the English world 'remedy'. Thus, the only remaining explanation is an application of the general rules of State responsibility.

A leap forward in legal thinking was made by the Security Council when it determined in Resolution 687 (1991) that Iraq 'is liable under international law for any direct loss, damage ... or injury to foreign Governments, nationals and corporations as a result of its unlawful invasion and occupation of Kuwait'. Here, for the first time, it was unequivocally recognised that grave breaches of international law may entail direct responsibility towards the individuals injured. However, Resolution 687 (1991) remains an isolated precedent as yet. In no event could it be extended to any kind of human rights violation. It should also be observed that its philosophy is based on traditional concepts of the law of aliens. Only foreign nationals are mentioned as being entitled to claim reparation, whereas Iraqi citizens are not taken into account.

THE REFUGEE PROBLEM—A MASS-SCALE PROBLEM

The ideas just developed rest on an analysis of configurations characterised by their individuality. Generally, however, refugees are not isolated individuals. When a tense political situation in a given country develops to the point of making departure an advisable option, many people will start leaving their homes at the same time. Mass migration sets in. The

October 1992, p. 78, at 83 para. 10 (with dissenting opinion by Prado Vallejo, Sadi, Wennergren, p. 84); *Collins v. Jamaica*, 25 March 1993, p. 85, at 90 para. 10.

question is whether the large-scale dimension of the phenomenon changes the terms under which it should be addressed.

... Refugees having left their country of origin and demanding compensation lay a claim against the remainder of the population which still lives under the regime responsible for giving rise to the mass departure for other countries. However, those staying back home may be exposed to even greater suffering. More often than not, refugees eventually enjoy much better opportunities for personal development than those choosing or involuntarily having to endure the mismanagement of public affairs by a government not in compliance with its human rights obligations. The complexity of this situation cannot be dealt with in accordance with relatively simple recipes of international law which seem to require full reparation for any injury caused to another nation. Within a national community, one would first have to establish a comprehensive balance sheet of all the damage resulting from the activity of a criminal regime; thereafter, one would have to make a determination on the extent to which reparation may seem feasible in light of the potential of the national economy. Lastly, it would also have to be determined how the financial burden for the damage caused should be distributed among all of the members of the national community, taking into account basic principles of just taxation.

We are not going to develop these arguments any further. Our aim is simply to recall that compensation for massive human rights violations raises a delicate problem of distributive justice. If one would grant a right of compensation to everyone having lived under an arbitrary system of governance, everyone would become debtor and creditor at the same time. Here, the model of international responsibility must yield to more subtle regimes which many countries have conceived of when trying to cope with a past that made victims of large numbers of the population. A good case in point is the situation in South Africa. During the last decades, many black South Africans were forced to leave their country because of the brutal strategies of repression resorted to by the white minority government. On the other hand, those who stayed behind lived under the daily harassment of blatant racial discrimination. Thus, both groups of the black population were victims of measures gravely violating universally accepted human rights standards. Yet, now to make the new democratic body politic accountable for the violations committed in the past would lead to an absurd result, since the victims would have to pay their own compensations.

The case of Palestine was different. Here, a national community, the Jewish people, took possession of the properties and other assets of the Arab population that had fled to neighbouring countries. Consequently, the issue of reparation could be stated in the classical terms by analogy with inter-State law, where the simple maxim applies that a population organised as a State may not unjustly enrich itself to the detriment of another similar group so that harm done must be repaired. A similar assessment is justified in cases of 'ethnic cleansing', when a specific ethnic group is the target of persecution intended to bring about a definitive expulsion from the former community of residents.

Responsibility towards Receiving States: Practice

... Although the legal reasoning may be developed ... one cannot ignore the fact that there is little practice confirming the existence of a duty to pay financial compensation. The international community has established the office of the UNHCR precisely because of its experience that source States are normally in such dire condition that any effort to squeeze the least amount of money out of them would be doomed beforehand. Germany is the one great exception to this lesson of the past, but it should not be overlooked that payments were made only by the new democratic regime after the fall of the Hitler dictatorship.

The same holds true with regard to the duty of cessation. It is logically most satisfactory to conclude that a government which submits its people to such abuses of power that large groups start leaving the country is under a duty to modify its conduct, returning to the path of legality. In a realistic perspective, however, one must acknowledge that to enforce such a duty belongs to the most challenging tasks ever imaginable.... Nothing can stop the murderous fighting other than sheer military might. In one instance only has the international community intervened with some success to stop merciless persecution of a minority. As is well known, in order to allay the plight of the Kurds in Northern Iraq the Security Council established a security zone (Resolution 688 of 5 April 1991). Given the many doubts concerning the role it can and should play within a new world order, the Security Council will certainly not repeat this experimental strategy in the near future. In any event, a hard look at realities shows again that there exists a wide discrepancy between theory and practice. It is precisely in recognition of the powerlessness of the international community vis-à-vis the collapse of civilised standards of conduct in a given society that refugee law has emerged. Because of the obvious lack of effectiveness of the ordinary rules of international law in such a situation, other States step in, motivated by considerations of human solidarity for the benefit of the victims. Still the basic parameters have changed. While 55 years ago R.Y. Jennings had to rely, in a somewhat strained fashion, on the doctrine of abuse of rights to show that States did not enjoy sovereign freedom to shove parts of their population out of their territories, well-established principles of human rights law now restrict the powers inherent in sovereign Statehood.

The lack of trust in the effectiveness of the traditional rules of international law is most conspicuously reflected in the relevant resolutions of the competent political bodies, the General Assembly and the Human

Rights Commission. Regarding the situation in Bosnia–Herzegovina, in particular, although 'ethnic cleansing' and other human rights violations are constantly deplored and unambiguously condemned, one does not find a single line that would suggest that the aggressor country involved could be under an obligation to defray at least part of the costs entailed by providing adequate care to the refugees expelled from their native towns and villages.

STATES ACTING AS GUARDIANS OF INTERNATIONAL LEGALITY

Even States that have not directly been affected by a flow of refugees may have legal claims against the State of origin. The jurisprudence of the ICJ on obligations *erga omnes* is too well known to have to be described here in any detail. What matters is the fact that according to the authoritative pronouncement in the *Barcelona Traction* case,[67] every State has legal standing to act—in some from—for the protection of basic human rights that have been breached. Generation of refugees is of course not an element of the indicative list given by the ICJ, and it would not fit therein. The criterion chosen by the ICJ is that of particular gravity. Hence, everything depends on the specific circumstances. If, for instance, a government engages in a policy of genocide, thereby terrorising the members of the persecuted group and inducing them to flee abroad, every member of the international community may be considered affected. The same is true with regard to a policy of apartheid, as explicitly emphasised by the ICJ in its advisory opinion on Namibia.[68] In the case of more subtle harassment, however, the threshold of gravity may not have been crossed.

The dictum of the ICJ has not remained an isolated incident. According to Article 5 of Part II of the draft articles of the ILC on State responsibility, in case of a violation of a human rights obligation under customary international law or if the breach attains by its seriousness the quality of an international crime, all other States are to be considered injured; in case of a human rights obligation based on treaty law, all other States parties. This gives them legal standing to participate in the enforcement process.

Unfortunately, the precise legal meaning of that position as *defensor legis* recognised for every State has not been fully clarified as yet. The Articles adopted by the ILC grant most generously all the rights to which an internationally wrongful act may give rise to the 'injured State' tout court, without drawing any distinction as to whether the State concerned has suffered tangible injury itself or whether its standing is solely justified *dans l'interet de la loi*. It is in this sense also that the special rapporteur on the topic, Gaetano Arangio-Ruiz, has suggested a new article 5 bis intended to do away with any legal differentiation between the two groups of

---

[67] ICJ Rep. (1970), p. 3 at p. 32.
[68] ICJ Rep. (1971), p. 16 at p. 57.

States. However, while nobody would have any doubt that the minimum content of a right of response to injury caused must include the right to make representations, it is a different matter altogether to acknowledge for any injured State a right to obtain compensation, as suggested by draft article 8, already adopted by the ILC. In the view of the present writer, this enlargement of the circle of right holders is simply wrong and would necessarily lead to utter confusion.

Responsibility towards the International Community

On more than one occasion the General Assembly has stressed that flows of refugees unleashed by one country affect the entire international community. Indeed, this simple truth finds confirmation in the fact that persons having lost the protection of their home State must be given a place to stay, food, shelter and medical care. To assist national governments in performing this task, the UN has created the office of the UNHCR, which for its part requires to be financed by the members of the international community.

In order to implement the responsibility of the State of origin, the international community can make use of the powers of the Security Council, provided that the requirements for action in accordance with Article 39 of the UN Charter—a threat to or a breach of the peace or an act of aggression—are met. Intervention by the Security Council can serve in particular to stop the actions that have set in motion a mass exodus. Almost unchallengeable in theory, this conclusion is hard to translate into concrete practice. Except in the case of the Kurds of Iraq, the Security Council has never taken the view that to generate a flow of refugees may constitute a threat to international peace and security. The guarded language of Resolution 918 (1994) of 17 May 1994 on Rwanda is most revealing. It is certainly not by sheer oversight that the Security Council confines itself to pointing out that 'the massive exodus of refugees to neighbouring countries constitutes a humanitarian crisis of enormous proportions.'

It goes without saying that the international community has additionally a vivid interest in recovering from a State of origin the costs it has defrayed for taking the requisite measures of protection. First of all, recovery would help replenish the budget of UNHCR which is constantly under threat inasmuch as it rests totally on voluntary contributions by interested States. On the other hand, if governments had to realise that monies spent for the benefit of refugees were recoverable from them, this might act as a deterrent in critical situations where fundamental policy determination are being made. In law, a good case can be made for a claim to reimbursement. If, in accordance with the judgement of the ICJ in *Barcelona Traction*, generation of large-scale flows of refugees in a given situation can be evaluated as a violation of an obligation *erga omnes*, then the international community as such must first and foremost be considered as the injured party. Indeed, the ICJ introduced the *omnes* only as a subsidiary construction to fill in the gap caused by the international community's lack of operative institutions. The office of the UNHCR, however, is a fully effective institution. It has been entrusted by all States with discharging the charitable functions which in a civilised world are owed to those having lost their homes. Thus, the international community is not a hollow word precisely in this connection. It has established appropriate mechanisms, and it continually spends important financial sums to counterbalance the wrongs inflicted on it by States that violate basic human rights of their citizens. Therefore, one is on safe ground in concluding that the UN, as the legal person to which UNHCR belongs, has a right to recover the costs disbursed by it from a State of origin that has wilfully caused massive departures of its citizens through a policy of systematic human rights violations.

The same result may also be obtained through a different line of reasoning. It is arguable that the international community, by taking care of the elementary vital needs of the citizens of a given country, engages in *negotiorum gestio*, an institution found in all major systems of law and whose rules can therefore be characterised as general principles of law. Normally, whoever supplies necessities to an indigent person who should have been taken care of by the principal, has a right to be compensated for his expenditure. This is precisely the situation at issue here where the international community through UNHCR provides shelter, food and medical care to refugees in order to save their lives and protect their physical integrity.

LIABILITY

State responsibility is not the only possible basis for a legal claim to compensation. One could also resort to objective liability in the sense that a State of origin, whatever its human rights record, is duty-bound to repair the damage caused to other States by a massive influx of its nationals into their territories. Some authors have suggested that the *Trail Smelter* case could be used as the starting point for this approach.... It could with some hesitation be applied to refugees as well. Quite obviously, it is rather embarrassing to compare refugees with toxic fumes, and the authors concerned have not failed to notice the qualitative difference, presenting their apologies for the equation. But even if one accepts that, viewed from the angle of the receiving State, the effect may have some similarity, one must note that to date the notion of objective liability, which does not require as one of its constitutive elements a breach of an international obligation, has not yet been generally accepted in international law. There is not a consistent practice, nor does the observer succeed in identifying a clear and unambiguous *opinio juris*. Ample proof for this lack of general consensus is provided by the ILC's inability to agree on a set of principles to deal with the issue of liability. The topic was put on the ILC's agenda back in 1978. To date, after 16 years, no more has been produced than a set of fairly innocuous principles of prevention with regard to activities involving risk. The general feeling of uneasiness with the topic results precisely from the fact that the ILC, instead of codifying time-honoured rules, would engage in progressive development in a highly sensitive field, the available practice of State failing to furnish any consolidated guiding criteria. It would be more than hazardous, therefore, to try to derive any rule concerning refugees from the *Trail Smelter* precedent.

F. International Law Association, 'The Cairo Declaration of Principles of International Law on Compensation to Refugees', *American Journal of International Law* (Vol. 87, No. 1, 1993), pp. 157–59.

The International Law Association

Recalling that the General Assembly in Resolution 41/70 of 3 December 1986 unanimously endorsed the Report of the Group of Governmental Experts on International Cooperation to Avert New Flows of Refugees (UN Doc. A/41/324), which calls upon Member States to respect as their 'obligations'" inter alia, 'the rights of refugees to be facilitated in returning voluntarily and safely to their homes in their homelands and to receive adequate compensation therefrom, where so established, in cases of those who do not wish to return' (paragraph 66 (f));

Recalling Further that the Generally Assembly in Resolution 194 (III) of 11 December 1948, which has since reaffirmed every year, resolved that:

> [T]he refugees wishing to return to their homes and live at peace with their neighbours should be permitted to do so at the earliest practical date, and that compensation should be paid for the property of those choosing not to return and for loss or damage to property which, under principles of international law or in equity, should be made good by the Governments or authorities responsible;... (paragraph 11);

Noting, however, that neither the 1986 nor the 1948 resolution identifies or elaborates upon specific principles of international law governing compensation to refugees;

Recognising the need to provide such elaboration with a view both to rendering justice to refugees and to averting new flows of refugees;

Bearing in Mind the significant contribution of the International Law Association in adopting by consensus at its 62nd Conference in Seoul, 24th–30th August 1986, the complementary Declaration of Principles of International Law on Mass Expulsion;

Declares the need for adopting the following principles, in the interest of the progressive development and codification of international law, in order to facilitate compensation, as appropriate, to persons who have been forced to leave their homes in their homelands and are unable to return to them.

Principle 1

The responsibility for caring for the world's refugees rests ultimately upon the countries that directly or indirectly force their own citizens to flee and/or remain abroad as refugees. The discharge of such responsibility by countries of asylum, international organisations (e.g., UNHCR, UNRWA, IOM) and donors (both governmental and nongovernmental), pending the return of refugees, their settlement in place, or their resettlement in third countries, shall not relieve the countries of origin of their basic responsibility, including that of paying adequate compensation to refugees.

Principle 2

Since refugees are forced directly or indirectly out of their homes in their homelands, they are deprived of the full and effective enjoyment of all articles in the Universal Declaration of Human Rights that presuppose a person's ability to live in the place chosen as home. Accordingly, the State that turns a person into a refugee commits an internationally wrongful act, which creates the obligation to make good the wrong done.

Principle 3

The act of generating refugees in some situations should be considered genocide if it is committed 'with intent to destroy, in whole or in part, a national ethnic, racial or religious group, as such....'

Principle 4

A State is obligated to compensate its own nationals forced to leave their homes to the same extent as it is obligated by international law to compensate an alien.

Principle 5

A State that has committed an 'internationally wrongful act' through the generation of refugees shall be required, as appropriate:

(*a*) to discontinue the act;

(*b*) to apply remedies provided under the municipal law;

(*c*) to restore the situation to that which existed prior to the act;

(*d*) to pay compensation in the event of the impossibility of the restoration of the pre-existing situation; and

(*e*) to provide appropriate guarantees against the repetition or recurrence of the act.

Principle 6

In implementing the right of refugees to compensation, States shall, directly or through the United Nations and intergovernmental organisations, tie the granting of economic or developmental assistance to countries of origin to their fulfillment of this right.

Principle 7

The United Nations may, in the discharge of its role as guardian of the interests of refugees, claim and administer compensation funds for refugees.

Principle 8

The possibility that refugees or UNHCR may one day successfully claim compensation from the country of origin should not serve as a pretext for withholding humanitarian assistance to refugees or refusing to join in international burden-sharing meant to meet the needs of refugees or otherwise to provide durable solutions, including mediation to facilitate voluntary repatriation in dignity and security, thereby removing or reducing the necessity to pay compensation.

Chapter 6

Durable Solutions

On Solutions

The meaning of the word 'solution' has rarely been explored in refugee studies literature. Yet, as Coles writes:

> curiously, everyone refers to solution as an accepted term of art in the approach to the refugee problem, but no one has considered in any depth what this concept means and entails.... The inadequate treatment of solution has been unfortunate, as solution is a notion fundamental to the formation of an approach to the refugee problem, and any misunderstanding where this concept is concerned is inevitably at the expense of the quality of the approach to the problem.[1]

The word 'solution' can have different meanings depending on how the problem to be addressed is defined. As Coles goes on to observe, 'in defining solution, a first step must be to define the problem that requires solving. Our ideas about solution will depend on how we perceive the problem.'[2] Thus, for example, the word 'solution' could be used either to refer to measures seeking to address the root causes of refugee flows or to measures which address the problem of individuals or groups who have found temporary refuge. In this chapter the word 'solution' is being used in the latter sense.

---

[1] G.J.L. Coles, 'The Human Rights Approach to the Solution of the Refugee Problem: A Theoretical and Practical Enquiry', in Alan E. Nash, ed., *Human Rights and the Protection of Refugees under International Law* (The Institute for Research on Public Policy, Nova Scotia, 1988), pp. 195–221 at pp. 195–96.

[2] Ibid., p. 197.

From Resettlement to Repatriation

There are three traditional durable solutions to the refugee problem: resettlement in third countries, local integration and voluntary repatriation.[3] In the past, the industrialised countries advocated resettlement as the principal solution, introducing an exile bias in international refugee law.[4] In **Reading I.A**, Stoessinger records how in the period after World War II it was the West which preferred resettlement to repatriation as a solution. Even when the policy of repatriation was formally adopted by the IRO at the insistence of the Soviet Union, the solution of resettlement prevailed in practice. For by then the question of solution to the international refugee problem had become an integral part of the Cold War.

Presently, great stress is laid on the solution of voluntary repatriation which is described as the ideal and the most desirable solution. As **Reading I.B** shows, the solution of third country resettlement is now proposed only in the context of refugees having special needs and is offered to less than 1 per cent of the world's refugees.[5] The Reading also explores the reasons why states are reluctant to offer resettlement places. Are these reasons persuasive? Should not the industrialised world, vide the principle of burden-sharing, accept a far larger number of refugees for resettlement? In this context interested readers may consider the validity of the reasons advanced by the affluent countries to accept fewer refugees today: these include security considerations, growing unemployment, preservation of cultural boundaries, etc.[6] Are these convincing reasons? Or is the reason simply the end of the Cold War and the fact that most refugees flee the poor world?

[3] According to Goodwin-Gill, 'a durable solution entails a process of integration into society; it will be successful and lasting only if it allows the refugee to attain a degree of self-sufficiency, to participate in the social and economic life of the community and to retain what might be described, too summarily, as a degree of personal identity and integrity.' Guy Goodwin-Gill, 'Refuge or Asylum: International Law and the Search for Solutions to the Refugee Problem', in H. Adelman and C.M. Lanphier, eds, *Refuge or Asylum: A Choice for Canada* (York Lanes Press, Toronto, 1990), pp. 27–43, at p. 38.

[4] 'Resettlement is about refugees moving from a transit or country of first asylum to another, or third, State.' Guy Goodwin-Gill, *The Refugee in International Law* (Clarendon Press, Oxford, 1996), second edition, p. 276. For example, nearly 1.2 million refugees have been resettled out of Southeast Asia.

[5] Gil Loescher, *Beyond Charity: International Cooperation and the Global Refugee Crisis* (Oxford University Press, New York, 1993), p. 148. See also UNHCR Executive Committee Conclusion No. 67 of 1991.

[6] See generally in this regard M. Walzer, *Spheres of Justice: A Defense of Pluralism and Equality* (Basic Books, New York, 1983); J.H. Carens, 'Aliens and Citizens: The Case for Open Borders', *Review of Politics* (Vol. 49, 1987), pp. 251–73; M. Gibney, *Open Border? Closed Societies? The Ethical and Political Questions* (Greenwood Press, Westport,Conn., 1988); E. Kamenka, 'On Being a Refugee', in A. Saikal, ed., *Refugees in the Modern World* (Australian National University, Canberra, 1989), pp. 11–15; J.H. Carens, 'Refugees and the

Local Integration

Like resettlement the solution of local integration is not viewed as a viable solution today. For, as Loescher explains:

> most first-asylum countries are very poor and unstable. A sudden influx of refugees can disrupt a fragile economy, exacerbate unemployment, and heighten ethnic tensions. Many countries of asylum are unwilling to settle refugees close to border areas if their presence is likely to raise diplomatic or security problems, or provoke popular resentment and domestic conflict. Few countries are willing to offer citizenship to refugees, although this would greatly facilitate their long-term integration into host societies.[7]

Therefore, it is not surprising that the idea of integration has received little theoretical attention. In **Reading II.A** Kuhlman, among the few to have written on the subject, offers a definition of the term 'integration'.

Voluntary Repatriation: The Most Desirable Solution?

The next section includes readings which debate the validity of projecting voluntary repatriation as the most desirable solution in all situations. A perusal of the relevant literature reveals that voluntary repatriation is recommended as the best solution from two different perspectives. The first is the statist perspective, particularly that of the industrialised states, which have dropped the exile bias in their approach and replaced it with *non-entrée* policies. Their favouring the durable solution of voluntary repatriation appears to be self-serving. The second is the liberal perspective, elaborated by Coles in **Reading III. A**, which contends that the exile bias in traditional Western thinking is not only unrealistic in the circumstances of the modern refugee problem, but also 'inhumane'. The problem with this understanding is that once the solution of voluntary repatriation is presented as *the* humane solution it is pursued even when it is relatively inappropriate. Moreover, an idealised image of the ultimate

---

Limits of Obligation', *Public Affairs Quarterly* (Vol. 6, 1992), pp. 31–44; G. Frankenberg, 'The Alchemy of Law and Strangeness', *Recht en Kritiek* (Vol. 19, 1993), pp. 362–72; J. Rawls, 'The Law of Peoples', *Critical Inquiry* (Vol. 30, 1993), pp. 37–68; A.H. Richmond, *Global Aparthied: Refugees, Racism, and the New World Order* (Oxford University Press, Toronto, 1994); M. Weiner, *The Global Migration Crisis: Challenges to States and Human Rights* (Harper Collins College Publishers, New York, 1995); J. Habermas, 'Citizenship and National Identity: Some Reflections on the Future of Europe', in R. Beiner, ed., *Theorizing Citizenship* (State University of New York Press, New York, 1995), pp. 255–81.

[7] Loescher, *Beyond Charity* (see footnote 5 earlier), pp. 148–49.

solution legitimises a degree of coercion since it is perceived as a solution which the refugees should themselves desire most.[8]

In **Readings III.B** and **III.C**, both Bascom and Rogge contend that the solution of voluntary repatriation has not been adequately researched and that there are situations and contexts in which it is not the ideal solution. They emphasise the need to listen to refugee voices and take cognisance of the experience of different refugee groups. Often, however, the refugee experience and wishes are subordinated to the interests of states. The need to guarantee the human rights of returnees and ensure sufficient opportunities to rebuild their lives are other factors to which they draw attention. The Bascom and Rogge Readings raise a series of questions which readers may reflect on. What makes repatriation appear a natural solution to the problem of refugees? What are the different push and pull factors which influence the decision of refugees? How can the different refugee experiences inform a system of rules, legal or administrative, regulating the return of refugees? How are the human rights of returnees best guaranteed? How are the special needs of women and other vulnerable groups to be taken into account? Should return take into account the concerns and expectations of the receiving communities? etc.

Voluntary Repatriation: Legal Framework

The solution of voluntary repatriation also raises a host of legal and policy issues. What is the meaning to be assigned to the word 'voluntary'? How is the voluntary nature of repatriation to be ascertained? Must it reflect the exercise of an individual will? Or can it be a part of a collective decision taken by a group of refugees to return? What kind of information of the country of origin must the refugees have access to if they are to make rational decisions? What are the minimum human rights standards that must be met in the country of origin? etc.

From the standpoint of international law it is interesting that Article V of the OAU Convention is the only multilateral treaty provision on the subject. However, there are two detailed conclusions adopted on the subject of voluntary repatriation by the Executive Committee of the UNHCR. Albeit these have the status of mere recommendations, in practice the conclusions have proved influential in shaping the practice of states and in defining the role of the UNHCR. **Readings IV.A** to **IV.C** reproduce the two Executive Committee conclusions and Article V of the OAU Convention.

The fact that there is no positive universal law on the question of voluntary repatriation may however become less critical if the right to return

---

[8] B.S. Chimni, 'Voluntary Repatriation: A Critical Note', *International Journal of Refugee Law* (Vol. 3, 1991), pp. 541–46.

is emphasised as a part of international human rights law. According to Goodwin-Gill, 'the legal context remains clear. Return is the objective to which international law aspires; it derives from the conception of nationality in international law, being coterminous with the notions of attachment and belonging; and is supported by the concept of fundamental human rights, now including the positive legal implications of the right to development.'[9] From a general perspective the right of repatriation has been upheld as a fundamental human right by Article 13(2) of the UDHR which states: 'Everyone has the right to leave any country including his own, and return to his country.'[10]

Organised Repatriation and the Role of UNHCR

Repatriation can either be organised or spontaneous. By organised repatriation is meant a situation in which:

> refugees return home under the terms of a plan that is worked out well in advance and has the support of both home and asylum governments, as well as that of UNHCR and the refugees themselves.... Such plans commonly include amnesties for political offences, assurances of safe passage for returning refugees, material assistance to help them re-establish themselves and provisions for international presence of some kind to monitor their safety.[11]

The UNHCR has therefore an important role to play in organised repatriation. The Statute of the Office of the UNHCR states that it should assist 'governments and ... private organisations to facilitate the voluntary repatriation of ... refugees...'. The legal framework laid down in Executive Committee conclusions provides the agreed basis for UNHCR's actions. The emphasis in these conclusions is squarely on ensuring that repatriation is voluntary and is undertaken in safety and dignity.

However, with pressure mounting from donor as well as host countries in recent years, the UNHCR is increasingly called upon to certify returns secured through questionable practices as being voluntary. This raises a whole host of questions. To whom is the UNHCR ultimately responsible,

---

[9] Guy Goodwin-Gill, 'Voluntary Repatriation: Legal and Policy Issues', in G. Loescher and L. Monahan, eds, *Refugees and International Relations* (Clarendon Press, Oxford, 1989), pp. 255–85 at p. 270.

[10] See generally M.Y.A. Zieck, 'Voluntary Repatriation: An Analysis of the Refugee's Rights to Return to his Own Country', *Austrian Journal of Public International Law* (Vol. 44, 1992), pp. 137–76; and R.J. Zedalis, 'Right to Return: A Closer Look', *Georgetown Immigration Law Journal* (Vol. 6, 1992), pp. 499–517.

[11] *The State of the World's Refugees: The Challenge of Protection* (Penguin, New York, 1993), p. 106.

to refugees under its charge or to the sovereign members of the United Nations? Should it stick to principles or should it accede to the harsh reality that states want refugees to return even when circumstances are less than ideal? What are the minimal conditions which must be satisfied before the UNHCR should assist repatriation? What is the manner in which it should verify the voluntary character of refugee repatriation? What should be its role in monitoring the status of returnees in the country of origin? In what ways can it intervene to ensure that the human rights of returnees are respected?

Organised repatriation can involve the UNHCR entering into legal arrangements with the concerned states. These can assume the form of tripartite or bipartite agreements which spell out the legal, technical and administrative arrangements which will be the basis of carrying out the repatriation. The complex nature of the role it may be called upon to play can be gleaned from the part it played in the repatriation of Cambodian refugees, which was an integral element of the 'Agreements on a Comprehensive Political Settlement of the Cambodian Conflict' arrived at in 1991.[12] In this regard the UNHCR entered into a tripartite Memorandum of Understanding with Thailand and Cambodia. **Reading V.A** provides a brief assessment of the role of the UNHCR in the Cambodian operation and the lessons which may be learnt from it.

Reading V.B reproduces an extract from the 'Concerted Plan of Action in Favour of Central American Refugees, Returnees and Displaced Persons' adopted by the International Conference on Central American Refugees (known by the Spanish acronym CIREFCA for the international conference). In the Plan of Action repatriation forms part of a complex process of sub-regional cooperation which involved a large number of actors (states of Central America, UNHCR, NGOs and donor countries). The welfare of returnees was made an integral part of the national development plans of the concerned states. At the same time, the Plan of Action considered the concerns of the receiving community along with those of the returnees. Unfortunately, the donor countries did not respond with enthusiasm once the plan was adopted.[13] Readers may examine the Action Plan to see whether it offers a model of cooperation for those parts of the world where the conditions are different.

[12] For the text see *Agreements on a Comprehensive Political Settlement of the Cambodian Conflict* (Department of Information, United Nations, 1991).

[13] See E. Mihalkanin, 'Refugee Aid, Displaced Persons, and Development in Central America', in Robert Gorman, ed., *Refugee Aid and Development: Theory and Practice* (Greenwood Press, Connecticut, 1993), pp. 83–111. On the CIREFCA process see also H.G. Espiell et al., 'Principles and Criteria for the Protection of and Assistance to Central American Refugees, Returnees and Displaced Persons in Central America', *International Journal of Refugee Law* (Vol. 83, 1990), p. 83.

Spontaneous Repatriation

Spontaneous repatriation takes place without any of the features of advanced planning which characterise organised repatriation. The decision-makers in this instance are refugees themselves. It is contended that a majority of the refugees who return to their home countries repatriate spontaneously. There is little legal guidance for the UNHCR in such cases other than the statement in Executive Committee Conclusion No. 40 that 'action taken to promote organised voluntary repatriation should not create obstacles to the spontaneous return of refugees.'

In **Reading VI.A** Stein and Cuny explain the phenomenon of spontaneous repatriation. In view of its increased involvement in recent years with voluntary repatriation operations, the Division of International Protection, UNHCR, prepared in 1996 a *Handbook* on the subject which attempts to consolidate the basic protection principles relating to voluntary repatriation as well as its operational experience in the field.[14] The *Handbook* is primarily intended for UNHCR staff and government and NGO partners working in the area. A brief excerpt from this *Handbook* is reproduced as **Reading VI.B** in the context of UNHCR facilitating and promoting spontaneous repatriation. It stresses that what the UNHCR needs to ensure above all is that what it is promoting in the name of spontaneous repatriation is not coerced repatriation.

Readers may raise the following questions in relation to spontaneous repatriation. Are there particular categories of refugees who tend to return even when conditions do not seem appropriate to outside observers? How does one determine whether refugees are repatriating spontaneously or whether they are doing so under pressure? Should the wishes of spontaneously repatriating refugees be respected under all circumstances? What should be the role of the UNHCR where spontaneous repatriation is concerned? Should it simply stand on the sidelines insisting on advance planning or facilitate the process on the ground? Does the fact that it is an intergovernmental organisation make any difference to the kind of role it can play?

The Ideas of Safe and Imposed Return

For some time now, in the context of the emerging temporary protection regime—discussed in Chapter 2—the concept of voluntary repatriation has been replaced with that of safe return.[15] Most recently, the idea of

---

[14] *Handbook on Voluntary Repatriation: International Protection* (UNHCR, Geneva, 1996).

[15] On safe return see Goodwin-Gill, *The Refugee in International Law* (see footnote 4 earlier), pp. 275–76; James C. Hathaway, 'The Meaning of Repatriation', *International Journal of Refugee Law* (Vol. 9, 1997), pp. 551–58.

imposed repatriation has been aired. It brings out in the open the discussion of circumstances in which involuntary return is justifiable.[16] It is not yet clear as to what those circumstances are to be. But be that as it may, it would appear to have negative implications for the principle of *non-refoulement* through legitimising involuntary return. These are worrisome developments which readers may note.[17]

Durable Solutions and Best Interests of the Child

In promoting durable solutions it is of utmost importance that the interests of the women, children and other vulnerable groups are adequately safeguarded. **Reading VII.A** lists certain guidelines in the instance of repatriating children with reference to all three durable solutions. The reading reveals the high degree of care and preparation necessary in promoting durable solutions for refugee children.

* * *

I. RESETTLEMENT

A. **John George Stoessinger,** *The Refugee and the World Community* **(The University of Minnesota Press, Minneapolis, 1963), pp. 61–62, 64–66, 81, 111–13.**

The question of refugees and displaced persons appeared as Item 17 on the agenda of the First Session of the General Assembly. There is little evidence to suggest that the United States, France, and the United Kingdom, in drawing the attention of that body to the remaining uprooted people, regarded the matter as one of major political import.... Item 17 seemed innocuous enough and was quietly referred to the Third Committee of the General Assembly, concerned with social, humanitarian and cultural questions. At the same time, the matter was placed on the agenda of the First Session of the Economic and Social Council.

---

[16] '... the UNHCR has somewhat abandoned the question of free choice and the rule of profound and lasting change in favour of a vague notion of safe return or return in dignity and safety. To replace the notion of voluntary repatriation with that of safe return is to replace the refugee's individual judgement with the discretion of the UNHCR or the states involved. This overruling of the will of refugees is all the more disquieting in that it increases the risk of pressure.' Francois Jean, 'The Plight of the World's Refugees: At the Crossroads of Protection', in Medicins Sans Frontieres, *World in Crisis* (Routledge, London, 1997), pp. 42–57 at pp. 50–51.

[17] For a critical perspective see B.S. Chimni, 'From Resettlement to Involuntary Repatriation: Towards a Critical History of Durable Solutions', Recent Issues in Refugee Research: Working Paper No. 2 (UNHCR, Geneva, May 1999).

An analysis of the discussions leading to the final adoption on 20 December 1946 of the Constitution for the International Refugee Organisation might be divided into two phases. The debate in the Third Committee of the General Assembly dealt mostly with the broad contours of the problem; the positions of the member governments toward the refugee question as a whole were explored and crystallised in the course of the session. During the two weeks from 28 January through 12 February 1946, the conversations ranged in tone from dogmatic rigidity to flexible compromise as the delegates in the Third Committee considered the two important issues confronting them: first, whether the refugee problem was a concern of the international community, and second, whether repatriation to the refugee's country of origin was a desirable solution. . . .

The issue now confronting the delegates was how the refugee problem could most equitably and speedily be settled. Mr. Arutiunian from the Soviet Union struck the keynote when he asked, 'What does every refugee expect from the organisation of the United Nations? . . . He expects help to be able to return to his native country.' V.N. Sassen, delegate of the Netherlands, while agreeing with the Soviet statement in part, took issue with the inclusiveness of the generalisation:

> A desire of an uprooted person not to return to his country of origin, should be respected by the authorities of his country of origin as well as by those of the country where he has found refuge, unless it is proved that—according to existing international agreements—such a person is liable to be extradited to his country of origin . . . in order to be brought to justice.

S.R. Stanczyk of Poland challenged the premise of the Dutch statement when he defended the view that the 'basic reasons which prevented the return of these persons to their countries have disappeared'. His view was supported by Dr. Bebler of Yugoslavia, who declared in effect that the only Yugoslavs outside the borders of his country refusing to be repatriated must by definition be war criminals, quislings and traitors. He pointed to the examples of the Ustashis, Zborachis, and the Chetniks as pro-Fascist elements who should be made to face justice at home without delay. His conclusions from these observations were logical enough:

> Has it ever been known in the history of international relations that a government contributed to the cost of maintaining its political enemies who have fled abroad or—*a fortiori*—emigrants who have in fact committed crimes against the people? No, nothing of the sort has ever been known.

The assumption implicit in the Yugoslav rhetorical question was challenged by A.M. Egeland, delegate from the Union of South Africa, who stated that 'the problem would be simple if the forced repatriation, actual or implied, which seems to me—I hope wrongly—implicit in the Yugo-slav proposals were resorted to.' The point was stated positively by Mr. Sassen: 'A person who has expressed his desire not to return to his coun-try of origin is entitled to resettlement elsewhere.'

Thus, the outlines of the two positions began to assume form and sub-stance. The majority and the minority were in agreement on the interna-tional character of the refugee problem, but a sharp cleavage emerged regarding the scope of operations to be assigned to the new organisation. The Western countries felt that political dissidence was a legitimate phe-nomenon; refugees were not necessarily composed only of war criminals, quislings and traitors, as the minority contended; in view of the fact that voluntary repatriation to the countries of origin had practically reached a standstill, the logical task of the new organ would be the resettlement and permanent re-establishment of the remaining refugees. The position of the countries of origin did not admit the existence of bona fide refugees not wishing to return. Such persons were ipso facto traitorous and repre-hensible. The only just course would therefore be speedy repatriation and retribution. As for genuine refugees, none would hesitate to return home, where they would be received with open arms.

In its broad implications, the Western position defended the right of the individual to differ politically from his government. The minority denied that right and considered it a punishable offense. The majority visualised the new organisation to be primarily a service organ for the re-establishment of the political dissident in a more friendly environment while, in the minds of the delegates from the countries of origin, the punitive element in the character of the projected refugee organ assumed top priority. The Western powers insisted that the alternative of repatria-tion must remain a voluntary one, while the Eastern governments repeat-edly stated and continuously implied the principle of enforced repatriation of all their dissident nationals. The West's conception of international organisation in this instance was a service organ for the benefit of individ-uals whereas that of the East was a service organ for the attainment of the political aims of states.

The debates on this controversial issue are masterpieces of parliamen-tary strategy hardly surpassed elsewhere in the annals of international organisation. Much patient search, some evidence of willingness to com-promise, as well as some flares of temper and impassioned oratory were characteristic of both sides. This painful process yielded a temporary solution but, finally, it too proved impracticable.

Thus, the United Nations Organisation, in its infancy, was already beginning to realise that social problems could not be divorced from politics. . . .

... The final result of the legislative debates was a somewhat paradoxical one. The influence of the Soviet bloc on the new organisation was manifest, despite the fact that the Eastern countries refused to become active participants in IRO. The heavy emphasis on repatriation as a preferable mode of settlement, reinforced by a poorly disguised bribe in the form of a three months' ration supply to repatriates, certainly stemmed from Soviet considerations of policy....

... In the last analysis, repatriation did not prove even a partial solution. During its lifetime the Organisation repatriated 72,834 refugees, a meager 5 percent of the total number of displaced persons registered with IRO. A great amount of energy was expended by the Organisation in adhering to the constitutional provision defining repatriation as its primary responsibility, but to little avail. It is possible, but improbable, that budgetary considerations motivated these efforts. Although it was evident to IRO officials that the cost of repatriation per refugee was but a fraction of the cost of resettlement, this argument never appeared in the discussions of the General Council. It seems that the Organisation was convinced of the inherent superiority of repatriation as a solution, provided freedom of choice was permitted. However, when resistance to repatriation reached such a degree that the Organisation began to fear for the welfare of its refugees and when the countries of origin themselves exhibited a slackening of interest, IRO reoriented its policy completely. In short, when the Organisation found itself confronted with a situation totally different from the one faced at the time of its birth, it met the new challenge in a pragmatic and realistic manner. Through a multiplicity of programmes ranging from the satisfaction of physical needs to intensive training of the mind, the refugee assembly centres had become more than mere 'camps for persons, asocial and unemployed, who had become superfluous and bothersome', and the majority of the uprooted were ready, when the time was ripe, for the first organised mass resettlement of refugees in history. That time came when the Organisation, untrammelled by the dead hand of the countries of origin and encouraged by increasingly positive attitudes in many nations of potential resettlement, directed its energies westward and across the sea.

... The absence of the Soviet Union and its satellites from the policy organ of the International Refugee Organisation made it possible for IRO to meet the challenge of the hour. Although the basic document of the Organisation had clearly stipulated the primacy of repatriation, resettlement had been left open as a possible alternative over the vigorous protests of the Eastern governments, and by the end of 1947, it had become abundantly clear that resettlement for over a million refugees was to be the major responsibility of IRO. In assuming this function, IRO became the first international organisation devoted to the mass reestablishment of refugees.

B. Rupert Colville, 'Resettlement: Still Vital after All These Years', *Refugees* (No. 94, December 1993), pp. 4–8.

Resettlement is geared to the special needs of an individual whose life, liberty, health or fundamental human rights are in jeopardy in the country where he or she first sought asylum. It is a highly complex, organised process that involves identifying those in urgent need and finding a suitable country prepared to accept them.

People eligible for resettlement include those who are essentially protection cases—refugees threatened with *refoulement* to their country of origin and people in physical danger in their first country of asylum. Resettlement is also used for 'vulnerable groups', such as torture and rape victims, the disabled and other injured or severely traumatised people in need of specialised treatment unavailable in their first country asylum, and for 'long-stayers' for whom no other solution is available. And it is often the only way to reunite refugee families who, through no fault of their own, find themselves divided by borders or, sometimes, by entire continents.

At first sight, history and terminology appear to have been conspiring to kill off resettlement, which has long been referred to as the 'least-preferred solution' and 'the last resort'. In 1980, a total of 267,000 people—3 percent of the world's refugees—were transported from one asylum country to another, many of them with the help of the Intergovernmental Committee for Migration. The agency, now known as the International Organisation for Migration (IOM), is UNHCR's long established partner in resettlement. Throughout the 1980s, the annual number of resettlement cases averaged 122,000 per year. By 1992, however, the number had plummeted to a mere 37,000, or 0.2 percent of the total number of refugees in the world.

Accepting people for resettlement is a mark of true generosity on the part of governments. No country is legally obliged to accept resettlement cases. Only 10 states do so on a regular basis, setting annual quotas. A further 10 or so states also regularly accept people for resettlement, sometimes in relatively large numbers, but do not commit themselves to quotas. However, the great majority of states rarely, if ever, offer resettlement places.

As a result, there has been a consistent shortfall in recent years between the number of places sought by UNHCR and those made available. In 1991, for example, there was a shortfall of 55 percent, and in 1992 one of 13 percent—despite the fact that the number of places sought had dropped from 75,600 to 42,300.

There are a variety of reasons why many states are reluctant to offer resettlement places, and why the numbers have been dropping over the past few years. While on the surface resettlement appears to be a straightforward humanitarian response to special, clearly identifiable needs, in reality it has always been problematic.

One reason for this is that resettlement is very expensive. It involves arranging international transport, as well as helping to integrate the refugees in the resettlement country and, in some cases, paying for costly follow-up treatment such as medical care and counselling. It is also labour-intensive and requires highly trained staff. In an age of overburdened asylum systems, and emergency and repatriation operations involving millions of refugees, donors tend to shy away from a solution which, on a per capita basis, far exceeds the cost of the other durable solutions—voluntary repatriation and local integration.

The difficulties are not confined to governments and the humanitarian agencies who process, transport and pay for resettlement. The refugees themselves may face immense problems adapting to a radically different culture far from home. There have been some particularly sad cases of people who have failed to adapt to life in their resettlement country, either because they themselves were unable to overcome the psychological and practical obstacles that they faced, or because they were not given enough, or the right type of support. . . .

Although the concept of resettlement was not clearly articulated until the mid-1960s, it had been undertaken in one form or another almost from the outset of the system of international protection for refugees. Between the two World Wars, resettlement was used as the principal or partial solution for a number of refugee situations. During the early 1920s, for example, around 45,000 White Russians who had fled to China after the Russian Revolution were subsequently resettled elsewhere. And in the 1930s a succession of international refugee organisations were charged with resettling Jews and others who were fleeing Nazi persecution in Germany and Austria.

UNHCR's immediate predecessor, the International Refugee Organisation (IRO), was primarily engaged in resettlement rather than repatriation. Over a period of five years from 1947 to 1951, the IRO resettled well over a million people (four-fifths of them outside Europe), while repatriating a mere 73,000. Similarly, UNHCR, during its early years, made extensive use of resettlement as a means of clearing the European refugee camps left over from World War II.

Over the next three decades, voluntary repatriation, local integration and resettlement enjoyed more or less equal status as durable solutions, depending on the circumstances. The Soviet invasion of Hungary in 1956 resulted in 200,000 refugees fleeing to Yugoslavia and Austria, many of whom were later resettled in other countries.

In 1972, President Idi Amin of Uganda peremptorily expelled most of the country's Asian minority, many of whom had lived there for decades and had no other country to go back to. With the help of UNHCR, IOM, the International Committee of the Red Cross (ICRC), and the United Nations Development Programme (UNDP), some 40,000 Ugandan Asians were resettled in a matter of a few months in a total of 25 different countries....

The largest and most dramatic example of resettlement in modern times occurred in South-East Asia. After the fall of Saigon in 1975, hundreds of thousands of refugees—mainly Vietnamese boat-people—fled to neighbouring countries. By 1979, a major protection crisis had developed as certain asylum countries refused to accept any more refugees and began preventing boats from landing and even started towing them out onto the pirate infested high seas.

The international community responded by agreeing to resettle new arrivals. In exchange, the asylum countries relented and agreed to allow the boat-people to land. Over the following decade, more than 700,000 Vietnamese were resettled.

In retrospect, it was clear that the decision to adopt blanket resettlement, while averting the immediate threat of massive loss of life, led to an additional problem as there was a risk that the number of economic migrants, attracted by automatic 'no-questions-asked' resettlement would outstrip genuine refugees. Meanwhile, elsewhere in the world, people who were in desperate need of resettlement were suffering from a lack of available places. By the late 1980s, resettlement—designed as an important solution and protection tool for individual refugees meeting certain very specific criteria—had itself become the chief pull-factor in a mass-migration movement.

The situation in South-East Asia has almost certainly had a long-term detrimental effect on resettlement that persists to the present day. It made potential resettlement countries extremely wary of triggering new economically-motivated outflows by over-generous offers of places.

II. LOCAL INTEGRATION

A. Tom Kuhlman, *Asylum or Aid? The Economic Integration of Ethiopian and Eritrean Refugees in the Sudan* (African Studies Centre, Leiden, 1994), pp. 51–52, 56–57.

... integration in the country of first refuge is one of the three possible durable solutions to refugee problems. It may thus be regarded as the goal of the settlement process: if it is achieved, the refugee problem can be considered solved. This makes it imperative to define integration; and it must be defined with sufficient rigour to permit assessing whether a refugee is truly integrated, comparing whether one group is more integrated than another, and measuring the progress of integration over time. Within the field of refugee studies we find ourselves here on relatively untrodden ground, as there has been little theoretical reflection on this issue. Most of the interest in refugee integration has come from practitioners, and few attempts have been made to define the term with any degree of precision.

The United Nations High Commissioner for Refugees defines integration as 'the process by which the refugee is assimilated into the social and economic life of a new national community'. This definition is clearly unsatisfactory; it is tautological, as it merely replaces the term to be defined with another word which is presumed to be synonymous. What then, is assimilation? The criticism can be moved a step further: is integration really the same as assimilation? As we shall see below a distinction between the two concepts makes sense.

It may be noted that integration is not formally defined in the principal legal instruments that govern UNHCR policies: the 1951 Convention and the UNHCR Statute. Article 8 of the Statute, which specifies the duties of the High Commissioner, includes promoting the 'admission [of refugees] to a new national community'. That can hardly mean anything else than their naturalisation, and this is confirmed in Article 34 of the Convention, which states that the state of asylum 'shall facilitate the naturalisation of refugees'. While this is an important aspect of refugee integration, it is not generally accepted.... Nor is it mentioned in UNHCR publications nowadays, undoubtedly because it would not carry any favour with countries of asylum. International hospitality has changed since the 1950s.

Among the few scholars who have grappled with defining refugee integration, Harrell-Bond suggests that it refers to

> a situation in which host and refugee communities are able to co-exist, sharing the same resources—both economic and social—with no greater mutual conflict than that which exists within the host community.[18]

However, she immediately rejects this definition as too simple: access to resources may be unequal; one group may be exploited by another; and conflict within the host society may have increased due to the pressure of the refugees' presence. Yet this definition has at least the merit that it looks at integration as something that happens not only to refugees, but also to the host society....

... When the migrants remain a group unto themselves, we could speak of *separation*; this could occur because they are settled in areas

[18] Barbara Harrell-Bond, *Imposing Aid: Emergency Assistance to Refugees* (Oxford University Press, Oxford, 1986), p. 7.

specifically set aside for them, because they are kept dependent on relief, or because they themselves wish to maintain their own identity and are able to do so. *Assimilation* would mean that the migrants as a group eventually become more or less indistinguishable from other members of the society that has adopted them. In the case of *marginalisation*, the relations they maintain with the other members of the new society permit them neither to live according to their own standards nor to attain those of the host country; instead, they become as a disadvantaged minority playing a subordinate role. *Integration*, finally, means that *the migrants maintain their own identity, yet become part of the host society to the extent that host population and refugees can live together in an acceptable way.*

... Our definition can now be made more specific. If refugees are able to participate in the host economy in ways commensurate with their skills and compatible with their cultural values; if they attain a standard of living which satisfies culturally determined minimum requirements (standard of living is taken here as meaning not only income from economic activities, but also access to amenities such as housing, public utilities, health services, and education); if the socio-cultural change they undergo permits them to maintain an identity of their own and to adjust psychologically to their new situation; if standards of living and economic opportunities for members of the host society have not deteriorated due to the influx of refugees; if friction between host population and refugees is not worse than within the host population itself; and if the refugees do not encounter more discrimination than exists between groups previously settled within the host society: then refugees are truly integrated. A durable solution to the problems arising from flight (but not those *causing* flight) can be said to have been achieved. This may seem a paradisiacal state seldom if ever attained in practice. What matters, however, is that it should give us a yardstick for measuring progress and for comparing the effects of alternative policies.

III. VOLUNTARY REPATRIATION:
THE MOST DESIRABLE SOLUTION?

**A. Gervase Coles, 'Approaching the Refugee Problem Today',
in Gil Loescher and Laila Monahan, eds, *Refugees and
International Relations* (Clarendon Press, Oxford, 1989),
pp. 387–93, 403–4.**

New Necessities for New Realities

If there is to be any hope of dealing effectively with the new realities today the first task is to free so much traditional Western thinking about the refugee problem of its 'exile' bias. This bias is inhumane and disastrously inappropriate in the circumstances of the modern refugee problem.

Because of the particular circumstances of the Cold War and because of the modern European history of the persecution of religious and racial groups, the assumption gained ground in the West that a refugee movement was a good thing. It provided the opportunity to attack an adversary, since the movement was the result of persecution, and it gave the persons involved the chance to find a new and better life. Sometimes too a refugee movement was a satisfactory way, though never proclaimed as such, of dealing with an internal problem. A refugee movement, however, is never a good thing: it may often be the lesser of two evils, but it remains an evil because it is, by definition, involuntary separation from the homeland—it is not voluntary migration.

It has even been asserted that refugees, unlike other human beings, do not want to return to their countries of origin. This could be true of only a relatively small number of refugees who have never had any real sense of belonging to their country of origin. For the vast majority of refugees the dream is of being able to return home one day. It is true that refugees normally have no desire to return to a country while the conditions that caused them to leave remain unchanged, but this far from saying that in no circumstances in the future would they wish to return home. Indeed, the contrary is true, as the magnitude and rapidity of the occurrence of spontaneous return when conditions permit well demonstrates. In the bleak and bitter moments of exile the hope of return can be the one factor which sustains the refugee in a moment of trial.

For the vast majority of refugees today, the conditions of exile are far from good, even by the standards which normally apply to them at home. In some situations the conditions of exile can prove worse than the conditions experienced at home. Many do not get beyond the threshold of their countries of first asylum. They are detained in camps or treated as irregular aliens, forced to live in makeshift accommodation or wherever a roof can be found, under constant fear of expulsion or *refoulement*, dependent on hand-outs or the sale of tourist artifacts for survival, separated from their families and friends, often deprived of all news of them, vulnerable to the intense pressure of military or political groups and, finally, with a better future not even a light at the end of a long, dark tunnel of terrestrial existence. For the many millions of these people, exile is a painful trial, the occasion for heroism for many and the occasion for despair for some. Even for those who pass beyond the threshold and are eventually settled in areas of peace and prosperity, many still remain socially marginalised, often without employment, and prone to depression engendered by their sense of alienation.

In addition flight or expulsion as a result of social conflict usually amounts to a deteriorating situation in the country of origin. Often this deterioration directly affects other states, either because of their sympathy for the refugees or because they do not welcome them, and see their entry into their territory as a danger to their own internal stability and external security. Refugee situations can become a notoriously potent source of international tension and conflict, creating new problems as well as rendering more difficult the resolution of old ones.

Addressing Kampuchean refugees on the border of Thailand in 1984, Pope John Paul II said:

> There is something repugnant and abnormal in the fact that thousands upon thousands of human beings are forced to leave their country ... transplantation cannot be a definite solution to the situation of refugees. They have a right to go back to their roots, to return to their native land with its national sovereignty and its right to independence and self-determination.

Accepting this view, therefore, it is unjustifiable—indeed it is profoundly wrong—that the prevailing international approach to the refugee problem should continue to have an exile bias. Yet this is unquestionably the case.

In the Western-inspired international instruments and documents on refugees and asylum, the emphasis has been mainly if not exclusively on exile. Although the UNHCR Statute mentioned voluntary repatriation as one of the durable solutions, it was only included, as the first High Commissioner Van Heuven Goedhart admitted, as 'the somewhat hypocritical compromise to which the interminable discussions in the United Nations had led'. In the 1951 Refugee Convention external settlement is the only solution contemplated, and there is no mention of the obligations (or rights) of the country of origin. When the United Nations General Assembly Declaration on Territorial Asylum was being debated in the Assembly's Sixth Committee in 1966, a proposal to include an article stating that 'nothing in the Declaration shall be interpreted to prejudice the right of everyone to return to his country as stated in Article 13, paragraph 2 of the Universal Declaration on Human Rights' was successfully opposed. And the draft Convention on Territorial Asylum prepared by a group of experts convened by the High Commissioner in the early 1970s included only a brief and passive provision on voluntary repatriation. In its own documentation, UNHCR refused consistently to accept the human right of return as the starting-point for a consideration of voluntary repatriation, and its documentation on protection persistently reflected its assumption that external settlement, not return, was the normal solution. The terminology employed revealed the exile bias; for example, 'exile' was always 'asylum' and 'homeland' was always the 'country of origin'. Expositions of international refugee law summarily dismissed the solution of return in a few platitudinous lines, which amounted to a complete evasion of the human rights issues involved, as well as of all the persistent promptings of some states; the subject of voluntary repatriation was considered and valuable recommendations were made, but some of them have yet to be implemented.

In addition UNHCR's operational weight has been primarily on care and maintenance and external settlement. A section existed for many years to deal with resettlement, but only ad hoc and often haphazard arrangements were made for voluntary repatriation. For much of the time UNHCR did not consider that it had any responsibility to take an initiative in favour of reconciliation or restoration. Whereas separation and alienation were humanitarian matters, reconciliation or restoration were political, and as such beyond UNHCR's mandate.

A New Approach to the Refugee Problem

In recent years, however, an increasing number of Western governments have called into question this traditional bias and have sought to promote a new and positive approach to prevention and voluntary repatriation. It seems that we may now be reaching a watershed, a reorientation towards the key issue of a solution leading to a new conception of the purposes and principles of the approach to the refugee problem. In its comments to the UN Secretary-General on the General Assembly item on 'International Co-operation to Avert Further Mass Flows of Refugees', inscribed on the Assembly's agenda, on the initiative of the Federal Republic of Germany, the Australian government stated in 1981 that the assumption of external settlement as the correct durable solution to a refugee situation could not be justified on either humanitarian or political grounds. It would effectively relieve the country of origin of its serious responsibility to take whatever measures were possible and necessary to enable people who had fled its territory to return; it would also undermine the right of people who had fled their homeland to seek the support of the international community in obtaining the conditions which would make possible their voluntary return; and it would institutionalise exile at the expense of the fundamental right of the individual to return home and to enjoy their basic human rights. In some cases it would place an unrealistic burden on the country of refuge and result in 'solutions' which were highly unsatisfactory.

The international bias in favour of exile has prevailed not only for political reasons but as a consequence of the equation of the refugee to the victim of persecution; for, if the refugee is a victim of persecution, which is normally the deliberate and often systematic violation of the rights of the individual by a government, then the co-operation of the country of origin is either undesirable or unrealistic. Another consequence of this equation of course is that it ensures that the country of origin loses any interest in co-operating with other countries or international organisations which have declared its citizens to be the victims of its own grave and deliberate violation of their rights.

The international political response to events involving persecution, whatever the motivation of that persecution, has always been principally directed towards external settlement. Resettlement, however, involves more than just political questions. The international community also should take into account victims, which involves questions of human rights. This exile bias simply cannot be defended today in cases where the transfrontier movement is the result of such events as armed conflict, serious internal disturbances, or natural disaster. It is also quite unrealistic in cases such as mass influx, which are seen as threatening external security as well as internal stability.

Normally displacements as a result of armed conflict or natural disaster are of relatively short duration. Return in these circumstances is usually the solution and it would be inappropriate therefore to postulate external settlement as the solution for such displacements. In defence of the exile bias, it has sometimes been maintained that external settlement is in fact the normal solution for refugee movements and that return is the rare exception. The facts, however, prove the contrary to be true. If the problem of external displacement is seen as one where armed conflict has been its principle cause, then it is external settlement which has been the exception, not return. For example, in the course of World War II, some thirty million people within Europe were displaced externally. Of this total, over nine-tenths returned to their homes. The problem of return concerned only a small percentage of this total. In the 1970s some fifteen million refugees returned to their countries of origin, including some ten million to the newly-formed state of Bangladesh.... Although the number of returns has not been nearly as high so far in this decade, return is nevertheless being considered on all sides as the eventual solution for the great majority of the refugees in the world. And, in all these cases, it is what the refugees themselves desire. It must be recognised that the available figures for return relate only to organised or assisted returns. No official figures are available for spontaneous (or non-assisted or non-organised) returns, but their number is clearly significant and over the last two decades runs into millions.

The exile bias of the traditional Western approach has been one of the main reasons why so many countries have kept their distance from it. In the case of Asia the bias poses grave political problems, since Asia is not much more than a geographic expression and, in an area which has been the birthplace of most of the world's religions and civilisations and where two-thirds of humanity is to be found, the problem of religious and racial discrimination is not one that can be easily solved by migration. It is in fact a highly complex and major political question.

Today it is of paramount importance that international co-operation in refugee situations be directed primarily towards the prevention of refugee movements and towards return. An approach to the refugee's problems, which amounts effectively to little more than one of separation and alienation, is not and has never been in anyone's long-term interest. Neither is it in accordance with the basic purposes and principles of the United Nations. Meaningful practical steps should be taken now to give effect to the primary concern for prevention and to the primary values of reconciliation and restoration. An invaluable first step would be to obtain a further objective and comprehensive study of the causes and dynamics of modern refugee movements....

International Law as Part of the Solution

A long overdue step would be to give more weight in international law and policy to the notion of belonging. Although the fact of belonging has not been mentioned explicitly in international human rights instruments as a source of rights, nonetheless, it basically underlies the proclamation of such rights as concerning return, as well as the related prohibitions contained in these instruments on expulsion, exile, and denationalisation. Such rights as self-determination or participation in the government of a country are closely connected with belonging. Belonging in the full sense is a pre-condition for the enjoyment of rights generally, since the exiled national or the national deprived of all national protection in a foreign country enjoys only that modicum of rights granted to refugees or to aliens. In addition, the fact of belonging, or of social attachment, is a basic criterion for determining national jurisdiction and protection and, as such, is a basic principle of international political organisation.

The human need to belong is more than a need for protection or for the means of individual development; it is also a need to be among one's own people. Although this latter need varies in degree according to individual circumstances and to such factors as age, it is normally a strong need, the satisfaction of which is conducive to individual and social well-being, and the denial of which is conducive to suffering and to social disorder.

One of the founders of modern international law, Francesco de Vittoria, rightly described exile as a capital penalty. To deny without justification an individual, a group, or a people the satisfaction of their need to belong by expelling or exiling, depriving of nationality or citizenship, by refusing return, or doing nothing to alleviate conditions which prevent return is to inflict a grievous injury on the persons concerned.

One possibility would be the preparation of a Protocol to the International Covenant on Civil and Political Rights which would deal more comprehensively than do the existing human rights instruments with the subject of belonging, including within itself provisions on such practices as expulsion, exile, de-nationalisation, and the denial by one means or another of the right to return.

... While not ruling out the necessity for some resettlement, an approach to the refugee problem which assumes that the normal solution should be external settlement and that the international approach should be directed primarily to this end is neither humane nor realistic. Until this concept is grasped, a more humane and effective approach to the international refugee problem will remain unattainable.

B. Jonathan Bascom, 'The Dynamics of Refugee Repatriation: The Case of Eritreans in Eastern Sudan', in W.T.S. Gould and A.M. Findlay, eds, *Population Migration and the Changing World Order* (John Wiley and Sons, New York, 1994), pp. 226–28, 244–46.

Repatriation, the return migration of refugees from a country of asylum, is commonly claimed to be the most desirable solution to mounting refugee crises worldwide. The fact that repatriation is 'en vogue' as the preferred policy solution is not at all surprising, given the growing burden that refugee populations place on poor African host countries and the negative reactions that prompts in the West. However, what is being promoted as the most desirable solution to refugee crises is a poorly understood social and spatial phenomenon.

Broadly speaking, the ongoing contributions of social scientists reflect the sequence of three basic phases that constitute the refugee experience—flight, resettlement, and repatriation. The literature of the 1970s focused on the initial phase of refugee experience—causality and patterns of flight.[19] During the 1980s the focus shifted to the process of refugee resettlement and integration in countries of asylum.[20] Most recently,

[19] E. Kunz, 'Exile and Resettlement: Refugee Theory', *International Migration Review*, (Vol. 15, 1981), pp. 125–46; P. Kolenic, 'African Refugees: Characteristics and Patterns of Movement' (unpublished Master's thesis, Ohio University, Department of Geography, 1974); L. Holborn, *Refugees: A Problem of our Time* (The Scarecrow Press Inc., Metuchen, New Jersey, 1975); J. Rogge, 'A Geography of Refugees: Some Illustrations from Africa', *Professional Geographer* (Vol. 29, 1977), pp. 186–89.

[20] A. Hansen, 'Self-settled Rural Refugees in Africa: The Case of Angolans in Zambian Villages', in A. Hansen and T. Oliver-Smith, eds, *Involuntary Migration and Resettlement: The Problems of Dislocated People* (Westview Press, Boulder, 1982), pp. 13–36; B. Harrell-Bond, *Imposing Aid* (see footnote 18 earlier); J. Rogge, *Too Many, Too Long: Sudan's Twenty-year Refugee Dilemma* (Rowman and Allanheld, Totowa, New Jersey, 1985); J. Desbarats, 'Indochinese Resettlement in the United States', *Annals of the Association of American Geographers* (Vol. 75, 1985), pp. 522–38; K. Conner, 'Rationales for the Movement of Afghan Refugees to

however, researchers in the field of refugee studies have drawn attention to the need for substantive work on repatriation. Rogge and Akol argue that the problems associated with repatriation, including the process of reintegration and rehabilitation upon return, are one of two main issues that remain relatively unresearched and poorly understood (the other being the integration of urban refugees).[21] Harrell-Bond goes further, suggesting that: 'in the case of voluntary repatriation in Africa there are no published research data which could be used to test the assumptions which govern current policies and practices of governments and international agencies'.[22] In sum, the literature on repatriation issues remains less developed relative to other aspects of refugee studies, and it should be stressed that research tends to be more concerned with official repatriation programmes rather than movements of refugees on their own accord.

... What is needed to explain the varied response by refugees to the repatriation option are analyses which delineate the factors that coalesce around their decisions to repatriate. Repatriation may be the solution that suits 'external parties', but whether repatriation becomes a normative behaviour or not largely depends on refugees themselves. This discussion poses the issue of repatriation to refugees themselves.

... The process of repatriation can be divided into as many as seven different stages on a time–space continuum—decision-making, preparation, departure, travel, arrival, dispersal and integration. The first and last stages are keeping with a fundamental distinction between the determinants and consequences of migration, while the middle five are associated with the migration event itself. This study examines the formation of an intention or disposition that will result in either repatriation or permanent settlement in the country of asylum. Hence, it focuses on the decision-making portion of the continuum.... There are three key variables—the differential in the economic opportunities afforded by the return economy versus the economy of asylum, the attributes of the potential repatriates and the attributes of the refugee population. These three components interact to provide an expected value of repatriation. Facilitators and constraints play an important role in mediating refugees' perception about repatriation. The approach of this study is to delineate the most important determinants of the repatriation decision from the perspective of the primary participant. This is particularly appropriate since most refugees chose to repatriate on their own accord....

Peshawar', in G. Farr and J. Merriam, eds, *Afghan Resistance: The Politics of Survival* (Westview Press, Boulder, 1986), pp. 151–90; G. Kibreab, *Refugees and Development in Africa: The Case of Eritrea* (The Red Sea Press, Trenton, New Jersey, 1987).

[21] J. Rogge and J. Akol, 'Repatriation: Its Role in Resolving Africa's Refugee Dilemma', *International Migration Review* (Vol. 23, 1989), pp. 184–200.

[22] Barbara Harrell-Bond, 'Repatriation: Under What Conditions is it the Most Desirable Solution for Refugees? An Agenda for Research', *African Studies Review* (Vol. 32, 1989), pp. 41–69 at p. 43.

Conclusions and Summary

This chapter has attempted to disaggregate key variables at the nexus of the repatriation decision. The summary discussion focuses on three main conclusions drawn from the study.

Firstly, refugee differentiation: most contemporary media images give the impression that refugees are undifferentiated 'masses' or 'flows' and that the return to their country of origin is a 'natural' and thus 'problem-free' process. Many forms of differentiation—ethnic, political, age, gender, and class—exist within each refugee population. This study has demonstrated how much differentiation affects the space and scale of repatriation. Table 6.1 summarises the relationship between different motivations for repatriation and different segments of the refugee population. Specifying the causal order of motives lies beyond the scope of the present study. The table does, however, underscore the evident need for relief agencies to apprehend clearly how different kinds of motivation are functioning in each refugee setting.

Table 6.1
Summary of Major Motives Related to Repatriation

Major Motive	Direction of Relationship	Estimated Strength	Potential Refugee Groups Most Affected
Economic opportunity	Positive	Strong	Males, working ages; middle-class strata
Political affinity	Positive	Strong	Majority identified; combatants
Location-specific capital to home country	Positive	Dependent on time	Older ages
Location-specific capital to asylum country	Negative	Dependent on time	Younger ages
Risk aversion	Negative	Moderate	Marginalised strata, capital-intensive strata
Responsive to authority structures	Positive	Moderate	Camp refugees

Source: Adapted from G. De Jong and J. Fawcett, 'Motivations for Migration: An Assessment and a Value-expectancy Research Model', in G. De Jong and R. Gardner, eds, *Migration Decision-making: Multidisciplinary Approaches to Microlevel Studies in Developed and Developing Countries* (Pergamon Press, New York, 1981), p. 40.

Second, authority and identification: a clear grasp of the authority structure at work within a given refugee community is an important key to helping ensure that refugee repatriation becomes a normative response. This study has highlighted the relationship of social transformation to decision-making authority, particularly as it relates to repatriation. The fact that camp refugees are buffered from the impact of host economies and subject to a more regimented way of life contributes to an ossification of authority structures. Among unassisted refugees, however, the locus of decision-making is more likely to shift away from traditional leaders. Beyond the specific people who hold an authoritative role in making repatriation decisions is the question of how much 'authority' specific *places* hold in the minds of would-be repatriates. By suggesting the likely possibility of a dominant 'myth of return' among many Eritreans, this study has questioned how 'authoritative' the homeland may be for refugees faced with the option to return. Those who design repatriation programme need to understand what points of identification with the homeland are most vivid to refugees. What meaning does 'home' hold? On what is the attachment to home based? Is it driven by identification with the cause for which they sought asylum, or are they alienated from that somewhat enduring means of identification?

Thirdly, decision-making frameworks: although the decision to migrate is never completely rational, a basic assumption common to all studies of microlevel migration decisions is that decision maker(s) are, at least to some degree, intentional in their choices.[23] This study demonstrates, however, the difficulty of devising a cost–benefit framework from refugees themselves. Generally speaking, refugees in this case study did not make explicit comparisons between the advantages and disadvantages afforded by their conditions in asylum versus those in their homeland. Part of the reason may be that they are still in a 'passive' mode toward the repatriation prospect rather than in the process of actualising the event itself. Nonetheless, this research illustrates how challenging a task it may be to access more 'submerged' intuitions about the repatriation decision, particularly if the focal point of the decision is constantly changing.

This study began with the proposition that refugee populations are both caused by and pose a serious threat to the established world order. Western nations are rapidly shifting from a 'welcome mode' into a 'protection mode'; all across Europe, boundaries are tightening against new influxes of refugees. As the prospect of third country resettlement diminishes, so too is the hospitality for refugees in neighbouring countries throughout the Third World. The pressure exerted by these two factors alone intensifies the importance of deploying repatriations successfully. This will require coming to a better understanding of the needs and motivations of the repatriates. Part of the dynamics of a changing world order is that refugees, even in remote rural locations, are increasingly cognisant of their rights and entitlements. All of this points to the need to close the gap between actors at large and refugees themselves. The history of repatriations is one characterised by collective approaches designed

---

[23] G. De Jong and R. Gardiner, 'Introduction and Overview', in G. De Jong and R. Gardiner, eds, *Migration Decision Making: Multidisciplinary Approaches to Microlevel Studies in Developed and Developing Countries* (Pergamon Press, New York, 1981), pp. 1–2.

to promote mass movements. Increasingly, however, refugees are resisting the 'herd' perspective and asserting their prerogatives in the process of repatriation. The ability of humanitarian organisations to promote repatriation as a normative behaviour will hinge more and more heavily in future upon their willingness and ability to understand the factors that affect the decisions that refugees make.

C. John R. Rogge, 'Repatriation of Refugees', in Tim Allen and Hubert Morsink, eds, *When Refugeees Go Home: African Experiences* (UNRISD, Geneva, 1994) pp. 14, 24, 31–34, 43–46.

Introduction

While many refugee repatriations have run their course without problems and have resulted in a total return of all refugees and their subsequent effective reintegration into their home regions, in other cases, repatriations have turned out to be a most difficult and problematic durable solution to implement. There have been instances where not all refugees have been willing to return; where a home government has been less than welcoming; where a host government has been too forceful in encouraging return; where there has been limited assistance to returnees creating difficulties in reintegration; and there have been cases where, after long periods in exile, returnees have encountered many and complex problems in re-establishing themselves their traditional areas and societies. For second-generation refugees, such as now exist in many parts of Africa, return to their country of 'origin' does not always necessarily mean 'going home'. Indeed, the Office of United Nations High Commissioner for Refugees (UNHCR) has conceded that repatriation is a most difficult durable solution to implement and that a successful and relatively problem-free return is more often the exception than the rule.[24] There is, therefore, much scope for each on repatriation so as to create a better understanding of potential problems and to facilitate better preparedness in the planning and implementation of return movements when circumstances permit.

The principal objective of this chapter is to provide a global overview of the problems arising from mass voluntary repatriations of refugees. It will explore some of the myths and realities associated with repatriations and critically evaluate an array of problems that have arisen from past repatriation exercise or which may be anticipated to arise in future return movements.... The questions which need addressing include:

(a) under what circumstances can and should refugees be returned to conflict zones?

[24] G. Coles, *Voluntary Repatriation: A Background Study*, report for UNHCR's Round Table on Voluntary Repatriation (International Institute of Humanitarian Law, San Remo, 1985).

(b)   who determines whether it is safe for refugees to return?

(c)   under what circumstances can or should people be 'forced' to participate in an 'organised' repatriation?

(d)   how does one define 'voluntariness' for repatriations?

(e)   what is the relationship between the success of a repatriation exercise and the length of exile?

(f)   under what conditions can or should services in refugee settlements be withdrawn in order to induce repatriation?

(g)   should refugees always be free to return to the destination of their choice?

(h)   what can be done to reduce the risks to people returning to former conflict zones where mines and other unexploded munitions abound?

The Desire to Return

... almost all refugees and host governments in Africa have assumed that their exile is temporary and that eventually all will be able to go home. This has produced an implicit acceptance of the fact that all of Africa's refugees desire to return. There are also many examples where refugees resist returning despite the fact that their home governments have extended an amnesty to them to return and their country of asylum wants them to go back. It is useful, therefore, to reflect on the extent to which such conditions of resistance, or even total opposition, to returning prevail among African refugees.

The desire to return to the country of origin is to a large extent a reflection of how refugees identify themselves vis-à-vis their home areas. In this context, Kunz suggested that there are three basic categories of refugees.[25] First, there are those who hold a firm conviction that their opposition or antagonism to events at home, which caused them to seek asylum, is shared by the majority of their compatriots. Thus, they are likely to retain a strong bond with their home areas—Kunz referred to such refugees as *majority identified refugees*. While Kunz did not address the issue of repatriation, it is suggested here that such refugees are clearly the ones most likely to want to repatriate when the cause of their exile is removed. It is also clear that many of Africa's refugees fall into this category. A second category is that of refugees who, on leaving their home areas, feel alienated from the rest of their homeland population, and probably also feel discriminated against. As such, they become irrevocably estranged from the fellow citizens. Such refugees may be referred to as *events related refugees*; they are less likely to have a strong desire to return home,

[25] E.F. Kunz, 'Exile and Resettlement: Refugee Theory', *International Migration Review* (Vol. 15, 1981), pp. 42–51.

especially if there have not been any fundamental changes to the social or political systems which alienated them on the one hand, or if they have become economically and/or socially integrated in their country of asylum on the other hand. In Africa, examples of such refugees can be drawn from areas where ethnic conflict was principal cause of exile, such as among Rwandan and Burundian refugees in Tanzania. A third category identified by Kunz—*self-alienated refugees*—is that of refugees who exile themselves rather than society alienating them; they are the least likely ever to want to return. This category is perhaps more relevant to non-African refugee situations.

Length of time in exile, degree of integration in the area of asylum, the pressures exerted by authorities for the refugee to return, the measure of physical disruption in home areas, and the extent to which political change has occurred in their country of origin are the principal sets of variables affecting attitudes regarding repatriation. The first two of these are often closely correlated. The third may be a reaction to the first two. The fourth may be downplayed or even ignored in attempts at governmental levels to achieve a repatriation, and, as has previously been suggested, there may be significant differences in perceptions among refugees vis-à-vis governments and international organisations regarding the fifth variable.

A key issue which needs to be examined for any impending massive repatriation is that of the information refugees have about their home areas and the sources of that information. Refugees in close proximity to the border, and where it is possible to make frequent visits into their home regions, will clearly be better informed about the safety or risks of returning than those at a distance from the border and wholly dependent upon secondary sources. When there are political motivations for having refugees return, or when the refugees are controlled by political fronts in opposition to the government in their country of origin, and who may be reluctant to see their population base reduced through some refugees repatriating, the information base provided the refugees may be limited or deliberately distorted. Refugees agreeing to repatriate 'voluntarily' on the basis of misinformation fed them are anything but voluntary returnees. Consequently, we need to understand much more about the basis on which refugees make their decisions to return, whether individually or collectively; what sets of information do refugees primarily base their decisions to return on and what are the sources of information they most depend upon?

The host government, the home government, the international community, and the political fronts in exile all play a role in influencing or even determining the refugees' desire to return. The manner in which a host government responds to a potential repatriation will depend greatly on the degree to which the refugees are believed to be positively or negatively impacting upon the asylum area. If the goal is to be rid of refugees but not be seen to be forcibly repatriating them, then an array of passive measures such as reducing services, restricting income-generating opportunities, limiting freedom of movement and association, etc., can all be implemented to influence the refugees' willingness to repatriate. Conversely, if the refugees are well integrated and making valuable contributions to regional economies—which might even be disrupted by the refugees' withdrawal—then the home governments may actively encourage refugees to remain.

With respect to the government in the country of origin, the type of signals it sends out to the refugees will greatly influence their desire to return. Clearly, the removal of a government whose activities caused the refugees to seek exile will usually be sufficient to attract refugees back; this is especially so when the new government is known to be sympathetic to the refugees or to their causes. But what if the political situation has not changed or if the fighting is over but the same authorities remain in control? Blanket amnesties for the refugees to return may be declared, but are these sufficient to entice reluctant returnees back? ... In most such cases, refugees tend to adopt a 'wait and see' attitude; a few courageous or desperate souls may return and the rest of the refugees wait to see how they fare. Again, this is where it is critical that an accurate flow of information to the remaining refugees is facilitated.

International agencies, whether large organisations or small-scale NGOs, have the potential of playing a major role in ensuring that good, reliable information flows are instituted and maintained. In theory at least, they have nothing to lose or gain from disseminating correct information. Also, refugees often place a high degree of trust in agency workers; they are often more likely to believe them than local officials or visiting officials from their home country. In reality, however, the information flows emanating from international agencies are sometimes contradictory or are based upon misguided philosophies. In extreme cases, they can also be self-serving. The personnel of some NGOs, especially among the smaller or missionary based agencies, is often relatively inexperienced or has only a limited understanding of the many complex underpinnings of a refugee movement; the very high turnover of agency personnel exacerbates this situation.

International agencies can also influence the desire to return by the scale and nature of the services they deliver. The levels of services available in refugee camps may sometimes be so superior to those available in their home areas that refugees are unwilling to leave the camps despite a strong desire to go home. Making the decision to wind down camp services when refugees are still present is not an easy task for an NGO nor is it easily justified to the distant population from whom funding for its humanitarian operations is derived. Yet such strategies may sometimes be necessary and desirable because of the longer-term benefits in achieving a durable solution for the refugees in their home country. Unfortunately, a few NGOs are extremely reluctant to let go of their refugee clients.

Exiled political fronts also have a significant influence on refugees' attitudes towards returning. This is especially the case when their credibility and international recognition as a political force are contingent upon the numbers of people the fronts are seen to represent, irrespective of whether the population is politically active or passive. The danger in such a situation is that political fronts may actively discourage refugees from returning, either indirectly by such activities as disseminating misinformation about the risk of returning, or directly by physically preventing their return. Such relationships between political fronts and populations under their control may even be extended when mass repatriations take place, in that returnees are forcibly channelled by the fronts into areas which they control in the home country....

Gender Issues and the Problems of Vulnerable Groups

An almost totally unresearched area in refugee studies is that of the diverse impacts of refugee experience, including repatriation, upon women and vulnerable groups. Both the adjustments women must make to life in exile and their subsequent needs to readjust on repatriation must be better understood by all involved in refugee assistance or administration. Women's traditional roles, responsibilities and supportive networks become dramatically altered by involuntary migration, especially when the migrations also mean separation from husbands and kin. Extended family networks from which women normally draw much of the strength and support for their onerous roles in traditional society may be completely lost; instead women become isolated, dependent upon themselves, solely responsible for children in the absence of fathers, subject to exploitation, and, in many cases, also to emotional and physical/sexual abuse. For many women, becoming a refugee sets in motion an almost continuous process of balancing traditional values with a new 'sense of self' imposed by the refugee experience.

Perhaps the single most important impact upon women refugees, and especially on those who become 'heads of households', is the change in family values, expectations and responsibilities. They are forced into completely new sets of decision-making roles. They gain new powers of determination regarding the allocation of resources. Their traditional roles as mothers are transformed by the need to survive; they are forced to become the sole providers of material and emotional stability for their children. The need to strive for economic self-sufficiency outside of a traditional system becomes an indispensable variable promoting their new 'sense of self'. Loneliness and a feeling of abandonment are common. The net effect of all these changes is that they are subject to much emotional and psychological upheaval.

Opportunities for self-support for women are usually very limited. On organised settlements they may, as heads of household, gain access to plots of land along with other refugees, but all too often they end up without the other means of support needed to become self-sufficient cultivators. Some engage in day labour if such options exist; others attempt to survive through informal sector activities such as marketing, running food stalls, or brewing (sometimes illegally) traditional beers and liquors. Domestic work among indigenous households is often the only form of permanent employment available, but exploitation is rife, wages are low, hours are long and physical abuse is common. Out of sheer desperation, and because of a total lack of other viable options, many refugee women are forced to resort to prostitution.

Such severe disruptions among women refugees clearly have serious implications when repatriation occurs. Alienation from traditional systems has often reached non-reversible levels. This is especially the case for younger, single women. Unlike their male counterparts, few women are likely to have learned readily applicable skills while in exile. Many will not even have had an opportunity for education, which, had they not gone into exile, they might well have had at home. Finding lost kin, and being accepted by them given the non-traditional attitudes, values and even manner of dress acquired while in exile, may also present a problem. As a result, many women may well drift into the anonymity of urban areas on return where they are forced to resort to marginalising activities.

The question of how to facilitate the reintegration of women refugees must be given a much higher priority in any repatriation plan. More attention must be paid to how better to prepare female refugees for repatriation through the provision of special skills-upgrading programmes before departure. Community and social support programmes must also be developed to assist women prior to departure as well as at their destinations. Effective programmes do exist in some refugee arenas; what is needed is a better sharing of experiences and ideas. Here is a niche where the NGOs can provide a valuable service.

Aside from women, there are several other groups which are made acutely vulnerable through the refugee experience. The elderly, especially those separated from their traditional extended family support networks, the orphaned or otherwise separated children, and the handicapped are all groups requiring special assistance and consideration in any repatriation exercise. In refugee settlements, effective support services for these groups are usually provided by NGOs; they allow the refugees to persevere. In most instances, the severely handicapped, such as quadriplegics (war injured), the blind, and the mentally incapacitated, are totally dependent upon NGO support services in the settlements. Once they repatriate, however, access to such services may not be possible and consequently their fingerhold on survival is lost. Only those able to return to villages where kinsfolk are able to provide the levels of assistance previously obtained from the NGOs are likely to survive. However, the demands this places upon kin may be too much for some to withstand, especially when they too are in the process of rehabilitation. Again, a sharing of experiences of how such vulnerable groups have been dealt with elsewhere will help develop more viable strategies for coping with vulnerable groups repatriating in Africa. Academic research in this area is also needed.

There is one additional group of returnees that need special consideration, namely, demobilised soldiers/resistance fighters. While not vulnerable in the same sense as the groups discussed above, these young adults often have a particularly traumatic experience in reintegrating. Their expectations are almost always much greater than the reality of the situation awaiting them on return. Lack of applicable skills is one problem, unless they are induced into the home army on return. They may be subjected to suspicion or even overt hostility on return, especially if they are returning to areas controlled by their former antagonists. In some cases they may have been members of undisciplined cadres and have become used to 'living off the land'; the possession of a gun gave them the 'right' to take what they needed. Rehabilitation of such returnees is thus as much a process of instilling new sets of values as it is of finding suitable means of income generation.

Implications and Conclusions

The chapter set out to summarise the diverse issues and problems that relate to repatriation of refugees. It has primarily drawn upon experiences with returnees in Africa and, to a lesser extent, in Asia. It has not attempted to address in any detail the question of programmes for returnees once back in their country of origin; this is clearly a subject for another chapter. However, by way of conclusion, it is useful to look at some of the policy implications of massive repatriations, and to establish the relationships between the needs of returnees as outlined in this paper and the factors governing the response to those needs once refugees are back in their home country.

Chart 6.1 attempts to summarise this relationship between need and response as it relates to the repatriation process. The levels of need which returnees have are a product of five sets of variables; all have been discussed in this chapter. Size of returnee populations is a self-evident issue; the larger the return, the greater are the pressures created and the needs that must be addressed. While repatriations of individuals are constantly being facilitated throughout the continent and elsewhere in the world by UNHCR, Africa has especially been required to deal with large-scale mass repatriations. The length of exile is a particularly critical variable. On the surface, long periods in exile may not change the underlying desire to go home, but do produce an array of personal adjustments to the conditions of life in exile, many of which may not even be perceived by the refugee, which, on return, exacerbate the process of reintegration. Resources and skills acquired in exile are clearly a positive force in the reintegration process if they can be transferred and adopted in the home areas. However, when no resources are transferred, or when the refugees return from conditions of long-term total dependency, the need for assistance with reintegration will be substantial. In turn, this variable relates to the extent to which returnees are required to reintegrate within areas that have been severely disrupted by conflict. While returnees may well have the capacity to adjust, they may not be able to do so, or do so quickly enough to be able to survive, due to a totally destroyed economic, social or physical infrastructure. In such cases the needs are for rehabilitating the home areas rather than specifically rehabilitating the refugees. Zonally targeted assistance is thus essential. Lastly, the question of degree of voluntariness among returnees must also be given more attention. Governments of countries of origin may want refugees to return for political reasons, governments of countries of asylum may want refugees to leave to reduce costs or localised tensions, the international agencies want to be seen to be effecting durable solutions and, in the process, the will and perceptions of the refugees are often relegated to secondary considerations. Success of any migration and settlement venture is in large part contingent upon the level of co-operation of the affected population; there have been few, if any, successful examples of relocation and resettlement programmes where the settler community was made up of reluctant participants. There is no indication that it is any different in the case of repatriations.

In the country of origin, the response to a repatriation exercise is also affected by several sets of variables. One set is the extent and effectiveness of the returnees' ability to articulate their needs. This is contingent upon many factors, including their distance from the centre of government, their numbers, their level of organisation and/or administration, and their past and present relationship with the powers in government, the

Chart 6.1
Determinants of Responses of Refugee Repatriations

Needs	Response
Size of returnee population	Returnees' demand articulation
Length of time in exile	
Level of resources	Local community's receptiveness
Community's skills transferred from exile	
Extent of disruption of home areas	Local governments' resources/interests
Degree of voluntariness in returning	National governments' sympathy/support for returnees

Source: Adapted from S. Pitterman 'Determinants of International Refugee Policy: A Comparative Study of UNHCR Material Assistance to Refugees in Africa, 1963–1981', in John Rogge, ed., *Refugees: A Third World Dilemma* (Totowa, 1987), pp. 15–36.

levels of assistance available to returnees at the local level is clearly a reflection of the resources available to local governments—usually very limited—and the interests and sympathies which local officials have in the returnees. In this context, there may be breakdowns in communicating the needs of the returnees to the authorities at the regional or national level who may have the capacity to mobilise appropriate interventions. On the other hand, when the national government is not overtly sympathetic to a repatriation it is unlikely to provide any meaningful response. Lastly, the receptiveness of the local population also affects the nature of responses returnees encounter. If local chiefs, for example, are supportive of the return, then an array of response strategies will be available from within the community. For rural refugees returning to their home areas, this is obviously the ideal scenario. If there is no support, or if local people are hostile to the returnees, then the reintegration process will be seriously impeded.

External interventions are also important in the reintegration process, especially when local resources are limited. International organisations and NGOs both have a role to play in monitoring the needs which returnees have and in sensitising the authorities to those needs. This is especially the case where repatriations have been spontaneous. They are also often the only ones with the appropriate resources and skills to be able to respond to those needs. The key issue here is one of how such assistance is best targeted—specifically at the refugees or zonally to regions where refuges are known to have returned. Given that many returnees are anxious to reintegrate as quickly as possible without being labelled 'refugees', or perhaps may even be fearful of such identification, zonal assistance strategies are often the most desirable. Moreover, zonally targeted responses benefit all the population in a region and thus may serve to foster the reintegration process by making local people more receptive and supportive of a repatriation. On the other hand, many returnees have very specific needs which can only be met through individually targeting them.

IV. VOLUNTARY REPATRIATION: LEGAL FRAMEWORK

A. UNHCR, Executive Committee Conclusion No. 18 (1980): Voluntary Repatriation

The Executive Committee,

(a) Recognised that voluntary repatriation constitutes generally, and in particular when a country accedes to independence, the most appropriate solution for refugee problems;

(b)   Stressed that the essentially voluntary character of repatriation should always be respected;

(c)   Recognised the desirability of appropriate arrangements to establish the voluntary character of repatriation, both as regards the repatriation of individual refugees and in the case of large-scale repatriation movements, and for UNHCR, whenever necessary, to be associated with such arrangements;

(d)   Considered that when refugees express the wish to repatriate, both the government of their country of origin and the government of their country of asylum should, within the framework of their national legislation and, whenever necessary, in co-operation with UNHCR take all requisite steps to assist them to do so;

(e)   Recognised the importance of refugees being provided with the necessary information regarding conditions in their country of origin in order to facilitate their decision to repatriate; recognised further that visits by individual refugees or refugee representatives to their country of origin to inform themselves of the situation there— without such visits automatically involving loss of refugee status— could also be of assistance in this regard;

(f)   Called upon governments of countries of origin to provide formal guarantees for the safety of returning refugees and stressed the importance of such guarantees being fully respected and of returning refugees not being penalised for having left their country of origin for reasons given rise to refugee situations;

(g)   Recommended that arrangements be adopted in countries of asylum for ensuring that the terms of guarantees provided by countries of origin and relevant information regarding conditions prevailing there are duly communicated to refugees, that such arrangements could be facilitated by the authorities of countries of asylum and that UNHCR should as appropriate be associated with such arrangements;

(h)   Considered that UNHCR could appropriately be called upon— with the agreement of the parties concerned—to monitor the situation of returning refugees with particular regard to any guarantees provided by the governments of countries of origin;

(i)   Called upon the governments concerned to provide repatriating refugees with the necessary travel documents, visas, entry permits and transportation facilities and, if refugees have lost their nationality, to arrange for such nationality to be restored in accordance with national legislation;

(*j*) Recognised that it may be necessary in certain situations to make appropriate arrangements in co-operation with UNHCR for the reception of returning refugees and/or to establish projects for their reintegration in their country of origin.

B. UNHCR, Executive Committee Conclusion No. 40 (1985): Voluntary Repatriation

The Executive Committee,

Reaffirming the significance of its 1980 conclusion on voluntary repatriation as reflecting basic principles of international law and practice, adopted the following further conclusions on this matter:

(*a*) The basic rights of persons to return voluntarily to the country of origin is reaffirmed and it is urged that international co-operation be aimed at achieving this solution and should be further developed;

(*b*) The repatriation of refugees should only take place at their freely expressed wish; the voluntary and individual character of repatriation of refugees and the need for it to be carried out under conditions of absolute safety, preferably to the place of residence of the refugee in his country of origin, should always be respected;

(*c*) The aspect of causes is critical to the issue of solution and international efforts should also be directed to the removal of the causes of refugee movements. Further attention should be given to the causes and prevention of such movements, including the co-ordination of efforts currently being pursued by the international community and in particular within the United Nations. An essential condition for the prevention of refugee flows is sufficient political will by the States directly concerned to address the causes which are at the origin of refugee movements;

(*d*) The responsibilities of States towards their nationals and the obligations of other States to promote voluntary repatriation must be upheld by the international community. International action in favour of voluntary repatriation, whether at the universal or regional level, should receive the full support and co-operation of all States directly concerned. Promotion of voluntary repatriation as a solution to refugee problems similarly requires the political will of States directly concerned to create conditions conducive to this solution. This is the primary responsibility of States;

(*e*) The existing mandate of the High Commissioner is sufficient to allow him to promote voluntary repatriation by taking initiatives to this end, promoting dialogue between all the main parties, facilitating communication between them, and by acting as an intermediary or channel of communication. It is important that he establishes, whenever possible, contact with all the main parties and acquaints himself with their points of view. From the outset of a refugee situation, the High Commissioner should at all times keep the possibility of voluntary repatriation for all or for part of a group under active review and the High Commissioner, whenever he deems that the prevailing circumstances are appropriate, should actively pursue the promotion of this solution;

(f) The humanitarian concerns of the High Commissioner should be recognised and respected by all parties and he should receive full support in his efforts to carry out his humanitarian mandate in providing international protection to refugees and in seeking a solution to refugee problems;

(g) On all occasions the High Commissioner should be fully involved from the outset in assessing the feasibility and, thereafter, in both the planning and implementation stages of repatriation;

(h) The importance of spontaneous return to the country of origin is recognised and it is considered that action to promote organised voluntary repatriation should not create obstacles to the spontaneous return of refugees. Interested States should make all efforts, including the provision of assistance in the country of origin, to encourage this movement whenever it is deemed to be in the interests of the refugees concerned;

(i) When, in the opinion of the High Commissioner, a serious problem exists in the promotion of voluntary repatriation of a particular refugee group, he may consider for that particular problem the establishment of an informal ad hoc consultative group which would be appointed by him in consultation with the Chairman and the other members of the Bureau of his Executive Committee. Such a group may, if necessary, include States which are not members of the Executive Committee and should in principle include the countries directly concerned. The High Commissioner may also consider invoking the assistance of other competent United Nations organs;

(j) The practice of establishing tripartite commission, which should consist of the countries of origin and of asylum and UNHCR, could concern itself with both the joint planning and the implementation of repatriation programme. It is also an effective means of securing consultations between the main parties concerned on any problems that might subsequently arise;

(*k*) International action to promote voluntary repatriation requires consideration of the situation within the country of origin as well as within the receiving country. Assistance for the reintegration of returnees provided by the international community in the country of origin is recognised as an important factor in promoting repatriation. To this end, UNHCR and other United Nations agencies as appropriate, should have funds readily available to assist returnees in the various stages of their reintegration and rehabilitation in their country of origin;

(*l*) The High Commissioner should be recognised as having a legitimate concern for the consequences of return, particularly where such return has been brought about as a result of an amnesty or other form of guarantee. The High Commissioner must be regarded as entitled to insist on his legitimate concern over the outcome of any return that he has assisted. Within the framework of close consultations with the State concerned, he should be given direct and unhindered access to returnees so that he is in a position to monitor fulfilment of the amnesties, guarantees or assurances on the basis of which the refugees have returned. This should be considered as inherent in his mandate;

(*m*) Consideration should be given to the further elaboration of an instrument reflecting all existing principles and guidelines relating to voluntary repatriation for acceptance by the international community as a whole.

C. Article V of the OAU Convention Governing the Specific Aspects of Refugee Problems in Africa, 1969.

Voluntary Repatriation

1. The essentially voluntary character of repatriation shall be respected in all cases and no refugee shall be repatriated against his will.

2. The country of asylum in collaboration with the country of origin, shall make adequate arrangements for the safe return of refugees who request repatriation.

3. The country of origin, on receiving back refugees, shall facilitate their resettlement and grant them the full rights and privileges of nationals of the country, and subject them to the same obligations.

4. Refugees who voluntarily return to their country shall in no way be penalised for having left it for any of the reasons giving rise to refugee situations. Whenever necessary, an appeal shall be made

through national information media and through the Administrative Secretary-General of the OAU, inviting refugees to return home and given assurance that the new circumstances prevailing in their country of origin will enable them to return without risk and to take up a normal and peaceful life without fear of being disturbed or punished, and that the text of such appeal should be given to refugees and clearly explained to them by their country of asylum.

5. Refugees who freely decide to return to their homeland, as a result of such assurances or on their own initiative, shall be given every possible assistance by the country of asylum, the country of origin, voluntary agencies and international and intergovernmental organisations, to facilitate their return.

V. ORGANISED REPATRIATION

A. US Committee for Refugees, 'Something Like Home Again': The Repatriation of Cambodian Refugees, May 1994, pp. 62–64, 67.

Insofar as much of the work of repatriation is completed, many of USCR's findings and recommendations are offered more as lessons learned in Cambodia to be applied elsewhere. . . .

Repatriation obviously was an integral and necessary part of the overall peacekeeping mission in Cambodia. . . . It would be naive to think that in a repatriation operation UNHCR would first and only serve the needs of refugees; it must also try to reconcile these needs with the interests of the host country and the country of origin. Repatriation in the context of a peacekeeping operation compels UNHCR to further accommodate its objectives to those of the broader UN mission. That is likely, on the one hand, to give UNHCR greater resources at its disposal in terms of protection, monitoring, and assistance, but it may also place added political pressures on the repatriation process.

In the case of Cambodia—and this may hold true for other complex UN missions that include a repatriation component—UNHCR was not an entirely neutral party, simply honouring the wishes of a refugee population to return home by brokering an agreement between Country A and Country B. It would be an obvious overstatement to say that, in this case, UNHCR *was* Country B but, as a component of UNTAC [United Nations Transitional Authority in Cambodia], UNHCR was invested in the success of the overall UN mission. For the peace plan to take shape, repatriation had to happen. It had to be voluntary and it had to be safe, but it had to happen. These three goals proved compatible in Cambodia, but UNHCR must recognise the tension between them....

Peacekeeping missions by definition operate in highly volatile situations. If the mission includes a repatriation component, UNHCR must be ready to be flexible, but readier still to stick to some of its most basic principles:

- Repatriation must be voluntary, safe, and in full possession of the facts.

- Political settlements that involve repatriation compel UNHCR to answer the question: when is it safe for refugees to return home? They may also raise another question; when should refugee status itself end? In order to invoke the cessation clause of the 1951 Refugee Convention, UNHCR must find that changes in a country of origin are 'fundamental, stable, and durable in character.' As a rule of thumb, it would seem prudent for UNHCR not to invoke that clause and terminate refugee status at least until a peacekeeping mission has successfully carried out its mandate.

- Without being too detailed or prescriptive, peace plans that include a repatriation component should spell out conditions under which return may be deemed safe and contingencies under which it is not.

... while repatriations often signal a successful end to a particular refugee situation, they do not necessarily preclude the possibility of future refugee outflows or the need for continued asylum in neighbouring countries. As such, repatriation agreements should not be cause to undermine or negate any previous commitments to refugee protection on the part of countries of asylum. UNHCR gave away too much by signing a Memorandum of Arrangement (MOA) in which UNHCR and Thailand concurred that new arrivals after March 30, 1992 had no basis to claim asylum and could all be deported. Repatriation was a very good reason to close the border camps but a poor excuse to close the border.

UNHCR officials argue that the MOA was intended solely to discourage the influx of thousands of Cambodians crossing into Thailand in early 1992, hoping to cash in on the repatriation assistance. Several dozen Khmer Rouge deserters who entered Thailand after the cut-off date, in fact, were given temporary protection and repatriation assistance. Nevertheless, the agreement supports the premise that, absent a fundamental breakdown in the peace agreements, there could be no such thing as a bona fide asylum seeker entering Thailand, either during or after repatriation. Without a Thai commitment to screen arrivals, unfortunately, that is the sort of prediction that can only be self-fulfilling....

Repatriation and Assistance

... following are several lessons on repatriation assistance that could be drawn from the Cambodian experience:

- UNHCR should employ any means possible to encourage and assist family reunification. This starts with early and active family tracing through ICRC or other appropriate agencies, but should be a benchmark for planning all facets of the operation from convoy manifests to options packages.

- Forced to abandon its land plan, UNHCR diversified with a vengeance, at one time considering as many as seven different options. Such variety is not likely to be replicated in other repatriation efforts, nor is it necessary. A per capita cash grant, coupled with food assistance, should prove to be the most convenient and flexible approach. More durable forms of in kind assistance—housing, land, etc.—if they are available at all, may need to be reserved for the most vulnerable groups.

- Identification of vulnerable groups must look beyond immediate needs for special transportation, medication, etc. to focus also on vulnerability in terms of the returnees' country of origin. Here again, family support, or the lack of it, is a critical factor. Having identified vulnerable groups, UNHCR should ensure that they have access to special assistance as well as necessary counselling, referral, and follow-up.

B. International Conference on Central American Refugees (CIREFCA), Guatemala City, 29–31 May 1989, Declaration and Concerted Plan of Action in Favour of Central American Refugees (CIREFCA/89/14, 31 May 1989), pp. 1–15.

The Governments of the States represented in the International Conference on Central American Refugees, held at Guatemala City from 29 to 31 May 1989,

Bearing in mind the significance of the Procedure for the Establishment of a Firm and Lasting Peace in Central America, signed by the Presidents of the five countries of Central America at Guatemala City on 7 August 1987, and especially the contents of its point 8,

Recalling the San Salvador Communique on Central American Refugees of 9 September 1988, resolution 43/118 of the General Assembly of the United Nations of 8 December 1988, entitled 'International Conference on Central American Refugees', and the resolution of the General Assembly of the Organisation of American States of 19 November 1988 entitled 'Central American Refugees and Regional Efforts to Resolve Their Problems', ...

Declare as follows:

...

3. *Reaffirm* their commitment to encourage the voluntary return of refugees and other persons displaced by the crisis, under conditions of personal security and dignity that would allow them to resume a normal life; ...

11. *Note with satisfaction* the willingness of the affected States to include in their national development plans, as a matter of priority, proposals for solutions for refugees, returnees and displaced persons submitted to the Conference; ...

15. *Recognise* the crucial role played by the tripartite commissions, made up of representatives of the country of asylum, the country of origin and the United Nations High Commissioner for Refugees, in facilitating and promoting the voluntary repatriation of refugees; ...

22. *Recognise* that solutions to the problems of refugees, returnees and displaced persons form an integral part of the efforts for peace, democracy and development taking place in the region;

And, therefore:

23. *Approve*, in accordance with the principle of international solidarity, the guidelines of the Concerted Plan of Action in Favour of Central American Refugees, Returnees and Displaced Persons, set forth below, support its principles and objectives, and consider it a promising initial framework for future activities and thus re-affirm their commitment to contribute to the establishment of a firm and lasting peace in Central America; ...

II. Concerted Plan of Action in Favour of Central American Refugees, Returnees and Displaced Persons

Introduction

1. The San Salvador Communique of 9 September 1988, which called for the International Conference on Central American Refugees, establishes the need for national plans and programmes of action in favour of Central American refugees, returnees and displaced persons, identifying concrete solutions to their serious problems to be formulated on a purely humanitarian and non-political basis.

2. In this context, the Governments of the affected countries have formulated, at the national level, detailed diagnostic studies of the massive population movements that have taken place in the region, on the basis of which the present Plan of Action has been prepared. In part one, which contains the strategy, the basic objectives, fundamentals and project proposals to identify solutions to the problems of Central American refugees, returnees and displaced persons are described. In part two, the mechanisms for follow-up and promotion of the Plan of Action are outlined.

Part One

STRATEGY

...

B. Basic Objectives

9. ... One of the objectives of the present Plan of Action is to identify durable solutions ...

10. From this fundamental objective follows the obligation to respect, in the first place, the right of refugees to return voluntarily to their countries of origin in order to resume a normal life. Consequently, voluntary repatriation, which is the best solution, will be facilitated above all. In those instances where conditions do not yet exist to make this possible, the Plan of Action proposes measures to help refugees play a larger and more positive role in the countries of asylum while awaiting voluntary repatriation, by opening camps—when conditions so permit—and promoting interaction with the local community. It also proposes that alternative solutions be identified for those refugees who are dispersed outside the camps. In exceptional cases, when some refugees cannot remain in the country of asylum, for protection reasons, the possibility of third country resettlement is considered.

...

C. Fundamentals of the Plan of Action

13. The Plan of Action is based on the following fundamental principles:

    ...

    (c) The problems of refugees, returnees and displaced persons and the proposals for solutions should continue to be treated on a strictly humanitarian and non-political basis; in this context, States are guided above all by considerations of solidarity with the individuals in need and the imperative of identifying humane solutions to their problems, giving priority to the preservation of life and personal safety above any other consideration.

...

PROGRAMMES IN FAVOUR OF RETURNEES

19. The voluntary repatriation programmes contain multisectoral projects aimed at facilitating the reintegration of returnees in their communities. These programmes address:

    (a) The needs of returnees who receive basic assistance, in some cases, rehabilitation assistance. The Plan of Action attempts to achieve their economic and social integration, benefiting the community where they return as well;

    (b) The needs of future returnees and the receiving communities, in an integrated approach, which begins with the process of return and ends with re-integration. The Plan of Action foresees support to communities in the country of origin in order to create minimum conditions for return, even before such movement starts. The rate of implementation of these programmes will depend on the actual return of returnees.

20. The projects submitted up to the time of formulation of the Plan of Action aim at facilitating the reintegration in El Salvador of some 13,000 returnees and another 8,000 future returnees (CIREFCA/ 89/4, projects 2 and 3); 3,500 returnees and 30,000 future returnees in Guatemala (CIREFCA/89/3, projects 1 and 2); and 35,000 returnees and 31,000 future returnees in Nicaragua (CIREFCA/ 89/8, projects 1 and 3 to 7).

21. These programmes reflect the commitment to continue respect for:

    (a) The right of refugees to return to their countires of origin as well as to receive information on the prevailing situation to allow them to reach a free decision concerning their return;

    (b) The voluntary and individually-manifested character of repatriation;

    (c) The necessity that repatriation take place in conditions of security and dignity;

    (d) The ability of the refugees to choose the destination in their countries, as well as freedom of movement and free choice of place of residence under the same conditions as other nationals of their countries;

    (e) Non-discrimination for having sought asylum;

    (f) Access to means of subsistence and to land under the same conditions as other nationals of their countries;

    (g) The respective cultural and ethnic values;

    (h) The work of the United Nations High Commissioner for Refugees in favour of returnees and his access to them.

    The rights referred to in this paragraph are to be implemented in the context of the prevailing legislation in each country.

22. The programmes also aim at regularising the situation of returnees with regard to the delivery of identity documents and the reg-
istry of births, marriages and deaths, and other events occurring
in the country of asylum and relating to the civil status of the individual. They also provide for access to citizenship for children of
returnees born abroad as well as for foreign spouses, when they
so desire and facilitate the recognition of studies undertaken in
the country of asylum.

23. The humanitarian and non-political character of international
assistance in favour of voluntary repatriation must be respected
by all parties involved throughout the repatriation process.

...

Part Two

FOLLOW-UP AND PROMOTION MECHANISMS

...

C. *Support of Tripartite Bodies*

39. The tripartite bodies which asylum countries, countries of origin
and the United Nations High Commissioner for Refugees have
formed to facilitate and promote voluntary repatriation will support those activities which in this context will be carried out
under the Plan of Action and will facilitate communication, coordination and evaluation as necessary.

VI. SPONTANEOUS REPATRIATION

A. Barry N. Stein and Fred C. Cuny, 'Repatriation under Conflict', *World Refugee Survey 1991*, pp. 15–21.

The contemporary international beliefs and principles regarding the
repatriation of refugees assume that return to one's homeland will be
purely voluntary, will be assisted and monitored by governments and
international agencies under the terms of a tripatriate agreement between the United Nations High Commissioner for Refugees (UNHCR)
and the governments of the refugees' country of origin and the country
of asylum, and that the refugees' complete safety and socio-economic
integration will be assured.

Unfortunately, it is the rare refugee situation that allows for such
orderly and organised return. International activities based on the above
assumptions may be irrelevant for most refugees' needs.

The changing nature of refugee problems has altered the contemporary practice of voluntary repatriation.... Today, most voluntary repatriations occur under conflict, without a decisive political event such as

national independence, without any change in the regime or the conditions that originally caused flight. Countless individual refugees and sizable groups of well-organised refugees return home in the face of continued risk, frequently without any amnesty, without a repatriation agreement or programme, without the permission of the authorities in either the country of asylum or of origin, without international knowledge or assistance, and without an end to the conflict that caused the exodus. The fact that refugees are returning to their homelands under these circumstances requires new thinking about voluntary repatriation and the ways of promoting it.

The refugees are the main actors in the contemporary practice of voluntary repatriation. They are the main decision-makers and participate in determining the means of their movement and the conditions under which they are received. In the absence of coercion, refugee-induced repatriation is a self-regulating process that takes place on the refugees' own terms. The refugees apply their own criteria to their situation in exile and to conditions in their homeland and will return home if it is safe and better by their standards.... We believe that many of the beliefs and principles commonly applied by governments, international assistance agencies and the public to the problem of voluntary repatriation do not fit the reality of contemporary repatriation—neither the situations in which it is likely to occur or the most common forms it will take.... The international system has failed to provide durable solutions for refugees. As a result some refugees are taking matters into their own hands and becoming major actors in the repatriation process.

In the last few years, UNHCR has intensified its efforts to promote voluntary repatriation. In several Central American repatriations, UNHCR undertook innovative measures to protect refugees, remain in contact with all parties, and promote return. Nonetheless, despite its importance as a durable solution, voluntary repatriation, particularly under conflict, is difficult for UNHCR to implement. Given the irregular nature of many contemporary refugee movements, many refugees never register with UNHCR while in an asylum country. The forces controlling the area to which the refugees return may not be those of the sovereign government recognised by the UN. Countries of origin often assume that returnees are part of an insurgent movement, and thus refuse to approve their return. Many refugees fear that going through official channels to repatriate and being 'turned over' to their government would put them in danger or mark them as suspect. Lastly, although UNHCR's tripartite approach to repatriation is useful and important, its pace is often slow and does not reflect the refugees' own pace and criteria for deciding to go home. Thus, refugees often return on their own rather than wait for formal action by UNHCR....

Varieties of Repatriation

Generally, if international agencies and governments do not initiate, manage, and organise a voluntary repatriation, the international agencies refer to it as 'unorganised' or 'spontaneous'. However ... the failure or inability to provide international repatriation assistance does not mean there is a lack of organisation....

To a degree, it is better to avoid labelling types of repatriation and to concentrate instead on examining the range of repatriation experiences. It is useful to think of types of repatriation as lying along several continuums or spectrums. Among the possible continuums would be (1) whether a repatriation is unassisted or organised and by which actors; (2) the degree to which a repatriation is purely voluntary, encouraged induced, or forced; (3) whether it is an individual, small group, or more sizable collective return; and (4) a political conflict spectrum reflecting the degree to which there has been a significant change in the original cause of flight.

Today, most repatriations occur under far from ideal conditions. Instead, they take place under conflict and raise serious questions of coercion and protection. A spectrum showing repatriation under political conflict would include several points: (1) return after fundamental political change such as independence (Zimbabwe, Namibia); (2) return after a political settlement or major political change (Nicaragua); (3) return after a political settlement that does not end the political conflict and that leaves the contending parties with substantial political and military power (Afghanistan, Sri Lanka, Angola); (4) return to areas controlled by a rival political force or by local forces rather than by the government of the country of origin (Tigray, Afghanistan, El Salvador, Cambodia); (5) return to a country controlled by the government that originally caused the flight (Guatemala); (6) return caused by deteriorating political security conditions in the host country (the post-1985 return from southern Sudan to Uganda, the 1989–1991 return from Somalia to Ethiopia); and (7) forced return of impressed refugees to a conflict zone (Khmer Rouge).

Repatriation Decisions and Patterns

In examining refugee-stimulated repatriation under conflict, it is necessary to take a split screen view of two interacting factors, the pattern of repatriation and the purpose of refugee decision-making. These two factors interact and drive the repatriation process.

The study's conceptual framework includes four main phases of repatriation: the 'ricochet' effect, relocation-stimulated repatriation, community and alienation and major repatriations. The pattern of these phases is not rigid, and the process may be drawn out or short-circuited. Progression through the phases may flow smoothly or be jumbled by events.

Key factors drive the events: the assistance decisions and attitudes of the host country, changing conditions within the homeland, the location of the refugees in exile and the evolution of refugee communities at sites where refugees are concentrated. The fact that most borders are relatively porous allowing refugees to visit and communicate with their homeland, also influence this process.

Decision-making

On one side of the split-screen are the nature and purpose of refugee decision-making, both of which interact with the pattern of repatriation. There are two points to note about refugee decision-making. First, not all refugees are alike; there will be different responses to forced location often rooted in different levels of mobility, urbanisation, education, and economic status among the refugees. Second, we are examining refugee responses during a long period of time. The refugee community will behave differently at the beginning, generally with a conservative risk-aversive response, than years later when greater initiative and risk-taking will occur.

Our analysis of refugee decision-making views the refugees as making 'rational' choices among unsatisfactory options, striving for an outcome that achieves relative security and some small degree of control over their lives. We assume that refugee actions are purposeful; their behaviour may be interpreted as directed toward attaining a goal. Refugees make choices for some purpose, and we must understand those purposes. Indicating that a choice is 'purposeful' or 'rational' does not necessarily mean that it is careful or conscious, that it lists all alternatives and consequences, or estimates and defines probabilities and preferences. Many people simplify complex decisions by relying on habit, instinct, simple cues, and trial and error....

Although refugees are commonly considered powerless, and they are certainly relatively powerless, it is important to remember that the decision to flee, or to stay, or to return home is an action and a choice. (The choice is often influenced by geography; those near the border cross it and become refugees; others, far from the border, flee to the cities and become internally displaced persons. Their status differs, but the cause of flight is often identical.) For almost everyone, the process of becoming a refugee is a transition from relative security and prosperity to uncertainty and poverty.

The decision to flee obviously reflects the refugee's belief that his or her power over others and level of self-control are now inadequate to provide protection from insult, injury, imprisonment or death. Thus, flight represents an attempt to use whatever power, control and mobility the person still possesses to escape from danger to safety. To stay or to flee internally are other alternatives usually available. Refugees make their moves to flee, to repatriate, to accept settlement or resettlement because of decisions that compare alternatives.

In comparing alternatives, refugees attempt to conserve and strengthen their control over their own lives and to reduce the possibility that further stress will occur. Their basic response is conservative, to limit change and disruption. Not surprisingly, refugees seek security. To cope with the stress of flight, they cling to old behavioural patterns, old institutions, and old goals. In clinging to the familiar, refugees attempt to move the shortest distance not only in space to remain in contact with a familiar habitat, but also in terms of the psychological and sociocultural context of their lives. They attempt to transfer old skills and farming practices, to relocate with kin, neighbours or their own ethnic groups of an encapsulating community with familiar institutions and symbols.

In the 'relocation' phase of repatriation, refugees scattered along the border consider the move to refugee camps or farther inland to settlements as a threat to their identity, a move from a known to an unknown world, farther away from kin and familiar territory.... Returning home to a previously established social identity with rights and obligations can be seen as allowing the refugee to retain more power and stability and control over his own life.

The passage of time is likely to alter the refugees' approach to decision-making, but not the goal of the decisions—security and control. Rarely will the transition stage, marked by a conservative response, be shorter than two years. Where refugees play an active role in reconstructing their lives and communities and so re-establish a positive image of themselves, the transition stage may be relatively short.

The later stage of decision-making is marked by increased initiative and risk-taking. Refugees reach this turning point when they have regained much of their former standard of living and degree of self-sufficiency. Local leaders emerge who are capable of pushing local interests with the hosts and government officials. The refugee community abandons its initial dependency, and an outward-looking and dynamic leadership emerges. Refugees organise themselves into more effective political units to obtain benefits from the external environment. This organisation requires the passage of time, but also gives the refugees a sense of control over their own community. Such organising can be encouraged by non-governmental organisations and by growing confidence in the international presence and delivery of supplies; it can be enhanced by the organisational skills of resistance-connected refugees. The refugees' willingness to take risks may focus on repatriation if the community's condition in the host country is hopeless, isolated, or precarious.

Refugees who are conservative and who have an aversion to taking risks will act as individuals and, suspicious of anything official, will avoid contact with government and international agencies. They will repatriate spontaneously. Over time, as initiative and risk-taking re-emerge in the refugee community, the refugees will be willing to confront their hosts, their homeland and the international community with requests for officially sanctioned, but refugee-stimulated repatriation.

Patterns of Repatriation

On the other side of the split-screen, actively interacting with the refugees' desire for security and some degree of control over their lives, are the events in exile: 'ricochet' repatriations; relocation-stimulated repatriation; return by refugees alienated from the emerging refugee community; secondary relocation-stimulated repatriation; and major repatriations.

Ricochet Repatriations: If the exodus was sudden, resulting from military action of a 'stampede' away from danger, a substantial number of people who might not have felt personally threatened or whose sympathies were not in line with the majority of the refugees will immediately seek ways to return. These initial 'ricochet repatriations' will be spontaneous and unassisted.

Relocation-stimulated Repatriation: The next phase is the host government's rounding up of refugees scattered along the border and moving them to refugee camps in order to assist and control them more easily. At this point, refugees must decide whether to accept host government control and reside in the camps or try to elude the authorities and find a place to live away from other refugees. For those who stay in the camps, repatriation will inevitably become a less immediate option. But for those refugees who settle outside the camps, repatriation is more likely to be a viable alternative, especially if they cannot find work in the asylum country.

Community and Alienation: One of the more interesting common denominators found in our case studies is the formation of politically organised, cohesive communities by uprooted people. Rounded up by the host government and relocated to refugee camps, refugees are placed in unaccustomed communal situations that may change their way of life and crowd them in among strangers. In these circumstances, refugees show an impressive ability to organise a coherent new community with its own mores and values. Frequently, refugee organisations are formed that ally with insurgent groups. Refugees come to believe that their situation is a key part of the political equation in the struggle of their group for social, cultural or economic change.

Some refugees will be indifferent to or alienated from the emerging refugee community, its values, and common cause. These aloof refugees, seeking control over their own lives, are candidates to move away from the camp or settlement or to repatriate.

As time passes, the available space for repatriation is likely to increase. At home, the locus of the conflict may change; the levels of violence may decrease; political or economic changes may occur. The border may become more porous as a result of internal changes in the homeland. Cross-border trade may normalise, providing an opportunity for families in the camps and spontaneously settled refugees to send 'scouts' back to check on conditions and to find out if it is feasible for small numbers of people to go back. If refugees learn than internally displaced people are returning to certain regions, that, too, may trigger some repatriation.

Inevitably, some scouts will report that people can return with relative safety. Gradually more and more people will begin to leave, primarily those who are on the periphery of the mainstream refugee community, or who feel they no longer 'belong'. The refugee organisations may oppose the return of these less committed refugees, feeling that repatriation somehow undercuts the political and/or moral position of the refugee community. Repatriations during this period may expand the political space at home, although not significantly.

Secondary Relocation-stimulated Repatriation: At some point, in almost every refugee situation, the host government will decide, or propose, to relocate or transfer refugees from camps near the border to camps or formal settlements farther inland. Political concerns may dictate this relocation.... Whatever the reason, the decision to relocate forces the refugees to decide whether to accept the transfer and its disruption of their lives and their established sense of community, or to leave the camps and either attempt to integrate into the surrounding communities or repatriate.

During this period, the perceived loss of the sense of community that has evolved in the camps becomes a key consideration. The emotional stress of having to move yet again and form still another community prompts many refugees to choose to repatriate. Few refugees may cite the relocation as the primary cause, but the fact that substantial numbers return home when transfers begin underscores the importance of this event. If more refugees show an interest in repatriation than the existing political conditions and organisation of assistance allow, then organisational attitudes start to change, and agencies working with the refugees actively begin to seek ways to expand the space for repatriation.

Refugee-controlled organisations are the first to actively assist repatriation. No longer are those who are repatriating deemed the 'alienated'; many represent the core of the refugee community. The fact that many mainstream refugees are returning, apparently successfully, enlarges the political space in the homeland and draws the attention of outside organisations to the repatriation process. Governments on both sides of the border must now make decisions about the limits of other involvement. The host country will naturally seek to encourage repatriation, while the country of origin may be unable to decide how to respond to the repatriation challenge.

In the country of origin, the civil government, the military and various political, social, ethnic and economic groups may have different political agendas. Inevitably, as the number of returnees increases, the government will seek to either control the repatriation or to benefit politically from the return. If the government wants to control the return, it will usually seek UNHCR participation.

Major Repatriations: UNHCR participation is the final stage in the repatriation process. Responding to governmental pressures (usually from the host government and then from the country of origin), UNHCR will begin to provide assistance, in some cases reluctantly due to concerns for the refugees' safety. Whether or not this is carried out as part of a formal tripartite agreement may depend on the way the international community perceives the repatriation.

Once repatriation becomes formalised under UNHCR, two very divergent patterns may emerge. In some cases, a formal agreement will lead to a decline in repatriation because some refugees fear being registered and being brought to their government's attention, while others may delay their return, waiting for assistance programmes to be established and implemented. In other cases, however, while formal repatriation agreements may produce little organised return, they can improve the political space for repatriation. Tripartite agreements enable UNHCR and non-governmental agencies to operate in the country of origin, they spur development of civilian refugee aid agencies in the homeland, and they facilitate the refugees' ability to communicate home and develop better information on conditions there. The large-scale unorganised returns to Mozambique and Afghanistan may reflect this process.

A Failure to Provide Durable Solutions

The ability of refugees to take matters into their own hands and organise repatriations is a hopeful sign. But often they are forced into this position by hopelessness, danger and lack of assistance. What is the connection between malnourished refugee children in Malawi and 'spontaneous repatriation' to Mozambique? The *masivas* to conflict zones in El Salvador grew out of the hostile, hopeless situation in the closed refugee camps in Honduras. Attacks on refugee settlements in southern Sudan have driven hundreds of thousands of refugees back to Uganda.

The international community has failed to provide durable solutions for millions of refugees. It compounds this failure by repeatedly declaring that voluntary repatriation is the most desirable solution, and by failing to effectively promote the other two solutions—resettlement and local integration. The international community also fails to effectively promote voluntary repatriation. At the 1990 Extraordinary Executive Committee of UNHCR, several countries of origin, such as Angola, Ethiopia and

Somalia, complained bitterly that 'refugees were awaiting the helping hand of the international community in order to return home', but that the funding crisis had reduced repatriation programmes.

We take the view that repatriation is not a panacea. Where is 'home' for those in exile for thirty years or for those born in exile? Hostile, ill-prepared homelands still embroiled in conflict are not ideal arenas for re-integration and protection. Nonetheless, despite significant protection worries, there is a need to actively promote voluntary repatriation—at times, even under conflict. In an imperfect world that only offers long-term temporary asylum to most refugees, there is a need to assist refugees to go home. Confronted with unsatisfactory options, one must search for the best that is available. Rather than passive international approach, there are circumstances where repatriation should be carefully and actively promoted even before the formal end of hostilities. And repatriation should be seen as a tool for reducing confrontations along tense borders, for expanding or securing zones of peace and stability for returnees, and possibly as an encouragement to talks between the adversaries.

Many of the almost one million refugees who returned home under imperfect conditions in the last few years have stayed at home. Many are in desperate circumstances, but they do not flee again. It is evident from a number of repatriations to date that the end of conflict is not a precondition for repatriation, and that suggest there are political possibilities that need to be explored.

B. *Handbook on Voluntary Repatriation: International Protection (UNHCR, Geneva, 1996), pp. 17–18.*

Facilitation

Respecting the refugees' right to return to their country at any time, UNHCR may *facilitate voluntary repatriation* when refugees indicate a strong desire to return voluntarily and/or have begun to do so on their own initiative, even where UNHCR does *not* consider that, objectively, it is safe for most refugees to return. This term should be used only when UNHCR is satisfied that refugees' wish to return is indeed voluntary and not driven by coercion.

While the condition of fundamental change of circumstances in the country of origin will usually not be met in such situations, UNHCR may consider facilitating return in order to have a positive impact on the safety of refugees/returnees as well as to render assistance which the refugees may require in order to return. Such assistance may have to be given in the absence of formal guarantees or assurances by the country of origin for the safety of repatriating refugees, and without any agreement or understanding having been concluded as to the basic terms and conditions of return.

In designing and carrying out its protection and assistance functions, UNHCR, however, has to make it clear to the authorities and, most importantly, to the refugees, that UNHCR support for such repatriations is based on respect for the refugees' decision to repatriate and cannot be interpreted as an indication of adequate security. UNHCR's role in facilitating such repatriations may include:

- providing information on conditions prevailing in the country of origin in general, and in areas of intended return in particular, which is both accurate and complete.

- providing those return with limited material assistance for their return.

- advising returnees of the limits of UNHCR protection and assistance in such situations (e.g., the lack of UNHCR presence in the country/area of origin or of agreement with the authorities of the country of origin).

- in addition to this, UNHCR should seek to make refugees aware of any obstacles which may exist to their re-entry to the present country of refuge.

- where possible, in the context of facilitating refugee-induced repatriation UNHCR should also try to seek ways to improve the safety of returnees in their country of origin. When return has become a fact, UNHCR should attempt to negotiate amnesties and guarantees, UNHCR presence in the areas of return and so on.

- If UNHCR is able to establish a presence in the areas of return, UNHCR should aim, to the extent possible, at exercising its returnee monitoring function, ... while still not promoting voluntary repatriation in the host country until such time as the conditions in the country of origin may allow UNHCR to consider moving from facilitation to promotion of repatriation.

VII. DURABLE SOLUTIONS AND REFUGEE CHILDREN

A. *Refugee Children: Guidelines on Protection and Care* (UNHCR, Geneva, 1994), pp. 137–48.

Durable Solutions

In seeking durable solutions, careful attention should be paid to the principles of family unity and the best interest of the child. Children may face specific difficulties in the process of moving and reintegrating. Some children—such as those who are unaccompanied or ill—require special protection and assistance to help them find and adjust to more permanent situations.

UNHCR defines durable solutions as voluntary repatriation, local settlement in the country of first asylum, and resettlement in a third country. In this chapter much attention is given to voluntary repatriation. It also contains certain rules and safeguards to keep in mind when resettlement of refugee children is considered.

Relocation and reintegration involve disrupting and, where possible, reconstituting the delicate fabric of social, community and cultural ties that are important to children. Where displacement has been prolonged, many children are born in the place of asylum. The camp, the shelter or the house of refuge will have become their primary reference. They may not share with their parents the same memories of 'home' or the same dreams for establishing life elsewhere. Children experience change of residence differently to adults; a child's age is a major determinant of his or her needs and response to the durable solution process.

Voluntary Repatriation

Voluntary repatriation . . . is the solution which in practice will be applicable to the highest number of refugee children. Overall planning of a repatriation operation, including logistics, must be geared towards reducing vulnerability and mainstreaming the special needs of those already vulnerable.

- **Link families together:** Family unity must be a key factor in planning. Ensure that pre-departure registration links nuclear families together and that the Family Books or other documentation given to the refugee do represent family units, including extended family networks. For example, two children living with grandparents should be flagged during the registration to ensure that they can all repatriate with the parents and other siblings. Also plan for flexibility if mistakes are identified so that last minute changes allow families to repatriate together.

- **No split families:** Parents should normally not be allowed to repatriate leaving a child in the country of asylum. Likewise, requests from minor children to repatriate leaving their parents in the country of asylum should be considered only in consultation and agreement with the parents and with an assurance that the child will be received by a responsible adult relative on return.

Preparatory Activities: Experience confirms the importance of actively involving repatriants in the planning and implementation of their return.

Identifying genuine representative voices who have only the best interests of children in mind is a key factor. It is important to be aware of political and peer pressure which may be detrimental to the well-being of vulnerable children.

- **Information:** Stimulate preparatory activities as early as possible in the country of asylum. Organise programmes and activities to assist children in the process of reorientation and psychological preparation. Children should be provided with accurate information. They should be given opportunities to express their questions, fears and insecurities, and they should be listened to. Information, video films and pictures of their home areas are helpful. Mini-surveys to determine the extent to which realities are understood may be helpful.

- **Focal point:** Ensure that there is a focal point for children's needs, for example an NGO with broad child experience. Setting up a counselling programme for children and adolescents that is pro-active in attempting to identify, understand and address children's needs is recommended. Such counselling has proved helpful not only improving decision-making but also in identifying children or families potentially in need of assistance upon repatriation.

- **Medical check-up and documentation:** Screen children's health and for sick or vulnerable children, prepare files to hand over to NGOs or government institutions in the areas of return or settlement, to ensure continued care and treatment.

Administrative Concerns: Ensure that adequate administrative systems are in place to move children efficiently and effectively and to minimise waiting time in transit centres. Often services for children are not available or not sufficient in such centres.

- **Travel permits:** Arrange cross-border travel permits for persons engaged in the movement of children in voluntary repatriation programmes. Experience confirms the importance of this arrangement.
- **Allocation of responsibilities:** Ensure that the responsibilities and mandate of personnel involved in the repatriation of children are clearly defined and understood by other parties in the voluntary repatriation programme.
- **Training:** Train registration, logistics and transport staff on the special needs of children and the need for the consideration of children in need of special assistance.

Especially Vulnerable Children: Give careful attention to safeguarding the best interests of each especially vulnerable child. Keep in mind that identifying possible problems and developing appropriate services and follow-up for especially vulnerable children is time-consuming and labour-intensive. Start early, and identify possible partners on the other side of the border.

- **Priority:** Ensure that vulnerable children are given priority for early voluntary repatriation. This is only feasible if adequate lead time and resources are available to ensure appropriate arrangements in the country of origin.

- **Children living with families other than their own:** With the aid of a child welfare specialist, identify children separated from their parents and ascertain: the family's plan upon repatriation and whether help is needed in linking up the parents; the child's degree of attachment to the family; the family's degree of commitment to care for the child on an ongoing basis; the child's views regarding a durable solution in relation to those of the family; the child's degree of mental maturity; and the child's immediate and developmental needs. Ensuring a healthy relationship can minimise the risk that such children are abandoned after movement.

- **Foster care:** Ensure that services exist to care for children abandoned before or during the repatriation process.

- **Accompaniment:** Involve trusted humanitarian organisations known to the children in accompanying and providing support to unaccompanied children in the process of their voluntary repatriation and reintegration.

Organisational Linkages: Establish administrative and operational linkages with social welfare services and humanitarian organisations in the refugees' country of origin. Ensure that a social welfare follow-up system is established to monitor children's well-being after their return. If the country of origin suffers from post-war devastation, institution-building will probably be required.

- **Share information:** Documentation on children with special needs should be made available to personnel in the country of origin prior to the commencement of the voluntary repatriation. Ensure that relevant information and documentation are shared with or available to implementing partners on both sides of the border.

- **Planning** for the re-integration of children with special needs should commence in the country of origin as early as possible. Resources necessary for the same repatriation and re-integration of vulnerable children should be allocated at an early stage or at least no later than the commencement of the actual movement phase.

- **Training:** Provide training support—through work-shops, seminars and educational tours—to agencies who will be assuming new responsibilities in working with children after their voluntary repatriation, particularly those working with children with special needs.

- **Sustain services:** Given the inevitable decline in camp services during the course of the repatriation process, ensure that essential services are sustained, including information dissemination and counselling for vulnerable children. Personnel working with at-risk children should also be retained because many vulnerable children will only be identified in the course of the movement process.

Movement and Reintegration: Ensure that social services are available to assess, monitor and assist repatriated families in their reintegration. Support may be required for institutional development activities.

- **Counter marginalisation:** Support activities to counter the marginalisation of vulnerable returnee families. This may include, for example, strengthening the capacity of groups assisting female-headed households, supporting family unit and income-generating activities.

Education: Advocate for the country of origin's recognition of comparable scholastic achievements of refugee children while they were away. Provide assistance as may be required to the existing educational system to absorb the repatriated children.

- **School certificates:** Ensure that repatriating children are provided with school certificates or other documentation of education obtained in the country of asylum. Even with appropriate documentation, returnee children often face problems in being accepted into schools or into the appropriate level.

- **Rebuilding schools:** Field staff must be prepared to negotiate admission into schools with local authorities. Financial assistance to reconstruct schools or to add new class-rooms may facilitate the swift admission of returnee children into schools.

- **Informal education:** Upon repatriation, children who have been living in camps for many years may suddenly find themselves thrown into new roles, such as breadwinners. Therefore, monitor returnee children's school attendance. Explore more informal ways of meeting the educational needs of such returnee children; creative approaches may be necessary.

Unaccompanied Children: Ensure that unaccompanied children are placed in foster families or grouped under the management of an assigned agency or responsible adults from the same community.

- **Stimulate involvement:** Encourage the involvement of communities, humanitarian agencies and other national organisations in the welfare of returning orphaned, abandoned or otherwise unaccompanied children. Ensure that placement and care arrangements are made in which the children are provided with love, protection and security. Encourage integration of unaccompanied children into local schools and village life; discourage segregation.

- **Tracing:** Ensure an assertive tracing programme to locate family members, a process to verify family links and assess family reunion possibilities.

- **Special cases:** Be prepared to help unaccompanied children reunite with their families who separated accidentally or for adventure during the repatriation process.

Local Settlement

If voluntary repatriation is not possible, refugees may benefit from assistance towards self-sufficiency and integration into the local community, planned or spontaneously. The main challenge to field staff may be to ensure refugee children the same access to services as national children. Areas of concern where intervention or assistance may be necessary in the integration phase are:

- access to adequate and balanced food and to health services
- access to education, including training in the language and the culture of the settlement country
- education grants or scholarships
- vocational training to adolescents and help to find work
- activities to strengthen the refugee community to enable adults to protect and assist their children.

Resettlement

Resettlement is sought when repatriation and local integration are considered impossible within an acceptable time-frame. It often involves the greatest upheaval for the individuals concerned, in view of the social, cultural and psychological adaptation required to integrate within a new community.

For individual children, resettlement with his or her parents, a viable guardian or relative should be the primary consideration. Every effort should be made to promote and facilitate reunification of children with their parents.

Resettlement may be considered if the child falls within the following categories:

- **Family reunification:** Children are resettled for family reunification, that is to join members of the family already resettled.

- **Physical safety:** If the physical safety of a child is under severe threat and local solutions are not available, immediate resettlement together with the family may be the only practical means to guarantee his or her protection.

    Physically and mentally disabled or sick children, and traumatised, tortured children or children victims of sexual violence are resettled with their families and given top priority, both for emergency and regular resettlement.

- **Disabled children** unable to get adequate treatment in their country of first asylum or with other health conditions that cannot be addressed due to lack of appropriate medical facilities, can in some exceptional cases be considered for resettlement with family members. Priority is given to serious cases in which the condition represents a significant obstacle to leading a normal life and achieving self-sufficiency....

Chapter 7

International Law and
Internally Displaced Persons

Refugees and IDPs Distinguished

There are an estimated 20 million IDPs in the world. There is a growing concern that despite the magnitude of the problem there is no special legal regime for IDPs. The challenge involves, it is said, both one of providing material assistance to those in need, as also ensuring protection and respect for their fundamental human rights.

In any discussion of the international law governing IDPs it is important at the outset to distinguish refugees from IDPs. It may be recalled that a refugee by definition is a person who crosses an international border whereas an IDP remains inside the territory of the concerned state of which he or she is a national. Critics contend that there is no justifiable reason for denying assistance and protection to a person simply because he or she has not succeeded in crossing a border.[1] In **Reading I.A** Hathaway reviews the historical and practical reasons which led to alienage being prescribed as a criteria for determining refugee status.

---

[1] '... alienage is an unnecessary condition for establishing refugee status. It ... is a subset of a broader category: the physical access of the international community to the unprotected person. The refugee need not necessarily cross an international frontier to gain such access. Thus, I shall argue that refugees are, in essence, persons whose basic needs are unprotected by their country of origin, who have no remaining recourse other than to seek international restitution of their needs, and who are so situated that their international assistance is possible.' Andrew Shacknove, 'Who is a Refugee', *Ethics* (Vol. 95, 1985), pp. 274–84 at p. 277. See also Patricia Tuitt, *False Images: Law's Construction of the Refugee* (Pluto Press, London, 1996), pp. 11–14.

Need for a Separate Legal Framework?

Scholarly opinion is divided on the need for evolving a specific legal framework to meet the assistance and protection needs of IDPs. One school of thought contends that the existing regime of international human rights and humanitarian laws offer a firm basis to enforce the accountability of states. Indeed, it argues that any attempt to produce a separate legal regime for IDPs could undercut the extensive legal framework which already exists.[2] The other school of thought believes that there is a need for a definitive legal statement of the principles and norms applicable to IDPs. In **Readings II.A** and **II.B** Francis Deng, the Special Representative of the UN Secretary-General on IDPs, and Roberta Cohen respectively argue that a specific framework would be more helpful. Readers are invited to consider the validity of the different reasons advanced, explicitly in the case of Cohen, in favour of a separate instrument.

Definition of IDPs

If there is to be a special regime for IDPs then its beneficiaries would need to be clearly identified. Any definition would need to avoid the twin pitfalls of being overly broad or too narrow. In the former case practically anyone would qualify as an IDP. The beneficiaries would include those displaced as a result of development projects, natural disasters, as also those who are victims of human rights violations. But should all categories of IDPs, irrespective of the cause of their displacement, be beneficiaries of a separate legal framework or only those who are the victims of human rights violations? On the other hand, if the definition were overly narrow it may leave too many people outside the protection net. In that case the purpose of having a separate regime would be lost. A special regime would also need to address the question as to when an individual ceases to be a displaced person. **Reading III.A** addresses the various issues involved.

The Law of Humanitarian Assistance

In **Reading I.A** Hathaway reviews some of the reasons for insisting on alienage as a criterion for defining refugees. But Hathaway, in my view,

---

[2] See UN Doc. E/CN.4/1996/52/Add.2: *Compilation and Analysis of Legal Norms*; and *International Legal Standards Applicable to the Protection of Internally Displaced Persons: A Reference Manual for UNHCR Staff* (UNHCR, Geneva, 1996).

does not sufficiently appreciate that the principal reason for the absence of a special regime for IDPs is the understanding that states are responsible for nationals inside their own territory. 'From an international law perspective, primary responsibility for the protection of and assistance to internally displaced persons rests with the territorial State, in virtue of its sovereignty and the principle of non-intervention.'[3] The principles of sovereignty and non-intervention have a special significance for formerly colonised peoples at a time when the threat of recolonisation looms large.[4] Any attempt to dilute them in the name of the defence and promotion of human rights is therefore viewed with understandable suspicion. Such an argument is, however, not to be read as supporting an absolute doctrine of sovereignty. It is not as if sovereignty cannot be trumped in favour of human rights under any circumstance.[5] The problem is 'that the invocation of human rights is selective, often a pretext for attaining incompatible ends, and is advocated by powers which author global policies irreconcilable with any conception of human rights'.[6]

But does the provision of humanitarian assistance violate the principles of sovereignty and non-intervention? Three key issues need to be addressed in this respect. First, what is the meaning to be assigned to the word

---

[3] Guy S. Goodwin-Gill, *The Refugee in International Law* (Clarendon Press, Oxford, 1996), second edition, p. 264.

[4] Decolonisation is today represented as a mistake, often in order to revive the notion of trusteeship. For example, Inis Claude writes:

> Trusteeship purported to offer careful preparation for colonial emancipation, and it is one of the tragedies of the twentieth-century international organization that such a scheme never caught on, gained the confidence of potential clients, or produced the promised results. For better or for worse, the colonial peoples rejected gradualism in favor of Freedom Now, and the United Nations became a party to the creation of so-called Third World of new states. Unfortunately, many of these entities were ill-prepared for independence, and their emergence accounts in considerable degree for the plethora of failed and uncertainly viable states that contribute so heavily to the global disorder of our time. The United Nations, having had some responsibility for the creation of these states, bears some responsibility for rescuing them from the chaos into which they all too frequently fall.

Inis Claude Jr, 'The United Nations of the Cold War: Contributions to the Post Cold War Situation', *Fordham International Law Journal* (Vol. 18, 1995), pp. 789–93 at p. 790.

[5] The Hegelian doctrine of absolute sovereignty has long been dead. The relative character of the principle of sovereignty has come to be accepted in several respects. It may suffice to mention two developments here. First, in contrast to the doctrine of absolute sovereignty which brooks no constraint on the actions of states, Article 2 para. 4 of the UN Charter prohibits the threat or use of force in international relations. Second, states are required to abide by voluntarily undertaken international obligations and the post-1945 period has seen a larger number of obligations assumed in the sphere of human rights with appropriate mechanisms to promote adherence to them.

[6] B.S. Chimni, 'Globalization and Refugee Blues', *Journal of Refugee Studies* (Vol. 8, 1995), pp. 298–99 at p. 299.

'humanitarian'? Second, can 'humanitarian' assistance be provided with-out the consent of the host state? Third, what are the principles which will regulate the provision of 'humanitarian' assistance?

According to Minear and Weiss, 'in international law, the term "human-itarian" seldom has been delineated with the precision accorded such concepts as "human rights" or "refugee"'.[7] Therefore, a wide range of acts can be classified as 'humanitarian'. For example, Minear and Weiss define 'humanitarian assistance' as 'encompassing activities covering a full spectrum, from the supplemental feeding of infants during famines to longer-term measures such as the strengthening of indigenous social and institutional coping mechanisms to avoid future crisis'.[8] But whatever the definition of 'humanitarian' that is adopted, it involves an intrusion into sovereign space. Whether such intrusions are deemed justified often depends upon the particular approach assumed towards the doctrines of sovereignty and non-intervention. **Readings IV.A** and **IV.B** offer two dif-ferent perspectives on them. In **Reading IV.A**, Reisman contends that the principle of sovereignty cannot be permitted to be used by violators of human rights to shield their regimes. On the other hand, in **Reading IV.B** the International Court of Justice in its judgement in the *Nicaragua* case emphasises the principle of non-intervention into the internal and external affairs of states.[9]

The most significant issue relating to the law of humanitarian assist-ance is whether the consent of the host state is a precondition in this regard.[10] In December 1991, the UNGA adopted Resolution 46/182 which lays down in an annex the guiding principles for the provision of emergency humanitarian assistance. **Reading IV.C** reproduces relevant parts of the text. The resolution *inter alia* states that such assistance must 'be provided with the consent of the affected country' and in principle be 'on the basis of an appeal by the affected country'. Western scholars either ignore this resolution or contend that the use of the word 'coun-try', as opposed to 'government', implies that only the tacit consent of authorities is required.[11] Also cited in this context are some Security Council resolutions which permitted humanitarian assistance to be given

---

[7] Larry Minear and Thomas G. Weiss, *Humanitarian Action in Times of War* (Lynn Reiner Publishers, Boulder, 1993), p. 7.

[8] Ibid., p. 9.

[9] For a discussion of the *Nicaragua* decision and the unlawful character of 'humanitarian intervention', see V.S. Mani, 'Humanitarian Intervention and International Law', *Indian Journal of International Law* (Vol. 33, 1993), pp. 1–26.

[10] Minear and Weiss, *Humanitarian Action in Times of War* (see footnote 7 earlier), p. 7.

[11] 'The resolution [i.e., 46/182] required only the tacit "consent" of authorities rather than their explicit "request" to activate UN responses. Moreover, consent could come from a "country" experiencing such a disaster instead of from the "government" itself'. Ibid., p. 14.

without the consent of the affected country.[12] These contentions raise a number of questions. Who can appeal on behalf of the 'country'? What form would such consent assume? Can the Security Council overstep the bounds of the UN Charter and peremptory principles of international law in departing from the principle of consent?[13] Can humanitarian assistance at a practical level be provided without the cooperation of the state concerned?

The reasons for the third world countries objecting to humanitarian assistance being provided without the consent of the concerned government is the possible pursuit of an hidden agenda. Even Minear and Weiss who support the idea that assistance can be given without the consent of the host state admit that 'elementary as appears the principle that humanitarian action should be directed toward the relief of immediate, life-threatening suffering, other agendas often have dominated.' This was without doubt true of the period of the Cold War.[14] Is the situation any different after the end of the Cold War? Have not new 'enemies'—Islam and the third world—already replaced communism? In the circumstances, the rare case apart, should not humanitarian assistance be provided with the consent of the government concerned? Further, is it not appropriate that states agree on what these rare cases are? Should not decisions

[12] For example, Minear and Weiss (ibid., p. 14) cite Security Council Resolution 688 which was the tenuous basis on which safe zones were created in Iraq. On safe zones see **Reading VII.A** in this chapter.

[13] Bedjaoui has framed the question thus: 'States are open to sanction for their internationally unlawful acts; it appears entirely illogical, therefore, that the universal organization which they set up should remain immune from any control over the legality of the acts of its organs and from any penalty for the wrongful exercise of power. It appears less acceptable than ever that sovereign States should have created an international organization equipped with broad powers of control and sanction vis-à-vis themselves but *itself* exempted from the duty to respect both the Charter which gave it birth and international law.' He further queries as to 'how can one conceivably imagine any real democratization of the United Nations without raising *inter alia* the fundamental problem of controlling the acts of the political organs, above all the kingpin, the Security Council.' Mohammed Bedjaoui, *The New World Order and the Security Council: Testing the Legality of its Acts* (Martinus Nijhoff Publishers, Dordrecht, 1994), p. 7. See also V.S. Mani, 'The Role of Law and Legal Considerations in the Functioning of the United Nations', *Indian Journal of International Law* (Vol. 36, 1996), pp. 91–118.

[14] 'During the Cold War when anti-communist fervor infiltrated long-standing humanitarian traditions, the United States provided tents, boots, and communications equipment to the Nicaraguan insurgents under the rubric of "humanitarian" aid. The United States also committed "humanitarian" aid to other insurgencies seeking to topple communist regimes in Afghanistan, Angola and Cambodia. Other major powers with less-established traditions of humanitarian assistance also aided selected regimes around the world to further their own political agendas.' Minear and Weiss, *Humanitarian Action in Times of War* (see footnote 7 earlier), pp. 20–21. They cite a 1985 editorial in *The Washington Post* which stated: 'Anyone who examines the historical record of communism must conclude that any aid directed at overthrowing communism is humanitarian aid.'

in such cases be taken by the General Assembly and not the Security Council? **Reading IV.D** does not pretend to answer these questions but offers a broad third world perspective on the politics of humanitarian assistance as a background against which to approach them. Among other things, it reveals the unhappiness of third world states with the choice of words in GA Resolution 46/182.

A third issue relates to the basis on which humanitarian assistance is to be dispensed. Resolution 46/182 states that 'humanitarian assistance must be provided in accordance with the principles of humanity, neutrality and impartiality'. This principle, as **Reading IV.E** notes, was approved by the ICJ in the *Nicaragua* case.[15] In this reading Plattner lists, in response to critics of the ICRC position, the elements which in her view should be the basis for formulating a definition of 'neutral humanitarian assistance'.[16]

The Guiding Principles on Internal Displacement (1998)

In April 1998, the Representative of the UN Secretary-General on IDPs presented to the UNCHR a set of *Guiding Principles on Internal Displacement*. The Commission in a unanimously adopted resolution took note of these principles whose text is reproduced in **Reading V.A**. It needs to be emphasised that the *Guiding Principles on Internal Displacement* is not binding on states. Its significance, according to Cohen, lies in the fact that

the *Guiding Principles* consolidate into one document all the international norms relevant to IDPs, otherwise dispersed in many different instruments. Although not a legally binding document, the principles reflect and are consistent with existing international human rights and humanitarian law. In re-stating existing norms, they also seek to address grey areas and gaps. An earlier study had found 17 areas of insufficient protection for IDPs and eight areas of clear gaps in the law.[17] No norm, for example, could be found explicitly prohibiting the forcible return of internally displaced persons to places of

[15] It may be noted that in the *Nicaragua* case, the Court did not consider whether the consent of the state concerned is a precondition for providing humanitarian assistance. It may also be pointed out that Resolution 46/182 was adopted after the judgement.

[16] The Plattner reading also raises, albeit indirectly, the issue of the role of different governmental and non-governmental agencies involved with providing humanitarian assistance. In this context readers' attention may be drawn to the discussion in the introduction to Chapter 4, where it was noted how humanitarian assistance has now become big business with NGOs having a stake in it, making them subservient to donor priorities and insensitive to the real needs of the people concerned.

[17] See *Compilation and Analysis of Legal Norms*, Report of the Representative of the Secretary-General on Internally Displaced Persons, E/CN/4/1996/52/Add.2, United Nations, December 1995.

danger. Nor was there a right to restitution of property lost as a consequence of displacement during armed conflict or to compensation for its loss. The law, moreover, was silent about internment of IDPs in camps. Special guarantees for women and children were needed.[18]

In the background of the discussion of issues relating to the need for a separate legal instrument for IDPs, the definition of IDPs and the law of humanitarian assistance, readers may like to critically examine the text of the *Guiding Principles*. A number of questions may be raised. First, would you agree with Cohen that the *Guiding Principles* serve a useful purpose through consolidating and filling the gaps in the international law relating to IDPs? Second, the *Guiding Principles* adopt a very broad definition of IDPs which includes peoples displaced by development projects. Is this the correct approach? Third, do the *Guiding Principles* depart in any way from G.A. Resolution 46/182 in stating the principles relating to humanitarian assistance? Fourth, an innovative feature of the *Guiding Principles* is said to be its emphasis on protection.[19] Besides providing assistance, humanitarian organisations are asked by Principle 27 to 'give due regard to the protection needs and human rights of internally displaced persons' and to 'take appropriate measures in this regard'. Would this lead to the greater politicisation of humanitarian organisations? Does the talk of protection clash with the principle of sovereignty on the one hand and neutrality on the other? Fifth, Principle 28 speaks of voluntary return of IDPs. Was it appropriate to borrow the concept from international refugee law which deals with those who have crossed an international border?

Institutional Measures: A New Agency?

In the last decade, a number of steps have been taken in the United Nations to enhance its capacity to respond to situations of internal displacement. In 1990, the General Assembly assigned to resident coordinators the function of coordinating assistance to IDPs. In 1991, the post of Emergency Relief Coordinator (ERC) was created to promote a more rapid and coherent response to emergency solutions. In 1992, the UN created the Inter-agency Standing Committee (IASC) chaired by the ERC and composed of the heads of the major UN humanitarian and development agencies, to strengthen coordination in emergency situations. Also chaired by the ERC since mid-1997 is a smaller body, the Executive Committee on Humanitarian Affairs (ECHA), which the Secretary-General created in

---

[18] Roberta Cohen, 'The Guiding Principles on Internal Displacement: A New Instrument for International Organizations and NGOs', *Forced Migration Review* (No. 2, August 1998), pp. 31–33 at p. 31.

[19] Ibid., p. 32.

1997, composed of the heads of humanitarian and development agencies and of the UN departments on peacekeeping and political affairs. In the same year it also created the Department of Humanitarian Affairs (DHA) to assist the ERC which was replaced in 1997 by a smaller office renamed the Office for the Coordination of Humanitarian Affairs (OCHA).

Despite these steps a persistent question which is asked is whether a new agency should be created for providing assistance and protection to IDPs. For at present no single operational agency in the international system has responsibility for IDPs. There appear to be many persuasive arguments against the establishment of a new agency. As Cohen and Deng point out:

> To begin with, it would duplicate the many existing resources and capacities that have already become involved with the internally displaced.... The cost of a new institution would be substantial.... There is also the concern that it would foster dependency by encouraging governments to call upon the new agency to address problems that should fall within their own purview.... A new agency for the internally displaced is certain to arouse considerable opposition from governments that believe the problem belongs within the domestic jurisdiction of states.[20]

In the alternative they suggest that

> assigning responsibility to an existing organization such as UNHCR could be an effective solution if it were assured the support of other agencies with skills needed to deal with the different phases of internal displacement, and if it received full back-up support from the UN system.[21]

The agencies which could lend support to the UNHCR include the ICRC, the United Nations Development Programme, the World Food Programme, the United Nations Children's Fund, the World Health Organisation, and the International Organisation for Migration.[22]

The Role of UNHCR

Against this background, **Reading VI.A** articulates the perspective of the UNHCR on the role it can play in providing assistance and protection to

[20] Roberta Cohen and Francis M. Deng, *Masses in Flight: The Global Crisis of Internal Displacement* (Brookings Institution Press, Washington, D.C., 1998), p. 169.
[21] Ibid., p. 185.
[22] For a review of the possible role these organisations can play see ibid., pp. 128–42.

IDPs. The Reading addresses a number of issues including UNHCR's competence with respect to the internally displaced; the criteria for UNHCR involvement; the legal norms applicable with respect to the persons displaced or at risk of displacement within their own country; the nature and content of UNHCR's involvement; and the complementary roles of other international organisations.

A number of questions may be raised to facilitate the critical evaluation of the guidelines which the UNHCR outlines for providing assistance and protection to IDPs: would UNHCR's increasing involvement with IDPs detract from the possibility of those displaced to seek and obtain asylum? Is its transformation from a refugee to a humanitarian organisation being dictated by the aim of the powerful donor states to keep potential refugees at home? Should it support standards which focus on IDPs without attempting to fill at first the gaps which exist in refugee protection? In all these respects the UNHCR may well find that 'the shield of IDP protection turns into a sword for undermining refugee protection.'[23]

The Law and Practice of Safety Zones

The idea of a safety zone or a safe haven is a simple one. It is an area within a country to which IDPs (and prospective refugees) can flee to secure assistance and protection. One can distinguish between three kinds of safe havens:

> One is a safe haven outside of the country from which individuals flee, a territory in a third country under the protection of an external power or the United Nations. The second involves the establishment of a large self-administered and economically viable internationally protected zone within the country whose citizens are at risk. And the third entails the establishment, also within the country whose citizens are at risk, of internationally protected safe havens whose populations are dependent on external support for their basic necessities.[24]

The first kind of safe haven or safety zone is the kind that the United States established in Guantanamo Bay, Cuba, for Haitian refugees inter-

[23] David Petrasek, 'New Standards for the Protection of Internally Displaced Persons: A Proposal for a Comprehensive Approach', *Refugee Survey Quarterly* (Vol. 14, Nos 1 and 2, 1995), pp. 285–90 at p. 286. Readers are referred here to the introduction to Chapter 4 in which a number of other questions have been raised in the context of the UNHCR's involvement with IDPs.

[24] *German and American Migration and Refugee Policies: Recommendations of the Joint German-American Project of the American Academy of Arts and Sciences* (American Academy of Arts and Sciences, Cambridge, Massachussetts, 1996), p. 23.

dicted on the high seas.[25] The second type of safe haven was created in Iraq for Kurds. And the last kind of safe havens were established in Bosnia. In **Reading VII.A** Chimni critically analyses at length the law and practice of safe havens or safety zones as they were established in Iraq and Bosnia. While sharply critical of them, Chimni offers reasons for not dismissing the concept of safety zones. Would you agree with the reasons offered for retaining the idea of safety zones? Chimni also appends a set of principles which must inform the creation of safety zones in future. Would you go along with them?

In **Reading VII.B** Bill Clarance of the UNHCR reflects on the lessons learnt in the process of creating and running Operation Relief Centres (ORCs) in Sri Lanka, a concept akin to safe havens.

* * *

I. REFUGEES AND IDPs DISTINGUISHED

A. James C. Hathaway, *The Law of Refugee Status* (Butterworths, Toronto, 1991), pp. 29–33.

Alienage

The first element of Convention refugee status is that the claimant must be outside her country of origin. There is nothing intuitively obvious about this requirement: many if not most of the persons forced to flee their homes in search of safety remain within the boundaries of their state. Their plight may be every bit as serious as that of individuals who cross borders, yet the Convention definition of refugee status excludes internal refugees from the scope of global protection.

The strict insistence on this territorial criterion has prompted concern that there is a mismatch between the definition and the human suffering consequent to involuntary migration. In one sense, the exclusion of internal refugees is clearly unfair: it does not recognise the existence of social, legal, and economic barriers which make it impossible for all to escape to international protection. The Convention definition of refugee status therefore responds in a less than even-handed way to the protection needs of persons similarly at risk of persecution.

---

[25] See the sensitive and brilliant critique of these safe havens by Professor Koh of the Yale Law School. Harold Hongju Koh, 'The Human Face of the Haitian Interdiction Program', *Virginia Journal of International Law* (Vol. 33, 1992–93), pp. 483–90; 'Refugees, the Courts, and the New World Order', *Utah Law Review* (No. 3, 1994), pp. 999–1027; 'America's Offshore Refugee Camps', *University of Richmond Law Review* (Vol. 29, 1995), pp. 139–73.

A brief excerpt from one of Koh's articles is reproduced as **Reading II.B** in Chapter 3.

There is a threefold historical rationale for the requirement that only persons outside their state be eligible for Convention refugee status. First, the Convention was drafted with a specific purpose in the context of limited international resources. Its intent was not to relieve the suffering of all involuntary migrants, but rather to deal 'only with the problem of legal protection and status'.[26] Its goal was to assist a subset of involuntary migrants composed of persons who were 'outside their own countries [and] who lacked the protection of a government',[27] and who consequently required short-term surrogate international rights until they acquired new or renewed national protection.[28] Internal refugee displacements, while of humanitarian note, 'were separate problems of a different character',[29] the alleviation of which would demand a more sustained commitment of resources than was available to the international community.[30]

Second, there was a very practical concern that the inclusion of internal refugees in the international protection regime might prompt states to attempt to shift responsibility for the well-being of large parts of their own population to the world community. The obligations of states under the Convention would thereby be increased, as a result of which fewer states would be likely to participate in the Convention regime.

Third and most fundamental, there was anxiety that any attempt to respond to the needs of internal refugees would constitute an infringement of the national sovereignty of the state within which the refugee resided. Refugee law, as a part of international human rights law, constitute a recent and carefully constrained exception to the long-standing rule of exclusive jurisdiction of states over their inhabitants. While it was increasingly accepted in the early 1950s that the world community had a legitimate right to set standards and scrutinise the human rights record of the various countries, it was unthinkable that refugee law would intervene in the territory of a state to protect citizens from their own government. The best that could be achieved within the context of the accepted

[26] Statement of Mr Henkin of the USA, UN Doc. E/AC.7/SR.161, at p. 7, 18 August 1950.

[27] Statement of Mrs Roosevelt of the United States of America, 5 UNGAOR at p. 473, 2 December 1949.

[28] 'The proposals of the Economic and Social Council were designed, however, to meet the needs of refugees who were outside their countries of origin for social, religious or political reasons, were unable to return thereto and required protection under international auspices until they acquired a new nationality or reassumed their former nationality'. Statement of Mrs Roosevelt of the United States of America, 5 UNGAOR at p. 363, 29 November 1950.

[29] Statement of Mrs Roosevelt, 5 UNGAOR at p. 473, 2 December 1949.

[30] '[W]hile he would like to see the Convention drafted to cover as many refugees as possible, he nevertheless appreciated how difficult it would be for governments to provide what the Ad Hoc Committee had described as a blank cheque...': Statement of Mr Van Heuven Goedhart, United Nations High Commissioner for Refugees, UN Doc. A/CONF.2/SR.21, at p. 12, 14 July 1951.

rules of international law was the sheltering of such persons as were able to liberate themselves from the territorial jurisdiction of a persecutory state.

None of the three factors which dictated the exclusion of internal refugees—limited resources, concern about state participation, or respect for sovereignty—was so much a matter of conceptual principle, as it was a reflection of the limited reach of international law. As Andrew Shacknove has observed, 'alienage is an unnecessary condition for establishing refugee status. It ... is a subject of a broader category: the physical access of the international community to the unprotected person.'[31] In other words, the physical presence of the unprotected person outside her country of origin is not a constitutive element of her refugeehood, but is rather a practical condition precedent to placing her within the effective scope of international protection.

The territorial dimension of the Convention definition of refugee status, then, was dictated by the extant authority of international law. Its purpose was not to divide involuntary migrants into those who are worthy of assistance and those who are not deserving, but was instead to define the scope of refugee law in a realistic, workable way.

II. NEED FOR A SEPARATE INSTRUMENT

A. UN Doc. E/CN.4/1994/44, 25 January 1994, 'Internally Displaced Persons: Report of the Representative of the Secretary-General, Mr Francis Deng, Submitted Pursuant to Commission on Human Rights Resolution 1993/95', paras 19–28.

19. Another task to be accomplished under the mandate is an assessment of the present situation with respect to existing international law to determine the degree to which it provides an adequate basis for the protection of the internally displaced. Controversy still prevails among lawyers as to the scope and applicability of existing legal doctrine. There are those who believe that the existing standards provide adequate protection and that the main challenge is one of implementation. The proponents of this view believe that to hold otherwise would be to put into question the legal foundation for accountability. In contrast, there are those who maintain that legal reform is necessary to ensure complete and adequate coverage. While both points of view emanate from the need to strengthen protection, the second implies that setting new standards would not only fill any existing gaps but would also focus international attention

[31] Shacknove, 'Who is a Refugee?' (see footnote 1 earlier), at p. 277.

and thereby raise the level of public awareness of the problem and the need for solutions....

20. The principal sources of the existing standards for protection, as well as the foundations for articulation of further protections, are found in international human rights law, specifically the Universal Declaration of Human Rights, the 1966 International Covenant on Civil and Political Rights and the 1966 International Covenant on Economic, Social and Cultural Rights; humanitarian law, which comprises the four Geneva Conventions of 1949 and the two Additional Protocols of 1977; and refugee law, embodied in the 1951 Convention relating to the Status of Refugees and the 1967 Protocol. The wide array of rights enshrined in the corpus of human rights law is applicable to situations common to the displaced. These rights cover the minimum standards of human existence and dignity: physical protection, shelter, food, clothing, basic health, work and the integrity of the person and the family as the most fundamental social unit.

21. The responsibility for meeting these needs for protection and assistance rests first and foremost with national Governments. However, in situations of displacement, the State may be required to take additional measures in order to safeguard these rights, which it might be unable or unwilling to do. Furthermore, human rights are subject to derogation during periods of public emergency, which often coincide with the times of greatest need for protecting the displaced. Finally, human rights law does not directly address some of the most critical situations affecting the displaced, such as forcible displacement or return to unsafe areas and access to humanitarian assistance.

22. A more elaborated right to humanitarian access and humanitarian assistance, including the right to food, has, therefore, been advocated. Since basic economic, social and cultural rights form part of international customary law, Governments unable to protect them adequately are obliged to avail themselves of international cooperation. It could be argued further that individuals are also entitled to receive international assistance when such rights are at risk, even if the Government concerned is unwilling to request such assistance.

23. It is also generally acknowledged that internally displaced persons face more risks with regard to their physical safety than the rest of the population. Standards to address these special protection needs may be appropriate. Special guidelines for the

protection problems that women and children face are also necessary. Such guidelines have already been developed within the United Nations system in order to deal with the protection needs of refugees and important principles could be derived from them and further elaborated.

24. Humanitarian law, which codifies the principle that those not directly participating in the hostilities shall be treated humanely, contains provisions which are of great value to the displaced. Particularly relevant is article 3, common to all four Geneva Conventions, which, in the case of armed conflicts not of an international character, categorically prohibits violence to life and/or person, the taking of hostages, and outrages upon the personal dignity of persons. Equally important is article 17 of Protocol II Additional to the Geneva Conventions (1977), which deals with displacement of civilian populations in internal conflicts and sets out restrictions on such movements. It provides guarantees to the civilian populations if these movements, for imperative reasons, have to take place and prohibits their being compelled to leave their territories for reasons related to the conflict. While useful, this provision applies only to persons displaced because of armed conflict, and only to States parties to Additional Protocol II.

25. Efforts to convince Governments to ratify the Geneva Conventions and the Additional Protocols are, consequently, essential. These legal instruments include important safeguards with regard to forcible displacements of civilian populations in the course of armed conflicts. . . .

26. Despite the fact that internally displaced persons have much in common with refugees, refugee law applies by definition only to persons who have crossed an international border. While some have argued that this is an arbitrary distinction, it is of enormous consequence, as a displaced person's presence in a country other than his or her own implicates a well-established protective regime, the core of which is the concept of *non-refoulement* (the right of non-return to a territory where the refugee's life or freedom would be threatened because of race, religion, nationality, membership of a particular social group or political opinion). For internally displaced persons, one of the most important rights provided for in refugee and human rights law is the right to seek asylum. It is important that this right not be undermined while efforts are being made to strengthen the standards for protection of internally displaced persons.

27. Given the similarities in the situations of internally displaced persons and refugees, many important principles can be drawn by analogy from refugee law for the protection of internally displaced persons. For instance, the articulation of a right not to be forcibly returned to areas where the life or freedom of the displaced person could be threatened could be vital in some cases.... Other similar rights could include the right to seek residence in a safe place, the right to be provided with adequate documentation, the right not to be identified as a displaced person if that would result in discrimination, the freedom of movement especially in and out of the camp or other shelter for the displaced, the right to benefit from measures towards family reunification and the right to voluntary return to the original area of residence.

28. Without prejudicing the issue of whether or not new normative standards are needed, it is generally recognised that even though the existing law appears to be adequate for the needs of internal displacement, a consolidation and evaluation of existing norms would be of value and would provide the basis for filling whatever gaps may exist.... This requires first a compilation/commentary of the existing norms and a further elaboration of the relevant standards (in the form, for instance, of a code of conduct) and, eventually, a declaration or other authoritative document.[32]

B. Roberta Cohen, 'Protecting the Internally Displaced', *World Refugee Survey 1996*, pp. 23–25.

International organisations and NGOs frequently complain that no legal instrument exists to guide their work with the internally displaced. Governments similarly find that there is no instrument to consult when drafting laws to protect the internally displaced. A myriad of provisions can be found in international human rights and humanitarian law, and in refugee law by analogy, but some are applicable in certain circumstances and not in others. And no one instrument sets forth these principles in a coherent fashion.

... international legal experts have worked to compile a set of appropriate provisions. They have found many gray areas and gaps in the law as it might apply to the internally displaced. Human rights law, for

---

[32] A compilation and analysis of legal norms was prepared in 1995. See UNHCR, E/CN.4/1996/52/Add.2, December 1995, *Compilation and Analysis of Legal Norms*. In 1998, a set of *Guiding Principles on Internal Displacement* was adopted by the UNHCR. Its text is reproduced here as **Reading V.A.**

example, can be derogated from in terms of public emergency or internal strife, leaving internally displaced persons without adequate protection. It also is not binding on insurgent forces. Humanitarian law applies only to armed conflict situations, not to lesser situations of civil strife in which many internally displaced persons are caught up.

Neither human rights nor humanitarian law is sufficiently explicit in its protection of the internally displaced. In some cases, it is possible to infer specific rights from existing general norms or by way of analogy. In others, however, inferences strain interpretation. For example, no explicit guarantee exists against the forcible return of internally displaced persons to places of danger. Governments are not explicitly obliged to accept international humanitarian assistance or to ensure the safe access of internally displaced persons to essential facilities and commodities needed for survival. Nor are there explicitly articulated protections for internally displaced women and children. Clear gaps exist in the law when it comes to personal documentation for the displaced or restitution or compensation for property lost during displacement. International lawyers have identified seventeen areas where there is insufficient protection owing to inexplicit articulation, and eight areas where there are significant gaps in the law.[33]

What is needed is a definitive statement of legal principles that recapitulates and clarifies in one coherent document the existing norms, makes explicit the gray areas in the law, and remedies identifiable gaps. The instrument should be non-derogable in all circumstances. It would have to apply both to governments and to insurgent forces. To obviate a need for ratification (and because the political reality is that many governments would not be willing to bind themselves through a convention), it should take the form of a declaration of principles whose moral force could, over time, achieve for it the status of customary law.

In addition to providing a modicum of legal protection for the internally displaced, such a declaration would serve the important educational purpose of raising the level of international public awareness of the needs of internally displaced persons. It would also serve the practical purpose of giving human rights and humanitarian agencies a document to point to when dealing with governments and insurgent forces to gain access to the internally displaced.

Arguments against a new legal instrument come mainly from those who believe in placing emphasis on implementing existing norms rather than creating new ones. The International Committee of the Red Cross (ICRC) in particular has expressed the fear that any attempt to develop new standards could risk undercutting the extensive coverage that already exists under the Geneva Conventions.

[33] Ibid.

Rather than undercutting existing protections, however, a new instrument would both reconfirm them and expand coverage for a group of persons insufficiently protected at present. Precedents abound in international law for the protection of disadvantaged groups—whether refugees, minorities, indigenous populations, the disabled or women and children. Drafting a non-binding declaration would be an incremental step toward establishing minimum conditions for the treatment of the displaced. Every effort should be made to encourage the UN Commission on Human Rights and the General Assembly to take that step.

III. DEFINITION

A. Roberta Cohen, 'Protecting the Internally Displaced', *World Refugee Survey 1996*, pp. 21–23.

At present, there exists no internationally agreed upon definition of who is an internally displaced person. Achieving one is essential both for the development of accurate statistics and information and for comprehensive and coherent action.

The UN's current working definition holds as internally displaced those

... persons who have been forced to flee their homes suddenly or unexpectedly in large numbers, as a result of armed conflict, internal strife, systematic violations of human rights or natural or man-made disasters, and who are within the territory of their own country.[34]

This definition has been described as both too broad and too narrow. Including victims of natural disasters is said to make it unduly broad. Persons fleeing armed conflict, internal strife, and systematic violations of human rights would, if they were to cross a border, qualify as refugees both under the Organisation of African Unity (OAU) Convention and the Cartagena Declaration, and, arguably, in many cases, under the narrower definition of the Refugee Convention as well. But persons uprooted by natural disasters would not; they generally are not in need of international protection of their human rights; moreover, their governments and the international community are usually willing—if not always able— to provide them with assistance. The argument for retaining them in the definition is based essentially on cases where governments respond to natural disasters by persecuting certain groups on political or ethnic grounds or by violating their human rights in other ways. For example,

---

[34] Analytical Report of the Secretary-General on Internally Displaced Persons, E/CN.4/ 1992/23, 14 February 1992, para. 17.

when drought and famine ravaged Ethiopia in the mid-1980s, the government forcibly relocated hundreds of thousands of Tigereans it regarded as political opponents, under the pretext of responding to a natural disaster. In other countries, persons have also been displaced because of a combination of natural causes and racial, social or political reasons. Maintaining natural disasters in the text, it is argued, would assure protection for such persons.

A better solution, however, might be to qualify the term so that it covers cases involving human rights violations and persecution but not all victims of natural disaster.

The same reasoning would apply to man-made disasters, for example ecological or nuclear disasters. Whereas displaced populations in many of these cases should readily receive assistance from their governments and/or from the international community, other cases may be complicated by persecution and systematic violations of human rights or the need for international protection. It is the latter cases that should be covered by the definition. The same would be true for development projects that cause displacement....

The quantitative and time qualifiers in the definition, on the other hand, make it unduly narrow. Restricting the internally displaced to those forced to leave 'suddenly or unexpectedly in large numbers' would exclude serious cases of internal displacement—such as in Colombia, where the displaced often flee in small numbers, making them less conspicuous, or in Iraq, where the government organised the uprooting of Kurds over a period of years in the late 1970s, 1980s and early 1990s.

The term 'forced to flee' is also too narrow. Countless numbers in Burma, Iraq and Ethiopia have been forcibly moved by their governments on political and ethnic grounds; they did not flee. Nor did Bosnian Muslims forcibly expelled from their homes in Banja Luka and other areas of Bosnia on ethnic and religious grounds. Such persons explicitly should be included as internally displaced.

The definition essentially should help identify persons who should be of concern to the international community because they are basically in refugee-like situations[35] within their own countries, and their own governments are unwilling or unable to protect and assist them. Some development agencies have proposed expanding the definition to encompass those who migrate because of poverty or other economic causes. But this would add millions of persons to the definition who have not fled or been forced from their homes and whose needs are best addressed by development programmes generated by national and international agencies.

The internally displaced should be defined as persons or groups of persons who have been forced to flee, or leave, their homes or places of

---

[35] Broadly defined as in the OAU Convention and the Cartagena Declaration as well as in the Refugee Convention.

habitual residence as a result of armed conflict, internal strife and systematic violations of human rights, as well as natural or man-made disasters involving one or more of these elements, and who have not crossed an internationally recognised state border. What should make internally displaced persons of concern to the international community should be the coercion that impels their movement, their subjection to human rights abuse as a result of this uprootedness, and the lack of protection available within their own countries.

When an internally displaced person ceases to be displaced also needs clarification. Conventional wisdom would have it that the voluntary return of the displaced to their homes or their reintegration elsewhere marks the end of internal displacement. But if protection is largely lacking in these areas and their land and homes are occupied by others, can internal displacement be said to be over? In Angola, for example, groups of internally displaced persons voluntarily transported back to their home areas found that they could not remain there because all infrastructure had been destroyed and they had no means of sustaining themselves. The mere act of return therefore did not end their internal displacement. Determining when internal displacement is ended should go beyond merely registering whether return or relocation has taken place. It should include whether the returns and relocations are reasonably viable and whether basic security and survival are assured.

IV. LAW OF HUMANITARIAN ASSISTANCE

A. Michael W. Reisman, 'Sovereignty and Human Rights in Contemporary International Law', *American Journal of International Law* (Vol. 84, 1990), pp. 866, 869–70, 872–74.

anachronism ... 1: an error in chronology; esp. a chronological misplacing of persons, events, objects or customs in regard to each other ... 2: a person or a thing that is chronologically out of place; esp: one that belongs to a former age and is incongruous if found in the present....

Webster's Third International Dictionary

Although the venerable term 'sovereignty' continues to be used in international legal practice, its referent in modern international law is quite different. International law still protects sovereignty, but—not surprisingly—it is the people's sovereignty rather than the sovereign's sovereignty. Under the old concept, even scrutiny of international human rights without the permission of the sovereign could arguably constitute a violation of sovereignty by its 'invasion' of the sovereign's *domaine reserve*. The United Nations Charter replicates the 'domestic jurisdiction–international concern' dichotomy, but no serious scholar still supports the contention that internal human rights are 'essentially within the domestic jurisdiction of any state' and hence insulated from international law.

This contemporary change in content of the term 'sovereignty' also changes the cast of characters who can violate that sovereignty. Of course, popular sovereignty is violated when an outside force invades and imposes its will on the people. One thinks of the invasion of Afghanistan in 1979 or of Kuwait in 1990. But what happens to sovereignty, in its modern sense, when it is not an outsider but some home-grown specialist in violence who seizes and purports to wield the authority of the government against the wishes of the people, by naked power, by putsch or by coup, by the usurpation of an election or by those systematic corruptions of the electoral process in which almost 100 percent of the electorate purportedly votes for the incumbent's list (often the only choice)? Is such a seizer of power entitled to invoke the international legal term 'national sovereignty' to establish or reinforce his own position in international politics?

Under the old international law, the internal usurper was so entitled, for the standard was *de facto* control: the only test was the effective power of the claimant. In the *Tinoco* case,[36] Costa Rica sought to defend itself by claiming a violation of its popular sovereignty. Tinoco, the erstwhile Minister of War, had seized power in violation of the Constitution. Therefore, the subsequent restorationist Costa Rican Government contended, his actions could not be deemed to have bound Costa Rica. But Chief Justice Taft decided that by virtue of his effective control, Tinoco had represented the legitimate government as long as he enjoyed that control.

The *Tinoco* decision was consistent with the law of its time. Were it applied strictly now, it would be anachronistic, for it stands in stark contradiction to the new constitutive, human rights-based conception of popular sovereignty. To be sure, there were policy reasons for *Tinoco*, which may still have some cogency, but the important point is that there was then no countervailing constitutive policy of international human rights and its conception of popular sovereignty.

... International law is still concerned with the protection of sovereignty, but, in its modern sense, the object of protection is not the power base of the tyrant who rules directly by naked power or through the apparatus of a totalitarian political order, but the continuing capacity of a population freely to express and effect choices about the identities and policies of its governors. ...

---

[36] *Tinoco* case (*Great Brit. v. Costa Rica*), 1 R.Int'l Arb. Awards 369 (1923).

In modern international law, sovereignty can be violated as effectively and ruthlessly by an indigenous as by an outside force, in much the same way that the wealth and natural resources of a country can be spoliated as thoroughly and efficiently by a native as by a foreigner. Sovereignty can be liberated as much by an indigenous as by an outside force. As in the interpretation of any other event in terms of policy, context and consequence must be considered.

The international human rights programme is more than a piecemeal addition to the traditional corpus of international law, more than another chapter sandwiched into traditional textbooks of international law. By shifting the fulcrum of the system from the protection of sovereigns to the protection of people, it works qualitative changes in virtually every component. Many of the old terms survive, but in using them in a modern context, one should bear in mind Holme's lapidary dictum: 'A word is not a crystal transparent and unchanged; it is the skin of a living thought and may vary greatly in color and content according to the circumstances and the time in which it is used.'[37]

When constitutive changes such as these are introduced into a legal system while many other struts of the system are left in place, appliers and interpreters of current cases cannot proceed in a piecemeal and mechanical fashion. Precisely because the human rights norms are constitutive, other norms must be reinterpreted in their light, lest anachronisms be produced.... Anachronism can only be avoided in legal decision by systematic actualisation, which considers inherited norms in the context of changed constitutive normative systems and makes sensitive assessments of the relative weight each is to be given and the various intensities with which each is demanded.

B. International Court of Justice, Case Concerning Military and Paramilitary Activities in and against Nicaragua (*Nicaragua v. United States of America*), Judgement of 27 June 1986, paras 202–3, 205–6, 209, 246, 263, 267–68.

202. The principle of non-intervention involves the right of every sovereign State to conduct its affairs without outside interference; though examples of trespass against this principle are not infrequent, the Court considers that it is part and parcel of customary international law. As the Court has observed: 'Between independent States, respect for territorial sovereignty is an essential foundation of international relations' (ICJ Reports 1949, p. 35), and international law requires political integrity also to be respected. Expressions of an *opinio juris* regarding the existence of the principle of non-intervention in customary international law are

[37] *Towne v. Eisner*, 245 US 372, 376 (1918).

numerous and not difficult to find. Of course, statements whereby States avow their recognition of the principles of international law set forth in the United Nations Charter cannot strictly be interpreted as applying to the principle of non-intervention by States in the internal and external affairs of other States, since this principle is not, as such, spelt out in the Charter. But it was never intended that the Charter should embody written confirmation of every essential principle of international law in force. The existence in the *opinio juris* of States of the principle of non-intervention is backed by established and substantial practice. It has moreover been presented as a corollary of the principle of the sovereign equality of States. A particular instance of this is General Assembly resolution 2625 (XXV), the Declaration on the Principles of International Law concerning Friendly Relations and Co-operation among States. In the *Corfu Channel* case, when a State claimed a right of intervention in order to secure evidence in the territory of another State for submission to an international tribunal (ICJ Reports 1949, p. 34), the Court observed that:

> the alleged right of intervention as the manifestation of a policy of force, such as has, in the past, given rise to most serious abuses and such as cannot, whatever be the present defects in international organisation, find a place in international law. Intervention is perhaps still less admissible in the particular form it would take here; for, from the nature of things, it would be reserved for the most powerful States, and might easily lead to preventing the administration of international justice itself. (ICJ Reports 1949, p. 35).

203. The principle has since been reflected in numerous declarations adopted by international organisations and conferences in which the United States and Nicaragua have participated, e.g., General Assembly resolution 2131 (XX), the Declaration on the Inadmissibility of Intervention in the Domestic Affairs of States and the Protection of their Independence and Sovereignty. It is true that the United States, while it voted in favour of General Assembly resolution 2131 (XX), also declared at the time of its adoption in the First Committee that it considered the declaration in that resolution to be 'only a statement of political intention and not a formulation of law' (Official Records of the General Assembly, twentieth Session, First Committee, A/C.1/SR.1423, p. 436). However, the essentials of resolution 2131 (XX) are repeated in the Declaration approved by resolution 2625 (XXV), which set out principles which the General Assembly declared to be 'basic principles' of international law and on the adoption of which no analogous statement was made by the United States representative.

205. Notwithstanding the multiplicity of declarations by States accepting the principle of non-intervention, there remain two questions: first, what is the exact content of the principle so accepted, and secondly, is the practice sufficiently in conformity with it for this to be a rule of customary international law? As regards the first problem—that of the content of the principle of non-intervention—the Court will define only those aspects of the principle which appear to be relevant to the resolution of the dispute. In this respect it notes that, in view of the generally accepted formulations, the principle forbids all States or groups of States to intervene directly or indirectly in internal or external affairs of other States. A prohibited intervention must accordingly be one bearing on matters in which each State is permitted, by the principle of State sovereignty, to decide freely. One of these is the choice of a political, economic, social and cultural system, and the formulation of foreign policy. Intervention is wrongful when it uses methods of coercion in regard to such choices, which must remain free ones. The element of coercion which defines, and indeed forms the very essence of, prohibited intervention, is particularly obvious in the case of an intervention which uses force, either in the direct form of military action, or in the direct form of support for subversive or terrorist armed activities within another State. . . . General Assembly resolution 2625 (XXV) equates assistance of this kind with the use of force by the assisting State when the acts committed in another State 'involve a threat or use of force'. These forms of action are therefore wrongful in the light of both the principle of non-use of force, and that of non-intervention. . . .

206. However, before reaching a conclusion on the nature of prohibited intervention, the Court must be satisfied that State practice justifies it. There have been in recent years a number of instances of foreign intervention for the benefit of forces opposed to the government of another State. The Court is not here concerned with the process of decolonisation; this question is not in issue in the present case. It has to consider whether there might be indications of a practice illustrative of belief in a kind of general right for States to intervene, directly or indirectly, with or without armed force, in support of an internal opposition in another State, whose cause appeared particularly worthy by reason of the political and moral values with which it was identified. For such a general right to come into existence would involve a fundamental modification of the customary law principle of non-intervention.

209. The Court therefore finds that no such general right of intervention, in support of an opposition within another State, exists in contemporary international law. The Court concludes that acts constituting a breach of the customary principle of non-intervention will also, if they directly or indirectly involve the use of force, constitute a breach of the principle of non-use of force in international relations.

246. Having concluded that the activities of the United States in relation to the activities of the contras in Nicaragua constitute *prima facie* acts

of intervention, the Court must next consider whether they may nevertheless be justified on some legal ground. As the Court has stated, the principle of non-intervention derives from customary international law. It would certainly lose its effectiveness as a principle of law if intervention were to be justified by a mere request for assistance made by an opposition group in another State—supposing such a request to have actually been made by an opposition to the regime in Nicaragua in this instance. Indeed, it is difficult to see what would remain of the principle of non-intervention in international law if intervention, which is already allowable at the request of the government of a State, were also to be allowed at the request of the opposition. This would permit any State to intervene at any moment in the internal affairs of another State, whether at the request of the government or at the request of its opposition. Such a situation does not in the Court's view correspond to the present state of international law.

263. ... the United States Congress ... expressed the view that the Nicaraguan Government had taken 'significant steps towards establishing a totalitarian Communist dictatorship'. However the regime in Nicaragua be defined, adherence by a State to any particular doctrine does not constitute a violation of customary international law; to hold otherwise would make nonsense of the fundamental principle of State sovereignty, on which the whole of international law rests, and the freedom of choice of the political, social, economic and cultural system of a State. Consequently, Nicaragua's domestic policy options, even assuming that they correspond to the description given of them by the Congress finding, cannot justify on the legal plane the various actions of the Respondent complained of. The Court cannot contemplate the creation of a new rule opening up a right to intervention by the one State against another on the ground that the latter has opted for some particular ideology or political system.

267. The Court also notes that Nicaragua is accused by the 1985 finding of the United States Congress of violating human rights. This particular point requires to be studied independently of the question of the existence of a 'legal commitment' by Nicaragua towards the Organisation of American States to respect these rights; the absence of such a commitment would not mean that Nicaragua could with impunity violate human rights. However, where human rights are protected by international conventions, that protection takes the form of such arrangements for monitoring or ensuring respect for human rights as are provided for in the conventions themselves....

268. In any event, while the United States might form its own appraisal of the situation as to respect for human rights in Nicaragua, the use of force could not be the appropriate method to monitor or ensure such respect. With regard to the steps actually taken, the protection of human rights, a strictly humanitarian objective, cannot be compatible with the mining of ports, the destruction of oil installations, or again with the training, arming and equipping of the contras. The Court concludes that the argument derived from the preservation of human rights in Nicaragua cannot afford a legal justification for the conduct of the United States....

C. G.A. Res 46/182: Strengthening of the Coordination of Humanitarian Emergency Assistance of the United Nations, 19 December 1991, adopted without a vote.

The General Assembly

Recalling its resolution 2816 (XXVI) of 14 December 1971, and its subsequent resolutions and decisions on humanitarian assistance, including its resolution 45/100 of 14 December 1990.

Recalling also its resolution 44/236 of 22 December 1989, the annex to which contains the International Framework of Action for the International Decade for Natural Disaster Reduction.

Deeply concerned about the suffering of the victims of disasters and emergency situations, the loss in human lives, the flow of refugees, the mass displacement of people and the material destruction.

Mindful of the need to strengthen further and make more effective the collective efforts of the international community, in particular the United Nations system, in providing humanitarian assistance.

Taking note with satisfaction of the report of the Secretary-General on the review of the capacity, experience and coordination arrangements in the United Nations system for humanitarian assistance.

1. *Adopts* the text contained in the annex to the present resolution for the strengthening of the coordination of emergency humanitarian assistance of the United Nations system;

2. *Requests* the Secretary-General to report to the General Assembly at its forty-seventh session on the implementation of the present resolution.

Annex

I. Guiding Principles

1. Humanitarian assistance is of cardinal importance for the victims of natural disasters and other emergencies.

2. Humanitarian assistance must be provided in accordance with the principles of humanity, neutrality and impartiality.

3. The sovereignty, territorial integrity and national unity of States must be fully respected in accordance with the Charter of the United Nations. In this context, humanitarian assistance should be provided with the consent of the affected country and in principle on the basis of an appeal by the affected country.

4. Each State has the responsibility first and foremost to take care of the victims of natural disasters and other emergencies occurring on its territory. Hence, the affected State has the primary role in the initiation, organisation, coordination and implementation of humanitarian assistance within its territory.

5. The magnitude and duration of many emergencies may be beyond the response capacity of many affected countries. International cooperation to address emergency situations and to strengthen the response capacity of affected countries is thus of great importance. Such cooperation should be provided in accordance with international law and national laws. Intergovernmental and non-governmental organisations working impartially and with strictly humanitarian motives should continue to make a significant contribution in supplementing national efforts.

6. States whose populations are in need of humanitarian assistance are called upon to facilitate the work of these organisations in implementing humanitarian assistance, in particular the supply of food, medicines, shelter and health care, for which access to victims is essential.

7. States in proximity to emergencies are urged to participate closely with the affected countries in international efforts, with a view to facilitating, to the extent possible, the transit of humanitarian assistance.

8. Special attention should be given to disaster prevention and preparedness by the Governments concerned, as well as by the international community.

9. There is a clear relationship between emergency, rehabilitation and development. In order to ensure a smooth transition from relief to rehabilitation and development, emergency assistance should be provided in ways that will be supportive of recovery and long-term development. Thus, emergency measures should be seen as a step towards long-term development.

10. Economic growth and sustainable development are essential for prevention of and preparedness against natural disasters and other emergencies. Many emergencies reflect the underlying crisis in development facing developing countries. Humanitarian

assistance should therefore be accompanied by a renewal of commitment to economic growth and sustainable development of developing countries. In this context, adequate resources must be made available to address their development problems.

11. Contributions for humanitarian assistance should be provided in a way which is not to the detriment of resources made available for international cooperation for development.

12. The United Nations has a central and unique role to play in providing leadership and coordinating the efforts of the international community to support the affected countries. The United Nations should ensure the prompt and smooth delivery of relief assistance in full respect of the above-mentioned principles, bearing in mind also relevant General Assembly resolutions, including resolutions 2816 (XXVI) and 45/100. The United Nations system needs to be adapted and strengthened to meet present and future challenges in an effective and coherent manner. It should be provided with resources commensurate with future requirements. The inadequacy of such resources has been one of the major constraints in the effective response of the United Nations to emergencies.

D. *For a Strong and Democratic United Nations: A South Perspective on UN Reform* (South Centre, Geneva, 1996), pp. 18–21.

The Increasing Need for Humanitarian Assistance: A Dilemma for the United Nations

Since the end of the Cold War, there has been a rapid expansion of UN humanitarian assistance in response to a growing number of armed conflicts in some parts of the world, mostly within national borders. Many of these crises are acute in the extreme, involving a breakdown in the prevailing systems of organisation and society. They involve widespread death, destruction, displacement, misery and human suffering.

Humanitarian assistance, in tandem with peace-keeping, has now become one of the principal activities of the United Nations and it is having a major impact on the Organisation's priorities, budget, staffing and operations. The current method of financing these emergency operations—which by nature are difficult to foresee—involves the UN in complex financial juggling and, due to the general shortage of UN financing, adds to the UN financial crisis and cuts into its other programmes and activities.

This itself is reason enough to suggest that the implications for the UN be assessed in the context of discussions of UN reform, as also the manner in which matters regarding humanitarian assistance are handled.

Indeed, from the perspective of the UN, as a universal and democratic organisation entrusted with a global agenda, and from the perspective of the countries of the South, which at present seem to be the countries that will most likely need humanitarian assistance, a number of major questions arise. These concern the increasing politicisation and militarisation of humanitarian assistance, the frequent predominance of military and security aims over humanitarian aspects, and the fact that humanitarian assistance is provided on a selective basis according to the interests and politics of the major powers, or as a result of pressures generated by the impact of media coverage on public opinion. The furnishing of humanitarian assistance is a factor perturbing North–South relations, because of the paternalistic and interventionist manner in which this issue is dealt with, and because of the fact that it disempowers developing countries.

If humanitarian assistance continues to be furnished in the current interventionist fashion it threatens to make further substantial inroads into developing countries' political, territorial and economic sovereignty. Taken together with various incursions such as the 'conditionalities' associated with external financial assistance and international trade, this raises the spectre of a 'post-colonial colonialism'. UN General Assembly Resolution 46/182, adopted by consensus, reflects the new realities. It specifies that humanitarian assistance should be delivered with the 'consent' (formerly it was at the 'request') of a country (formerly always 'government'). A number of the legal, political and military precedents established recently in specific cases could be put to use for selective intervention in the name of humanitarian assistance but with a view also to achieving political, military, security and other strategic objectives of Northern powers.

A further reason for concern is that crises with important humanitarian implications are generally regarded as individual, isolated events, to be dealt with on an emergency basis to stem the damage. Yet, the need to extend humanitarian assistance to populations in dire trouble is evidence of the failure of local social, political and economic processes and of socio-economic development policies. In addition to reflecting the inadequacy of inappropriateness of development policies themselves, it signals the past inability or unwillingness of the international community to help create the broader conditions that would help prevent such crises and conflicts, as well as its failure to take practical steps to pre-empt or help defuse such crises.

In many, if not most, of the countries experiencing acute crises development policies have failed to provide for the basic economic needs of all sectors of society and have generated or exacerbated social cleavages. Structural adjustment policies have tended to aggravate the divisive nature of conventional development policies, and the debt burden, resulting as much from external as internal factors, has diminished the ability of many countries to maintain the necessary growth to sustain development.

When the economic bed-rock founders and people feel threatened, sectoral, ethnic and regional differences easily develop into complex conflicts, frequently with the involvement of external factors. Had governments and the international community paid proper attention to the nurturing of development in the past, much of this could have been avoided. States could have spared themselves paying for humanitarian assistance, moneys which usually cut into their overseas aid budgets and thus undermine current development efforts. Less is therefore done to create the conditions in the South to help avert future crises with severe humanitarian implications.

The frequency and seriousness of emergencies and the shortage of resources tend to rivet attention on immediate needs, thus diverting UN energies even further away from the search for integrated, longer term strategies and solutions, which should be at the core of the UN mandate.

Yet, any real humanitarian concern and sense of solidarity with populations in the South would extend beyond acting promptly to relieve the situation of persons whose immediate existence is threatened by deprivation and violence. It would also ensure that the international community, including the multilateral financial institutions, made strenuous efforts to devise economic and social policies and take appropriate action to make the right to development a reality through broad-based growth. Multilateral efforts would also be needed to create an international policy framework and external economic environment that are more conducive to the development efforts of developing countries.

Any discussion of how these policies and approaches can best be developed and of the role of the international community necessarily involves discussing one of the most important and sensitive issues regarding the respective roles of the Organisation's foremost organs, but also of the position of the UN itself vis-à-vis the major powers. Indeed, humanitarian assistance more than any other area of UN activity reflects the new trend and ambiguities regarding the respective roles of the General Assembly and the Security Council.

The UN Security Council has taken up humanitarian assistance matters in a fairly vigorous way, with policy-making and action relating to complex structural breakdowns concentrated in its hand, despite the fact that its mandate under the UN Charter is restricted to dealing with conflicts between countries and does not directly empower it to deal with matters of humanitarian assistance. The General Assembly, on the other hand, plays a marginal role and refrains from exercising its mandates in this field. It has not used its powers to analyse the implications for the UN of the new types of emergencies calling for humanitarian assistance, nor has it debated fully or decided on changes in UN policy on these matters. This situation constitutes a serious erosion of the democratic process.

As a result, the views of the overwhelming majority of UN members—often including those directly affected or concerned are not sought or taken into account. In effect, therefore, they have allowed themselves to become powerless and passive spectators.

The Security Council's assumption of exclusive responsibility for emergencies automatically gives a dominant role to those countries from the North with a permanent seat. Moreover, it reduces the range of possible approaches to dealing with the complex crises, since Security Council members and particularly its key permanent members tend to see such matters essentially in military terms and on the basis of their own strategic considerations. Experience also shows that giving the Security Council responsibility for these matters has allowed a handful of major powers with the adequate resources and capabilities to assume effective control of operations, either under the UN flag or simply by subcontracting missions to themselves.

In sum, the scope and implications of humanitarian assistance, and related operations, go far beyond the narrow perceptions commonly held. They have major implications for developing countries and they establish legal and political precedents which can easily be abused by external interests. They introduce a major new asymmetry in North–South relations, vitally affecting the future of those relations. For that reason too, they have significant implications for the United Nations.

E. Denise Plattner, 'ICRC Neutrality and Neutrality in Humanitarian Assistance', *International Review of the Red Cross* (No. 311, March–April 1996), pp. 171–73, 175–77.

It is only fairly recently that experts in international relations have started focusing on neutrality as it pertains to humanitarian assistance. Their interest is closely related to the favourable light in which all things humanitarian are regarded and, above all, to the development of coordination of humanitarian action within the United Nations system. Their thinking has sometimes strayed beyond the bounds of the actual provision of relief to cover everything intended to protect the individual from threats to his or her life, physical integrity and dignity.[38] Seen from that angle, neutrality is divested of its legal meaning and becomes a criterion for distinguishing between different forms of international action.

Even the neutrality of humanitarian law is sometimes invoked;[39] here, the implementation of humanitarian law cannot be regarded as detrimental

---

[38] For instance, 'The Mohonk Criteria for Humanitarian Assistance in Complex Emergencies' (published by the World Conference on Religion and Peace, February 1994), which mention neutrality and impartiality among their principles are guidelines covering a field of activity far wider than the mere provision of relief.

[39] See, for example, T.A. von Baarda, 'The Involvement of the Security Council in Maintaining International Humanitarian Law', *Netherlands Quarterly of Human Rights* (Vol. 12, No. 2, 1994), pp. 137–52 at p. 146.

to the military or political positions of the parties to a conflict[40] because its rules have been adopted by States as an acceptable compromise between military necessity and humanitarian imperatives. That case apart, scrutiny of other branches of international law in the light of the concept of neutrality seems inappropriate and likely to lead to misunderstandings. Impartiality, on the other hand, is a relevant principle for application of the law and, more specifically, for the administration of justice. However, it has a very precise meaning and only a remote bearing on neutrality.

In considering neutrality as applied to assistance, a distinction must be made between activities related to the distribution of relief, which are designated by the word 'assistance', and other forms of action which may be undertaken by organisations operating in the sphere of food and medical relief. As Professor Torrelli points out, the impact that the denunciation of alleged violations of the applicable rules might have on relief operations must be considered.[41] This distinction is similar to that which must be drawn between the neutrality of an entity and neutrality as applied to a given form of international action.

Abstention and impartiality as applied to the action of United Nations forces has recently come in for criticism by several writers. 'Humanitarian aid may rest upon universalist motives and principles, but in its implementation it inevitably takes on a partisan political character, long considered inappropriate for peacekeepers under the UN banner as a threat to their impartiality.'[42] 'If impartiality and neutrality are compromised, an ongoing humanitarian operation should be reconsidered, scaled down or terminated.'[43] Then again, 'in intra-State conflicts impartiality has often failed to restore peace and, in some cases such as Bosnia, may have actually prolonged suffering.'[44] 'Is the conclusion, then, that being neutral and impartial is not enough?'[45]

---

[40] J. Pictet, *Humanitarian Law and the Protection of War Victims* (A.W. Sijthoff, Leyden/ Henry Dunant Institute, Geneva, 1975), p. 44.

[41] M. Torrelli, 'From Humanitarian Assistance to Intervention on Humanitarian Grounds', *IRRC* (No. 288, May–June 1992), pp. 228–48 at p. 241.

[42] See M. Pugh, *International Peacekeeping* (Vol. 1, No. 4, Winter 1994), pp. 503–5 at p. 503; T.G. Weiss and L. Minear, *Humanitarian Aid Across Borders: Sustaining Civilians in Times of War* (Lynne Rienner Publishers, Colorado and London, 1993).

[43] See 'Military Support for Humanitarian Aid Operations: HSS—Strategic Comments', *IISS* No. 2 (International Institute for Strategic Studies, 22 February 1995).

[44] See S. Duke, 'The United Nations and Intra-state Conflict', *International Peacekeeping* (Vol. 1, No. 4, Winter 1994), pp. 375–93 at p. 389. Similarly, see R.K. Betts, 'The Delusions of Impartiality', *Foreign Affairs* (November-December 1994), pp. 20–33 at p. 20.

[45] See A. Donini, 'Beyond Neutrality: On the Compatibility of Military Intervention and Humanitarian Assistance', *The Fletcher Forum of World Affairs* (Vol. 19, No. 2, Summer/Fall 1995), pp. 31–45 at p. 44.

In theory, the objections raised in regard to discrepancies between the objectives of United Nations forces and observance of abstention and impartiality should not compromise the position of the ICRC. However, since these objections do not always draw a distinction between the military and the humanitarian applications of the concept of neutrality, they may be construed as blanket criticism of the principle, covering all the fields to which it may be applied.

As to the application of the principle of neutrality among non-governmental organisations, one such organisation has claimed that 'the devaluation of the ICRC's concepts, symbols and procedures through their adoption by other less scrupulous relief organisations has profound implications for the integrity of the ICRC itself.'[46] While we do not fully share the pessimism of that organisation, much less its severity, we do think that a clarification of terms is needed and could prove helpful to those studying certain forms of international action in the light of the principle of neutrality....

... none of the texts to which we have referred offers a definition of neutral humanitarian assistance. In our view ... such a definition can be formulated only on the basis of a number of elements drawn from current law and thinking on the matter, as outlined below.

1. *Neutral assistance is assistance whose validity is grounded in international humanitarian law.* Article 70 of Protocol I and Article 18, para 2, of Protocol II mention two conditions closely associated with neutrality, i.e., impartiality and non-discrimination. Moreover, neutrality is regarded as a principle of humanitarian law, which implies inter alia that 'humanitarian assistance is never interference in a conflict.'[47]

2. *Neutral assistance does not constitute interference in an armed conflict or an unfriendly act.* This arises from the very letter of Article 70 of Protocol I, Protocol II states more generally that none of its provisions can justify direct or indirect intervention in an armed conflict.[48]

3. *Assistance imposed by armed force as part of a unilateral action is interference and therefore does not meet the criterion of neutrality.* Two authors who have studied the right to intervene, namely O. Corten and

[46] 'Humanitarianism Unbound', *African Rights*, Discussion Paper No. 5 (November 1994), p. 25.

[47] J. Pictet, *Humanitarian Law and the Protection of War Victims* (see footnote 40 earlier [note 3]), p. 44.

[48] Article 3, para. 2; see also Article 5 of the Resolution of the Institute of International Law on 'The Protection of Human Rights and the Principle of Non-intervention in Internal Affairs of States', *Yearbook of the Institute of International Law* (1990), Vol. 63-II, p. 339 et seq.

P. Klein, contrast unarmed humanitarian operations undertaken following arbitrary refusal by a State with unilateral armed reactions which they consider prohibited by international law.[49] As an example of the former, they cite the 1987 parachuting of food and medicines by Indian aircraft into Jaffna, in the Tamil-controlled area of Sri Lanka, although they conclude that the operation remained of dubious legality because the civilian aircraft used were escorted by Mirages.[50]

4. *Only assistance of an exclusively humanitarian nature is neutral.* Unlike Article 70 of Protocol I, Article 18, para 2, of Protocol II contains no reference to interference but it does stipulate that relief actions must be 'of an exclusively humanitarian (...) nature'.

5. *Neutral assistance is confined to the purposes hallowed in the practice of the Red Cross.* In its ruling on the military and paramilitary activities in and against Nicaragua, the International Court of Justice took the view that 'if the provision of "humanitarian assistance" is to escape condemnation as an intervention in the internal affairs of [another State], not only must it be limited to the purposes hallowed in the practice of the Red Cross, namely "to prevent and alleviate human suffering", and "to protect life and health and to ensure respect for the human being"; it must also, and above all, be given without discrimination to all in need.'[51]

6. *The fact that assistance is provided even though a State or another party to the conflict has arbitrarily refused an offer of relief does not divest it of its neutral character, as long as it is not accompanied by the use of armed force.* As indicated earlier, an offer of relief which, meets the terms of Article 70 of Protocol I and Article 18, para 2, of Protocol II does not amount to interference. If the arbitrary refusal persists after fruitless negotiations, any relief action undertaken despite that refusal can, at least when undertaken by a third-party State, be regarded as a legitimate counter-measure and therefore does not constitute interference.[52]

7. *The fact that assistance provided by one or other of the components of the International Red Cross and Red Crescent Movement is protected by armed escorts does not divest it of its neutral character, provided that the parties (or authorities) controlling the territory through which the convoy must pass and to which the humanitarian assistance is to be delivered have fully*

---

[49] O. Corten and P. Klein, *Droit d'ingerence ou obligation de reaction?* (University of Brussels, 1992), p. 220.

[50] Ibid., pp. 144–45.

[51] Reports of Judgements, Advisory Opinions and Orders, 1986, p. 125, para. 243.

[52] O. Corten and P. Klein, *Droit d'ingerence ou obligation de reaction?* (see footnote 49 earlier), p. 144.

approved the principles and procedures of the armed escort, and that the purpose of the latter is to protect the relief supplies against bandits and common criminals. Such were the conclusions reached by a joint working group of the ICRC and the Federation pursuant to Resolution 5 adopted by the Council of Delegates in 1993.[53] The same working group also stressed that the use of armed escorts should be decided upon only in exceptional cases, as a last resort and after careful weighing of the advantages and disadvantages of such a measure.

8. *In order to be neutral, assistance must not be discriminatory.* Article 70 of Protocol I and Article 18, para 2, of Protocol II both use the term 'without any adverse distinction'. In the instruments of humanitarian law, the most comprehensive list of adverse distinctions is contained in Article 75 of Protocol I.

9. *In order to be neutral, assistance must be aimed at relieving the suffering of individuals, being guided solely by their needs, and to give priority to the most urgent cases of distress.*[54] That requirement is laid down in particular by the International Red Cross and Red Crescent Movement's principle of impartiality.[55]

10. In order to be neutral, assistance must not favour certain groups or individual over others.[56] Distinctions other than those contained in the list of adverse distinctions and which are not justified having regard to the needs of victims therefore do not meet the condition of impartiality.

11. Unilateral assistance is not necessarily non-neutral.[57] Subject to other factors, assistance provided to victims belong to only one party to the conflict is not contrary to the terms of humanitarian law.

V. GUIDING PRINCIPLES ON INTERNAL DISPLACEMENT

A. Office for the Coordination of Humanitarian Affairs (OCHA), *Guiding Principles on Internal Displacement*

Introduction—Scope and Purpose

1. These Guiding Principles address the specific needs of internally displaced persons worldwide. They identify rights and guarantees

[53] See 'Resolutions of the Council of Delegates', *IRRC* (No. 297, November–December 1993), pp. 477–78.

[54] Commentary on the Additional Protocols of 8 June 1977 to the Geneva Conventions of 12 August 1949, Y. Sandoz, C. Swinarski and B. Zimmermann, eds, *ICRC* (Geneva, 1986), p. 818, para. 2801.

[55] See Section 2B above (not included in this extract—editor).

[56] Commentary on the Additional Protocols (note 64), p. 818, para. 2802.

[57] Ibid., para. 2803, and p. 820, para. 2812.

relevant to the protection of persons from forced displacement and to their protection and assistance during displacement as well as during return or resettlement and reintegration.

2. For the purposes of these Principles, internally displaced persons are persons or groups of persons who have been forced or obliged to flee or to leave their homes or places of habitual residence, in particular as a result of or in order to avoid the effects of armed conflict, situations of generalised violence, violations of human rights or natural or human-made disasters, and who have not crossed an internationally recognised State border.

3. These Principles reflect and are consistent with international human rights law and international humanitarian law. They provide guidance to:

   (a) The Representative of the Secretary-General on internally displaced persons in carrying out his mandate,

   (b) States when faced with the phenomenon of internal displacement;

   (c) All other authorities, groups and persons in their relations with internally displaced persons; and

   (d) Intergovernmental and non-governmental organisations when addressing internal displacement.

4. These Guiding Principles should be disseminated and applied as widely as possible.

Section I. General Principles

Principle 1

1. Internally displaced persons shall enjoy, in full equality, the same rights and freedoms under international and domestic law as do other persons in their country. They shall not be discriminated against in the enjoyment of any rights and freedoms on the ground that they are internally displaced.

2. These Principles are without prejudice to individual criminal responsibility under international law, in particular relating to genocide, crimes against humanity and war crimes.

Principle 2

1. These Principles shall be observed by all authorities, groups and persons irrespective of their legal status and applied without any adverse distinction. The observance of these Principles shall not affect the legal status of any authorities, groups or persons involved.

2. These Principles shall not be interpreted as restricting, modifying or impairing the provisions of any international human rights or international humanitarian law instrument or rights granted to persons under domestic law. In particular, these Principles are without prejudice to the right to seek and enjoy asylum in other countries.

Principle 3

1. National authorities have the primary duty and responsibility to provide protection and humanitarian assistance to internally displaced persons within their jurisdiction.

2. Internally displaced persons have the right to request and to receive protection and humanitarian assistance from these authorities. They shall not be persecuted or punished for making such a request.

Principle 4

1. These Principles shall be applied without discrimination of any kind, such as race, colour, sex, language, religion or belief, political or other opinion, national, ethnic or social origin, legal or social status, age, disability, property, birth, or any other similar criteria.

2. Certain internally displaced persons, such as children, especially unaccompanied minors, expectant mothers, mothers with young children, female heads of household, persons with disabilities and elderly persons, shall be entitled to protection and assistance required by their condition and to treatment which takes into account their special needs.

Section II. Principles Relating to Protection from Displacement

Principle 5

All authorities and international actors shall respect and ensure respect for their obligations under international law, including human rights and humanitarian law, in all circumstances, so as to prevent and avoid conditions that might lead to displacement of persons.

Principle 6

1. Every human being shall have the right to be protected against being arbitrarily displaced from his or her home or place of habitual residence.

2. The prohibition of arbitrary displacement includes displacement:

   (a) When it is based on policies of apartheid, 'ethnic cleansing' or similar practices aimed at/or resulting in altering the ethnic, religious or racial composition of the affected population;

    (b) In situations of armed conflict, unless the security of the civilians involved or imperative military reasons so demand;

    (c) In cases of large-scale development projects, which are not justified by compelling and overriding public interests;

    (d) In cases of disasters, unless the safety and health of those affected requires their evacuation; and

    (e) When it is used as a collective punishment.

3. Displacement shall last no longer than required by the circumstances.

Principle 7

1. Prior to any decision requiring the displacement of persons, the authorities concerned shall ensure that all feasible alternatives are explored in order to avoid displacement altogether. Where no alternatives exist, all measures shall be taken to minimise displacement and its adverse effects.

2. The authorities undertaking such displacement shall ensure, to the greatest practicable extent, that proper accommodation is provided to the displaced persons, that such displacements are effected in satisfactory conditions of safety, nutrition, health and hygiene, and that members of the same family are not separated.

3. If displacement occurs in situations other than during the emergency stages of armed conflicts and disasters, the following guarantees shall be complied with:

    (a) A specific decision shall be taken by a State authority empowered by law to order such measures;

    (b) Adequate measures shall be taken to guarantee to those to be displaced full information on the reasons and procedures for their displacement and, where applicable, on compensation and relocation;

    (c) The free and informed consent of those to be displaced shall be sought;

    (d) The authorities concerned shall endeavour to involve those affected, particularly women, in the planning and management of their relocation;

    (e) Law enforcement measures, where required shall be carried out by competent legal authorities; and

    (f) The right to an effective remedy, including the review of such decisions by appropriate judicial authorities, shall be respected.

Principle 8

Displacement shall not be carried out in a manner that violates the rights to life, dignity, liberty and security of those affected.

Principle 9

States are under a particular obligation to protect against the displacement of indigenous peoples, minorities, peasants, pastoralists and other groups with a special dependency on and attachment to their lands.

Section III. Principles Relating to Protection during Displacement

Principle 10

1. Every human being has the inherent right to life which shall be protected by law. No one shall be arbitrarily deprived of his or her life. Internally displaced persons shall be protected in particular against:

   (*a*) Genocide;

   (*b*) Murder;

   (*c*) Summary or arbitrary executions; and

   (*d*) Enforced disappearances, including abduction or unacknowledged detention, threatening or resulting in death.

   Threats and incitement to commit any of the foregoing acts shall be prohibited.

2. Attacks or other acts of violence against internally displaced persons who do not or no longer participate in hostilities are prohibited in all circumstances. Internally displaced persons shall be protected, in particular, against:

   (*a*) Direct or indiscriminate attacks or other acts of violence, including the creation of areas wherein attacks on civilians are permitted;

   (*b*) Starvation as a method of combat;

   (*c*) Their use to shield military objectives from attack or to shield, favour or impede military operations;

   (*d*) Attacks against their camps or settlements; and

   (*e*) The use of anti-personnel landmines.

Principle 11

1. Every human being has the right to dignity and physical, mental and moral integrity.

2. Internally displaced persons, whether or not their liberty has been restricted, shall be protected in particular against:

(a) Rape, mutilation, torture, cruel, inhuman or degrading treatment or punishment, and other outrages upon personal dignity, such as acts of gender-specific violence, forced prostitution and any form of indecent assault;

(b) Slavery or any contemporary form of slavery, such as sale into marriage, sexual exploitation, or forced labour of children; and

(c) Acts of violence intended to spread terror among internally displaced persons.

Threats and incitement to commit any of the foregoing acts shall be prohibited.

Principle 12

1. Every human being has the right to liberty and security of person. No one shall be subjected to arbitrary arrest or detention.

2. To give effect to this right for internally displaced persons, they shall not be interned in or confined to a camp. If in exceptional circumstances such internment or confinement is absolutely necessary, it shall not last longer than required by the circumstances.

3. Internally displaced persons shall be protected from discriminatory arrest and detention as a result of their displacement.

In no case shall internally displaced persons be taken hostage.

Principle 13

1. In no circumstances shall displaced children be recruited nor be required or permitted to take part in hostilities.

2. Internally displaced persons shall be protected against discriminatory practices of recruitment into any armed forces or groups as a result of their displacement. In particular any cruel, inhuman or degrading practices that compel compliance or punish non-compliance with recruitment are prohibited in all circumstances.

Principle 14

1. Every internally displaced person has the right to liberty of movement and freedom to choose his or her residence.

2. In particular, internally displaced persons have the right to move freely in and out of camps or other settlements.

Principle 15

Internally displaced persons have:

(a) The right to seek safety in another part of the country;

(b) The right to leave their country;

(c) The right to seek asylum in another country; and

(d) The right to be protected against forcible return to or resettlement in any place where their life, safety, liberty and/or health would be at risk.

Principle 16

1. All internally displaced persons have the right to know the fate and whereabouts of missing relatives.

2. The authorities concerned shall endeavour to establish the fate and whereabouts of internally displaced persons reported missing, and cooperate with relevant international organisations engaged in this task. They shall inform the next of kin on the progress of the investigation and notify them of any result.

3. The authorities concerned shall endeavour to collect and identify the mortal remains of those deceased, prevent their despoliation or mutilation, and facilitate the return of those remains to the next of kin or dispose of them respectfully.

4. Grave sites of internally displaced persons should be protected and respected in all circumstances. Internally displaced persons should have the right of access to the grave sites of their deceased relatives.

Principle 17

1. Every human being has the right to respect of his or her family life.

2. To give effect to this right for internally displaced persons, family members who wish to remain together shall be allowed to do so.

3. Families which are separated by displacement should be reunited as quickly as possible. All appropriate steps shall be taken to expedite the reunion of such families, particularly when children are involved. The responsible authorities shall facilitate inquiries made by family members and encourage and cooperate with the work of humanitarian organisations engaged in the task of family reunification.

4. Members of internally displaced families whose personal liberty has been restricted by internment or confinement in camps shall have the right to remain together.

Principle 18

1. All internally displaced persons have the right to an adequate standard of living.

2. At the minimum, regardless of the circumstances, and without discrimination, competent authorities shall provide internally displaced persons with and ensure safe access to:

   (a) Essential food and potable water;

   (b) Basic shelter and housing;

   (c) Appropriate clothing; and

   (d) Essential medical services and sanitation.

3. Special efforts should be made to ensure the full participation of women in the planning and distribution of these basic supplies.

Principle 19

1. All wounded and sick internally displaced persons as well as those with disabilities shall receive to the fullest extent practicable and with the least possible delay, the medical care and attention they require, without distinction on any grounds other than medical ones. When necessary, internally displaced persons shall have access to psychological and social services.

2. Special attention should be paid to the health needs of women, including access to female health care providers and services, such as reproductive health care, as well as appropriate counselling for victims of sexual and other abuses.

3. Special attention should also be given to the prevention of contagious and infectious diseases, including AIDS, among internally displaced persons.

Principle 20

1. Every human being has the right to recognition everywhere as a person before the law.

2. To give effect to this right for internally displaced persons, the authorities concerned shall issue to them all documents necessary for the enjoyment and exercise of their legal rights, such as passports, personal identification documents, birth certificates and marriage certificates. In particular, the authorities shall facilitate the issuance of new documents or the replacement of documents lost in the course of displacement, without imposing unreasonable conditions, such as requiring the return to one's area of habitual residence in order to obtain these or other required documents.

3. Women and men shall have equal rights to obtain such necessary documents and shall have the right to have such documentation issued in their own names.

Principle 21

1. No one shall be arbitrarily deprived of property and possessions.

2. The property and possessions of internally displaced persons shall in all circumstances be protected, in particular, against the following acts:

   (a) Pillage;

   (b) Direct or indiscriminate attacks or other acts of violence;

   (c) Being used to shield military operations or objectives;

   (d) Being made the object of reprisal; and

   (e) Being destroyed or appropriated as a form of collective punishment.

3. Property and possessions left behind by internally displaced persons should be protected against destruction and arbitrary and illegal appropriation, occupation or use.

Principle 22

1. Internally displaced persons, whether or not they are living in camps, shall not be discriminated against as a result of their displacement in the enjoyment of the following rights;

   (a) The rights to freedom of thought, conscience, religion or belief, opinion and expression;

   (b) The right to seek freely opportunities for employment and to participate in economic activities;

   (c) The right to associate freely and participate equally in community affairs;

   (d) The right to vote and to participate in governmental and public affairs, including the right to have access to the means necessary to exercise this right; and

   (e) The right to communicate in a language they understand.

Principle 23

1. Every human being has the right to education.

2. To give effect to this right for internally displaced persons, the authorities concerned shall ensure that such persons, in particular displaced children, receive education which shall be free and compulsory at the primary level. Education should respect their cultural identity, language and religion.

3. Special efforts should be made to ensure the full and equal participation of women and girls in educational programmes.

4. Education and training facilities shall be made available to internally displaced persons, in particular adolescents and women, whether or not living in camps, as soon as conditions permit.

Section IV: *Principles Relating to Humanitarian Assistance*

Principle 24

1. All humanitarian assistance shall be carried out in accordance with the principles of humanity and impartiality and without discrimination.

2. Humanitarian assistance to internally displaced persons shall not be diverted, in particular for political or military reasons.

Principle 25

1. The primary duty and responsibility for providing humanitarian assistance to internally displaced persons lies with national authorities.

2. International humanitarian organisations and other appropriate actors have the right to offer their services in support of the internally displaced. Such an offer shall not be regarded as an unfriendly act or an interference in a State's internal affairs and shall be considered in good faith. Consent thereto shall not be arbitrarily withheld, particularly when authorities concerned are unable or unwilling to provide the required humanitarian assistance.

3. All authorities concerned shall grant and facilitate the free passage of humanitarian assistance and grant persons engaged in the provision of such assistance rapid and unimpeded access to the internally displaced.

Principle 26

Persons engaged in humanitarian assistance, their transport and supplies shall be respected and protected. They shall not be the object of attack or other acts of violence.

Principle 27

1. International humanitarian organisations and other appropriate actors when providing assistance should give due regard to the protection needs and human rights of internally displaced persons and take appropriate measures in this regard. In so doing, these organisations and actors should respect relevant international standards and codes of conduct.

2. The preceding paragraph is without prejudice to the protection responsibilities of international organisations mandated for this purpose, whose services may be offered or requested by States.

Section V. Principles Relating to Return, Resettlement and Reintegration

Principle 28

1. Competent authorities have the primary duty and responsibility to establish conditions, as well as provide the means, which allow internally displaced persons to return voluntarily, in safety and with dignity, to their homes or places of habitual residence, or to resettle voluntarily in another part of the country. Such authorities shall endeavour to facilitate the reintegration of returned or resettled internally displaced persons.

2. Special efforts should be made to ensure the full participation of internally displaced persons in the planning and management of their return or resettlement and reintegration.

Principle 29

1. Internally displaced persons who have returned to their homes or places of habitual residence or who have resettled in another part of the country shall not be discriminated against as a result of their having been displaced. They shall have the right to participate fully and equally in public affairs at all levels and have equal access to public services.

2. Competent authorities have the duty and responsibility to assist returned and/or resettled internally displaced persons to recover, to the extent possible, their property and possessions which they left behind or were dispossessed of upon their displacement. When recovery of such property and possessions is not possible, competent authorities shall provide or assist these persons in obtaining appropriate compensation or another form of just reparation.

Principle 30

All authorities concerned shall grant and facilitate for international humanitarian organisations and other appropriate actors, in the exercise of their respective mandates, rapid and unimpeded access to internally displaced persons to assist in their return or resettlement and reintegration.

VI. ROLE OF UNHCR

A. UNHCR, Executive Committee, 45th Session, EC/SCP/87, 17 August 1994, 'Protection Aspects of UNHCR Activities on Behalf of Internally Displaced Persons', pp. 176–91.

Introduction

1. The Office of the United Nations High Commissioner for Refugees has frequently been called upon to address the needs of persons who had

been forced to flee their homes for the same reasons as refugees, but who have not left their own countries and are therefore not considered 'refugees' under the UNHCR Statute (General Assembly res./428 (v)) or under relevant international or regional instruments. In the past, and still to a large extent today, UNHCR's involvement with the internally displaced has often been in the context of the voluntary repatriation of refugees, where return movements and rehabilitation and reintegration programmes have included both returning refugees and displaced persons in circumstances where it was neither reasonable nor feasible to treat the two categories differently. Thus, for example, in 1972 the Economic and Social Council (ECOSOC), in the context of the voluntary repatriation of refugees to southern Sudan, called upon the High Commissioner, as well as other agencies and organisations, to extend rehabilitation measures both to refugees returning from abroad and to 'persons displaced within the country'.

2. In other cases, UNHCR activities in countries of asylum on behalf of refugees from neighbouring countries also include people displaced in their own country who are victims of the same regional conflict. This was the case in Indo-China from the 1950s through 1975, as [was] in Croatia.... Frequently returnees, refugees and internally displaced populations are present together in the same region, and a growing number of UNHCR operations have encompassed all three categories, together with local residents who have not left their homes, often as part of comprehensive regional schemes aiming both to solve refugee problems and to address the causes of forced displacement. Finally, at times the Office has been asked, on the basis of its humanitarian expertise, to undertake activities on behalf of persons displaced within their own country in certain situations which involve neither refugees nor returnees, and sometimes with little or no prospect of flight across national boundaries. Typically these cases have involved the de facto division of a country along a cease-fire line, which placed persons who had been forcibly displaced across that line in a situation very similar to that of refugees.

3. The importance of addressing the problems of the internally displaced has become increasingly apparent in the light of UNHCR's focus on the prevention and solution of refugee problems. To the extent that refugee flows and internal displacement have the same causes, it makes little sense to deal only with the trans-frontier aspects of coerced population moments, either in responding to immediate humanitarian needs or in seeking solutions. From the vantage point of UNHCR, as the international agency responsible for refugees, it is clearly preferable, where possible, to obviate the need for people to leave their country—and thus to become refugees—in order to find safety and to obtain vital humanitarian assistance. For the international community as a whole, there are clear advantages in adopting a global approach to situations of coerced displacement, actual or potential. The measures necessary to solve a refugee problem through voluntary repatriation are the same as those

required to relieve the plight of the internally displaced and of those at risk of displacement; and preventing internal displacement by removing the factors that force people to flee their homes will also remove the immediate cause of refugee flows.

4. By recognising that the problems of the internally displaced and of refugees are manifestations of the same phenomenon of coerced displacement, UNHCR has increasingly considered activities on behalf of the internally displaced to be indispensable components of an overall strategy of prevention and solutions. In Sri Lanka, Tajikistan, Azerbaijan, Georgia, the countries of the former Yugoslavia, the Horn and Central Africa, Liberia, Mozambique, and Central America, to cite some current examples of UNHCR involvement with the internally displaced, the link between internal and external displacement is obvious and the need to address the internal situation in order to satisfactorily resolve the external refugee problem seems equally clear.

II. Issues arising out of UNHCR's involvement with IDPs

8. The present note will ... briefly review certain issues arising in connection with UNHCR's activities in this field.... These issues are:

(a) UNHCR's competence (or mandate) with respect to the internally displaced;

(b) the criteria for UNHCR involvement

(c) the legal norms applicable with respect to the persons displaced or at risk of displacement within their own country;

(d) the nature and content of UNHCR's involvement;

(e) the complementary roles of other international organisations.

A. To what extent, and under what conditions, does the High Commissioner have a mandate to undertake activities on behalf of persons displaced within their own country?

9. Although it remains correct to say that the basic mandate of the High Commissioner under the Statute of the Office (General Assembly res. 428 (v)) does not include any general competence for persons displaced within their own country, the effect of various General Assembly resolutions has been to confer upon UNHCR a selective and limited mandate to undertake humanitarian assistance and protection activities on behalf of the displaced, provided certain specific conditions are met....

11. ... [The] two mandatory requirements for UNHCR action in favour of the internally displaced [are]: a specific request from the Secretary-General or a competent principal organ of the United Nations (i.e., the General Assembly, the Security Council or ECOSOC), and the

consent of the concerned State.... Since UNHCR's 'particular expertise' lies in providing international protection and humanitarian assistance to refugees and seeking solutions to refugee problems ... the internally displaced who are of potential concern to the Office are those in a refugee-like situation, i.e., persons fleeing persecution, armed conflict or civil strife, rather than victims of physical disasters, such as earthquakes, floods or nuclear power-plant expositions. Persons displaced for the latter reasons may well require humanitarian assistance from the international community, but their situation does not normally require UNHCR's 'particular expertise'.

B. In which situations is it appropriate for UNHCR to undertake activities on behalf of the internally displaced?

12. The High Commissioner's limited mandate to undertake activities on behalf of the internally displaced is both conditional and, in principle, discretionary ... the Executive Committee has called for due regard to be paid to the availability of sufficient resources ... which must be understood to include not only funds but also institutional capacity and the possibility of deploying sufficient qualified staff....

14. ... [Further] there are certain preconditions that UNHCR considers essential for its involvement. These are:

(a) UNHCR's involvement must not in any way detract from the possibility to seek and to obtain asylum;

(b) UNHCR must have full and unhindered access to the affected population;

(c) adequate provision must be made for the security of staff of UNHCR and its operating partners and for acceptable operating conditions; and

(d) UNHCR's involvement should have the consent of all concerned parties and enjoy the support of the international community.

15. ... [The] UNHCR considers that it should give favourable consideration to assuming primary responsibility for international action on behalf of the internally displaced in situations where there is a direct link with UNHCR's activities under its basic mandate to protect refugees and to seek solutions to refugee problems. Such situations include those where:

(a) internally displaced populations are present in or returning to the same areas as repatriating refugees, or areas to which refugees are expected to return;

(b) refugees and displaced persons in similar circumstances are present and in need of humanitarian assistance and/or protection in the same area of a country of asylum;

(c) the same causes have produced both internal displacement and refugee flows and there are operational or humanitarian advantages in addressing the problems within a single operation, including for example a 'cross-border' component; or

(d) there is a potential for cross-border movement, and the provision of humanitarian assistance and/or protection to internally displaced persons may enable them to remain in safety in their own country.

C. What legal norms are applicable for the protection of persons forcibly displaced or at risk of being displaced within their own country?

19. Since they remain within their own country, the internally displaced cannot benefit from the protection accorded to refugees in international law. . . .

23. The absence of a single body of principles and norms specifically for the protection of the internally displaced, equivalent to internal refugee law, has [. . .] been mentioned as a·deficiency in the present legal situation. It should be noted, however, that refugees have been granted a particular status because they are foreigners who do not enjoy the protection of any Government. Internally displaced persons, as nationals within their own country, require above all respect for and enforcement by the authorities of their rights as full citizens, including the right to liberty of movement and freedom of residence, whether in the place from which they were displaced or elsewhere. A specific legal status different from their fellow citizens would perhaps not be to their advantage. On the other hand, codification of legal protections against displacement as well as of remedies and protections for persons who have suffered displacement, including the right if they so wished to return to their homes, could be of value. . . .

24. While the further development of international legal norms against forcible displacement and for the protection of the displaced, building on the protection already provided by international human rights and humanitarian law, would be most welcome, it must be recognised that the most serious problems with respect to the protection of persons who are either displaced or threatened with displacement in their own country result not from an absence or deficiency of legal norms but from the failure of the parties concerned to respect and to enforce those norms, and, even more fundamentally, from the failure of warring parties, and of the international community as a whole, to achieve a peaceful resolution of the murderous conflicts that are the major cause of forced displacement. Any effective legal system must include both norms of conduct and some mechanism to ensure their observance or enforcement. The existing international mechanisms for ensuring observance of human rights principles and of humanitarian law are clearly not fully adequate to the task.

D. The content of UNHCR's activities on behalf of internally displaced persons

28. With regard to the specific protection aspects of UNHCR's activities, it is to be noted that protection and solutions are at the core of UNHCR's mandate, and displacement together with the need for protection provide the basis and rationale for UNHCR's competence for refugees. When UNHCR is called upon to assume responsibility for the internally displaced on the basis of its particular expertise, its activities must be consistent with its basic mandate for protection and solutions. While the provision of humanitarian assistance is normally a major component of UNHCR programmes for the internally displaced, these also include, wherever necessary and feasible, protection activities aimed at enhancing their safety and ensure respect for the human rights of the persons concerned.

29. ... The specifically protection-related tasks that UNHCR staff have recently been called upon to perform in various situations include monitoring, at the request of the Governments concerned, the treatment of members of threatened minority (or majority) groups, reporting violations of fundamental rights, and intervening with the relevant authorities to request protective action, as well as investigation and prosecution of specific cases of abuse; assistance and de facto protection to displaced persons in temporary relief centres; promoting tracing and family reunion of unaccompanied children; and assisting Governments to provide personal documentation. In circumstances of armed conflict and/or massive violations of human rights, UNHCR activities have involved assisting the safe passage of civilians through front lines; facilitating, in acute life-threatening situations, in cooperation with the International Committee of the Red Cross (ICRC), the organised evacuation of civilians; intervening with local authorities to prevent the involuntary return of the internally displaced to areas of danger; facilitating genuine freedom of movement, including the possibility for persons in danger to seek asylum; and promoting the right of the internally displaced to return—or not to return—voluntarily to their homes. Elsewhere ... UNHCR has participated in mediation and reconciliation efforts between returning displaced persons and local residents. The Office has also participated in negotiating, been a party to, and/or taken part in ensuring compliance with repatriation agreements involving internally displaced persons as well as refugees.

E. Interagency cooperation in activities on behalf of internally displaced persons

32. In virtually all situations where UNHCR is involved with the internally displaced, the Office works closely with other United Nations, intergovernmental and non-governmental organisations and agencies, often as part of comprehensive multisectoral programmes. ...

34. With respect to the appropriate apportionment of responsibilities for the internally displaced as between UNHCR and other international organisations, it has been noted that the High Commissioner's involvement is subject to certain conditions and criteria, including the recommendation that there be a link with the protection or solution of refugee problems and the requirement that adequate resources be available....

35. When there is a predominant refugee element, as when the internally displaced are mixed with large numbers of refugees or returnees for whom UNHCR has a mandatory responsibility, it is natural for UNHCR to assume responsibility also for the displaced. Thus when large numbers of refugees are going back to a particular area which will also receive large numbers of displaced returning, UNHCR has often been requested by the Secretary-General to assume the lead role. In situations where there are few refugees or returnees, but where activities on behalf of the displaced could contribute to the prevention of a refugee situation by relieving their plight in their own country, UNHCR involvement will depend, besides the availability of resources, upon the readiness and capacity of other agencies to meet the need. In situations of armed conflict which include a strong link to refugee problems, such as actual or potential cross-border movements, UNHCR will have to reach agreement with ICRC on the most effective way to share the task of assisting and protecting the internally displaced. Despite the potential for overlap, however, the magnitude of humanitarian tasks in conflict areas is such that regular consultation and coordination between UNHCR and ICRC result in complementary action and fruitful collaboration. It should be noted that ICRC and UNHCR are the only international organisations to combine humanitarian assistance and protection mandates. When neither is present, the protection needs of the internally displaced may be addressed by associating international or regional human rights organisations in a comprehensive programme with humanitarian assistance agencies.

VII. SAFETY ZONES

A. B.S. Chimni, 'The Incarceration of Victims: Deconstructing Safety Zones', in N. Al-Nauimi and R. Meese, eds, *International Legal Issues Arising under the United Nations Decade of International Law* (Kluwer Law International, The Hague, 1995), pp. 823–54.

Introduction

The past two decades have seen the reassertion of space in critical social theory. Henry Lefebvre, Michel Foucault and John Berger have, each in his own way, emphasised that it is 'space more than time that hides things from us, that the demystification of spatiality and its veiled instrumentality of power is the key to making practical, political, and theoretical sense of the contemporary era'.[58] Further, along with Nicos Poulantzas, Anthony Giddens and David Harvey they have revealed that 'spatial fragmentation as well as the appearance of spatial coherence and homogeneity are social products and often integral part of the instrumentality of political power.'[59] In other words, spatial practices are socially constructed and are implicated in power. The absence of innocent space can only be grasped if we understand that spatial practices cannot be assigned meaning independently of the material or social processes which produce them. New spatial categories, like the concept of 'safety zone', must therefore necessarily be deconstructed in the matrix of changing configurations of material and social processes. The growing concern with 'internal asylum' (for example, through establishing safety zones for the internally displaced) as opposed to 'external asylum' (refugee status) has, in other words, to be grounded in contemporary realities.

Refugees in the post Cold War era, particularly from the developing world, no longer possess any ideological or strategic value. In the face of the phenomenon of disintegrating 'national' space, the growing number of refugees, the synchronised recession and accompanying xenophobia, it has metamorphosed the refugee policy of the developed countries. According to Bill Frelick of the United States Committee for Refugees (USCR), 'a new paradigm is emerging by which refugee flows are prevented before asylum seekers cross an international border, the definitional trip-wire that heretofore marked the threshold step in the world's response to refugees.'[60] It is concerned with the need to contain the problem within states. Thus the idea to create distinct spaces in which displaced people can be accommodated.

The paradigm shift has taken place in two separate but overlapping stages which have quickly succeeded, and therefore continue to complement, each other. In the first phase the language of protection was replaced by the reality of rejection. A whole host of restrictive laws and practices were/are being put in place: visa restrictions, carrier sanctions, restrictive interpretations of the 1951 UN definition, etc. The ensuing contradiction which stared states in the face, and which concerned institutions could not but bring to their notice, necessitated the second phase of couching the reality of rejection in a language which conceals the discourse of power in humanitarian concepts and phrases. It has spawned a

---

[58] Edward W. Soja, *Post Modern Geographies: The Reassertion of Space in Critical Social Theory* (Verso, London, 1989), p. 61.

[59] Ibid., p. 126.

[60] Bill Frelick, 'Preventing Refugee Flows: Protection or Peril?' *World Refugee Survey* (1993), pp. 5–13 at p. 5.

new vocabulary: the right to remain, on-site assistance, on-site inspection, relief corridors, and of course 'safety zone'. The shift in the terms of discourse may be exemplified with reference to the emphasis which is now being placed on the 'right to remain'.

Till only a few years back progressive refugee lawyers and activists recommended that the definition of a refugee contained in the 1951 UN Convention be brought in accord with the broader definition contained in the 1969 OAU Convention so that more people could be given refuge in the Western world.[61] Today, the High Commissioner *for Refugees* is talking about the right to remain. That is to say, even the 1951 definition is being viewed as overly burdensome in the post Cold War era. It is not the argument here that the High Commissioner is no longer concerned with asylum. Indeed, she almost always states that the right to remain is not to be at the expense of the right to seek asylum. However, it is not sufficiently appreciated that for the High Commissioner *for Refugees* to stress the right to remain is to offer space and justification for the dilution of the institution of asylum. States will tend to rationalise measures to stop the outflow of refugees on the pretext that they are necessary to defend the right of people to exercise their right to remain. In other words, states will ensure that people do not flee. That they remain at any cost. The concept of a 'safety zone' understood amidst this policy matrix has been conceived and executed in Northern Iraq and former Yugoslavia. However, a review of these two cases ... needs to be preceded by some preliminary reflections on the concept of a safety zone. The aim will be to identify some relevant issues which invite consideration in the context of establishing a 'safety zone'. The case studies will draw the real world into the discussion.

Clarifying the Concept

Inappropriate Parallels

A 'safety zone' may, in formal terms, be defined as a clearly demarcated space in which individuals fleeing danger can seek safety within their own country. Parallels are drawn with the establishment of hospital and safety zones, as well as neutralised zones, under the Fourth Geneva Convention relative to the Protection of Civilian Persons in Time of War and the 1977 Additional Protocol I. Such zones are created with the consent of the parties concerned.

The aim of creating hospital and safety zones is to establish areas removed from the effects of the armed conflict for the safety of wounded,

[61] See, for example, Guy S. Goodwin-Gill, 'Refugees and Human Rights: Challenge for the 1990s', *International Journal of Refugee Law* (Special Issue, September 1990), pp. 29–38 at pp. 34–35.

sick and aged persons, children under the age of 15, expectant mothers and mothers of children under the age of seven.[62] The purpose of setting up a neutralised zone is also intended to afford shelter to the wounded and sick, whether combatant or non-combatant and to civilians who do not take part in the hostilities and who perform no military work whilst in the zone. The agreement creating the neutralised zone is required to state its location, the duration of its status, and the arrangements made for supervision and provisioning.[63]

However, the parallels are misleading in several respects. First, the purposes for which a 'safety zone' and zones established under the Geneva Conventions may be created are different, albeit there is a moment of identity. In theory a 'safety zone' can serve three purposes: first, it can, by insulating this space from unsafe space(s) offer protection to those present in it; second, it can facilitate orderly movement of those wishing to seek asylum abroad; and third, it can help reduce the outflow of refugees, whether by eliminating the need for flight or otherwise. Hospital and neutralised zones were conceived to serve the first purpose, albeit they can also be made to serve the latter two purposes. That this was not the intention of the international community is testified to by the creation of a parallel refugee regime in 1951 with its emphasis on exile; the creation of separate regimes to deal with different circumstances is in other words significant.

Second, the Geneva Convention zones offer protection to those displaced by an armed conflict. That too essentially to victims of an international armed conflict. In other words, they are created to deal with only one category of internally displaced. On the other hand, 'safety zones' may be established to meet the concerns of those internally displaced due to a whole host of causes including gross human rights violations, civil conflicts, and natural or man made disasters. However, the appropriateness of such zones for other categories of internally displaced cannot be presumed. For instance, any notion that an asylum seeker or groups thereof, fleeing persecution in the country of origin should be required to delay the asylum request and to remain in the country where they had genuine fear of persecution runs against both refugee and human rights law.

Third, while neutralised zones, etc. can only be created with the consent of the parties concerned, a 'safety zone' has been established through multilateral action. Indeed, multilateral action is the likely mode through which such zones are going to be established. An observation of the UN Secretary-General in his recent report on the work of the Organisation is

---

[62] Hilaire McCoubrey, *International Humanitarian Law* (Dartmouth, Aldershot, 1990), p. 125.

[63] Ibid. See Article 15 of the Fourth Geneva Convention, 1949 as expanded by Article 60 of its Protocol I.

a pointer in this direction: 'Humanitarian emergencies, by causing the mass exodus of people, may constitute threats to international peace and security, or aggravate existing threats;...'[64] And for the envisaged multi-lateral action the consent of the state in whose territory such a zone is created may not be deemed a precondition. Given the present constitution of international relations and organisations this is problematic.

Still on consent, the Geneva Convention zones cannot be created through the unilateral intervention of an outside state(s). On the other hand, a 'safety zone' may be created through what is termed humanitarian intervention. While the legal basis of such intervention is tenuous and may raise a number of practical problems (for example, the UNHCR does not, or at least did not, like it)[65] the possibility cannot be ruled out in an unequal world. What is more, if the concept of a 'safety zone' is given respectability the legality of humanitarian intervention may acquire some legitimacy.

Fourth, since a 'safety zone' may be, as it has been, created without the consent of the concerned state it raises the problem of ensuring the security and effectiveness of such zones in the face of the possibility of non-cooperation of the state or parties concerned.

To summarise, two points are being made. First, it is not correct to compare the concept of a 'safety zone' with similar concepts in the Geneva Conventions. Second, the appropriateness and feasibility of creating a safety zone, and its meaning in practice, will depend upon a number of factors. These—some of which I have indicated above—include: who has the authority to create a safety zone, the length of time for which it is established, the parties which will guarantee its safe character, the category of people to be protected, their rights in this zone, the agencies which will be involved in the relief and assistance effort, and finally which of the stated purposes represents the predominant motive for creating the safety zone. Even at the cost of repetition some of these factors may be considered in some detail.

Establishing the Safety Zone

The most sensitive issue with regard to the creation of a safety zone is whether it can be created without the consent of the country of origin. In

---

[64] Boutros Boutros Ghali, *Report on the Work of the Organisation from the Forty-seventh to the Forty-eighth Session of the General Assembly* (United Nations, New York, September 1993), p. 165.

[65] See *Report of the UNHCR Working Group on International Protection* (Geneva, July 1992). The Working Group distinguished between 'humanitarian intervention in its classical sense from the collective action creating a Safety Zone which may have been sanctioned by the United Nations in line with its responsibilities for the maintenance of international peace and security. It clarified that as a part of the UN system the UNHCR cannot refuse to provide humanitarian assistance in such situations, if it is requested to do so either by the General Assembly or the Security Council.'

general it is conceded that a safety zone should be established with the consent of the country of origin vide the principles of sovereignty and non-intervention into the internal affairs of states. In fact, the legal and political basis to explain the absence to date of a regime on behalf of internally displaced persons is that states are responsible for citizens inside their territory, and the state system generally precludes all forms of intervention.[66] In this context it may be mentioned that in 1992, in the Commission of Human Rights, India, Bangladesh and a number of other developing countries expressed serious reservations with respect to the proposal that an independent expert study human rights issues related to the internally displaced.[67] To put it differently, it is no mere accident that the refugee regime posits alienage as an essential criteria for seeking protection; only when an individual crosses a border can she seek international protection and claim refugee status.

However, where the interests of the powerful states are involved the requirement of consent may be seen as an unnecessary constraint on action and its waiver justified with reference to the need for urgent humanitarian action. This is no longer an abstract and exaggerated fear in the post Cold War era. It is not at all surprising, for example, that safety zones were established for Kurds in Northern Iraq without the consent of the concerned state. On the other hand, where consent is secured it may be at the expense of the individual right to seek asylum. This, as I argue below, is what has happened in the instance of Bosnia and Herzegovina. Furthermore, as Bosnia exemplifies, force will be committed to defend such zones only when they serve non-humanitarian interests. In other words, the concept of a 'safety zone' may often represent a single edged sword.

The question however remains whether the UN Security Council, the organ of the United Nations which it is contended has such power, has the general authority to create a safety zone without the consent of the state concerned? Insofar as the developing countries are concerned, the answer to the question can be inferred from the fact that China and India abstained from, and Cuba, Yemen, and Zimbabwe voted against Security Council Resolution 688 concerning the Iraqi civilian population, which was the basis on which safety zones were later established in Iraq. As the Indian delegate stressed, the Security Council should have concentrated on the aspect of peace and security in contrast to concentrating 'on the factors that have created the present situation'.[68] It may be noted that this

[66] Charles P. Keely, 'Filling a Critical Gap in the Refugee Protection Regime: The Internally Displaced', *World Refugee Survey 1991*, pp. 22–27 at p. 24.

[67] Guy S. Goodwin-Gill, 'UNHCR and International Protection: New Directions', *World Refugee Survey 1993*, pp. 14–20 at p. 17.

[68] S.C. Doc. S/PV.2982, 5 April 1991, Provisional Verbal Record of the 2892nd Meeting, p. 63.

reaction was against a resolution which recalled Article 2 para (7) of the Charter, did not suggest in any way the creation of safety zones but talked of 'immediate access by international humanitarian organisations to all those in need of assistance in all parts of Iraq...'; it was later unjustifiedly interpreted to allow the establishment of safety zones.[69]

In the *Nicaragua* case the World Court observed that 'there can be no doubt that the provision of strictly humanitarian aid to persons or forces in another country, whatever their policy objectives, cannot be regarded as unlawful intervention, or as in any other way contrary to international law.'[70] It however added that such assistance, if it were not to tantamount to intervention, should be given without discrimination of any kind and in accordance with the purposes hallowed in the practice of the Red Cross.[71] It did not talk of the consent of the state concerned. However, on 20 December 1991, the General Assembly adopted Resolution 46/182 which elaborates the principles which must be applied in the case of humanitarian assistance. Para (3) of the principles states:

> The sovereignty, territorial integrity and national unity of States must be fully respected in accordance with the Charter of the United Nations. In this context, humanitarian assistance should be provided with the consent of the affected country and in principle on the basis of an appeal by the affected country.

The Security Council has, in any case, to abide by Article 2 para (7) which only excepts 'the application of enforcement measures under Chapter VII' from the domestic jurisdiction proscription. Herein, it is often overlooked that the exception extends not to any decision of the Security Council but only to 'application of enforcement measures'. As Goodrich and Hambro point out:

> the Council's actions under Article 41 and 42 are exempt from the 'domestic jurisdiction' clause, but this exception *does not extend to all actions* by the Council under Chapter VII.[72]

In other words, the Security Council appears to have exceeded its authority in passing Resolution 688, and without doubt in establishing

[69] 'In the case of Kurds, legislative history reveals no Security Council intent to authorise the use of force in Iraq. Responding to public pressure and a Senate resolution, President Bush interpreted Resolution 688 as allowing for the use of force to protect Kurds.' Mark R. Hutchinson, 'Restoring Hope: UN Security Council Resolutions for Somalia and an Expanded Doctrine of Humanitarian Intervention', *Harvard International Law Journal* (Vol. 34, 1993), pp. 624–40 at p. 633.

[70] ICJ Rep. (1986), p. 124.

[71] Ibid., p. 125.

[72] Leland Goodrich, Eduard Hambro and Ann Patricia Simons, *Charter of the United Nations: Commentary and Documents* (New York, 1969), third revised edition, p. 292.

and organising the coercive defense of safety zones in Iraq without its consent.[73] Finally, it may be pointed out that Article 60 of the UN Charter gives the General Assembly, and, under its authority, the Economic and Social Council the exclusive competence to act with regard to all matters relating to human rights and their violation. Be it as it may, the phrase 'international peace' occurring in Article 24 para (1) which describes the functions of the Security Council in essentially security terms cannot be interpreted to permit 'humanitarian' intervention.

The form in which the use of force for the protection of humanitarian assistance is being recommended is also unacceptable. This led to China, India and Zimbabwe abstaining on Security Council Resolutions 770 and 776 adopted in September 1992 when it, acting explicitly under Chapter VII of the UN Charter, empowered states to use force for the protection of humanitarian assistance and convoys of released detainees in former Yugoslavia. The statement of the Delegate of Zimbabwe summed up their objection. He noted that the Resolution 770:

> seeks to empower any State which feels able and so inclined to use military force in any part of Bosnia and Herzegovina in the name of the United Nations but without any control from or accountability to the United Nations. What is even more disturbing to my delegation is the fact that it is left entirely to the individual states so intervening to define the scope of the said humanitarian operation. My delegation has serious difficulties in accepting a proposition that calls upon the Security Council to authorise unidentified States to use military force after which the Council is likely to assume the role of a helpless spectator in a military operation it has so authorised.[74]

In other words, not only was the objection to the concern with internal matters, but also the manner in which the Security Council sought to protect its intervention....

Safety Zones for Kurds in Iraq: The Hidden Agenda

Soon after the end of the Gulf War came widespread civil fighting in Iraq. Shia Muslims in the South and the Kurdish population in the North were instigated to rebel by Western democracies to overthrow a weakened

---

[73] This is particularly unfortunate in view of the charges of selectivity, discrimination, excess of coercion and lack of sensitivity to people offered humanitarian assistance, which can be levied against it on the basis of even the most perfunctory historical analysis. V.S. Mani, 'Humanitarian Intervention and International Law' (mimeo). Some of these charges are sustainable, as we shall see later, even in the instance of the Iraqi people.

[74] S.C. Doc. S/PV.3106, 13 August 1992: Provisional Verbal Record of the 3106th Meeting, pp. 16–17.

regime. By the first week of April both the Shi'ite revolt and the Kurdish uprising were suppressed by Saddam Hussein. Some 700,000 Iraqi refugees stampeded into Iran and about half that number toward Turkey. Turkey decided not to admit the Kurds but to provide 'humanitarian aid' at the border. The USCR has described the scene thus:

> In early April 1991, the landscape on the sides of those mountains was one of chaos—mud, smoke, crowds, litter. Following days of walking under extremely harsh conditions, the refugees congregated in places exposed to the wind and cold with no sanitary facilities or fresh water other than the pounding, cold rain that froze at night. Most were concentrated in two areas, near Uludere and Cukurca. South of the town of Uludere, they huddled on the side of a steep mountain, nearly inaccessible to relief convoys because the dirt roads leading to it had been washed away in heavy rains. Any who ventured more than a hundred yards or so into Turkey were pushed back by Turkish soldiers, firing warning shots in the air.[75]

A staff report issued by the U.S. Senate Subcommittee on Immigration and Refugee Affairs in May said:

> If the refugees had been permitted to cross the border—even by half a mile—to enter more hospitable Turkish valleys and facilities, some of the tragic loss of life could have been minimised during those desperate early days in April.[76]

But instead of persuading Turkey to temporarily take in the refugees on humanitarian grounds the Western coalition came to the rescue of its ally rather than to that of the refugees.[77]

The attitude of Turkey to its Kurd minority is well known. The Kurdish population in Turkey has historically enjoyed fewer rights than Iraqi Kurds. So much so they have been described as mountain Turks rather than Kurds. The Turkish President Turgut Ozal was also fearful of feeding the separatist movement within the country; almost half of the 25 million Kurd population in the region is present in Turkey. It was perhaps he who first mooted the idea of creating safety zones.[78] The British Prime Minister John Major however took the initiative. The idea did not at first find acceptance. President Bush was reluctant to be drawn into a 'Vietnam-style quagmire'. The result was the adoption on 5 April 1991 of

---

[75] *World Refugee Survey 1992*, p. 82.
[76] Ibid.
[77] Turkey has only acceded to the 1951 UN Convention on Refugees which carries a geographical limitation. It recognises as refugees only those who have fled from Europe.
[78] *Times*, London (21 April 1991).

Security Council Resolution 688 which, as we have noted before, did not contain a word about the creation of safe havens or zones. On the other hand, it especially mentioned Article 2 para (7) of the Charter of the United Nations and reaffirmed 'the commitment of all Member States to the sovereignty, territorial integrity and political independence of Iraq...'. The resolution certainly did not permit military intervention on behalf of the Kurds.

However, the resolution did decide that the massive flow of refugees towards and across international frontiers threatened international peace and security in the region. In other words, the concern was less with the suffering of the Kurdish people as with the Turkish sensitivities to letting in Kurdish refugees.[79] In fact, the immediate effect of denying asylum outside Iraq was widespread death and suffering.[80]

It is difficult to accept the assessment that the granting of temporary asylum to the refugees would have threatened the international peace and security of the region. Massive refugee flows are hardly a new phenomenon, and how massive was it anyway.[81] Can all such movements be perceived to be a threat to the peace and security of the particular region? Were there any peculiar reasons present for arriving at this understanding in this instance? At least none that are evident.

On April 18 Iraq concluded a Memorandum of Understanding with the UN Secretary General's Executive Delegate, Prince Saddrudin Aga Khan, allowing the UN to provide humanitarian assistance to displaced persons and returnees.[82] However, two days before the UN operations could begin the United States, France and Britain began sending troops into Northern Iraq to create a safe haven zone for refugees about 100 miles long and 25 miles deep stretching along the western end of the Turkish–Iraqi border and including the city of Zakho.[83] The move achieved, among other things, the objective of preventing refugee flows.

---

[79] 'Refugee flows . . . were the obvious foundation for the Security Council's pivotal decision to condemn Iraq's repression of the Kurds. . .'. David A. Martin, 'Strategies for a Resistant World: Human Rights Initiatives and the Need for Alternatives to Refugee Interdiction', *Cornell International Law Journal* (Vol. 26, 1993), pp. 753–71 at p. 765.

[80] Astri Suhrke, 'Safeguarding the Right to Asylum', paper written for the Expert Group Meeting on Population Distribution and Migration, Santacruz, Bolivia, 18–22 January 1993, p. 22.

[81] Turkey, it would appear, deliberately exaggerated the figures in its statement at the Security Council that, other than the 300,000 already at the borders, there were 600,000 people on the move and that therefore 'a million people might be forced to move from that country [i.e., Iraq] to Turkey.' S.C. Doc. S/PV.2982, 5 April 1991: Provisional Verbal Record of the 2982nd Meeting, p. 6.

[82] For the text of the Memorandum of Understanding see *International Legal Materials* (Vol. 30, 1991), p. 860.

[83] *World Refugee Survey 1992*, p. 99.

It is my submission that alternative policy options were available to handle the Kurdish problem. First of all the instigation to revolt should not have taken place. Second, Turkey should have been asked to offer temporary protection to refugees. Eminent exponents of refugee law have argued that the principle of temporary protection is a customary norm of international law.[84] Instead, Resolution 688 'served to legitimise Turkey's decision to close its border and that an undesirable precedent had thereby been set'.[85] Third, a weakened Iraq could have been persuaded through other means to stop the gross violation of human rights of the Iraqi people, including that of Shi'ite Muslims and Kurds. As it happened the rights of Iraqi people was never paid any attention. In fact, sanctions have been kept in place even when they have proved disastrous for the Iraqi populace.

Fourth, the humanitarian intervention option should have been openly debated and all its ramifications seriously considered, including the need to avoid selective application. However, ever since the end of the Cold War, in particular since the Gulf crisis, there has been a lack of transparency in the decisions of the Security Council. Even Michael Reisman admits:

> Like a parliamentary matryoshka (doll), it now contains ever-smaller 'mini-councils', each meeting behind closed doors without keeping records, and each taking decisions secretly.... Decisions that appear to go further than at any time in the history of the United Nations are now ultimately being taken, it seems, by a small group of states [the United States, United Kingdom and France] separately meeting in secret.[86]

But a momentous change in the normative structure of international law cannot surely be brought about in secret. Particularly when the resolution is opposed by the most populous countries in the world and with the pretension of being leaders of the developing world. It also cannot be brought about through what may be described at best as an extremely tenuous interpretation of Resolution 688. The seriousness of these charges is driven home when it is recalled that the Western democracies, led by the United States, had hitherto, for the sake of commercial and

---

[84] Guy S. Goodwin Gill, 'Non-refoulement and the New Asylum Seekers', *Virginia Journal of International Law* (Vol. 26, 1986), pp. 897–918; Deborah Perluss and Joan F. Hartman, 'Temporary Refuge: Emergence of a Customary Norm', *Virginia Journal of International Law* (Vol. 26, 1986), pp. 551–626.

[85] Astri Suhrke, 'A Crisis Diminished: Refugees in the Developing World', *International Journal of Refugee Law* (Vol. 48, No. 2, Spring 1993), pp. 215–40 at p. 235.

[86] W. Michael Reisman, 'The Constitutional Crisis in the United Nations', *American Journal of International Law* (Vol. 87, 1993), pp. 83–100 at pp. 85–86.

geopolitical advantages, turned a blind eye to the oppression heaped on the minorities by Saddam Hussein.[87]

Former Yugoslavia: The Policy of Refugee Containment

The meaning and implications of establishing safety zones or sister concepts becomes abundantly clear when the case of former Yugoslavia is considered. The idea of a safety zone was first mooted in the middle of 1992. On July 29 1992, at the invitation of the High Commissioner for Refugees, donor countries attended in Geneva an International Meeting on Humanitarian Aid to the Victims of the Conflict in the Former Yugoslavia to arrive at a consensus on the handling of the refugee crisis. At that time the count of refugees and displaced persons stood at 2.2 million, more than 1.4 million of whom were from Bosnia, with most of the remainder displaced by earlier fighting in Croatia.[88] Among the several proposals which were mooted were the German proposal calling for burden sharing of asylum through instituting quotas, and the Slovenian proposal for the establishment of four safe haven zones within Bosnia.

The Slovenian statement was distributed under the title *Proposals Concerning the Measures for Voluntary Return Home of the Displaced Persons and Refugees from Bosnia and Hercegovina*. It declared that 'the basic task ahead and the principal solutions of the problem are to promote the voluntary return home of displaced persons and to take humanitarian measures to avert new flows of refugees and displaced persons from Bosnia and Hercegovina'.[89] While the German proposal was cold shouldered the Slovenian one received an enthusiastic response, particularly from Britain and France which had together admitted no more than 3,000 refugees. The view was expressed that everything must be done to keep the refugees in the former Yugoslavia for to resettle refugees abroad 'is

[87] As Richard Falk has pointed out:

> The revealed character of Saddam's criminality—launching an aggressive war against Iran, introducing poison gas onto the battlefield, using poison gas and chemical weapons against Kurdish villages in Iraq—did nothing at all to impair Iraq's status as a privileged customer for Western technology and long-term credits. Bush, who claimed to be appalled by Saddam in August 1990, was the same Bush who only weeks earlier had intervened with the US Congress to discourage terminating a $200 million credit in Iraq's favor, and a few months before that, had used his influence in Geneva to discourage investigation of flagrant human rights abuses in Iraq. Bush reminded law-makers prior to August 2nd that Saddam was a fact-of-life in the region, better to befriend than to alienate.

Richard Falk, 'Democracy Died at the Gulf' (mimeo), pp. 10–11.

[88] Frelick, 'Preventing Refugee Flows' (see footnote 60 earlier), p. 9.

[89] US Committee for Refugees, *Croatia's Crucible: Providing Asylum for Refugees from Bosnia and Hercegovina* (October 1992), p. 18.

perhaps the best way of supporting the policy of ethnic cleansing'.[90] Thus a humanitarian twist was given to what Frelick has called 'collusion with genocide'.[91] The proposal was also endorsed by Croatia which was besieged by refugees while already burdened with nearly 260,000 internally displaced people. In fact, it soon prevented refugees from entering the country.[92]

Interestingly, the proposal also had the support of Bosnia, drawing attention to the possibility that safety zones may be endorsed by the 'host' state to meet its own objectives. In this case the aim was to increase the number of persons under arms opposing Serb aggression and to keep the Bosnian economy alive by keeping productive Bosnians in Bosnia.[93] It raises the question whether a state has the right to prevent people from fleeing persecution even when the objective is the survival of the state itself. Those concerned about the negative implications of the principle of sovereignty, and committed to the cause of human rights, do not seem to have paid any attention to this consequence.

The plan to create safety zones fell through because the Western powers were not willing to commit the necessary resources to protect them. On August 13, 1992 the UN Security Council passed Resolution 770 calling on states to take 'all measures necessary' to facilitate the delivery of relief supply to civilians. With Resolution 770 the debate shifted from safety zones to 'safe corridors' for humanitarian assistance. UN peacekeeping forces were ordered to prevent people from fleeing Sarajevo. 'The apparent quid pro quo reached with the Serb militias was that the UN would only be permitted to deliver humanitarian assistance if it agreed not to allow any would-be refugees to escape.'[94] It is hardly surprising that powers which supported this policy were not forthcoming with more offers of asylum.

In mid-December 1992, the International Committee of Red Cross (ICRC) issued its well known statement calling for the creation of safety zones in Bosnia:

> As no third country seems to be ready, even on a provisional basis,
> to grant asylum to one hundred thousand Bosnian refugees ... an

---

[90] The French foreign ministry spokesman Daniel Bernard cited by Frelick, 'Preventing Refugee Flows' (see footnote 60 earlier), p. 9.

[91] As Frelick (ibid., p. 11) has aptly pointed out:

By analogy, it would be like refusing refuge to the victims of the Nazi Holocaust by saying that one did not want to contribute to Hitler's 'ethnic cleansing' of the Jews, all the while barring their escape so that rather than lose their homes and countries, they would lose their lives.

[92] US Committee for Refugees, *Croatia's Crucible* (see footnote 89 earlier), p. 2.

[93] Ibid., p. 18.

[94] Frelick, 'Preventing Refugee Flows' (see footnote 60 earlier), p. 10.

original concept must be devised to create protected zones ... which are equal to the particular requirements and the sheer scale of the problem.[95]

This was open admission that since states were only interested in stopping the flow of refugees from former Yugoslavia the only way out was to create safety zones inside the country. In other words, in the case of former Yugoslavia the equation *safety zones = collusion with genocide* is justified.

On 16 April 1993 the Security Council, in the background of the rapidly deteriorating situation in Srebrenica resulting from continuous armed attacks on civilians by Bosnian Serb paramilitary units, adopted Resolution 819 which demanded that 'all parties and others concerned treat Srebrenica and its surroundings as a *safe area* which should be free from any armed attack or any other hostile act.' It also decided to send a mission of members of the Council to ascertain the situation and report back to it. The Mission submitted its Report on 30 April, 1993. I reproduce below some excerpts:

Srebrenica is today the equivalent of an open jail in which its people can wander around but are controlled and terrorised by the increasing presence of Serb tanks and other heavy weapons in its immediate surroundings. The UNHCR representative described the town as a 'bad refugee camp'.

Even though Security Council Resolution 819 (1993) declared the city a safe area, the actual situation obviously does not correspond to either the spirit or the intent of the resolution.... The town is practically under siege with Serbian forces controlling access to it.... Inhuman conditions prevail, with potentially catastrophic consequences.[96]

The Mission concluded that the Serbs had put into effect, through denial of humanitarian assistance, 'a slow-motion process of genocide'. It however called for the declaration of the towns of Gorazde, Zepa, Tuzla and Sarajevo as safe areas.

On 6 May 1993 the Security Council unanimously adopted Resolution 824 declaring Sarajevo, Tuzla, Zepa, Gorazde, Bihac as well as Srebrenica as safe areas. It *inter alia* demanded that all armed attacks against these areas should cease and humanitarian agencies be allowed free and unimpeded access. Resolutions 836 adopted on 4 June 1993, and 844 of 18 June 1993 endorsed Resolution 824 and affirmed 'that these safe areas

[95] Ibid., p. 11.
[96] S.C. Doc. S/25700, 30 April 1993: *Report of the Security Council Mission Established Pursuant to Resolution 819 (1993)*, pp. 6–8.

are a temporary measure'. It authorised the United Nations Protection Force (UNPROFOR) to, acting in self defence, take necessary measures, including the use of force, in reply to bombardments against the safe areas. Later on 24 August, 1993 the Security Council adopted Resolution 859 which demanded that 'all concerned facilitate the unhindered flow of humanitarian assistance, including the provision of food, water, electricity, fuel and communications, in particular to the 'safe areas' in Bosnia and Herzegovina'. However, the attacks on 'safe areas' continued.[97] Air strikes never took place partly because Britain cited fears of Serb reprisals against its peacekeeping troops. In September 1993 the UN Secretary General reported:

> The conditions for the international community's humanitarian efforts have steadily deteriorated [...]. In Bosnia and Hercegovina there is currently widespread fighting. Relief operations are obstructed, sabotaged or diverted for military purposes, while the personnel of UNPROFOR, UNHCR and other organisations are increasingly targeted deliberately by members of the armed forces of all parties. Meanwhile, the support of the international community for humanitarian operations is dwindling and the sums actually received fall far short of requirements.... The ultimate consequences would be further large population displacements, which would have serious destabilising effects on neighboring countries and the region as a whole, and a humanitarian catastrophe.[98]

In November, 1993 Mr. Tadeusz Mazowiecki submitted to the Commission on Human Rights the fifth report on the situation of human rights in the territory of former Yugoslavia. He noted:

> The purpose of the 'safe areas' was to provide people with the food and medicines they needed in places where their security was guaranteed. Relentless military action by Bosnian Serb forces, however, has turned them into areas under siege.

> Sometimes the parties to the conflict instigate or use movements of large numbers of peoples in order to achieve 'ethnic cleansing'.[99]

The situation had not changed substantially till July 1994 despite the threat of air strikes—or actual air strikes, of the most limited kind. The

[97] S.C. Doc. S/26601, 19 October 1993: *Letter From the Permanent Representative of Bosnia and Herzegovina to the United Nations Addressed to the President of the Security Council.*

[98] Boutros Boutros Ghali, *Report* (see footnote 64 earlier), pp. 154–55.

[99] ECOSOC Doc. E/CN.4/1994/47, 17 November 1993: *Fifth Periodic Report on the Situation of Human Rights in the Territory of Former Yugoslavia Submitted by Mr. Tadeusz Mazowiecki, Special Rapporteur of the Commission on Human Rights, pursuant to para 32 of Commission Resolution 1993/7 of 23 February, 1993*, p. 4.

February market massacre in Sarajevo and the Serb offensive against Gorazde through April testified to the unchanged ground realities, although there was some improvement in the case of Sarajevo after March. On 22 April, 1994, the Security Council adopted Resolution 913 condemning the Serb offensive against Gorazde. It demanded the withdrawal of Bosnian Serb forces and their weapons to a distance to be agreed by UNPROFOR wherefrom they ceased to constitute a threat to the status of Gorazde as a safe area. It also called for an 'end to any provocative action by whomsoever committed to and around the safe areas'. But on 25 May 1994 the President of the Security Council was still demanding the immediate and full compliance with Resolution 913.[100]

The lesson is that the need to protect safe areas will not be seriously considered in the absence of geopolitical and commercial interests. In other words, 'humanitarian interventions' are unlikely without a hidden geopolitical or commercial agenda. Is this judgement too harsh and cynical? It may be readily conceded that one aim of establishing 'safe areas' was a humanitarian one. For instance, the declaration of Srebrenica as a safe area did prevent a massacre. However, there is little doubt that a principal end aim was to prevent refugee flows. Even those who recommended firmer action against the Serbs stressed the need to stop 'the floods of refugees that would cross Europe'.[101]

An important question remains as to why was the UNPROFOR unable to secure the safe areas. In a report on the question to the Security Council, the United Nations Secretary-General in May 1994 identified some of the problems. These deserve notice. In evaluating the experience the first lesson the report underlined was that 'the effective implementation of the safe-area concept depends on the degree of consent by the parties on the ground.'[102] Its implementation is facilitated in areas where agreement is reached on the precise obligations that each party has to abide by. This was the case with Srebrenica and Zepa.[103] Second, there is a need for a clear definition of a 'safe area'. The geography of a 'safe area' needed to be clearly delineated in contrast to a description like 'towns and sorroundings' contained in Resolution 824 because its absence created obvious difficulties in a civil conflict.[104] Third, there must be clear specification of what is to be safeguarded. For instance, is the objective to defend a geographically defined safe area or is it to deter attacks on the civilian

---

[100] S.C. Doc. S/PRST/26, 25 May 1994: Statement of the President of the Security Council on Bosnia and Herzegovina.

[101] Margaret Thatcher, 'Stop the Serbs with Air Strikes and Arms for their Adversaries', *The International Herald Tribune* (5 May 1994).

[102] S.C. Doc. S/1994/555, 9 May 1994: Report of the Secretary-General Pursuant to Resolution 844 (1993), p. 3.

[103] Ibid., p. 2.

[104] Ibid., p. 5.

population living therein? The report recommended that safe areas were created primarily to protect people and not to defend territory. Fourth, safe areas must not be allowed to be used as a base for pursuing the conflict. For such use would provoke retaliation and make its defense difficult. Fifth, the force present to enforce a safe area must have sufficient resources and the appropriate mandate. Finally, the concept of a safe area should be regarded as a 'temporary mechanism' to protect vulnerable populations pending a comprehensive negotiated political settlement.[105] These practical lessons, among others, will have to be taken into account in any implementation of the concept of safety zones in the future....

Summation

What then is a 'safety zone'? As conceived and applied in Iraq and former Yugoslavia, it may be described as a vast prison house in whose confines individuals stay or 'voluntarily' go for it protects them from the outside world. Thus the internally displaced, those who need rather than those from whom refuge is sought, go to prison. It is a prison because escape into the world 'outside' is not a serious possibility; the choice that it offers is between the confines of the zone and an unsafe world in which survival is a distinct impossibility. There is no available space which is 'outside' the 'outside'. Rather, the prison house is constructed and maintained by those outside the outside.

The concept of a safety zone offers an excellent example of how language can constitute our practices. By calling the particular space a 'safety' zone, despite its contrary nature, it contrives to remove all other spaces, genuinely safer, from view. Instead, attention is riveted on a predefined space. Counter-discourse is thereby entrapped in a polarity—of safe and unsafe zones—which the discourse to be countered posits and reproduces, eliminating possibilities of introducing other spaces into the debate.

We are dealing here with a new architecture of control which is being constructed in the aftermath of the Cold War. In it the UN Security Council, dominated by two or three states, seeks to operate the loom of power which generates 'knowledge' and the mechanisms for the execution of innovative solutions to old problems. In fact, it defines the new field of institutional life. Ideally nothing will escape its surveillance. In fact, the Security Council is, I submit, the modern day Benthamite Panopticon. It hopes to regulate individuals and appropriately created subjects, be it geographical (safe area being one), in a bid to establish a new world order whose distinguishing feature is a spatial divide (North–South/Rich–Poor) which must be prevented from bridging. Thus we have

[105] Ibid., p. 8.

preventive protection and, not to forget, the right to remain. Those on the wrong side of the divide are increasingly becoming objects of information—on-site investigation, on-site assistance etc., rather than subjects in communication about information and spaces transcending the divide. The body of the oppressed, the refugee, is coming to be enmeshed in an international division of labour in which only goods, capital, and services are permitted mobility.[106]

Yet, disturbing as the concept of a safety zone is, should it be rejected out of hand? There is the point that in a cynical world moral judgements do not translate into practical intervention. What is more, when the world is as unjust as it is today, the victims of the international system (in this case the host countries) themselves often end up, for the opposite but nevertheless what often appear to be, and sometimes are, good reasons, to seek answer in responses which are proposed by hegemonic powers for their own reasons. Thus it is that even some developing countries find the concept of a safety zone attractive. In 1985 it was Thailand which proposed to the Asian–African Legal Consultative Committee (AALCC) that it study the possibility of establishing safety zones for refugees and displaced persons in the country of origin. The proposal emanated out of the experience of a developing country faced with massive refugee flows, albeit in this instance for other, and not so good, reasons as well.[107] The African countries with one lost decade behind them, and another staring them in the face, are also beginning to dilute their traditional hospitality to refugees when faced with mass influx. In brief, it needs to be appreciated that today the concept of a safety zone may be advanced in diverse contexts. On the one hand, there are the poorest of countries which are faced with mass influx of refugees and cannot cope with it. In there case the very misery of the world that they inhabit is conspiring to break the bonds of solidarity with the more immediate victims of the inequitous

---

[106] This is clear from the outcome of the GATT Uruguay Round of Trade Negotiations which enhances the global mobility of capital, technology and services without offering parallel concessions to labour. For a critique of the negotiations see B.S. Chimni, 'The Political Economy of Uruguay Round Negotiations: A Perspective', *International Studies* (Vol. 29, 1992), pp. 135–58.

The coerced immobility of the oppressed body amidst shrinking *dignity zones* in the underdeveloped world however forecasts a future which is devoid of hope. Will it come to pass? In my view confinement can do no more than delay the inevitable: the rebellion of the subaltern and the creation of a just world order. The developed world must try and understand this. But to quote the philosopher Wittgenstein: 'It is difficult to tell a short-sighted man how to get somewhere. Because you cannot say to him: "Look at the Church tower ten miles away and go in that direction".' Ludwig Wittgenstein, *Culture and Value*, p. 1e.

[107] See Court Robinson, 'Buying Time: Refugee Repatriation from Thailand', *World Refugee Survey 1992*, pp. 18–25; and John R. Rogge, 'Thailand's Refugee Policy: Some Thoughts on its Origin and Future Directions', in Howard Adelman and C. Michael Lanphier, eds, *Refuge or Asylum* (York Lanes Press, Toronto, 1990), pp. 150–72.

international system. On the other, there are the affluent countries which advance the concept in order to eliminate the need for burden sharing at the level of asylum, in this way hoping to protect unbelievable privileges.[108] Only in the former instance should the idea of creating a safety zone be considered with sympathy.

In the matrix of this understanding, and taking into account the hitherto experience, the following general principles can be stated as having application to the concept of a safety zone:

1. Since each refugee situation is unique, the need for, and the possibility of, creating a safety zone must be considered on a case by case basis.

2. The decision to establish a safety zone shall be taken in strict accordance with the Charter of the United Nations. Subsequent to its creation it shall remain under the supervision of the United Nations.

3. A safety zone shall be established and maintained with the consent of the state concerned.

4. The establishment and maintenance of a safety zone shall in no way derogate from the territorial integrity and political independence of the state in which it is established.

5. No individual or group of individuals shall be prevented from leaving the safety zone in order to seek asylum in a third country.

6. The developed countries shall undertake to share the burden of asylum, if need be, through establishing a quota system.

7. A safety zone must be viewed as a temporary mechanism pending a comprehensive political settlement and the restoration of the democratic process in the country of origin.

8. The mandate of the force assigned the task to defend the safety zone must be clearly defined both in terms of territory and function. The focus must be essentially on protecting people and not the defense of territory.

9. In creating and maintaining the safety zone troops of those countries should not be deployed which have had in the past a special, in particular military, relationship with one of the parties to the conflict.

[108] There is of course a third situation where parochial perceptions rooted in tradition and history dictate policies which seek to avoid sharing the burden of asylum. The international community should sensitise states holding such a narrow perspective to the need to express solidarity with the refugee community.

10. Agreements should be entered into with the involved parties to ensure protection to the people in the safety zone.

11. The force protecting people in the safety zone must operate on the basis of complete neutrality and impartiality.

12. The territory of the safety zone should not be allowed to be used in any way for the purpose of the continuance of the conflict.

13. The role of United Nations agencies such as the UNHCR must be in conformity with their mandate. They must not be involved in any process which leads to losing sight of the fundamental object-ives of the agency.

14. The status and protection of personnel engaged in providing humanitarian assistance in safety zones shall be regulated on the basis of the applicable principles of international humanitarian law.

B. Bill Clarance, 'Protective Structure, Strategy and Tactics: International Protection in Ethnic Conflicts', *International Journal of Refugee Law* (Vol. 5, No. 4, 1993), pp. 586–92.

What follows is neither a comprehensive explanation of how interna-tional protection works in a situation of conflict, nor a detailed evaluation of protective mechanisms for field reference. Although there is need for both, all that is possible here is a brief note for Sri Lankan experience in the short, but intensely challenging period from mid-1990, when hostil-ities abruptly resumed between the Government security forces and the LTTE, until the end of 1991, together with an evaluation of its relevance to the international approach to ethnic conflicts. . . .

Background

. . . From June 1990, the situation of civilian Tamils in the North and East was dramatic. Those who could, were already fleeing their homes to dis-tance themselves from the fighting. The roads and jungle tracks were filled with displaced families, travelling by lorry, bullock cart, bicycle and on foot. Others remaining behind in conditions of insecurity and fre-quently hunger, were awaiting the chance to get away.

Those Tamils already on the move were heading for Mannar district in the North-West, where the conflict as yet was of relatively low intensity and, most importantly, where Mannar Island provided the shortest, safest and cheapest crossing to South India. During June–September 1990, well over 100,000 asylum-seekers embarked on small fishing boats to take this route.

Institutional Reluctance

Mannar Relief Operation

From early on, the very modest project to provide emergency relief in Mannar for such refugees, the displaced and other conflict-affected persons aroused stiff opposition in Geneva, mainly because of restrictive interpretation of the UNHCR mandate and limited resources. Initially approved by the then High Commissioner, Thorvald Stoltenberg, on the basis of the submission of the UNHCR office in Sri Lanka, the project immediately came under fire when he abruptly resigned after only a few months in office. In the interregnum and until the new High Commissioner, Sadako Ogata, had fully taken over all her new functions and decided in favour of the programme as a useful innovative model, it was permitted to continue only under the strictest constraints.

Traditional Mandate

Opposition to the Mannar relief operation revolved principally around the central question of the mandate: Why should UNHCR concern itself with internally displaced persons when its Statute stated that the High Commissioner's competence was for refugees who were clearly outside their country of origin? Why should UNHCR take on extra mandatory commitments when some of its existing programmes were underfunded? If internally displaced persons needed international relief, the argument went, then this could be provided by the International Committee of the Red Cross (ICRC) and/or international NGOs. If the UN had to be involved, then UNDP, UNICEF or some other agency should take up the burden. In the event, the Sri Lanka programme survived this opposition. Ironically, the strength of the criticism served eventually to highlight both the need for and the capacity of UNHCR to play an essential role in situations of conflict and, in so doing, helped clear away some of the institutional inhibitions in that regard.

Immediate Causes of Refugee Exodus

The related concepts of prevention and containment of refugee producing situations, now widely discussed and increasingly accepted, were then regarded as unorthodox and unwelcome extensions of the traditional UNHCR mandate. The imperative challenge of the ground situation in Mannar helped change this position. On the one hand, was the raw humanitarian need to relieve the suffering of those who were fleeing to India to escape the conflict, and on the other hand, the fact that the pressures to leave could be reduced within Sri Lanka, most significantly without prejudice to the right to seek asylum.

In such conditions, UNHCR intervention was cogent common sense. Thenceforth, it was clear that similar initiatives to come to grip with the immediate causes of mass refugee exodus would be widely supported in the international community.

Internally Displaced/Conflict Affected Persons

Notwithstanding the opposition, there was more than enough in law and humanitarian equity to make it imperative for UNHCR to intervene, even for 'non-refugees' such as internally displaced and other conflict-affected persons. Thus, they were shown to be entitled to UNHCR relief on the same basis as returnees within the traditional mandate in circumstances where they were living together and suffering the same hardships. In humanitarian equity, distribution could not have been otherwise than even-handed....

Protection through Relief Mechanisms

Without in any way impeding the fundamental human right to seek asylum, protection strategy on the ground was implemented largely through operational relief mechanisms, such as food convoys and the Open Relief Centres. Thus, the organisation, transport and escort of *food convoys*— invariably without armed escorts—not only fed displaced persons who were hungry, but also established a regular channel for UNHCR access to them.

Two *Open Relief Centres* (ORCs) were established in Mannar, one at Pesalai on Government-held Mannar Island, and the other at Madhu on the mainland, in an area dominated by the LTTE. The ORCs operated on the principle that basic necessities such as shelter, food, sanitation and medical care were provided for displaced persons, who were free to move in and out at will. But of at least equal importance was the fact that they were under UNHCR protection, with resident field officers and frequent back-up missions from Colombo.

At Madhu ORC, the sense of security of people living in the surrounding area was illustrated by a remark of a nearby Tamil resident: 'You don't have to live in Madhu (ORC) to feel the benefit of having UNHCR there—you can be in a village fifty miles away.' Indeed, the open nature of the centre meant that the surrounding population could seek safety there whenever they felt threatened, and leave when the situation improved. Some brought their livestock. Others slept in the ORC and made occasional visits back home to keep an eye on their property or to cultivate their crops.

From its early days, the ORC mechanism attracted particular interest and support, initially from European NGOs and later from diplomats in Colombo. Thus in March 1991, when the British Refugee Council wrote to the High Commissioner expressing strong support for the UNHCR programme, it referred to the Madhu ORC as 'a genuine place of safety in the North, after attacks by both sides on other areas holding high concentrations of displaced people'.[109] Moreover, in the following month, when there was a mass exodus of Kurdish refugees from Northern Iraq in the aftermath of the Gulf War, ORCs in Sri Lanka were considered as possible models for the safe havens then being advocated by British Prime Minister John Major....[110]

Conclusions

Broadly, the Sri Lankan experience helped establish the conceptual and practical basis for UNHCR intervention in situations of conflict which were actually or potentially refugee producing. Very briefly, the principal points were as follows:

Justification for intervention: There was more than enough in law, humanitarian equity and pragmatic common sense to justify UNHCR intervention on behalf of the internally displaced and other conflict-affected persons. Moreover, in similar conditions where the right to seek asylum is not thereby endangered, UNHCR initiatives to come to grips with the immediate causes of refugee exodus would be widely supported in the international community.

UNHCR's role: There was an essential, but largely vacant role for an international organisation in conflict situations, which UNHCR was uniquely well qualified to fill.

With respect to the *protective structure*, direct representation by UNHCR at the political level of central government was essential, both to maintain ongoing working relations with key departments, such as Defence and Rehabilitation, and to facilitate immediate access to the top in times of protection crisis.

In addition, it was possible for UNHCR to implement a *protective strategy*, largely by means of operational tactics that satisfied some of the more basic material needs of the affected population and, in so doing, had a dynamic protective impact. Certain of the *protective mechanisms and tactics* adopted could be considered as models for adaptation in similar situations of conflict elsewhere.

The earliest *deployment of international field staff* on the ground is a fundamental prerequisite for any significant role in situations of ethnic conflict. Given close liaison with ICRC and NGOs on the ground, UNHCR interventions could be undertaken on a strictly limited territorial basis, and with due regard to the *complementarity of mandates*.

⁊ԣ
⁊ԣ

[109] Letter from the British Refugee Council, 20 March 1991.
[110] Reuters Library Report, 10 April 1991.

Chapter 8

Legal Condition of Refugees in India

The Story of Partition Refugees

The story of refugees in independent India must begin with the partition
of the country in 1947. This is for two reasons. First, the human dimension of partition, which saw the displacement of millions of people, has
not received sufficient attention from historians who have confined themselves to an analysis of its causes.[1] Second, in the ordinary consciousness,
the story of partition refugees has come to be separated from that of refugee flows to free India. While the two stories have different trajectories
and endings, the two experiences are united by the enormous sufferings
they recount. Recalling and reliving the traumatic passage of partition
refugees helps empathise with the problems of refugee populations present in India today who, unlike the partition refugees, have lost not only

[1] As one observer notes: 'The Partition, related massacres and migrations, represented
an unfolding human tragedy of enormous proportions. Nevertheless, historical studies
have tended to focus on the causes of Partition rather than its impact. Sustained treatment
of its consequences has largely been limited to accounts whose main purpose is to apportion blame for the related massacres. In this great human event, human voices are
strangely silent.' Ian Talbot, 'Literature and the Human Drama of the 1947 Partition',
South Asia (Vol. 18, Special Issue, 1995), pp. 37–56. Pandey likewise points out that 'the
horror of Partition, the anguish and sorrow, pain and brutality of the "riots" of 1946–47
has been left almost entirely to creative writers and filmmakers.' He notes the outstanding
contributions of the short stories of Sa'adat Hasan Manto, the films of Ritwik Ghatak and
M.S. Sathyu's *Garam Hawa* in this regard. See Gyanendra Pandey, 'The Prose of Otherness', in David Arnold and David Hardiman, eds, *Subaltern Studies VIII: Essays in Honour of
Ranajit Guha* (Oxford University Press, New Delhi, 1994), pp. 188–222 at p. 205. For a
good collection of creative writing on partition see Mushirul Hasan, ed., *India Partitioned:
The Other Face of Freedom* (Roli Books, Delhi, 1997), jubilee edition, vols 1–2. For a non-
fictional account see Urvashi Butalia, *The Other Side of Silence: Voices from the Partition of India*
(Viking Penguin India, New Delhi, 1998).

their homes but have also been uprooted from their nationhood and culture. In **Reading I.A**, Schechtman offers a glimpse into the tragic exodus from East to West Panjab which was conducted principally on foot and which he describes as 'the greatest single refugee trek in world history'. **Reading I.B** however tells a more detailed story of how successive waves of refugees from East Bengal coped with their life situation in the city of Calcutta and the state of West Bengal. Chatterjee challenges therein what she terms the 'official discourse' 'which perceives refugees as objects of assistance and as such a "problem" group'.

But can the millions displaced in the course of partition be categorised as 'refugees' in accordance with the 1951 Convention definition? In **Readings I.C** and **I.D**, Pakrasi and Vernant consider the question and conclude that they were not 'refugees'. Would readers agree?

Newly independent India not only provided prompt relief to partition refugees but also successfully rehabilitated them.[2] A large number of laws were passed to deal with the problem of refugees and evacuee property.[3] The rich experience that India acquired in the sphere of relief and rehabilitation of refugees deserves to be recalled for at least two reasons. First, it can be drawn upon, in so far as it is relevant, to frame current refugee policies. Second, India's experience in handling the problem of evacuee property could be of much practical use in similar situations prevailing in the world, such as in former Yugoslavia. In the latter context, **Reading I.E** narrates a small episode from the story of the payment of compensation to refugees for property left behind.

Post-independence Refugees: Legal Framework

India is not a party to the 1951 Convention or the 1967 Protocol. Neither has it passed any domestic legislation on the subject of refugees. The fate of the individual refugee is essentially determined by the protections available under the Constitution of India. **Reading II.A** briefly describes the status of refugees in the Indian legal system.[4] It also offers a critique

[2] For sociological and psychological studies of the process of rehabilitation see R.N. Saxena, *Refugees: A Study in Changing Attitudes* (Asia Publishing House, Bombay, 1961); Kanti B. Pakrasi, *The Uprooted: A Sociological Study of the Refugees of West Bengal, India* (S. Ghatack, Calcutta, 1971); Stephen L. Keller, *Uprooting and Social Change: The Role of Refugees in Development* (Manohar Book Service, Delhi, 1975).

[3] These included *inter alia* the Administration of Evacuee Property Act, 1950; the Evacuee Interest (Separation) Act, 1951; the Displaced Persons (Debt Adjustment) Act, 1951; The Displaced Persons (Claims) Supplementary Act, 1954; The Displaced Persons (Compensation and Rehabilitation) Act, 1954 and the Transfer of Evacuee Deposits Act, 1954.

[4] See also Smrithi Talwar, 'Building a Regional Consensus on Asylum—An Indian Perspective', *Bulletin on IHL and Refugee Law* (Vol. 1, No. 2, July–December 1996), pp. 251–64; and Sumbul Rizvi, 'Response of the Indian Judicial System to the Refugee Problem', *Bulletin on IHL and Refugee Law* (Vol. 2, No. 1, January–June 1997), pp. 65–77.

of the decision of the Supreme Court of India in *Louis de Raedt v. Union of India* (1991) in which it held that the government had an absolute right to deport aliens under the 1946 Foreigners Act.

In the past Indian courts were rarely approached to determine the obligations of the state with respect to refugees or to pronounce on their rights and duties. More recently, however, courts have considered these matters. Generally speaking, as **Reading II.A** notes, the courts have been helpful when dealing with the problem of individual refugees or refugee groups. However, as J.S. Verma, the former Chief Justice of the Supreme Court of India, argues in **Reading II.B**, this does not occlude the need for establishing a firm legal framework for the protection, rehabilitation and repatriation of refugees in India and other countries of South Asia. In his view, 'the attempt to fill the void by judicial creativity can only be a temporary phase. Legislation alone will provide permanent solution.'

Refugees from Tibet

In **Reading III.A**, Chimni reviews India's record with respect to Tibetan refugees and the rights extended to them. In comparison with other refugee groups in the country Tibetan refugees have received far better treatment. Readers may query as to what accounts for this differential treatment? Can it be explained by the fact that in the case of the Tibetan refugees the possibility of repatriation was non-existent from the very beginning? But then how does one explain the relatively better treatment of the Sri Lankan Tamil refugees when compared to the Chakma refugees from Bangladesh? Can in this case the differential treatment be accounted for by the existence or absence of ethnic ties? Do the resources of the state in which the refugees are located make a difference? For example, Tripura where the camps of the now repatriated Chakma refugees were located is among the poorest regions in the country. Was that a reason for the refugees receiving, as we shall see presently, less than humane treatment? Should then the central government have the responsibility for looking after the welfare of refugees? More generally, is there a need to formulate and pursue a uniform policy towards different refugee groups? If so, what should be the core elements of this policy?

Refugees from Bangladesh

Reading IV.A describes the two major refugee flows from Bangladesh: the 10 million refugees who sought refuge in India in 1971 and the Chakma refugees who later fled persecution in the Chittagong Hill Tracts and who repatriated in 1998.

While India's response to the mass influx in 1971 is a matter of pride, the treatment of Chakma refugees left much to be desired: food, medical and education facilities in the camps were inadequate. The sorry state of affairs was confirmed by the National Human Rights Commission (NHRC) in May 1996 when it sent an investigation team to Tripura to report on the conditions in the camps. The report which it submitted noted:

the shortage of water, inadequacy of accommodation and woefully inadequate medical facilities in the camps. The report also pointed out that the scale of ration was meagre and its supply was often suspended. During the visit, the team found that many of the tubewells were out of order and that the inmates of the camps were bringing water from far-off places. The camps were also unclean and bore signs of neglect. The report noted that refugee children suffered from malnutrition, water-borne diseases and malaria, while there was no visible effort to improve their living conditions. It also outlined various other problems faced by the refugees.[5]

The last batch of Chakma refugees returned to Bangladesh at the end of February, 1998. **Reading IV.B** deals briefly with the the peace accord signed on 2 December 1997 between the Government of Bangladesh and the Hill Tracts People's Solidarity Association leading to the repatriation of Chakma refugees.

The Chakmas, as **Reading IV.A** points out, had sought refuge in India even *prior* to the creation of Bangladesh. **Reading IV.C** reproduces the important decision of the Supreme Court of India in *National Human Rights Commission v. State of Arunachal Pradesh and Anr* (1996) which was concerned with the threat to life and liberty to the approximately 65,000 Chakma refugees settled in Arunachal Pradesh since 1965. Several features of the case invite attention. First, it is significant that it was the NHRC, established in 1993,[6] which brought the matter before the Supreme Court through a public interest petition, asserting its right to take up the cause of aliens and refugees present in the country.[7] Second, the Union of India opposed the action of the state government of Arunachal Pradesh showing that it was aware of its responsibilities towards aliens and refugees. Third, in deciding that it was the duty of the state of Arunachal Pradesh to protect the life and liberty of the Chakma refugees the Supreme Court did not give any weight to the argument that the settlement of such large numbers of them would disturb 'its ethnic balance and

---

[5] *Human Rights Newsletter* (published by NHRC) (Vol. 3, No. 7, July 1996).
[6] See *The Protection of Human Rights Act, 1993* (NHRC, New Delhi).
[7] See *NHRC Annual Report 1995–96*, pp. 61–62.

destroy its culture and identity'. Fourth, it clarified that the earlier decision of the Court in the *Khudiram Chakma* case did not foreclose the consideration of the grant of citizenship to the Chakmas.[8] Finally, the Supreme
Court affirmed, endorsing earlier decisions, that 'the State is bound to
protect the life and liberty of every human being, be he a citizen or otherwise.'

Sri Lankan Tamil Refugees

In **Reading V.A** Chandrahasan—a Sri Lankan Tamil refugee herself—
notes how despite not being a party to the 1951 Convention or the 1967
Protocol, or having an official refugee determination process, India has
in practice complied with the principle of *non-refoulement*.[9] In **Reading
V.B**, Asha Hans critically reviews the different phases of the repatriation
of Sri Lankan Tamil refugees. Her focus is on the question of voluntariness. In this regard the attention of readers is drawn to the conflicting
conclusions which have often been reached with respect to the same
phase of repatriation. For example, with respect to refugees repatriated
in the period 1992–93 Hans reaches mixed conclusions, while a report by
Asia Watch at this time states that the repatriations were forced.[10] On the

---

[8] *State of Arunachal Pradesh v. Khudiram Chakma* 1994 Supp. (1) SCC 615. See in this
regard **Reading IV.A**.

[9] As a study of the USCR put it: 'despite the curbs on international assistance and monitoring, India has accorded a welcome to asylum seekers that is as generous as for any refugee group in Asia. The record is not unblemished, to be sure. There have been instances of
pushbacks and coercive measures to promote repatriation, but it has largely been the case,
as Chandrahasan (former legal counsel for Tamil United Liberation Front in Sri Lanka
and now a refugee and human rights activist in Madras) put it, that "every person who has
landed on the shore and asked for refuge has been granted refuge".... India, in fact, sent
a ship to Sri Lanka in September 1983 to pick up about 1,000 Plantation Tamils who were
living in camps in Colombo following the ethnic riots of that year.' US Committee for Refugees, *Sri Lanka: Island of Refugees* (Washington, D.C., October 1991), p. 11. Zolberg et al.
support this view in observing that '...India maintained a completely open admissions policy for Sri Lankan Tamils.' A. Zolberg et al., *Escape from Violence* (Oxford University Press,
New York, 1989), p. 148.

[10] 'The Indian government should not proceed with repatriation of Sri Lankan refugees
until it is willing to guarantee full access by the UNHCR to all refugees and refugee facilities. Interviewing potential repatriates at the point of departure, after registration to
return has already taken place, is not sufficient.

'The ban on NGOs working in the refugee camps in Tamil Nadu should be lifted. The
barring of organisations which provide essential protection and support for refugees, and
the deliberate denial of relief are forms of implicit coercion.

'It is essential that refugees be provided with full and up-to-date information about the
nature of the ongoing conflict in Sri Lanka. Mail deliveries to the camps in Tamil Nadu
should be facilitated, not hindered, in the interests of ensuring that such information
reaches the refugees. (Lifting the ban on NGOs would also improve the information flow.)
At present, refugees do not have the facts to be able to make informed decisions.

other hand, a USCR report lends support to the view that refugees returned voluntarily, a conclusion endorsed by the UNHCR.[11] To what factors can we trace the different evaluations of the voluntariness of the 1992–93 repatriations? Can it be attributed to the lack of understanding of the process and/or of particular conditions prevailing in this part of the world? Or can the different evaluations be traced to the separate concerns of those undertaking it? For example, in **Reading V.B**, Hans notes the significance of the UNHCR certification of voluntariness to the return of refugees from Europe and North America.[12] Could this concern have compelled Asia Watch to conclude that the return was involuntary in nature?

Reading V.C reproduces an unreported decision of the Madras High Court in *P. Nedumaran and Dr. S. Ramadoss v. The Union of India and the State of Tamil Nadu* (1992) in which it was asked to decide if Sri Lankan Tamil refugees were being forced to repatriate by the Indian government. The significance of the decision—even though confined to considering a specific situation—lies in the standards it sets for the repatriation of refugees, in particular its stress on its voluntary character. In its decision the Madras High Court relied heavily on the presence of the UNHCR, albeit not in the camps, to oversee the repatriation of refugees. Was it correct in placing so much faith in the UNHCR?

The final reading in this section reproduces an unreported decision of the Karnataka High Court in *Digvijay Mote v. Government of India* (1994) which shows that it was only when the attention of authorities was drawn to the pathetic condition of refugee children living in Karnataka that the government agreed to do the needful. It underlines the important role

---

'Sri Lankan refugees in Tamil Nadu face implicit, and sometimes explicit, coercion to return. That pressure, which includes keeping the camps in a deliberate state of disrepair and withholding stipends and food rations, makes repatriation more attractive. If the refugees knew that they would be returning to the kind of camps described in this report, providing free labour for police, threatened by the LTTE and pro-government paramilitary organisations, fleeing from bombing and shelling, many would decide not to go.

'Until the voluntariness of their return can be assured, any repatriation would be tantamount to *refoulement*.' Asia Watch: *Halt Repatriation of Sri Lankan Tamils* (Vol. 5, No. 11, 11 August 1993).

[11] 'USCR interviewed more than two dozen Tamil families who returned from India during the recent repatriation. A large majority of those interviewed said that they had made their decision to repatriate voluntarily, largely free of external pressure.... Some families mentioned varying degrees of pressures in India—including threats of rations being cut off, or not being allowed to continue working—as contributing to their decision, but only one family cited those pressures as the primary reason for their return.

'UNHCR's field officer in Trincomalee had made a similar assessment. He told USCR that, based on his interviews with recent returnees, he was satisfied that the repatriation had been voluntary ....' US Committee for Refugees, *'People Want Peace': Repatriation and Reintegration in War-torn Sri Lanka* (January 1994), p. 26.

[12] See in this regard USCR, ibid., pp. 20–21.

that individuals and the judiciary can play in the defence of the rights of refugees.

India, 1951 Convention and the UNHCR

Reading VI.A briefly considers some of the reasons which have prevented India from ratifying the 1951 Convention or the 1967 Protocol. In its light readers may address the following questions: are the reasons advanced for non-ratification valid? In what ways will the legal situation change if India were to become a party to the Convention? Will India be able to protect its national interests if it ratifies the Convention? Would it have to alter its relationship with the UNHCR if it did so? Is there a need to become a party to the Convention if India passes a domestic legislation? Finally, is the fact that the 1951 Convention is being dismantled in the West a good enough reason for India and other countries in South Asia to not become parties to it?

I have elsewhere advanced the doctrine of constructive linkage and argued that the most significant reason why states in the South Asian region should refuse to accede to the 1951 Convention is the fact that it is being dismantled by the very states which adopted it.[13] In other words:

> any talk of accession should also be linked to the withdrawal of measures which constitute the *non-entrée* and temporary protection regimes. That is to say, the countries of the region should collectively argue that they would consider acceding to the Convention only if the Western world was willing to withdraw those measures which violate the principle of burden sharing and instead practise burden shifting.[14]

Would readers agree with this perspective? In response to the doctrine of constructive linkage critics contend that there is no reason why states in the region should not fulfil their moral obligations towards refugees just because the West is not doing so. But if the core objective is to offer assistance and protection to refugees can it not be effectively realised through the passage of domestic legislations even as pressure is brought on Western states to fulfil their obligations? Or is the worry that domestic legislations will be more restrictive than the 1951 Convention? In this respect readers may consider the following. First, as the US Supreme Court decision in *Sale v. Haitian Centers* shows, the 1951 Convention can also be very

---

[13] B.S. Chimni, *The Law and Politics of Regional Solution of the Refugee Problem: The Case of South Asia*, RCSS Policy Studies 4 (Regional Centre for Strategic Studies, Colombo, July 1998).

[14] Ibid.

restrictively interpreted.[15] Thus, the mere ratification of the 1951 Convention does not ensure that asylum-seekers will not be kept out. Second, Article 42 of the 1951 Convention permits reservations with respect to the rights of refugees. Third, in its recent decision in *Apparel Export Promotion Council v. A.K. Chopra* the Supreme Court of India observed:

> This Court has in numerous cases emphasised that while discussing constitutional requirements, courts and counsel must never forget the core principle embodied in the International Conventions and Instruments and so far as possible give effect to the principles contained in those international instruments. The Courts are under an obligation to give due regard to International Conventions and Norms for construing domestic laws more so when there is no inconsistency between them and there is a void in domestic law.[16]

The ruling opens up the possibility that the courts in India can refer to the 1951 Convention in interpreting the domestic legislation. Indeed, in *Vishaka and others v. State of Rajasthan and others* (1997 6 SCC 241) the Supreme Court went further and relied upon an 'official commitment' made by the Government of India at the Fourth World Conference on Women in Beijing. The Court observed that 'reliance can be placed on the above for the purpose of construing the nature and ambit of constitutional guarantee of gender equality in our Constitution.' Thus, an official statement made in the Executive Committee of the UNHCR that India intended to incorporate the basic provisions of the 1951 Convention into the domestic law would enable the Supreme Court to consult the Convention. In the circumstances, should India and the countries in South Asia ratify the 1951 Convention?

Readings VI.B and **VI.C** are concerned with India's relationship with the UNHCR. They offer by way of background two readings on an episode in the course of the Bangladesh liberation war which may have shaped India's relationship with the Office of the High Commissioner for Refugees. The negative perception of the role which the then High Commissioner played is seen as at least one reason which inhibited India for long from developing a constructive relationship with the UNHCR. **Reading VI.D** touches on this episode and goes on to record the positive direction in which it has evolved in recent years culminating with India becoming a member of the Executive Committee of the UNHCR in 1995. It is hoped that it will play its due role in this body. But what is the role India should play in the Executive Committee? Should it be solely concerned with the protection of its national interests or should it also

---

[15] For the text of relevant parts of the decision see Chapter 2, **Reading III. B.**
[16] 1999 (1) Scale (Vol. 1, No. 3, 18–24 January), para. 27.

attempt to articulate, in close coordination with other third world countries in the Committee, a Southern response to the global refugee problem?

Reading VI.E reproduces a brief excerpt from *The World Refugee Survey 1997* on the urban refugees living in and around New Delhi who are recognised by the UNHCR.

Rights of Refugees in India: Further Questions

In the background of the readings in this chapter and Chapter 3 on the 'Rights and Duties of Refugees' readers may also address the following questions: why does the Government of India not allow NGOs and the UNHCR access to the camps? What is the government's policy in relation to detention? How does it compare to the global policy on detention? Is confinement to camps tantamount to detention? What rights does a detainee possess? Are unreasonable restrictions placed on the right of movement of refugees within the country? What are the kinds of identification and travel papers that are provided to them? Can they travel abroad with the same? What steps can be taken by the government, in cooperation with NGOs and the UNHCR, to ensure that refugees live a life of dignity?

* * *

I. THE STORY OF PARTITION REFUGEES

A. Joseph B. Schechtman, *The Refugee in the World: Displacement and Integration* (A.S. Barnes and Co., New York, 1963), pp. 103–5.

By and large [...] the tragic exodus was conducted in the simplest and oldest way—on foot. Like the Children of Israel, but in ten to twenty times their number, millions of Hindus, Moslems, and Sikhs began their self-evacuation over footpaths and bullock-cart roads. Sometimes the caravans were relatively small, considering the danger they faced, sometimes they were unwieldy columns of hundreds of thousands of people. Forming what may be called the greatest single refugee trek in the world's history, 800,000 Hindus and Sikhs, coming on foot from Pakistan, were reported by the middle of October [1947] as being within twenty-five miles of the Indian border. The procession was forty-five miles long, with 400,000 in a single column and the rest in smaller groups. New Delhi newspaper correspondents reported on October 16 that the immense convoy had been attacked twice and suffered about 1,000 casualties. The exact whereabouts of the marchers was kept as a military secret to avoid further attacks. A month later, ten Moslem foot convoys, totalling 570,000, were reported moving across the Punjab toward Pakistan. In December, foot convoys, 30,000 to 40,000 strong, marched 150 miles from the rich agricultural lands of the Lyallpur and Montgomery districts of Pakistani West Punjab with thousands of head of cattle and hundreds of bullock carts carrying the migrants' meagre possessions.

Large or small, Moslem or Hindu–Sikh, all these convoys shared common emotions—misery and fear. For those individuals among them who had not been driven out by violence and had had ample time to make preparations before they left their homes, the food problems presented no great difficulty; people who joined the convoys with their bullock carts were generally able to carry sufficient supplies with them to last them for, say, a month. But in many cases the refugees carried only their clothing and a few pounds of food. Moving at the slow pace of the bullocks, ten to twelve miles a day, they had to forage or starve. Often the old and the very young dropped from hunger and exhaustion. Some were fortunate enough to have relatives who could aid them when they fell, but others were simply left behind by the roadside, alone and helpless in a hostile land.

The hardships of the trek, common to most migrations, were compounded by disease and mass murder. From the beginning, cholera flourished in the filthy camps and accompanied the travellers on the road. Armed bands of Moslem, Sikh and Hindu zealots preyed upon each other's convoys, and sometimes caravans were massacred in miniature wars between groups of refugees bound in opposite directions:

> From a high altitude or from a distance these caravans may have resembled a medieval army on the march. On a closer view, however, these columns appeared to lack both the buoyancy of a victorious army and the desperate energy of a retreating rabble. Men, women and children, even the cattle, stared as they trudged along. There was no anger and no vindictiveness on their faces—not yet; they moved forward as if they wore leaden shoes. The endless journey may have been tiring, but the fatigue somehow added to the chill of the nights under the sky. Mentally these people were just a blank.

The scope of this migration, as well as its hardships, was almost beyond imagination.

B. Nilanjana Chatterjee, 'The East Bengal Refugees: A Lesson in Survival', in Sukanta Chaudhuri, ed., *Calcutta: The Living City*, Vol. 2: *The Present and Future* (Oxford University Press, Delhi, 1990), pp. 70–76.

Since the history of Calcutta has been inextricably bound up with the refugees' struggles for survival, the city itself as a physical entity and a cultural process can be read as a text for some understanding of the dynamics of post-Partition reconstruction. Among the varied signifiers of refugee experiences are the urban topography of squatter colonies and pavement shanties; West Bengal party politics and the interlocutory activism of organisations such as the United Central Refugee Council; the films of Ritwik Ghatak; enduring folk memories of post-Partition inflation, rationing, black-marketing and the nightmare that was Sealdah Station; compelling evocations of *Sonar Bangla* in the lilt of a dialect and the taste of a fish curry; acts of introduction that involve genealogies extending beyond the Padma River. These signifiers suggest at least as many narratives of displacement and rehabilitation as there are refugees, each one a reminder of human suffering and enterprise.

This article presents an interpretative version of two representative accounts. One may be called the official discourse, which perceives the refugees as objects of assistance and as such a 'problem' group. The other may be called a refugee counter-discourse that assigns centrality to the displaced themselves in reconstructing their lives, and may even hold the government responsible for exacerbating the refugee 'problem'....

Defining the Refugees

The minorities who fled from East Pakistan through fear of the actual event of discrimination and violence were all equally refugees by experience. But they were not a homogeneous group. They were differentiated by period or wave of migration; reason for flight; place of origin and subsequent trajectory; caste, class, occupation; and status vis-à-vis the government's assistance programme.

The time of displacement was crucial to the last factor. Refugees were classified as 'old' or 'new' migrants. The 'old migrants' were the 41.17 lakh people who escaped to India from former East Bengal between October 1946 and March 1958 in different waves. 31.32 lakh of them are estimated to have remained in West Bengal, while the rest dispersed throughout India. Those who migrated between April 1958 and December 1963 were not considered eligible for Government help. The unofficial figures for refugees who settled of their own accord in West Bengal in this liminal period is in the region of 2.5 lakh.

January 1964 and March 1971 bracket the period of 'new migrants'. Responding to a sharp rise in migration, the Indian Government took a policy decision that relief and rehabilitation benefits would only be extended to those 'new migrants' who agreed to be resettled outside West Bengal. In spite of this, of the 11.14 lakh displaced between 1964 and 1970, about 6 lakh chose to stay in West Bengal. Finally, the 80-lakh wave during the Bangladesh War of 1971 left behind, on a conservative estimate, about 2 lakh refugees as human flotsam in West Bengal.

It must be remembered that most of these statistics are unreliable. In 1981, the Government of West Bengal estimated the total number of displaced people from East Bengal in the State to be about 80 lakh, or one-sixth the total population of West Bengal. . . .

Rethinking Stereotypes

Refugees are helped for humanitarian reasons and because they present a long-term development problem. But ironically, the assistance paradigm casts the refugees in a supplicatory, helpless position, perpetuating a vicious spiral. East Bengal refugees have long been negatively stereotyped as victims and trouble-makers—indolent, obstructive, reasonably demanding and unwilling to adapt to new environments. These canards are refuted by abundant evidence of self-reliance and the will to survive against tremendous odds. The displaced tended to take refuge in West Bengal seemingly regardless of specific Government policy. Individually and as groups they projected a survivor mentality, manipulating and, where necessary, resisting official assumptions about dependence. They dynamically influenced the outcome of organised assistance, though many of their survival strategies were considered illegal or anti-social by the host Government and population. While they might have presented a 'problem', they also testified to a unique potential for positive change and development. . . .

The 'Old Migrants': 1946–1949

After Partition, 258,000 migrants sought shelter in West Bengal in 1947 alone. This number increased by 590,000 in 1948 and 182,000 in 1949. Interestingly, there was no overt communal conflict in East Pakistan during these years; but as Kiranshankar Ray, leader of the Congress Party in the Pakistan Constituent Assembly, pointed out in 1948, there were many and widespread instances of harassment, extortion and persecution of the minorities, which in turn fed their fears—of physical annihilation, political powerlessness, social and economic deterioration, and loss of identity.

On the Indian side, certain emergency governmental relief measures were supplemented by an immense public relief effort. At the same time, the Government clearly did not wish to encourage migration by offering attractive relief. It was also feared that too great an exodus would strain Hindu–Muslim relations in India. These and a number of other political factors led to an agreement at the Inter-Dominion Conference of April 1948 that the responsibility for the protection of minorities would rest exclusively with the government of the country concerned. A fall in the influx subsequent to the agreement allowed Nehru to believe, prematurely as it turned out, that the worst of the exodus was over. It was even anticipated that the migration was temporary and could be reversed. Hence the emphasis was on relief rather than rehabilitation: measures for the latter were limited and piecemeal.

Many of these early refugees had pre-Partition ties, of occupation or kinship, with West Bengal and specifically Calcutta. Others were civil servants who opted to work in India. Hence most of these early migrants had some resources in West Bengal and could find niches for themselves. Of the 13.78 lakh persons displaced by December 1949, only 1.06 lakhs sought admission to relief camps. The vast majority who did not were surveyed around this time by the Indian Statistical Institute: they were found to belong to the 'upper' and 'middle' castes, who tended to gravitate to urban areas including Calcutta. (The 'lower' and scheduled castes preferred resettlement in villages.) Significantly, 60 percent of the migrants up to 1949 were non-agriculturists.

As these *bhadralok* migrants converged on Calcutta, there resulted an acute housing shortage in an already congested city. Some refugees who had the means bought property or exchanged it with evacuee Muslims: this could happen as a group effort, creating 'private colonies'. A considerable number rented houses, in middle-class localities or slums. But it was the squatters who made East Bengali refugees famous or infamous.

Squatting ranged from the forcible occupation of barracks in the Dhakuria Lake area and New Alipur by individual families and of empty country villas in suburban Calcutta, to the collective take-over of private, government and wastelands and the establishment of 'colony' communities. This happened as early as 1948 with middle-class refugees in the Jadabpur area: first on government land, then on private property, leading to violent clashes. Having won the battle, the elated squatters named their colony 'Bijaygarh', the Fort of Victory. By 1949 there were over forty such colonies in the south-east of the Calcutta Metropolitan District, in Jadabpur, Kasba, Santoshpur, Garia and Behala, and about sixty-five in the Dumdum and Panihati zone in the north.

There was a pattern to the squatter movement: *jabardakhal* (seizure and settlement) came to acquire the quality of a myth. The land, identified in advance, would usually be occupied under cover of night; plots would be marked off, and shacks erected with incredible speed, thatched with the hogla leaves that became an emblem of squatter life. Young girls were often left in charge of a newly-set-up hearth to forestall violent eviction. Subscriptions and joint labour, supervised by the colony committee, went into clearing the land and laying down roads, drains and a water supply.

Not only were the refugees themselves proud of having built these settlements almost entirely from their own assistance; their pioneer spirit was lauded by government rehabilitation authorities like N.B. Maiti and Rameshwari Nehru. Property owners were naturally—and often violently—

hostile, but public opinion was generally favourable. The refugees themselves asserted the 'respectable' nature of their formally illegal acts, driven
by dire necessity for shelter, and looked to the Government to legalise
their claim in the extraordinary circumstances....

The 'Old Migrants': 1950

Communal conflict broke out in Khulna in December 1949, and had
spread all over East Pakistan by February 1950, setting off a new wave of
migration. This led to counter-violence in Calcutta and a counter-wave of
Muslim migration from West Bengal, making the passage unsafe for all
the displaced. This time the refugees from East Pakistan were chiefly
rural—peasant proprietors, traders and artisans.

As tension mounted, there was pressure on the Government of India
for either a military or a negotiated solution. In April 1950, Prime Minister Nehru signed a pact with his Pakistani counterpart Liaquat Ali Khan,
which guaranteed equality of citizenship to minorities irrespective of religion. It also guaranteed freedom of movement, with the right to move
personal property across the frontier. Migrants who returned home by
the end of 1950 would have their immovable property restored; others
could continue to hold it or dispose of it through trustees.

The immediate result of the pact was a drop in migration and even a
small but much publicised repatriation. But by August 1950, it was
already being argued in Parliament that the pact was being implemented
by India alone. The notional retention by the refugees of the title to their
abandoned property also prevented them from receiving the compensation which would have helped to rehabilitate them in their new homes.

Meanwhile, a Branch Secretariat of the Rehabilitation Ministry was set
up at Calcutta in 1950. Its optimistic estimates allowed for only 2 lakh
assistance-seekers, just half of them in West Bengal. In fact, 75,000 were
admitted to refugee camps, pending planned rehabilitation, in March
alone; about 25,000 per month from April to September, and nearly
10,000 per month thereafter. Tent colonies, empty warehouses and even
sewers were set up as temporary shelters. Those who sought admission to
camps were taken to special reception centres like Shealdah Station prior
to dispersal. Delays caused thousands of refugees to become a fixture
there, and transit camps were opened in and around Calcutta to reduce
the pressure—in the jute godowns of Ultadanga, Kashipur, Ghusuri and
Babu Ghat.

Families which could be resettled were sent temporarily to regular
camps like Dhubulia, the largest in West Bengal with a capacity of 60,000,
and Cooper's Camp which was meant for refugees to be rehabilitated
outside West Bengal. Long-term responsibilities such as widows, orphans
and the old and infirm were sent to 'permanent liability' camps. Camp

inmates were given maintenance doles of foodgrains and cash; they also had access to the camp medical facilities and schools. The target date for closing all regular camps was set for 30 April 1950.

Of the 11.82 lakh refugees who were supposed to have entered West Bengal in 1950, only 23 percent actually took shelter in the camps. But the figure in real terms was too large for the camp facilities in the state and critics soon pointed to the overcrowding, insanitary conditions, inadequate rations and water supply, disease, high death rates, corruption among camp personnel and demoralising delays in dispersal. In the early days of 1950 the city itself seemed to be converted into a relief camp. The refugees received aid from voluntary and charitable organisations, college students and concerned private citizens. But as the migrations continued, concern gave way to resigned inertia and then to competition over shrinking economic resources.

All studies suggest that the refugees responded to the inadequate relief and rehabilitation resources with enterprise and flexibility. In the process of self-settlement, caste rules were bent, traditional occupations were abandoned in the search for employment, families became more nuclear and women came out of the home to work....

The 'Old Migrants': 1951–1958

The migration from East Pakistan continued unabated through the 1950s. In 1951, threatened by unrest in Pakistan over the Kashmir issue, 1.40 lakh people fled to West Bengal. Passports were introduced in 1951 as a check to migration, yet 1.52 lakhs came that year and 1.64 lakhs in 1953–54. In 1955, Pakistan declared Urdu to be its official language; in 1956 it adopted an Islamic constitution. The migration to West Bengal mounted to 2.12 lakhs and 2.47 lakhs respectively. In a last attempt to stem the influx, all assistance was stopped to migrants after March 1958.

The pressure of refugees forced the Government of West Bengal to reopen its camps in 1951. As the new migrants were chiefly from the depressed sections of Hindus, often totally pauperised by displacement, increasingly larger numbers came to the camps—as much as 50 percent of the total inflow in 1955–56. By 1958, there were about 8 lakh refugees in some 150 camps and homes in West Bengal. One-third of them had spent six to ten years in camps. Dispersal was slow because 60 percent of the inmates were agriculturists. There was an acute shortage of land in West Bengal, and acceptable sites elsewhere were difficult to find.

Official attempts at rehabilitation crystallised in the 1950s. Only around 1955 did the Government begin replacing ad hoc assistance measures by planned rehabilitation on a rational or economic basis. From about 1958, such programmes were sought to be integrated into comprehensive regional development programmes. The Government's overall effort did help stimulate some economic growth in Calcutta and West Bengal, but in the process highlighted the lost opportunities for progress.

In general, rehabilitation schemes were divided into rural and urban categories. The rural assistance programmes were gradually geared to a search for land in other states, especially Orissa, Andhra Pradesh, Madhya Pradesh and the Andaman Islands. Such attempts pointed the way to the Dandakaranya Project initiated in 1958....

At the end of 1958–59, the government reported that it had spent 48.5 crores on the non-camp refugees and only 18 crores on those in its own camps. Looking back at the 1950s, it might be argued that more 'old migrants' rebuilt their lives successfully, with or without assistance, than refugees belonging to later waves. Resettlement in West Bengal and Calcutta since the 1960s was, by definition, self-settlement, and shrinking resources tended to make marginalisation a persistent condition for 'new migrants'.

C. Kanti B. Pakrasi, *The Uprooted: A Sociological Study of the Refugees of West Bengal, India* (S. Ghatack, Calcutta, 1971), pp. 49–52.

The present study concerns mainly with some interesting sociological problems of the migrated families from erstwhile East Bengal.... The refugees in question have been distinguished as a *special group* from the ordinary alien or usual migrant groups in that *they had left their territory of regular residence because of political developments there and not because of economic conditions or because of the economic attractions of another territory*. It has been already stated that 'before a man can be described as a refugee, the political events which caused him to leave, or to break with, the State to which he owed allegiance must be defined. The political events which in the country of origin led to his departure must be accompanied by persecution or the threat of persecution against himself or at least against a section of the population with which he identified himself'.[17]

But, in case of the displaced persons under study it was a different issue. Though a *forced movement of population* results invariably in loss of citizenship to the refugees, yet in the case of East Bengal refugees there was certainly no question of granting them *new nationality*. They simply moved away from the troubled spots in East Bengal to join their co-religionists, blood relatives and inmates in West Bengal. Truly speaking, they were no refugee, *they were displaced people from one socio-political environment to another*....

The sociologists are concerned in general with the *consequences* of the conditions under which the minorities were forced to become a *problem*

[17] Jacques Vernant, *The Refugee in the Post-war World* (Yale University Press, London, 1953), p. 7.

group as refugees in the receiving countries. The refugees are generally thought to represent a symbol of instability and isolation and thereby they continue to remain to be a problem group till they are able to identify and integrate themselves completely with other social groups of the receiving country. But in the case of the refugees of West Bengal they were (or are) no foreigners, rather their 'social co-ordinates' got temporarily distorted and disorganised. They lost their natal homes and hearths, yet in general they met 'neither with hostility, nor coolness or reserve' in their new places of settlement. As a Bengali-speaking group the non-Muslim migrants from the Muslim state of East Bengal found no ostensible difficulty in meeting the *mores* of their co-religionists of West Bengal. Territorial separation was there but that was never a factor to snap the cultural and linguistic semblances between the non-Muslim refugees and Hindu non-migrants of the State. Thus, it may be understood that the refugees under study were not exclusively unstable and isolated in their new abodes within West Bengal. They were never *an unknown entity* in the receiving States of India. As each country has its own situation and problems the question of West Bengal refugees has to be merited in consonance with the objective societal situation that was prevailing in West Bengal of 1947–48.

Sociological perspective of the present study should, therefore, not be confused or equated with those which are met with in several brilliant studies made on the refugees concerned outside India.[18] Displaced persons (refugees) of India deserve special attention of the sociologists since they created a new history of forced migration under political cum religious mandates. The displaced persons of West Bengal or of any State of Indian Union are not in a position to satisfy the definition of the refugees found in international laws which, on the other hand, treat a refugee as an alien for the State where he preferred to reside. The refugees of India were and are never considered socially or legally as aliens, rather they have been accepted as lawful citizens of the country and Indian nationality has been accorded to them unquestionably. The fact remains clear that in consequence of communal disturbances in the areas which now constitute Pakistan they were compelled to migrate from their homeland and overnight reduced themselves to the status of 'refugee' in India.

For security, shelter and self-preservation, non-Muslim inhabitants of Pakistan migrated to several states of India and under circumstances beyond their control they became eventually uprooted and displaced from their natal homes in Pakistan. Such displaced persons have been grouped under a specific *social category* of refugee for the mere purpose of general description. It should be noted clearly that the integration of

---

[18] Ibid.; John Hope Simpson, *The Refugee Problem* (London, 1939); and M.J. Proudfoot, *European Refugees, 1939–52: A Study in Forced Population Movements* (London, 1957).

such displaced persons with the general population of India was and is in the long run inevitable and immediately after Partition and migration the only trait they had in common with *true* refugees (as defined in international laws) was that they had no home, or work or that they were awaiting some sort of settlement with official and non-official help and co-operation. It is, of course, a fact that these displaced persons were once in the position of refugee when they were displaced from one country to another as a result of communal disturbances and solicited admission to a new country. Thus, in the present study of the migrant families whenever the term 'refugee' would occur the same shall mean unquestionably the displaced persons from East Pakistan who migrated in West Bengal immediately after the act of Partition during 1947–48.

D. Jacques Vernant, *The Refugee in the Post-war World* (Yale University Press, New Haven, 1953), pp. 740–41.

The question whether those who are called refugees in India and Pakistan are refugees in the precise sense that we have given to the term calls for very careful consideration. It is true that in the countries in which they sought refuge, the refugees met with neither hostility, nor coldness, nor reserve. They were welcomed on either side as co-religionists, as compatriots re-entering the fold. They were integrated almost at once in either country. Their integration was, moreover, a right to which they were entitled by the laws introduced during or after the Partition. Consequently, those who were termed refugees are now fully fledged citizens[19] of either India or Pakistan. The only trait they still have in common with refugees is that they have no home or work or land, or that they are awaiting the settlement of their claims for their abandoned property. It is, however, unquestionable that they were once in the position of refugees, that is to say, that they were displaced from one country to another as a result of religious disturbances and solicited admission to a new country. The fact that their position has now ceased to be that of refugees both in the legal sense and also, as is true of millions, from the material point of view, is due to the promptitude and the intense energy shown by the two Governments in solving the problem. That problem has now, to a large extent, been solved, but it would be wrong on that account alone to deny its existence or to minimise its magnitude. It would be wrong to overlook the fact that these two States, which are among the youngest in the world, had to face a refugee problem of gigantic dimensions and have gained in this field experience from which much may doubtless be learnt.

[19] Hence the very apt title of the book by Horace Alexander, *New Citizens of India* (Oxford University Press, Oxford, 1951), a masterly and extremely vivid presentation of the refugee problem in India.

E. U. Bhaskar Rao, *The Story of Rehabilitation* **(Department of Rehabilitation, Government of India, New Delhi, 1967), pp. 112–15, 121–25, 128–34.**

Compensation

As early as in 1949 [...] the Government of India pledged itself to the payment of compensation ... But there was a long way to go before a scheme could be worked out and payment made, months of wearisome waiting, of frustration....

... Early in 1950 the Claims Act was passed and displaced persons were invited to present claims in respect of immovable property they had abandoned in West Pakistan. Agricultural land, which was dealt with under a separate scheme, was excluded from the scope of these operations. By the middle of the year, hundreds of thousands of claims had been filed. Outside every regional rehabilitation centre one saw a cluster of refugees squatting in front of petition-writers to get their claims recorded. To the large number of illiterate or semi-literate property owners such help was indispensable. On 1 July 1950, the Ministry [the Ministry of Rehabilitation] was able to start on the registration of these claims. More than 300 regional centres were established in the various States to handle the job. By the end of November, except for stragglers, the entire work of registration had been completed.

Immediately thereafter, the Ministry swung into the most complicated part of the task—the verification of more than 535,000 registered claims involving over 10 lakhs of houses, among other property. A vast organisation came into being under a Chief Claims Commissioner. Besides a large establishment at the New Delhi headquarters were 264 Claims Officers, each with his own administrative and clerical staff. It took nearly three years to complete those colossal operations. Hundreds of thousands of claimants had to be heard patiently and diligently cross-examined before the claims could be verified. By 1953, some 3,90,000 claims had been verified. The total value of those verified claims was of the staggering order of Rs. 500 crores.

The Ministry had now before it a fairly accurate picture of the financial burden of payment of full compensation. But where was the money to meet the obligations to come from? The total value of evacuate property in India was a bare Rs. 100 crores, pitifully inadequate for anything like a satisfactory compensation scheme....

... The framers of the Interim Compensation Scheme, sanctioned on 5 November 1953, were guided by certain fundamental principles. First, that compensation is the culmination of the process of rehabilitation. Second, that certain vulnerable categories of displaced persons needed immediate assistance. Third, that in consonance with social justice, the smaller claimants should receive a proportionately larger measure of relief.

The five priority categories of claimants to benefit from the Interim Scheme were:

(a) Widows, old and infirm persons in receipt of maintenance allowance.

(b) Inmates of women's homes and infirmaries and unattached women and children, aged and infirm persons in receipt of gratuitous relief outside homes (including recipients of doles).

(c) Other widows with claims in their own names.

(d) Persons living in certain Government-built townships and colonies.

(e) Residents of mud huts in the Punjab.

The smaller the claim the greater the consideration it deserved. This principle was inherent in the human approach to the problem. In its practical application there were two separate strands. The total amount due to a claimant was split up into two components. One, the compensation, which declined gradually from 20 per cent of verified claims up to Rs. 37,000 to 16 per cent in the case of claims of Rs. 50,000 and above; the other the rehabilitation grant, intended to cover the claimant's need for adequate rehabilitation. This was as high as 40 per cent of the verified claim in the lower brackets, and tapered down progressively to nothing in respect of claims beyond the stage of Rs. 37,000. It was the latter, of course, that really served to redress the balance in favour of the small claimant. For instance, a person with a claim of Rs. 2,000 received Rs. 400 as compensation plus twice that sum, that is, Rs. 800 as rehabilitation grant. He was awarded under the Scheme altogether Rs. 1,200, as much as 60 per cent of his claim. A person with a claim of Rs. 37,000 received only compensation, calculated at 20 per cent. The maximum compensation one was entitled to under this Scheme was Rs. 8,000, that is, persons with claims of Rs. 50,000 and over received just Rs. 8,000 and no more.

The fairness of this scale is apparent from the following rough breakdown: 32 per cent of the claimants had claims up to Rs. 5,000; another 28 per cent claims between Rs. 5,000 and Rs. 10,000; a further 24 per cent were in the Rs. 10,000–20,000 bracket; those between Rs. 20,000 and Rs. 50,000 comprised nearly 13 per cent; only 3 per cent had claims of more than Rs. 50,000.

Claimants living in homes and infirmaries were eligible for rehabilitation grants on an even more generous scale. In the case of such persons with claims up to Rs. 5,000, to the normal rehabilitation grant was added another 75 per cent of it. Thus a person in this category with a claim of Rs. 2,000 or less was entitled to as much as 90 per cent of his verified claim. In the case of persons with claims ranging from Rs. 5,000 to Rs. 10,000 the additional payment by way of rehabilitation grant declined progressively from 75 per cent to 37.5 per cent. Rehabilitation grant was admissible to claimants in this group up to the stage of Rs. 39,000.

Claimants living in homes and infirmaries had the option of receiving payment under this scheme and quitting the institutions, or of staying on. If they chose to stay on, their dues were kept in deposit and their expenses met out of them.

The first distribution of compensation took place at Delhi on 28 November 1953, Mr. Ajit Prasad Jain, then Rehabilitation Minister, handing over bank drafts to several old men and women at a formal ceremony....

... The Rehabilitation Ministry was in no mood to rest on its oars. The Interim Scheme, excellent as it was, attacked only the hard core of the problem. On the periphery were thousands and thousands of displaced persons excluded from its beneficence. Every effort was, therefore, directed towards enlarging its scope so that it swept every one of them into its fold as quickly as might be. Rehabilitation, to be effective, had to be timely. Otherwise long-suffering patience turned to despair, sullenness and resentment. Besides, there was the missionary enthusiasm that had come to permeate everyone in the Ministry. Compensation was reorganised as the cornerstone to the edifice of rehabilitation.

The legal impediments were largely cleared away with the passing of the Displaced Persons (Compensation and Rehabilitation) Act on October 9, 1954. This enactment conferred on the central government powers to acquire evacuee property for the relief and rehabilitation of displaced persons and for the payment of compensation. It provided for the constitution of a Compensation Pool out of which payment of such compensation could be made, and also for the setting up of machinery for purposes of implementing the Compensation Scheme. The Act only set out in broad outline the principles that must govern the scheme, leaving the quantum of payment and the manner of disbursement, as well as the other multitudinous procedural details, to be covered by Rules. A Statutory Advisory Board constituted under the Act examined the Rules as soon as they had been drafted, and then referred them to a conference of the Rehabilitation Ministers of various States. In their final shape, the rules were promulgated on 27 June 1955, and in a slightly modified form, received Parliamentary approval towards the end of September.

Naturally, the new scheme evolved was a considerable improvement on the interim one. In the first place, its benefits were extended to persons outside the five priority categories. The scale of payments was liberalised. New concessions were also announced. The experience gained in the administration of the Interim Scheme proved invaluable in the formulation of a better and more comprehensive plan.

The upgrading of the scale of compensation conferred substantial additional benefits on claimants. But the principle of awarding a proportionately larger share to the smaller claimant was not abandoned. So long as it was impossible to meet every claim in full some adjustment of this kind was imperative in the interests of social justice....

For joint families, which had been treated as a single unit under the Interim Scheme, there was now special relief. Members of a Hindu joint family entitled to claim partition were allowed to file separate individual claims for compensation, each in respect of his share. This splitting up ensured the family as a whole larger quantum of compensation. The concession was particularly appreciated by joint families with verified claims in excess of Rs. 2 lakhs.

The distinction made under the Interim Scheme between urban and rural claims disappeared with the promulgation of the Rules. If a claimant for a rural house was given cash or allotted urban property, the value of the rural claim was, before the new scheme came into force, reduced by half. This was done with a view to ensuring justice as between rural and urban house owners. But now the two sets of claims were accorded equality of treatment.

There was quite a large number of displaced persons who, for one reason or another beyond their control, had been unable to take advantage of the Displaced Persons (Claims) Act of 1950. The Rules made provision for payment of rehabilitation grants to recompense such persons for property they had abandoned in Pakistan. Rehabilitation grants were paid also to certain categories of displaced persons who had been allotted land and who, in view of such allotment, had not been permitted to submit claims for small rural houses. Such claims had been disallowed on the ground that along with the land allotted invariably went a small rural house. There were, besides, refugees who had been allotted less than four acres of agricultural land, but had either declined the offer or had had the allotment cancelled. In order to mitigate their hardships similar grants were paid to them, too. Yet another category of land claimants, those in the lowest bracket, who had been allotted two standard acres or less in the Punjab (PEPSU included) but had refused to accept such allotments were afforded relief in the shape of ex-gratia grants at the rate of Rs. 450 per standard acre of the area allotted to them.

No sooner was the task of paying the compensation launched in earnest than it became apparent that the greater proportion of the claimants would have to be content with property. The cash resources of the pool, as we have seen, were severely restricted. It was, therefore, necessary to lay down specifically which categories of claimants should be given compensation in cash, and which in the form of property. The transfer of evacuee and government-built property against verified claims thus came to be regarded as the cardinal feature of the pattern of compensation.

II. LEGAL FRAMEWORK

A. B.S. Chimni, 'The Legal Condition of Refugees in India', *Journal of Refugee Studies* (Vol. 7, No. 4, 1994), pp. 378–81[20]

International Obligations

India is not a party to the 1951 Convention . . . [or the 1967 Protocol] . . . . However, it acceded in March 1979 to the two 1966 Covenants on Civil and Political Rights and Economic, Social and Cultural rights. . . . Albeit it may be noted that India has reserved its right to apply its own municipal law in relation to foreigners.[21] Moreover, since the Covenants have not been enacted into Indian law they do not have the force of law in India and are therefore not enforceable in Indian courts. But as has been pointed out, 'this does not relieve India of its international obligations under the Covenants. . . . The courts may take them into account in appropriate cases while interpreting the statue law'.[22] India has also acceded to the Convention on the Rights of the Child on 11 December 1992. While it entered certain reservations these are not concerning Article 22 which deals with the refugee child.[23]

---

[20] The article is a slightly abridged version of a report written for the International Academy of Comparative Law. However, I have reproduced here excerpts from the original report as it contains material of interest to the reader in India.

[21] India's reservation reads:

With respect to Article 13 of the International Covenants on Civil and Political Rights, the Government of the Republic of India reserves its right to apply its law relating to foreigners.

For the text of India's Declaration of Accession see *Indian Journal of International Law* (Vol. 20, 1980), pp. 118–19. Article 13 of the Civil and Political Rights Covenant reads:

An alien lawfully in the territory of a State Party to the present Covenant may be expelled therefrom only in pursuance of a decision reached in accordance with law and shall, except where compelling reasons of national security otherwise require, be allowed to submit the reasons against his expulsion and to have his case reviewed by, and be represented for the purpose before, the competent authority or a person or persons especially designated by the competent authority.

[22] P. Chandrasekhara Rao, *The Indian Constitution and International Law* (Taxman, Delhi, 1993), p. 143.

[23] Article 2 para. (1) states:

States Parties shall take appropriate measures to ensure that a child who is seeking refugee status or who is considered a refugee in accordance with applicable international or domestic law and procedures shall, whether unaccompanied or accompanied by his or her parents or by any other person, receive appropriate protection and humanitarian

The Indian Supreme Court, the highest court of the land, has had occasion to refer to India's international obligations in many cases. For instance, ... the Supreme Court made the following observations in the context of preventive detention of a foreign national:

> Preventive detention of a foreign national who is not resident of the country involves an element of international law and human rights and the appropriate authorities ought not to be seen to have been oblivious of its international obligations in this regard. The universal declaration of human rights include the right to life, liberty and security of person, freedom of arbitrary arrest and detention; the right to fair trial by an independent and impartial tribunal; and the right to presume to be an innocent man until proved guilty. When an act of preventive detention involves a foreign national, though from the national point of view the municipal law alone counts in its application and interpretation, it is generally a recognised principle in national legal system that in the event of doubt the national rule is to be interpreted in accordance with the State's international obligations.... There is a need for harmonisation whenever possible bearing in mind the spirit of the covenants.[24]

Refugees and the Domestic Legal System

India has a federal set up and is described as a Union of States.[25] It is the Union which is a state in the sense of international law. The Union legislature, i.e., the Parliament, alone is given the right to deal with the subject of citizenship, naturalisation and aliens. Generally speaking, the executive power of the Union is co-extensive with its legislative power.[26] India has not passed a refugee specific legislation which regulates the entry and status of refugees. It has handled the influx of refugees at the political and administrative levels. The result is that refugees are treated under the law applicable to aliens in India, unless a specific provision is made as in the case of Ugandan refugees (of Indian origin) when it passed the Foreigners from Uganda Order, 1972.[27]

---

assistance in the enjoyment of applicable rights set forth in this Convention and in other human rights or humanitarian instruments to which the said States are Parties.

For India's Declaration Acceding to the Convention see *Multilateral Treaties Deposited with the Secretary-General, Status as at 31 December 1992* (UN, New York, 1993), p. 187.

[24] *Kubic Dariusz v. Union of India*, All India Reporter (A.I.R.) 1990 SC 605 at pp. 614–15.

[25] Article 1 (1) of the Constitution of India.

[26] Rao, *The Indian Constitution and International Law* (see footnote 22 earlier), pp. 12–13.

[27] J.N. Saxena, 'Legal Status of Refugees: India's Position', *Indian Journal of International Law* (Vol. 26, 1986), pp. 501–15 at p. 508. For the text of Foreigners from Uganda Order,

The word 'alien' is nowhere defined though it appears in the Constitution of India (Article 22 para 3 and Entry 17, List I, Schedule 7), in Section 83 óf the Indian Civil Procedure Code, and in Section 3 (2) (b) of the Indian Citizenship Act, 1955, as well as some other statues. The following enactments have relevance to the regulation of aliens in India: the Foreigners Act, 1946 under which the central government is empowered to regulate the entry of aliens into India, their presence and departure therefrom; it defines a 'foreigner' to mean 'a person who is not a citizen of India'.[28] The Registration Act, 1939 deals with the registration of foreigners entering, being present in, and departing from India. Besides these two principal enactments there is the Passport (Entry into India) Act, 1920 and the Passport Act, 1967 dealing with the powers of the government to impose conditions of passport for entry into India, and the issue of passports and travel documents to regulate departure from India of citizens of India and applies in certain instances to other cases to.

What rights do foreigners or aliens possess in the territory of India? The Indian Supreme Court has taken the view that even a foreigner possesses rights but it is confined to the right of life and liberty contained in Article 21 of the Indian Constitution[29] which reads:

> *Protection of Life and Personal Liberty*—No person shall be deprived of his life or personal liberty except by procedure established by law.

1972, see Vijay Kumar Diwan, *Law of Citizenship, Foreigners and Passports* (Orient Law House, Allahabad, 1984), first edition, p. 291.

[28] Since the words 'alien' and 'foreigner' are used interchangeably in Indian legislations it should be deemed the definition of 'alien' as well.

[29] *Louis De Raedt v. Union of India* (1991 [3] SCC 554 at p. 562); and *State of Arunachal Pradesh v. Khudiram Chakma*, (JT 1993 [3] S.C. 546 at p. 552). In the *Louis De Raedt* case, the Supreme Court observed:

> The fundamental right of the foreigner is confined to Article 21 for life and liberty and does not include the right to reside and settle in this country, as mentioned in Article 19 (1) (e), which is applicable only to citizens of this country.

It is difficult to understand how the Supreme Court has confined, at least in its observations in some cases, the right of aliens to Article 21 alone when clearly other articles, Article 14, for example, which deals with equal protection of the laws, is extended to both aliens and non-nationals alike. It would appear that the alien possesses rights also under Articles 20 and 22 of the Indian Constitution which deal with issues like double jeopardy and preventive detention. The rationale for granting the latter rights to aliens has been explained by eminent Indian constitutional law expert H.M. Seervai: 'as a civilised country valuing the dignity of the individuals, the founding fathers decided that when it came to depriving a person of his life or putting his person under restraint by imprisonment, justice required that safeguards provided by Articles 20, 21 and 22 (1) and (2) should be available to citizen and non-citizen alike before anyone is held guilty of committing a crime, and before he is sentenced to death or imprisonment.' H.M. Seervai, *Constitutional Law of India: A Critical Commentary* (N.M. Tripathi and Co. Ltd., Bombay, 1991), fourth edition, p. 989.

Thus, a foreigner does not have the right to move freely throughout and to reside and stay in any part of the territory of India as conferred under Article 19 (1) (d) and (e). Such a right is available only to citizens, and thus not to aliens, including refugees.[30] The Indian Supreme Court has also held that the government's right to deport is absolute:

> the power of the Government in India to expel foreigners is absolute and unlimited and there is no provision in the Constitution fettering this discretion ... the executive Government has unrestricted right to expel a foreigner.[31]

But do refugees as a special class of aliens possess any more rights than aliens in general? That is to say, to the extent that the existence of refugees as a class is known to and defined by general international law as a special category of aliens, does it import legal consequences for the Indian government in the absence of any legislation on the subject? The answer to this question depends on the constraints customary international law imposes on the Indian judicial system, for every state, whether a member of the 1951 Convention or not, is obliged to respect the principle of *non-refoulement* which is a customary norm of international law.[32]

It is well established in India that the principles of customary international law cannot be enforced by courts if they are in conflict with statutes.[33] Indian courts have accepted and applied the doctrine of incorporation according to which customary rules are to be considered part of the law of the land and enforced as such, with the qualification that they are incorporated only so far as is not inconsistent with Acts of Parliament.[34] In *Gramophone Co. of India v. Birendra Bahadur Pandey* the Indian Supreme Court observed:

> The Comity of Nations requires that Rules of international law may be accommodated in the Municipal Law even without express legislative sanction provided they do not run into conflict with Acts of Parliament. But when they do run into such conflict, the sovereignty and the integrity of the Republic and the supremacy of the constituted legislatures in making the laws may not be subjected to external rules except to the extent legitimately accepted by the constituted

---

[30] *Khudiram Chakma* case (see footnote 29 earlier).

[31] *Louis de Raedt v. Union of India*, A.I.R. 1991 SC 1886 at p. 1890.

[32] According to Goodwin-Gill, 'the principle forms part of general international law.... There is substantial, if not conclusive, authority that the principle is binding on all states, independently of specific assent.' Guy S. Goodwin-Gill, *The Refugee in International Law* (Clarendon Press, Oxford, 1983), first edition, p. 97.

[33] Rao, *The Indian Constitution and International Law* (see footnote 22 earlier), p. 179.

[34] Ian Brownlie, *Principles of Public International Law* (Oxford University Press, Oxford, 1990), fourth edition, p. 43.

legislatures themselves. The doctrine of incorporation also recognises the position that the rules of international law are incorporated into national law and considered to be part of the national law, unless they are in conflict with an Act of Parliament. Comity of Nations or no, Municipal Law must prevail in case of conflict.[35]

Since the 1946 Foreigners Act has been interpreted to grant absolute and unfettered rights to the Indian Government to expel a foreigner the principles of customary international law cannot impose any limitation on its powers in this regard.[36]

However, the Supreme Court appears to have erred in concluding in *Louis de Raedt v. Union of India* that there is no provision in the Constitution fettering the 'absolute' and 'unlimited' power of the Government to expel foreigners. In actuality, Article 21 of the Indian Constitution does impose certain constraints: any action of the State which deprives an alien of his or her life and personal liberty without a procedure established by law would fall foul of it, and such action would certainly include the *refoulement* of refugees.

The reason the Supreme Court did not so hold was that it affirmed a thirty-five-year-old judgement of the Court without taking into account either the developments in international human rights law or the different and liberal interpretation given by the Court to Article 21 since; in fact it simply repeated verbatim the words of the 1955 decision.[37] While

---

[35] A.I.R. 1984 SC 667 at p. 671. For a contrary opinion see Rao, *The Indian Constitution and International Law* (see footnote 22 earlier), p. 185. According to him, 'since the [Indian] Constitution and other laws do not stipulate [as in some countries] that international law is *per se* part of the law of the land, there is no valid reason as to why customary international law should be deemed to be part of Indian law or be placed on a favored footing than conventional international law.' I prefer Brownlie's view that 'when a municipal court applies a rule of international law because it is appropriate, it is pointless to ask if the rule applied has been "transformed", except insofar as "transformation" describes a special process required by a particular municipal system before certain organs are permitted, or are willing, to apply rules of international law.' Brownlie, *Principles of Public International Law* (see footnote 34 earlier), p. 57.

[36] For interested readers I reproduce below para. (1) of Section 3 of the 1946 Foreigners Act which defines the overall powers of the Central Government:

Power to make orders.(1) The Central Government may by order make provision either generally or with respect to all foreigners or with respect to any particular foreigner or any prescribed class or description of foreigner, for prohibiting, regulating or restricting the entry of foreigners into India or their departure therefrom or their presence or continued presence therein.

[37] It was in *Hans Muller of Nurenburg v. Suprintendent, Presidency Jail, Calcutta* that the Supreme Court had observed:

The Foreigners Act confers the power to expel foreigners from India. It vests the Central Government with absolute and unfettered discretion and, as there is no provision

till 1978 Article 21 of the Indian Constitution was construed narrowly as a mere guarantee against executive action unsupported by law it is now clear that it imposes a limitation upon law-making as well. In *Mithun v. State of Panjab* decided in 1983 the Supreme Court after citing recent decisions[38] of the Court observed:

These decisions have expanded the scope of Article 21 in a significant way and it is now too late in the day to contend that it is for the legislature to prescribe the procedures and for the Court to follow it, that it is for the legislature to provide the punishment and for the courts to impose it ... the last word on the question of justice does not rest with the legislature. It is for the courts to decide whether the procedure prescribed by a law for depriving a person of his life or liberty is fair, just and reasonable.[39]

In other words, while in 1955 the Court only had to consider whether an action taken complied with the procedure laid down in the Foreigners Act it has now to consider whether the same was fair, just and reasonable. Therefore, the Court was wrong in concluding that there was no provision in the Constitution which fettered the 'absolute' and 'unlimited' discretion of the government. Indeed, it should have proceeded to test the validity of the Foreigners Act as against Article 21.[40] In the context of refugee rights it can be argued that Article 21 encompasses the principle of *non-refoulement* which requires that a State shall not expel or return a refugee 'in any manner whatsoever to the frontiers of territories where his life or freedom would be threatened on account of his race, religion, nationality, membership of a particular social group or political opinion'.[41]

---

fettering this discretion in the Constitution, an unrestricted right to expel remains...
[It] gives an unfettered right to the Union Government to expel.

A.I.R. 1955 SC 367 at pp. 374 and 375.

[38] *Maneka Gandhi v. Union of India* (1978) 2 SCR 621; *Sunil Batra v. Delhi Administration* (1979) 1 SCR 392; and *Bachan Singh v. State of Panjab* (1980) 2 SCC 684. On the interpretation of Article 21 see in general V.N. Shukla, *Constitution of India* (Eastern Book Company, Lucknow, 1994), ninth edition, pp. 164–79.

[39] (1983) 2 SCR 690 at pp. 698 and 699.

[40] Article 21 containing the right to life and personal liberty is contained in Part III of the Indian Constitution entitled 'Fundamental Rights'. Article 13 of this Part makes it clear that all laws inconsistent with Part III will be void to the extent of the contravention.

[41] Article 33 para. (1) of the 1951 Convention on the Status of Refugees. It is to be emphasised that even the principle of *non-refoulement* is not an absolute principle. Para. (2) of Article 33 states:

The benefit of the present provision may not, however, be claimed by a refugee who there are reasonable grounds for regarding as a danger to the security of the country

That is to say, any procedure which disregards the principle of *non-refoulement* cannot be deemed fair, just and reasonable.[42] This interpretation is consistent with the international obligations India has assumed through ratifying the two 1966 Covenants and the Convention on the Rights of the Child. In the light of the highest court's reading of Article 21 the reservation India appended to Article 13 of the Civil and Political Rights Covenant would also appear to have lost much of its rationale.

In practice Indian courts have been generally helpful when approached with respect to individual cases, albeit they have done so without discussing in any manner the content of international refugee law. Courts have stayed the deportation of individuals when an application for the determination of refugee status is pending with the UNHCR.[43] In some instances leave has been sought and granted by courts to detenus to travel to New Delhi, where the Office of the UNHCR is located, in order to seek determination of refugee status.[44]

---

in which he is, or who, having been convicted by a final judgement of a particularly serious crime, constitutes a danger to the community of that country.

[42] It may be clarified that in none of the cases was refugee rights an issue.

[43] Supreme Court of India, *Dr. Malavika Karlekar v. Union of India*, Writ Petition (Criminal) No. 583, 25.9.92. This case concerned Burmese refugees. The brief decision of the Supreme Court stated:

It is submitted by counsel that 21 persons. . . are likely to be deported from Andaman Islands to Burma tomorrow. We are informed that their applications for refugee status are pending determination. The authorities may check whether these statements are true and that the refugee status claimed by them is pending determination and a prima facie case is made out for the grant of refugee status and further that these individuals pose no danger or threat to the security of the country, they may not be deported till question of their status can be determined.

[44] See the following unreported cases: *Shri Khy-Htoon and Others v. The State of Manipur*, Gauhati High Court, Civil Rule No. 515 of 1990, Order dated 11th September 1990; *Mr. Bogyi v. Union of India*, Gauhati High Court, Civil Rule No. 1847/89, Order dated 17th November 1989; and *Ms. Zothansangpuli v. The State of Manipur*, Gauhati High Court Civil Rule No. 981 of 1989, Order dated 20th September 1989. In the first case eight Burmese refugees under detention in Manipur Central Jail, Imphal invoked the writ jurisdiction of the court praying that the State of Manipur be directed to produce the petitioners before the Office of the UNHCR to enable them to seek the status of refugees. The Gauhati High Court directed that they be released on interim bail for a period of three months on furnishing personal bonds of Rs. 5,000 (about US$ 200) in order that they could go to Delhi to seek refugee status. The same decision was given in the second case where the Gauhati High Court added that 'If he is successful in obtaining necessary permission to qualify as a refugee, he shall be released forthwith and need not serve out the sentence, if any'. In the final case the petitioner, Ms. Zothansangpuli, had already served out a 195-day sentence for illegal entry. She was allowed to travel to Delhi and seek asylum after she completed her sentence.

B. Justice J.S. Verma, former Chief Justice of India, Inaugural Address delivered at the Conference on Refugees in SAARC Region: Building a Legal Framework, New Delhi, 2 May 1997, pp. 3–9.

The legal framework for the protection of refugees requires provision to be made for their protection during their status as refugees; to find solutions for their problems; to enable them to return to their home country; and for protecting the returnees in their home countries. Provision is necessary also to implement the principle of *non-refoulement* which means protection against compulsion to return to their home country while the threats for persecution continue. The 1951 Convention relating to the Status of Refugees and its 1967 Protocol ought to be given legal sanction in the SAARC region by enacting domestic laws which can be enforced in the national courts. The legal framework in the SAARC region must satisfy this need.

In the absence of national laws satisfying the need, the provisions of the Convention and its Protocol can be relied on when there is no conflict with any provision in the Municipal Laws. This is a cannon of construction, recognised by the courts in enforcing the obligations of the State for the protection of the basic human rights of individuals. It is more so when the country is a signatory to the international convention which implies its consent and obligation to be bound by the international convention, even in the absence of expressly enacted Municipal Laws to that effect. However, to ensure uniformity in the application of legal principles and to avoid any uncertainty, building of legal framework to implement the international convention which recognise the collective responsibility of the community of the States for the protection of refugees is a felt need and should be met expeditiously. The efficacy of enacted laws is the justification for prompt action by the SAARC countries to discharge their obligation in this sphere.

The zeal of the judiciary to find a solution under the Municipal Laws for protection of human rights is a healthy trend. To some extent, the existing legal framework provides solution, which may be taken into account while enacting new laws. In India, Articles 14, 21 and 25 guarantee the Right to Equality, Right to Life and Liberty and Freedom of Religion to everyone. These provisions have been held to apply to the aliens also and not merely to the citizens. In addition, the Directive Principle of State Policy in Article 51(c) requires that the State shall endeavour to foster respect for international law and treaty obligations. Even without being a party to the 1951 Convention relating to the Status of Refugees or the 1967 Protocol, in India, the rights of the refugees to this extent are protected by the provisions made in the Constitution.

In 1979, India acceded to the 1966 International Covenant on Civil and Political Rights (ICPR) and the 1966 International Covenant on Economic, Social and Cultural Rights. In 1992 India acceded to the 1989 Convention on the Rights of the Child which deals with Refugee Children and refugee family reunification (Article 22). The 1963 Convention on the Elimination of all Forms of Racial Discrimination was ratified in 1969. The Convention on the Elimination of all Forms of Discrimination Against Women was ratified in 1993. In the absence of incorporation of the provisions of the said international human rights instruments into Municipal Laws by the Parliament, the Judiciary has attempted to enforce obedience of the treaty obligations by the executive through the medium of Fundamental Rights under Articles 14, 21 and 25 which are available also to the non-citizens. The need, however, is for the incorporation of the treaty obligations in the Municipal Law of the land to make their obedience by the executive enforceable directly. For the purpose of determining the ambit of the Fundamental Rights, the Directive Principles of State Policy in Part IV of the Constitution which are fundamental to the governance of the country have been read to enlarge the scope of these Fundamental Rights. By the method of judicial interpretation in the absence of specific legislation, the judiciary has read the provisions in Part IV of the Constitution as complementary to the Fundamental Rights in Part III. The policy of humane treatment to the refugees in India has received fillip from a number of executive orders passed under the Foreigners Act, 1946.

The result is that the rights accruing to the refugees in India are those available to all aliens under the Indian Constitution, namely, the Right to Equality (Article 14), Right to Life and Liberty (Article 21) and Freedom to Practice and Propagate their own Religion (Article 25). Any violation of these Rights can be remedied by the enforcement of these Fundamental Rights in the Supreme Court under Article 32 and in the High Court under Article 226 of the Constitution.

The National Human Rights Commission in India has functioned effectively as a watchdog for the protection of Refugees. It approached the Supreme Court under Article 32 of the Constitution and obtained protection for the Chakma Refugees living in the North-East ... when their expulsion was threatened by an activist students union. Relief was granted on the basis of the rights of aliens under Articles 14 and 21 (see: *National Human Rights Commission v. Union of India*, [(1996) 1 SCC 295; *Khudiram Chakma v. Union of India*, (1994) Supp. 1 SCC 614].

Protection against expulsion orders issued even by the Government of India has been given by Courts by staying the deportation. The Court stayed the deportation orders to enable the asylum-seekers to approach UNHCR for refugee status. However, these orders being 'adhoc' in nature, the exact legal position in this area has remained nebulous with regard to *non-refoulement*. The indication is that international obligations influence the Courts in making orders in areas of existing gaps.

The zeal to protect refugees and to prevent their deportation by means of the activist approach of the Courts, National Human Rights Commission and NGOs has its limitations. There is need for the enactment of clear laws to provide for the refugees to give certainty in the field. The UNHCR has an important role to play because of its impartial third party status in determination of genuine refugee status of such persons and its emphasis on the need for uniform legal framework in all countries.

Legal framework is needed to provide for the protection, rehabilitation and repatriation of the refugees. The attempt to fill the void by judicial creativity can only be a temporary phase. Legislation alone will provide permanent solution.

III. TIBETAN REFUGEES

A. B.S. Chimni, 'The Legal Condition of Refugees in India', *Journal of Refugee Studies* (Vol. 7, No. 4, 1994), pp. 381, 389, 391, 393.

The Principle of Non-refoulement

In the 1950s, culminating with the arrival of the Dalai Lama in 1959, nearly a hundred thousand Tibetan refugees were granted asylum. Even though India did not support the independence or autonomy of Tibet, and the continued presence of the Dalai Lama and his followers has always been a thorn in the side of Indian–Chinese relations, it has scrupulously respected the principle of *non-refoulement....*

General Welfare

Alerted of the arrival of refugees the Indian Government set up transit camps at Misamari in Assam and Buxa in West Bengal. 'Three hundred bamboo huts were hastily constructed, and food, clothing and medical supplies were rushed in, often from great distances. When the refugees arrived at the camps they were provided with rations, clothing, and cooking utensils, as well as some medical care. Serious cases were sent to hospitals in nearby towns.'[45] The Dalai Lama and his followers were eventually not put up in camps but settled in different parts of India, especially near the hill stations. Misamari, which had nearly 15,000 inmates between May–June 1959, was wound up in July 1960. The refugees were dispersed to the colder regions, including some 4,000 to Sikkim.

[45] Louise W. Holborn, *Refugees: A Problem of Our Time* (The Scarecrow Press Inc., Metuchen, New Jersey, 1975), p. 718.

In the beginning the Tibetan refugees 'resisted efforts to settle them permanently in the country of asylum'.[46] Later, they were willing to consider permanent settlement only if India 'would permit them to settle in large, relatively isolated communities'.[47] This would allow them to protect and maintain their separate cultural and religious traditions. By 1962, the year of hostilities between India and China, the refugees realised that there stay was going to be a prolonged one. In this background the Government of India proposed three approaches. These were first, resettlement in agriculture, horticulture and animal husbandry. Second, the establishment of centres for training refugees in the production and sale of Tibetan handicrafts. Finally, the establishment of small industries to be run and operated by Tibetans.[48] This plan was put into action from the early 1960s itself although it was extensively tried only after 1965.[49]

Over the last three decades the Tibetan community has lived peacefully side-by-side with local communities.[50] However, in recent times some tension has arisen between local residents and the Tibetan community in places like Dharamsala in the state of Himachal Pradesh which is the headquarters of the Dalai Lama. The local community appears to resent the fact that there are two Dharamsalas: one of the Tibetans and the other of Himachalis.[51] It has also alleged that the Tibetans were buying large tracts of land through unlawful *benami* transactions.[52] In May, 1994 after a local youth was allegedly killed by a Tibetan, following which there were incidents of violence against the Tibetan community, the situation had reached a point where the Dalai Lama threatened to shift his base to another part of India. The crisis blew over after the Chief Minister of Himachal Pradesh apologised to the Dalai Lama and requested him to continue in Dharamsala.[53] The incident has in no way affected the relationship of the Dalai Lama with the Indian Government. He reiterated that it had 'helped Tibetans culturally, in education and resettlement. There can be no doubt that without India's help, we would not be in this position today'.[54]

[46] Ibid., p. 721.
[47] Ibid.
[48] Ibid., p. 722.
[49] For details see ibid., pp. 722–33. For a brief review of the implementation of this plan see John S. Conway, 'The Tibetan Community in Exile', *Pacific Affairs* (Vol. 48, 1975), pp. 75–87.
[50] In 1975 Conway wrote that 'relations with the local populations have so far been harmonious. . .', ibid., p. 80.
[51] S.K. Pande, 'Story of Strife: In the Dalai Lama's Headquarters', *Frontline* (17 June 1994), p. 122.
[52] *The Times of India* (10 May 1994). It may be mentioned that under the local Himachal Pradesh Tenancy Act only the Himachalis can buy land in the state of Himachal Pradesh.
[53] *The Sunday Times of India* (8 May 1994).
[54] Interview with the Dalai Lama, *The Sunday Times of India* (8 May 1994).

Public Education

After 1961 a special subdivision in the Ministry of Education was created, the Tibetan Schools Society, which was funded by the Indian Government. The Society 'developed and administered an outstanding programme for Tibetan refugee education'.[55] Tibetan refugees also have access to institutions of higher education in India. However, they are faced with certain problems in this regard. Education being a state—as opposed to federal—responsibility in India one of the requirements of admission into any of the state colleges is a 'domicile certificate' which confirms that his or her parents are legal residents of that state.[56] If you are not a legal resident of the state you are not eligible to apply for admission.[57] Furthermore, it is pointed out, to be able to get a domicile certificate a Tibetan student must first take Indian citizenship, a highly sensitive and emotional issue with Tibetan refugees for it is felt that 'taking Indian citizenship and forsaking refugee status negates the very purpose of fleeing one's own country'.[58] Where institutions run by the federal or central government are concerned it has been felt that it is difficult to get admission because the level of competition is very high.[59] These problems need

[55] Holborn, *Refugees* (see footnote 45 earlier), p. 735. See also Conway, 'The Tibetan Community in Exile' (see footnote 49 earlier), pp. 76 and 78.

[56] Thondup Tsering, 'Should Tibetan Students in India become Indian Citizens?' *Tibetan Review* (February 1990), pp. 12–14 at p. 12. It perhaps needs to be clarified here that in geographical terms the word 'domicile' is used in two senses in India. In one sense it is used to mean residence anywhere in the territory of India, and in another sense it means residence in any particular state (province) within India. In the early years, the Supreme Court of India held that the word 'domicile' was appropriately used in both these contexts. *D.P. Joshi v M.B.* (1955) 1 SCR 1215. However, more recently the Court held that there is only one domicile, namely domicile in the territory of India. *Pradeep Jain v Union of India* A.I.R. 1984 SC 1420. Yet it may be noted that in this case it still held that 'a certain percentage of reservation on the basis of residence requirements may legitimately be made in order to equalise opportunities...to bring about real and not formal, actual and not merely legal, equality', p. 1433. For a critique of the Court's judgement see Seervai, *Constitutional Law of India* (see footnote 29 earlier), pp. 316–28.

[57] Ibid.

[58] Ibid., p. 13. Tibetan refugees born in India are entitled to Indian citizenship under Section 3 of the Indian Citizenship Act, 1955 whose relevant part reads:

(1) Except as provided in sub-section (2) of this section, every person born in India on or after the 26th January, 1950, shall be a citizen of India by birth.

(2) A person shall not be such a citizen by virtue of this section if at the time of his birth—(a) his father possesses such immunity from suits and legal process as is accorded to an envoy of a foreign sovereign power accredited to the President of India and is not a citizen of India; or (b) his father is an enemy alien and the birth occurs in a place then under occupation by the enemy.

[59] Ibid., p. 12.

to be looked into. But even as these problems are pointed out the contribution of India in the area of education is acknowledged. In the words of Dawa Norbu,

> India's patronage of Tibetan education since the early 1960s represents one of the biggest investments she has made in the Tibetan refugees.... This unprecedented generosity has to be appreciated all the more because India is not without her economic problems.[60]

Employment

Tibetan refugees have been issued certificates of identity which enables them to engage themselves in gainful employment, economic activities and even travel abroad and return to India.[61] However, since they are not Indian citizens most employment opportunities are closed to them.[62] The only avenues open to a vast majority of Tibetan students are the Dalai Lama's administration in exile.[63]

IV. REFUGEES FROM BANGLADESH

A. B.S. Chimni, 'The Legal Condition of Refugees in India', *Journal of Refugee Studies* (Vol. 7, No. 4, 1994), pp. 381–83, 389–90, 392.

Principle of Non-refoulement

i. **Refugees from East Pakistan:** In 1971 East Pakistan, now Bangladesh, seceded from Pakistan in what has been described as 'a classic case of national liberation from a colonial political economy that was sustained in the postcolonial period, with relations of dominance and dependence further reinforced by ethnic divisions'.[64] Brutal repression was unleashed by Pakistan in present day Bangladesh in March 1971. With the result that nearly 10 million refugees entered India between March and December 1971; as of 1971 there were at least 71 countries that had a population of less than ten million. Most of the refugees were Bengali Hindus

---

[60] Dawa Norbu, 'Motivational Crisis in Tibetan Education System: Some Personal Reflections', *Tibetan Review* (May 1994), pp. 13–14 at p. 13.

[61] Saxena, 'Legal Status of Refugees' (see footnote 27 earlier), p. 504.

[62] Tsering, 'Should Tibetan Students in India become Indian Citizens?' (see footnote 56 earlier), p. 12.

[63] Norbu, 'Motivational Crisis' (see footnote 60 earlier), p. 15.

[64] Zolberg et al., *Escape from Violence* (see footnote 9 earlier), p. 142.

who were especially open to attack by the armed forces. Of the 10 million nearly 7 million were put up in camps while the other 3 million stayed with friends and relatives outside the camps. There was no question of turning any refugee back. Even Zolberg et al. who note that 'the refugees were an important part of the conflict'[65] concede that 'India's ability to derive political mileage from the refugee situation does not deny its objective reality'.[66]

The refugees returned quickly home after the liberation of Bangladesh.[67] But thousands remained in neighbouring Indian states (i.e., other than West Bengal, Tripura and Assam) where migration and refugee trails already had created sizable Bengali communities.[68]

ii. **The Chakma Refugees:** Since the creation of Bangladesh, and even prior to that, the Chakma refugees have been seeking refuge in India from persecution at home. In the year 1964 thousands of Chakma families entered India fleeing the then East Pakistan. They were initially sheltered in government camps in Assam. They were later shifted to a camp within the State of Arunachal Pradesh which was then known as North-East Frontier Agency (NEFA). In the years 1966–68 the then government drew up the Chakma resettlement schemes. Altogether 5 schemes were sanctioned for the resettlement of 3100 families.[69] The refugees numbered 81,000 by 1981. According to the All Arunachal Pradesh Students Union (AAPSU)—which has been agitating for their repatriation to Bangladesh—their number at present is 100,000.[70] The AAPSU stand has been supported by the state assembly which has passed resolutions to this effect. In September 1992, the then Union Minister of State for Home said in a letter to a local Member of Parliament that the refugees who came to India between 1964 and 1971 were eligible for the grant of citizenship and ruled out deportation of these refugees.[71] However, the Indian Supreme Court has ruled that they are not entitled to citizenship under Section 6–A of Citizenship Act of 1955 which contains certain special provisions with regard to persons of Indian origin who came to Assam before 1966.[72] Meanwhile, the agitation to oust the Chakmas from

[65] Ibid., p. 144.

[66] Ibid.

[67] 'In comparison to the prospects of a free life in a newly independent country, camp life appeared to be like a bondage which had suddenly become intolerable. The impatience with which they awaited release was notable.' Partha Nath Mukherji, 'The Great Migration of 1971: Return', *Economic and Political Weekly* (Vol. 9, No. 11, 16 March 1974), pp. 449–51 at p. 449.

[68] Zolberg et al., *Escape from Violence* (see footnote 9 earlier), p. 144.

[69] *Khudiram Chakma* case, footnote 29 earlier, p. 556.

[70] *The Times of India*, (9 May 1994).

[71] Ibid.

[72] *Khudiram Chakma* case, footnote 29 earlier, p. 558. See, however, **Reading IV.C.**

the State of Arunachal Pradesh has gained momentum leading to tension in the area.[73]

Insofar as the flow in recent years is concerned, in 1992 there were an estimated 56,000 refugees, primarily Buddhist Chakmas, from Bangladesh's Chittagong Hill Tracts (CHT) living in camp's in India's Tripura state. In 1993, which was declared the Year of Indigenous Peoples, there was considerable pressure on Bangladesh to bring home the Chakma refugees.[74] But a parliamentary team from Bangladesh which visited India in May, 1993 failed to convince the refugees to return despite promises of 'improved' conditions in the CHT.[75] Mr. Upendralal Chakma, the President of the Refugee Welfare Association and a former Bangladeshi minister, has stated time and again that the refugees would not go back unless a 13-point Charter of Demands was accepted which included the withdrawal of army, the eviction of Muslim settlers from tribal land and more political autonomy for the tribals.[76]

On its part the Indian authorities have ruled out any forcible repatriation of refugees. In July 1993 the Chief Minister of Tripura Mr. Dasareth Deb categorically stated: 'We will try to convince them to go back to their homes but will never allow the state apparatus to be used for the forcible deportation of the refugees.'[77]

On 16 January 1994 a 10-member delegation of refugees along with Indian officials left for CHT to hold a high-level meeting with the Bangladesh government regarding repatriation.[78] This was the second such delegation. The first one was led, as this one, by Mr. Upendralal Chakma. On return he announced that repatriation of the first batch of about 400 families would begin from 15 February 1994. Bangladesh had agreed to sympathetically consider the demands of the refugees and pay Rs. 1,600 (about US $50) as subsistence allowance per family for the first six months.[79] But on 31 January 1994 Mr. Bhagya Chandra Chakma, President of the Humanity Protection Forum (HPF), a Chakma human rights

[73] *The Times of India* (19 September 1994).

[74] Rajashri Dasgupta, 'Victims of an Unforgotten Past and Unforgiving Nation', *The Economic Times* (29 August 1993), p. 8.

[75] The Bangladesh government maintained that it was committed to the repatriation of the Chakma refugees. It claimed that it had plans for the overall development of the CHT and offered to increase householding and agricultural grants and prolonged periods of free ration for the refugees. But the promises failed to move the refugees. *The Times of India* (20 July 1993).

[76] *The Times of India* (17 January 1994). The other demands include: a government guarantee of security; a high-level judicial enquiry into past 'ethnocides'; compensation to the affected people; end to religious persecution; rehabilitation of refugees under the auspices of the United Nations, the Red Cross, Amnesty International and other human rights bodies. 'Back to Bangladesh: Chakma Repatriation and After', *Frontline* (11 March 1994), pp. 13–17 at p. 15.

[77] *The Times of India* (20 July 1993).

[78] *The Times of India* (17 January 1994).

[79] *The Times of India* (24 January 1994).

organisation said that the refugees were unwilling to go back unless a political solution was found and the 13-point Charter of Demands accepted. He said that the claim that the repatriation was voluntary was 'totally false' and that refugees were being 'pressurised' to go back to Bangladesh.[80]

However, a little after noon on February 15, 284 Chakma men, women and children crossed a makeshift wood-and-bamboo bridge over river Feni which marks India's border with Bangladesh. The second batch comprising 540 people left on 17 February. In the first phase of the repatriation 2,500 people returned. On a balanced view the refugees appeared to have going back voluntarily, albeit there were apprehensions as to the treatment which would be meted out to them. The rest of the refugee community closely followed the fates of those who left in this first phase of repatriation.[81]

From all accounts the apprehensions of the first batch of returnees proved to be true.[82] A large number of the families were not given back their homes and lands and suffered from a sense of insecurity because of the existence of numerous camps of the Bangladesh army close to their ancestral homes.[83] Despite this the Chakma leadership agreed to the return of a second batch of refugees in July 1994. A total of 752 families consisting of 3,767 members were repatriated by August. The Indian Government offered Rs. 2,500 (approx US $ 80) to each family returning home. Mr. Chandra Shekar Chattopadhyay, the District Magistrate supervising the process in Tripura claimed: 'We are not putting any pressure on the refugees to go back to their country.'[84] But doubts have been expressed about the voluntary nature of the repatriation process.[85] The India-based Humanity Protection Forum president Mr. Bhagya Chandra Chakma claimed that the refugees were being forced to return.[86] There was a core of truth in the allegation.[87]

General Welfare

i. **Refugees from East Pakistan:** In 1971, refugees were put up in camps which were as a rule run by the federal or state governments. The number

[80] *The Times of India* (1 February 1994).

[81] For, as Hongshadoz Chakma, who played a key role in the repatriation negotiations, said: 'if the returnees under the first phase are not properly rehabilitated and not allowed to live in peace and security, this will be the first and last batch.' *Frontline* (11 March 1994), p. 19.

[82] Sumit Sen, 'Return to Bangladesh Upsets Chakmas', *The Statesman* (26 July 1994).

[83] Ibid.

[84] *The Statesman* (22 July 1994).

[85] Suhas Chakma, 'Pawns in the Game', *The Pioneer* (29 July 1994).

[86] *The Times of India* (25 July 1994).

[87] The growing pressure on the refugees to return was noted by *The Statesman* in an editorial entitled 'Unwanted Chakmas' (9 August 1994).

of refugee camps reached a record figure of 1,200 in June 1971. They were later consolidated into 827 camps in seven states in India: West Bengal, Tripura, Meghalaya, Assam, Madhya Pradesh, Uttar Pradesh and Bihar. Some 35,000 government functionaries were employed on the entire refugee relief programme.[88] The refugee relief work centred around five major necessities. These were requirements of space, the construction of shelters on this space, provision of medical cover, supply of water and the supply of food.[89] Refugees were later given utensils, mats and blankets.[90] The resources of the Indian Government were taxed to the extreme. According to Holborn:

> The resources of the Indian Government ... were soon strained to the utmost, and the extraordinary heavy burden imposed by the flow of refugees came to threaten India's own prospects for economic, political and social development.[91]

In order to provide medical facilities the Central Government created new facilities in the camps. For a camp of 50,000 refugees a 25-bed hospital was set up as well as two health centres and dispensaries. The personnel was provided in the initial period from existing medical establishments or from medical colleges and other medical institutions.[92] Later the Government welcomed the cooperation of voluntary agencies.

In the administration of relief, foreign relief agencies were not allowed to function at the level of camps. However, some 30 voluntary organisations were operating in various states to assist the administration of camps. A significant contribution these organisations made was the running of orphanages and training homes for girls. However, insofar as the refugee was concerned he/she was economically isolated and according to one view 'hardly had any rights'.[93]

ii. **The Chakma Refugees:** The Chakma refugees have been put up in camps which have been variously described as 'squalid' and 'ill equipped'. They are, it is reported, given a daily ration of 400 gms rice, 15 grams of salt, and a dole of 20 paise per day.[94] Refugees in camps stay in long sheds in which there is little privacy. The sheds have no kitchen or latrines

---

[88] P.N. Luthra, 'Problem of Refugees from East Bengal', *Economic and Political Weekly* (Vol. 6, No. 50, 1971), pp. 2467–72 at p. 2472.

[89] Ibid., p. 2471.

[90] Ibid.

[91] Holborn, *Refugees* (see footnote 45 earlier), p. 757.

[92] Ibid., p. 773.

[93] Partha Nath Mukherji, 'The Great Migration of 1971: Reception', *Economic and Political Weekly* (Vol. 9, No. 10, 1974), pp. 399–408 at p. 399.

[94] *The Times of India* (20 July 1993); *Frontline* (2 July 1993), pp. 26–28 at p. 27. Thus, financially the refugees' presence on Indian soil has cost the government a relatively small amount—Rs 45 crore in about eight years. *Frontline* (11 March 1994).

attached to them. Food is cooked in the open air on the roadside. Drinking water is not readily available. Though tubewells have been dug a large number of them reportedly do not work. Since fuel is scarce in the camps the women have had to go to the nearby forests for collecting firewood. This has exposed them to sexual assaults—seven to eight cases are said to be reported each year. The culprits have been rarely apprehended.[95] Finally, health care for the inmates is virtually non-existent.[96] There are only five doctors and five dispensaries for the six camps. The supply of medicines is irregular and often the medicine prescribed is not available and has to be bought from private medical shops. The nearest hospital is hundred odd kilometres away in Agartala, the capital of Tripura.[97]

Public Education

i. **Refugees from East Pakistan:** The question of education did not arise in 1971 as the refugees soon returned back. However, in 18 orphanages which were set up by voluntary organisations boys and girls received residential education and training in handicrafts.[98] Additionally, according to Holborn, 'homes and vocational training centres were established for unattached women and social education centres were opened in various camps, where refugees were taught health measures to prevent spreading diseases and children were given elementary education'.[99]

ii. **The Chakma Refugees:** Insofar as Chakma refugees are concerned there is a lack of adequate educational facilities. However, there are primary schools in all the six camps, where 57 teachers render voluntary service and eight work for an allowance of Rs. 100 each. There are secondary schools (up to Class X) where teachers are paid Rs. 100 each.[100] Even these sums are a heavy burden for the inmates of the camps. The refugees' request that their children be allowed to take the state of Tripura's *madhyamik* examination has been turned down.[101]

Employment

i. **Refugees from East Pakistan:** In 1971 the Indian government made it clear: 'Refugees will not be given any employment in India as apart from

[95] *Frontline* (2 July 1993), p. 27.
[96] Ibid.
[97] See LLM Dissertation, 'Chakma: A Case Study in the Right of Refugee and Humanitarian Law', submitted to the National Law School of India University, Bangalore, 1993.
[98] Luthra, 'Problem of Refugees from East Bengal' (see footnote 88 earlier), p. 2472.
[99] Holborn, *Refugees* (see footnote 45 earlier), p. 757.
[100] *Frontline* (2 July 1993), p. 27.
[101] Ibid.

being foreign nationals, such employment will lead to social and economic tensions within this country'.[102]

The refugees were not expected to engage in any economic activity. 'The reason why the host system imposed such restrictions is easy to discern. It tried to minimise the deleterious impact of an immigrant population of such magnitude on its own system. Struggling to manage its own inner strains, the host system attempted to isolate the new problem rather than allow it to combine with the already existing complex of problems. More specifically, the evacuees were allowed to remain as a non-competitive group in the economy, thus keeping the balance of the labour market undisturbed'.[103] The state of West Bengal which took in 7 million refugees had unemployment to the tune of 2.5 million. Consequently, as one observer queried, 'how can they look kindly at the foreign refugees'.[104]

However, the refugees were often involved in economic activities. Since their labour could be purchased at a level lower than the market price for agricultural labour there services were hired by local landlords.[105] This led to some tension with host labourers. The other major economic activity was fishing and marketing fish.[106]

ii. **The Chakma Refugees:** As for the Chakma refugees because of the almost non-existent dole camp inmates have had to find ways of earning some money. Usually it means manual labour. While the local rate is Rs. 25 to Rs. 30 a day in the farming season, the refugees work for as little as Rs. 10 or even Rs. 5. This has often caused tension with the local people. Some refugees are involved in selling essential commodities, vegetables and other items grown inside relief camps.

B. K.C. Saha, 'Landmark Chakma Peace Accord—A Model for Permanent Solution of Refugee Problem', *Bulletin on IHL and Refugee Law* (Vol. 3, No. 2, 1998), pp. 255, 265–68.

On 2 December 1997, a landmark peace accord aimed at ending the decades old insurgency in the Chittagong Hill Tract (CHT) in Bangladesh, was signed by the Government of Bangladesh and the Hill Tracts Peoples' Solidarity Association (Parbottiya Chattogram Jana Shangati Samiti or PCJSS). The accord was widely acclaimed by the international community as a major peace initiative. . . .

---

[102] Government of India, Ministry of Labour and Rehabilitation, Branch Secretariat, *Administrative Instructions for Transit Relief Camps for Refugees from East Bengal* (Calcutta, 1971), p. 12.

[103] Mukherji, 'The Great Migration of 1971' (see footnote 93 earlier), p. 399.

[104] Luthra, 'Problem of Refugees from East Bengal' (see footnote 88 earlier), p. 2472.

[105] Ibid., p. 407.

[106] Ibid.

The Chakma peace accord is an attempt to find a solution to the insurgency problem in the CHT within the framework of the Constitution. The disturbed condition in CHT continued for a long period because, on the one hand, the insurgents who claimed to fight for the cause of tribals carried on their activities and, on the other hand, the police and the army carried on the counter insurgency operations. There were serious violations of the human rights of the hill peoples causing massive refugee flow to India. The accord is expected to reverse such trend and is supposed to assure the hill people that their human rights would be protected. The accord is recognition of the fact that the life and property of the ethnic minority groups need to be protected by special legal provisions and institutional changes in the political and administrative systems. The accord emphasises the fact that the political, economic, civil, social and cultural rights would be maintained by necessary legal and administrative measures.

... There had been peace initiatives by the Government of Bangladesh in the past also but the real transition point came during the June 1996 parliamentary elections. The Awami League in its election manifesto declared that it would earnestly try for a military solution to the CHT insurgency problem, if voted to power. The Awami League got overwhelming majority in the parliamentary elections. Negotiation with the new government in power became easy for the tribal leaders. The Awami League government immediately after coming to power initiated important measures like reconsitution of the National Committee on CHT which started dialogue with the tribal leaders and visited the refugee camps in the State of Tripura in India. The Government of India, being the host country of refugees, played a very important role in convincing the refugee leaders that they should cooperate with the Bangladesh authorities in finding a permanent solution in CHT. The previous governments in Bangladesh maintained a very rigid attitude towards the insurgents and it was made very clear that there should be no compromise with the insurgents in finding solution to the CHT. The approach followed was to intensify police and army action against the insurgents and find a solution without their involvement. The Awami League government, on the other hand, realised that no meaningful solution can be achieved without the involvement of insurgents thus making a complete departure from the past, decided to bring the insurgents under the legal and constitutional bounds. The tribal leaders who were rigid in their demand regarding self-determination with separate legislature in the CHT to protect the rights of the hill people changed their stand and reconciled to the establishment of local self governments of the Regional Council and the Hill District Councils with adequate powers. The local self-governments are legal entities derived either from the Constitution or by an Act of Parliament. The Government made it very clear from the beginning that any solution had to be within the framework of the constitution. The Government while conceding the demands of the tribal leaders for setting up of local self-governments, bargained on the issue that the insurgents would have to surrender arms which was agreed to by them....

It is important to consider the contents of the peace accord. The most important aspect of the peace accord relates to measures for creating peace and security. Decisions such as granting of general amnesty, surrender of arms, withdrawal of criminal cases against insurgents are very difficult ones.... But such major decisions alone can bring about reconciliation. The accord details the power of the Regional Council and the Hill District Councils. The Regional Council has been given vast powers to oversee all aspects of administration and development activities in CHT. The Hill District Councils' power to recruit local police and control all matters relating to land and land administration, including power to collect revenue, would really make the Councils effective. The Hill District Councils will be able to prevent future transfer of tribal land. In CHT the issue of land alienation by tribals was the root cause of unrest The accord proposes through a land commission to restore land to the tribals illegally captured and allotted to the non-tribals. The accord mentions about the package of welfare measures to be taken for the rehabilitation of refugees as well as insurgents. Measures such as reinstatement in jobs, preference of tribals in the government jobs, making available soft loans through banks would enable quick rehabilitation. The power of the Hill District Councils on other subjects such as youth welfare, environmental protection, industry and commerce, development of infrastructure would encourage local initiative and lead to the integrated development of the region.

Though the accord and the subsequent legislations have addressed the root causes of insurgency and the refugee flow, much would depend on the actual implementation of the terms of the accord. The rehabilitation and resettlement of refugees and insurgents would call for not only assistance to meet their immediate requirements for dwelling houses and such other requirements but also to provide substantial assistance so that they could engage themselves in economic activities. The refugees who have spent more than a decade in refugee camps are not in a position to take up any economic activity of their own whether it is agriculture, or otherwise. Further, it would not be possible for the government also to create so many jobs to gainfully employ them. The Bangladesh government has projected a need of assistance of $100 million from external sources to provide such assistance and develop infrastructure in CHT. It is important that such external assistance is mobilised so that package of assistance could be made available to the refugees without much delay, otherwise it would lead to resentment amongst the tribals and some tribals may again organise themselves to take up insurgency....

In the final conclusion, it can be said that a political settlement within the framework of the Constitution of the country such as the Chakma accord which addresses the root causes of insurgency and also takes into account the aspirations of ethnic minorities can bring about a permanent solution to the refugee problem. Such political settlements bring about not only repatriation of refugees living in other countries but also ensure that no future refugee outflow takes place. Violations of human rights can be prevented only through such political settlements. The Chakma accord is in a way a model peace accord which can be adopted in many refugee situations and also in situations of internally displaced persons.

C. In the Supreme Court of India Original Civil Jurisdiction, Writ Petition (Civil) No. 720 of 1995. (1) Supreme Court 295, 1996, 49435, pp. 1–20. *National Human Rights Commission ... Petitioner v. State of Arunachal Pradesh and Union of India ... Respondents*

Ahmadi, CJI

This public interest petition, being a writ petition under Article 32 of the Constitution, has been filed by the National Human Rights Commission (hereinafter called 'NHRC') and seeks to enforce the rights, under Article 21 of the Constitution, of about 65,000 Chakma/Hajong tribals (hereinafter called 'Chakmas'). It is alleged that these Chakmas, settled mainly in the State of Arunachal Pradesh, are being persecuted by sections of the citizens of Arunachal Pradesh. The first respondent is the State of Arunachal Pradesh and the second respondent is the Union of India.

The NHRC has been set up under the Protection of Human Rights Act, 1993 (No. 10 of 1994) Section 18 of this Act empowers the NHRC to approach this Court in appropriate cases.

The factual matrix of the case may now be referred to. A large number of Chakmas from erstwhile East Pakistan (now Bangladesh) were displaced by the Kaptai Hydel Power Project in 1964. They had taken shelter in Assam and Tripura. Most of them were settled in these States and became Indian citizens in due course of time. Since a large number of refugees had taken shelter in Assam, the State Government had expressed its inability to rehabilitate all of them and requested assistance in this regard from certain other States. Therefore, in consultation with the erstwhile NEFA administration (North-East Frontier Agency—now Arunachal Pradesh), about 4,012 Chakmas were settled in parts of NEFA. They were also allotted some land in consultation with local tribals. The Government of India had also sanctioned rehabilitation assistance @Rs. 4,200 per family. The present population of Chakmas in Arunachal Pradesh is estimated to be around 65,000.

The issue of conferring citizenship on the Chakmas was considered by the second respondent from time to time. The Minister of State for Home Affairs has on several occasions expressed the intention of the second respondent in this regard. Groups of Chakmas have represented to the petitioner that they have made representations for the grant of citizenship under Section 5(1)(a) of the Citizenship Act, 1955 (hereinafter called 'The Act') before their local Deputy Commissioners but no decision has been communicated to them. In recent years, relations between citizens of Arunachal Pradesh and the Chakmas have deteriorated, and the latter have complained that they are being subjected to repressive measures with a view to forcibly expelling them from the State of Arunachal Pradesh.

On September 9, 1994, the People's Union for Civil Liberties, Delhi brought this issue to the attention of the NHRC which issued letters to the Chief Secretary, Arunachal Pradesh and the Home Secretary, Government of India making enquiries in this regard. On September 30, 1994, the Chief Secretary of Arunachal Pradesh faxed a reply stating that the situation was totally under control and adequate police protection had been given to the Chakmas.

On October 15, 1994, the Committee for Citizenship Rights of the Chakmas (hereinafter called 'The CCRC') filed a representation with the NHRC complaining of the persecution of the Chakmas. The petition contained a press report carried in *The Telegraph* dated August 26, 1994 stating that the All Arunachal Pradesh Students Union (hereinafter called 'AAPSU') had issued 'quit notices' to all alleged foreigners, including the Chakmas, to leave the State by September 30, 1995. The AAPSU had threatened to use force if its demand was not acceded to. The matter was treated as a formal complaint by the NHRC and on October 28, 1994, it issued notices to the first and the second respondents calling for their reports on the issue.

On November 22, 1994, the Ministry of Home Affairs sent a note to the petitioner reaffirming its intention of granting citizenship to the Chakmas. It also pointed out that Central Reserve Forces had been deployed in response to the threat of the AAPSU and that the State Administration had been directed to ensure the protection of the Chakmas. On December 7, 1994, the NHRC directed the first and second respondents to appraise it of the steps taken to protect the Chakmas. This direction was ignored till September, 1995, despite the sending of reminders. On September 25, 1995, the first respondent filed an interim reply and asked for time of four weeks' duration to file a supplementary report. The first respondent did not, however, comply with its own deadline.

On October 12, 1995 and again on October 28, 1995 the CCRC sent urgent petitions to the NHRC alleging immediate threats to the lives of the Chakmas. On October 29, 1995, the NHRC recorded a *prima facie* conclusion that the officers of the first respondent were acting in coordination with the AAPSU with a view to expelling the Chakmas from the State of Arunachal Pradesh. The NHRC stated that since the first respondent was delaying the matter, and since it had doubts as to whether its own efforts would be sufficient to sustain the Chakmas in their own habitat, it had decided to approach this Court to seek appropriate reliefs.

On November 2, 1995, this Court issued an interim order directing the first respondent to ensure that the Chakmas situated in its territory are not ousted by any coercive action, not in accordance with law.

We may now refer to the stance of the Union of India, the second respondent, on the issue. It has been pointed out that, in 1964, pursuant to extensive discussions between the Government of India and the NEFA administration, it was decided to send the Chakmas for the purposes of their resettlement to the territory of the present day Arunachal Pradesh. The Chakmas have been residing in Arunachal Pradesh for more than three decades, having developed close social, religious and economic ties. To uproot them at this stage would be both impracticable and inhuman. Our attention has been drawn to a Joint Statement issued by the Prime Ministers of India and Bangladesh at New Delhi in February 1972, pursuant to which the Union Government had conveyed to all the States concerned, its decision to confer citizenship on the Chakmas, in accordance with Section 5(1)(a) of the Act. The second respondent further states that the children of the Chakmas who were born in India prior to the amendment of the Act in 1987, would have legitimate claims to citizenship. According to the Union of India, the first respondent has been expressing reservations on this account by not forwarding the applications submitted by the Chakmas along with their reports for grant of citizenship as required by Rule 9 of the Citizenship Rules, 1955. The officers of the first respondent are preventing the Union of India is actively considering the issue of citizenship and has recommended to the first respondent that it take all necessary steps for providing security to the Chakmas. To this end, central para-military forces have been made available for deployment in the strife-ridden areas. The Union Government favours a dialogue between the State Government, the Chakmas and all concerned within the State to amicably resolve the issue of granting citizenship to the Chakmas while also redressing the genuine grievances of the citizens of Arunachal Pradesh.

The first respondent, in its counter to its petition, has contended before us that the allegations of violation of human rights are incorrect; that it has taken *bona fide* and sincere steps towards providing the Chakmas with basic amenities and has, to the best of its ability, protected their lives and properties. It is further contended that the issue of citizenship of the Chakmas has been conclusively determined by the decision of this Court in *State of Arunachal Pradesh v. Khudiram Chakma* (1994 Supp. (1) SCC 615—hereinafter called *Khudiram Chakma's case*). It is therefore contended that since the Chakmas are foreigners, they are not entitled to the protection of fundamental rights except Article 21. This being so, the authorities may, at any time, ask the Chakmas to move. They also have the right to ask the Chakmas to move. They also have the right to ask the Chakmas to quit the state, if they so desire. According to the first respondent, having lost their case in this Court, the Chakmas have 'raised a bogey of violation of human rights'.

The first respondent has filed a counter to the stand taken by the Union of India. The first respondent denies that the Union of India had sent the CRPF Battalions of its own accord; according to it, they were sent pursuant to its letter dated 20.9.1994 asking for assistance. It has also denied that certain Chakmas were killed on account of economic blockades effected by the AAPSU; according to it, these casualties were the result of a malarial epidemic. The first respondent reiterates that the *sui generis* Constitutional position of the State debars it from permitting outsiders to be settled within its territory, that it has limited resources and that its economy is mainly dependent on the vagaries of nature; and that it has no financial resources to tend to the needs of the Chakmas having already spent approximately Rs. 100 crores on their upkeep. It has also been stated that the Union of India has refused to share its financial responsibility for the upkeep of the Chakmas.

Referring to the issue of grant of citizenship it is submitted as follows:

It is submitted that under the Citizenship Act, 1955 and the Rules made thereunder a specific procedure is provided for forwarding the application for grant of citizenship. According to that after receiving the application, the DC of the area makes necessary enquiries about the antecedents of the applicant and after getting a satisfactory report forwards the case to the State Government which in turn forwards it to the Central Government. It is submitted that on enquiry if the report is adverse the DC would not forward it further. It is submitted that the applications, if any, made in this regard have already been disposed of after necessary enquiry. There is no application pending before the DC.

It may be pointed out that this stand of the first respondent is in direct contravention of the stand adopted by it in the representation dated September 25, 1995, submitted by it to the NHRC where it had stated:

The question of grant of citizenship is entirely governed by the Citizenship Act, 1955, and the Central Government is the sole authority to grant citizenship. The State Government has no jurisdiction in the matter.

It is further submitted by the first respondent that under the Constitution, the State of Arunachal Pradesh enjoys a special status and, bearing in mind its ethnicity, it has been declared that it would be administered under Part X of the Constitution. That is the reason why laws and regulations applicable during the British Regime continue to apply even today. The settlement of Chakmas in large numbers in the State would disturb its ethnic balance and destroy its culture and identity. The special provisions made in the Constitution would be set at naught if the State's tribal population is allowed to be invaded by people from outside. The tribals, therefore, consider Chakmas as a potential threat to their tradition and culture and are, therefore, keen that the latter do not entrench themselves in the State. Besides, the financial resources of the State without Central assistance, which is ordinarily not forthcoming, would throw a heavy burden on the State which it would find well nigh impossible to bear. In the circumstances, contends the first respondent, it is unfair and unconstitutional to throw the burden of such a large number of Chakmas on the State.

We are unable to accept the contention of the first respondent that no threat exists to the life and liberty of the Chakmas guaranteed by Article 21 of the Constitution, and that it has taken adequate steps to ensure the protection of the Chakmas. After handling the present matter for more than a year, the NHRC recorded a *prima facie* finding that the service of quit notices and their admitted enforcement appeared to be supported by the officers of the first respondent. The NHRC further held that the first respondent had, on the one hand, delayed the disposal of the matter by not furnishing the required response and had, on the other hand, sought to enforce the eviction of the Chakmas through its agencies. It is to be noted that, at no time, has the first respondent sought to condemn the activities of the AAPSU. However, the most damning facts against the first respondent are to be found in the counter affidavit of the second respondent. In the assessment of the Union of India, the threat posed by the AAPSU was grave enough to warrant the placing of two additional battalions of CRPF at the disposal of the State Administration. Whether it was done at the behest of the state government or by the union on its own is of no consequence; the fact that it had become necessary speaks for itself. The second respondent further notes that after the expiry of the deadline of October 30, 1994, the AAPSU and other tribal student organisations continued to agitate and press for the expulsion of all foreigners including the Chakmas. It was reported that the AAPSU had started enforcing economic blockade on the refugee camps, which adversely affected the supply of rations, medical and essential facilities, etc. to the

Chakmas. Of course the State Government has denied the allegation, but the independent inquiry of the NHRC shows otherwise. The fact that the Chakmas were dying on account of the blockade for want of medicines is an established fact. After reports regarding lack of medical facilities and the spread of malaria and dysentery in Chakma settlements were received, the Union Government advised the first respondent to ensure normal supplies of essential commodities to the Chakma settlement. On September 20, 1995 the AAPSU, once again, issued an ultimatum ousting of Chakmas. This is yet another threat which the first respondent has not indicated how it proposes to counter.

It is, therefore, clear that there exists a clear and present danger to the lives and personal liberty of the Chakmas. In *Louis De Raedt v. Union of India* [(1991) 3 SCC 554] and *Khudiram Chakma's* this court held that foreigners are entitled to the protection of Article 21 of the Constitution.

The contention of the first respondent that the ruling of this Court in *Khudiram Chakma's* case has foreclosed the consideration of the citizenship of Chakmas is misconceived. The facts of that case reveal that the appellant and 56 families migrated to India in 1964 from erstwhile East Pakistan and were lodged in the Government Refugee Camp at Ledo. They were later shifted to another camp at Miao. In 1966, the State Government drew up the Chakma Resettlement Scheme for refugees and the Chakmas were allotted lands in two villages. The appellant, however, strayed out and secured land in another area by private negotiations. The State questioned the legality of the said transaction since, under the Regulations then in force, no person other than a native of that District could acquire land in it. Since there were complaints against the appellant and others who had settled on this land, the State by order dated February 15, 1984, directed that they shift to the area earmarked for them. This order was challenged on the ground that Chakmas who had settled there were citizens of India and by seeking their forcible eviction, the State was violating their fundamental rights and, in any case, the order was arbitrary and illegal as violative of the principles of natural justice. On the question of citizenship, they invoked Section 6-A of the Act which, inter alia, provides that all persons of Indian origin who came before January 1, 1966 to Assam from territories included in Bangladesh immediately before the commencement of the Citizenship (Amendment) Act, 1985, and who had been ordinarily resident in Assam since their entry into Assam shall be deemed to be citizens of India as from 1 January 1966. Others who had come to Assam after that date and before May 25, 1971, and had been ordinarily resident in Assam since then and had been detected to be foreigners, could register themselves. It will thus be seen that the appellant and others claimed citizenship under this special provision made pursuant to the Assam Accord. The High Court held that the appellant and others did not fall under the said category as they had stayed in Assam for a short period in 1964 and had strayed away therefrom in the area now within the State of Arunachal Pradesh. On appeal, this Court affirmed that view. It is, therefore, clear that in that case, the Court was required to consider the claim of citizenship based on the language of Section 6-A of the Act. Thus, in *Khudiram Chakma's case*, this Court was seized of a matter where 57 Chakma families were seeking to challenge an order requiring them to vacate land bought by them in direct contravention of Clause 7 of the Bengal Eastern Frontier Regulation, 1873. The issue of citizenship was raised in a narrower context and was limited to Section 6-A(2) of the Act. The Court observed that the Chakmas in that case, who were resident in Arunachal Pradesh, could not avail of the benefit of Section 6-A of the Act which is a special provision for the citizenship of persons covered by the Assam Accord in the present case the Chakmas are seeking to obtain citizenship under Section 5 (1) (a) of the Act, where the considerations are entirely different. That section provides for citizenship by registration. It says that the prescribed authority may, on receipt of an application in that behalf, register a person who is not a citizen of India, as a citizen of India if he/she satisfies the conditions set out therein. This provision is of general application and is not limited to persons belonging to a certain group only as in the case of Section 6–A. Section 5, therefore, can be invoked by persons who are not citizens of India but are seeking citizenship by registration. Such applications would have to be in the form prescribed by part II of the Citizenship Rules, 1956 (hereinafter called 'The Rules'). Under Rule 7, such application has to be made to the Collector within whose jurisdiction the applicant is ordinarily resident. Rule 8 describes the authority to register a person as a citizen of India under Section 5 (1) of the Act. It says that the authority to register a person as a citizen of India shall be an officer not below the rank of a Deputy Secretary to the Government of India in the Ministry of Home Affairs, and also includes such officer as the Central Government may, by a notification in the Official Gazette, appoint and in any other case falling under the Rules, any officer not below the rank of a Joint Secretary to the Government of India in the Ministry of Home Affairs, and also includes such other officer as the Central Government may, by notification in the Official Gazette, appoint. Rule 9 next enjoins the Collector to transmit every application received by him under Section 5 (1) (a) to the Central Government through the State Government or the Union Territory administration, as the case may be, along with a report on matters set out in clauses (a) to (e) thereof. Rule 10 provides for issuance of a certificate to be granted to persons registered as citizens and Rules 11 and 12 provide for maintenance of registers. These are the relevant rules in regard to registration of persons as citizens of India.

From what we have said hereinbefore, there is no doubt that the Chakmas who migrated from East Pakistan (now Bangladesh) in 1964, first settled down in the State of Assam and then shifted to areas which now fall within the State of Arunachal Pradesh. They have settled there since the last about two and a half decades and have raised their families in the said State. Their children have married and they too have had children. Thus, a large number of them were born in the State itself. Now it is proposed to uproot them by force. The AAPSU has been giving out threats to forcibly drive them out to the neighbouring State which in turn is unwilling to accept them. The residents of the neighbouring State have also threatened to kill them if they try to enter their State. They are thus sandwiched between two forces, each pushing in opposite direction which can only hurt them. Faced with the prospect of annihilation the NHRC was moved which, finding it impossible to extend protection to them, moved this Court for certain reliefs.

By virtue of their long and prolonged stay in the State the Chakmas who migrated to, and those born in the State, seek citizenship under the Constitution read with Section 5 of the Act. We have already indicated earlier that if a person satisfies the requirements of Section 5 of the Act, he/she can be registered as a citizen of India. The procedure to be followed in processing such requests has been outlined in Part II of the Rules. We have adverted to the relevant rules hereinbefore. According to these rules, the application for registration has to be made in the prescribed form, duly affirmed, to the Collector within whose jurisdiction he resides. After the application is so received, the authority to register a person as a citizen of India, is vested in the officer named under Rule 8 of the Rules. Under Rule 9, the Collector is expected to transmit every application under Section 5 (1) (a) of the Act to the Central Government. On a conjoint reading of Rules 8 and 9 it becomes clear that the Collector has merely to receive the application and forward it to the Central Government. It is only the authority constituted under Rule 8 which is empowered to register a person as a citizen of India. It follows that only that authority can refuse to entertain an application made under Section 5 of the Act. Yet it is an admitted fact that after receipt of the application, the Deputy Collector (DC) makes an enquiry and if the report is adverse, the DC refuses to forward the application; in other words, he rejects the application at the threshold and does not forward it to the Central Government. The grievance of the Central Government is that since the DC does not forward the applications, it is not in a position to take a decision whether or not to register the person as a citizen of India. That is why it is said that the DC or Collector, who receives the application should be directed to forward the same to the Central Government to enable it to decide the request on merits. It is obvious that by refusing to forward the applications of the Chakmas to the Central Government, the DC is failing in his duty and is also preventing the Central Government from performing its duty under the Act and the Rules.

We are a country governed by the Rule of Law. Our Constitution confers certain rights to every human being and certain other rights on citizens. Every person is entitled to equality before the law and equal protection of the laws. So also, no person can be deprived of his life or personal liberty except according to procedure established by law. Thus the State is bound to protect the life and liberty of every human being, be he a citizen or otherwise, and it cannot permit anybody or group of persons, e.g., the AAPSU, to threaten the Chakmas to leave the State, failing which they would be forced to do so. No State Government worth the name can tolerate such threats by one group of persons to another group of persons; it is duty bound to protect the threatened group from such assaults and if it fails to do so, it will fail to perform its Constitutional as well as statutory obligations. Those giving such threats would be liable to be dealt with in accordance with law. The State Government must act impartially and carry out its legal obligations to safeguard the life, health and well-being of Chakmas residing in the State without being inhibited by local politics. Besides, by refusing to forward their applications, the Chakmas are denied rights, Constitutional and statutory, to be considered for being registered as citizens of India.

In view of the above, we allow this petition and direct the first and second respondents, by way of a writ of mandamus, as under:

1. the first respondent, the State of Arunachal Pradesh, shall ensure that the life and personal liberty of each and every Chakma residing within the State shall be protected and any attempt to forcibly evict or drive them out of the State by organised groups, such as the AAPSU, shall be repelled, if necessary by requisitioning the service of para-military or police force, and if additional forces are considered necessary to carry out this direction, the first respondent will request the second respondent, the Union of India, to provide such additional force, and the second respondent shall provide such additional force as is necessary to protect the lives and liberty of the Chakmas;

2. except in accordance with law, the Chakmas shall not be evicted from their homes and shall not be denied domestic life and comfort therein;

3. the quit notices and ultimatums issued by the AAPSU and any other group which tantamount to threats to the life and liberty of each and every Chakma should be dealt with by the first respondent in accordance with law;

4. the application made for registration as citizen of India by the Chakma or Chakmas under Section 5 of the Act, shall be entered

in the register maintained for the purpose and shall be forwarded by the Collector or the DC who receives them under the relevant rule, with or without enquiry, as the case may be, to the Central Government for its consideration in accordance with law; even returned applications shall be called back or fresh ones shall be obtained from the concerned persons and shall be processed and forwarded to the Central Government for consideration;

5. while the application of any individual Chakma is pending consideration, the first respondent shall not evict or remove the concerned person from his occupation on the ground that he is not a citizen of India until the competent authority has taken a decision in that behalf; and

6. the first respondent will pay to the petitioner cost of this petition which we quantify of Rs. 10,000 within six weeks from today by depositing the same in the office of the NHRC, New Delhi.

The petition shall stand so disposed of.

V. SRI LANKAN TAMIL REFUGEES

A. Nirmala Chandrahasan, 'A Precarious Refuge: A Study of the Reception of Tamil Asylum Seekers into Europe, North America and India', *Harvard Human Rights Yearbook* (Vol. 2, 1989), pp. 92–94.

As a legal matter, the actual status of Tamil asylum seekers in India is ambiguous. India is not a party to the 1951 Convention nor the 1967 Protocol and has no formal refugee determination procedures, nor did India provide any ad hoc determination procedures for the Tamil refugees as a group. Nonetheless, the Tamils from Sri Lanka were commonly referred to as 'refugees' both in the media and in communications from the central government of India and the state government of Tamil Nadu. More importantly, India recognised the Tamils' need for asylum, and admitted them with a good deal of sympathy. In fact, in many respects, the government treated the Tamils as if they were Convention refugees, and in general did not subject them to arbitrary detention or restrictions on movement. The Sri Lankan Tamils received the same elementary education in Tamil Nadu schools as Indian nationals, and in the universities, the state government made special allocations for the Sri Lanka Tamil students. The students were also issued a certificate of Refugee Status, describing them as persons affected by the ethnic violence in Sri Lanka; however, this certificate was only valid for application to the university college or higher educational institute specified in the document.

... Thus, although the Indian government had no official refugee determination process, it in fact recognised the Tamil asylum seekers as refugees in various documents. In addition, the government also recognised that the Tamils could not be sent back until conditions in Sri Lanka improved. Hence, the Indian government regarded the Tamil asylum seekers as *de facto* refugees, giving them temporary asylum and protection from forcible deportation to Sri Lanka.

The temporary refuge given to the Tamil refugees in India accords with the practice of Asian and African states over the last few decades ... this practice of receiving mass influxes and granting temporary refuge or asylum may have evolved into a rule of customary international law, binding on nonparties to the 1951 Convention. India's response to the influx of Sri Lankan Tamils could thus represent an application of the broad principle of *non-refoulement* and observance of a legal norm. Of course, India's actions also could have been motivated by humanitarian concerns or political and ethnic considerations. However, while ethnic affinities of foreign policy may act as incentives to conform to a legal norm, they do not necessarily imply the absence of such a norm. Moreover, in the case of India, overall national considerations, regional relations and India's role as a mediator in the ethnic conflict in Sri Lanka may well have acted as disincentives. A desire to conform with a legal norm may thus have tipped the balance toward accepting the refugees.

In addition, acknowledging the role of humanitarian considerations does not make them a substitute for legal obligations. Refugee law itself is grounded in humanitarian principles; the two are interrelated, not exclusive. Conformity with a legal norm does not necessarily require public statements of legal obligation but can be expressed by nonaction, such as *non-refoulement* or non-repatriation. Thus, India's response can be understood as having a legal basis in the norm of *non-refoulement*.

B. Asha Hans, 'Repatriation of the Sri Lankan Refugees from India', *Bulletin on IHL and Refugee Law* (Vol. 2, No. 1, January–June 1997), pp. 96–108.

On 29 July 1987, India and Sri Lanka signed an agreement to establish peace and normalcy in Sri Lanka. Article 2.16 (D) of the Accord, stated that the Government of India would expedite repatriation from Sri Lanka of Indians who are resident there concurrently with the repatriation of Sri Lankan refugees from Tamil Nadu. In an annexure to the agreement the Prime Minister of India also agreed to deport all Sri Lankan citizens who were engaging in terrorist activities or advocating separatism.... The Sri Lankan Government and UNHCR signed a Memorandum of Understanding on 31 August 1987 under which UNHCR agreed to provide rehabilitation assistance to refugees and the displaced in Sri Lanka.

By 31 January 1987, 128,564 refugees had come into India. Of these 34,429 persons who were destitute were admitted into the refugee camps. 171 temporary camps were set up in Tamil Nadu for the accommodation of these refugees. Of these 9,350 refugees voluntarily left the camp after admission. The population of refugees in various refugee camps in Tamil Nadu at the time of repatriation was about 25,000. They were ready for return with the announcement of the 1987 Accord between India and Sri Lanka.

As per the agreement, all Sri Lankan Tamils in India were asked to register for repatriation. Repatriation began on 24 December 1987. The first trip reached Talaimannar with 252 Sri Lankan repatriates on board. By January 1989, 25,065 persons returned officially. These included camp and noncamp refugees. Together with organised repatriation, spontaneous repatriation also took place. According to the UNHCR records in this repatriation process a total of 25,610 returned through organised channels and 17,290 spontaneously.[107] The nearly equivalent spontaneous repatriation indicated that the return back was not forced. In this first attempt at repatriation though UNHCR was not involved from the Indian side there were thus no forcible departures. People had volunteered to go back, even to Jaffna which was still under the LTTE siege....

... In 1990 as fighting increased, the Government of India for the first time tried to find a new solution to stop refugee flows. *Refoulement* was not attempted. The concept of 'safe havens' provided the alternative. The UNHCR agreed to set up a 'safe haven' on Mannar Island with its financial assistance. The project was not implemented. In its place the UNHCR started a Programme of Immediate Relief Assistance to Returnees and Displaced Persons in Sri Lanka. This was an ambitious programme which was to meet not only immediate needs but also restore communication links (roads, etc.), housing and agriculture. It was not surprising that these plans failed to materialise. Sri Lanka was in the grip of conflict and UNHCR could not do more than provide immediate assistance programmes.

The UNHCR programme in Sri Lanka signalled that the time was appropriate for the return of Tamil asylum-seekers in the West to Sri Lanka. UNHCR envisaged the return of all Sri Lankans, including asylees in Europe. In April 1988 UNHCR sent a telex to all its field officers advising them that 'since the signing of the Indo-Sri Lanka Peace Accord in July 1987 there has been appreciable improvement in the situation in Sri Lanka and that rejected applications for asylum in Europe

---

[107] United Nations High Commissioner for Refugees, 1989 E/1989/64:32

and other countries could be returned to the Mannar District.'[108] The European countries guided by the first part of the telex which suited it, argues Varman, ignored the second part which stated that the UNHCR 'could not undertake any responsibility to ensure the safety of the return-ees in Sri Lanka'.[109] In June 1988, the intergovernmental consultations with UNHCR in Geneva and in Semmering in Austria in 1989 took place, and plans were drawn up for a return programme for Sri Lankan Tamils. The UNHCR decision provided the European States the justifi-cation for returning asylum-seekers.

... Refugees continued to trickle into India till May 1991. Tamil Nadu which had been protesting against the presence of Sri Lankan Tamil mili-tants now saw the common refugee as a potentially destabilising factor, and persuaded New Delhi, that they should be sent back quickly. The focus of Indian diplomacy then shifted towards persuading Colombo to receive them back. No attempt was made to force the refugees to go back. The assassination of former Indian Prime Minister Rajiv Gandhi by a Sri Lankan Tamil suicide bomber changed Indian policy completely.

In the aftermath of Rajiv Gandhi's assassination ... no large-scale riot-ing took place. The Congress (I) party in Tamil Nadu took up a restrained position. The attacks by party members were not against the refugees but against the DMK, for having provided support to the LTTE. Thus, although two camps were set on fire by mobs, the reaction was subdued, but in the days following the hostility faced by the Sri Lankan Tamils liv-ing in Tamil Nadu was unprecedented.

The psychological impact on the refugees [was] tremendous due to arbitrary arrests accompanied by the government's response to consoli-date the camps. The official stand was that it was no longer safe to keep refugees in small isolated camps. Security could only be provided if the number of camps was decreased. The Tamil Nadu government consoli-dated the existing 237 camps to about 132 in 1993. The camps along the coastline such as those in Thanjavur and Cuddalore districts were closed down. These camps according to refugee sources had been havens for militants and provided support in smuggling weapons to Sri Lanka.

The public in Tamil Nadu has viewed with apprehension the refugees because of the narrow divide that seemingly exists between the refugee and the militant. The assassin of Rajiv Gandhi and her associates were no gun-toting warriors, but simply dressed persons. Six of the accused in the assassination were registered refugees. The refugees themselves began to fear public reaction and as they themselves say suffered a guilt complex, and confined themselves to the camps....

---

[108] M.K. Varman, *Repatriation of Sri Lankan Asylum Seekers: Journey into Peril* (Tamil Refu-gee Group, London, 1989), p. 5.

[109] Ibid.

... Repatriation started in June 1991. The Government notified all Sri Lankan Tamils on 28 June 1991 and 29 June 1991 to register so as to facilitate the process of repatriation....

Repatriation II

The second repatriation process was not as simple or as easy as the first. It was complicated by the change in India's political environment in which the Sri Lankan Tamils had played a major role. It encompassed not only new policies but also new actors. The UNHCR made its presence felt from the Indian side. It was complicated and so solutions were not easy to find. It was composed of both a spontaneous and organised repatriation process....

Organised Repatriation

The large scale repatriation has been organised in character. It was carried out by the Government of India only, from June 1991–January 1992. From then onwards it was with the consent of the Government of Sri Lanka. The UNHCR was not present on the Indian side till July 1992....

... In an enumeration of refugees done in August 1991, 30,000 refugees expressed their willingness to return. Since, there were irregularities in the enumeration process, and the refugees complained, a second enumeration was carried out in December 1991. At this round refugees were required to confirm their willingness to return by the head of each family signing a form that was both in English and Tamil. About 15,000 of the 1,13,000 refugees accommodated in government camps confirmed their willingness to return. In January 1992, a new form offering third country asylum was also issued, though no follow up action was taken on it. During January to March 1992, 15,000 refugees had returned. When more refused to do so, pressure to return was increased by certain local officials and the public. The methods have been classified below. At the same time I would argue that ... the issue was politicised and blown out of all proportion by many refugees with access to international human rights agencies.

The Push Process

The excellent Indian record of providing refuge to numerous neighbours, has been blemished by the push factors used in repatriating the Sri Lankan refugees. It must be made clear that no Central Government policy to this effect was taken. It was basically a local factor. In a majority of cases junior Tamil officials and public were responsible for this policy. Many different methods were tried to enforce the operation.

Returnee Forms were Issued in English and without the Confirmation of Voluntariness

Returnee forms as per the refugees were handed over to some camps to the refugees by government officials. These forms were in English, a language all refugees are not familiar with. The forms did not confirm voluntariness. It did not offer the optional clause as to whether the refugee wished to return or did not wish to return.

Drawing up of Unrealistic Schedules

Camp authorities drew up unrealistic time schedules for departure. Refugees were given three to five days in many camps to leave for the Transit camps. The refugees were thus neither psychologically nor otherwise prepared for departure.

Misinformation Strategies

Refugees were read out news items of the problems facing Sri Lankans in Tamil Nadu and the peace process initiated by the Indian and Sri Lankan governments. They were then made to sign on forms giving their assent to return confirming their voluntariness.

Withdrawal of Ration Cards and Educational Facilities

Ration cards were withdrawn from many camps. The impact of Rajiv Gandhi's assassination has been felt most on education. Higher educational facilities provided to Sri Lankans were the best India could afford. In 1991 all these special facilities in education were withdrawn by the government, followed by withdrawal of facilities to Sri Lankan refugee children in schools. Though government officials when interviewed asserted, that only higher educational facilities were withdrawn and school facilities were restored within a very short span, the problems remained till 1996. When refugees were shifted for instance to new camps to prepare for repatriation, in some areas such as T. Sambuvaryar district, new schools refused to take them in. In Salvanakuppam such children had to wait for two months and then a nearby Jesuit school took them in. According to the refugees even some Jesuit schools renowned for their services in the education sector, refused to take in children unless a government circular cancelling the above order was produced.... In 1997, finally higher educational facilities [were] restored.

Security and its Impact on Employment

In the aftermath of Rajiv Gandhi's assassination, certain other problems were noticed. Among these were increased security within and outside the camps. Though, the security in the camps was looked after by camp volunteers, the state security system was fortified to check militancy. This resulted in strict surveillance and restriction on refugee movement.

Strict surveillance in camps has meant that some refugees are not allowed to go to work at whatever time their job requires them to do so. Industrial workers working on shifts, fishermen, and those working outside regular working hours were worse hit....

... On 6 January 1992, the Indian Government announced a bilateral agreement with the Sri Lankan Government to begin repatriation of refugees from 20 January 1992. The response of the refugees was poor. Since the assassination of Rajiv Gandhi the Government at the centre had not interfered with the repatriation process. The only time it did so blemishing an overall excellent record in refugee management was when the Rehabilitation Division of the Home Ministry issued orders in March 1992, to 'Persuade and Advise' the unwilling refugees also to return. This order was telexed by the Tamil Nadu Rehabilitation Department to all the District officers. Force began to be overtly used though on being questioned by S. Ramachandran (PMK), the Finance Minister V.R. Nedunchezian denied its use....

... The use of force was carried out as earlier mentioned by junior officials, party workers and the public. Except in one instance there is no proof that the Indian Government was a party to the use of force. This was proved when UNHCR stepped in to monitor 'voluntariness' in refugee repatriation and found a minimal use of force by the Government.

The Role of UNHCR in Repatriation II

As reports of forced repatriation took ground, UNHCR and the Indian Government opened discussions on ways to overcome these concerns. The UNHCR was critical of forced repatriation. The UNHCR representative Hasheed Furkhan who visited India had stated that the repatriation did not take place according to an 'internationally accepted procedure'. As coercion in some camps continued, the Head of UNHCR, Sadako Ogata took up the issue directly with the Government. Consequently repatriation was suspended for the time being. UNHCR made no comment on the situation existing in Sri Lanka. In a surprise move on 27 July 1992 India signed a Memorandum of Understanding with the UNHCR.

In July 1992, UNHCR opened its Madras office. The five conditions of UNHCR operations are: ascertaining the willingness of the refugees to return, the provision of a list of repatriates and completed repatriation forms, giving the list of camps in which sample checking is to be done, review cases of repatriates who want to postpone their departure or decide to stay in India and permit UNHCR to give the refugees details of assistance the organisation is rendering to those returning to Sri Lanka.

In India, UNHCR's major work has been to see that repatriation is not forced. All those who have signed the returnee forms are interviewed in Transit camps, by UNHCR to ascertain whether the repatriation is forced or voluntary. UNHCR has no access to camps except by invitation. It also has no financial commitment. All financial assistance to the Tamil Nadu State Government for repatriation of the refugees comes from the Government of India....

... By May 1995, as per the UNHCR records 51,188 refugees had returned to Sri Lanka from India, leaving 54,746 in camps. 31,062 of these had returned before UNHCR entry. Fifty two percent of these refugees have gone back for reasons of family reunification, seventeen for reasons of employment and some for education. Some gave their reasons as being the bad conditions in Indian camps.... The last batch of 10,013 refugees left India in May 1995. This was before the war and takeover of Jaffna when repatriation was finally suspended.... In 1997, more than seven thousand refugees have returned, mostly from Mannar District as conditions worsened....

Durable solutions such as repatriation, promoted by the international community, have to be dependent on voluntariness and return to safety and in dignity. To resettle refugees in the home of origin implies an environment of safety is assured. This presumes that the refugees go back to areas where their human rights are protected. In the years that the refugee has been going back to Sri Lanka this has not been the case. The human rights situation in Sri Lanka needs to be strengthened....

Another issue which needs attention is linking of the return of refugees in India with that of asylum seekers in Europe. The Sri Lankan Tamils reach Europe, as they reach India, after great difficulties and spending all that they own. As asylum laws in Europe tighten, there is slight chances of returning to Europe after repatriation if conflict in Sri Lanka breaks out again. Fearing for their lives and no possibility of return to these countries, the Sri Lankans would definitely not volunteer to go back.... Sending them back then constitutes the contravention of voluntariness.... In the case of asylum-seekers in distant countries the return to conflict zones has to be considered differently than from neighbouring countries with open borders and policies.

Conclusion

Repatriation under any circumstances is not an easy solution. Criticism of India's repatriation of Sri Lankans in 1991-1993 and classification of methods used was easy, but the reasons for these actions were mixed. Growing local impatience with militancy, social changes as well as economic hardships due to the presence of rich Sri Lankan refugees who stayed outside the camps were obvious reasons. More than this, it is the lack of a refugee policy in India which resulted in the creation of this situation.... Under the existing circumstances India does follow a generally good policy, but the deviations from this cannot be overlooked. Measures must be taken to see that these do not recur. Countries such as India if they continue a humanitarian policy can perhaps push the international regime towards a more humanitarian path, and in the process review its own policy and build more humane guidelines.

C. *P. Nedumaran and Dr. S. Ramadoss v. The Union of India* and another Unreported Judgement in the High Court of Judicature at Madras, dt. 27.8.1992.

... The prayer of the writ petitioners in the first two writ miscellaneous petitions is for an injunction restraining the respondents from repatriating the refugees in Tamil Nadu till the disposal of the writ petitions. The prayer in the main writ petitions is almost the same excepting with regard to one prayer in W.P.No. 12343 of 1992. In the earlier writ petition, the prayer is for a direction to the respondents to permit United Nations High Commissioner for Refugees (UNHCR) officials to check the voluntariness of the refugees in going back to Sri Lanka, directing the respondents to permit the refugees who do not want to be repatriated to continue their stay in camps in India and directing the respondents to provide all facilities to the refugees as they are entitled according to international laws. The additional prayer in W.P.No. 12343 of 1992 is to direct the respondents to nominate the respective District Judges to verify the voluntariness of the refugees to go back to their country....

3. It is not in dispute that there has been an influx of refugees from Sri Lanka from August, 1989 and they have been given shelter and accommodation in various camps.... It is also stated in the counter affidavit that the Sri Lankan Government has agreed to take back the willing refugees and they have furnished a list of assistance to be provided to the refugees on arrival in Sri Lanka.

4. The complaint of the petitioners in the writ petitions as well as in the interlocutory applications is that the respondents are repatriating refugees against their will and they are coercing the refugees to sign letters of consent. It is also alleged that the respondents are adopting certain unlawful methods in order to force the refugees to go back to Sri Lanka after executing letters of consent ...

5. In the other writ petition filed by Dr. Ramadoss it is stated that several refugees have brought to his notice that they are forced to sign the so called voluntary consent statements and force is used directly and indirectly by stoppage of rations, cash doles and curb on their movements. It is further alleged that politics is playing without considering the humanitarian aspects and inmates of the refugee camps are being packed off to Sri Lanka without ascertaining their willingness.

The following statement is found in his affidavit:

'I state that I have received several letters and telegrams from the refugee camps requesting my efforts to prevent the involuntary deportation. They are apprehending danger to life and liberty and they have expressed the same as if they are being sent to the slaughter houses. We do not have any apprehension for those opting voluntarily for their return to Sri Lanka. This petition is only in respect of those who are being compelled to sign and forced to go back to their country against their wishes and preferences.'

6. The crux of the matter is found in the above passage in the affidavit of Dr. Ramadoss. Those two petitions are concerned only with the persons who are being repatriated against their willingness and the petitioners are not interested in persons who voluntarily wish to go back to Sri Lanka. Thus, the crucial question is whether the respondents have taken appropriate steps to ascertain the willingness of the refugees before repatriating them to Sri Lanka. Several documents have been filed by the petitioners in the typed sets comprising of certain newspaper reports and letters purporting to have been written by the refugees. It is not possible for the Court to ascertain the genuineness and reliability of these documents at this stage without any further materials. But, however, it is clear from the various documents placed before the court that some of the refugees are not willing to go and some others are happened to go back to their country. In fact, one of the newspaper reports filed by Dr. Ramadoss, viz., *Frontline* contains a report, a reading of which shows that all the refugees interviewed by the reporter except one declared that they were returning to Sri Lanka on their own accord. The report also quotes one of the refugees as saying that he was going back with full satisfaction. In the same report, another person, a lady, is said to have expressed her unwillingness and dissatisfaction in going back.

7. Reliance is placed on the reports as well as the letters to show that the Government is adopting unfair means to force the refugees to go back to Sri Lanka and that some pamphlets containing objectionable language are being circulated in the refugee camp. The respondents have denied the same. As at present, since there is no material to show that the Government had caused circulation of the said pamphlets, it is not possible to draw any inference from the said pamphlet. Based on the records produced before me, it is seen that one section of the refugees is willing to go back to Sri Lanka and another section is not so willing. The question is what should be done at this stage.

8. In the counter affidavit the following averments are set out. In paragraph 3 of the counter affidavit it is stated as follows:

'The willingness to go back to Sri Lanka or otherwise were obtained in writing both in English and Tamil. As a result of discussion with the

Government of Sri Lanka, the Government of India have decided to send back the willing Sri Lankan Tamil refugees to Sri Lanka. Nearly 30,000 refugees have expressed their written willingness both in English and Tamil to go back to Sri Lanka. Accordingly, the Government of India have arranged for the reverse flow of the willing refugees and charted the vessels M.V. Akbar and M.V. Ramanujam.'....

Thus, as on 15.5.92, 23,126 willing refugees were repatriated back to Sri Lanka. Due to non-availability of either ship or aircraft the reverse flow has been temporarily suspended on 15.5.92. The Government of India have since placed one aircraft for repatriating the willing refugees. The reverse flow has been recommenced from 3.8.92 (one trip on every Monday and Thursday). So far 777 willing refugees have been air lifted from Madras to Trincomalee. Next air lifting will be on 24.8.92, 28.8.92 and 31.8.92 and the willing refugees are accommodated in two transit camps at Tambaram and they are ready to reach their land. If the repatriation is stopped there will be agitation in the Transit Camps.

In paragraph 4 it is stated as follows:

'These representatives are satisfied during the interview with the refugees accommodated in the temporary transit camp that the repatriation of refugees is done on their own willingness and the UNHCR team have thus cleared for the repatriation, of the willing refugees. Mr. Fazhul Karim, Chief of Mission, UNHCR office and his representatives met the refugees at the Transit Camp near Meenambakkam Airport before their departure. Out of 556 refugees ready to return, 42 refugees said that they would like to get back to Sri Lanka but not now. They constituted 8%. Accordingly, they were not repatriated to Sri Lanka but sent back to various camps in Tamil Nadu, similarly, another team of the UNHCR led by Ms. W.M. Lim interviewed about 250 families out of 340 families at Mandapam Transit camp willing to go back to Sri Lanka. It is learnt that all those interviewed were willing to go back. Therefore, no force or any compulsion is thrust on the refugees. All the refugees who are now staying in the transit camp, Madras are urging to send them back to Sri Lanka immediately. It would be pertinent to mention here that certain willing refugees are threatening to resort to hunger strike/commit suicide if they are not sent back to Sri Lanka immediately. No pressure or coercion is being attributed on the Sri Lankan refugees at any level as alleged by the writ petitioner. In fact, 8904 more refugees are still willing to go back to Sri Lanka. It may thus be seen that the willing refugees alone are being sent back to Sri Lanka.'

9. It is repeated in the counter affidavit in several paragraphs that the willing refugees are alone sent back to Sri Lanka and not the others.

10. The fact that the representatives of UNHCR are camping here and interviewing the refugees to ascertain whether they are willing to go back

to Sri Lanka is not in dispute. The main complaint made in the writ petition is that the Government is repatriating the refugees without ascertaining their consent. That loses its force once it is seen that the representatives of the world organisation are present here to ascertain whether the refugees are willing to go back or not. The details furnished in the counter affidavit show that the representatives of UNHCR are ascertaining whether the refugees have given their consent voluntarily before they are actually repatriated. In fact, the averments in paragraph 4 of the counter affidavit show that even after coming to the transit camp 42 refugees out of a total of 556 refugees expressed their unwillingness to go back to Sri Lanka and they were retained here. The counter affidavit shows that even at their stage the refugees are permitted to express their willingness or otherwise to go back. The facts set out in the counter affidavit are enough to show that an outside agency is present to ascertain whether the refugees are voluntarily going back to their country.

11. Learned counsel for the petitioners submitted that the very fact that 42 persons out of 556 persons who are brought to the Transit Camps expressed their unwillingness at that stage throws considerable doubt as to the original consent said to have been given by them. According to learned counsel for the petitioners, there is no verification in the camps themselves whether the refugees are subjected to coercion and whether they are giving consent voluntarily or not. It is also stated by learned counsel for the petitioners that newspaper reports disclose that the consent is obtained only in English forms and not in Tamil forms. According to him most of the refugees do not understand English and they have been made to sign the consent forms. It is further contended that the respondents are adopting intimidation tactics to get the signatures of the refugees by stopping supplies and other materials. The last arguments of learned counsel for the petitioners is that even in Sri Lanka these refugees are only going to be placed in refugee camps and they are not going to be sent back to their original places of abode and there is no purpose to send them back at this stage.

12. Insofar as the consent of the refugees is concerned, when there is a world agency to ascertain whether the consent is voluntary or not, it is not for this court to consider whether the consent is voluntary or not. Nothing has been suggested as against the competence or impartiality of the representatives of the UNHCR in ascertaining the willingness of the refugees to go back. The allegation that it is only in the English forms the signatures of the refugees are obtained is not correct. Learned Special Government Pleader has produced the file containing the consent forms. Each person who signs the form has signed not only in the English form but also in the Tamil form. The willingness is obtained in both the forms. Hence, it is not correct to state that willingness is obtained only in the English form. The forms in which signatures have been obtained are

produced before me. I do not find anything to suspect the genuineness of the same at this stage. Apart from that, the Special Government Pleader has also produced the file containing the forms in which the refugees have expressed their unwillingness to go back. In those forms several refugees have refused to go back and their signatures have also been obtained in the forms expressing their unwillingness. Thus, the Government has adopted the proper procedure to ascertain whether the refugees are willing to go back. There is no substance in the argument that the fact that the refugees have refused to go back after coming to the transit camps shows that their consent was initially obtained by unfair means. After all, human mind is known to be fickle and it may change due to various factors: It only shows that the refugees are given a chance even at the last stage to express their unwillingness and if they do so, they are retained here and sent back to their camps. This court cannot assume that the refugees who expressed refusal to go back after coming to the transit camps were forced to give their consent earlier. The question whether the original consent was obtained by force or not is not very material inasmuch as the voluntary nature of the consent is ascertained by the representatives of the UNHCR before the actual expatriation of the refugees.

13. There is nothing at present to show that intimidation tactics are being adopted by the Government. The records produced by the petitioner show that the refugees are having correspondence with the petitioners and other Organisations in the country and it is not as if the refugees are kept in a prison without any contact with the outside world. Mr. Nedumaran has produced a copy of the letter addressed to the Director of Rehabilitation Department said to have been written by certain refugees. He has also produced similar letters addressed to other persons including the Organisation for Rehabilitation of Eelam Refugees. Thus, the refugees are admittedly having contact with prominent persons in the country. Hence, it cannot be said that the refugees are so helpless as to sign in the forms at the places indicated by the Government. The contention that refugees are going to be placed in a camp at Sri Lanka is not relevant. It is beyond the purview of this Court to enquire whether the Sri Lankan Government is acting in accordance with the norms prescribed by the United Nations Organisation in the matter of rehabilitation of refugees returning to that country.

14. The only question before me is whether the refugees are voluntarily going out of this country. If they have expressed willingness to go back, they cannot be stopped by the petitioners herein, as rightly pointed out by the petitioner in W.P.No. 12343 of 1992, these petitions are concerned only with the persons who are compelled to sign the forms forcibly to go out of this country against their will. As at present, there are

no materials to show that persons who have expressed their unwillingness are compelled to go out of this country. I am satisfied by the records produced by the Special Government Pleader that the consent of the refugees is obtained in proper manner and only those refugees who have expressed their consent are being sent back and the voluntariness of consent is being verified by the representatives of the UNHCR.

15. It is not necessary for me at this stage to consider the questions raised under the provisions of the Foreigners Act by the learned Senior Counsel appearing for the Central Government and the answers given thereto by the petitioners' counsel. Even assuming that the Sri Lankan refugees can be expatriated without their consent, the respondents have not now raised a plea that refugees are not entitled to continue here and they can be forcibly sent out. On the other hand, the only plea of the respondents is that the refugees who are sent out of this country are only those who have expressed their willingness to go back.

16. Learned counsel for the petitioners submitted that it is better to depute the District Judge of each District to verify whether the consent is voluntary or not. It is not necessary as the representatives of the world organisation are verifying whether the consent is voluntary. The files produced by the Special Government Pleader relate to North Arcot and Dharmapuri Districts. Learned Special Government Pleader states that similar files are available for all the other Districts, though they are not produced before me.

17. In the circumstances, I am of the view that no prima facie case has been made out for grant of injunction as the respondents are acting properly in accordance with international conventions. Consequently, W.M.P. Nos. 17372 and 17242 of 1992 are dismissed and interim orders are vacated. W.M.P. Nos. 18085 and 18086 of 1992 are allowed.

18. After the conclusion of the dictation of the order, learned counsel for the petitioners submits that directions may be issued to the respondents to (1) translate this order in Tamil and circulate the same in the refugee camps and (2) issue a circular in Tamil to the refugees that they will not be expatriated unless they expressed their consent voluntarily. Learned Special Government Pleader agrees to do so. Hence, the second respondent is directed to (1) translate this order in Tamil and circulate it in the refugee camps and (2) to issue a circular in Tamil that the refugees will not be expatriated unless they express their willingness voluntarily. These directions shall be carried out on or before 14.9.1992. The Special Government Pleader shall file a report as to compliance with the above direction in this Court....

Sd/- V.V. Kannan,
Asstt. Registrar (R).

D. *Digvijay Mote v. Government of India and Government of Karnataka.* **Unreported Decision in the High Court of Karnataka at Bangalore dt. 17.2.1994.**

1. This appeal is directed against the order passed by the learned Single Judge in a pending Writ Petition moved by the appellant (party-in-person) as a public interest litigation for enforcing the rights of 150 children of refugees being Srilanka Tamilians. They are staying in residential School in Karnataka which is situated in Jakkur near Bangalore. These children are said to have come for studies in Primary and Secondary Education courses in Tamil and English. They were earlier staying in refugee camps with their parents in Tamil Nadu and Orissa. From these two camps these children have come to the aforesaid place for prosecuting their studies. In the Writ Petition various reliefs were prayed for and at the stage of notice ad interim order was not granted. The petitioner has, therefore, filed this appeal.

2. The appellant (party-in-person) submitted before us that some ad interim order is required to be issued in this connection so that these children who are otherwise starving may keep their body and soul together because they are studying in a residential school where there are no funds to maintain them and it was likely that some of them may die out of starvation and therefore, the learned Single Judge should have passed some ad interim on ad hoc basis so that these children can avoid starvation deaths.

3. In this appeal we have issued notice to the respondents i.e., Government of India and Government of Karnataka. We are happy to note that pursuant to the notice issued by us, on humanitarian grounds, respondent-2 has agreed to provide, without prejudice to the rights and contentions of both the sides, some basic requirements such as food, tea etc., to these children subject to further orders in the Writ Petition. Mr. Farooq, the learned Government Advocate produced before us a photostat copy of the proceedings of the meeting held in the Chambers of Chief Secretary to Government at 12-30 p.m. on 5-2-1994. On humanitarian grounds the following decision was taken:

'Department of Women and Children Welfare through the Social Welfare Department will be requested to take appropriate measures to provide basic amenities to the children lodged in the camp on humanitarian consideration.'

4. Mr. Farooq informed us that he has been instructed to submit, subject to the orders of this Court, that the Social Welfare Department will see to it that an ad hoc arrangement is made on spot in the said residential school to provide food on the same line as provided in the Government hostels and ashrams which will include, tea twice a day, morning

breakfast, lunch and dinner. It is made clear that these arrangements will be made on ad hoc basis with a view to see that the concerned inmates do not starve. Mr. Farooq made it clear that the food will be provided on spot from Sunday i.e., 20-2-1994. We highly appreciate this good gesture on the part of the State Government. It is made clear that this arrangement is purely on humanitarian grounds and it is voluntarily made by the State Government without prejudice to the rights and contentions of both the sides and subject to the further orders which the learned Single Judge may pass after hearing both the sides in the Writ Petition which we are told is at the stage of admission. In the light of the above, this arrangement will continue for some time. We should not be understood to have expressed any opinion on the merits of the Writ Petition. In short, all questions are kept open.

5. It is obvious that respondent 2 will carry out the directions as contained in this order and as agreed to before us. It will be open to the Departmental Authorities who will be supplying the food on spot to take co-operation of any of the inmates in this regard.

6. This appeal is disposed of subject to the directions issued as aforesaid with the consent of both sides.

VI. INDIA AND THE 1951 CONVENTION

A. B.S. Chimni, 'The Legal Condition of Refugees in India', *Journal of Refugee Studies* (Vol. 7, No. 4, 1994), pp. 394–96.

The question is often asked why India—like most countries in South Asia—is not a member of the 1951 UN Convention. In a recent article Weiner has offered, without directly addressing the issue, important insights into the question.[110] He identifies some of the peculiar features of the South Asian region which need to be borne in mind in discussing the problem. First, none of the states in South Asia have the capacity to control population entry. Borders are porous, and governments lack the administrative, military, or political capacity to enforce rules of entry.[111]

Second, cross-border population movements in South Asia are regarded as issues that affect internal security, political stability, and international relations, not simply the structure and composition of the labour market, or the provision of services to newcomers.[112] Third, there is the possibility of a refugee flow changing the linguistic or religious composition of the receiving area within the country. Local anxieties are acute when there is a perceived threat of being culturally and/or economically swamped. For

---

[110] Myron Weiner, 'Rejected Peoples and Unwanted Migrants in South Asia', *Economic and Political Weekly* (Vol. 28, No. 34, 21 August 1993), pp. 1737–46.

[111] Ibid., p. 1743.

[112] Ibid., p. 1745.

instance, in 1971, given the already substantial Bengali presence, some of the states in North-East India (Meghalaya, Assam, and Tripura) were concerned that the influx from Bangladesh would result in the indigenous population becoming a minority in their own land.

For these reasons, governments in South Asia have concluded that unwanted migrations, including refugees, are a matter of bilateral not multilateral relations, and that international agreements could constrict their freedom of action[113] ... Indicative of the desire to deal bilaterally with the entire gamut of problems is the fact that the paramount regional organisation, South Asian Association for Regional Co-operation (SAARC), has chosen to exclude the issue of population movements from its purview for 'fear that it would disrupt the organisation'.

Within this context we can identify other possible reasons why India has been reluctant to accede to the 1951 Convention. First, since India has been willing host to refugees it sees no reason for becoming party to the Convention, especially when it has allowed UNHCR to open a office in New Delhi. Second, ... because of its experience with what it regarded as the unhelpful role played by UNHCR during the Bangladesh crisis of 1971, India has been wary of what may be described as the non-humanitarian or political role of UNHCR.[114] Indeed, until recently UNHCR was perceived as an institution established and financed by the West to serve its geopolitical interests.

Third, the rights incorporated in the 1951 Convention are seen as being unrealistic for a poor country. While India can invoke the reservation clause of the Convention, this will not provide sufficient protection against criticism coming from UNHCR and the NGO community. Fourth, a general lack of knowledge and understanding of international refugee law in official circles has prevented a deeper consideration of the issues involved; in particular, of the discretionary powers which would still be vested in the state on becoming party to the 1951 Convention. Finally, insofar as the current situation is concerned, the restrictive policies of the Western countries towards refugees do not provide the climate in which any state can be persuaded to become a party to the Convention.

VII. INDIA AND THE UNHCR

A. UN Secretary-General's Aide Memoire of 19 July 1971, to Governments of India and Pakistan. *Bangladesh Documents* (Ministry of External Affairs, New Delhi, n.d.), p. 657.

The repatriation of the refugees from East Pakistan now in India is a matter of the utmost concern and urgency. The Secretary-General is

---

[113] Ibid.
[114] Ibid., p. 1743. See in this regard **Readings VII.A to VII.C.**

anxious to do everything possible, in co-operation with the Governments concerned and complementary to their own efforts, to facilitate the voluntary repatriation of the refugees in a secure and orderly manner which takes due account of their welfare. One possible method of doing this might be to establish a limited representation of the High Commissioner for Refugees on both sides of the border. The High Commissioner for Refugees is already acting as a focal point for the United Nations effort on behalf of these refugees. The representatives of the High Commissioner would be stationed at collecting points on the Indian side, at border crossing points on both sides, and in reception centres on the Pakistan side. It is the feeling of the Secretary-General that before attempting to make such an arrangement on a large scale, it would be desirable to test it in a limited way in order to ascertain whether in practice it would serve a useful purpose in facilitating the process of repatriation.

The Secretary-General therefore wishes to suggest to both Governments concerned that representatives of the High Commissioner for Refugees be accepted in two or three selected areas on both sides of the border, the areas to be suggested by the Governments in consultation with the High Commissioner. Were this arrangement to prove useful, it would then be possible to expand it gradually to include most, or all, of the repatriation points....

B. India's Reply to UN Secretary-General's Aide Memoire, delivered on 2 August 1971. *Bangladesh Documents* (Ministry of External Affairs, New Delhi, n.d.) pp. 660–63.

Government of India shares the view of the Secretary-General that the repatriation of the refugees from East Pakistan, now in India, is a matter of utmost concern and urgency. Of even greater concern and urgency is the need to stop military atrocities in East Pakistan and the consequent daily flow of refugees into India at the rate of 40,000 to 50,000 a day. The refugees already in India are unlikely to return as long as this further exodus continues. Government of India has noted with infinite dismay and grave concern that far from encouraging return of refugees or stopping or reducing the further flow of refugees from East Pakistan to India, their number has increased by nearly four million since President Yahya Khan made his statement on the 25th May that he would agree to allow these Pakistani citizens to return to their own country.

The root cause of the inflow of over seven million refugees into India and the daily exodus that still continues can only be explained by the total absence of such conditions in East Pakistan as would encourage or enable the refugees to return to their homes. The chaos and the systematic military repression and the decimation of the Bengali-speaking people in East Pakistan continue unabated, as indeed is clear to any objective reader of the international press. This has been further corroborated by the recent reports of the World Bank and the public statements made by independent foreign observers who have visited East Pakistan and heard the tales of woe from refugees themselves in their camps in India. . . .

Prince Sadruddin told the Prime Minister of India in New Delhi some time ago that the process and organisation of repatriation would be hampered by posting a number of personnel drawn from different parts of the world, speaking various languages with diverse backgrounds and following an assortment of techniques. UNHCR made no suggestion in the ECOSOC meeting held in Geneva on 16th July that the establishment of a limited representation of High Commissioner for Refugees on both sides of the border would in any way encourage the return of refugees to their homes in East Pakistan.

In these circumstances, the Government of India are unable to understand what purpose the posting of a few men on the Indian side of the border will fulfil. Our conviction is that they can in no way help or encourage the refugees to return home and face indiscriminate and deliberate massacre by the West Pakistan military authorities. . . .

India has no desire to prevent the refugees from returning to their homeland, indeed we are most anxious that they should go back as soon as possible and as a first step, conditions must be created in East Pakistan to prevent the further arrival of refugees into India. In this context, the Secretary-General must have seen the report and statement of 30th June by the UNHCR refuting Pakistani allegation that India is obstructing the return of refugees. Prince Sadruddin is further reported to have said there was absolutely no evidence for the host Government having obstructed the refugees if they wanted to go. Again in Paris on 10th July the Prince in reply to a question said that it would not be logical to say that India was in any way holding back their return. . . . Apart from these and many other statements of this nature, not even a single responsible and reputable report has ever indicated that the return of refugees or their continued inflow is due to any other cause except the intolerable and tragic conditions prevailing in East Bengal.

In this background, Government of India must express their total opposition to the suggestion for the induction of a 'limited representation of the High Commissioner for Refugees on both sides' and must categorically state that they resent any insinuation that they are preventing the refugees from returning to East Bengal. They allowed them to enter India purely on humanitarian grounds in spite of the most serious impact on her social, political and economic structure. Government of India are anxious that they return as soon as possible. The presence of the United Nations or UNHCR representatives cannot help in this. On the other hand, it would only provide a facade of action to divert world attention from the root cause of the problem which is the continuation of military atrocities, leading to further influx of refugees and absence of political settlement acceptable to the people of East Pakistan and their already elected leaders.

The UNHCR has a fairly strong team of senior officers located in Delhi and they have been given every facility to visit refugee camps. In fact, Mr. Thomas Jaimeson, Director of Operations of the UNHCR who is the Chief Representative of the UNHCR's office in India, has recently returned from a second tour of the refugee camps. He was allowed access to all the refugee camps and was given facilities to visit these camps including those in the border areas. Apart from this, 1,000 foreign observers have visited these refugee camps and most of them have publicly stated that the refugees have taken shelter in India from the military oppression in Bangladesh and are not willing to return unless suitable conditions are created ensuring their safe return through a political settlement with Sheikh Mujibur Rahman, the acknowledged leader of East Pakistan and his already elected colleagues. In the light of the information available to Government of India and to the interested Governments and organisations, they have painfully come to the conclusion, that the time is past when international community can continue to stand by, watching the situation deteriorate and merely hoping that the relief programmes, humanitarian efforts, posting of a few people here and there, and good intentions would be enough to turn the tide of human misery and potential disaster.

While, therefore, the Government of India have no wish to lend their support to any proposal which will deflect attention from the basic problem or diffuse concern from the fate of the unfortunate refugees, they would welcome any action by the United Nations which would ensure and guarantee, under adequate international supervision, that the refugees lands, houses and property will be returned to them in East Pakistan and that conditions are created there to ensure the safe return under credible international guarantees without threat of reprisal or other measures of repression from the military authorities of West Pakistan. It is painful to note that even the handful of refugees who ventured to return to East Bengal have not only been not allowed to go back to their homes and villages but have been subjected to endless indignities and inequities and even made to do forced labour and face many other difficulties. Government of India should like to draw the Secretary-General's attention in this context to the *New York Times* report and photographs published on the 27th July, 1971. In these circumstances it is unrealistic to hope that these circumstances will begin to be changed by the posting of any personnel on the Indian side of the border. The Government of India cannot support such a facade of action in the full knowledge that it is unrealistic, unhelpful and even dangerous. They find therefore the proposal totally unacceptable.

The crux of the problem is the situation inside East Bengal where an army from a distant territory is exercising control by sheer force and brutality. If the international community is serious about the need for return of refugees to East Bengal the first step that has to be taken is to restore conditions of normalcy inside East Pakistan through a political settlement acceptable to the people of East Bengal and their already elected leaders, and take such internationally credible measures as would assure the refugees their safe return without reprisals, etc.

C. B.S. Chimni, 'The Legal Condition of Refugees in India', *Journal of Refugee Studies* (Vol. 7, No. 4, 1994), pp. 396–98.

India has long maintained a general policy of not internationalising refugee problems and thus not seeking assistance from the international community. When the stay of the Tibetan refugees became prolonged the Government began a tentative reconsideration of this position. Initially, UNHCR's involvement was rejected because the continued tensions with China meant that the Indian Government preferred not to have an official representative of UNHCR based in the country.[115] However, in February 1969 a Branch Office was officially opened in Delhi, and Mr. Frederik L. Pijnacker-Hordijk of the Netherlands was appointed UNHCR representative. In October 1969, India for the first time designated an observer to attend the sessions of the Executive Committee of UNHCR. In 1970 the role of UNHCR assumed new importance as attempts were made to speed up and consolidate the permanent settlement of Tibetan refugees. All this led to 'a close working relationship between UNHCR and the government'.[116]

In April 1971, with the flood of refugees from East Pakistan, India called upon the United Nations for assistance; it was motivated to do so both because of the size of the problem as well as, in this case, the need and desire to internationalise the issue. Despite the initial protest of Pakistan, on 29 April 1971 the UN Secretary-General designated UNHCR as the focal point to coordinate assistance from all Organisations and Programmes. The High Commissioner, Prince Sadruddin Aga Khan, visited India and Pakistan in June to consult with the respective governments on relief measures and the problem of voluntary repatriation. The position of the High Commissioner was from the beginning 'a delicate one'.[117] However, to the extent that the relief programme was seen as palliative and repatriation the only solution, 'the activities of the High Commissioner

[115] Holborn, *Refugee,* (see footnote 45 earlier), p. 737.
[116] Ibid. at p. 738.
[117] Ibid. at p. 764.

and the means by which implementation of his programmes occurred threaded constantly through and around the political framework of the problem'.[118]

Pakistan was seeking a UN presence on the eastern border with India so that it could control the situation inside East Pakistan by claiming the protective safeguards of domestic jurisdiction under the UN Charter.[119] As a part of this general strategy, 'Pakistan attempted to make use of the proposal of the Secretary-General that the voluntary repatriation of the refugees should be promoted under the auspices of UNHCR. Expectedly India refused to be trapped.'[120] In November, the High Commissioner made a second journey to India and Pakistan. The issue of voluntary repatriation came up once again. The fact of the matter was that it was inextricably tied up with the military and political situation on the ground. This led to the feeling in India that UNHCR was not confining itself to playing its non-political and humanitarian role but was transgressing traditional boundaries.

Nevertheless, since 1981, when a significant number of refugees arrived from Afghanistan and Iran, the Government of India has allowed a UNHCR presence in India.... However, UNHCR is only allowed a nominal presence; the UNHCR mission in New Delhi is required to function under the banner of the UNDP. But the relationship between the Indian Government and the Office of the UNHCR is evolving in a positive direction. In 1993, India agreed to allow UNHCR to oversee the voluntary nature of the repatriation of Sri Lankan Tamils, although denying it the same role in the case of the Chakma refugees. Finally, there is much greater interaction and cooperation between the Government and UNHCR and thus reason to believe that the relationship between the two will significantly improve in the coming years.

Indeed, by the time this article appears in print India would have taken its rightful place in the Executive Committee of UNHCR. India's initiative to become a member of the Executive Committee was dictated by several factors. First is, of course, its more positive experience with UNHCR in recent years. Second, the fact that Pakistan has been a member of the Executive Committee since 1988 and could use the body to agitate against India's national interests. Finally, India is seeking to become a member of the UN Security Council. It can hardly hope to see its urging taken seriously if it does not play its due role in an important UN organisation such as UNHCR.

[118] Ibid.
[119] C.S.R. Murthy, *India's Diplomacy in the United Nations* (Lancer Books, New Delhi, 1993), p. 53.
[120] Ibid.

D. US Committee for Refugees, *World Refugee Survey 1997* (Washington, D.C., 1997).

Urban Refugees

UNHCR [...] recognised some 18,600 Afghans and 600 persons of various other nationalities, including 243 Somalis, 195 Iranians, and 84 Sudanese, as refugees. These 19,200 so-called urban refugees, who mostly lived in and around Delhi (reportedly at the Indian Government's insistence) were the only refugees in India to whom the UNHCR had full access. In part because India had no national legislation regarding refugees, the Indian Government did not grant even the UNHCR-recognised refugees any legal status, nor did it permit them to work. It did, however, permit them to stay, though it required them to renew their residence permits yearly....

More than 14,000 of the Afghans arrived in India in 1993 and early 1994. An estimated 60 percent were Hindi-speakers whose families had migrated to Afghanistan from present-day India. UNHCR initially provided cash assistance to 12,500 of the refugees and arranged for 6,200 of the refugees, some of whom it gave a one-time, lump-sum grant intended to help them develop their own income generating activities. UNHCR based its decision to terminate assistance to many of the urban refugees on a study that the agency conducted in 1993 that indicated that many of the refugees were living in good conditions. During 1996, UNHCR began terminating assistance to some non-Afghan refugees. SAHRDAC (South Asian Human Rights Documentation Centre) reported that two refugees whose assistance was terminated committed suicide in despair. It said that one, a 27-year-old Afghan woman, burned herself to death at the back gate of the UNHCR Office in New Delhi. In April and May, a number of Burmese urban refugees staged a sit-in and hunger strike outside the UNHCR office to protest the agency's plan to terminate their assistance and give them lump-sum grants.

According to a 1995 report by SAHRDC, UNHCR's cash assistance was 'insufficient to meet basic necessities'.[121] The report added, 'Rent rates are high and consume a considerable amount of ... [refugees' cash assistance] leaving very little for food, clothing, and other necessities'.[122] SAHRDC also criticised the lump-sum selfsufficiency grants, saying that the sum offered was 'too meager to establish any business or develop selfsufficiency'.[123]

---

[121] *The Status of Refugees under the Protection of the UNHCR in New Delhi* (South Asia Human Rights Documentation Centre, New Delhi, 1995).

[122] Ibid.

[123] Ibid.

UNHCR said that one year after giving the lump-sum grants, it reviewed the progress of refugees who received them. It found that many had done well, that some needed extra help, which UNHCR gave, and that others were not doing well and UNHCR had reinstated their assistance. UNHCR said that 5,000 urban refugees continued to receive assistance at the end of the year.

Annexures

Annexures

I

STATUTE OF THE OFFICE OF THE UNITED NATIONS HIGH COMMISSIONER FOR REFUGEES

GENERAL ASSEMBLY RESOLUTION 428 (V)
of 14 December 1950

The General Assembly
In view of its resolution 319 A (IV) of 3 December 1949,

1. Adopts the annex to the present resolution, being the Statute of the Office of the United Nations High Commissioner for Refugees;

2. Calls upon Governments to co-operate with the United Nations High Commissioner for Refugees in the performance of his functions concerning refugees falling under the competence of his Office, especially by:

(a) Becoming parties to international conventions providing for the protection of refugees, and taking the necessary steps of implementation under such conventions;

(b) Entering into special agreements with the High Commissioner for the execution of measures calculated to improve the situation of refugees and to reduce the number requiring protection;

(c) Admitting refugees to their territories, not excluding those in the most destitute categories;

(d) Assisting the High Commissioner in his efforts to promote the voluntary repatriation of refugees;

(e) Promoting the assimilation of refugees, especially by facilitating their naturalisation;

(f) Providing refugees with travel and other documents such as would normally be provided to other aliens by their national authorities, especially documents which would facilitate their resettlement;

(g) Permitting refugees to transfer their assets and especially those necessary for their resettlement;

(h) Providing the High Commissioner with information concerning the number and condition of refugees, and laws and regulations concerning them.

3. Requests the Secretary-General to transmit the present resolution, together with the annex attached thereto, also to States non-members of the United Nations, with a view to obtaining their co-operation in its implementation.

STATUTE OF THE OFFICE OF THE UNITED NATIONS HIGH COMMISSIONER FOR REFUGEES

CHAPTER I

General Provisions

1. The United Nations High Commissioner for Refugees, acting under the authority of the General Assembly, shall assume the function of providing international protection, under the auspices of the United Nations, to refugees who fall within the scope of the present Statute and of seeking permanent solutions for the problem of refugees by assisting Governments and, subject to the approval of the Governments concerned, private organisations to facilitate the voluntary repatriation of such refugees, or their assimilation within new national communities.

In the exercise of his functions, more particularly when difficulties arise, and for instance with regard to any controversy concerning the international status of these persons, the High Commissioner shall request the opinion of the advisory committee on refugees if it is created.

2. The work of the High Commissioner shall be of an entirely non-political character; it shall be humanitarian and social and shall relate, as a rule, to groups and categories of refugees.

3. The High Commissioner shall follow policy directives given him by the General Assembly or the Economic and Social Council.

4. The Economic and Social Council may decide, after hearing the views of the High Commissioner on the subject, to establish an advisory committee on refugees, which shall consist of representatives of States Members and States non-members of the United Nations, to be selected by the Council on the basis of their demonstrated interest in and devotion to the solution of the refugee problem.

5. The General Assembly shall review, not later than at its eighth regular session, the arrangements for the Office of the High Commissioner

with a view to determining whether the Office should be continued beyond 31 December 1953.

CHAPTER II

Functions of the High Commissioner

6. The competence[1] of the High Commissioner shall extend to:

A. (i) Any person who has been considered a refugee under the Arrangements of 12 May 1926 and of 30 June 1928 or under the Conventions of 28 October 1933 and 10 February 1938, the Protocol of 14 September 1939 or the Constitution of the International Refugee Organisation.

(ii) Any person who, as a result of events occurring before 1 January 1951 and owing to well-founded fear of being persecuted for reasons of race, religion, nationality or political opinion, is outside the country of his nationality and is unable or, owing to such fear or for reasons other than personal convenience, is unwilling to avail himself of the protection of that country; or who, not having a nationality and being outside the country of his former habitual residence, is unable or, owing to such fear or for reasons other than personal convenience, is unwilling to return to it.

Decisions as to eligibility taken by the International Refugee Organisation during the period of its activities shall not prevent the status of refugee being accorded to persons who fulfil the conditions of the present paragraph;

The competence of the High Commissioner shall cease to apply to any person defined in section A above if:

(a) He has voluntarily re-availed himself of the protection of the country of his nationality; or

(b) Having lost his nationality, he has voluntarily re-acquired it; or

---

[1] In addition to refugees as defined in the Statute, other categories of persons finding themselves in refugee-like situations, have in the course of the years come within the concern of the High Commissioner in accordance with the subsequent General Assembly and ECOSOC Resolutions.

General Assembly Resolutions: 1167 (XII)—1388 (XIV)—1501 (XV)—1671 (XVI)—1673 (XVI)—1783 (XVII)—1784 (XVII)—1959 (XVIII)—2958 (XXVII)—3143 (XXVIII)—3454 (XXX)—3455 (XXX), and ECOSOC Resolutions: 1655 (LII)—1705 (LIII)—1741 (LIV)—1799 (LV)—1877 (LVII)—2011 (LXI).

(c) He has acquired a new nationality, and enjoys the protection of the country of his new nationality; or

(d) He has voluntarily re-established himself in the country which he left or outside which he remained owing to fear of persecution; or

(e) He can no longer, because the circumstances in connexion with which he has been recognised as a refugee have ceased to exist, claim grounds other than those of personal convenience for continuing to refuse to avail himself of the protection of the country of his nationality. Reasons of a purely economic character may not be invoked; or

(f) Being a person who has no nationality, he can no longer, because the circumstances in connexion with which he has been recognised as a refugee have ceased to exist and he is able to return to the country of his former habitual residence, claim grounds other than those of personal convenience for continuing to refuse to return to that country;

B. Any other person who is outside the country of his nationality, or if he has no nationality, the country of his former habitual residence, because he has or had well-founded fear of persecution by reason of his race, religion, nationality or political opinion and is unable or, because of such fear, is unwilling to avail himself of the protection of the government of the country of his nationality, or, if he has no nationality, to return to the country of his former habitual residence.

7. Provided that the competence of the High Commissioner as defined in paragraph 6 above shall not extend to a person:

(a) Who is a national of more than one country unless he satisfies the provisions of the preceding paragraph in relation to each of the countries of which he is a national; or

(b) Who is recognised by the competent authorities of the country in which he has taken residence as having the rights and obligations which are attached to the possession of the nationality of that country; or

(c) Who continues to receive from other organs or agencies of the United Nations protection or assistance; or

(d) In respect of whom there are serious reasons for considering that he has committed a crime covered by the provisions of treaties of extradition or a crime mentioned in article VI of the London Charter of the International Military Tribunal or by the provisions of article 14, paragraph 2, of the Universal Declaration of Human Rights.[2]

8. The High Commissioner shall provide for the protection of refugees falling under the competence of his Office by:

(a) Promoting the conclusion and ratification of international conventions for the protection of refugees, supervising their application and proposing amendments thereto;

(b) Promoting through special agreements with Governments the execution of any measures calculated to improve the situation of refugees and to reduce the number requiring protection;

(c) Assisting governmental and private efforts to promote voluntary repatriation or assimilation within new national communities;

(d) Promoting the admission of refugees, not excluding those in the most destitute categories, to the territories of States;

(e) Endeavouring to obtain permission for refugees to transfer their assets and especially those necessary for their resettlement;

(f) Obtaining from Governments information concerning the number and conditions of refugees in their territories and the laws and regulations concerning them;

(g) Keeping in close touch with the Governments and inter-governmental organisations concerned;

(h) Establishing contact in such manner as he may think best with private organisations dealing with refugee questions;

(i) Facilitating the co-ordination of the efforts of private organisations concerned with the welfare of refugees.

9. The High Commissioner shall engage in such additional activities, including repatriation and resettlement, as the General Assembly may determine, within the limits of the resources placed at his disposal.

10. The High Commissioner shall administer any funds, public or private, which he receives for assistance to refugees, and shall distribute them among the private and, as appropriate, public agencies which he deems best qualified to administer such assistance.

The High Commissioner may reject any offers which he does not consider appropriate or which cannot be utilised.

The High Commissioner shall not appeal to Governments for funds or make a general appeal, without the prior approval of the General Assembly.

[2] See UN General Assembly Resolution 217 A (III) of 10 December 1948.

The High Commissioner shall include in his annual report a statement of his activities in this field.

11. The High Commissioner shall be entitled to present his views before the General Assembly, the Economic and Social Council and their subsidiary bodies.

The High Commissioner shall report annually to the General Assembly through the Economic and Social Council; his report shall be considered as a separate item on the agenda of the General Assembly.

12. The High Commissioner may invite the co-operation of the various specialised agencies.

CHAPTER III

Organisation and Finances

13. The High Commissioner shall be elected by the General Assembly on the nomination of the Secretary-General. The terms of appointment of the High Commissioner shall be proposed by the Secretary-General and approved by the General Assembly. The High Commissioner shall be elected for a term of three years, from 1 January 1951.

14. The High Commissioner shall appoint, for the same term, a Deputy High Commissioner of a nationality other than his own.

15. (a) Within the limits of the budgetary appropriations provided, the staff of the Office of the High Commissioner shall be appointed by the High Commissioner and shall be responsible to him in the exercise of their functions.

   (b) Such staff shall be chosen from persons devoted to the purposes of the Office of the High Commissioner.

   (c) Their conditions of employment shall be those provided under the staff regulations adopted by the General Assembly and the rules promulgated thereunder by the Secretary-General.

   (d) Provision may also be made to permit the employment of personnel without compensation.

16. The High Commissioner shall consult the Government of the countries of residence of refugees as to the need for appointing representatives therein. In any country recognising such need, there may be appointed a representative approved by the Government of that country. Subject to the foregoing, the same representative may serve in more than one country.

17. The High Commissioner and the Secretary-General shall make appropriate arrangements for liaison and consultation on matters of mutual interest.

18. The Secretary-General shall provide the High Commissioner with all necessary facilities within budgetary limitations.

19. The Office of the High Commissioner shall be located in Geneva, Switzerland.

20. The Office of the High Commissioner shall be financed under the budget of the United Nations. Unless the General Assembly subsequently decides otherwise, no expenditure other than administrative expenditures relating to the functioning of the Office of the High Commissioner shall be borne on the budget of the United Nations and all other expenditures relating to the activities of the High Commissioner shall be financed by voluntary contributions.

21. The administration of the Office of the High Commissioner shall be subject to the Financial Regulations of the United Nations and to the financial rules promulgated thereunder by the Secretary-General.

22. Transactions relating to the High Commissioner's funds shall be subject to audit by the United Nations Board of Auditors, provided that the Board may accept audited accounts from the agencies to which funds have been allocated. Administrative arrangements for the custody of such funds and their allocation shall be agreed between the High Commissioner and the Secretary-General in accordance with the Financial Regulations of the United Nations and rules promulgated thereunder by the Secretary-General.

II

CONVENTION RELATING TO THE STATUS OF REFUGEES, 1951

Done at Geneva on 28 July 1951[1]

Entry into force: 22 April 1954, in accordance with Article 43
Text: United Nations Treaty Series No. 2545, Vol. 189, p. 137

PREAMBLE

The High Contracting Parties

Considering that the Charter of the United Nations and the Universal Declaration of Human Rights approved on 10 December 1948 by the General Assembly have affirmed the principle that human beings shall enjoy fundamental rights and freedoms without discrimination,

Considering that the United Nations has, on various occasions, manifested its profound concern for refugees and endeavoured to assure refugees the widest possible exercise of these fundamental rights and freedoms,

Considering that it is desirable to revise and consolidate previous international agreements relating to the status of refugees and to extend the scope of and the protection accorded by such instruments by means of a new agreement,

Considering that the grant of asylum may place unduly heavy burdens on certain countries, and that a satisfactory solution of a problem of

[1] The Convention was adopted by the United Nations Conference of Plenipotentiaries on the Status of Refugees and Stateless Persons, held at Geneva from 2 to 25 July 1951. The Conference was convened pursuant to Resolution 429 (V), adopted by the General Assembly of the United Nations on 14 December 1950. For the text of this resolution, see Official Records of the General Assembly, Fifth Session, Supplement No. 20 (A/1775), p. 48. The Text of the Final Act of the Conference is reproduced in Appendix.

which the United Nations has recognised the international scope and nature cannot therefore be achieved without international co-operation,

Expressing the wish that all States, recognising the social and humanitarian nature of the problem of refugees, will do everything within their power to prevent this problem from becoming a cause of tension between States,

Noting that the United Nations High Commissioner for Refugees is charged with the task of supervising international conventions providing for the protection of refugees, and recognising that the effective co-ordination of measures taken to deal with this problem will depend upon the co-operation of States with the High Commissioner,

Have agreed as follows:

CHAPTER I

General Provisions

Article 1

Definition of the term 'Refugee'

A. For the purposes of the present Convention, the term "refugee" shall apply to any person who:

(1) Has been considered a refugee under the Arrangements of 12 May 1926 and 30 June 1928 or under the Conventions of 28 October 1933 and 10 February 1938, the Protocol of 14 September 1939 or the Constitution of the International Refugee Organisation;

Decisions of non-eligibility taken by the International Refugee Organisation during the period of its activities shall not prevent the status of refugee being accorded to persons who fulfil the conditions of paragraph 2 of this section;

(2) As a result of events occurring before 1 January 1951 and owing to well-founded fear of being persecuted for reasons of race, religion, nationality, membership of a particular social group or political opinion, is outside the country of his nationality and is unable or, owing to such fear, is unwilling to avail himself of the protection of that country; or who, not having a nationality and being outside the country of his former habitual residence as a result of such events, is unable or, owing to such fear, is unwilling to return to it.

In the case of a person who has more than one nationality, the term "the country of his nationality" shall mean each of the countries of which he is a national, and a person shall not be deemed to be lacking the protection of the country of his nationality if, without any valid reason based on well-founded fear, he has not availed himself of the protection of one of the countries of which he is a national.

B. (1) For the purposes of this Convention, the words 'events occurring before 1 January 1951' in Article 1, Section A, shall be understood to mean either

(a) 'events occurring in Europe before 1 January 1951'; or

(b) 'events occurring in Europe or elsewhere before 1 January 1951', and each Contracting State shall make a declaration at the time of signature, ratification or accession, specifying which of these meanings it applies for the purpose of its obligations under this Convention.

(2) Any Contracting State which has adopted alternative (a) may at any time extend its obligations by adopting alternative (b) by means of a notification addressed to the Secretary-General of the United Nations.

C. This Convention shall cease to apply to any person falling under the terms of section A if:

(1) He has voluntarily re-availed himself of the protection of the country of his nationality; or

(2) Having lost his nationality, he has voluntarily re-acquired it, or

(3) He has acquired a new nationality, and enjoys the protection of the country of his new nationality; or

(4) He has voluntarily re-established himself in the country which he left or outside which he remained owing to fear of persecution; or

(5) He can no longer, because the circumstances in connexion with which he has been recognised as a refugee have ceased to exist, continue to refuse to avail himself of the protection of the country of his nationality;

Provided that this paragraph shall not apply to a refugee falling under section A(1) of this Article who is able to invoke compelling reasons arising out of previous persecution for refusing to avail himself of the protection of the country of nationality;

(6) Being a person who has no nationality he is, because the circumstances in connexion with which he has been recognised as a refugee have ceased to exist, able to return to the country of his former habitual residence,

Provided that this paragraph shall not apply to a refugee falling under section A(1) of this Article who is able to invoke compelling reasons arising out of previous persecution for refusing to return to the country of his former habitual residence.

D. This Convention shall not apply to persons who are at present receiving from organs or agencies of the United Nations other than the United Nations High Commissioner for Refugees protection or assistance.

When such protection or assistance has ceased for any reason, without the position of such persons being definitively settled in accordance with the relevant resolutions adopted by the General Assembly of the United Nations, these persons shall *ipso facto* be entitled to the benefits of this Convention.

E. This Convention shall not apply to a person who is recognised by the competent authorities of the country in which he has taken residence as having the rights and obligations which are attached to the possession of the nationality of that country.

F. The provisions of this Convention shall not apply to any person with respect to whom there are serious reasons for considering that:

(a) he has committed a crime against peace, a war crime, or a crime against humanity, as defined in the international instruments drawn up to make provision in respect of such crimes;

(b) he has committed a serious non-political crime outside the country of refuge prior to his admission to that country as a refugee;

(c) he has been guilty of acts contrary to the purposes and principles of the United Nations.

Article 2

General obligations

Every refugee has duties to the country in which he finds himself, which require in particular that he conform to its laws and regulations as well as to measures taken for the maintenance of public order.

Article 3

Non-discrimination

The Contracting States shall apply the provisions of this Convention to refugees without discrimination as to race, religion or country of origin.

Article 4

Religion

The Contracting States shall accord to refugees within their territories treatment at least as favourable as that accorded to their nationals with respect to freedom to practise their religion and freedom as regards the religious education of their children.

Article 5

Rights granted apart from this Convention

Nothing in this Convention shall be deemed to impair any rights and benefits granted by a Contracting State to refugees apart from this Convention.

Article 6

The term 'in the same circumstances'

For the purpose of this Convention, the term "in the same circumstances" implies that any requirements (including requirements as to length and conditions of sojourn or residence) which the particular individual would have to fulfil for the enjoyment of the right in question, if he were not a refugee, must be fulfilled by him, with the exception of requirements which by their nature a refugee is incapable of fulfilling.

Article 7

Exemption from reciprocity

1. Except where this Convention contains more favourable provisions, a Contracting State shall accord to refugees the same treatment as is accorded to aliens generally.

2. After a period of three years' residence, all refugees shall enjoy exemption from legislative reciprocity in the territory of the Contracting States.

3. Each Contracting State shall continue to accord to refugees the rights and benefits to which they were already entitled, in the absence of reciprocity, at the date of entry into force of this Convention for that State.

4. The Contracting States shall consider favourably the possibility of according to refugees, in the absence of reciprocity, rights and benefits beyond those to which they are entitled according to paragraphs 2 and 3, and to extending exemption from reciprocity to refugees who do not fulfil the conditions provided for in paragraphs 2 and 3.

5. The provisions of paragraphs 2 and 3 apply both to the rights and benefits referred to in Articles 13, 18, 19, 21 and 22 of this Convention and to rights and benefits for which this Convention does not provide.

Article 8

Exemption from exceptional measures

With regard to exceptional measures which may be taken against the person, property or interests of nationals of a foreign State, the Contracting States shall not apply such measures to a refugee who is formally a national of the said State solely on account of such nationality. Contracting States which, under their legislation, are prevented from applying the general principle expressed in this Article, shall, in appropriate cases, grant exemptions in favour of such refugees.

Article 9

Provisional measures

Nothing in this Convention shall prevent a Contracting State, in time of war or other grave and exceptional circumstances, from taking provisionally measures which it considers to be essential to the national security in the case of a particular person, pending a determination by the Contracting State that that person is in fact a refugee and that the continuance of such measures is necessary in his case in the interests of national security.

Article 10

Continuity of residence

1. Where a refugee has been forcibly displaced during the Second World War and removed to the territory of a Contracting State, and is resident there, the period of such enforced sojourn shall be considered to have been lawful residence within that territory.

2. Where a refugee has been forcibly displaced during the Second World War from the territory of a Contracting State and has, prior to the date of entry into force of this Convention, returned there for the purpose of taking up residence, the period of residence before and after such enforced displacement shall be regarded as one uninterrupted period for any purposes for which uninterrupted residence is required.

Article 11

Refugee seamen

In the case of refugees regularly serving as crew members on board a ship flying the flag of a Contracting State, that State shall give sympathetic consideration to their establishment on its territory and the issue of travel documents to them or their temporary admission to its territory particularly with a view to facilitating their establishment in another country.

CHAPTER II

Juridical Status

Article 12

Personal status

1. The personal status of a refugee shall be governed by the law of the country of his domicile or, if he has no domicile, by the law of the country of his residence.

2. Rights previously acquired by a refugee and dependent on personal status, more particularly rights attaching to marriage, shall be respected by a Contracting State, subject to compliance, if this be necessary, with the formalities required by the law of that State, provided that the right in question is one which would have been recognised by the law of that State had he not become a refugee.

Article 13

Movable and immovable property

The Contracting States shall accord to a refugee treatment as favourable as possible and, in any event, not less favourable than that accorded to aliens generally in the same circumstances, as regards the acquisition of movable and immovable property and other rights pertaining thereto, and to leases and other contracts relating to movable and immovable property.

Article 14

Artistic rights and industrial property

In respect of the protection of industrial property, such as inventions, designs or models, trade marks, trade names, and of rights in literary, artistic and scientific works, a refugee shall be accorded in the country in which he has his habitual residence the same protection as is accorded to nationals of that country. In the territory of any other Contracting State, he shall be accorded the same protection as is accorded in that territory to nationals of the country in which he has his habitual residence.

Article 15

Right of association

As regards non-political and non-profit-making associations and trade unions the Contracting States shall accord to refugees lawfully staying in their territory the most favourable treatment accorded to nationals of a foreign country, in the same circumstances.

Article 16

Access to courts

1. A refugee shall have free access to the courts of law on the territory of all Contracting States.

2. A refugee shall enjoy in the Contracting State in which he has his habitual residence the same treatment as a national in matters pertaining to access to the Courts, including legal assistance and exemption from *cautio judicatum solvi.*

3. A refugee shall be accorded in the matters referred to in paragraph 2 in countries other than that in which he has his habitual residence the treatment granted to a national of the country of his habitual residence.

CHAPTER III

Gainful Employment

Article 17

Wage-earning employment

1. The Contracting State shall accord to refugees lawfully staying their territory the most favourable treatment accorded to nationals of a foreign country in the same circumstances, as regards the right to engage in wage-earning employment.

2. In any case, restrictive measures imposed on aliens or the employment of aliens for the protection of the national labour market shall not be applied to a refugee who was already exempt from them at the date of entry into force of this Convention for the Contracting State concerned, or who fulfils·one of the following conditions:

   (a) He has completed three years' residence in the country,

   (b) He has a spouse possessing the nationality of the country of residence. A refugee may not invoke the benefits of this provision if he has abandoned his spouse, *(c)* He has one or more children possessing the nationality of the country of residence.

3. The Contracting States shall give sympathetic consideration to assimilating the rights of all refugees with regard to wage-earning employment to those of nationals, and in particular of those refugees who have entered their territory pursuant to programmes of labour recruitment or under immigration schemes.

Article 18

Self-employment

The Contracting States shall accord to a refugee lawfully in their territory treatment as favourable as possible and, in any event, not less favourable than that accorded to aliens generally in the same circumstances, as regards the right to engage on his own account in agriculture, industry, handicrafts and commerce and to establish commercial and industrial companies.

Article 19

Liberal professions

1. Each Contracting State shall accord to refugees lawfully staying in their territory who hold diplomas recognised by the competent authorities of that State, and who are desirous of practising a liberal profession, treatment as favourable as possible and, in any event, not less favourable than that accorded to aliens generally in the same circumstances.

2. The Contracting States shall use their best endeavours consistently with their laws and constitutions to secure the settlement of such refugees in the territories, other than the metropolitan territory, for whose international relations they are responsible.

CHAPTER IV

Welfare

Article 20

Rationing

Where a rationing system exists, which applies to the population at large and regulates the general distribution of products in short supply, refugees shall be accorded the same treatment as nationals.

Article 21

Housing

As regards housing, the Contracting States, in so far as the matter is regulated by laws or regulations or is subject to the control of public authorities, shall accord to refugees lawfully staying in their territory treatment as favourable as possible and, in any event, not less favourable than that accorded to aliens generally in the same circumstances.

Article 22

Public education

1. The Contracting States shall accord to refugees the same treatment as is accorded to nationals with respect to elementary education.

2. The Contracting States shall accord to refugees treatment as favourable as possible, and, in any event, not less favourable than that accorded to aliens generally in the same circumstances, with respect to education other than elementary education and, in particular, as regards access to studies, the recognition of foreign school certificates, diplomas and degrees, the remission of fees and charges and the award of scholarships.

Article 23

Public relief

The Contracting States shall accord to refugees lawfully staying in their territory the same treatment with respect to public relief and assistance as is accorded to their nationals.

Article 24

Labour legislation and social security

1. The Contracting States shall accord to refugees lawfully staying in their territory the same treatment as is accorded to nationals in respect of the following matters:

   (a) Insofar as such matters are governed by laws or regulations or are subject to the control of administrative authorities: remuneration, including family allowances where these form part of remuneration, hours of work, overtime arrangements, holidays with pay, restrictions on home work, minimum age of employment, apprenticeship and training, women's work and the work of young persons, and the enjoyment of the benefits of collective bargaining:

(b) Social security (legal provisions in respect of employment injury, occupational diseases, maternity, sickness, disability, old age, death, unemployment, family responsibilities and any other contingency which, according to national laws or regulations, is covered by a social security scheme), subject to the following limitations:

(i) There may be appropriate arrangements for the maintenance of acquired rights and rights in course of acquisition;

(ii) National laws or regulations of the country of residence may prescribe special arrangements concerning benefits or portions of benefits which are payable wholly out of public funds, and concerning allowances paid to persons who do not fulfil the contribution conditions prescribed for the award of a normal pension.

2. The right to compensation for the death of a refugee resulting from employment injury or from occupational disease shall not be affected by the fact that the residence of the beneficiary is outside the territory of the Contracting State.

3. The Contracting States shall extend to refugees the benefits of agreements concluded between them, or which may be concluded between them in the future, concerning the maintenance of acquired rights and rights in the process of acquisition in regard to social security, subject only to the conditions which apply to nationals of the States signatory to the agreements in question.

4. The Contracting States will give sympathetic consideration to extending to refugees so far as possible the benefits of similar agreements which may at any time be in force between such Contracting States and non-contracting States.

CHAPTER V

Administrative Measures

Article 25

Administrative assistance

1. When the exercise of a right by a refugee would normally require the assistance of authorities of a foreign country to whom he cannot have recourse, the Contracting States in whose territory he is residing shall arrange that such assistance be afforded to him by their own authorities or by an international authority.

2. The authority or authorities mentioned in paragraph 1 shall deliver or cause to be delivered under their supervision to refugees such

documents or certifications as would normally be delivered to aliens by or through their national authorities.

3. Documents or certifications so delivered shall stand in the stead of the official instruments delivered to aliens by or through their national authorities, and shall be given credence in the absence of proof to the contrary.

4. Subject to such exceptional treatment as may be granted to indigent persons, fees may be charged for the services mentioned herein, but such fees shall be moderate and commensurate with those charged to nationals for similar services.

5. The provisions of this Article shall be without prejudice to Articles 27 and 28.

Article 26

Freedom of movement

Each Contracting State shall accord to refugees lawfully in its territory the right to choose their place of residence and to move freely within its territory, subject to any regulations applicable to aliens generally in the same circumstances.

Article 27

Identity papers

The Contracting States shall issue identity papers to any refugee in their territory who does not possess a valid travel document.

Article 28

Travel documents

1. The Contracting States shall issue to refugees lawfully staying in their territory travel documents for the purpose of travel outside their territory unless compelling reasons of national security or public order otherwise require, and the provisions of the Schedule to this Convention shall apply with respect to such documents. The Contracting States may issue such a travel document to any other refugee in their territory, they shall in particular give sympathetic consideration to the issue of such a travel document to refugees in their territory who are unable to obtain a travel document from the country of their lawful residence.

2. Travel documents issued to refugees under previous international agreements by parties thereto shall be recognised and treated by the

Contracting States in the same way as if they had been issued pursuant to this article.

Article 29

Fiscal charges

1. The Contracting States shall not impose upon refugees duties, charges or taxes, of any description whatsoever, other or higher than those which are or may be levied on their nationals in similar situations.

2. Nothing in the above paragraph shall prevent the application to refugees of the laws and regulations concerning charges in respect of the issue to aliens of administrative documents including identity papers.

Article 30

Transfer of assets

1. A Contracting State shall, in conformity with its laws and regulations, permit refugees to transfer assets which they have brought into its territory, to another country where they have been admitted for the purposes of resettlement.

2. A Contracting State shall give sympathetic consideration to the application of refugees for permission to transfer assets wherever they may be and which are necessary for their resettlement in another country to which they have been admitted.

Article 31

Refugees unlawfully in the country of refuge

1. The Contracting States shall not impose penalties, on account of their illegal entry or presence, on refugees who, coming directly from a territory where their life or freedom was threatened in the sense of Article 1, enter or are present in their territory without authorisation, provided they present themselves without delay to the authorities and show good cause for their illegal entry or presence.

2. The Contracting States shall not apply to the movements of such refugees restrictions other than those which are necessary and such restrictions shall only be applied until their status in the country is regularised or they obtain admission into another country. The Contracting States shall allow such refugees a reasonable period and all the necessary facilities to obtain admission into another country.

Article 32

Expulsion

1. The Contracting States shall not expel a refugee lawfully in their territory save on grounds of national security or public order.

2. The expulsion of such a refugee shall be only in pursuance of a decision reached in accordance with due process of law. Except where compelling reasons of national security otherwise require, the refugee shall be allowed to submit evidence to clear himself, and to appeal to and be represented for the purpose before competent authority or a person or persons specially designated by the competent authority.

3. The Contracting States shall allow such a refugee a reasonable period within which to seek legal admission into another country. The Contracting States reserve the right to apply during that period such internal measures as they may deem necessary.

Article 33

Prohibition of expulsion or return ("refoulement")

1. No Contracting State shall expel or return ("refouler") a refugee in any manner whatsoever to the frontiers of territories where his life or freedom would be threatened on account of his race, religion, nationality, membership of a particular social group or political opinion.

2. The benefit of the present provision may not, however, be claimed by a refugee whom there are reasonable grounds for regarding as a danger to the security of the country in which he is, or who, having been convicted by a final judgment of a particularly serious crime, constitutes a danger to the community of that country.

Article 34

Naturalisation

The Contracting States shall as far as possible facilitate the assimilation and naturalisation of refugees. They shall in particular make every effort to expedite naturalisation proceedings and to reduce as far as possible the charges and costs of such proceedings.

CHAPTER VI

Executory and Transitory Provisions

Article 35

Co-operation of the national authorities with the United Nations

1. The Contracting States undertake to co-operate with the Office of the United Nations High Commissioner for Refugees, or any other agency of the United Nations which may succeed it, in the exercise of its functions, and shall in particular facilitate its duty of supervising the application of the provisions of this Convention.

2. In order to enable the Office of the High Commissioner or any other agency of the United Nations which may succeed it, to make reports to the competent organs of the United Nations, the Contracting States undertake to provide them in the appropriate form with information and statistical data requested concerning:

   (a) the condition of refugees,

   (b) the implementation of this Convention, and

   (c) laws, regulations and decrees which are, or may hereafter be, in force relating to refugees.

Article 36

Information on national legislation

The Contracting States shall communicate to the Secretary-General of the United Nations the laws and regulations which they may adopt to ensure the application of this Convention.

Article 37

Relation to previous Conventions

Without prejudice to Article 28, paragraph 2, of this Convention, this Convention replaces, as between parties to it, the Arrangements of 5 July 1922, 31 May 1924, 12 May 1926, 30 June 1928 and 30 July 1935, the Conventions of 28 October 1933 and 10 February 1938, the Protocol of 14 September 1939 and the Agreement of 15 October 1946.

CHAPTER VII

Final Clauses

Article 38

Settlement of disputes

Any dispute between parties to this Convention relating to its interpretation or application, which cannot be settled by other means, shall be referred to the International Court of Justice at the request of any one of the parties to the dispute.

Article 39

Signature, ratification and accession

1. This Convention shall be opened for signature at Geneva on 28 July 1951 and shall thereafter be deposited with the Secretary-General of the United Nations. It shall be open for signature at the European Office of the United Nations from 28 July to 31 August 1951 and shall be re-opened for signature at the Headquarters of the United Nations from 17 September 1951 to 31 December 1952.

2. This Convention shall be open for signature on behalf of all States Members of the United Nations, and also on behalf of any other State invited to attend the Conference of Plenipotentiaries on the Status of Refugees and Stateless Persons or to which an invitation to sign will have been addressed by the General Assembly. It shall be ratified and the instruments of ratification shall be deposited with the Secretary-General of the United Nations.

3. This Convention shall be open from 28 July 1951 for accession by the States referred to in paragraph 2 of this Article. Accession shall be effected by the deposit of an instrument of accession with the Secretary-General of the United Nations.

Article 40

Territorial application clause

1. Any State may, at the time of signature, ratification or accession, declare that this Convention shall extend to all or any of the territories for the international relations of which it is responsible. Such a declaration shall take effect when the Convention enters into force for the State concerned.

2. At any time thereafter any such extension shall be made by notification addressed to the Secretary-General of the United Nations and shall take effect as from the ninetieth day after the day of receipt by the Secretary-General of the United Nations of this notification, or as from the date of entry into force of the Convention for the State concerned, whichever is the later.

3. With respect to those territories to which this Convention is not extended at the time of signature, ratification or accession, each State concerned shall consider the possibility of taking the necessary steps in order to extend the application of this Convention to such territories, subject, where necessary for constitutional reasons, to the consent of the governments of such territories.

Article 41

Federal clause

In the case of a Federal or non-unitary State, the following provisions shall apply:

(a) With respect to those Articles of this Convention that come within the legislative jurisdiction of the federal legislative authority, the obligations of the Federal Government shall to this extent be the same as those of Parties which are not Federal States,

(b) With respect to those Articles of this Convention that come within the legislative jurisdiction of constituent States, provinces or cantons which are not, under the constitutional system of the federation, bound to take legislative action, the Federal Government shall bring such Articles with a favourable recommendation to the notice of the appropriate authorities of States, provinces or cantons at the earliest possible moment.

(c) A Federal State Party to this Convention shall, at the request of any other Contracting State transmitted through the Secretary-General of the United Nations, supply a statement of the law and practice of the federation and its constituent units in regard to any particular provision of the Convention showing the extent to which effect has been given to that provision by legislative or other action.

Article 42

Reservations

1. At the time of signature, ratification or accession, any State may make reservations to articles of the Convention other than to Articles 1,3,4,16 (1), 33, 36-46 inclusive.

2. Any State making a reservation in accordance with paragraph 1 of this article may at any time withdraw the reservation by a communication to that effect addressed to the Secretary-General of the United Nations.

Article 43

Entry into force

1. This Convention shall come into force on the ninetieth day following the day of deposit of the sixth instrument of ratification or accession.

2. For each State ratifying or acceding to the Convention after the deposit of the sixth instrument of ratification or accession, the Convention shall enter into force on the ninetieth day following the date of deposit by such State of its instrument of ratification or accession.

Article 44

Denunciation

1. Any Contracting State may denounce this Convention at any time by a notification addressed to the Secretary-General of the United Nations.

2. Such denunciation shall take effect for the Contracting State concerned one year from the date upon which it is received by the Secretary-General of the United Nations.

3. Any State which has made a declaration or notification under Article 40 may, at any time thereafter, by a notification to the Secretary-General of the United Nations, declare that the Convention shall cease to extend to such territory one year after the date of receipt of the notification by the Secretary-General.

Article 45

Revision

1. Any Contracting State may request revision of this Convention at any time by a notification addressed to the Secretary-General of the United Nations.

2. The General Assembly of the United Nations shall recommend the steps, if any, to be taken in respect of such request.

Article 46

Notifications by the Secretary-General of the United Nations

The Secretary-General of the United Nations shall inform all Members of the United Nations and non-member States referred to in Article 39:

(a) of declarations and notifications in accordance with Section B of Article 1;

(b) of signatures, ratifications and accessions in accordance with Article 39;

(c) of declarations and notifications in accordance with Article 40;

(d) of reservations and withdrawals in accordance with Article 42;

(e) of the date on which this Convention will come into force in accordance with Article 43;

(f) of denunciations and notifications in accordance with Article 44;

(g) of requests for revision in accordance with Article 45.

In Faith whereof the undersigned, duly authorised, have signed this Convention on behalf of their respective Governments.

Done at Geneva, this twenty-eighth day of July, one thousand nine hundred and fifty-one, in a single copy, of which the English and French texts are equally authentic and which shall remain deposited in the archives of the United Nations, and certified true copies of which shall be delivered to all Members of the United Nations and to the non-member States referred to in Article 39.

SCHEDULE

Paragraph 1

1. The travel document referred to in Article 28 of this Convention shall be similar to the specimen annexed hereto.

2. The document shall be made out in at least two languages, one of which shall be English or French.

Paragraph 2

Subject to the regulations obtaining in the country of issue, children may be included in the travel document of a parent or, in exceptional circumstances, of another adult refugee.

Paragraph 3

The fees charged for issue of the document shall not exceed the lowest scale of charges for national passports.

Paragraph 4

Save in special or exceptional cases, the document shall be made valid for the largest possible number of countries.

Paragraph 5

The document shall have a validity of either one or two years, at the discretion of the issuing authority.

Paragraph 6

1. The renewal or extension of the validity of the document is a matter for the authority which issued it, so long as the holder has not established lawful residence in another territory and resides lawfully in the territory of the said authority. The issue of a new document is, under the same conditions, a matter for the authority which issued the former document.

2. Diplomatic or consular authorities, specially authorised for the purpose, shall be empowered to extend, for a period not exceeding six months, the validity of travel documents issued by their Governments.

3. The Contracting States shall give sympathetic consideration to renewing or extending the validity of travel documents or issuing new documents to refugees no longer lawfully resident in their territory who are unable to obtain a travel document from the country of their lawful residence.

Paragraph 7

The Contracting States shall recognise the validity of the documents issued in accordance with the provisions of Article 28 of this Convention.

Paragraph 8

The competent authorities of the country to which the refugee desires to proceed shall, if they are prepared to admit him and if a visa is required, affix a visa on the document of which he is the holder.

Paragraph 9

1. The Contracting States undertake to issue transit visas to refugees who have obtained visas for a territory of final destination.

2. The issue of such visas may be refused on grounds which would justify refusal of a visa to any alien.

Paragraph 10

The fees for the issue of exit, entry or transit visas shall not exceed the lowest scale of charges for visas on foreign passports.

Paragraph 11

When a refugee has lawfully taken up residence in the territory of another Contracting State, the responsibility for the issue of a new document, under the terms and conditions of Article 28, shall be that of the competent authority of that territory, to which the refugee shall be entitled to apply.

Paragraph 12

The authority issuing a new document shall withdraw the old document and shall return it to the country of issue, if it is stated in the document that it should be so returned; otherwise it shall withdraw and cancel the document.

Paragraph 13

1. Each Contracting State undertakes that the holder of a travel document issued by it in accordance with Article 28 of this Convention shall be re-admitted to its territory at any time during the period of its validity.

2. Subject to the provisions of the preceding sub-paragraph, a Contracting State may require the holder of the document to comply with such formalities as may be prescribed in regard to exit from or return to its territory.

3. The Contracting States reserve the right, in exceptional cases, or in cases where the refugee's stay is authorised for a specific period, when issuing the document, to limit the period during which the refugee may return to a period of not less than three months.

Paragraph 14

Subject only to the terms of paragraph 13, the provisions of this Schedule in no way affect the laws and regulations governing the conditions of admission to, transit through, residence and establishment in, and departure from, the territories of the Contracting States.

Paragraph 15

Neither the issue of the document nor the entries made thereon determine or affect the status of the holder, particularly as regards nationality.

Paragraph 16

The issue of the document does not in any way entitle the holder to the protection of the diplomatic or consular authorities of the country of issue, and does not confer on these authorities a right of protection.

ANNEX

Specimen Travel Document

The document will be in booklet form (approximately 15 × 10 centimetres).

It is recommended that it be so printed that any erasure or alteration by chemical or other means can be readily detected, and that the words 'Convention of 28 July 1951' be printed in continuous repetition on each page, in the language of the issuing country.

(Cover of booklet)
TRAVEL DOCUMENT
(Convention of 28 July 1951)

No. ....

(1)
TRAVEL DOCUMENT
(Convention of 28 July 1951)

This document expires on ....
unless its validity is extended or renewed.
Name ....
Forename(s) ....
Accompanied by.. child (children)

1. This document is issued solely with a view to providing the holder with a travel
document which can serve in lieu of a national passport. It is without prejudice to
and in no way affects the holder's nationality.

2. The holder is authorized to return to ....
[state here the country whose authorities are issuing the document] on or before
.... unless some later date is hereafter specified.
[The period during which the holder is allowed to return must not be less than
three months]

3. Should the holder take up residence in a country other than that which issued
the present document, he must, if he wishes to travel again, apply to the competent
authorities of his country of residence for a new document. [The old travel document shall be withdrawn by the authority issuing the new document and returned
to the authority which issued it.][1]

(This document contain   pages, exclusive of cover.)

---

[1] The sentence in brackets to be inserted by Governments which so desire.

---

(2)

Place and date of birth ....
Occupation ....
Present residence ....
* Maiden name and forename(s) of wife ....
....
* Name and forename(s) of husband ....
....

Description
Height ....
Hair ....
Colour of eyes ....
Nose ....
Shape of face ....
Complexion ....
Special peculiarities ....

Children accompanying holder

Name	Forename(s)	Place and date of birth	Sex
....	....	....	....
....	....	....	....
....	....	....	....
....	....	....	....

* Strike out whichever does not apply.

(This document contains .... pages, exclusive of cover.)

---

(3)

Photograph of holder and stamp of issuing authority
Finger-prints of holder (if required)

Signature of holder ....

(This document contains .... pages, exclusive of cover.)

---

(4)

1. This document is valid for the following countries:

....
....
....
....

2. Document or documents on the basis of which the present document is issued:

....
....
....

Issued at ....

Date ....

Signature and stamp of authority
issuing the document:

Fee paid:

(This document contains .... pages, exclusive of cover.)

---

(5)

Extension or renewal of validity

Fee paid: ....   From ....
To ....

Done at ....   Date ....

Signature and stamp of authority
extending or renewing the validity
of the document:

Extension or renewal of validity

Fee paid: ....   From ....
                                                         To ....
Done at ....   Date ....

Signature and stamp of authority
extending or renewing the validity
of the document:

(This document contains .... pages, exclusive of cover.)

---

(6)

Extension or renewal of validity

Fee paid: ....   From ....
                                                        To..
Done at ....   Date ....

Signature and stamp of authority
extending or renewing the validity
of the document:

Extension or renewal of validity

Fee paid: ....   From ....
                                                        To ....
Done at ....   Date ....

Signature and stamp of authority
extending or renewing the validity
of the document:

(This document contains .... pages, exclusive of cover.)

(7–32)

Visas

The name of the holder of the document must be repeated in each visa.

(This document contains .... pages, exclusive of cover.)

APPENDIX

Final Act of the 1951 United Nations Conference of Plenipotentiaries on the Status of Refugees and Stateless Persons

I

The General Assembly of the United Nations, by Resolution 429 (V) of 14 December 1950, decided to convene in Geneva a Conference of Plenipotentiaries to complete the drafting of, and to sign, a Convention relating to the Status of Refugees and a Protocol relating to the Status of Stateless Persons.

The Conference met at the European Office of the United Nations in Geneva from 2 to 25 July 1951.

The Governments of the following twenty-six States were represented by delegates who all submitted satisfactory credentials or other communications of appointment authorising them to participate in the Conference:

Australia	Italy
Austria	Luxembourg
Belgium	Monaco
Brazil	Netherlands
Canada	Norway
Colombia	Sweden
Denmark	Switzerland (the Swiss delegation
Egypt	also represented Liechtenstein)
France	Turkey
Germany, Federal Republic of	United Kingdom of Great Britain
Greece	and Northern Ireland
Holy See	United States of America
Iraq	Venezuela
Israel	Yugoslavia

The Governments of the following two States were represented by observers

Cuba
Iran

Pursuant to the request of the General Assembly, the United Nations High Commissioner for Refugees participated, without the right to vote, in the deliberations of the Conference.

The International Labour Organisation and the International Refugee Organization were represented at the Conference without the right to vote.

The Conference invited a representative of the Council of Europe to be represented at the Conference without the right to vote.

Representatives of the following Non-Governmental Organisations in consultative relationship with the Economic and Social Council were also present as observers:

Category A

International Confederation of Free Trade Unions
International Federation of Christian Trade Unions
Inter-Parliamentary Union

Category B

Agudas Israel World Organisation
Caritas Internationalis
Catholic International Union for Social Service
Commission of the Churches on International Affairs
Consultative Council of Jewish Organisations
Co-ordinating Board of Jewish Organisations
Friends' World Committee for Consultation
International Association of Penal Law
International Bureau for the Unification of Penal Law
International Committee of the Red Cross
International Council of Women
International Federation of Friends of Young Women
International League for the Rights of Man
International Social Service
International Union for Child Welfare
International Union of Catholic Women's Leagues
Pax Romana
Women's International League for Peace and Freedom
World Jewish Congress
World Union for Progressive Judaism
World Young Women's Christian Association

Register

International Relief Committee for Intellectual Workers
League of Red Cross Societies
Standing Conference of Voluntary Agencies
World Association of Girl Guides and Girl Scouts
World University Service

Representatives of Non-Governmental Organisations which have been granted consultative status by the Economic and Social Council as well as those entered by the Secretary-General on the Register referred to in Resolution 288 B (X) of the Economic and Social Council, paragraph 17, had under the rules of procedure adopted by the Conference the right to submit written or oral statements to the Conference.

The Conference elected Mr. Knud Larsen, of Denmark, as President, and Mr. A. Herment, of Belgium, and Mr. Talat Miras, of Turkey, as Vice-Presidents.

At its second meeting, the Conference, acting on a proposal of the representative of Egypt, unanimously decided to address an invitation to the Holy See to designate a plenipotentiary representative to participate in its work. A representative of the Holy See took his place at the Conference on 10 July 1951.

The Conference adopted as its agenda the Provisional Agenda drawn up by the Secretary-General (A/CONF.2/2/Rev.1). It also adopted the Provisional Rules of Procedure drawn up by the Secretary-General, with the addition of a provision which authorised a representative of the Council of Europe to be present at the Conference without the right to vote and to submit proposals (A/CONF.2/3/Rev.1).

In accordance with the Rules of Procedure of the Conference, the President and Vice-Presidents examined the credentials of representatives and on 17 July 1951 reported to the Conference the results of such examination, the Conference adopting the report.

The Conference used as the basis of its discussions the draft Convention relating to the Status of Refugees and the draft Protocol relating to the Status of Stateless Persons prepared by the *ad hoc* Committee on Refugees and Stateless Persons at its second session held in Geneva from 14 to 25 August 1950, with the exception of the preamble and Article 1 (Definition of the term 'refugee') of the draft Convention. The text of the preamble before the Conference was that which was adopted by the Economic and Social Council on 11 August 1950 in Resolution 319B II (XI). The text of Article 1 before the Conference was that recommended by the General Assembly on 14 December 1950 and contained in the Annex to Resolution 429 (V). The latter was a modification of the text as it had been adopted by the Economic and Social Council in Resolution 319B II (XI).[1]

The Conference adopted the Convention relating to the Status of Refugees in two readings. Prior to its second reading it established a Style Committee composed of the President and the representatives of Belgium, France, Israel, Italy, the United Kingdom of Great Britain and Northern Ireland and the United States of America, together with the High Commissioner for Refugees, which elected as its Chairman Mr. G. Warren,

---

[1] The texts referred to in the paragraph above are contained in document A/CONF.2/1.

of the United States of America. The Style Committee re-drafted the text which had been adopted by the Conference on first reading, particularly from the point of view of language and of concordance between the English and French texts.

The Convention was adopted on 25 July by 24 votes to none with no abstentions and opened for signature at the European Office of the United Nations from 28 July to 31 August 1951. It will be re-opened for signature at the permanent headquarters of the United Nations in New York from 17 September 1951 to 31 December 1952.

The English and French texts of the Convention, which are equally authentic, are appended to this Final Act.

II

The Conference decided, by 17 votes to 3 with 3 abstentions, that the titles of the chapters and of the articles of the Convention are included for practical purposes and do not constitute an element of interpretation.

III

With respect to the draft Protocol relating to the Status of Stateless Persons, the Conference adopted the following resolution:

The Conference

Having considered the draft Protocol relating to the Status of Stateless Persons,

Considering that the subject still requires more detailed study,

Decides not to take a decision on the subject at the present Conference and refers the draft Protocol back to the appropriate organs of the United Nations for further study.

IV

The Conference adopted unanimously the following recommendations:

A.
(Facilitation of refugee travels)[1]

The Conference

Considering that the issue and recognition of travel documents is necessary to facilitate the movement of refugees, and in particular their resettlement,

---

[1] Headline added.

Urges Governments which are parties to the Inter-Governmental Agreement on Refugee Travel Documents signed in London on 15 October 1946, or which recognise travel documents issued in accordance with the Agreement, to continue to issue or to recognise such travel documents, and to extend the issue of such documents to refugees as defined in Article 1 of the Convention relating to the Status of Refugees or to recognise the travel documents so issued to such persons, until they shall have undertaken obligations under Article 28 of the said Convention.

B.
(Principle of unity of the family)[1]

The Conference

Considering that the unity of the family, the natural and fundamental group unit of society, is an essential right of the refugee, and that such unity is constantly threatened, and

Noting with satisfaction that, according to the official commentary of the *ad hoc* Committee on Statelessness and Related Problems (E/1618, p. 40) the rights granted to a refugee are extended to members of his family,

Recommends Governments to take the necessary measures for the protection of the refugee's family, especially with a view to:

(1) Ensuring that the unity of the refugee's family is maintained particularly in cases where the head of the family has fulfilled the necessary conditions for admission to a particular country,

(2) The protection of refugees who are minors, in particular unaccompanied children and girls, with special reference to guardianship and adoption.

C.
(Welfare services)[2]

The Conference

Considering that, in the moral, legal and material spheres, refugees need the help of suitable welfare services, especially that of appropriate non-governmental organisations,

Recommends Governments and inter-governmental bodies to facilitate, encourage and sustain the efforts of properly qualified organisations.

---

[1] Headline added.
[2] Headline added.

D.
(International co-operation in the field of asylum and resettlement)[1]

The Conference

Considering that many persons still leave their country of origin for reasons of persecution and are entitled to special protection on account of their position,

Recommends that Governments continue to receive refugees in their territories and that they act in concert in a true spirit of international co-operation in order that these refugees may find asylum and the possibility of resettlement.

E.
(Extension of treatment provided by the Convention)[2]

The Conference

Expresses the hope that the Convention relating to the Status of Refugees will have value as an example exceeding its contractual scope and that all nations will be guided by it in granting so far as possible to persons in their territory as refugees and who would not be covered by the terms of the Convention, the treatment for which it provides.

In witness whereof the President, Vice-Presidents and the Executive Secretary of the Conference have signed this Final Act.

Done at Geneva this twenty-eighth day of July one thousand nine hundred and fifty-one in a single copy in the English and French languages, each text being equally authentic. Translations of this Final Act into Chinese, Russian and Spanish will be prepared by the Secretary-General of the United Nations, who will, on request, send copies thereof to each of the Governments invited to attend the Conference.

The President of the Conference:	KNUD LARSEN
The Vice-Presidents of the Conference:	A. HERMENT
	TALAT MIRAS
The Executive Secretary of the Conference:	JOHN P. HUMPHREY

---

[1] Headline added.
[2] Headline added.

III

PROTOCOL RELATING TO THE STATUS OF REFUGEES OF 31 JANUARY 1967[1]

Entry into force: 4 October 1967, in accordance with Article VIII
Text: United Nations Treaty Series No. 8791, Vol. 6)6, p. 267

The States Parties to the present Protocol

Considering that the Convention relating to the Status of Refugees done at Geneva on 28 July 1951 (hereinafter referred to as the Convention) covers only those persons who have become refugees as a result of events occurring before 1 January, 1951,

Considering that new refugee situations have arisen since the Convention was adopted and that the refugees concerned may therefore not fall within the scope of the Convention,

Considering that it is desirable that equal status should be enjoyed by all refugees covered by the definition in the Convention irrespective of the dateline 1 January 1951,

Have agreed as follows:

Article I

General provision

1. The States Parties to the present Protocol undertake to apply Articles 2 to 34 inclusive of the Convention to refugees as hereinafter defined.

2. For the purpose of the present Protocol, the term "refugee" shall, except as regards the application of paragraph 3 of this Article, mean any person within the definition of Article 1 of the Convention as if the words

[1] The Protocol was signed by the President of the General Assembly and by the Secretary-General on 31 January 1967. The text of the General Assembly Resolution 2198 (XXI) of 16 December 1966 concerning the accession to the 1967 Protocol relating to the Status of Refugees is reproduced in Appendix.

'As a result of events occurring before 1 January 1951 and ...' and the words '...as a result of such events', in Article 1A (2) were omitted.

3. The present Protocol shall be applied by the States Parties hereto without any geographic limitation, save that existing declarations made by States already Parties to the Convention in accordance with Article 1B (1) *(a)* of the Convention, shall, unless extended under Article 1B (2) thereof, apply also under the present Protocol.

Article II

Co-operation of the national authorities with the United Nations

1. The States Parties to the present Protocol undertake to co-operate with the Office of the United Nations High Commissioner for Refugees, or any other agency of the United Nations which may succeed it, in the exercise of its functions, and shall in particular facilitate its duty of supervising the application of the provisions of the present Protocol.

2. In order to enable the Office of the High Commissioner, or any other agency of the United Nations which may succeed it, to, make reports to the competent organs of the United Nations, the States Parties to the present Protocol undertake to provide them with the information and statistical data requested, in the appropriate form, concerning:

(a) The condition of refugees;

(b) The implementation of the present Protocol;

(c) Laws, regulations and decrees which are, or may hereafter be, in force relating to refugees.

Article III

Information on national legislation

The States Parties to the present Protocol shall communicate to the Secretary-General of the United Nations the laws and regulations which they may adopt to ensure the application of the present Protocol.

Article IV

Settlement of disputes

Any dispute between States Parties to the present Protocol which relates to its interpretation or application and which cannot be settled by other means shall be referred to the International Court of Justice at the request of any one of the parties to the dispute.

Article V

Accession

The present Protocol shall be open for accession on behalf of all States Parties to the Convention and of any other State Member of the United Nations or member of any of the specialised agencies or to which an invitation to accede may have been addressed by the General Assembly of the United Nations. Accession shall be effected by the deposit of an instrument of accession with the Secretary-General of the United Nations.

Article VI

Federal clause

In the case of a Federal or non-unitary State, the following provisions shall apply:

(a) With respect to those articles of the Convention to be applied in accordance with Article I, paragraph 1, of the present Protocol that come within the legislative jurisdiction of the federal legislative authority, the obligations of the Federal Government shall to this extent be the same as those of States Parties which are not Federal States;

(b) With respect to those articles of the Convention to be applied in accordance with Article I, paragraph 1, of the present Protocol that come within the legislative jurisdiction of constituent States, provinces or cantons which are not, under the constitutional system of the federation, bound to take legislative action, the Federal Government shall bring such articles with a favourable recommendation to the notice of the appropriate authorities of States, provinces or cantons at the earliest possible moment;

(c) A Federal State Party to the present Protocol shall, at the request of any other State Party hereto transmitted through the Secretary-General of the United Nations, supply a statement of the law and practice of the Federation and its constituent units in regard to any particular provision of the Convention to be applied in accordance with Article I, paragraph 1, of the present Protocol, showing the extent to which effect has been given to that provision by legislative or other action.

Article VII

Reservations and declarations

1. At the time of accession, any State may make reservations in respect of Article IV of the present Protocol and in respect of the application in

accordance with Article I of the present Protocol of any provisions of the Convention other than those contained in Articles 1, 3, 4, 16(1) and 33 thereof, provided that in the case of a State Party to the Convention reservations made under this Article shall not extend to refugees in respect of whom the Convention applies.

2. Reservations made by States Parties to the Convention in accordance with Article 42 thereof shall, unless withdrawn, be applicable in relation to their obligations under the present Protocol.

3. Any State making a reservation in accordance with paragraph 1 of this Article may at any time withdraw such reservation by a communication to that effect addressed to the Secretary-General of the United Nations.

4. Declarations made under Article 40, paragraphs 1 and 2, of the Convention by a State Party thereto which accedes to the present Protocol shall be deemed to apply in respect of the present Protocol, unless upon accession a notification to the contrary is addressed by the State Party concerned to the Secretary-General of the United Nations. The provisions of Article 40, paragraphs 2 and 3, and of Article 44, paragraph 3, of the Convention shall be deemed to apply *mutatis mutandis* to the present Protocol.

Article VIII

Entry into force

1. The present Protocol shall come into force on the day of deposit of the sixth instrument of accession.

2. For each State acceding to the Protocol after the deposit of the sixth instrument of accession, the Protocol shall come into force on the date of deposit by such State of its instrument of accession.

Article IX

Denunciation

1. Any State Party hereto may denounce this Protocol at any time by a notification addressed to the Secretary-General of the United Nations.

2. Such denunciation shall take effect for the State Party concerned one year from the date on which it is received by the Secretary-General of the United Nations.

Article X

Notifications by the Secretary-General of the United Nations

The Secretary-General of the United Nations shall inform the States referred to in Article V above of the date of entry into force, accessions, reservations and withdrawals of reservations to and denunciations of the present Protocol, and of declarations and notifications relating hereto.

Article XI

Deposit in the archives of the Secretariat of the United Nations

A copy of the present Protocol, of which the Chinese, English, French, Russian and Spanish texts are equally authentic, signed by the President of the General Assembly and by the Secretary-General of the United Nations, shall be deposited in the archives of the Secretariat of the United Nations. The Secretary-General will transmit certified copies thereof to all States Members of the United Nations and to the other States referred to in Article V above.

APPENDIX

General Assembly Resolution 2198 (XXI)

Protocol relating to the Status of Refugees

The General Assembly

Considering that the Convention relating to the Status of Refugees, signed at Geneva on 28 July 1951,[1] covers only those persons who have become refugees as a result of events occurring before 1 January 1951,

Considering that new refugee situations have arisen since the Convention was adopted and that the refugees concerned may therefore not fall within the scope of the Convention,

Considering that it is desirable that equal status should be enjoyed by all refugees covered by the definition in the Convention, irrespective of the date-line of 1 January 1951,

Taking note of the recommendation of the Executive Committee of the Programme of the United Nations High Commissioner for Refugees[2] that the draft Protocol relating to the Status of Refugees should be submitted to the General Assembly after consideration by the Economic and Social Council, in order that the Secretary-General might be authorised to open the Protocol for accession by Governments within the shortest possible time,

Considering that the Economic and Social Council, in its resolution 1186 (XLI) of 18 November 1966, took note with approval of the draft Protocol contained in the addendum to the report of the United Nations High Commissioner for Refugees and concerning measures to extend the personal scope of the Convention[3] and transmitted the addendum to the General Assembly,

[1] United Nations, *Treaty Series*, vol. 189 (1954), No. 2545.
[2] See A/6311/Rev. 1/Add. 1, part two, para. 38.

1. *Takes note* of the Protocol relating to the Status of Refugees, the text of which[3] is contained in the addendum to the report of the United Nations High Commissioner for Refugees;

2. *Requests* the Secretary-General to transmit the text of the Protocol to the States mentioned in article V thereof, with a view to enabling them to accede to the Protocol.[4]

1495th plenary meeting,
16 December 1966.

---

[3] *Ibid.*, part one, para. 2.
[4] The Protocol was signed by the President of the General Assembly and by the Secretary-General on 31 January 1967.

Bibliography

Books

Adelman, H., ed., *Refugee Policy: Canada and the United States* (York Lanes Press, Toronto, 1991).

Adelman H. and J. Sorenson, eds, *African Refugees: Development Aid and Repatriation* (York Lanes Press, Toronto, 1994).

Aleinikoff, T.H., et al., eds, *Immigration: Process and Policy* (West Publishing Co., Minnesota, 1995), third edition.

Alston, P., *The United Nations and Human Rights: A Critical Appraisal* (Clarendon Press, Oxford, 1992).

An-Na'im, A.A., *Human Rights in Cross-cultural Perspectives: A Quest for Consensus* (University of Pennsylvania Press, Philadelphia, 1992).

Asbjorn, E., et al., eds, *Economic, Social and Cultural Rights: A Textbook* (Martinus Nijhoff Publishers, Dordrecht, 1995).

Bedjaoui, M., *Toward a New International Economic Order* (Homes and Meir Publishers, New York, 1979).

——, *The New World Order and the Security Council: Testing the Legality of its Acts* (Martinus Nijhoff Publishers, Dordrecht, 1994).

Bello, W. et al., *Dark Victory: The United States, Structural Adjustment, and Global Poverty* (Pluto Press, London, 1994).

Bhabha, J. and G. Col, eds, *Asylum Law and·Practice in Europe and North America* (Federal Publications, Washington, D.C., 1992).

Brownlie, I., *Principles of Public International Law* (Clarendon Press, Oxford, 1993), third edition.

Chimni, B.S., *International Law and World Order: A Critique of Contemporary Approaches* (Sage Publications, New Delhi, 1993).

Cook, R.J., *Human Rights of Women: National and International Perspectives* (University of Pennsylvania Press, Philadelphia, 1994).

Cornea, G.A., ed., *Africa's Recovery in the 1990s: From Stagnation to Human Development* (St. Martin's Press, New York, 1992).

Cornea, G.A., et al., *Adjustment with a Human Face* (Clarendon Press, Oxford, 1987).

Cox, R.W., *Production, Power and World Order: Social Forces in the Making of History* (Columbia University Press, New York, 1987).

Cruz, A., *Shifting Responsibility: Carriers' Liability in the Member States of the European Union and North America* (Trentham Books, Staffordshire, 1995).

Cuny, F.C., B.N. Stein and P. Reed, *Repatriation During Conflict in Africa and Asia* (Center for the Study of Societies in Crisis, Dallas, 1992).

Daniel, E.V. and C.K. Knudsen, *Mistrusting Refugees* (University of California Press, Berkeley, 1995).

Davies, W., ed., *Rights Have No Borders: Worldwide Internal Displacement* (Norwegian Refugee Council, Oxford, 1998).

Deng. F., *Protecting the Dispossessed: A Challenge for the International Community* (The Brookings Institution, Washington, D.C., 1993).

Deng, F. and R. Cohen, *Masses in Flight: The Global Crisis of Internal Displacement* (Brookings Institution Press, Washington, D.C., 1998).

——, *The Forsaken People: Case Studies of the Internally Displaced* (Brookings Institution Press, Washington, D.C., 1998).

Frelic, B. and B. Kohnen, *Filling the Gap: Temporary Protected Status* (US Committee for Refugees, Washington, D.C., December 1994).

Gibney, M., *Open Border? Closed Societies? The Ethical and Political Questions* (Greenwood Press, Westport, 1988).

Goodwin-Gill, G.S., *Child Soldiers: The Role of Children in Armed Conflicts* (Clarendon Press, Oxford, 1994).

——, *The Refugee in International Law* (Clarendon Press, Oxford, 1996), second edition.

Gordenker, L., *Refugees in International Politics* (Croom Helm, London, 1987).

Gorman, R.F., ed., *Refugee Aid and Development: Theory and Practice* (Greenwood Press, Westport, 1993).

——, *Historical Dictionary of Refugee and Disaster Relief Organizations* (Scarecrow Press, Methuen, 1994).

Grahl-Madsen, A., *The Status of Refugees in International Law*, vols 1 and 2 (Sijthoff, Leiden, 1966–72).

——, *Territorial Asylum* (Swedish Institute of International Affairs, Uppsala, 1979).

Harrell-Bond, B., *Imposing Aid* (Oxford University Press, Oxford, 1986).

Hathaway, J., *The Law of Refugee Status* (Butterworths, Toronto, 1991).

——, *Reconceiving International Refugee Law* (Martinus Nijhoff Publishers, The Hague, 1997).

Heinze, E., *Sexual Orientation: A Human Right. An Essay on International Human Rights Law* (Martinus Nijhoff Publishers, Dordrecht, 1995).

Henckaerts, J.M., *Mass Expulsion in Modern International Law and Practice* (Martinus Nijhoff Publishers, The Hague, 1995).

Hoffman, S., *Duties Beyond Borders: On the Limits and Possibilities of Ethical International Policy* (Syracuse University Press, Syracuse, 1981).

Holborn, L.W., *The International Refugee Organisation: A Specialised Agency of the United Nations: Its History and Work 1946–1952* (Oxford University Press, London, 1956).

Holborn, L.W., *Refugees: A Problem of Our Time. The Work of the UNHCR, 1951–72*, vols 1 and 2 (Scarecrow Press, Methuen, 1975).

Hui, O.J., et al., eds, *Crossing Borders: Transmigration in Asia Pacific* (Prentice-Hall, New York, 1995).

Independent Commission on International Humanitarian Issues, *Refugees: The Dynamics of Displacement* (Zed Books, London, 1986).

Keller, S.L., *Uprooting and Social Change: The Role of Refugees in Development* (Manohar Book Service, Delhi, 1975).

Kibreab, G., *African Refugees: Reflections on the African Refugee Problem* (The Red Sea Press, Trenton, 1985).

Koehn, P., *Refugees from Revolution: US Policy and Third World Migration* (Westview Press, Boulder, 1991).

Kymlicka, W., ed., *The Rights of Minority Cultures* (Oxford University Press, Oxford, 1995).

Lawyers Committee for Human Rights, *The Human Rights of Refugees and Displaced Persons: Protection Afforded Refugees, Asylum Seekers and Displaced persons under International Human Rights, Humanitarian and Refugee Law* (May 1991).

——, *African Exodus: Refugee Crisis, Human Rights, and the 1969 OAU Convention* (1994).

Lillich, R.B., *The Human Rights of Aliens in Contemporary International Law* (Manchester University Press, Manchester, 1984).

Loescher, G., *Beyond Charity: International Cooperation and the Global Refugee Crisis* (Oxford University Press, New York, 1993).

Loescher, G., and Laila Monahan, eds, *Refugees and International Relations* (Clarendon Press, Oxford, 1989).

Macalister-Smith, P., *International Humanitarian Assistance: Disaster Relief Actions in International Law and Organization* (Martinus Nijhoff Publishers, Dordrecht, 1985).

Malkki, L.H., *Purity and Exile: Violence, Memory, and National Cosmology Among Hutu Refugees in Tanzania* (The University of Chicago Press, Chicago, 1995).

Mani, V.S., *Basic Principles of Modern International Law* (Lancer Books, New Delhi, 1993).

McGoldrick, D., *The Human Rights Committee: Its Role in the Development of the International Covenant on Civil and Political Rights* (Clarendon Press, Oxford, 1991).

Mihevc, J., *The Market Tells Them So: The World Bank and Economic Fundamentalism in Africa* (Third World Network, Penang, 1995).

Muntarbhorn, V., *The Status of Refugees in Asia* (Clarendon Press, Oxford, 1992).

Nicholson, F., and Twomey, P., eds, *Refugee Rights and Realities: Evolving International Concepts and Regimes* (Cambridge University Press, Cambridge, 1999).

Pakrasi, K.B., *The Uprooted: A Sociological Study of the Refugees of West Bengal, India* (Editions Indian, Calcutta, 1971).

Rao, P.C., *The Indian Constitution and International Law* (Taxman, Delhi, 1993).

Richmond, A.H., *Global Apartheid: Refugees, Racism, and the New World Order* (Oxford University Press, Toronto, 1994).

Rogge, J., ed., *Refugee: A Third World Dilemma* (Rowman and Littlefield, Lanham, 1987).

Ruthstrom-Ruin, C., *Beyond Europe: The Globalization of Refugee Aid* (Lund University Press, Lund, 1993).

Salomon, K., *Refugees in the Cold War: Toward a New International Refugee Regime in the Early Postwar Era* (Lund University Press, Lund, 1991).

Saxena, R.N., *Refugees: A Study in Changing Attitudes* (Asia Publishing House, Bombay, 1961).

Scarry, E., *The Body in Pain: The Making and Unmaking of the World* (New York, 1985).

Simpson, J. Hope, *The Refugee Problem* (OUP, London, 1939).

Sinha, S.P., *Asylum and International Law* (Martinus Nijhoff Publishers, The Hague, 1971).

Skran, C.M., *Refugees in Inter-war Europe: The Emergence of a Regime* (Clarendon Press, Oxford, 1995).

Spencer, M., *States of Injustice: A Guide to Human Rights and Civil Liberties in the European Union* (Pluto Press, London, 1995).

Stoessinger, J.G., *The Refugee and the World Community* (The University of Minnesota Press, Minneapolis, 1956).

Takkenberg, A., *The Status of Palestinian Refugees in International Law* (Clarendon Press, Oxford, 1998).

Takkenberg, A. and C.C. Tahbaz, eds, *The Collected Travaux Preparatoires of the 1951 Geneva Convention Relating to the Status of Refugees* (Dutch Refugee Council, Amsterdam, 1990), vol. III.

Tuitt, P., *False Images: Law's Construction of the Refugee* (Pluto Press, London, 1996).

UNDP, *Human Development Report* (OUP, New York, 1990–1999).

UNHCR, *Handbook on Procedures and Criteria for Determining Refugee Status* (Geneva, September 1979).

——, *Report of the Working Group on Current Problems in the International Protection of Refugees and Displaced Persons in Asia* (Geneva, March 1981).

——, *Guidelines on the Protection of Refugee Women* (Geneva, July 1991).

——, *Guidelines on Assistance to Disabled Refugees* (Geneva, 1992).

——, *Directory of Non-Governmental Organizations* (Geneva, 1992).

——, *Sexual Violence Against Refugees: Guidelines on Prevention and Response* (Geneva, March 1995).

——, *Human Rights and Refugee Protection*, parts I and II (Geneva, October 1995).

——, *On Accession to the 1951 Convention and the 1967 Protocol Relating to the Status of Refugees* (Geneva, November 1995).

——, *International Legal Standards Applicable to the Protection of Internally Displaced Persons: A Reference manual for UNHCR Staff* (Division of International Protection, Geneva, 1996).

UNHCR, *Handbook. Voluntary Repatriation: International Protection* (Geneva, 1996).

——, *International Legal Standards Applicable to the Protection of Internally Displaced Persons: A Reference Manual for UNHCR Staff* (Geneva, 1996).

——, *Rebuilding a War-Torn Society: A Review of the UNHCR Reintegration Programme for Mozambican Returnees* (July 1996).

U.S. Committee for Refugees, *Sri Lanka: Island of Refugees* (October 1991).

——, *Left out in the Cold: The Perilous Homecoming of Afghan Refugees* (December 1992).

——, *"People Want Peace": Repatriation and Reintegration in War-Torn Sri Lanka* (January 1994).

——, *The People in Between: Sri Lankans Face Long-Term Displacement as Conflict Escalates* (March 1996).

——, *Conflict and Displacement in Sri Lanka* (March 1997).

Van Bueren, G., *The International Law on the Rights of the Child* (Martinus Nijhoff Publishers, Dordrecht, 1995).

Vernant, J., *The Refugee in the Post-war World* (Yale University Press, New Haven, 1953).

Walters, F.P., *A History of the League of Nations* (Oxford University Press, London, 1960).

Walzer, M., *Spheres of Justice: A Defense of Pluralism and Equality* (Basic Books, New York, 1983).

Weiner, M., *The Global Migration Crisis: Challenges to States and Human Rights* (Harper Collins Publishers, New York, 1995).

Weiss, P., *Nationality and Statelessness in International Law* (Sijthoff, Leiden, 1979), second edition.

Working with Refugees and Asylum Seekers (League of Red Cross and Red Crescent, Geneva, 1991).

Zieck, M., *UNHCR and Voluntary Repatriation of Refugees: A Legal Analysis* (Martinus Nijhoff Publishers, Dordrecht, 1997).

Zolberg, A., A. Suhrke and S. Aguayo, *Escape from Violence: Conflict and Refugee Crisis in the Developing World* (Oxford University Press, Oxford, 1989).

Articles

Achermann, A. and M. Gattiker, 'Safe Third Countries: European Developments', *International Journal of Refugee Law* (Vol. 7, 1995), pp. 19–37.

Adelman, H., 'Ethnicity and Refugees', *World Refugee Survey 1992*, pp. 6–12.

——, 'Humanitarian Intervention: The Case of the Kurds', *International Journal of Refugee Law* (Vol. 4, 1992), pp. 4–38.

Aleinikoff, A., 'State-Centered Refugee Law: From Resettlement to Containment', *Michigan Journal of International Law* (Vol. 14, 1992), pp. 120–39.

Anon, 'The UNHCR Note on International Protection You Won't See', *International Journal of Refugee Law* (Vol. 9, 1997), pp. 267–73.

Arboleda, E., 'The Cartagena Declaration of 1984 and its Similarities to the 1969 OAU Convention—A Comparative Perspective', *International Journal of Refugee Law* (Special Issue, 1995), pp. 87–101.

Bari, S., 'The right to development and refugee protection', in S.R. Chowdhury et al., eds, *The Right to Development in International Law* (Martinus Nijhoff Publishers, Dordrecht, 1992), pp. 167–77.

——., 'Refugee Status Determination under the Comprehensive Plan of Action (CPA): A Personal Assessment', *International Journal of Refugee Law* (Vol. 4, 1992), p. 487.

Barutciski, M., 'Tensions between the refugee concept and the IDP debate', *Forced Migration Review* (No. 3, December 1998), pp. 11–15.

Berlin, I., 'Two Concepts of Liberty', in M.J. Sandel, ed., *Liberalism and its Critics* (Basil Blackwell, Oxford, 1984), pp. 15–36.

Beyani, C., 'A Political and Legal Analysis of the Problem of the Return of Forcibly Transferred Populations', *Refugee Survey Quarterly* (Vol. 16, No. 3, 1997), pp. 1–26.

Black, R., 'Environmental Change in Refugee-Affected Areas of the Third World: The Role of Policy and Research', *Disasters* (Vol. 18, 1994), pp. 107–39.

——, 'Forced Migration and Environmental Change: The Impact of Refugees on Host Environments', *Journal of Environmental Management* (Vol. 42, 1994), pp. 261–77.

——, 'Putting Refugees in Camps', *Forced Migration Review* (No. 2, August 1998), pp. 4–7.

Bolten, J.J., 'From Schengen to Dublin: The New Frontiers of Refugee Law', in H. Meijers et al., eds, *Schengen: Internationalization of Central Chapters of the Law on Aliens, Refugees, Privacy, Security and the Police* (Kluwer Law and Taxation, W.E.J. Tjeenk Willink, 1991), pp. 8–36.

Boothby, N., 'Displaced Children: Psychological Theory and Practice from the Field', *Journal of Refugee Studies* (Vol. 5, 1992), pp. 106–22.

Carens, J.H., 'Aliens and Citizens: The Case for Open Borders', *Review of Politics* (Vol. 49, 1987), pp. 251–73.

——, 'Refugees and the Limits of Obligation', *Public Affairs Quarterly* (Vol. 6, 1992), pp. 31–44.

Chimni, B.S., 'Voluntary Repatriation: A Critical Note', *International Journal of Refugee Law* (Vol. 3, 1991), pp. 541–50.

——, 'The Meaning of Words and the Role of UNHCR in Voluntary Repatriation', *International Journal of Refugee Law* (Vol. 5, 1993), pp. 442–59.

——, 'The Legal Condition of Refugees in India', *Journal of Refugee Studies* (Vol. 7, 1994), pp. 378–401.

——, 'The Language of Protection and the Reality of Rejection: End of Cold War and Crisis in Refugee Law', in K.P. Saksena, ed., *Human Rights: Perspective and Challenges* (Lancer Books, New Delhi, 1994), pp. 322–37.

——, 'Globalization and Refugee Blues', *Journal of Refugee Studies* (Vol. 8, 1995), pp. 298–99.

Chimni, B.S., 'The Law and Politics of Regional Solution of Refugee Problem; The Case of South Asia', *RCSS Policy Studies*, 4 (Regional Centre for Strategic Studies, Colombo, 1998).

——, 'The Global Refugee Problem in the 21st Century and the Emerging Security Paradigm' in Antony Anghie and Gary Sturgess, eds, *Legal Visions of the 21st Century: Essays in Honour of Judge Weeramantry* (Kluwer Law International, The Hague, 1998), pp. 283–301.

——, 'The Geopolitics of Refugee Studies: A View from the South', *Journal of Refugee Studies* (Vol. 11, 1998), pp. 350–75.

——, 'From Resettlement to Involuntary Repatriation: Toward a Critical History of Durable Solutions', *UNHCR Working Paper No. 2* (Geneva, May 1999).

——, 'Globalization, Humanitarianism and the Erosion of Refugee Protection', First Harrell-Bond Lecture, 17 November 1999 (forthcoming).

Coles, G.J.L., 'The Human Rights Approach to the Solution of the Refugee problem: A Theoretical and Practical Enquiry', in Alan E. Nash, ed., *Human Rights and the Protection of Refugees under International Law* (Nova Scotia: Institute for Research on Public Policy, 1988), pp. 195–221.

——, 'Refugees and Human Rights', *Bulletin of Human Rights* (Vol. 91, UN, New York, 1992), pp. 63–74.

Crisp, J., and K. Jacobsen, 'Refugee camps reconsidered', *Forced Migration Review* (No. 3, December 1998), pp. 27–30.

Cunliffe, S.A. and M. Pugh, 'The Politicization of UNHCR in the Former Yugoslavia', *Journal of Refugee Studies* (Vol. 10, 1997), pp. 134–53.

David, U., 'Refugees from Bosnia and Herzegovina: Are they Genuine?', *Suffolk International Law Review* (Vol. 18, 1995), pp. 53–131.

Feliciano, F.P., 'The Principle of *Non-Refoulement*: A Note on International Legal Protection of Refugees and Displaced Persons', *Phillipine Law Journal* (Vol. 57, 1982), p. 598.

Frankenberg, G., 'The Alchemy of Law and Strangeness', *Recht en Kritiek* (Vol. 19, 1993), pp. 362–72.

Frelick, B., 'Preventing Refugee Flows: Protection or Peril?', *World Refugee Survey 1993*, pp. 5–14.

——, 'Safe haven: Safe for Whom?', *World Refugee Survey 1995*, pp. 18–28.

Garvey, J., 'Toward a Reformulation of International Refugee Law', *Harvard International Law Journal* (Vol. 26, 1985), pp. 483–500.

Gassmann, P., 'International Humanitarian Action: Growing Dilemmas and New Perspectives for the Twenty-first Century', in Medicins Sans Frontieres, *World in Crisis: The Politics of Survival at the End of the 20th Century* (Routledge, London, 1997), pp. 37–42.

Gibney, M., 'A "Well-Founded Fear" of Persecution', *Human Rights Quarterly* (Vol. 10, 1988), pp. 109–121.

——, 'United States Immigration Policy and the "Huddled Masses" Myth', *Georgetown Immigration Law Journal* (Vol. 3, 1989), pp. 361–86.

Gibney, M.J., 'Liberal Democratic States and Responsibilities to Refugees', *American Political Science Review* (Vol. 93, 1999), pp. 169–81.

Gilbert, G., 'Root Causes and International Law: Flow in the 1990's', *Netherlands Quarterly of Human Rights* (Vol. 11, 1993), pp. 413–36.

Goodwin-Gill, G., 'The Benigno Aquino Lecture in Human Rights. Refugees and Human Rights: Challenges for the 1990s', *International Journal of Refugee Law* (Vol. 2, 1990), Special Issue, pp. 29–37.

——, 'International Law and the Detention of Refugees and Asylum Seekers', *International Migration Review* (Vol. 20, 1986), pp. 193–219.

——, 'The Right to Leave, the Right to Return and the Question of a Right to Remain', in V. Gowlland-Debbas, ed., *The Problem of Refugees in the Light of Contemporary International Law* (Kluwer Law International, The Hague, 1995), pp. 93–106.

Habermas, J., 'Citizenship and National Identity: Some Reflections on the Future of Europe', in R. Beiner, ed., *Theorizing Citizenship* (State University of New York Press, New York, 1995), pp. 255–81.

Hans, Asha, 'Sri Lankan Tamil Refugees in India', *Refuge* (Vol. 13, No. 3, June 1993), pp. 30–33.

Harrell-Bond, B., 'Humanitarianism in a Straightjacket', *African Affairs* (Vol. 84, No. 334, January 1985), pp. 3–15.

——, 'Repatriation: Under What Conditions is it the Most Desirable Solution for Refugees? An Agenda for Research', *African Studies Review* (Vol. 31, 1988), pp. 41–69.

Harrell-Bond, B.E., and E. Voutira, 'Anthropology and the Study of Refugees', *Anthropology Today* (Vol. 8, No. 4, 1992), pp. 6–10.

Harvey, C.J., 'Talking about Refugee Law', *Journal of Refugee Studies* (Vol. 12, No. 2, 1999), pp. 101–35.

Hathaway, J., 'A Reconsideration of the Underlying Premise of Refugee Law', *Harvard International Law Journal* (Vol. 31, 1990), pp. 129–83.

——, 'Reconceiving Refugee Law as Human Rights Protection', *Journal of Refugee Studies* (Vol. 4, 1991), pp. 113–31.

——, 'Harmonizing for Whom? The Devaluation of Refugee Protection in the Era of European Economic Integration', *Cornell International Law Journal* (Vol. 26, 1993), pp. 719–35.

——, 'The Meaning of Repatriation', *International Journal of Refugee Law* (Vol. 9, No. 4, 1997), pp. 551–58.

Helton, A., 'UNHCR and Protection in the 90s', *International Journal of Refugee Law* (Vol. 6, 1994), pp. 1–6.

Hofmann, R., 'Refugee Law in Africa', *Law and State* (Vol. 39, 1989), pp. 79–99.

Hyndman, P., 'Asylum and *Non-Refoulement*—Are these Obligations Owed to Refugees under International Law?', *Philippines Law Journal* (Vol. 57, 1982), p. 43.

——, 'Developing International Refugee Law in the Asian Pacific Region: Some Issues and Prognosis', *Asian Yearbook of International Law, 1993*, pp. 19–44.

Jacobsen, K., 'Refugees' Environmental Impact: The Effect of Patterns of Settlement', *Journal of Refugee Studies* (Vol. 10, 1997), pp. 19–37.

Jennings, R.Y., 'Some International Law Aspects of the Refugee Question', *The British Yearbook of International Law* (Vol. 20, 1939), p. 20.

Joly, D., 'The Porous Dam: European Harmonization on Asylum in the Nineties', *International Journal of Refugee Law* (Vol. 6, 1994), pp. 159–94.

Kamenka, E., 'On Being a Refugee', in A. Saikal, ed., *Refugees in the Modern World* (Australian National University, Canberra, 1989), pp. 11–15.

Kiernan, V., 'The Separation of India and Pakistan', in R. Cohen, ed., *The Cambridge Survey of India and Pakistan* (Cambridge University Press, Cambridge, 1995), pp. 356–59.

Kimminich, O., 'The Present International Law of Asylum', *Law and State* (Vol. 32, 1985), pp. 25–47.

Kjaergaard, E., 'The Concept of "Safe Third Country" in Contemporary European Refugee Law', *International Journal of Refugee Law* (Vol. 6, 1994), pp. 649–55.

Kjaerum, M., 'Temporary Protection in Europe in the 1990s', *International Journal of Refugee Law* (Vol. 6, 1994), pp. 444–56.

Koh, H.H., 'The Human Face of the Haitian Interdiction Program', *Virginia Journal of International Law* (Vol. 33, 1993), pp. 483–90.

——, 'Refugees, the Courts, and the New World Order', *Utah Law Review* (No. 3, 1994), pp. 999–1027.

——, 'America's Offshore Refugee Camps', *University of Richmond Law Review* (Vol. 29, 1995), pp. 139–73.

Kunz, B.P., 'The Refugee in Flight: Kinetic Models and Forms of Displacement', *International Migration Review* (Vol. 7, 1973), p. 7.

Kyoichi, 'The "Non-Political and Humanitarian" Clause in UNHCR's Statute', *Refugee Survey Quarterly* (Vol. 17, No. 1, 1998), pp. 33–60.

Landgren, K., 'The Future of Refugee Protection: Four Challenges', *Journal of Refugee Studies* (Vol. 4, 1998), pp. 416–33.

Lewis, C.E., 'Dealing with the Problem of Internally Displaced Persons', *Georgetown Immigration Law Journal* (Vol. 6, 1992), pp. 693–720.

Luca, D., 'Questioning Temporary Protection, together with a Selected Bibliography on Temporary Refuge/Temporary Protection', *International Journal of Refugee Law* (Vol. 6, 1994), p. 535.

Macklin, A., 'Refugee Women and the Imperative of Categories', *Human Rights Quarterly* (Vol. 17, 1995), pp. 213–77.

Mani, V.S., 'Humanitarian Intervention and International Law', *Indian Journal of International Law* (Vol. 33, 1993), pp. 1–27.

Martin, D.A., 'Large Scale Migrations of Asylum Seekers', *American Journal of International Law* (Vol. 76, 1982), p. 598.

Massey, D., 'A Global Sense of Place', *Marxism Today*, June 1991, pp. 24–29.

Mahmood, S., 'The Schengen Information System: An Inequitable Data Protection System: An Inequitable Data Protection Regime', *International Journal of Refugee Law* (Vol. 7, 1995), pp. 188–200.

McCalmon, B.K., 'States, Refugees and Self-defense', *Georgetown Immigration Law Journal* (Vol. 10, 1996), pp. 215–39.

McCarron, K.E., 'The Schengen Agreement as a Violation of International Law and the Need for Centralized Adjudication on the Validity of National Asylum Policies for Members of the United Nations', *Boston College International Nad Comparative Law Review* (Vol. 17, 1995), pp. 401–28.

Mendiluce, J., 'War and Disaster in the Former Yugoslavia: The Limits of Humanitarian Action', *World Refugee Survey 1994*, pp. 10–20.

Neuman, G.L., 'Buffer Zones Against Refugees: Dublin, Schengen, and the German Asylum Amendment', *Virginia Journal of International Law* (Vol. 33, 1993), pp. 503–26.

Okoth-Obbo, G., 'Coping with a Complex Refugee Crisis in Africa: Issues, Problems and Constraints for Refugee and International Law', in V. Gowlland-Debbas, ed., *The Problem of Refugees in the Light of Contemporary International Law* (Kluwer Law International, The Hague, 1995), pp. 7–17.

Oloka-Onyango, J., 'The Place and Role of the OAU Bureau for Refugees in the African Refugee Crisis', *International Journal of Refugee Law* (Vol. 6, 1994), pp. 34–52.

Parish, T.D., 'Membership in a Particular Social Group under the Refugee Act of 1980: Social Identity and the Legal Concept of a Refugee', *Columbia Law Review* (Vol. 92, 1992), pp. 923–53.

Perluss, D. and J. Hartman, 'Temporary Refuge: Emergence of a Customary International Law Norm', *Virginia Journal of International Law* (Vol. 26, 1986), p. 551.

Perruchoud, 'Persons falling under the Mandate of the International Organization for Migration (IOM) and to Whom the Organization may Provide Migration Services', *International Journal of Refugee Law* (Vol. 4, 1992), pp. 205–16.

Plattner, D., 'ICRC Neutrality and Neutrality in Humanitarian Assistance', *International Review of the Red Cross* (Vol. 36, 1996), pp. 161–79.

——, 'The protection of displaced persons in non-international armed conflicts', *International Review of the Red Cross* (No. 291, November–December 1992), pp. 567–80.

Plender, R., 'The Legal Basis of International Jurisdiction to Act with Regard to the Internally Displaced', *International Journal of Refugee Law* (Vol. 6, 1994), pp. 345–60.

Porter, G.S., 'Persecution based on Political Opinion: Interpretation of the Refugee Act of 1980', *Cornell International Law Journal* (Vol. 25, 1992), pp. 231–76.

Quigley, J., 'Family Reunion and the Right to Return to Occupied Territory', *Georgetown Immigration Law Journal* (Vol. 6, 1992), pp. 223–51.

——, 'Displaced Palestinians and a Right to Return', *Harvard International Law Journal* (Vol. 39, No. 1, Winter 1998), pp. 171–229.

Rawls, J., 'The Law of Peoples', *Critical Inquiry* (Vol. 30, 1993), pp. 37–68.

Robinson, V., 'Into the Next Millennium: An Agenda for Refugee Studies. A Report on the First Annual Meeting of the International Advisory Panel, January 1990', *Journal of Refugee Studies* (Vol. 3, 1990), pp. 3–15.

Rusu, S., 'Refugees, Information and Solutions: The Need for Informed Decision-making', *Refugee Studies Quarterly* (Vol. 13, 1994), pp. 4–11.

Rutinwa, B., 'Beyond Durable Solutions: An Appraisal of the New Proposals for Prevention and Solution of Refugee Crisis in the Great Lakes Region', *Journal of Refugee Studies* (Vol. 9, 1996), pp. 312–26.

Saxena, J.N., 'Legal Status of Refugees: Indian Position', *Indian Journal of International Law* (Vol. 26, 1986), pp. 501–15.

Shacknove, A., 'Who is a Refugee?', *Ethics* (Vol. 95, 1985), pp. 274–84.

——, 'From Asylum to Containment', *International Journal of Refugee Law* (Vol. 5, 1993), pp. 516–33.

Simpson, J. Hope, *The Refugee Problem* (Oxford University Press, London, 1939).

The Polity Reader in Gender Studies (Polity Press, Cambridge, 1994).

Thorburn, J., 'Transcending Boundaries: Temporary Protection and Burden-Sharing in Europe', *International Journal of Refugee Law* (Vol. 7, 1995), p. 459.

Walzer, M., 'The Politics of Rescue', *Social Research* (Vol. 62, 1995), pp. 53–66.

Warner, D., 'The Dynamics of Community', *Peace Review* (Vol. 5, 1993), pp. 329–34.

Weiner, M., 'The Clash of Norms: Dilemmas in Refugee Policies', *Journal of Refugee Studies* (Vol. 11, 1998), pp. 433–53.

Weiss, P., 'Territorial Asylum', *Indian Journal of International Law* (Vol. 6, 1966), p. 173.

——, 'The United Nations Declaration on Territorial Asylum', *The Canadian Yearbook of International Law* (Vol. 7, 1969), pp. 92–149.

——, 'The Draft United Nations Convention on Territorial Asylum', *British Yearbook of International Law* (Vol. 50, 1980), p. 151.

Widgren, J., 'International Migration and Regional Stability', *International Affairs* (Vol. 60, 1990), pp. 749–66.

Zedalis, R.J., 'Right to Return: A Closer Look', *Georgetown Immigration Law Journal* (Vol. 6, 1992), pp. 499–517.

Zetter, R., 'Refugee Survival and NGO Project Assistance: Mozambican Refugees in Malawi', *Community Development Journal* (Vol. 31, 1996), pp. 214–29.

Zieck, M.Y.A., 'Voluntary Repatriation: An Analysis of the Refugee's Rights to Return to his own Country', *Austrian Journal of Public International Law* (Vol. 44, 1992), pp. 137–76.

Zolberg, A.R., 'The Roots of U.S. Refugee Policy', in R.W. Tucker, C.B. Keely and L. Wrigley, eds, *Immigration and U.S. Foreign Policy* (Westview Press, Boulder, 1990).

Journals

Forced Migration
Georgetown Immigration Law Journal

International Journal of Refugee Law
International Migration Review
Journal of Refugee Studies
Refuge
Refugee
Refugee Survey Quarterly
South Asian Refugee Watch
The Global IDP Survey
World Refugee Survey

Refugee-related Web sites

For addresses of Web sites related to refugee issues see *Refugee Survey Quaterly* (Vol. 16, 1997), Special Issue on Refugee-related sites on the World Wide Web.

About the Editor

B.S. Chimni is Professor of International Law at the School of International Studies, Jawaharlal Nehru University, New Delhi. He has been Fulbright Visiting Scholar at the Harvard Law School (1995–96) and Law Fellow, Centre for Refugee Studies, University of York, Canada (1993). Professor Chimni is a member of the External Research Advisory Committee of the Office of the United Nations High Commissioner for Refugees, and is on the international advisory boards of the *Journal of Refugee Studies*, *Refugee Survey Quarterly*, *Georgetown Immigration Law Journal* and *South Asian Refugee Watch*. He has published two books and numerous articles on a range of subjects concerning international law, including refugee law.

Index